The Black Book
of
Federal Courts

Scott Dodson

2021 Edition

About *The Black Book* and Acknowledgements

This book is designed for the course most law schools call Federal Courts. I have selected and edited the material and priced the book with students in mind. The first edition (2018) was under 550 pages and priced at just $39 on Amazon, and I expect future annual editions—which I intend to make available each July—to be comparable.

The casebook's no-nonsense, minimalist style—without additional notes or commentary, except for a brief preliminary statement setting out some general themes at the start of each topic—preserves instructor flexibility without sacrificing economy. Federal Courts instruction varies in both style and coverage. Some instructors may prefer to use this casebook as a primary foundation and to supplement with their own hypotheticals, commentary, additional cases, or other materials. At the book's price point, I hope those instructors find the casebook a useful part of their own assembled materials for their particular preferences in teaching the course.

A few notes about editing. I have used ellipses to indicate excised material except for the removal of footnotes, case citations, some separate opinions, and some authorship material. I have cleaned up certain quotations in the text and eliminated some quotation marks and citations for readability. I have modified certain stylistic choices in the cases—by, for example, making "Congress's" the possessive of Congress—for purposes of uniformity. I have modernized some of the archaic spelling and punctuation used in older opinions. Unless otherwise indicated, all opinions are from the United States Supreme Court.

I am indebted to my wife Ami, without whose persistent and tireless support of my work this book would not exist.

Table of Contents

Introduction to Federal Courts

Cases and Controversies

Standing

Ripeness & Mootness

Political-Question Doctrine

Federal-Question Jurisdiction

Diversity Jurisdiction

Supplemental Jurisdiction

Erie

Federal Common Law

Abstention

Substance-Based Exceptions to Jurisdiction

State Sovereign Immunity

Federal Review of State Decisions

Habeas Corpus

Introduction to Federal Courts

Introduction

The jurisdiction and powers of the federal courts are fundamental matters that go to the very heart of our constitutional system. In some respects, the Constitution speaks directly to them. For example, Article III sets out with some specificity the matters over which the federal courts can exercise subject-matter jurisdiction and the division of the Supreme Court's appellate and original jurisdiction. But other issues are far more oblique, such as what is outside the "judicial power," what the role of the federal courts could or should be in the structure of the federal government, what federalism or separation-of-powers limitations constrain or counsel hesitation in the exercise of federal judicial power, and what practical implications affect the scope or interpretation of federal-court jurisdiction.

This first topic introduces some of the larger themes of the course. It begins with the Constitution's text covering the federal judicial power and then turns to some of the foundational cases. As you read these materials, consider the following questions:

- Why is it important, if at all, for federal courts to have the "province and duty" to say authoritatively what federal law means?

- What factors or situations might counsel avoidance of that duty?

- What does it mean for something to be "jurisdictional," and what are the practical implications of that determination?

- How does the judicial branch "talk" to the other branches, and is that "communication" effective?

United States Constitution

Article III, section 1. The judicial power of the United States, shall be vested in one Supreme Court, and in such inferior courts as the Congress may from time to time ordain and establish. . . .

Article III, section 2. The judicial power shall extend to all cases, in law and equity, arising under this Constitution, the laws of the United States, and treaties made, or which shall be made, under their authority; . . . to controversies between two or more states;—between a state and citizens of another state;—between citizens of different states. . . , and between a state, or the citizens thereof, and foreign states, citizens or subjects. In all cases affecting ambassadors, other public ministers and consuls, and those in which a state shall be party, the Supreme Court shall have original jurisdiction. In all the other cases before mentioned, the Supreme Court shall have appellate jurisdiction, both as to law and fact, with such exceptions, and under such regulations as the Congress shall make.

Amendment XI. The Judicial power of the United States shall not be construed to extend to any suit in law or equity, commenced or prosecuted against one of the United States by Citizens of another State, or by Citizens or Subjects of any Foreign State.

Marbury v. Madison (1803)

. . . . At the last term on the affidavits then read and filed with the clerk, a rule was granted in this case, requiring the secretary of state to show cause why a mandamus should not issue, directing him to deliver to William Marbury his commission as a justice of the peace for the county of Washington, in the district of Columbia.

No cause has been shewn, and the present motion is for a mandamus. The peculiar delicacy of this case, the novelty of some of its circumstances, and the real difficulty attending the points which occur in it, require a complete exposition of the principles, on which the opinion to be given by the court, is founded. . . .

In the order in which the court has viewed this subject, the following questions have been considered and decided.

1st. Has the applicant a right to the commission he demands? 2dly. If he has a right, and that right has been violated, do the laws of his country afford him a remedy? 3dly. If they do afford him a remedy, is it a *mandamus* issuing from this court?

[The Court concluded that Mr. Marbury had a right to the commission and that the law afforded him a remedy.] . . . . It remains to be inquired whether, 3dly, he is entitled to the remedy for which he applies. This depends on, 1st, the nature of the writ applied for, and, 2dly, the power of this court.

[The Court concluded that mandamus was the appropriate writ.] . . . . This, then, is a plain case for a mandamus, either to deliver the commission, or a copy of it from the record; and it only remains to be inquired, [w]hether it can issue from this court.

The act to establish the judicial courts of the United States authorizes the supreme court "to issue writs of mandamus, in cases warranted by the principles and usages of law, to any courts appointed, or persons holding office, under the authority of the United States."

The secretary of state, being a person holding an office under the authority of the United States, is precisely within the letter of the description; and if this court is not authorized to issue a writ of mandamus to such an officer, it must be because the law is unconstitutional, and therefore absolutely incapable of conferring the authority, and assigning the duties which its words purport to confer and assign.

The constitution vests the whole judicial power of the United States in one supreme court, and such inferior courts as congress shall, from time to time, ordain and establish. This power is expressly extended to all cases arising under the laws of the United States; and consequently, in some form, may be exercised over the present case; because the right claimed is given by a law of the United States.

In the distribution of this power it is declared that "the supreme court shall have original jurisdiction in all cases affecting ambassadors, other public ministers and consuls, and those in which a state shall be a party. In all other cases, the supreme court shall have appellate jurisdiction."

It has been insisted, at the bar, that as the original grant of jurisdiction, to the supreme and inferior courts, is general, and the clause, assigning original jurisdiction to the supreme court, contains no negative or restrictive words; the power remains to the legislature, to assign original jurisdiction to that court in other cases than those specified in the article which has been recited; provided those cases belong to the judicial power of the United States.

If it had been intended to leave it in the discretion of the legislature to apportion the judicial power between the supreme and inferior courts according to the will of that body, it would certainly have been useless to have proceeded further than to have defined the judicial power, and the tribunals in which it should be vested. The subsequent part of the section is mere surplusage, is entirely without meaning, if such is to be the construction. If congress remains at liberty to give this court appellate jurisdiction, where the constitution has declared their jurisdiction shall be original; and original jurisdiction where the constitution has declared it shall be appellate; the distribution of jurisdiction, made in the constitution, is form without substance.

Affirmative words are often, in their operation, negative of other objects than those affirmed; and in this case, a negative or exclusive sense must be given to them or they have no operation at all.

It cannot be presumed that any clause in the constitution is intended to be without effect; and therefore such a construction is inadmissible, unless the words require it.

If the solicitude of the convention, respecting our peace with foreign powers, induced a provision that the supreme court should take original jurisdiction in cases which might be supposed to affect them; yet the clause would have proceeded no further than to provide for such cases, if no further restriction on the powers of congress had been intended. That they should have appellate jurisdiction in all other cases, with such exceptions as congress might make, is no restriction; unless the words be deemed exclusive of original jurisdiction.

When an instrument organizing fundamentally a judicial system, divides it into one supreme, and so many inferior courts as the legislature may ordain and establish; then enumerates its powers, and proceeds so far to distribute them, as to define the jurisdiction of the supreme court by declaring the cases in which it shall take original jurisdiction, and that in others it shall take appellate jurisdiction; the plain import of the words seems to be, that in one class of cases its jurisdiction is original, and not appellate; in the other it is appellate, and not original. If any other construction would render the clause inoperative, that is an additional reason for rejecting such other construction, and for adhering to their obvious meaning.

To enable this court then to issue a mandamus, it must be shown to be an exercise of appellate jurisdiction, or to be necessary to enable them to exercise appellate jurisdiction. . . . It is the essential criterion of appellate jurisdiction, that it revises and corrects the proceedings in a cause already instituted, and does not create that cause. Although, therefore, a mandamus may be directed to courts, yet to issue such a writ to an officer for the delivery of a paper, is in effect the same as to sustain an original action for that paper, and therefore seems not to belong to appellate, but to original jurisdiction. Neither is it necessary in such a case as this, to enable the court to exercise its appellate jurisdiction.

The authority, therefore, given to the supreme court, by the act establishing the judicial courts of the United States, to issue writs of mandamus to public officers, appears not to be warranted by the constitution; and it becomes necessary to enquire whether a jurisdiction, so conferred, can be exercised.

[The Court determined that a statute contrary to the Constitution cannot be given effect.] . . . . If an act of the legislature, repugnant to the constitution, is void, does it, notwithstanding its invalidity, bind the courts, and oblige them to give it effect? Or, in other words, though it be not law, does it constitute a rule as operative as if it was a law? This would be to overthrow in fact what was established in theory; and would seem, at first view, an absurdity too gross to be insisted on. It shall, however, receive a more attentive consideration.

It is emphatically the province and duty of the judicial department to say what the law is. Those who apply the rule to particular cases, must of necessity expound and interpret that rule. If two laws conflict with each other, the courts must decide on the operation of each.

So if a law be in opposition to the constitution; if both the law and the constitution apply to a particular case, so that the court must either decide that case conformably to the law, disregarding the constitution; or conformably to the constitution, disregarding the law; the court must determine which of these conflicting rules governs the case. This is of the very essence of judicial duty.

If then the courts are to regard the constitution; and the constitution is superior to any ordinary act of the legislature; the constitution, and not such ordinary act, must govern the case to which they both apply. . . .

The judicial power of the United States is extended to all cases arising under the constitution. Could it be the intention of those who gave this power, to say that, in using it, the constitution should not be looked into? That a case arising under the constitution should be decided without examining the instrument under which it arises? This is too extravagant to be maintained.

In some cases then, the constitution must be looked into by the judges. And if they can open it at all, what part of it are they forbidden to read, or to obey?

. . . . Thus, the particular phraseology of the constitution of the United States confirms and strengthens the principle, supposed to be essential to all written constitutions, that a law repugnant to the constitution is void; and that *courts,* as well as other departments, are bound by that instrument.

The rule must be discharged.

Cohens v. Virginia (1821)

This is a writ of error to a judgment rendered in the Court of Hustings for the borough of Norfolk, on an information for selling lottery tickets, contrary to an act of the Legislature of Virginia. In the State Court, the defendant claimed the protection of an act of Congress. A case was agreed between the parties, which states the act of Assembly on which the prosecution was founded, and the act of Congress on which the defendant relied, and concludes in these words: "If upon this case the Court shall be of opinion that the acts of Congress before mentioned were valid, and, on the true construction of those acts, the lottery tickets sold by the defendants as aforesaid, might lawfully be sold within the State of Virginia, notwithstanding the act or statute of the general assembly of Virginia prohibiting such sale, then judgment to be entered for the defendants; And if the Court should be of opinion that the statute or act of the General Assembly of the State of Virginia, prohibiting such sale, is valid, notwithstanding the said acts of Congress, then judgment to be entered that the defendants are guilty, and that the Commonwealth recover against them one hundred dollars and costs."

Judgment was rendered against the defendants; and the Court in which it was rendered being the highest Court of the State in which the cause was cognizable, the record has been brought into this Court by writ of error.

The defendant in error moves to dismiss this writ, for want of jurisdiction. . . .

The first question to be considered is, whether the jurisdiction of this Court is excluded by the character of the parties, one of them being a State, and the other a citizen of that State?

The second section of the third article of the constitution defines the extent of the judicial power of the United States. Jurisdiction is given to the Courts of the Union in two classes of cases. In the first, their jurisdiction depends on the character of the cause, whoever may be the parties. This class comprehends "all cases in law and equity arising under this constitution, the laws of the United States, and treaties made, or which shall be made, under their authority." This clause extends the jurisdiction of the Court to all the cases described, without making in its terms any exception whatever, and without any regard to the condition of the party. If there be any exception, it is to be implied against the express words of the article.

In the second class, the jurisdiction depends entirely on the character of the parties. In this are comprehended "controversies between two or more States, between a State and citizens of another State," "and between a State and foreign States, citizens or subjects." If these be the parties, it is entirely unimportant what may be the subject of controversy. Be it what it may, these parties have a constitutional right to come into the Courts of the Union.

The counsel for the defendant in error have stated that the cases which arise under the constitution must grow out of those provisions which are capable of self-execution; examples of which are to be found in the 2d section of the 4th article, and in the 10th section of the 1st article.

A case which arises under a law of the United States must, we are likewise told, be a right given by some act which becomes necessary to execute the powers given in the constitution, of which the law of naturalization is mentioned as an example.

The use intended to be made of this exposition of the first part of the section, defining the extent of the judicial power, is not clearly understood. If the intention be merely to distinguish cases arising under the constitution, from those arising under a law, for the sake of precision in the application of this argument, these propositions will not be controverted. If it be to maintain that a case arising under the constitution, or a law, must be one in which a party comes into Court to demand something conferred on him by the constitution or a law, we think the construction too narrow. A case in law or equity consists of the right of the one party, as well as of the other, and may truly be said to arise under the constitution or a law of the United States, whenever its correct decision depends on the construction of either. Congress seems to have intended to give its own construction of this part of the constitution in the 25th section of the judiciary act; and we perceive no reason to depart from that construction.

The jurisdiction of the Court, then, being extended by the letter of the constitution to all cases arising under it, or under the laws of the United States, it follows that those who would withdraw any case of this description from that jurisdiction, must sustain the exemption they claim on the spirit and true meaning of the constitution, which spirit and true meaning must be so apparent as to overrule the words which its framers have employed.

The counsel for the defendant in error have undertaken to do this; and have laid down the general proposition, that a sovereign independent State is not suable, except by its own consent. . . .

The constitution gave to every person having a claim upon a State, a right to submit his case to the Court of the nation. However unimportant his claim might be, however little the community might be interested in its decision, the framers of our constitution thought it necessary for the purposes of justice, to provide a tribunal as superior to influence as possible, in which that claim might be decided. Can it be imagined, that the same persons considered a case involving the constitution of our country and the majesty of the laws, questions in which every American citizen must be deeply interested, as withdrawn from this tribunal, because a State is a party?

While weighing arguments drawn from the nature of government, and from the general spirit of an instrument, and urged for the purpose of narrowing the construction which the words of that instrument seem to require, it is proper to place in the opposite scale those principles, drawn from the same sources, which go to sustain the words in their full operation and natural import. One of these, which has been pressed with great force by the counsel for the plaintiffs in error, is, that the judicial power of every well constituted government must be co-extensive with the legislative, and must be capable of deciding every judicial question which grows out of the constitution and laws. . . .

It is most true that this Court will not take jurisdiction if it should not: but it is equally true, that it must take jurisdiction if it should. The judiciary cannot, as the legislature may, avoid a measure because it approaches the confines of the constitution. We cannot pass it by because it is doubtful. With whatever doubts, with whatever difficulties, a case may be attended, we must decide it, if it be brought before us. We have no more right to decline the exercise of jurisdiction which is given, than to usurp that which is not given. The one or the other would be treason to the constitution. Questions may occur which we would gladly avoid; but we cannot avoid them. All we can do is, to exercise our best judgment, and conscientiously to perform our duty. In doing this, on the present occasion, we find this tribunal invested with appellate jurisdiction in *all* cases arising under the constitution and laws of the United States. We find no exception to this grant, and we cannot insert one. . . .

We think, then, that, as the constitution originally stood, the appellate jurisdiction of this Court, in all cases arising under the constitution, laws, or treaties of the United States, was not arrested by the circumstance that a State was a party. . . .

Judgment affirmed.

Insurance Corp. of Ireland v. Compagnie des Bauxites (1982)

. . . . Federal courts are courts of limited jurisdiction. The character of the controversies over which federal judicial authority may extend are delineated in Art. III, § 2, cl. 1. Jurisdiction of the lower federal courts is further limited to those subjects encompassed within a statutory grant of jurisdiction. Again, this reflects the constitutional source of federal judicial power: Apart from this Court, that power only exists "in such inferior Courts as the Congress may from time to time ordain and establish." Art. III, § 1.

Subject-matter jurisdiction, then, is an Art. III as well as a statutory requirement; it functions as a restriction on federal power, and contributes to the characterization of the federal sovereign. Certain legal consequences directly follow from this. For example, no action of the parties can confer subject-matter jurisdiction upon a federal court. Thus, the consent of the parties is irrelevant, principles of estoppel do not apply, and a party does not waive the requirement by failing to challenge jurisdiction early in the proceedings. Similarly, a court, including an appellate court, will raise lack of subject-matter jurisdiction on its own motion. The rule, springing from the nature and limits of the judicial power of the United States is inflexible and without exception, which requires this court, of its own motion, to deny its jurisdiction, and, in the exercise of its appellate power, that of all other courts of the United States, in all cases where such jurisdiction does not affirmatively appear in the record. . . .

Arbaugh v. Y & H Corp. (2006)

This case concerns the distinction between two sometimes confused or conflated concepts: federal-court "subject-matter" jurisdiction over a controversy; and the essential ingredients of a federal claim for relief. Title VII of the Civil Rights Act of 1964 makes it unlawful for an employer to discriminate, *inter alia*, on the basis of sex. The Act's jurisdictional provision empowers federal courts to adjudicate civil actions "brought under" Title VII. Covering a broader field, the Judicial Code gives federal courts subject-matter jurisdiction over all civil actions "arising under" the laws of the United States. Title VII actions fit that description. In a provision defining 13 terms used in Title VII, Congress limited the definition of "employer" to include only those having "fifteen or more employees." The question here presented is whether the numerical qualification contained in Title VII's definition of "employer" affects federal-court subject-matter jurisdiction or, instead, delineates a substantive ingredient of a Title VII claim for relief.

The question arises in this context. Jenifer Arbaugh, plaintiff below, petitioner here, brought a Title VII action in federal court against her former employer, defendant-respondent Y & H Corporation (hereinafter Y & H), charging sexual harassment. The case was tried to a jury, which returned a verdict for Arbaugh in the total amount of $40,000. Two weeks after the trial court entered judgment on the jury verdict, Y & H moved to dismiss the entire action for want of federal subject-matter jurisdiction. For the first time in the litigation, Y & H asserted that it had fewer than 15 employees on its payroll and therefore was not amenable to suit under Title VII.

Although recognizing that it was unfair and a waste of judicial resources to grant the motion to dismiss, the trial court considered itself obliged to do so because it believed that the 15-or-more-employees requirement was jurisdictional. We reject that categorization and hold that the numerical threshold does not circumscribe federal-court subject-matter jurisdiction. Instead, the employee-numerosity requirement relates to the substantive adequacy of Arbaugh's Title VII claim, and therefore could not be raised defensively late in the lawsuit, *i.e.*, after Y & H had failed to assert the objection prior to the close of trial on the merits.

I

We set out below statutory provisions and rules that bear on this case. Title VII makes it "an unlawful employment practice for an employer . . . to fail or refuse to hire or to discharge any individual, or otherwise to discriminate against any individual with respect to his compensation, terms, conditions, or privileges of employment, because of such individual's race, color, religion, sex, or national origin." To spare very small businesses from Title VII liability, Congress provided that: "[t]he term 'employer' means a person engaged in an industry affecting commerce who has fifteen or more employees for each working day in each of twenty or more calendar weeks in the current or preceding calendar year, and any agent of such a person."

This employee-numerosity requirement appears in a section headed "Definitions," which also prescribes the meaning, for Title VII purposes, of 12 other terms used in the Act.[3]

[3] The other terms defined in § 2000e are: "person," "employment agency," "labor organization," "employee," "commerce," "industry affecting commerce," "State," "religion," "because of sex," "complaining party," "demonstrates," and "respondent."

Congress has broadly authorized the federal courts to exercise subject-matter jurisdiction over "all civil actions arising under the Constitution, laws, or treaties of the United States." Title VII surely is a "law[] of the United States." In 1964, however, when Title VII was enacted, § 1331's umbrella provision for federal-question jurisdiction contained an amount-in-controversy limitation: Claims could not be brought under § 1331 unless the amount in controversy exceeded $10,000. Title VII, framed in that light, assured that the amount-in-controversy limitation would not impede an employment-discrimination complainant's access to a federal forum. The Act thus contains its own jurisdiction-conferring provision, which reads: "Each United States district court and each United States court of a place subject to the jurisdiction of the United States shall have jurisdiction of actions brought under this subchapter."

Congress amended 28 U.S.C. § 1331 in 1980 to eliminate the amount-in-controversy threshold. Since that time, Title VII's own jurisdictional provision has served simply to underscore Congress's intention to provide a federal forum for the adjudication of Title VII claims. . . .

The objection that a federal court lacks subject-matter jurisdiction may be raised by a party, or by a court on its own initiative, at any stage in the litigation, even after trial and the entry of judgment. Rule 12(h)(3) instructs: "Whenever it appears by suggestion of the parties or otherwise that the court lacks jurisdiction of the subject matter, the court shall dismiss the action." By contrast, the objection that a complaint "fail[s] to state a claim upon which relief can be granted," Rule 12(b)(6), may not be asserted post trial. Under Rule 12(h)(2), that objection endures up to, but not beyond, trial on the merits: A defense of failure to state a claim upon which relief can be granted may be made in any pleading or by motion for judgment on the pleadings, or at the trial on the merits.

From May 2000 through February 2001, Jenifer Arbaugh worked as a bartender and waitress at the Moonlight Cafe, a New Orleans restaurant owned and operated by Y & H. Arbaugh alleged that Yalcin Hatipoglu, one of the company's owners, sexually harassed her and precipitated her constructive discharge. In November 2001, Arbaugh filed suit against Y & H in the United States District Court for the Eastern District of Louisiana. Her complaint asserted claims under Title VII and Louisiana law.

Arbaugh's pleadings alleged that her federal claim arose under Title VII and that the Federal District Court had jurisdiction over this claim under § 1331 plus supplemental jurisdiction over her state-law claims under § 1367. Y & H's responsive pleadings admitted Arbaugh's jurisdictional allegations but denied her contentions on the merits. The pretrial order submitted and signed by the parties, and later subscribed by the presiding judge, reiterated that the court was vested with jurisdiction over Arbaugh's Title VII claim pursuant to 28 U.S.C. § 1331, and had supplemental jurisdiction over her state law claims pursuant to 28 U.S.C. § 1367. The order listed "Uncontested Material Facts," including: "Plaintiff was employed as a waitress/bartender at the Moonlight for Defendants from May 2000 through February 10, 2001 when she terminated her employment with the company." It did not list among "Contested Issues of Fact" or "Contested Legal Issues" the question whether Y & H had the requisite number of employees . . . . Nor was the issue raised at any other point pretrial or at trial.

. . . . After a two-day trial, the jury found that Arbaugh had been sexually harassed and constructively discharged in violation of Title VII and Louisiana antidiscrimination law. The verdict awarded Arbaugh $5,000 in backpay, $5,000 in compensatory damages, and $30,000 in punitive damages. The trial court entered judgment for Arbaugh on November 5, 2002.

Two weeks later, Y & H filed a motion under Federal Rule 12(h)(3) to dismiss Arbaugh's complaint for lack of subject-matter jurisdiction. As sole ground for the motion, Y & H alleged, for the first time in the proceedings, that it did not employ fifteen or more employees during the relevant period and thus is not an employer for Title VII purposes. The trial court commented that "[i]t is unfair and a waste of judicial resources to permit [Y & H] to admit Arbaugh's allegations of jurisdiction, try the case for two days and then assert a lack of subject matter jurisdiction in response to an adverse jury verdict." Nevertheless, reciting the text of Rule 12(h)(3), the trial court allowed Y & H to plead that it did not qualify as an "employer" under Title VII's definition of that term.

Discovery ensued. The dispute over the employee count turned on the employment status of Y & H's eight drivers, engaged to make deliveries for the restaurant, and the company's four owners (the Moonlight Cafe's two managers and their shareholder spouses). As the trial court noted, if either the delivery drivers or the four owners are counted with the persons shown on the payroll journals, then Y & H employed fifteen or more persons for the requisite time. After reviewing the parties' submissions, however, the trial court concluded that neither the delivery drivers nor the owner-managers nor their shareholder spouses qualified as "employees" for Title VII purposes. Based on that determination, the trial court vacated its prior judgment in favor of Arbaugh, dismissed her Title VII claim with prejudice, and her state-law claims without prejudice.

The Court of Appeals for the Fifth Circuit affirmed . . . . We granted certiorari to resolve conflicting opinions in Courts of Appeals on the question whether Title VII's employee-numerosity requirement is jurisdictional or simply an element of a plaintiff's claim for relief.

III

Jurisdiction, this Court has observed, is a word of many, too many, meanings. This Court, no less than other courts, has sometimes been profligate in its use of the term. For example, this Court and others have occasionally described a nonextendable time limit as mandatory and jurisdictional. But in recent decisions, we have clarified that time prescriptions, however emphatic, are not properly typed "jurisdictional."

. . . . On the subject-matter jurisdiction/ingredient-of-claim-for-relief dichotomy, this Court and others have been less than meticulous. Subject matter jurisdiction in federal-question cases is sometimes erroneously conflated with a plaintiff's need and ability to prove the defendant bound by the federal law asserted as the predicate for relief—a merits-related determination. Judicial opinions, the Second Circuit incisively observed, often obscure the issue by stating that the court is dismissing for lack of jurisdiction when some threshold fact has not been established, without explicitly considering whether the dismissal should be for lack of subject matter jurisdiction or for failure to state a claim. We have described such unrefined dispositions as "drive-by jurisdictional rulings" that should be accorded no precedential effect on the question whether the federal court had authority to adjudicate the claim in suit. . . .

A plaintiff properly invokes § 1331 jurisdiction when she pleads a colorable claim "arising under" the Constitution or laws of the United States. . . . Arbaugh invoked federal-question jurisdiction under § 1331, but her case "aris[es]" under a federal law, Title VII, that specifies, as a prerequisite to its application, the existence of a particular fact, *i.e.*, 15 or more employees. We resolve the question whether that fact is "jurisdictional" or relates to the "merits" of a Title VII claim mindful of the consequences of typing the 15-employee threshold a determinant of subject-matter jurisdiction, rather than an element of Arbaugh's claim for relief.

First, subject-matter jurisdiction, because it involves the court's power to hear a case, can never be forfeited or waived. Moreover, courts, including this Court, have an independent obligation to determine whether subject-matter jurisdiction exists, even in the absence of a challenge from any party. Nothing in the text of Title VII indicates that Congress intended courts, on their own motion, to assure that the employee-numerosity requirement is met.

Second, in some instances, if subject-matter jurisdiction turns on contested facts, the trial judge may be authorized to review the evidence and resolve the dispute on her own. If satisfaction of an essential element of a claim for relief is at issue, however, the jury is the proper trier of contested facts.

Third, when a federal court concludes that it lacks subject-matter jurisdiction, the court must dismiss the complaint in its entirety. Thus in the instant case, the trial court dismissed, along with the Title VII claim, pendent state-law claims, fully tried by a jury and determined on the merits. In contrast, when a court grants a motion to dismiss for failure to state a federal claim, the court generally retains discretion to exercise supplemental jurisdiction, pursuant to 28 U.S.C. § 1367, over pendent state-law claims.

Of course, Congress could make the employee-numerosity requirement "jurisdictional," just as it has made an amount-in-controversy threshold an ingredient of subject-matter jurisdiction in delineating diversity-of-citizenship jurisdiction under 28 U.S.C. § 1332. But neither § 1331, nor Title VII's jurisdictional provision, specifies any threshold ingredient akin to 28 U.S.C. § 1332's monetary floor. Instead, the 15-employee threshold appears in a separate provision that does not speak in jurisdictional terms or refer in any way to the jurisdiction of the district courts. Given the unfairness and waste of judicial resources, entailed in tying the employee-numerosity requirement to subject-matter jurisdiction, we think it the sounder course to refrain from constricting § 1331 or Title VII's jurisdictional provision, and to leave the ball in Congress's court. If the Legislature clearly states that a threshold limitation on a statute's scope shall count as jurisdictional, then courts and litigants will be duly instructed and will not be left to wrestle with the issue. But when Congress does not rank a statutory limitation on coverage as jurisdictional, courts should treat the restriction as nonjurisdictional in character. Applying that readily administrable bright line to this case, we hold that the threshold number of employees for application of Title VII is an element of a plaintiff's claim for relief, not a jurisdictional issue. . . .

For the reasons stated, the judgment of the Court of Appeals is reversed, and the case is remanded for further proceedings consistent with this opinion.

Cases and Controversies

Introduction

The case-or-controversy requirement stems from the Constitution's delegation of judicial power to the judicial branch over "cases" and "controversies." Those two words are limiting. In other words, the judicial power does not extend to something that is neither a "case" nor a "controversy." But the proscriptive force of those two words, coupled with the delegation of a "judicial" power, is difficult to define. Consider the following questions in this topic:

- What are the essential features of a "case" or "controversy"?

- What policies underlie the limitation of the judicial power to "cases" and "controversies"?

- What counterpolicies are affected by that limitation?

United States Constitution

Article III, section 2. The judicial power shall extend to all cases, in law and equity, arising under this Constitution, the laws of the United States, and treaties made, or which shall be made, under their authority; . . . to controversies between two or more states;—between a state and citizens of another state;—between citizens of different states . . . , and between a state, or the citizens thereof, and foreign states, citizens or subjects.

Golden v. Zwickler (1969)

. . . . New York Election Law § 457. . . . makes it a crime to distribute anonymous literature in connection with an election campaign. Zwickler had been convicted of violating this provision by distributing anonymous handbills in connection with the 1964 congressional election. That conviction was reversed, on state law grounds, by the New York Supreme Court, Appellate Term. The New York Court of Appeals affirmed in 1965 and filed a memorandum which stated that constitutional questions had not been reached. A few months thereafter, on April 22, 1966, Zwickler brought this suit.

The complaint sets forth the facts regarding the prosecution and its termination. A Congressman standing for re-election in 1964 was criticized in [Zwickler's] anonymous handbill for opposing two amendments to the 1964 Foreign Aid bill. The complaint alleged that the Congressman "will become a candidate in 1966 for reelection . . . and has been a political figure and public official for many years," and that Zwickler "desires and intends to distribute . . . at the place where he had previously done so and at various places in said (Kings) County, the anonymous leaflet herein described . . . and similar anonymous leaflets . . . at any time during the election campaign of 1966 and in subsequent election campaigns or in connection with any election of party officials, nomination for public office and party position that may occur subsequent to said election campaign of 1966."

It was disclosed . . . that the Congressman had left the House of Representatives [in mid-1966] for a place on the Supreme Court of New York. . . .

The federal courts established pursuant to Article III of the Constitution do not render advisory opinions. For adjudication of constitutional issues, concrete legal issues, presented in actual cases, not abstractions, are requisite. This is as true of declaratory judgments as any other field. . . . Basically, the question in each case is whether the facts alleged, under all the circumstances, show that there is a substantial controversy, between parties having adverse legal interests, of sufficient immediacy and reality to warrant the issuance of a declaratory judgment.

We think that under all the circumstances of the case the fact that it was most unlikely that the Congressman would again be a candidate for Congress precluded a finding that there was sufficient immediacy and reality here.[4] The allegations of the complaint focus upon the then forthcoming 1966 election when, it was alleged, the Congressman would again stand for re-election. The anonymous handbills which the complaint identified as to be distributed in the 1966 and subsequent elections were the 1964 handbill and similar anonymous leaflets. On the record therefore the only supportable conclusion was that Zwickler's sole concern was literature relating to the Congressman and his record. Since the New York statute's prohibition of anonymous handbills applies only to handbills directly pertaining to election campaigns, and the prospect was neither real nor immediate of a campaign involving the Congressman, it was wholly conjectural that another occasion might arise when Zwickler might be prosecuted for distributing the handbills referred to in the complaint. His assertion in his brief that the former Congressman can be a candidate for Congress again is hardly a substitute for evidence that this is a prospect of immediacy and reality. . . .

[4] The . . . term of office as a State Supreme Court Justice is 14 years.

It was not enough to say, as did the District Court, that nevertheless Zwickler has a "further and far broader right to a general adjudication of unconstitutionality . . . (in) (h)is own interest as well as that of others who would with like anonymity practice free speech in a political environment . . . ." The constitutional question, First Amendment or otherwise, must be presented in the context of a specific live grievance. . . .

The judgment of the District Court is reversed, and the case is remanded with direction to enter a new judgment dismissing the complaint.

Muskrat v. United States (1911)

These cases arise under an act of Congress undertaking to confer jurisdiction upon the court of claims, and upon this court, on appeal, to determine the validity of certain acts of Congress hereinafter referred to.

Case No. 330 was brought by David Muskrat and J. Henry Dick, in their own behalf, and in behalf of others in a like situation, to determine the constitutional validity of the act of Congress of April 26, 1906, and to have the same declared invalid in so far as the same undertook to increase the number of persons entitled to share in the final distribution of lands and funds of the Cherokees beyond those enrolled on September 1, 1902, in accordance with the act of Congress passed July 1, 1902. The acts subsequent to that of July 1, 1902, have the effect to increase the number of persons entitled to participate in the division of the Cherokee lands and funds, by permitting the enrollment of children who were minors, living on March 4, 1906, whose parents had theretofore been enrolled as members of the Cherokee tribe, or had applications pending for that purpose.

Case No. 331 was brought by Brown and Gritts on their own behalf and on behalf of other Cherokee citizens having a like interest in the property allotted under the act of July 1, 1902. Under this act, Brown and Gritts received allotments. The subsequent act of March 11, 1904, empowered the Secretary of the Interior to grant rights of way for pipe lines over lands allotted to Indians under certain regulations. Another act, that of April 26, 1906, purported to extend to a period of twenty-five years the time within which full-blooded Indians of the Cherokee, Choctaw, Chickasaw, Creek, and Seminole tribes were forbidden to alienate, sell, dispose of, or encumber certain of their lands.

The object of the petition of Brown and Gritts was to have the subsequent legislation of 1904 and 1906 declared to be unconstitutional and void, and to have the lands allotted to them under the original act of July 1, 1902, adjudged to be theirs free from restraints upon the rights to sell and convey the same. From this statement it is apparent that the purpose of the proceedings instituted in the court of claims, and now appealed to this court, is to restrain the enforcement of such legislation subsequent to the act of July 1, 1902, upon the ground that the same is unconstitutional and void. The court of claims sustained the validity of the acts and dismissed the petitions. . . .

These proceedings were begun under the supposed authority of an act of Congress passed March 1, 1907 (a part of the Indian appropriation bill). As that legislation is important in this connection, so much of the act as authorized the beginning of these suits is here inserted in full:

That William Brown and Levi B. Gritts, on their own behalf and on behalf of all other Cherokee citizens, having like interests in the property allotted under the act of July first, nineteen hundred and two, entitled, 'An Act to Provide for the Allotment of Lands of the Cherokee Nation, for the Disposition of Town Sites Therein, and for Other Purposes,' and David Muskrat and J. Henry Dick, on their own behalf, and on behalf of all Cherokee citizens enrolled as such for allotment as of September first, nineteen hundred and two, be, and they are hereby, authorized and empowered to institute their suits in the court of claims to determine the validity of any acts of Congress passed since the said act of July first, nineteen hundred and two, in so far as said acts, or any of them, attempt to increase or extend the restrictions upon alienation, encumbrance, or the right to lease the allotments of lands of Cherokee citizens, or to increase the number of persons entitled to share in the final distribution of lands and funds of the Cherokees beyond those enrolled for allotment as of September first, nineteen hundred and two, and provided for in the said act of July first, nineteen hundred and two.

And jurisdiction is hereby conferred upon the court of claims, with the right of appeal, by either party, to the Supreme Court of the United States, to hear, determine, and adjudicate each of said suits.

The suits brought hereunder shall be brought on or before September first, nineteen hundred and seven, against the United States as a party defendant, and, for the speedy disposition of the questions involved, preference shall be given to the same by said courts, and by the Attorney General, who is hereby charged with the defense of said suits.

Upon the rendition of final judgment by the court of claims or the Supreme Court of the United States, denying the validity of any portion of the said acts authorized to be brought into question, in either or both of said cases, the court of claims shall determine the amount to be paid the attorneys employed by the above-named parties in the prosecution thereof for services and expenses, and shall render judgment therefor, which shall be paid out of the funds in the United States Treasury belonging to the beneficiaries, under the said act of July first, nineteen hundred and two.

This act is the authority for the maintenance of these two suits.

The first question in these cases, as in others, involves the jurisdiction of the court to entertain the proceeding, and that depends upon whether the jurisdiction conferred is within the power of Congress, having in view the limitations of the judicial power, as established by the Constitution of the United States. . . .

The subject underwent a complete examination [when] an act of Congress was held invalid which undertook to confer jurisdiction upon the court of claims, and thence by appeal to this court, the judgment, however, not to be paid until an appropriation had been estimated therefore by the Secretary of the Treasury; and, as was said by the chief justice, the result was that neither court could enforce its judgment by any process, and whether it was to be paid or not depended on the future action of the Secretary of the Treasury and of Congress. "The Supreme Court," says the Chief Justice, "does not owe its existence or its powers to the legislative department of the government. It is created by the Constitution, and represents one of the three great divisions of power in the government of the United States, to each of which the Constitution has assigned its appropriate duties and powers, and made each independent of the other in performing its appropriate functions. The power conferred on this court is exclusively judicial, and it cannot be required or authorized to exercise any other." . . .

It therefore becomes necessary to inquire what is meant by the judicial power thus conferred by the Constitution upon this court, and, with the aid of appropriate legislation, upon the inferior courts of the United States. "Judicial power," says Mr. Justice Miller, in his work on the Constitution, "is the power of a court to decide and pronounce a judgment and carry it into effect between persons and parties who bring a case before it for decision."

As we have already seen, by the express terms of the Constitution, the exercise of the judicial power is limited to "cases" and "controversies." Beyond this it does not extend, and unless it is asserted in a case or controversy within the meaning of the Constitution, the power to exercise it is nowhere conferred.

What, then, does the Constitution mean in conferring this judicial power with the right to determine "cases" and "controversies." A "case" was defined by Mr. Chief Justice Marshall as early as the leading case of *Marbury v. Madison* to be a suit instituted according to the regular course of judicial procedure. And what more, if anything, is meant in the use of the term "controversy?" That question was dealt with by Mr. Justice Field, at the circuit, in the case of *Re Pacific R. Commission*. Of these terms that learned justice said:

> The judicial article of the Constitution mentions cases and controversies. The term "controversies," if distinguishable at all from "cases," is so in that it is less comprehensive than the latter, and includes only suits of a civil nature. *Chisholm v. Georgia*. By cases and controversies are intended the claims of litigants brought before the courts for determination by such regular proceedings as are established by law or custom for the protection or enforcement of rights, or the prevention, redress, or punishment of wrongs. Whenever the claim of a party under the Constitution, laws, or treaties of the United States takes such a form that the judicial power is capable of

acting upon it, then it has become a case. The term implies the existence of present or possible adverse parties, whose contentions are submitted to the court for adjudication.

The power being thus limited to require an application of the judicial power to cases and controversies, is the act which undertook to authorize the present suits to determine the constitutional validity of certain legislation within the constitutional authority of the court? This inquiry in the case before us includes the broader question, when may this court, in the exercise of the judicial power, pass upon the constitutional validity of an act of Congress? That question has been settled from the early history of the court, the leading case on the subject being *Marbury v. Madison*.

In that case Chief Justice Marshall, who spoke for the court, was careful to point out that the right to declare an act of Congress unconstitutional could only be exercised when a proper case between opposing parties was submitted for judicial determination; that there was no general veto power in the court upon the legislation of Congress; and that the authority to declare an act unconstitutional sprang from the requirement that the court, in administering the law and pronouncing judgment between the parties to a case, and choosing between the requirements of the fundamental law established by the people and embodied in the Constitution and an act of the agents of the people, acting under authority of the Constitution, should enforce the Constitution as the supreme law of the land. The Chief Justice demonstrated, in a manner which has been regarded as settling the question, that with the choice thus given between a constitutional requirement and a conflicting statutory enactment, the plain duty of the court was to follow and enforce the Constitution as the supreme law established by the people. And the court recognized, in *Marbury v. Madison* and subsequent cases, that the exercise of this great power could only be invoked in cases which came regularly before the courts for determination . . . .

Again, in the case of *Cohen v. Virginia*, Chief Justice Marshall, amplifying and reasserting the doctrine of *Marbury v. Madison*, recognized the limitations upon the right of this court to declare an act of Congress unconstitutional, and granting that there might be instances of its violation which could not be brought within the jurisdiction of the courts, and referring to a grant by a state of a patent of nobility as a case of that class, and conceding that the court would have no power to annul such a grant, said:

This may be very true; but by no means justifies the inference drawn from it. The article does not extend the judicial power to every violation of the Constitution which may possibly take place, but to "a case in law or equity" in which a right under such law is asserted in a court of justice. If the question cannot be brought into a court, then there is no case in law or equity, and no jurisdiction is given by the words of the article. But if, in any controversy depending in a court, the cause should depend on the validity of such a law, that would be a case arising under the Constitution, to which the judicial power of the United States would extend. The same observation applies to the other instances with which the counsel who opened the cause has illustrated this argument. Although they show that there may be violations of the Constitution of which the courts can take no cognizance, they do not show that an interpretation more restrictive than the words themselves import ought to be given to this article. They do not show that there can be "a *case* in law or equity" arising under the Constitution, to which the judicial power does not extend. . . .

Applying the principles thus long settled by the decisions of this court to the act of Congress undertaking to confer jurisdiction in this case, we find that William Brown and Levi B. Gritts . . . are authorized and empowered to institute suits in the court of claims to determine the validity of acts of Congress passed since the act of July 1, 1902 . . . .

The jurisdiction was given for that purpose first to the court of claims, and then upon appeal to this court. That is, the object and purpose of the suit is wholly comprised in the determination of the constitutional validity of certain acts of Congress; and furthermore, in the last paragraph of the section, should a judgment be rendered in the court of claims or this court, denying the constitutional validity of such acts, then the amount of compensation to be paid to attorneys employed for the purpose of testing the constitutionality of the law is to be paid out of funds in the Treasury of the United States belonging to the beneficiaries, the act having previously provided that the United States should be made a party, and the Attorney General be charged with the defense of the suits.

It is therefore evident that there is neither more nor less in this procedure than an attempt to provide for a judicial determination, final in this court, of the constitutional validity of an act of Congress. Is such a determination within the judicial power conferred by the Constitution, as the same has been interpreted and defined in the authoritative decisions to which we have referred? We think it is not. That judicial power, as we have seen, is the right to determine actual controversies arising between adverse litigants, duly instituted in courts of proper jurisdiction. The right to declare a law unconstitutional arises because an act of Congress relied upon by one or the other of such parties in determining their rights is in conflict with the fundamental law. The exercise of this, the most important and delicate duty of this court, is not given to it as a body with revisory power over the action of Congress, but because the rights of the litigants in justiciable controversies require the court to choose between the fundamental law and a law purporting to be enacted within constitutional authority, but in fact beyond the power delegated to the legislative branch of the government. This attempt to obtain a judicial declaration of the validity of the act of Congress is not presented in a "case" or "controversy," to which, under the Constitution of the United States, the judicial power alone extends. It is true the United States is made a defendant to this action, but it has no interest adverse to the claimants. The object is not to assert a property right as against the government, or to demand compensation for alleged wrongs because of action upon its part. The whole purpose of the law is to determine the constitutional validity of this class of legislation, in a suit not arising between parties concerning a property right necessarily involved in the decision in question, but in a proceeding against the government in its sovereign capacity, and concerning which the only judgment required is to settle the doubtful character of the legislation in question. Such judgment will not conclude private parties, when actual litigation brings to the court the question of the constitutionality of such legislation In a legal sense the judgment could not be executed, and amounts in fact to no more than an expression of opinion upon the validity of the acts in question. Confining the jurisdiction of this court within the limitations conferred by the Constitution, which the court has hitherto been careful to observe, and whose boundaries it has refused to transcend, we think the Congress exceeded the limitations of legislative authority, so far as it required of this court action not judicial in its nature within the meaning of the Constitution.

Nor can it make any difference that the petitioners had brought suits in the supreme court of the District of Columbia to enjoin the Secretary of the Interior from carrying into effect the legislation subsequent to the act of July 1, 1902, which suits were pending when the jurisdictional act here involved was passed. The latter act must depend upon its own terms and be judged by the authority which it undertakes to confer. If such actions as are here attempted, to determine the validity of legislation, are sustained, the result will be that this court, instead of keeping within the limits of judicial power, and deciding cases or controversies arising between opposing parties, as the Constitution intended it should, will be required to give opinions in the nature of advice concerning legislative action,—a function never conferred upon it by the Constitution, and against the exercise of which this court has steadily set its face from the beginning.

The questions involved in this proceeding as to the validity of the legislation may arise in suits between individuals, and when they do and are properly brought before this court for consideration they, of course, must be determined in the exercise of its judicial functions. For the reasons we have stated, we are constrained to hold that these actions present no justiciable controversy within the authority of the court, acting within the limitations of the Constitution under which it was created. As Congress, in passing this act, as a part of the plan involved, evidently intended to provide a review of the judgment of the court of claims in this court, as the constitutionality of important legislation is concerned, we think the act cannot be held to intend to confer jurisdiction on that court separately considered.

The judgments will be reversed and the cases remanded to the Court of Claims, with directions to dismiss the petitions for want of jurisdiction.

MedImmune, Inc. v. Genentech, Inc. (2007)

Justice SCALIA delivered the opinion of the Court.

We must decide whether Article III's limitation of federal courts' jurisdiction to "Cases" and "Controversies," reflected in the "actual controversy" requirement of the Declaratory Judgment Act, 28 U.S.C. § 2201(a), requires a patent licensee to terminate or be in breach of its license agreement before it can seek a declaratory judgment that the underlying patent is invalid, unenforceable, or not infringed.

I

. . . . Petitioner MedImmune, Inc., manufactures Synagis, a drug used to prevent respiratory tract disease in infants and young children. In 1997, petitioner entered into a patent license agreement with respondent Genentech, Inc. . . . Petitioner agreed to pay royalties on sales of "Licensed Products," and respondents granted petitioner the right to make, use, and sell them. . . . [Later,] Genentech delivered petitioner a letter expressing its belief that Synagis was covered by [its] . . . patent and its expectation that petitioner would pay royalties beginning March 1, 2002. Petitioner did not think royalties were owing, believing that the . . . patent was invalid and unenforceable, and that its claims were in any event not infringed by Synagis. Nevertheless, petitioner considered the letter to be a clear threat to enforce the . . . patent, terminate the 1997 license agreement, and sue for patent infringement if petitioner did not make royalty payments as demanded. If respondents were to prevail in a patent infringement action, petitioner could be ordered to pay treble damages and attorney's fees, and could be enjoined from selling Synagis, a product that has accounted for more than 80 percent of its revenue from sales since 1999. Unwilling to risk such serious consequences, petitioner paid the demanded royalties under protest and with reservation of all of its rights. This declaratory-judgment action followed.

Petitioner sought the declaratory relief discussed in detail in Part II below. Petitioner also requested damages and an injunction with respect to other federal and state claims not relevant here. The District Court granted respondents' motion to dismiss the declaratory-judgment claims for lack of subject-matter jurisdiction . . . . The Federal Circuit affirmed . . . . . We granted certiorari. . . .

III

The Declaratory Judgment Act provides that, "[i]n a case of actual controversy within its jurisdiction . . . any court of the United States . . . may declare the rights and other legal relations of any interested party seeking such declaration, whether or not further relief is or could be sought." There was a time when this Court harbored doubts about the compatibility of declaratory-judgment actions with Article III's case-or-controversy requirement. We dispelled those doubts, however, holding (in a case involving a declaratory judgment rendered in state court) that an appropriate action for declaratory relief *can* be a case or controversy under Article III. The federal Declaratory Judgment Act was signed into law the following year, and we upheld its constitutionality in *Aetna Life Ins. Co. v. Haworth*. Our opinion explained that the phrase "case of actual controversy" in the Act refers to the type of "Cases" and "Controversies" that are justiciable under Article III.

Aetna and the cases following it do not draw the brightest of lines between those declaratory-judgment actions that satisfy the case-or-controversy requirement and those that do not. Our decisions have required that the dispute be definite and concrete, touching the legal relations of parties having adverse legal interests; and that it be real and substantial and admit of specific relief through a decree of a conclusive character, as distinguished from an opinion advising what the law would be upon a hypothetical state of facts. Basically, the question in each case is whether the facts alleged, under all the circumstances, show that there is a substantial controversy, between parties having adverse legal interests, of sufficient immediacy and reality to warrant the issuance of a declaratory judgment.[7]

> [7] The dissent asserts that the declaratory judgment procedure cannot be used to obtain advanced rulings on matters that would be addressed in a future case of actual controversy. As our preceding discussion shows, that is not so. If the dissent's point is simply that a defense cannot be raised by means of a declaratory judgment action where there is no "actual controversy" or where it would be "premature," phrasing that argument as the dissent has done begs the question: whether this is an actual, ripe controversy. . . .

There is no dispute that these standards would have been satisfied if petitioner had taken the final step of refusing to make royalty payments under the 1997 license agreement. Respondents claim a right to royalties under the licensing agreement. Petitioner asserts that no royalties are owing because the . . . patent is invalid and not infringed; and alleges (without contradiction) a threat by respondents to enjoin sales if royalties are not forthcoming. The factual and legal dimensions of the dispute are well defined and, but for petitioner's continuing to make royalty payments, nothing about the dispute would render it unfit for judicial resolution. Assuming (without deciding) that respondents here could not claim an anticipatory breach and repudiate the license, the continuation of royalty payments makes what would otherwise be an imminent threat at least remote, if not nonexistent. As long as those payments are made, there is no risk that respondents will seek to enjoin petitioner's sales. Petitioner's own acts, in other words, eliminate the imminent threat of harm.[8] The question before us is whether this causes the dispute no longer to be a case or controversy within the meaning of Article III.

[8] The justiciability problem that arises, when the party seeking declaratory relief is himself preventing the complained-of injury from occurring, can be described in terms of standing (whether plaintiff is threatened with "imminent" injury in fact fairly . . . traceable to the challenged action of the defendant, or in terms of ripeness (whether there is sufficient hardship to the parties [in] withholding court consideration until there is enforcement action, *Abbott Laboratories v. Gardner*). As respondents acknowledge, standing and ripeness boil down to the same question in this case.

Our analysis must begin with the recognition that, where threatened action by *government* is concerned, we do not require a plaintiff to expose himself to liability before bringing suit to challenge the basis for the threat-for example, the constitutionality of a law threatened to be enforced. The plaintiff's own action (or inaction) in failing to violate the law eliminates the imminent threat of prosecution, but nonetheless does not eliminate Article III jurisdiction. . . . The dilemma posed by that coercion—putting the challenger to the choice between abandoning his rights or risking prosecution—is a dilemma that it was the very purpose of the Declaratory Judgment Act to ameliorate. *See Abbott Laboratories.*

Supreme Court jurisprudence is more rare regarding application of the Declaratory Judgment Act to situations in which the plaintiff's self-avoidance of imminent injury is coerced by threatened enforcement action of *a private party* rather than the government. Lower federal courts, however (and state courts interpreting declaratory judgment Acts requiring "actual controversy"), have long accepted jurisdiction in such cases. The only Supreme Court decision in point is, fortuitously, close on its facts to the case before us. . . .

Lastly, respondents urge us to affirm the dismissal of the declaratory-judgment claims on discretionary grounds. The Declaratory Judgment Act provides that a court "*may* declare the rights and other legal relations of any interested party," not that it *must* do so. This text has long been understood to confer on federal courts unique and substantial discretion in deciding whether to declare the rights of litigants. We have found it more consistent with the statute, however, to vest district courts with discretion in the first instance, because facts bearing on the usefulness of the declaratory judgment remedy, and the fitness of the case for resolution, are peculiarly within their grasp. . . . Respondents have raised the issue for the first time before this Court, exchanging competing accusations of inequitable conduct with petitioner. Under these circumstances, it would be imprudent for us to decide whether the District Court should, or must, decline to issue the requested declaratory relief. We leave the equitable, prudential, and policy arguments in favor of such a discretionary dismissal for the lower courts' consideration on remand. Similarly available for consideration on remand are any merits-based arguments for denial of declaratory relief.

* * *

We hold that petitioner was not required, insofar as Article III is concerned, to break or terminate its 1997 license agreement before seeking a declaratory judgment in federal court that the underlying patent is invalid, unenforceable, or not infringed. The Court of Appeals erred in affirming the dismissal of this action for lack of subject-matter jurisdiction.

The judgment of the Court of Appeals is reversed, and the cause is remanded for proceedings consistent with this opinion.

Justice THOMAS, dissenting.

We granted certiorari in this case to determine whether a patent licensee in good standing must breach its license prior to challenging the validity of the underlying patent pursuant to the Declaratory Judgment Act. The answer to that question is yes. We have consistently held that parties do not have standing to obtain rulings on matters that remain hypothetical or conjectural. We have also held that the declaratory judgment procedure cannot be used to obtain advanced rulings on matters that would be addressed in a future case of actual controversy. MedImmune has sought a declaratory judgment for precisely that purpose, and I would therefore affirm the Court of Appeals's holding that there is no Article III jurisdiction over MedImmune's claim. . . .

I

. . . . In the context of declaratory judgment actions, this Court's cases have provided a uniform framework for assessing whether an Article III case or controversy exists. In the constitutional sense, a "Controversy" is distinguished from a difference or dispute of a hypothetical or abstract character; from one that is academic or moot. The controversy must be definite and concrete, touching the legal relations of parties having adverse legal interests. Finally, it must be a real and substantial controversy . . . as distinguished from an opinion advising what the law would be upon a hypothetical state of facts.

The Declaratory Judgment Act did not (and could not) alter the constitutional definition of "case or controversy" or relax Article III's command that an actual case or controversy exist before federal courts may adjudicate a question. Thus, this Court has held that the operation of the Declaratory Judgment Act is procedural only. In other words, the Act merely provides a different procedure for bringing an actual case or controversy before a federal court. . . . We have also held that no controversy exists when a declaratory judgment plaintiff attempts to obtain a premature ruling on potential defenses that would typically be adjudicated in a later actual controversy. . . . These principles apply with equal force in the patent licensing context.

II

Against the foregoing background, the case before us is not a justiciable case or controversy under Article III. . . .

B

The facts before us present no case or controversy under Article III. When MedImmune filed this declaratory judgment action challenging the validity of the Cabilly II patent, it was under no threat of being sued by Genentech for patent infringement. This was so because MedImmune was a licensee in good standing that had made all necessary royalty payments. Thus, by voluntarily entering into and abiding by a license agreement with Genentech, MedImmune removed any threat of suit. MedImmune's actions in entering into and continuing to comply with the license agreement deprived Genentech of any cause of action against MedImmune. Additionally, MedImmune had no cause of action against Genentech. Patent invalidity is an affirmative defense to patent infringement, not a freestanding cause of action. Therefore, here, the Declaratory Judgment Act must be something more than an alternative procedure for bringing on otherwise actual case or controversy before a federal court.

Because neither Genentech nor MedImmune had a cause of action, MedImmune's prayer for declaratory relief can be reasonably understood only as seeking an advisory opinion about an affirmative defense it might use in some future litigation. MedImmune wants to know whether, if it decides to breach its license agreement with Genentech, and if Genentech sues it for patent infringement, it will have a successful affirmative defense. Presumably, upon a favorable determination, MedImmune would then stop making royalty payments, knowing in advance that the federal courts stand behind its decision. Yet as demonstrated above, the Declaratory Judgment Act does not allow federal courts to give advisory rulings on the potential success of an affirmative defense before a cause of action has even accrued. MedImmune has therefore asked the courts to render an opinion advising what the law would be upon a hypothetical state of facts. A federal court cannot, consistent with Article III, provide MedImmune with such an opinion.

Finally, as this Court has plainly stated in the context of a counterclaim declaratory judgment action challenging the validity of a patent, to hold a patent valid if it is not infringed is to decide a hypothetical case. Of course, MedImmune presents exactly that case. Based on a clear reading of our precedent, I would hold that this case presents no actual case or controversy.

III

. . . . The majority explains that the coercive nature of the exaction preserves the right to challenge the legality of the claim. The coercive nature of what "exaction"? The answer has to be the voluntarily made license payments because there was no threat of suit here. By holding that contractual obligations are sufficiently coercive to allow a party to bring a declaratory judgment action, the majority has given every patent licensee a cause of action and a free pass around Article III's requirements for challenging the validity of licensed patents. But the reasoning of today's opinion applies not just to patent validity suits. Indeed, today's opinion contains no limiting principle whatsoever . . . .

For the foregoing reasons, I respectfully dissent.

Standing

Introduction

The constitutional case-or-controversy doctrine has spawned a number of related doctrines, or perhaps subspecies, including standing, ripeness, and mootness. Standing can be seen as a requirement focused on the particular plaintiff: does *this* plaintiff have a sufficient stake in the case to produce a "case" or "controversy" fit for judicial resolution? Beyond the constitutional dimensions, standing also has practical implications, for an insufficiently interested plaintiff who fails to zealously advocate can impoverish a federal court's decisionmaking process. Standing doctrine thus implements—but also goes beyond the bare textual source of—the case-or-controversy doctrine. Consider the opinions below in light of the following questions:

- What policies support, and what policies undermine, standing?

- What are the requirements of standing? Are they workable? Do they effectively implement its policies?

- Which components of standing are constitutional and which are prudential? Why?

- Could there be cases in which no one has standing? If so, is that acceptable?

Allen v. Wright (1984)

Justice O'CONNOR delivered the opinion of the Court.

Parents of black public school children allege in this nation-wide class action that the Internal Revenue Service (IRS) has not adopted sufficient standards and procedures to fulfill its obligation to deny tax-exempt status to racially discriminatory private schools. They assert that the IRS thereby harms them directly and interferes with the ability of their children to receive an education in desegregated public schools. The issue before us is whether plaintiffs have standing to bring this suit. We hold that they do not.

I

The IRS denies tax-exempt status . . . and hence eligibility to receive charitable contributions deductible from income taxes . . . to racially discriminatory private schools. . . . The IRS policy requires that a school applying for tax-exempt status show that it admits the students of any race to all the rights, privileges, programs, and activities generally accorded or made available to students at that school and that the school does not discriminate on the basis of race in administration of its educational policies, admissions policies, scholarship and loan programs, and athletic and other school-administered programs. To carry out this policy, the IRS has established guidelines and procedures for determining whether a particular school is in fact racially nondiscriminatory. . . . Failure to comply with the guidelines will ordinarily result in the proposed revocation of tax-exempt status. . . .

The IRS rules require a school applying for tax-exempt status to give a breakdown along racial lines of its student body and its faculty and administrative staff, as well as of scholarships and loans awarded. They also require the applicant school to state the year of its organization, and to list incorporators, founders, board members, and donors of land or buildings, and state whether any of the organizations among these have an objective of maintaining segregated public or private school education. The rules further provide that, once given an exemption, a school must keep specified records to document the extent of compliance with the IRS guidelines. Finally, the rules announce that any information concerning discrimination at a tax-exempt school is officially welcomed.

In 1976 respondents challenged these guidelines and procedures in a suit filed in Federal District Court against the Secretary of the Treasury and the Commissioner of Internal Revenue. The plaintiffs named in the complaint are parents of black children who, at the time the complaint was filed, were attending public schools in seven States in school districts undergoing desegregation. They brought this nationwide class action on behalf of themselves and their children, and on behalf of all other parents of black children attending public school systems undergoing, or which may in the future undergo, desegregation pursuant to court order or HEW regulations and guidelines, under state law, or voluntarily. They estimated that the class they seek to represent includes several million persons.

Respondents allege in their complaint that many racially segregated private schools were created or expanded in their communities at the time the public schools were undergoing desegregation. According to the complaint, many such private schools, including 17 schools or school systems identified by name in the complaint (perhaps some 30 schools in all), receive tax exemptions either directly or through the tax-exempt status of "umbrella" organizations that operate or support the schools. Respondents allege that, despite the IRS policy of denying tax-exempt status to racially discriminatory private schools and despite the IRS guidelines and procedures for implementing that policy, some of the tax-exempt racially segregated private schools created or expanded in desegregating districts in fact have racially discriminatory policies. Respondents allege that the IRS grant of tax exemptions to such racially discriminatory schools is unlawful.

Respondents allege that the challenged Government conduct harms them in two ways. The challenged conduct (a) constitutes tangible federal financial aid and other support for racially segregated educational institutions, and (b) fosters and encourages the organization, operation and expansion of institutions providing racially segregated educational opportunities for white children avoiding attendance in desegregating public school districts and thereby interferes with the efforts of federal courts, HEW and local school authorities to desegregate public school districts which have been operating racially dual school systems.

Thus, respondents do not allege that their children have been the victims of discriminatory exclusion from the schools whose tax exemptions they challenge as unlawful. Indeed, they have not alleged at any stage of this litigation that their children have ever applied or would ever apply to any private school. Rather, respondents claim a direct injury from the mere fact of the challenged Government conduct and, as indicated by the restriction of the plaintiff class to parents of children in desegregating school districts, injury to their children's opportunity to receive a desegregated education. The latter injury is traceable to the IRS grant of tax exemptions to racially discriminatory schools, respondents allege, chiefly because contributions to such schools are deductible from income taxes under . . . the Internal Revenue Code and the deductions facilitate the raising of funds to organize new schools and expand existing schools in order to accommodate white students avoiding attendance in desegregating public school districts.

Respondents request only prospective relief. They ask for a declaratory judgment that the challenged IRS tax-exemption practices are unlawful. They also ask for an injunction requiring the IRS to deny tax exemptions to a considerably broader class of private schools than the class of racially discriminatory private schools. . . . Finally, respondents ask for an order directing the IRS to replace its 1975 guidelines with standards consistent with the requested injunction. . . .

The District Court . . . granted the defendants' motion to dismiss the complaint, concluding that respondents lack standing, that the judicial task proposed by respondents is inappropriately intrusive for a federal court, and that awarding the requested relief would be contrary to the will of Congress expressed in the 1979 ban on strengthening IRS guidelines.

The United States Court of Appeals for the District of Columbia Circuit reversed, concluding that respondents have standing to maintain this lawsuit. The court . . . observed [that] the sole injury respondents claim is the denigration they suffer as black parents and schoolchildren when their government graces with tax-exempt status educational institutions in their communities that treat members of their race as persons of lesser worth. The court held this denigration injury enough to give respondents standing . . . . The court accordingly remanded the case to the District Court for further proceedings, enjoining the defendants meanwhile from granting tax-exempt status to any racially discriminatory school . . . .We granted certiorari, and now reverse.

II
A

Article III of the Constitution confines the federal courts to adjudicating actual "cases" and "controversies." [T]he "case or controversy" requirement defines with respect to the Judicial Branch the idea of separation of powers on which the Federal Government is founded. The several doctrines that have grown up to elaborate that requirement are founded in concern about the proper—and properly limited—role of the courts in a democratic society.

All of the doctrines that cluster about Article III—not only standing but mootness, ripeness, political question, and the like—relate in part, and in different though overlapping ways, to an idea, which is more than an intuition but less than a rigorous and explicit theory, about the constitutional and prudential limits to the powers of an unelected, unrepresentative judiciary in our kind of government. The case-or-controversy doctrines state fundamental limits on federal judicial power in our system of government.

The Art. III doctrine that requires a litigant to have "standing" to invoke the power of a federal court is perhaps the most important of these doctrines. In essence the question of standing is whether the litigant is entitled to have the court decide the merits of the dispute or of particular issues. Standing doctrine embraces several judicially self-imposed limits on the exercise of federal jurisdiction, such as the general prohibition on a litigant's raising another person's legal rights, the rule barring adjudication of generalized grievances more appropriately addressed in the representative branches, and the requirement that a plaintiff's complaint fall within the zone of interests protected by the law invoked. The requirement of standing, however, has a core component derived directly from the Constitution. A plaintiff must allege personal injury fairly traceable to the defendant's allegedly unlawful conduct and likely to be redressed by the requested relief.

Like the prudential component, the constitutional component of standing doctrine incorporates concepts concededly not susceptible of precise definition. The injury alleged must be, for example, distinct and palpable, and not abstract or conjectural or hypothetical. The injury must be fairly traceable to the challenged action, and relief from the injury must be likely to follow from a favorable decision. These terms cannot be defined so as to make application of the constitutional standing requirement a mechanical exercise.

The . . . . law of Art. III standing is built on a single basic idea—the idea of separation of powers. It is this fact which makes possible the gradual clarification of the law through judicial application. . . .

Determining standing in a particular case may be facilitated by clarifying principles or even clear rules developed in prior cases. Typically, however, the standing inquiry requires careful judicial examination of a complaint's allegations to ascertain whether the particular plaintiff is entitled to an adjudication of the particular claims asserted. Is the injury too abstract, or otherwise not appropriate, to be considered judicially cognizable? Is the line of causation between the illegal conduct and injury too attenuated? Is the prospect of obtaining relief from the injury as a result of a favorable ruling too speculative? These questions and any others relevant to the standing inquiry must be answered by reference to the Art. III notion that federal courts may exercise power only in the last resort, and as a necessity, and only when adjudication is consistent with a system of separated powers and the dispute is one traditionally thought to be capable of resolution through the judicial process.

B

Respondents allege two injuries in their complaint to support their standing to bring this lawsuit. First, they say that they are harmed directly by the mere fact of Government financial aid to discriminatory private schools. Second, they say that the federal tax exemptions to racially discriminatory private schools in their communities impair their ability to have their public schools desegregated.

In the Court of Appeals, respondents apparently relied on the first injury. Thus, the court below asserted that the sole injury respondents claim is the denigration they suffer as a result of the tax exemptions. In this Court, respondents have not focused on this claim of injury. Here they stress the effect of the tax exemptions on their equal educational opportunities.

Because respondents have not clearly disclaimed reliance on either of the injuries described in their complaint, we address both allegations of injury. We conclude that neither suffices to support respondents' standing. The first fails under clear precedents of this Court because it does not constitute judicially cognizable injury. The second fails because the alleged injury is not fairly traceable to the assertedly unlawful conduct of the IRS.

1

Respondents' first claim of injury can be interpreted in two ways. It might be a claim simply to have the Government avoid the violation of law alleged in respondents' complaint. Alternatively, it might be a claim of stigmatic injury, or denigration, suffered by all members of a racial group when the Government discriminates on the basis of race. Under neither interpretation is this claim of injury judicially cognizable.

This Court has repeatedly held that an asserted right to have the Government act in accordance with law is not sufficient, standing alone, to confer jurisdiction on a federal court. . . . Assertion of a right to a particular kind of Government conduct, which the Government has violated by acting differently, cannot alone satisfy the requirements of Art. III without draining those requirements of meaning. Respondents here have no standing to complain simply that their Government is violating the law.

Neither do they have standing to litigate their claims based on the stigmatizing injury often caused by racial discrimination. There can be no doubt that this sort of noneconomic injury is one of the most serious consequences of discriminatory government action and is sufficient in some circumstances to support standing. Our cases make clear, however, that such injury accords a basis for standing only to those persons who are personally denied equal treatment by the challenged discriminatory conduct. . . . Insofar as their first claim of injury is concerned, respondents are in exactly the same position: . . . they do not allege a stigmatic injury suffered as a direct result of having personally been denied equal treatment.

The consequences of recognizing respondents' standing on the basis of their first claim of injury illustrate why our cases plainly hold that such injury is not judicially cognizable. If the abstract stigmatic injury were cognizable, standing would extend nationwide to all members of the particular racial groups against which the Government was alleged to be discriminating by its grant of a tax exemption to a racially discriminatory school, regardless of the location of that school. All such persons could claim the same sort of abstract stigmatic injury respondents assert in their first claim of injury. A black person in Hawaii could challenge the grant of a tax exemption to a racially discriminatory school in Maine. Recognition of standing in such circumstances would transform the federal courts into no more than a vehicle for the vindication of the value interests of concerned bystanders. Constitutional limits on the role of the federal courts preclude such a transformation.

2

It is in their complaint's second claim of injury that respondents allege harm to a concrete, personal interest that can support standing in some circumstances. The injury they identify— their children's diminished ability to receive an education in a racially integrated school— is, beyond any doubt, not only judicially cognizable but, as shown by cases . . . , one of the most serious injuries recognized in our legal system. Despite the constitutional importance of curing the injury alleged by respondents, however, the federal judiciary may not redress it unless standing requirements are met. In this case, respondents' second claim of injury cannot support standing because the injury alleged is not fairly traceable to the Government conduct respondents challenge as unlawful.[22]

> [22] Respondents' stigmatic injury, though not sufficient for standing in the abstract form in which their complaint asserts it, is judicially cognizable to the extent that respondents are personally subject to discriminatory treatment. The stigmatic injury thus requires identification of some concrete interest with respect to which respondents are personally subject to discriminatory treatment. That interest must independently satisfy the causation requirement of standing doctrine. . . . In this litigation, respondents identify only one interest that they allege is being discriminatorily impaired—their interest in desegregated public school education. Respondents' asserted stigmatic injury, therefore, is sufficient to support their standing in this litigation only if their school-desegregation injury independently meets the causation requirement of standing doctrine.

The illegal conduct challenged by respondents is the IRS's grant of tax exemptions to some racially discriminatory schools. The line of causation between that conduct and desegregation of respondents' schools is attenuated at best. From the perspective of the IRS, the injury to respondents is highly indirect and results from the independent action of some third party not before the court. As the Court pointed out . . . , the indirectness of the injury . . . may make it substantially more difficult to meet the minimum requirement of Art. III. . . .

The diminished ability of respondents' children to receive a desegregated education would be fairly traceable to unlawful IRS grants of tax exemptions only if there were enough racially discriminatory private schools receiving tax exemptions in respondents' communities for withdrawal of those exemptions to make an appreciable difference in public school integration. Respondents have made no such allegation. It is, first, uncertain how many racially discriminatory private schools are in fact receiving tax exemptions. Moreover, it is entirely speculative, as respondents themselves conceded in the Court of Appeals, whether withdrawal of a tax exemption from any particular school would lead the school to change its policies. It is just as speculative whether any given parent of a child attending such a private school would decide to transfer the child to public school as a result of any changes in educational or financial policy made by the private school once it was threatened with loss of tax-exempt status. It is also pure speculation whether, in a particular community, a large enough number of the numerous relevant school officials and parents would reach decisions that collectively would have a significant impact on the racial composition of the public schools.

The links in the chain of causation between the challenged Government conduct and the asserted injury are far too weak for the chain as a whole to sustain respondents' standing. . . . It involves numerous third parties (officials of racially discriminatory schools receiving tax exemptions and the parents of children attending such schools) who may not even exist in respondents' communities and whose independent decisions may not collectively have a significant effect on the ability of public school students to receive a desegregated education.

The idea of separation of powers that underlies standing doctrine explains why our cases preclude the conclusion that respondents' alleged injury fairly can be traced to the challenged action of the IRS. That conclusion would pave the way generally for suits challenging, not specifically identifiable Government violations of law, but the particular programs agencies establish to carry out their legal obligations. Such suits, even when premised on allegations of several instances of violations of law, are rarely if ever appropriate for federal-court adjudication.

Carried to its logical end, respondents' approach would have the federal courts as virtually continuing monitors of the wisdom and soundness of Executive action; such a role is appropriate for the Congress acting through its committees and the power of the purse; it is not the role of the judiciary, absent actual present or immediately threatened injury resulting from unlawful governmental action. . . . Animating this Court's holdings was the principle that a federal court . . . is not the proper forum to press general complaints about the way in which government goes about its business. . . .

When transported into the Art. III context, that principle, grounded as it is in the idea of separation of powers, counsels against recognizing standing in a case brought, not to enforce specific legal obligations whose violation works a direct harm, but to seek a restructuring of the apparatus established by the Executive Branch to fulfill its legal duties. The Constitution, after all, assigns to the Executive Branch, and not to the Judicial Branch, the duty to take

Care that the Laws be faithfully executed. U.S. Const., Art. II, § 3. We could not recognize respondents' standing in this case without running afoul of that structural principle.[26] . . .

[26] We disagree with Justice Stevens's suggestions that separation of powers principles merely underlie standing requirements, have no role to play in giving meaning to those requirements, and should be considered only under a distinct justiciability analysis. Moreover, our analysis of this case does not rest on the more general proposition that no consequence of the allocation of administrative enforcement resources is judicially cognizable. Rather, we rely on separation of powers principles to interpret the fairly traceable component of the standing requirement.

III

The necessity that the plaintiff who seeks to invoke judicial power stand to profit in some personal interest remains an Art. III requirement. Respondents have not met this fundamental requirement. The judgment of the Court of Appeals is accordingly reversed, and the injunction issued by that court is vacated. It is so ordered.

Justice BRENNAN, dissenting.

Once again, the Court uses standing to slam the courthouse door against plaintiffs who are entitled to full consideration of their claims on the merits. And once again, the Court does so by waxing eloquent on considerations that provide little justification for the decision at hand. This time, however, the Court focuses on "the idea of separation of powers," as if the mere incantation of that phrase provides an obvious solution to the difficult questions presented by these cases.

One could hardly dispute the proposition that Art. III of the Constitution, by limiting the judicial power to "Cases" or "Controversies," embodies the notion that each branch of our National Government must confine its actions to those that are consistent with our scheme of separated powers. But simply stating that unremarkable truism provides little, if any, illumination of the standing inquiry that must be undertaken by a federal court faced with a particular action filed by particular plaintiffs. The question whether a particular person is a proper party to maintain the action does not, by its own force, raise separation of powers problems related to improper judicial interference in areas committed to other branches of the Federal Government.

The Court's attempt to obscure the standing question must be seen, therefore, as no more than a cover for its failure to recognize the nature of the specific claims raised by the respondents in these cases. By relying on generalities concerning our tripartite system of government, the Court is able to conclude that the respondents lack standing to maintain this action without acknowledging the precise nature of the injuries they have alleged. In so doing, the Court displays a startling insensitivity to the historical role played by the federal courts in eradicating race discrimination from our Nation's schools—a role that has played a prominent part in this Court's decisions . . . . Because I cannot join in such misguided decisionmaking, I dissent. . . .

Persons seeking judicial relief from an Art. III court must have standing to maintain their cause of action. At a minimum, the standing requirement is not met unless the plaintiff has such a personal stake in the outcome of the controversy as to assure that concrete adverseness which sharpens the presentation of issues upon which the court so largely depends. . . . Under the Court's cases, this "personal stake" requirement is satisfied if the person seeking redress has suffered, or is threatened with, some distinct and palpable injury, and if there is some causal connection between the asserted injury and the conduct being challenged. . . .

In these cases, the respondents have alleged at least one type of injury that satisfies the constitutional requirement of distinct and palpable injury.[3] In particular, they claim that the IRS's grant of tax-exempt status to racially discriminatory private schools directly injures their children's opportunity and ability to receive a desegregated education. As the complaint specifically alleges, the IRS action being challenged "fosters and encourages the organization, operation and expansion of institutions providing racially segregated educational opportunities for white children avoiding attendance in desegregating public school districts and thereby interferes with the efforts of federal courts, HEW and local school authorities to desegregate public school districts which have been operating racially dual school systems."

> [3] Because I conclude that the second injury alleged by the respondents is sufficient to satisfy constitutional requirements, I do not need to reach what the Court labels the "stigmatic injury." . . .

The Court acknowledges that this alleged injury is sufficient to satisfy constitutional standards. It does so only grudgingly, however, without emphasizing the significance of the harm alleged. Nonetheless, we have consistently recognized throughout the last 30 years that the deprivation of a child's right to receive an education in a desegregated school is a harm of special significance; surely, it satisfies any constitutional requirement of injury in fact. Just last Term . . . , for example, we acknowledged that an unbroken line of cases following *Brown v. Board of Education* establishes beyond doubt this Court's view that racial discrimination in education violates a most fundamental national public policy, as well as rights of individuals. The right of a student not to be segregated on racial grounds in schools . . . is indeed so fundamental and pervasive that it is embraced in the concept of due process of law.

In the analogous context of housing discrimination, the Court has similarly recognized that the denial of an opportunity to live in an integrated community is injury sufficient to satisfy the constitutional requirements of standing. In particular, we have recognized that injury is properly alleged when plaintiffs claim a deprivation of the social and professional benefits of living in an integrated society. Noting the importance of the benefits obtained from interracial associations, as well as the oft-stated principle that noneconomic injuries may suffice to provide standing, we have consistently concluded that such an injury is sufficient to satisfy the constitutional standing requirement of actual or threatened harm. . . . .

Fully explicating the injury alleged helps to explain why it is fairly traceable to the governmental conduct challenged by the respondents. As the respondents specifically allege in their complaint: "Defendants have fostered and encouraged the development, operation and expansion of many of these racially segregated private schools by recognizing them as 'charitable' organizations described in Section 501(c)(3) of the Internal Revenue Code, and exempt from federal income taxation under Section 501(a) of the Code. Once the schools are classified as tax-exempt . . ., contributions made to them are deductible from gross income on individual and corporate income tax returns. . . . Moreover, [the] organizations . . . are also exempt from federal social security taxes . . . and from federal unemployment taxes. . . . The resulting exemptions and deductions provide tangible financial aid and other benefits which support the operation of racially segregated private schools. In particular, the resulting deductions facilitate the raising of funds to organize new schools and expand existing schools in order to accommodate white students avoiding attendance in desegregating public school districts. Additionally, the existence of a federal tax exemption amounts to a federal stamp of approval which facilitates fund raising on behalf of racially segregated private schools. Finally, by supporting the development, operation and expansion of institutions providing racially segregated educational opportunities for white children avoiding attendance in desegregating public schools, defendants are thereby interfering with the efforts of courts, HEW and local school authorities to desegregate public school districts which have been operating racially dual school systems."

Viewed in light of the injuries they claim, the respondents have alleged a direct causal relationship between the Government action they challenge and the injury they suffer: their inability to receive an education in a racially integrated school is directly and adversely affected by the tax-exempt status granted by the IRS to racially discriminatory schools in their respective school districts. Common sense alone would recognize that the elimination of tax-exempt status for racially discriminatory private schools would serve to lessen the impact that those institutions have in defeating efforts to desegregate the public schools.

The Court admits that the diminished ability of respondents' children to receive a desegregated education would be fairly traceable to unlawful IRS grants of tax exemptions if there were enough racially discriminatory private schools receiving tax exemptions in respondents' communities for withdrawal of those exemptions to make an appreciable difference in public school integration, but concludes that respondents have made no such allegation. With all due respect, the Court has either misread the complaint or is improperly requiring the respondents to prove their case on the merits in order to defeat a motion to dismiss. For example, the respondents specifically refer by name to at least 32 private schools that discriminate on the basis of race and yet continue to benefit illegally from tax-exempt status. Eighteen of those schools—including at least 14 elementary schools, 2 junior high schools, and 1 high school—are located in the city of Memphis, Tenn., which has been the subject of several court orders to desegregate. Similarly, the respondents cite two private schools in Orangeburg, S.C. that continue to benefit from federal tax exemptions even though they practice race discrimination in school districts that are desegregating pursuant to judicial and administrative orders. At least with respect to these school districts, as well as the others specifically mentioned in the complaint, there can be little doubt that the respondents have identified communities containing enough racially discriminatory private schools receiving tax exemptions . . . to make an appreciable difference in public school integration.

. . . . The respondents in these cases do not challenge the denial of any service by a tax-exempt institution; admittedly, they do not seek access to racially discriminatory private schools. Rather, the injury they allege, and the injury that clearly satisfies constitutional requirements, is the deprivation of their children's opportunity and ability to receive an education in a racially integrated school district. This injury, as the Court admits, and as we have previously held, is a of a kind that is directly traceable to the governmental action being challenged. The relationship between the harm alleged and the governmental action cannot simply be deemed "purely speculative." . . .

Justice STEVENS, with whom Justice BLACKMUN joins, dissenting.

Three propositions are clear to me: (1) respondents have adequately alleged injury in fact; (2) their injury is fairly traceable to the conduct that they claim to be unlawful; and (3) the "separation of powers" principle does not create a jurisdictional obstacle to the consideration of the merits of their claim. . . .

In final analysis, the wrong respondents allege that the Government has committed is to subsidize the exodus of white children from schools that would otherwise be racially integrated. The critical question in these cases, therefore, is whether respondents have alleged that the Government has created that kind of subsidy.

In answering that question, we must of course assume that respondents can prove what they have alleged. Furthermore, at this stage of the litigation we must put to one side all questions about the appropriateness of a nationwide class action. The controlling issue is whether the causal connection between the injury and the wrong has been adequately alleged.

An organization that qualifies for preferential treatment under § 501(c)(3) of the Internal Revenue Code, because it is operated exclusively for charitable purposes, is exempt from paying federal income taxes, and under § 170 of the Code, persons who contribute to such organizations may deduct the amount of their contributions when calculating their taxable income. Only last Term we explained the effect of this preferential treatment: "Both tax exemptions and tax deductibility are a form of subsidy that is administered through the tax system. A tax exemption has much the same effect as a cash grant to the organization of the amount of tax it would have to pay on its income. Deductible contributions are similar to cash grants of the amount of a portion of the individual's contributions."

The purpose of this scheme, like the purpose of any subsidy, is to promote the activity subsidized; the statutes seek to achieve the same basic goal of encouraging the development of certain organizations through the grant of tax benefits. If the granting of preferential tax treatment would encourage private segregated schools to conduct their charitable activities, it must follow that the withdrawal of the treatment would discourage them, and hence promote the process of desegregation.[2]

[2] Respondents' complaint is premised on precisely this theory. The complaint describes a number of private schools which receive preferential tax treatment and which allegedly discriminate on the basis of race, providing white children with a racially segregated alternative to attendance in the public schools which respondents' children attend. The complaint then states:

"There are thousands of other racially segregated private schools which operate or serve desegregating public school districts and which function under the umbrella of organizations which have received, applied for, or will apply for, federal tax exemptions. Moreover, many additional public school districts will in the future begin desegregating pursuant to court order or [government] regulations and guidelines, under state law or voluntarily. Additional racially segregated private schools may be organized or expanded, many of which will be operated by organizations which have received, applied for, or will apply for federal tax exemptions. As in the case of those representative organizations and private schools described in paragraphs 39-48, such organizations and schools provide, or will provide, white children with a racially segregated alternative to desegregating public schools. By recognizing these organizations as exempt from federal taxation, defendants facilitate their development, operation and expansion and the provision of racially segregated educational opportunities for white children avoiding attendance in desegregating public school systems. Defendants thereby also interfere with the efforts of federal courts, [the Federal Government] and local school authorities to eliminate racially dual school systems." Thus, like Justice Brennan, I do not understand why the Court states that the complaint contains no allegation that the tax benefits received by private segregated schools make an appreciable difference in public school integration, unless the Court requires intricacies of pleading that would have gladdened the heart of Baron Parke.

We have held that when a subsidy makes a given activity more or less expensive, injury can be fairly traced to the subsidy for purposes of standing analysis because of the resulting increase or decrease in the ability to engage in the activity. . . .

This causation analysis is nothing more than a restatement of elementary economics: when something becomes more expensive, less of it will be purchased. Sections 170 and 501(c)(3) are premised on that recognition. If racially discriminatory private schools lose the "cash grants" that flow from the operation of the statutes, the education they provide will become more expensive and hence less of their services will be purchased. Conversely, maintenance of these tax benefits makes an education in segregated private schools relatively more attractive, by decreasing its cost. Accordingly, without tax-exempt status, private schools will either not be competitive in terms of cost, or have to change their admissions policies, hence reducing their competitiveness for parents seeking a racially segregated alternative to public schools, which is what respondents have alleged many white parents in desegregating school districts seek.[5]

[5] It is this racially segregated alternative to public schools—the availability of schools that receive tax exemptions merely on the basis of adopting and certifying—but not implementing—a policy of nondiscrimination, which respondents allege white parents have found attractive, and which would either lose their cost advantage or their character as a segregated alternative if denied tax-exempt status because of their discriminatory admissions policies.

In either event the process of desegregation will be advanced in the same way that it was advanced in Gilmore and Norwood—the withdrawal of the subsidy for segregated schools means the incentive structure facing white parents who seek such schools for their children will be altered. Thus, the laws of economics, not to mention the laws of Congress embodied in §§ 170 and 501(c)(3), compel the conclusion that the injury respondents have alleged—the increased segregation of their children's schools because of the ready availability of private schools that admit whites only—will be redressed if these schools' operations are inhibited through the denial of preferential tax treatment. . . .

Considerations of tax policy, economics, and pure logic all confirm the conclusion that respondents' injury in fact is fairly traceable to the Government's allegedly wrongful conduct. The Court therefore is forced to introduce the concept of "separation of powers" into its analysis. The Court writes that the separation of powers explains why our cases preclude the conclusion that respondents' injury is fairly traceable to the conduct they challenge.

The Court could mean one of three things by its invocation of the separation of powers. First, it could simply be expressing the idea that if the plaintiff lacks Art. III standing to bring a lawsuit, then there is no "case or controversy" within the meaning of Art. III and hence the matter is not within the area of responsibility assigned to the Judiciary by the Constitution. As we have written in the past, through the standing requirement Art. III limits the federal judicial power to those disputes which confine federal courts to a role consistent with a system of separated powers and which are traditionally thought to be capable of resolution through the judicial process. While there can be no quarrel with this proposition, in itself it provides no guidance for determining if the injury respondents have alleged is fairly traceable to the conduct they have challenged.

Second, the Court could be saying that it will require a more direct causal connection when it is troubled by the separation of powers implications of the case before it. That approach confuses the standing doctrine with the justiciability of the issues that respondents seek to raise. The purpose of the standing inquiry is to measure the plaintiff's stake in the outcome, not whether a court has the authority to provide it with the outcome it seeks: The standing question is whether the plaintiff has alleged such a personal stake in the outcome of the controversy as to warrant his invocation of federal-court jurisdiction and to justify the exercise of the court's remedial powers on his behalf.

Thus, the fundamental aspect of standing is that it focuses primarily on the party seeking to get his complaint before the federal court rather than on the issues he wishes to have adjudicated. The strength of the plaintiff's interest in the outcome has nothing to do with whether the relief it seeks would intrude upon the prerogatives of other branches of government; the possibility that the relief might be inappropriate does not lessen the plaintiff's stake in obtaining that relief. If a plaintiff presents a nonjusticiable issue, or seeks relief that a court may not award, then its complaint should be dismissed for those reasons, and not because the plaintiff lacks a stake in obtaining that relief and hence has no standing. . . .

Third, the Court could be saying that it will not treat as legally cognizable injuries that stem from an administrative decision concerning how enforcement resources will be allocated. This surely is an important point. Respondents do seek to restructure the IRS's mechanisms for enforcing the legal requirement that discriminatory institutions not receive tax-exempt status. Such restructuring would dramatically affect the way in which the IRS exercises its prosecutorial discretion. The Executive requires latitude to decide how best to enforce the law, and in general the Court may well be correct that the exercise of that discretion, especially in the tax context, is unchallengeable.

However, as the Court also recognizes, this principle does not apply when suit is brought to enforce specific legal obligations whose violation works a direct harm. . . . Here, respondents contend that the IRS is violating a specific constitutional limitation on its enforcement discretion. . . .

In short, I would deal with the question of the legal limitations on the IRS's enforcement discretion on its merits, rather than by making the untenable assumption that the granting of preferential tax treatment to segregated schools does not make those schools more attractive to white students and hence does not inhibit the process of desegregation. I respectfully dissent.

California v. Texas (2021)

As originally enacted in 2010, the Patient Protection and Affordable Care Act required most Americans to obtain minimum essential health insurance coverage. The Act also imposed a monetary penalty, scaled according to income, upon individuals who failed to do so. In 2017, Congress effectively nullified the penalty by setting its amount at $0.

Texas and 17 other States brought this lawsuit against the United States and federal officials. They were later joined by two individuals (Neill Hurley and John Nantz). The plaintiffs claim that without the penalty the Act's minimum essential coverage requirement is unconstitutional. Specifically, they say neither the Commerce Clause nor the Tax Clause (nor any other enumerated power) grants Congress the power to enact it. They also argue that the minimum essential coverage requirement is not severable from the rest of the Act. Hence, they believe the Act as a whole is invalid. We do not reach these questions of the Act's validity, however, for Texas and the other plaintiffs in this suit lack the standing necessary to raise them. . . .

Neither the individual nor the state plaintiffs have shown that the injury they will suffer or have suffered is "fairly traceable" to the "allegedly unlawful conduct" of which they complain.

We begin with the two individual plaintiffs. They claim a particularized individual harm in the form of payments they have made and will make each month to carry the minimum essential coverage that [the coverage requirement] requires. The individual plaintiffs point to the statutory language, which, they say, commands them to buy health insurance. . . .

Their problem lies in the fact that the statutory provision, while it tells them to obtain that coverage, has no means of enforcement. With the penalty zeroed out, the IRS can no longer seek a penalty from those who fail to comply. Because of this, there is no possible Government action that is causally connected to the plaintiffs' injury—the costs of purchasing health insurance. Or to put the matter conversely, that injury is not "fairly traceable" to any "allegedly unlawful conduct" of which the plaintiffs complain. They have not pointed to any way in which the defendants, the Commissioner of Internal Revenue and the Secretary of Health and Human Services, will act to enforce [the coverage requirement]. They have not shown how any other federal employees could do so either. In a word, they have not shown that any kind of Government action or conduct has caused or will cause the injury they attribute to [the coverage requirement]. . . .

[O]ur cases have consistently spoken of the need to assert an injury that is the result of a statute's actual or threatened *enforcement*, whether today or in the future. In the absence of contemporary enforcement, we have said that a plaintiff claiming standing must show that the likelihood of future enforcement is "substantial."

The plaintiffs point out that these and other precedents concern injuries anticipated in the future from a statute's later enforcement. Here, the plaintiffs say, they have already suffered a pocketbook injury, for they have already bought health insurance. . . . But critically, . . . here no unlawful Government action "fairly traceable" to [the coverage requirement] caused the plaintiffs' pocketbook harm. Here, there is no action—actual or threatened—whatsoever. There is only the statute's textually unenforceable language.

To consider the matter from the point of view of another standing requirement, namely, redressability, makes clear that the statutory language alone is not sufficient. To determine whether an injury is redressable, a court will consider the relationship between "the judicial relief requested" and the "injury" suffered. The plaintiffs here sought injunctive relief and a declaratory judgment. . . . Remedies, however, ordinarily operate with respect to specific parties. In the absence of any specific party, they do not simply operate on legal rules in the abstract. . . . There is no one, and nothing, to enjoin. They cannot enjoin the Secretary of Health and Human Services, because he has no power to enforce [the coverage requirement] against them. And they do not claim that they might enjoin Congress. In these circumstances, injunctive relief could amount to no more than a declaration that the statutory provision they attack is unconstitutional, *i.e.*, a declaratory judgment. But once again, that is the very kind of relief that cannot alone supply jurisdiction otherwise absent.

The matter is not simply technical. To find standing here to attack an unenforceable statutory provision would allow a federal court to issue what would amount to an advisory opinion without the possibility of any judicial relief. It would threaten to grant unelected judges a general authority to conduct oversight of decisions of the elected branches of Government. Article III guards against federal courts assuming this kind of jurisdiction. . . .

Next, we turn to the state plaintiffs. We conclude that Texas and the other state plaintiffs have similarly failed to show that they have alleged an injury fairly traceable to the defendant's allegedly *unlawful* conduct. . . .

[T]he state plaintiffs claim that the minimum essential coverage provision has led state residents subject to it to enroll in state-operated or state-sponsored insurance programs such as Medicaid, the Children's Health Insurance Program (CHIP), and health insurance programs for state employees. The state plaintiffs say they must pay a share of the costs of serving those new enrollees. As with the individual plaintiffs, the States also have failed to show how this injury is directly traceable to any actual or possible unlawful Government conduct in enforcing [the coverage requirement]. That alone is enough to show that they, like the individual plaintiffs, lack Article III standing.

But setting aside that pure issue of law, we need only examine the initial factual premise of their claim to uncover another fatal weakness: The state plaintiffs have failed to show that the challenged minimum essential coverage provision, without any prospect of penalty, will harm them by leading more individuals to enroll in these programs.

We have said that, where a causal relation between injury and challenged action depends upon the decision of an independent third party (here an individual's decision to enroll in, say, Medicaid), standing is not precluded, but it is ordinarily substantially more difficult to establish. . . . The programs to which the state plaintiffs point offer their recipients many benefits that have nothing to do with the minimum essential coverage provision [like no-cost Medicaid services furnished to children and pregnant women, prohibiting Medicaid premiums for low-income families, and providing tax credits for health insurance]. Given these benefits, neither logic nor intuition suggests that the presence of the minimum essential coverage requirement would lead an individual to enroll in one of those programs that its absence would lead them to ignore. A penalty might have led some inertia-bound individuals to enroll. But without a penalty, what incentive could the provision provide?

The evidence that the state plaintiffs introduced in the District Court does not show the contrary. That evidence consists of 21 statements (from state officials) about how new enrollees will increase the costs of state health insurance programs . . . . Of the 21 statements, we have found only 4 that allege that added state costs are attributable to the minimum essential coverage requirement. And all four refer to that provision as it existed *before Congress removed the penalty* effective beginning tax year 2019, *i.e.*, while a penalty still existed to be enforced. . . . Unsurprisingly, the States have not demonstrated that an unenforceable mandate will cause their residents to enroll in valuable benefits programs that they would otherwise forgo. It would require far stronger evidence than the States have offered here to support their counterintuitive theory of standing, which rests on a highly attenuated chain of possibilities.

Therefore, we reverse the Fifth Circuit's judgment in respect to standing, vacate the judgment, and remand the case with instructions to dismiss.

It is so ordered.

Carney v. Adams (2020)

. . . . The Delaware Constitution contains a political balance requirement applicable to membership on all five of its courts: the Supreme Court, the Chancery Court, the Superior Court, the Family Court, and the Court of Common Pleas. The provision says that no more than a bare majority of judges on any of these courts "shall be of the same political party." The Delaware Constitution also contains a second requirement applicable only to the Supreme Court, the Chancery Court, and the Superior Court. It says that the remaining members of those three courts (those not in the bare majority) "shall be of the other major political party." Thus, all five courts are subject to the "bare majority" requirement, and three of the five courts are additionally subject to the "major party" requirement.

On February 21, 2017, plaintiff-respondent James R. Adams sued Delaware's Governor, John Carney, in Federal District Court. Adams, then a newly registered political independent, claimed that both of Delaware's political balance requirements violated his First Amendment right to freedom of association by making him ineligible to become a judge unless he rejoined a major political party. . . .

[The lower courts held for Adams on the merits. The Governor sought certiorari, which the Supreme Court granted and directed the parties to brief the question of whether Adams had standing.]

Two aspects of standing doctrine are relevant here. First, standing requires an "injury in fact" that must be "concrete and particularized," as well as "actual or imminent." It cannot be "conjectural or hypothetical." Second, a grievance that amounts to nothing more than an abstract and generalized harm to a citizen's interest in the proper application of the law does not count as an "injury in fact." And it consequently does not show standing. In other words, a plaintiff cannot establish standing by asserting an abstract general interest common to all members of the public, no matter how sincere or deeply committed a plaintiff is to vindicating that general interest on behalf of the public. . . .

And we conclude that Adams did not show the necessary "injury in fact." Adams suffered a "generalized grievance" of the kind we have just described. He, like all citizens of Delaware, must live and work within a State that (in his view) imposes unconstitutional requirements for eligibility on three of its courts. Lawyers, such as Adams, may feel sincerely and strongly that Delaware's laws should comply with the Federal Constitution. But that kind of interest does not create standing. Rather, the question is whether Adams will suffer a "personal and individual" injury beyond this generalized grievance—an injury that is concrete, particularized, and imminent rather than "conjectural or hypothetical."

Adams says he has. He claims that Delaware's major party requirement in fact prevents him, a political independent, from having his judicial application considered for three of Delaware's courts. To prove this kind of harm, however, Adams must at least show that he is likely to apply to become a judge in the reasonably foreseeable future if Delaware did not bar him because of political affiliation. And our cases make clear that he can show this only if he is "able and ready" to apply. We have examined the summary judgment record to determine whether Adams made this showing. And, as we have said, we conclude that he has not.

The only evidence supporting Adams is two statements he made in his deposition and in his answer to interrogatories that he wants to be, and would apply to be, a judge on any of Delaware's five courts. He said: "I would apply for any judicial position that I thought I was qualified for, and I believe I'm qualified for any position that would come up . . . [o]n any of the courts. I would feel less comfortable on Chancery than any other court. I would feel most comfortable on Superior Court, Family Court, Court of Common Pleas, state Supreme Court based on my background, experience, and what I have done in my career."

He added in his answer to interrogatories: "Adams . . . would seriously consider and apply for any judicial position for which he feels he is qualified.... Adams believes that he meets the minimum qualifications to apply for any judicial officer position."

Those statements, however, must be considered in the context of the record, which contains evidence showing that, at the time he brought this lawsuit, Adams was not "able and ready" to apply.

First, the record showed that, between 2012 and 2016, during which time Adams was a practicing lawyer and a registered Democrat, Delaware's five courts had a combined total of 14 openings for which Adams, then a Democrat, would have been eligible. Yet he did not apply for any of them. When deposed during discovery, Adams said that in 2014 he had wanted to apply for a Supreme Court or Superior Court judgeship. Adams said that he could not do so because only Republicans were eligible for those positions that year. He was wrong about that. In particular, there were three vacancies on those two courts in 2014 for which he, as a Democrat, was eligible. Adams later conceded that he had indeed been eligible to apply for those vacancies, but he had not done so.

Second, on December 31, 2015, after roughly 12 years as a lawyer for the Delaware Department of Justice, Adams retired. In February 2016, Adams changed his bar membership from "Active" to "Emeritus" status. He then returned to "Active" status in January 2017. In his deposition, he stated that at about that same time in the "[b]eginning of the year, January/February," he read a law review article arguing that Delaware's judicial eligibility requirements were unconstitutional because they excluded independents. Adams called the article's author and said, "I just read your Law Review . . . article. I'd like to pursue this." The author suggested several attorneys who might handle the matter.

Third, shortly thereafter, on February 13, 2017, Adams changed his political affiliation from Democrat to unaffiliated independent. Before that, he had been a Democrat his "whole life" and actively involved in the Delaware Democratic Party. Leaving the party made it less likely that he would become a judge. But doing so made it possible for him to vindicate his view of the law as set forth in the article.

Fourth, after Adams became a political independent on February 13, 2017, he filed this lawsuit eight days later on February 21.

Fifth, Adams said in his answer to interrogatories that he "has no knowledge of what judicial positions may become open in the next year."

Sixth, other than the act of filing the lawsuit itself, the summary judgment record contains no evidence of conversations or other actions taken by Adams suggesting that he was "able and ready" to apply for a judgeship. . . .

This is a highly fact-specific case. In our view, three considerations, taken together, convince us that the record evidence fails to show that, at the time he commenced the lawsuit, Adams was "able and ready" to apply for a judgeship in the reasonably foreseeable future. First, as we have just laid out, Adams' words "I would apply . . . " stand alone without any actual past injury, without reference to an anticipated timeframe, without prior judgeship applications, without prior relevant conversations, without efforts to determine likely openings, without other preparations or investigations, and without any other supporting evidence.

Second, the context offers Adams no support. It suggests an abstract, generalized grievance, not an actual desire to become a judge. Indeed, Adams' failure to apply previously when he was eligible, his reading of the law review article, his change of party affiliation, and his swift subsequent filing of the complaint show a desire to vindicate his view of the law, as articulated in the article he read.

Third, if we were to hold that Adams' few words of general intent—without more and against all contrary evidence—were sufficient here to show an "injury in fact," we would significantly weaken the longstanding legal doctrine preventing this Court from providing advisory opinions at the request of one who, without other concrete injury, believes that the government is not following the law. Adams did not show that he was "able and ready" to apply for a vacancy in the reasonably imminent future. Adams has not sufficiently differentiated himself from a general population of individuals affected in the abstract by the legal provision he attacks. We do not decide whether a statement of intent alone under other circumstances could be enough to show standing. But we are satisfied that Adams' words alone are not enough here when placed in the context of this particular record.

Precedent supports the conclusion that an injury in fact requires an intent that is concrete. In *Lujan v. Defenders of Wildlife*, for example, organizations dedicated to wildlife conservation sought to enjoin enforcement of a federal regulation that they believed would unlawfully harm endangered species. The organizations' members had previously visited the species' habitats abroad, and they said that they intended to return to those foreign habitats in the future. This Court recognized that having to view a species-impoverished habitat could constitute a cognizable injury. But it pointed out that the plaintiffs had not described any concrete plans to visit those habitats, nor had they said when they would do so. The Court said that the organizations had set forth only "some day intentions." And "some day intentions" do "not support a finding of the 'actual or imminent' injury that our cases require."

For another thing, arguably similar cases in which this Court has found standing all contained more evidence that the plaintiff was "able and ready" than Adams has provided here. In *Adarand Constructors, Inc. v. Pena*, for example, a subcontractor challenging a race-based program for allocating contracts established standing by showing that it "bids on every guardrail project in Colorado," that the defendant "is likely to let contracts involving guardrail work . . . at least once per year in Colorado," and that the plaintiff "is very likely to bid on each such contract." . . . The contractors showed that they were "able and ready to bid on [future] contracts," for it was undisputed that they had "regularly bid on construction contracts in Jacksonville, and that they would have bid on contracts set aside pursuant to the city's ordinance were they so able."

In *Gratz v. Michigan*, we held that a plaintiff had standing to attack as unlawful a university's affirmative action admissions policy. The plaintiff had applied for admission to the university as a freshman applicant in the recent past and been rejected. He said he intended to apply to transfer to the university in the near future, should the university cease using affirmative action in its transfer admissions process. And the university had a "rolling" transfer program open for application each year, so there was no doubt that the plaintiff's injury was imminent. The Court therefore concluded that he was "able and ready" to apply as a transfer student. Unlike Adams, none of these plaintiffs relied on a bare statement of intent alone against the context of a record that shows nothing more than an abstract generalized grievance. Rather, each introduced at least some evidence that, e.g., they had applied in the past, there were regular opportunities available with relevant frequency, and they were "able and ready" to apply for them.

. . . . Adams has not shown that he was "able and ready" to apply in the imminent future. Consequently, he has failed to show that "personal," "concrete," and "imminent" injury upon which our standing precedents insist.

For these reasons, we reverse the Third Circuit's decision in respect to standing, vacate the judgment, and remand with instructions to dismiss the case.

TransUnion LLC v. Ramirez (2021)

Justice KAVANAUGH delivered the opinion of the Court.

To have Article III standing to sue in federal court, plaintiffs must demonstrate, among other things, that they suffered a concrete harm. . . .

I

. . . [T]he Fair Credit Reporting Act . . . . seeks to promote "fair and accurate credit reporting" and to protect consumer privacy. To achieve those goals, the Act regulates the consumer reporting agencies that compile and disseminate personal information about consumers. . . . Three of the Act's requirements are relevant to this case. *First*, the Act requires consumer reporting agencies to "follow reasonable procedures to assure maximum possible accuracy" in consumer reports. *Second*, the Act provides that consumer reporting agencies must, upon request, disclose to the consumer "[a]ll information in the consumer's file at the time of the request." *Third*, the Act compels consumer reporting agencies to "provide to a consumer, with each written disclosure by the agency to the consumer," a "summary of rights" prepared by the Consumer Financial Protection Bureau. The Act creates a cause of action for consumers to sue and recover damages for certain violations. The Act provides: "Any person who willfully fails to comply with any requirement imposed under this subchapter with respect to any consumer is liable to that consumer" for actual damages or for statutory damages not less than $100 and not more than $1,000, as well as for punitive damages and attorney's fees.

TransUnion is one of the "Big Three" credit reporting agencies, along with Equifax and Experian. As a credit reporting agency, TransUnion compiles personal and financial information about individual consumers to create consumer reports. TransUnion then sells those consumer reports for use by entities such as banks, landlords, and car dealerships that request information about the creditworthiness of individual consumers.

Beginning in 2002, TransUnion introduced an add-on product called OFAC Name Screen Alert. OFAC is the U. S. Treasury Department's Office of Foreign Assets Control. OFAC maintains a list of "specially designated nationals" who threaten America's national security. Individuals on the OFAC list are terrorists, drug traffickers, or other serious criminals. It is generally unlawful to transact business with any person on the list. TransUnion created the OFAC Name Screen Alert to help businesses avoid transacting with individuals on OFAC's list.

When this litigation arose, Name Screen worked in the following way: When a business opted into the Name Screen service, TransUnion would conduct its ordinary credit check of the consumer, and it would also use third-party software to compare the consumer's name against the OFAC list. If the consumer's first and last name matched the first and last name of an individual on OFAC's list, then TransUnion would place an alert on the credit report indicating that the consumer's name was a "potential match" to a name on the OFAC list. TransUnion did not compare any data other than first and last names. Unsurprisingly, TransUnion's Name Screen product generated many false positives. Thousands of law-abiding Americans happen to share a first and last name with one of the terrorists, drug traffickers, or serious criminals on OFAC's list of specially designated nationals.

Sergio Ramirez learned the hard way that he is one such individual. On February 27, 2011, Ramirez visited a Nissan dealership in Dublin, California, seeking to buy a Nissan Maxima. Ramirez was accompanied by his wife and his father-in-law. After Ramirez and his wife selected a color and negotiated a price, the dealership ran a credit check on both Ramirez and his wife. Ramirez's credit report, produced by TransUnion, contained the following alert: "***OFAC ADVISOR ALERT - INPUT NAME MATCHES NAME ON THE OFAC DATABASE." A Nissan salesman told Ramirez that Nissan would not sell the car to him because his name was on a "terrorist list." Ramirez's wife had to purchase the car in her own name.

The next day, Ramirez called TransUnion and requested a copy of his credit file. TransUnion sent Ramirez a mailing that same day that included his credit file and the statutorily required summary of rights . . . . The mailing did not mention the OFAC alert in Ramirez's file. The following day, TransUnion sent Ramirez a second mailing—a letter alerting him that his name was considered a potential match to names on the OFAC list. The second mailing did not include an additional copy of the summary of rights. Concerned about the mailings, Ramirez consulted a lawyer and ultimately canceled a planned trip to Mexico. TransUnion eventually removed the OFAC alert from Ramirez's file.

In February 2012, Ramirez sued TransUnion and alleged three violations of the Fair Credit Reporting Act. *First*, he alleged that TransUnion, by using the Name Screen product, failed to follow reasonable procedures to ensure the accuracy of information in his credit file. *Second*, he claimed that TransUnion failed to provide him with *all* the information in his credit file upon his request. In particular, TransUnion's first mailing did not include the fact that Ramirez's name was a potential match for a name on the OFAC list. *Third*, Ramirez asserted that TransUnion violated its obligation to provide him with a summary of his rights "with each written disclosure," because TransUnion's second mailing did not contain a summary of Ramirez's rights. Ramirez requested statutory and punitive damages.

Ramirez also sought to certify a class of all people in the United States to whom TransUnion sent a mailing during the period from January 1, 2011, to July 26, 2011, that was similar in form to the second mailing that Ramirez received. TransUnion opposed certification. The U.S. District Court for the Northern District of California rejected TransUnion's argument and certified the class.

Before trial, the parties stipulated that the class contained 8,185 members, including Ramirez. The parties also stipulated that only 1,853 members of the class (including Ramirez) had their credit reports disseminated by TransUnion to potential creditors during the period from January 1, 2011, to July 26, 2011. The District Court ruled that all 8,185 class members had Article III standing.

At trial, Ramirez testified about his experience at the Nissan dealership. But Ramirez did not present evidence about the experiences of other members of the class.

After six days of trial, the jury returned a verdict for the plaintiffs. The jury awarded each class member $984.22 in statutory damages and $6,353.08 in punitive damages for a total award of more than $60 million. The District Court rejected all of TransUnion's post-trial motions.

The U.S. Court of Appeals for the Ninth Circuit affirmed in relevant part. . . . We granted certiorari.

II

. . . The question in this case focuses on the Article III requirement that the plaintiff's injury in fact be "concrete"—that is, real, and not abstract. What makes a harm concrete for purposes of Article III? . . . [C]ourts should assess whether the alleged injury to the plaintiff has a "close relationship" to a harm "traditionally" recognized as providing a basis for a lawsuit in American courts. . . .

[C]ertain harms readily qualify as concrete injuries under Article III. The most obvious are traditional tangible harms, such as physical harms and monetary harms. If a defendant has caused physical or monetary injury to the plaintiff, the plaintiff has suffered a concrete injury in fact under Article III. Various intangible harms can also be concrete. . . . Those include, for example, reputational harms, disclosure of private information, and intrusion upon seclusion. And those traditional harms may also include harms specified by the Constitution itself [including First Amendment violations].

In determining whether a harm is sufficiently concrete to qualify as an injury in fact, . . . Congress's views may be instructive. Courts must afford due respect to Congress's decision to impose a statutory prohibition or obligation on a defendant, and to grant a plaintiff a cause of action to sue over the defendant's violation of that statutory prohibition or obligation. In that way, Congress may elevate to the status of legally cognizable injuries concrete, *de facto* injuries that were previously inadequate in law. But . . . it may not simply enact an injury into existence, using its lawmaking power to transform something that is not remotely harmful into something that is.

Importantly, this Court has rejected the proposition that a plaintiff automatically satisfies the injury-in-fact requirement whenever a statute grants a person a statutory right and purports to authorize that person to sue to vindicate that right. . . . Article III standing requires a concrete injury even in the context of a statutory violation.

Congress's creation of a statutory prohibition or obligation and a cause of action does not relieve courts of their responsibility to independently decide whether a plaintiff has suffered a concrete harm under Article III any more than, for example, Congress's enactment of a law regulating speech relieves courts of their responsibility to independently decide whether the law violates the First Amendment.

For standing purposes, therefore, an important difference exists between (i) a plaintiff's statutory cause of action to sue a defendant over the defendant's violation of federal law, and (ii) a plaintiff's suffering concrete harm because of the defendant's violation of federal law. Congress may enact legal prohibitions and obligations. And Congress may create causes of action for plaintiffs to sue defendants who violate those legal prohibitions or obligations. But under Article III, an injury in law is not an injury in fact. Only those plaintiffs who have been *concretely harmed* by a defendant's statutory violation may sue that private defendant over that violation in federal court. . . .

To appreciate how the Article III "concrete harm" principle operates in practice, consider two different hypothetical plaintiffs. Suppose first that a Maine citizen's land is polluted by a nearby factory. She sues the company, alleging that it violated a federal environmental law and damaged her property. Suppose also that a second plaintiff in Hawaii files a federal lawsuit alleging that the same company in Maine violated that same environmental law by polluting land in Maine. The violation did not personally harm the plaintiff in Hawaii.

Even if Congress affords both hypothetical plaintiffs a cause of action (with statutory damages available) to sue over the defendant's legal violation, Article III standing doctrine sharply distinguishes between those two scenarios. The first lawsuit may of course proceed in federal court because the plaintiff has suffered concrete harm to her property. But the second lawsuit may not proceed because that plaintiff has not suffered any physical, monetary, or cognizable intangible harm traditionally recognized as providing a basis for a lawsuit in American courts. An uninjured plaintiff who sues in those circumstances is, by definition, not seeking to remedy any harm to herself but instead is merely seeking to ensure a defendant's compliance with regulatory law (and, of course, to obtain some money via the statutory damages). Those are not grounds for Article III standing.

As those examples illustrate, if the law of Article III did not require plaintiffs to demonstrate a "concrete harm," Congress could authorize virtually any citizen to bring a statutory damages suit against virtually any defendant who violated virtually any federal law. Such an expansive understanding of Article III would flout constitutional text, history, and precedent. In our view, the public interest that private entities comply with the law cannot be converted into an individual right by a statute that denominates it as such, and that permits all citizens (or, for that matter, a subclass of citizens who suffer no distinctive concrete harm) to sue.[2] . . .

[2] A plaintiff must show that the injury is not only concrete but also particularized. But if there were no concrete-harm requirement, the requirement of a particularized injury would do little or nothing to constrain Congress from freely creating causes of action for vast classes of *unharmed* plaintiffs to sue any defendants who violate any federal law. (Congress might, for example, provide that everyone has an individual right to clean air and can sue any defendant who violates any air-pollution law.) That is one reason why the Court has been careful to emphasize that concreteness and particularization are separate requirements.

III

. . . . We first address the plaintiffs' claim that TransUnion failed to "follow reasonable procedures to assure maximum possible accuracy" of the plaintiffs' credit files maintained by TransUnion. In particular, the plaintiffs argue that TransUnion did not do enough to ensure that OFAC alerts labeling them as potential terrorists were not included in their credit files.

Assuming that the plaintiffs are correct that TransUnion violated its obligations under the Fair Credit Reporting Act to use reasonable procedures in internally maintaining the credit files, we must determine whether the 8,185 class members suffered concrete harm from TransUnion's failure to employ reasonable procedures.

Start with the 1,853 class members (including the named plaintiff Ramirez) whose reports were disseminated to third-party businesses. The plaintiffs argue that the publication to a third party of a credit report bearing a misleading OFAC alert injures the subject of the report. The plaintiffs contend that this injury bears a "close relationship" to a harm traditionally recognized as providing a basis for a lawsuit in American courts—namely, the reputational harm associated with the tort of defamation.

We agree with the plaintiffs. Under longstanding American law, a person is injured when a defamatory statement that would subject him to hatred, contempt, or ridicule is published to a third party. TransUnion provided third parties with credit reports containing OFAC alerts that labeled the class members as potential terrorists, drug traffickers, or serious criminals. The 1,853 class members therefore suffered a harm with a "close relationship" to the harm associated with the tort of defamation. We have no trouble concluding that the 1,853 class members suffered a concrete harm that qualifies as an injury in fact.

TransUnion counters that those 1,853 class members did not suffer a harm with a "close relationship" to defamation because the OFAC alerts on the disseminated credit reports were only misleading and not literally false. TransUnion points out that the reports merely identified a consumer as a "*potential* match" to an individual on the OFAC list—a fact that TransUnion says is not technically false.

In looking to whether a plaintiff's asserted harm has a "close relationship" to a harm traditionally recognized as providing a basis for a lawsuit in American courts, we do not require an exact duplicate. The harm from being labeled a "potential terrorist" bears a close relationship to the harm from being labeled a "terrorist." In other words, the harm from a misleading statement of this kind bears a sufficiently close relationship to the harm from a false and defamatory statement.

In short, the 1,853 class members whose reports were disseminated to third parties suffered a concrete injury in fact under Article III.

The remaining 6,332 class members are a different story. To be sure, their credit files, which were maintained by TransUnion, contained misleading OFAC alerts. But the parties stipulated that TransUnion did not provide those plaintiffs' credit information to any potential creditors during the class period from January 2011 to July 2011. Given the absence of dissemination, we must determine whether the 6,332 class members suffered some other concrete harm for purposes of Article III.

The initial question is whether the mere existence of a misleading OFAC alert in a consumer's internal credit file at TransUnion constitutes a concrete injury. . . . Publication is essential to liability in a suit for defamation. And there is no historical or common-law analog where the mere existence of inaccurate information, absent dissemination, amounts to concrete injury. . . .

The standing inquiry in this case thus distinguishes between (i) credit files that consumer reporting agencies maintain internally and (ii) the consumer credit reports that consumer reporting agencies disseminate to third-party creditors. The mere presence of an inaccuracy in an internal credit file, if it is not disclosed to a third party, causes no concrete harm. In cases such as these where allegedly inaccurate or misleading information sits in a company database, the plaintiffs' harm is roughly the same, legally speaking, as if someone wrote a defamatory letter and then stored it in her desk drawer. A letter that is not sent does not harm anyone, no matter how insulting the letter is. So too here.

Because the plaintiffs cannot demonstrate that the misleading information in the internal credit files itself constitutes a concrete harm, the plaintiffs advance a separate argument based on an asserted *risk of future harm*. They say that the 6,332 class members suffered a concrete injury for Article III purposes because the existence of misleading OFAC alerts in their internal credit files exposed them to a material risk that the information would be disseminated in the future to third parties and thereby cause them harm. . . .

As this Court has recognized, a person exposed to a risk of future harm may pursue forward-looking, injunctive relief to prevent the harm from occurring, at least so long as the risk of harm is sufficiently imminent and substantial. But a plaintiff must demonstrate standing separately for each form of relief sought. Therefore, a plaintiff's standing to seek injunctive relief does not necessarily mean that the plaintiff has standing to seek retrospective damages.

TransUnion advances a persuasive argument that in a suit for damages, the mere risk of future harm, standing alone, cannot qualify as a concrete harm—at least unless the exposure to the risk of future harm itself causes a *separate* concrete harm.[7] TransUnion contends that if an individual is exposed to a risk of future harm, time will eventually reveal whether the risk materializes in the form of actual harm. If the risk of future harm materializes and the individual suffers a concrete harm, then the harm itself, and not the pre-existing risk, will constitute a basis for the person's injury and for damages. If the risk of future harm does *not* materialize, then the individual cannot establish a concrete harm sufficient for standing, according to TransUnion.

---

[7] For example, a plaintiff's knowledge that he or she is exposed to a risk of future physical, monetary, or reputational harm could cause its own current emotional or

psychological harm. We take no position on whether or how such an emotional or psychological harm could suffice for Article III purposes . . . .

Consider an example. Suppose that a woman drives home from work a quarter mile ahead of a reckless driver who is dangerously swerving across lanes. The reckless driver has exposed the woman to a risk of future harm, but the risk does not materialize and the woman makes it home safely. As counsel for TransUnion stated, that would ordinarily be cause for celebration, not a lawsuit. But if the reckless driver crashes into the woman's car, the situation would be different, and (assuming a cause of action) the woman could sue the driver for damages.

The plaintiffs note that . . . libel and slander *per se* a[re] examples of cases where, as the plaintiffs see it, a mere risk of harm suffices for a damages claim. But . . . libel and slander *per se* require evidence of *publication*. And for those torts, publication is generally presumed to cause a harm, albeit not a readily quantifiable harm. But there is a significant difference between (i) an actual harm that has occurred but is not readily quantifiable, as in cases of libel and slander *per se*, and (ii) a mere risk of future harm. . . .

Here, the 6,332 plaintiffs did not demonstrate that the risk of future harm materialized—that is, that the inaccurate OFAC alerts in their internal TransUnion credit files were ever provided to third parties or caused a denial of credit. Nor did those plaintiffs present evidence that the class members were independently harmed by their exposure to the risk itself—that is, that they suffered some other injury (such as an emotional injury) from the mere risk that their credit reports would be provided to third-party businesses. Therefore, the 6,332 plaintiffs' argument for standing for their damages claims based on an asserted risk of future harm is unavailing. . . .

We next address the plaintiffs' standing to recover damages for two other claims in the complaint: the disclosure claim and the summary-of-rights claim. Those two claims are intertwined. . . .

[T]he plaintiffs have not demonstrated that the format of TransUnion's mailings caused them a harm with a close relationship to a harm traditionally recognized as providing a basis for a lawsuit in American courts. In fact, they do not demonstrate that they suffered any harm *at all* from the formatting violations. The plaintiffs presented no evidence that, other than Ramirez, a single other class member so much as *opened* the dual mailings, nor that they were confused, distressed, or relied on the information in any way. The plaintiffs put forth no evidence, moreover, that the plaintiffs would have tried to correct their credit files—and thereby prevented dissemination of a misleading report—had they been sent the information in the proper format. Without any evidence of harm caused by the format of the mailings, these are bare procedural violations, divorced from any concrete harm. . . .

We reverse the judgment of the U.S. Court of Appeals for the Ninth Circuit and remand the case for further proceedings consistent with this opinion. . . .

Justice THOMAS, with whom Justice BREYER, Justice SOTOMAYOR, and Justice KAGAN join, dissenting.

. . . . The principle that the violation of an individual right gives rise to an actionable harm was widespread at the founding, in early American history, and in many modern cases. In light of this history, tradition, and common practice, our test should be clear: So long as a statute fixes a minimum of recovery, there would seem to be no doubt of the right of one who establishes a technical ground of action to recover this minimum sum without any specific showing of loss. . . . [C]ourts for centuries held that injury in law to a private right was enough to create a case or controversy.

Here, each class member established a violation of his or her private rights. The jury found that TransUnion violated three separate duties created by statute. All three of those duties are owed to individuals, not to the community writ large. . . . The plaintiffs thus have a sufficient injury to sue in federal court. . . .

Never before has this Court declared that legal injury is *inherently* insufficient to support standing. And never before has this Court declared that legislatures are constitutionally precluded from creating legal rights enforceable in federal court if those rights deviate too far from their common-law roots. According to the majority, courts alone have the power to sift and weigh harms to decide whether they merit the Federal Judiciary's attention. In the name of protecting the separation of powers, this Court has relieved the legislature of its power to create and define rights. . . .

I respectfully dissent.

Craig v. Boren (1976)

Mr. Justice BRENNAN delivered the opinion of the Court.

The interaction of two sections of an Oklahoma statute prohibits the sale of "nonintoxicating" 3.2% beer to males under the age of 21 and to females under the age of 18. The question to be decided is whether such a gender-based differential constitutes a denial to males 18-20 years of age of the equal protection of the laws in violation of the Fourteenth Amendment.

This action was brought in the District Court for the Western District of Oklahoma on December 20, 1972, by appellant Craig, a male then between 18 and 21 years of age, and by appellant Whitener, a licensed vendor of 3.2% beer. The complaint sought declaratory and injunctive relief against enforcement of the gender-based differential on the ground that it constituted invidious discrimination against males 18-20 years of age. A three-judge court convened under 28 U.S.C. § 2281 sustained the constitutionality of the statutory differential and dismissed the action. We noted probable jurisdiction of appellants' appeal. We reverse. . . .

We first address a preliminary question of standing. Appellant Craig attained the age of 21 after we noted probable jurisdiction. Therefore, since only declaratory and injunctive relief against enforcement of the gender-based differential is sought, the controversy has been rendered moot as to Craig. *DeFunis v. Odegaard*.[2] The question thus arises whether appellant Whitener, the licensed vendor of 3.2% beer, who has a live controversy against enforcement of the statute, may rely upon the equal protection objections of males 18-20 years of age to establish her claim of unconstitutionality of the age-sex differential. We conclude that she may.

> [2] Appellants did not seek class certification of Craig as representative of other similarly situated males 18-20 years of age.

. . . . Whitener[] reli[es] upon the claimed unequal treatment of 18-20-year-old males as the premise of her equal protection challenge to Oklahoma's 3.2% beer law. . . . [O]ur decisions have settled that limitations on a litigant's assertion of jus tertii are not constitutionally mandated, but rather stem from a salutary rule of self-restraint designed to minimize unwarranted intervention into controversies where the applicable constitutional questions are ill-defined and speculative. These prudential objectives[are] thought to be enhanced by restrictions on third-party standing . . . .

In any event, we conclude that appellant Whitener has established independently her claim to assert jus tertii standing. The operation of §§ 241 and 245 plainly has inflicted injury in fact upon appellant sufficient to guarantee her concrete adverseness and to satisfy the constitutionally based standing requirements imposed by Art. III. The legal duties created by the statutory sections under challenge are addressed directly to vendors such as appellant. She is obliged either to heed the statutory discrimination, thereby incurring a direct economic injury through the constriction of her buyers' market, or to disobey the statutory command and suffer, in the words of Oklahoma's Assistant Attorney General, sanctions and perhaps loss of license. This Court repeatedly has recognized that such injuries establish the threshold requirements of a case or controversy mandated by Art. III.

As a vendor with standing . . . , appellant Whitener is entitled to assert those concomitant rights of third parties that would be diluted or adversely affected should her constitutional challenge fail and the statutes remain in force. Otherwise, the threatened imposition of governmental sanctions might deter appellant Whitener and other similarly situated vendors from selling 3.2% beer to young males, thereby ensuring that enforcement of the challenged restriction against the (vendor) would result indirectly in the violation of third parties' rights. Accordingly, vendors and those in like positions have been uniformly permitted to resist efforts at restricting their operations by acting as advocates of the rights of third parties who seek access to their market or function.[4]

> [4] The standing question presented here is not answered by the principle . . . that one to whom application of a statute is constitutional will not be heard to attack the statute on the ground that impliedly it might also be taken as applying to other persons or other situations in which its application might be unconstitutional. . . . [That rule remains germane] where the interests of the litigant and the rights of the proposed third parties are in no way mutually interdependent. . . . . [The] principle has also been relaxed where legal action against the claimant threatens to chill the First Amendment rights of third parties.

We therefore hold that Whitener has standing to raise relevant equal protection challenges to Oklahoma's gender-based law. . . .

Mr. Chief Justice BURGER, dissenting.

. . . . I cannot agree that appellant Whitener has standing arising from her status as a saloonkeeper to assert the constitutional rights of her customers. In this Court a litigant may only assert his own constitutional rights or immunities. There are a few, but strictly limited exceptions to that rule; despite the most creative efforts, this case fits within none of them.

. . . [T]here is here no barrier whatever to Oklahoma males 18-20 years of age asserting, in an appropriate forum, any constitutional rights they may claim to purchase 3.2% beer. Craig's successful litigation of this very issue was prevented only by the advent of his 21st birthday. There is thus no danger of interminable dilution of those rights if appellant Whitener is not permitted to litigate them here.

Nor is this controlled by *Griswold v. Connecticut*. It borders on the ludicrous to draw a parallel between a vendor of beer and the intimate professional physician-patient relationship which undergirded relaxation of standing rules in that case.

Even in *Eisenstadt*, the Court carefully limited its recognition of third-party standing to cases in which the relationship between the claimant and the relevant third party was not simply the fortuitous connection between a vendor and potential vendees, but the relationship between one who acted to protect the rights of a minority and the minority itself. This is plainly not the case here.

Elk Grove Unified School District v. Newdow (2004)

Each day elementary school teachers in the Elk Grove Unified School District (School District) lead their classes in a group recitation of the Pledge of Allegiance. Respondent, Michael A. Newdow, is an atheist whose daughter participates in that daily exercise. Because the Pledge contains the words "under God," he views the School District's policy as a religious indoctrination of his child that violates the First Amendment. A divided panel of the Court of Appeals for the Ninth Circuit agreed with Newdow. . . . We conclude that Newdow lacks standing and therefore reverse the Court of Appeals's decision.

. . . . Under California law, every public elementary school must begin each day with "appropriate patriotic exercises." The statute provides that the giving of the Pledge of Allegiance to the Flag of the United States of America shall satisfy this requirement. The Elk Grove Unified School District has implemented the state law by requiring that each elementary school class recite the pledge of allegiance to the flag once each day. Consistent with our case law, the School District permits students who object on religious grounds to abstain from the recitation.

In March 2000, Newdow filed suit in the United States District Court for the Eastern District of California against the United States Congress, the President of the United States, the State of California, and the School District and its superintendent. At the time of filing, Newdow's daughter was enrolled in kindergarten in the School District and participated in the daily recitation of the Pledge. Styled as a mandamus action, the complaint explains that Newdow is an atheist who was ordained more than 20 years ago in a ministry that espouses the religious philosophy that the true and eternal bonds of righteousness and virtue stem from reason rather than mythology. The complaint seeks a declaration that the . . . words "under God" violated the Establishment and Free Exercise Clauses of the United States Constitution, as well as an injunction against the School District's policy requiring daily recitation of the Pledge. It alleges that Newdow has standing to sue on his own behalf and on behalf of his daughter as "next friend."

. . . . After the Court of Appeals's initial opinion was announced, Sandra Banning, the mother of Newdow's daughter, filed a motion for leave to intervene, or alternatively to dismiss the complaint. She declared that although she and Newdow shared physical custody of their daughter, a state-court order granted her exclusive legal custody of the child, including the sole right to represent [the daughter's] legal interests and make all decision[s] about her education and welfare. Banning further stated that her daughter is a Christian who believes in God and has no objection either to reciting or hearing others recite the Pledge of Allegiance, or to its reference to God. Banning expressed the belief that her daughter would be harmed if the litigation were permitted to proceed, because others might incorrectly perceive the child as sharing her father's atheist views. Banning accordingly concluded, as her daughter's sole legal custodian, that it was not in the child's interest to be a party to Newdow's lawsuit. On September 25, 2002, the California Superior Court entered an order enjoining Newdow from including his daughter as an unnamed party or suing as her "next friend." . . .

In every federal case, the party bringing the suit must establish standing to prosecute the action. In essence the question of standing is whether the litigant is entitled to have the court decide the merits of the dispute or of particular issues. . . . The command to guard jealously and exercise rarely our power to make constitutional pronouncements requires strictest adherence when matters of great national significance are at stake. Even in cases concededly within our jurisdiction under Article III, we abide by a series of rules under which [we have] avoided passing upon a large part of all the constitutional questions pressed upon [us] for decision. Always we must balance the heavy obligation to exercise jurisdiction, against the deeply rooted commitment not to pass on questions of constitutionality unless adjudication of the constitutional issue is necessary.

Consistent with these principles, our standing jurisprudence contains two strands: Article III standing, which enforces the Constitution's case-or-controversy requirement, and prudential standing, which embodies judicially self-imposed limits on the exercise of federal jurisdiction. The Article III limitations are familiar: The plaintiff must show that the conduct of which he complains has caused him to suffer an injury in fact that a favorable judgment will redress. Although we have not exhaustively defined the prudential dimensions of the standing doctrine, we have explained that prudential standing encompasses the general prohibition on a litigant's raising another person's legal rights, the rule barring adjudication of generalized grievances more appropriately addressed in the representative branches, and the requirement that a plaintiff's complaint fall within the zone of interests protected by the law invoked. *Allen.* Without such limitations—closely related to Art. III concerns but essentially matters of judicial self-governance—the courts would be called upon to decide abstract questions of wide public significance even though other governmental institutions may be more competent to address the questions and even though judicial intervention may be unnecessary to protect individual rights.

One of the principal areas in which this Court has customarily declined to intervene is the realm of domestic relations. Long ago we observed that the whole subject of the domestic relations of husband and wife, parent and child, belongs to the laws of the States and not to the laws of the United States. So strong is our deference to state law in this area that we have recognized a "domestic relations exception" that divests the federal courts of power to issue divorce, alimony, and child custody decrees. *Ankenbrandt v. Richards.* We have also acknowledged that it might be appropriate for the federal courts to decline to hear a case involving elements of the domestic relationship, even when divorce, alimony, or child custody is not strictly at issue . . . . Thus, while rare instances arise in which it is necessary to answer a substantial federal question that transcends or exists apart from the family law issue, in general it is appropriate for the federal courts to leave delicate issues of domestic relations to the state courts.

. . . . Newdow contends that despite Banning's final authority, he retains an unrestricted right to inculcate in his daughter—free from governmental interference—the atheistic beliefs he finds persuasive. The difficulty with that argument is that Newdow's rights, as in many cases touching upon family relations, cannot be viewed in isolation. This case concerns not merely Newdow's interest in inculcating his child with his views on religion, but also the rights of the child's mother as a parent generally and under the Superior Court orders specifically. And most important, it implicates the interests of a young child who finds herself at the center of a highly public debate over her custody, the propriety of a widespread national ritual, and the meaning of our Constitution.

The interests of the affected persons in this case are in many respects antagonistic. Of course, legal disharmony in family relations is not uncommon, and in many instances that disharmony poses no bar to federal-court adjudication of proper federal questions. What makes this case different is that Newdow's standing derives entirely from his relationship with his daughter, but he lacks the right to litigate as her next friend. In marked contrast to our case law on *jus tertii*, the interests of this parent and this child are not parallel and, indeed, are potentially in conflict.

Newdow's parental status is defined by California's domestic relations law. . . . Animated by a conception of family privacy that includes not simply a policy of minimum state intervention but also a presumption of parental autonomy, the state cases create a zone of private authority within which each parent, whether custodial or noncustodial, remains free to impart to the child his or her religious perspective.

Nothing that either Banning or the School Board has done, however, impairs Newdow's right to instruct his daughter in his religious views. Instead, Newdow . . . . wishes to forestall his daughter's exposure to religious ideas that her mother, who wields a form of veto power, endorses, and to use his parental status to challenge the influences to which his daughter may be exposed in school when he and Banning disagree. The California cases simply do not stand for the proposition that Newdow has a right to dictate to others what they may and may not say to his child respecting religion. . . . A next friend surely could exercise such a right, but the Superior Court's order has deprived Newdow of that status.

In our view, it is improper for the federal courts to entertain a claim by a plaintiff whose standing to sue is founded on family law rights that are in dispute when prosecution of the lawsuit may have an adverse effect on the person who is the source of the plaintiff's claimed standing. When hard questions of domestic relations are sure to affect the outcome, the prudent course is for the federal court to stay its hand rather than reach out to resolve a weighty question of federal constitutional law. There is a vast difference between Newdow's right to communicate with his child—which both California law and the First Amendment recognize—and his claimed right to shield his daughter from influences to which she is exposed in school despite the terms of the custody order. We conclude that, having been deprived under California law of the right to sue as next friend, Newdow lacks prudential standing to bring this suit in federal court.

The judgment of the Court of Appeals is reversed.

Lexmark International v. Static Control Components (2014)

This case requires us to decide whether respondent, Static Control Components, Inc., may sue petitioner, Lexmark International, Inc., for false advertising under the Lanham Act.

I. Background

Lexmark manufactures and sells laser printers. It also sells toner cartridges for those printers (toner being the powdery ink that laser printers use to create images on paper). Lexmark designs its printers to work only with its own style of cartridges, and it therefore dominates the market for cartridges compatible with its printers. That market, however, is not devoid of competitors. Other businesses, called "remanufacturers," acquire used Lexmark toner cartridges, refurbish them, and sell them in competition with new and refurbished cartridges sold by Lexmark.

Lexmark would prefer that its customers return their empty cartridges to it for refurbishment and resale, rather than sell those cartridges to a remanufacturer. So Lexmark introduced what it called a "Prebate" program, which enabled customers to purchase new toner cartridges at a 20-percent discount if they would agree to return the cartridge to Lexmark once it was empty. Those terms were communicated to consumers through notices printed on the toner-cartridge boxes, which advised the consumer that opening the box would indicate assent to the terms—a practice commonly known as "shrinkwrap licensing." To enforce the Prebate terms, Lexmark included a microchip in each Prebate cartridge that would disable the cartridge after it ran out of toner; for the cartridge to be used again, the microchip would have to be replaced by Lexmark.

Static Control is not itself a manufacturer or remanufacturer of toner cartridges. It is, rather, the market leader in making and selling the components necessary to remanufacture Lexmark cartridges. In addition to supplying remanufacturers with toner and various replacement parts, Static Control developed a microchip that could mimic the microchip in Lexmark's Prebate cartridges. By purchasing Static Control's microchips and using them to replace the Lexmark microchip, remanufacturers were able to refurbish and resell used Prebate cartridges.

Lexmark did not take kindly to that development. In 2002, it sued Static Control, alleging that Static Control's microchips violated both the Copyright Act of 1976 and the Digital Millennium Copyright Act. Static Control counterclaimed, alleging, among other things, violations of § [1125](a) of the Lanham Act, ... which provides:

(1) Any person who, on or in connection with any goods or services, or any container for goods, uses in commerce any word, term, name, symbol, or device, or any combination thereof, or any false designation of origin, false or misleading description of fact, or false or misleading representation of fact, which—

(A) is likely to cause confusion, or to cause mistake, or to deceive as to the affiliation, connection, or association of such person with another person, or as to the origin, sponsorship, or approval of his or her goods, services, or commercial activities by another person, or

(B) in commercial advertising or promotion, misrepresents the nature, characteristics, qualities, or geographic origin of his or her or another person's goods, services, or commercial activities,

shall be liable in a civil action by any person who believes that he or she is or is likely to be damaged by such act.

. . . . As relevant to its Lanham Act claim, Static Control alleged two types of false or misleading conduct by Lexmark. First, it alleged that through its Prebate program Lexmark purposefully misleads end-users to believe that they are legally bound by the Prebate terms and are thus required to return the Prebate-labeled cartridge to Lexmark after a single use. Second, it alleged that upon introducing the Prebate program, Lexmark sent letters to most of the companies in the toner cartridge remanufacturing business falsely advising those companies that it was illegal to sell refurbished Prebate cartridges and, in particular, that it was illegal to use Static Control's products to refurbish those cartridges. Static Control asserted that by those statements, Lexmark had materially misrepresented the nature, characteristics, and qualities of both its own products and Static Control's products. It further maintained that Lexmark's misrepresentations had proximately caused and were likely to cause injury to Static Control by diverting sales from Static Control to Lexmark, and had substantially injured its business reputation by leading consumers and others in the trade to believe that Static Control is engaged in illegal conduct. Static Control sought treble damages, attorney's fees and costs, and injunctive relief.

The District Court granted Lexmark's motion to dismiss Static Control's Lanham Act claim. It held that Static Control lacked "prudential standing" to bring that claim . . . . The Sixth Circuit reversed . . . .

II. "Prudential Standing"

The parties' briefs treat the question on which we granted certiorari as one of "prudential standing." Because we think that label misleading, we begin by clarifying the nature of the question at issue in this case.

From Article III's limitation of the judicial power to resolving "Cases" and "Controversies," and the separation-of-powers principles underlying that limitation, we have deduced a set of requirements that together make up the irreducible constitutional minimum of standing. The plaintiff must have suffered or be imminently threatened with a concrete and particularized "injury in fact" that is fairly traceable to the challenged action of the defendant and likely to be redressed by a favorable judicial decision. Lexmark does not deny that Static Control's allegations of lost sales and damage to its business reputation give it standing under Article III to press its false-advertising claim, and we are satisfied that they do.

Although Static Control's claim thus presents a case or controversy that is properly within federal courts' Article III jurisdiction, Lexmark urges that we should decline to adjudicate Static Control's claim on grounds that are "prudential," rather than constitutional. That request is in some tension with our recent reaffirmation of the principle that a federal court's obligation to hear and decide cases within its jurisdiction is virtually unflagging. *Sprint Communications, Inc. v. Jacobs* (quoting *Colorado River Water Conservation Dist. v. United States*). In recent decades, however, we have adverted to a "prudential" branch of standing, a doctrine not derived from Article III and not exhaustively defined but encompassing (we have said) at least three broad principles: the general prohibition on a litigant's raising another person's legal rights, the rule barring adjudication of generalized grievances more appropriately addressed in the representative branches, and the requirement that a plaintiff's complaint fall within the zone of interests protected by the law invoked. *Elk Grove Unified School Dist. v. Newdow* (quoting *Allen v. Wright*).

. . . . Static Control . . . argues that we should measure its "prudential standing" by using the zone-of-interests test. Although we admittedly have placed that test under the "prudential" rubric in the past, it does not belong there . . . . Whether a plaintiff comes within the zone of interests is an issue that requires us to determine, using traditional tools of statutory interpretation, whether a legislatively conferred cause of action encompasses a particular plaintiff's claim. . . .[3]

[3] The zone-of-interests test is not the only concept that we have previously classified as an aspect of "prudential standing" but for which, upon closer inspection, we have found that label inapt. Take, for example, our reluctance to entertain generalized grievances—*i.e.,* suits claiming only harm to the plaintiff's and every citizen's interest in proper application of the Constitution and laws, and seeking relief that no more directly and tangibly benefits him than it does the public at large. While we have at times grounded our reluctance to entertain such suits in the counsels of prudence (albeit counsels closely related to the policies reflected in Article III), we have since held that such suits do not present constitutional "cases" or "controversies." They are

barred for constitutional reasons, not "prudential" ones. The limitations on third-party standing are harder to classify; we have observed that third-party standing is closely related to the question whether a person in the litigant's position will have a right of action on the claim, but most of our cases have not framed the inquiry in that way. This case does not present any issue of third-party standing, and consideration of that doctrine's proper place in the standing firmament can await another day.

In sum, the question this case presents is whether Static Control falls within the class of plaintiffs whom Congress has authorized to sue under § 1125(a). In other words, we ask whether Static Control has a cause of action under the statute. That question requires us to determine the meaning of the congressionally enacted provision creating a cause of action. In doing so, we apply traditional principles of statutory interpretation.

. . . . Static Control has adequately pleaded both elements. The judgment of the Court of Appeals is affirmed.

Ripeness & Mootness

Introduction

Ripeness and mootness have been called "standing in time" by some commentators, but the Court has not adopted that moniker. Instead, the Court has treated them differently, including by differentiating how closely connected they are to constitutional standing. The Court also has identified exceptions. Consider the following questions:

- How are ripeness and mootness different from standing, if at all?

- Are ripeness and mootness jurisdictional? Are they constitutional? Prudential?

- What power, if any, do the federal courts have to create exceptions to these doctrines?

Abbott Laboratories v. Gardner (1967)

In 1962 Congress amended the Federal Food, Drug, and Cosmetic Act to require manufacturers of prescription drugs to print the "established name" of the drug "prominently and in type at least half as large as that used thereon for any proprietary name or designation for such drug," on labels and other printed material. . . . The underlying purpose of the 1962 amendment was to bring to the attention of doctors and patients the fact that many of the drugs sold under familiar trade names are actually identical to drugs sold under their "established" or less familiar trade names at significantly lower prices. The Commissioner of Food and Drugs, exercising authority delegated to him by the Secretary, . . . promulgated the following regulation for the efficient enforcement of the Act: "If the label or labeling of a prescription drug bears a proprietary name or designation for the drug or any ingredient thereof, the established name, if such there be, corresponding to such proprietary name or designation, shall accompany each appearance of such proprietary name or designation." 21 CFR § 1.104(g)(1). A similar rule was made applicable to advertisements for prescription drugs, § 1.105(b)(1).

The present action was brought by a group of 37 individual drug manufacturers and by the Pharmaceutical Manufacturers Association, of which all the petitioner companies are members, and which includes manufacturers of more than 90% of the Nation's supply of prescription drugs. They challenged the regulations on the ground that the Commissioner exceeded his authority under the statute by promulgating an order requiring labels, advertisements, and other printed matter relating to prescription drugs to designate the established name of the particular drug involved every time its trade name is used anywhere in such material.

The District Court, on cross motions for summary judgment, granted the declaratory and injunctive relief sought, finding that the statute did not sweep so broadly as to permit the Commissioner's "every time" interpretation. The Court of Appeals for the Third Circuit reversed without reaching the merits of the case. It held . . . that no actual case or controversy existed and, for that reason, that no relief under the Administrative Procedure Act, or under the Declaratory Judgment Act, was in any event available. Because of the general importance of the question, . . . we granted certiorari. . . .

The injunctive and declaratory judgment remedies are discretionary, and courts traditionally have been reluctant to apply them to administrative determinations unless these arise in the context of a controversy "ripe" for judicial resolution. Without undertaking to survey the intricacies of the ripeness doctrine, it is fair to say that its basic rationale is to prevent the courts, through avoidance of premature adjudication, from entangling themselves in abstract disagreements over administrative policies, and also to protect the agencies from judicial interference until an administrative decision has been formalized and its effects felt in a concrete way by the challenging parties. The problem is best seen in a twofold aspect, requiring us to evaluate both the fitness of the issues for judicial decision and the hardship to the parties of withholding court consideration.

As to the former factor, we believe the issues presented are appropriate for judicial resolution at this time. First, all parties agree that the issue tendered is a purely legal one: whether the statute was properly construed by the Commissioner to require the established name of the drug to be used every time the proprietary name is employed. Both sides moved for summary judgment in the District Court, and no claim is made here that further administrative proceedings are contemplated. It is suggested that the justification for this rule might vary with different circumstances, and that the expertise of the Commissioner is relevant to passing upon the validity of the regulation. This of course is true, but the suggestion overlooks the fact that both sides have approached this case as one purely of congressional intent, and that the Government made no effort to justify the regulation in factual terms.

Second, the regulations in issue we find to be final agency action within the meaning of § 10 of the Administrative Procedure Act, as construed in judicial decisions. An agency action includes any rule, defined by the Act as an agency statement of general or particular applicability and future effect designed to implement, interpret, or prescribe law or policy. The cases dealing with judicial review of administrative actions have interpreted the "finality" element in a pragmatic way. . . .

The regulation challenged here, promulgated in a formal manner after announcement in the Federal Register and consideration of comments by interested parties is quite clearly definitive. There is no hint that this regulation is informal, or only the ruling of a subordinate official, or tentative. It was made effective upon publication, and the Assistant General Counsel for Food and Drugs stated in the District Court that compliance was expected.

The Government argues, however, that the present case can be distinguished . . . on the ground that . . . here the Attorney General must authorize criminal and seizure actions for violations of the statute. In the context of this case, we do not find this argument persuasive. These regulations are not meant to advise the Attorney General, but purport to be directly authorized by the statute. Thus, if within the Commissioner's authority, they have the status of law and violations of them carry heavy criminal and civil sanctions. Also, there is no representation that the Attorney General and the Commissioner disagree in this area; the Justice Department is defending this very suit. It would be adherence to a mere technicality to give any credence to this contention. Moreover, the agency does have direct authority to enforce this regulation in the context of passing upon applications for clearance of new drugs, or certification of certain antibiotics.

This is also a case in which the impact of the regulations upon the petitioners is sufficiently direct and immediate as to render the issue appropriate for judicial review at this stage. These regulations purport to give an authoritative interpretation of a statutory provision that has a direct effect on the day-to-day business of all prescription drug companies; its promulgation puts petitioners in a dilemma that it was the very purpose of the Declaratory Judgment Act to ameliorate. As the District Court found on the basis of uncontested allegations, "Either they must comply with the every time requirement and incur the costs of changing over their promotional material and labeling or they must follow their present course and risk prosecution." The regulations are clear-cut, and were made effective immediately upon publication; as noted earlier the agency's counsel represented to the District Court that immediate compliance with their terms was expected. If petitioners wish to comply they must change all their labels, advertisements, and promotional materials; they must destroy stocks of printed matter; and they must invest heavily in new printing type and new supplies. The alternative to compliance—continued use of material which they believe in good faith meets the statutory requirements, but which clearly does not meet the regulation of the Commissioner—may be even more costly. That course would risk serious criminal and civil penalties for the unlawful distribution of misbranded drugs.

It is relevant at this juncture to recognize that petitioners deal in a sensitive industry, in which public confidence in their drug products is especially important. To require them to challenge these regulations only as a defense to an action brought by the Government might harm them severely and unnecessarily. Where the legal issue presented is fit for judicial resolution, and where a regulation requires an immediate and significant change in the plaintiffs' conduct of their affairs with serious penalties attached to noncompliance, access to the courts under the Administrative Procedure Act and the Declaratory Judgment Act must be permitted, absent a statutory bar or some other unusual circumstance, neither of which appears here.

The Government does not dispute the very real dilemma in which petitioners are placed by the regulation, but contends that mere financial expense is not a justification for pre-enforcement judicial review. It is of course true that cases in this Court dealing with the standing of particular parties to bring an action have held that a possible financial loss is not by itself a sufficient interest to sustain a judicial challenge to governmental action. But there is no question in the present case that petitioners have sufficient standing as plaintiffs: the regulation is directed at them in particular; it requires them to make significant changes in their everyday business practices; if they fail to observe the Commissioner's rule they are quite clearly exposed to the imposition of strong sanctions. . . .

The Government further contends that the threat of criminal sanctions for noncompliance with a judicially untested regulation is unrealistic; the Solicitor General has represented that if court enforcement becomes necessary, the Department of Justice will proceed only civilly for an injunction or by condemnation. We cannot accept this argument as a sufficient answer to petitioners' petition. This action at its inception was properly brought and this subsequent representation of the Department of Justice should not suffice to defeat it.

Finally, the Government urges that to permit resort to the courts in this type of case may delay or impede effective enforcement of the Act. We fully recognize the important public interest served by assuring prompt and unimpeded administration of the Pure Food, Drug, and Cosmetic Act, but we do not find the Government's argument convincing. First, in this particular case, a pre-enforcement challenge by nearly all prescription drug manufacturers is calculated to speed enforcement. If the Government prevails, a large part of the industry is bound by the decree; if the Government loses, it can more quickly revise its regulation. . . . Reversed and remanded.

United Public Workers v. Mitchell (1947)

The Hatch Act, enacted in 1940, declares unlawful certain specified political activities of federal employees. Section 9 forbids officers and employees in the executive branch of the Federal Government, with exceptions, from taking any active part in political management or in political campaigns. Section 15 declares that the activities theretofore determined by the United States Civil Service Commission to be prohibited to employees in the classified civil service of the United States by the civil service rules shall be deemed to be prohibited to federal employees covered by the Hatch Act. . . .

For many years before the Hatch Act the Congress had authorized the exclusion of federal employees in the competitive classified service from active participation in political management and political campaigns. In June, 1938, the Congressional authorization for exclusion had been made more effective by a Civil Service Commission disciplinary rule. . . .

The present appellants sought an injunction before a statutory three judge district court of the District of Columbia against appellees, members of the United States Civil Service Commission to prohibit them from enforcing against petitioners the provisions of the second sentence of § 9(a) of the Hatch Act for the reason that the sentence is repugnant to the Constitution of the United States. A declaratory judgment of the unconstitutionality of the sentence was also sought. The sentence referred to reads, "No officer or employee in the executive branch of the Federal Government . . . shall take any active part in political management or in political campaigns."

Various individual employees of the federal executive civil service and the United Public Workers of America, a labor union with these and other executive employees as members, as a representative of all its members, joined in the suit. It is alleged that the individuals desire to engage in acts of political management and in political campaigns. From the affidavits it is plain, and we so assume, that these activities will be carried on completely outside of the hours of employment. Appellants challenge the second sentence of § 9(a) as unconstitutional for various reasons. They are set out below in the language of the complaint.

None of the appellants, except George P. Poole, has violated the provisions of the Hatch Act. They wish to act contrary to its provisions and those of § 1 of the Civil Service Rules and desire a declaration of the legally permissible limits of regulation. Defendants moved to dismiss the complaint for lack of a justiciable case or controversy. The District Court determined that each of these individual appellants had an interest in their claimed privilege of engaging in political activities, sufficient to give them a right to maintain this suit. The District Court further determined that the questioned provision of the Hatch Act was valid and that the complaint therefore failed to state a cause of action. It accordingly dismissed the complaint and granted summary judgment to defendants.

. . . . At the threshold of consideration, we are called upon to decide whether the complaint states a controversy cognizable in this Court. We defer consideration of the cause of action of Mr. Poole until section Three of this opinion. . . . The assumed controversy between affiant and the Civil Service Commission as to affiant's right to act as watcher at the polls on November 2, 1943, had long been moot when this complaint was filed. We do not therefore treat this allegation separately. The affidavits, it will be noticed, follow the generality of purpose expressed by the complaint. They declare a desire to act contrary to the rule against political activity but not that the rule has been violated. In this respect, we think they differ from the type of threat adjudicated in [other cases involving] the refusal to admit an applicant to membership in a labor union on account of race [or involving] an injunction . . . forbidding [a party] from acting as the business agent of the union and the Union from further functioning as a union until it complied with the state law. The threats which menaced the affiants of these affidavits in the case now being considered are closer to a general threat by officials to enforce those laws which they are charged to administer, than they are to the direct threat of punishment against a named organization for a completed act that made [those] cases justiciable.

As is well known the federal courts established pursuant to Article III of the Constitution do not render advisory opinions. For adjudication of constitutional issues concrete legal issues, presented in actual cases, not abstractions, are requisite. This is as true of declaratory judgments as any other field. These appellants seem clearly to seek advisory opinions upon broad claims of rights protected by the First, Fifth, Ninth and Tenth Amendments to the Constitution. As these appellants are classified employees, they have a right superior to the generality of citizens, but the facts of their personal interest in their civil rights, of the general threat of possible interference with those rights by the Civil Service Commission under its rules, if specified things are done by appellants, does not make a justiciable case or controversy. Appellants want to engage in "political management and political campaigns, to persuade others to follow appellants' views by discussion, speeches, articles and other acts reasonably designed to secure the selection of appellants' political choices. Such generality of objection is really an attack on the political expediency of the Hatch Act, not the presentation of legal issues. It is beyond the competence of courts to render such a decision.

The power of courts, and ultimately of this Court to pass upon the constitutionality of acts of Congress arises only when the interests of litigants require the use of this judicial authority for their protection against actual interference. A hypothetical threat is not enough. We can only speculate as to the kinds of political activity the appellants desire to engage in or as to the contents of their proposed public statements or the circumstances of their publication. It would not accord with judicial responsibility to adjudge, in a matter involving constitutionality, between the freedom of the individual and the requirements of public order except when definite rights appear upon the one side and definite prejudicial interferences upon the other.[22]

[22] It has long been this Court's considered practice not to decide abstract, hypothetical or contingent questions, . . . or to decide any constitutional question in advance of the necessity for its decision, . . . or to formulate a rule of constitutional law broader than is required by the precise facts to which it is to be applied, . . . or to decide any constitutional question except with reference to the particular facts to which it is to be applied . . . .

The Constitution allots the nation's judicial power to the federal courts. Unless these courts respect the limits of that unique authority, they intrude upon powers vested in the legislative or executive branches. Judicial adherence to the doctrine of the separation of powers preserves the courts for the decision of issues, between litigants, capable of effective determination. Judicial exposition upon political proposals is permissible only when necessary to decide definite issues between litigants. When the courts act continually within these constitutionally imposed boundaries of their power, their ability to perform their function as a balance for the people's protection against abuse of power by other branches of government remains unimpaired. Should the courts seek to expand their power so as to bring under their jurisdiction ill-defined controversies over constitutional issues, they would become the organ of political theories. Such abuse of judicial power would properly meet rebuke and restriction from other branches. By these mutual checks and balances by and between the branches of government, democracy undertakes to preserve the liberties of the people from excessive concentrations of authority. No threat of interference by the Commission with rights of these appellants appears beyond that implied by the existence of the law and the regulations. We should not take judicial cognizance of the situation presented on the part of the appellants considered in this subdivision of the opinion. These reasons lead us to conclude that the determination of the trial court, that the individual appellants, other than Poole, could maintain this action, was erroneous. . . .

The judgment of the District Court is accordingly affirmed.

. . . . Mr. Justice BLACK, dissenting.

. . . . [W]hatever opinions employees may dare to express, even secretly, must be at their peril. They cannot know what particular expressions may be reported to the Commission and held by it to be a sufficient political activity to cost them their jobs. Their peril is all the greater because of another warning by the Commission that "Employees are . . . accountable for political activity by persons other than themselves, including wives or husbands, if, in fact, the employees are thus accomplishing by collusion and indirection what they may not lawfully do directly and openly." Thus are the families of public employees stripped of their freedom of political action. The result is that the sum of political privilege left to government and state employees, and their families, to take part in political campaigns seems to be this: They may vote in silence; they may carefully and quietly express a political view at their peril; and they may become "spectators" (this is the Commission's word) at campaign gatherings, though it may be highly dangerous for them to "second a motion" or let it be known that they agree or disagree with a speaker.

. . . . [S]ince I agree with Mr. Justice Douglas that all the petitioners' complaints state a case or controversy, and show threats of imminent irreparable damages, I think that the contention that the challenged provision is unconstitutional on its face should be sustained as to all of them. . . .

Mr. Justice DOUGLAS, dissenting in part.

. . . . It is clear that the declaratory judgment procedure is available in the federal courts only in cases involving actual controversies and may not be used to obtain an advisory opinion in a controversy not yet arisen. The requirement of an actual controversy, which is written into the statute and has its roots in the Constitution (Article III, § 2) seems to me to be fully met here.

What these appellants propose to do is plain enough. If they do what they propose to do, it is clear that they will be discharged from their positions. The analysis of the situation by the District Court seems to me to be accurate and conclusive:

> The mere existence of the statute, saying that they shall not engage in political activity, the penalty in the statute that they shall be dismissed if they do, and the warning addressed to them by the Civil Service Commission in their posters certainly prevent them from engaging in such activity, if the statute is constitutional. If the statute is unconstitutional, they are being prevented from things which they have the right to do. If the statute is constitutional, it is mandatory that they be dismissed for doing such things. . . . The provisions of Civil Service Rule XV that in case of any violation of the Civil Service Act or Rules or of any Executive Order or any regulation of the Commission the Commission shall certify the facts to the proper appointing officer with specific instructions as to discipline or dismissal is now

controlled by the provisions of the Hatch Act that in case of violation of Section 9(a) of that Act, dismissal is mandatory.

Their proposed conduct is sufficiently specific to show plainly that it will violate the Act. The policy of the Commission and the mandate of the Act leave no lingering doubt as to the consequences.[2]

> [2] The case is, therefore, unlike those situations where the Court refused to entertain actions for declaratory judgments, the state of facts being hypothetical in the sense that the challenge was to statutes which had not as yet been construed or their specific application known.

On a discharge these employees would lose their jobs, their seniority, and other civil service benefits. They could, of course, sue in the Court of Claims. But the remedy there is a money judgment, not a restoration to the office formerly held. Of course, there might be other remedies available in these situations to determine their rights to the offices from which they are discharged. But to require these employees first to suffer the hardship of a discharge is not only to make them incur a penalty; it makes inadequate, if not wholly illusory, any legal remedy which may have. Men who must sacrifice their means of livelihood in order to test their rights to their jobs must either pursue prolonged and expensive litigation as unemployed persons or pull up their roots, change their life careers, and seek employment in other fields. . . .

. . . . The declaratory judgment procedure is designed to declare rights and other legal relations of any interested party . . . whether or not further relief is or could be prayed. The fact that equity would not restrain a wrongful removal of an office holder but would leave the complainant to his legal remedies is, therefore, immaterial. A judgment which, without more, adjudicates the status of a person is permissible under the Declaratory Judgment Act. The declaration of a status was perhaps the earliest exercise of this procedure. The right to hold an office or public position against such threats is a common example of its use. Declaratory relief is the singular remedy available here to preserve the status quo while the constitutional rights of these appellants to make these utterances and to engage in these activities are determined. The threat against them is real not fanciful, immediate not remote. The case is therefore an actual not a hypothetical one. And the present case seems to me to be a good example of a situation where uncertainty, peril, and insecurity result from imminent and immediate threats to asserted rights. . . .

DeFunis v. Odegaard (1974)

In 1971 the petitioner Marco DeFunis, Jr., applied for admission as a first-year student at the University of Washington Law School, a state-operated institution. The size of the incoming first-year class was to be limited to 150 persons, and the Law School received some 1,600 applications for these 150 places. DeFunis was eventually notified that he had been denied admission. He thereupon commenced this suit in a Washington trial court, contending that the procedures and criteria employed by the Law School Admissions Committee invidiously discriminated against him on account of his race in violation of the Equal Protection Clause of the Fourteenth Amendment to the United States Constitution.

DeFunis brought the suit on behalf of himself alone, and not as the representative of any class, against the various respondents, who are officers, faculty members, and members of the Board of Regents of the University of Washington. He asked the trial court to issue a mandatory injunction commanding the respondents to admit him as a member of the first-year class entering in September 1971, on the ground that the Law School admissions policy had resulted in the unconstitutional denial of his application for admission. The trial court agreed with his claim and granted the requested relief. DeFunis was, accordingly, admitted to the Law School and began his legal studies there in the fall of 1971. On appeal, the Washington Supreme Court reversed the judgment of the trial court and held that the Law School admissions policy did not violate the Constitution. By this time DeFunis was in his second year at the Law School.

He then petitioned this Court for a writ of certiorari, and Mr. Justice Douglas, as Circuit Justice, stayed the judgment of the Washington Supreme Court pending the final disposition of the case by this Court. By virtue of this stay, DeFunis has remained in law school, and was in the first term of his third and final year when this Court first considered his certiorari petition in the fall of 1973. Because of our concern that DeFunis's third-year standing in the Law School might have rendered this case moot, we requested the parties to brief the question of mootness before we acted on the petition. In response, both sides contended that the case was not moot. The respondents indicated that, if the decision of the Washington Supreme Court were permitted to stand, the petitioner could complete the term for which he was then enrolled but would have to apply to the faculty for permission to continue in the school before he could register for another term.

We granted the petition for certiorari . . . .

In response to questions raised from the bench during the oral argument, counsel for the petitioner has informed the Court that DeFunis has now registered for his final quarter in law school. Counsel for the respondents have made clear that the Law School will not in any way seek to abrogate this registration. In light of DeFunis's recent registration for the last quarter of his final law school year, and the Law School's assurance that his registration is fully effective, the insistent question again arises whether this case is not moot, and to that question we now turn.

The starting point for analysis is the familiar proposition that federal courts are without power to decide questions that cannot affect the rights of litigants in the case before them. The inability of the federal judiciary to review moot cases derives from the requirement of Art. III of the Constitution under which the exercise of judicial power depends upon the existence of a case or controversy. Although as a matter of Washington state law it appears that this case would be saved from mootness by the great public interest in the continuing issues raised by this appeal, the fact remains that under Art. III even in cases arising in the state courts, the question of mootness is a federal one which a federal court must resolve before it assumes jurisdiction.

The respondents have represented that, without regard to the ultimate resolution of the issues in this case, DeFunis will remain a student in the Law School for the duration of any term in which he has already enrolled. Since he has now registered for his final term, it is evident that he will be given an opportunity to complete all academic and other requirements for graduation, and, if he does so, will receive his diploma regardless of any decision this Court might reach on the merits of this case. In short, all parties agree that DeFunis is now entitled to complete his legal studies at the University of Washington and to receive his degree from that institution. A determination by this Court of the legal issues tendered by the parties is no longer necessary to compel that result, and could not serve to prevent it. DeFunis did not cast his suit as a class action, and the only remedy he requested was an injunction commanding his admission to the Law School. He was not only accorded that remedy, but he now has also been irrevocably admitted to the final term of the final year of the Law School course. The controversy between the parties has thus clearly ceased to be definite and concrete and no longer touches the legal relations of parties having adverse legal interests.

It matters not that these circumstances partially stem from a policy decision on the part of the respondent Law School authorities. The respondents, through their counsel, the Attorney General of the State, have professionally represented that in no event will the status of DeFunis now be affected by any view this Court might express on the merits of this controversy. And it has been the settled practice of the Court, in contexts no less significant, fully to accept representations such as these as parameters for decision.

There is a line of decisions in this Court standing for the proposition that the "voluntary cessation" of allegedly illegal conduct does not deprive the tribunal of power to hear and determine the case, i.e., does not make the case moot. These decisions and the doctrine they reflect would be quite relevant if the question of mootness here had arisen by reason of a unilateral change in the admissions procedures of the Law School. For it was the admissions procedures that were the target of this litigation, and a voluntary cessation of the admissions practices complained of could make this case moot only if it could be said with assurance that there is no reasonable expectation that the wrong will be repeated. Otherwise, the defendant is free to return to his old ways, and this fact would be enough to prevent mootness because of the public interest in having the legality of the practices settled. But mootness in the present case depends not at all upon a "voluntary cessation" of the admissions practices that were the subject of this litigation. It depends, instead, upon the simple fact that DeFunis is now in the final quarter of the final year of his course of study, and the settled and unchallenged policy of the Law School to permit him to complete the term for which he is now enrolled.

It might also be suggested that this case presents a question that is capable of repetition, yet evading review, and is thus amenable to federal adjudication even though it might otherwise be considered moot. But DeFunis will never again be required to run the gantlet of the Law School's admission process, and so the question is certainly not capable of repetition so far as he is concerned. Moreover, just because this particular case did not reach the Court until the eve of the petitioner's graduation from Law School, it hardly follows that the issue he raises will in the future evade review. If the admissions procedures of the Law School remain unchanged, there is no reason to suppose that a subsequent case attacking those procedures will not come with relative speed to this Court, now that the Supreme Court of Washington has spoken. This case, therefore, in no way presents . . . a departure from the usual rule in federal cases . . . that an actual controversy must exist at stages of appellate or certiorari review, and not simply at the date the action is initiated.

Because the petitioner will complete his law school studies at the end of the term for which he has now registered regardless of any decision this Court might reach on the merits of this litigation, we conclude that the Court cannot, consistently with the limitations of Art. III of the Constitution, consider the substantive constitutional issues tendered by the parties.[5] Accordingly, the judgment of the Supreme Court of Washington is vacated, and the cause is remanded for such proceedings as by that court may be deemed appropriate.

> [5] It is suggested in dissent that any number of unexpected events—illness, economic necessity, even academic failure—might prevent his graduation at the end of the term. But such speculative contingencies afford no basis for our passing on the substantive issues the petitioner would have us decide, in the absence of evidence that this is a prospect of immediacy and reality.

It is so ordered.

Mr. Justice BRENNAN, with whom Mr. Justice DOUGLAS, Mr. Justice WHITE, and Mr. Justice MARSHALL concur, dissenting.

I respectfully dissent. Many weeks of the school term remain, and petitioner may not receive his degree despite respondents' assurances that petitioner will be allowed to complete this term's schooling regardless of our decision. Any number of unexpected events—illness, economic necessity, even academic failure—might prevent his graduation at the end of the term. Were that misfortune to befall, and were petitioner required to register for yet another term, the prospect that he would again face the hurdle of the admissions policy is real, not fanciful; for respondents warn that DeFunis would have to take some appropriate action to request continued admission for the remainder of his law school education, and some discretionary action by the University on such request would have to be taken. Thus, respondents' assurances have not dissipated the possibility that petitioner might once again have to run the gantlet of the University's allegedly unlawful admissions policy. The Court therefore proceeds on an erroneous premise in resting its mootness holding on a supposed inability to render any judgment that may affect one way or the other petitioner's completion of his law studies. For surely if we were to reverse the Washington Supreme Court, we could insure that, if for some reason petitioner did not graduate this spring, he would be entitled to re-enrollment at a later time on the same basis as others who have not faced the hurdle of the University's allegedly unlawful admissions policy. In these circumstances, and because the University's position implies no concession that its admissions policy is unlawful, this controversy falls squarely within the Court's long line of decisions holding that the mere voluntary cessation of allegedly illegal conduct does not moot a case. Since respondents' voluntary representation to this Court is only that they will permit petitioner to complete this term's studies, respondents have not borne the heavy burden, of demonstrating that there was not even a mere possibility that petitioner would once again be subject to the challenged admissions policy. On the contrary, respondents have positioned themselves so as to be free to return to their old ways.

I can thus find no justification for the Court's straining to rid itself of this dispute. While we must be vigilant to require that litigants maintain a personal stake in the outcome of a controversy to assure that the questions will be framed with the necessary specificity, that the issues will be contested with the necessity adverseness and that the litigation will be pursued with the necessary vigor to assure that the constitutional challenge will be made in a form traditionally thought to be capable of judicial resolution, there is no want of an adversary contest in this case. Indeed, the Court concedes that, if petitioner has lost his stake in this controversy, he did so only when he registered for the spring term. But appellant took that action only after the case had been fully litigated in the state courts, briefs had been filed in this Court, and oral argument had been heard. The case is thus ripe for decision on a fully developed factual record with sharply defined and fully canvassed legal issues. . . .

Political-Question Doctrine

Introduction

Some disputes may present actual "cases" or "controversies" within the jurisdiction of the federal courts but nevertheless ask for resolution of questions that are not appropriate for judicial determination, perhaps because they are questions whose resolution is committed to a different body, or perhaps because they are questions whose answer depends upon heuristics that courts are not equipped to consider. The result is the misnamed "political-question doctrine." Consider the following questions as you read the opinions below:

- What policies underlie the political-question doctrine?

- How has the doctrine evolved over time?

- Are the factors that the Court has used to define the contours of the doctrine workable and useful?

- Has the Court applied those factors in ways that balance both the duty of the Court to decide cases and the need to ensure that the Court does so properly?

- Is the doctrine jurisdictional or prudential? Does its character depend upon the basis by which it is invoked in a particular case?

Baker v. Carr (1962)

This civil action was brought under 42 U.S.C. §§ 1983 and 1988 to redress the alleged deprivation of federal constitutional rights. The complaint, alleging that by means of a 1901 statute of Tennessee apportioning the members of the General Assembly among the State's 95 counties, these plaintiffs and others similarly situated are denied the equal protection of the laws accorded them by the Fourteenth Amendment to the Constitution of the United States by virtue of the debasement of their votes, was dismissed by a three-judge court convened under 28 U.S.C. § 2281 in the Middle District of Tennessee. The court held that it lacked jurisdiction of the subject matter and also that no claim was stated upon which relief could be granted. . . . We hold that the dismissal was error, and remand the cause to the District Court for trial and further proceedings consistent with this opinion.

The General Assembly of Tennessee consists of the Senate with 33 members and the House of Representatives with 99 members. The Tennessee Constitution provides in Art. II as follows:

> Sec. 3. Legislative authority—Term of office.—The Legislative authority of this State shall be vested in a General Assembly, which shall consist of a Senate and House of Representatives, both dependent on the people; who shall hold their offices for two years from the day of the general election.

> Sec. 4. Census.—An enumeration of the qualified voters, and an apportionment of the Representatives in the General Assembly, shall be made in the year one thousand eight hundred and seventy-one, and within every subsequent term of ten years.

> Sec. 5. Apportionment of representatives.—The number of Representatives shall, at the several periods of making the enumeration, be apportioned among the several counties or districts, according to the number of qualified voters in each; and shall not exceed seventy-five, until the population of the State shall be one million and a half, and shall never exceed ninety-nine; Provided, that any county having two-thirds of the ratio shall be entitled to one member.

> Sec 6. Apportionment of senators.—The number of Senators shall, at the several periods of making the enumeration, be apportioned among the several counties or districts according to the number of qualified electors in each, and shall not exceed one-third the number of representatives. In apportioning the Senators among the different counties, the fraction that may be lost by any county or counties, in the apportionment of members to the House of Representatives, shall be made up to such county or counties in the Senate, as near as may be practicable. When a district is

composed of two or more counties, they shall be adjoining; and no county shall be divided in forming a district.

Thus, Tennessee's standard for allocating legislative representation among her counties is the total number of qualified voters resident in the respective counties, subject only to minor qualifications. Decennial reapportionment in compliance with the constitutional scheme was effected by the General Assembly each decade from 1871 to 1901. The 1871 apportionment was preceded by an 1870 statute requiring an enumeration. . . . In 1901 the General Assembly abandoned separate enumeration in favor of reliance upon the Federal Census and passed the Apportionment Act here in controversy. . . .

Between 1901 and 1961, Tennessee has experienced substantial growth and redistribution of her population. . . . The relative standings of the counties in terms of qualified voters have changed significantly. It is primarily the continued application of the 1901 Apportionment Act to this shifted and enlarged voting population which gives rise to the present controversy.

Indeed, the complaint alleges that the 1901 statute, even as of the time of its passage, "made no apportionment of Representatives and Senators in accordance with the constitutional formula . . . , but instead arbitrarily and capriciously apportioned representatives in the Senate and House without reference . . . to any logical or reasonable formula whatever." It is further alleged that because of the population changes since 1900, and the failure of the Legislature to reapportion itself since 1901, the 1901 statute became unconstitutional and obsolete. Appellants also argue that, because of the composition of the legislature effected by the 1901 Apportionment Act, redress in the form of a state constitutional amendment to change the entire mechanism for reapportioning, or any other change short of that, is difficult or impossible. The complaint concludes that these plaintiffs and others similarly situated, are denied the equal protection of the laws accorded them by the Fourteenth Amendment to the Constitution of the United States by virtue of the debasement of their votes. They seek a declaration that the 1901 statute is unconstitutional and an injunction restraining the appellees from acting to conduct any further elections under it. . . .

Of course the mere fact that the suit seeks protection of a political right does not mean it presents a political question. Such an objection is little more than a play upon words. Rather, it is argued that apportionment cases, whatever the actual wording of the complaint, can involve no federal constitutional right except one resting on the guaranty of a republican form of government,[30] and that complaints based on that clause have been held to present political questions which are nonjusticiable.

30 "The United States shall guarantee to every State in this Union a Republican Form of Government, and shall protect each of them against Invasion; and on Application of the Legislature, or of the Executive (when the Legislature cannot be convened) against domestic Violence." U.S. Const. Art. IV, § 4.

We hold that the claim pleaded here neither rests upon nor implicates the Guaranty Clause and that its justiciability is therefore not foreclosed by our decisions of cases involving that clause. . . .

The nonjusticiability of a political question is primarily a function of the separation of powers. Much confusion results from the capacity of the "political question" label to obscure the need for case-by-case inquiry. Deciding whether a matter has in any measure been committed by the Constitution to another branch of government, or whether the action of that branch exceeds whatever authority has been committed, is itself a delicate exercise in constitutional interpretation, and is a responsibility of this Court as ultimate interpreter of the Constitution. . . .

It is apparent that several formulations which vary slightly according to the settings in which the questions arise may describe a political question, although each has one or more elements which identify it as essentially a function of the separation of powers. Prominent on the surface of any case held to involve a political question is found a textually demonstrable constitutional commitment of the issue to a coordinate political department; or a lack of judicially discoverable and manageable standards for resolving it; or the impossibility of deciding without an initial policy determination of a kind clearly for nonjudicial discretion; or the impossibility of a court's undertaking independent resolution without expressing lack of the respect due coordinate branches of government; or an unusual need for unquestioning adherence to a political decision already made; or the potentiality of embarrassment from multifarious pronouncements by various departments on one question.

Unless one of these formulations is inextricable from the case at bar, there should be no dismissal for non-justiciability on the ground of a political question's presence. . . .

We come, finally, to the ultimate inquiry whether our precedents as to what constitutes a nonjusticiable "political question" bring the case before us under the umbrella of that doctrine. A natural beginning is to note whether any of the common characteristics which we have been able to identify and label descriptively are present. We find none: The question here is the consistency of state action with the Federal Constitution. We have no question decided, or to be decided, by a political branch of government coequal with this Court. Nor do we risk embarrassment of our government abroad, or grave disturbance at home if we take issue with Tennessee as to the constitutionality of her action here challenged. Nor need the appellants, in order to succeed in this action, ask the Court to enter upon policy determinations for which judicially manageable standards are lacking. Judicial standards under the Equal Protection Clause are well developed and familiar, and it has been open to courts since the enactment of the Fourteenth Amendment to determine, if on the particular facts they must, that a discrimination reflects no policy, but simply arbitrary and capricious action.

This case does, in one sense, involve the allocation of political power within a State, and the appellants might conceivably have added a claim under the Guaranty Clause. Of course, as we have seen, any reliance on that clause would be futile. But because any reliance on the Guaranty Clause could not have succeeded it does not follow that appellants may not be heard on the equal protection claim which in fact they tender. True, it must be clear that the Fourteenth Amendment claim is not so enmeshed with those political question elements which render Guaranty Clause claims nonjusticiable as actually to present a political question itself. But we have found that not to be the case here. . . . We conclude then that the nonjusticiability of claims resting on the Guaranty Clause which arises from their embodiment of questions that were thought "political," can have no bearing upon the justiciability of the equal protection claim presented in this case. . . .

We conclude that the complaint's allegations of a denial of equal protection present a justiciable constitutional cause of action upon which appellants are entitled to a trial and a decision. The right asserted is within the reach of judicial protection under the Fourteenth Amendment.

The judgment of the District Court is reversed and the cause is remanded for further proceedings consistent with this opinion.

Nixon v. United States (1993)

Chief Justice REHNQUIST delivered the opinion of the Court.

Petitioner Walter L. Nixon, Jr., asks this Court to decide whether Senate Rule XI, which allows a committee of Senators to hear evidence against an individual who has been impeached and to report that evidence to the full Senate, violates the Impeachment Trial Clause, Art. I, § 3, cl. 6. That Clause provides that the "Senate shall have the sole Power to try all Impeachments." But before we reach the merits of such a claim, we must decide whether it is justiciable, that is, whether it is a claim that may be resolved by the courts. We conclude that it is not.

Nixon, a former Chief Judge of the United States District Court for the Southern District of Mississippi, was convicted by a jury of two counts of making false statements before a federal grand jury and sentenced to prison. The grand jury investigation stemmed from reports that Nixon had accepted a gratuity from a Mississippi businessman in exchange for asking a local district attorney to halt the prosecution of the businessman's son. Because Nixon refused to resign from his office as a United States District Judge, he continued to collect his judicial salary while serving out his prison sentence.

On May 10, 1989, the House of Representatives adopted three articles of impeachment for high crimes and misdemeanors. The first two articles charged Nixon with giving false testimony before the grand jury and the third article charged him with bringing disrepute on the Federal Judiciary.

After the House presented the articles to the Senate, the Senate voted to invoke its own Impeachment Rule XI, under which the presiding officer appoints a committee of Senators to "receive evidence and take testimony." The Senate committee held four days of hearings, during which 10 witnesses, including Nixon, testified. Pursuant to Rule XI, the committee presented the full Senate with a complete transcript of the proceeding and a Report stating the uncontested facts and summarizing the evidence on the contested facts. Nixon and the House impeachment managers submitted extensive final briefs to the full Senate and delivered arguments from the Senate floor during the three hours set aside for oral argument in front of that body. Nixon himself gave a personal appeal, and several Senators posed questions directly to both parties. The Senate voted by more than the constitutionally required two-thirds majority to convict Nixon on the first two articles. The presiding officer then entered judgment removing Nixon from his office as United States District Judge.

Nixon thereafter commenced the present suit, arguing that Senate Rule XI violates the constitutional grant of authority to the Senate to "try" all impeachments because it prohibits the whole Senate from taking part in the evidentiary hearings. See Art. I, § 3, cl. 6. Nixon sought a declaratory judgment that his impeachment conviction was void and that his judicial salary and privileges should be reinstated. The District Court held that his claim was nonjusticiable, and the Court of Appeals for the District of Columbia Circuit agreed. We granted certiorari.

A controversy is nonjusticiable—*i.e.*, involves a political question—where there is a textually demonstrable constitutional commitment of the issue to a coordinate political department; or a lack of judicially discoverable and manageable standards for resolving it. . . . But the courts must, in the first instance, interpret the text in question and determine whether and to what extent the issue is textually committed. As the discussion that follows makes clear, the concept of a textual commitment to a coordinate political department is not completely separate from the concept of a lack of judicially discoverable and manageable standards for resolving it; the lack of judicially manageable standards may strengthen the conclusion that there is a textually demonstrable commitment to a coordinate branch.

In this case, we must examine Art. I, § 3, cl. 6, to determine the scope of authority conferred upon the Senate by the Framers regarding impeachment. It provides: "The Senate shall have the sole Power to try all Impeachments. When sitting for that Purpose, they shall be on Oath or Affirmation. When the President of the United States is tried, the Chief Justice shall preside: And no Person shall be convicted without the Concurrence of two thirds of the Members present."

The language and structure of this Clause are revealing. The first sentence is a grant of authority to the Senate, and the word "sole" indicates that this authority is reposed in the Senate and nowhere else. The next two sentences specify requirements to which the Senate proceedings shall conform: The Senate shall be on oath or affirmation, a two-thirds vote is required to convict, and when the President is tried the Chief Justice shall preside.

Petitioner argues that the word "try" in the first sentence imposes by implication an additional requirement on the Senate in that the proceedings must be in the nature of a judicial trial. From there petitioner goes on to argue that this limitation precludes the Senate from delegating to a select committee the task of hearing the testimony of witnesses, as was done pursuant to Senate Rule XI. "'Try' means more than simply 'vote on' or 'review' or 'judge.' In 1787 and today, trying a case means hearing the evidence, not scanning a cold record." Petitioner concludes from this that courts may review whether or not the Senate "tried" him before convicting him.

There are several difficulties with this position which lead us ultimately to reject it. The word "try," both in 1787 and later, has considerably broader meanings than those to which petitioner would limit it. Older dictionaries define try as "to examine" or "to examine as a judge." In more modern usage the term has various meanings. For example, try can mean "to examine or investigate judicially," "to conduct the trial of," or "to put to the test by experiment, investigation, or trial." . . . Based on the variety of definitions, . . . we cannot say that the Framers used the word "try" as an implied limitation on the method by which the Senate might proceed in trying impeachments. . . .

The conclusion that the use of the word "try" in the first sentence of the Impeachment Trial Clause lacks sufficient precision to afford any judicially manageable standard of review of the Senate's actions is fortified by the existence of the three very specific requirements that the Constitution does impose on the Senate when trying impeachments: The Members must be under oath, a two-thirds vote is required to convict, and the Chief Justice presides when the President is tried. These limitations are quite precise, and their nature suggests that the Framers did not intend to impose additional limitations on the form of the Senate proceedings by the use of the word "try" in the first sentence.

Petitioner devotes only two pages in his brief to negating the significance of the word "sole" in the first sentence of Clause 6. As noted above, that sentence provides that "[t]he Senate shall have the sole Power to try all Impeachments." We think that the word "sole" is of considerable significance. Indeed, the word "sole" appears only one other time in the Constitution—with respect to the House of Representatives's "*sole* Power of Impeachment." The commonsense meaning of the word "sole" is that the Senate alone shall have authority to determine whether an individual should be acquitted or convicted. The dictionary definition bears this out. "Sole" is defined as "having no companion," "solitary," "being the only one," and "functioning . . . independently and without assistance or interference." If the courts may review the actions of the Senate in order to determine whether that body "tried" an impeached official, it is difficult to see how the Senate would be "functioning . . . independently and without assistance or interference." . . .

The history and contemporary understanding of the impeachment provisions support our reading of the constitutional language. The parties do not offer evidence of a single word in the history of the Constitutional Convention or in contemporary commentary that even alludes to the possibility of judicial review in the context of the impeachment powers. This silence is quite meaningful in light of the several explicit references to the availability of judicial review as a check on the Legislature's power with respect to bills of attainder, *ex post facto* laws, and statutes.

The Framers labored over the question of where the impeachment power should lie. Significantly, in at least two considered scenarios the power was placed with the Federal Judiciary. Indeed, James Madison and the Committee of Detail proposed that the Supreme

Court should have the power to determine impeachments. Despite these proposals, the Convention ultimately decided that the Senate would have "the sole Power to try all Impeachments." According to Alexander Hamilton, the Senate was the most fit depositary of this important trust because its Members are representatives of the people. The Supreme Court was not the proper body because the Framers doubted whether the members of that tribunal would, at all times, be endowed with so eminent a portion of fortitude as would be called for in the execution of so difficult a task or whether the Court would possess the degree of credit and authority to carry out its judgment if it conflicted with the accusation brought by the Legislature—the people's representative. In addition, the Framers believed the Court was too small in number: "The awful discretion, which a court of impeachments must necessarily have, to doom to honor or to infamy the most confidential and the most distinguished characters of the community, forbids the commitment of the trust to a small number of persons."

There are two additional reasons why the Judiciary, and the Supreme Court in particular, were not chosen to have any role in impeachments. First, the Framers recognized that most likely there would be two sets of proceedings for individuals who commit impeachable offenses—the impeachment trial and a separate criminal trial. In fact, the Constitution explicitly provides for two separate proceedings. The Framers deliberately separated the two forums to avoid raising the specter of bias and to ensure independent judgments: "Would it be proper that the persons, who had disposed of his fame and his most valuable rights as a citizen in one trial, should in another trial, for the same offence, be also the disposers of his life and his fortune? Would there not be the greatest reason to apprehend, that error in the first sentence would be the parent of error in the second sentence? That the strong bias of one decision would be apt to overrule the influence of any new lights, which might be brought to vary the complexion of another decision?"

Certainly judicial review of the Senate's "trial" would introduce the same risk of bias as would participation in the trial itself.

Second, judicial review would be inconsistent with the Framers' insistence that our system be one of checks and balances. In our constitutional system, impeachment was designed to be the *only* check on the Judicial Branch by the Legislature. On the topic of judicial accountability, Hamilton wrote: "The precautions for their responsibility are comprised in the article respecting impeachments. They are liable to be impeached for mal-conduct by the house of representatives, and tried by the senate, and if convicted, may be dismissed from office and disqualified for holding any other. This is the only provision on the point, which is consistent with the necessary independence of the judicial character, and is the only one which we find in our own constitution in respect to our own judges."

Judicial involvement in impeachment proceedings, even if only for purposes of judicial review, is counterintuitive because it would eviscerate the important constitutional check placed on the Judiciary by the Framers. Nixon's argument would place final reviewing authority with respect to impeachments in the hands of the same body that the impeachment process is meant to regulate.

Nevertheless, Nixon argues that judicial review is necessary in order to place a check on the Legislature. Nixon fears that if the Senate is given unreviewable authority to interpret the Impeachment Trial Clause, there is a grave risk that the Senate will usurp judicial power. The Framers anticipated this objection and created two constitutional safeguards to keep the Senate in check. The first safeguard is that the whole of the impeachment power is divided between the two legislative bodies, with the House given the right to accuse and the Senate given the right to judge. This split of authority avoids the inconvenience of making the same persons both accusers and judges; and guards against the danger of persecution from the prevalence of a factious spirit in either of those branches. The second safeguard is the two-thirds supermajority vote requirement. Hamilton explained that "as the concurrence of two-thirds of the senate will be requisite to a condemnation, the security to innocence, from this additional circumstance, will be as complete as itself can desire."

In addition to the textual commitment argument, we are persuaded that the lack of finality and the difficulty of fashioning relief counsel against justiciability. We agree with the Court of Appeals that opening the door of judicial review to the procedures used by the Senate in trying impeachments would expose the political life of the country to months, or perhaps years, of chaos. This lack of finality would manifest itself most dramatically if the President were impeached. The legitimacy of any successor, and hence his effectiveness, would be impaired severely, not merely while the judicial process was running its course, but during any retrial that a differently constituted Senate might conduct if its first judgment of conviction were invalidated. Equally uncertain is the question of what relief a court may give other than simply setting aside the judgment of conviction. Could it order the reinstatement of a convicted federal judge, or order Congress to create an additional judgeship if the seat had been filled in the interim?

Petitioner finally contends that a holding of nonjusticiability cannot be reconciled with our opinion in *Powell v. McCormack*. The relevant issue in *Powell* was whether courts could review the House of Representatives's conclusion that Powell was "unqualified" to sit as a Member because he had been accused of misappropriating public funds and abusing the process of the New York courts. We stated that the question of justiciability turned on whether the Constitution committed authority to the House to judge its Members' qualifications, and if so, the extent of that commitment. Article I, § 5, provides that "Each House shall be the Judge of the Elections, Returns and Qualifications of its own Members."

In turn, Art. I, § 2, specifies three requirements for membership in the House: The candidate must be at least 25 years of age, a citizen of the United States for no less than seven years, and an inhabitant of the State he is chosen to represent. We held that, in light of the three requirements specified in the Constitution, the word "qualifications"—of which the House was to be the Judge—was of a precise, limited nature.

Our conclusion in *Powell* was based on the fixed meaning of "[q]ualifications" set forth in Art. I, § 2. The claim by the House that its power to "be the Judge of the Elections, Returns and Qualifications of its own Members" was a textual commitment of unreviewable authority was defeated by the existence of this separate provision specifying the only qualifications which might be imposed for House membership. The decision as to whether a Member satisfied these qualifications *was* placed with the House, but the decision as to what these qualifications consisted of was not.

In the case before us, there is no separate provision of the Constitution that could be defeated by allowing the Senate final authority to determine the meaning of the word "try" in the Impeachment Trial Clause. We agree with Nixon that courts possess power to review either legislative or executive action that transgresses identifiable textual limits. As we have made clear, whether the action of either the Legislative or Executive Branch exceeds whatever authority has been committed, is itself a delicate exercise in constitutional interpretation, and is a responsibility of this Court as ultimate interpreter of the Constitution. But we conclude, after exercising that delicate responsibility, that the word "try" in the Impeachment Trial Clause does not provide an identifiable textual limit on the authority which is committed to the Senate.

For the foregoing reasons, the judgment of the Court of Appeals is *Affirmed.*

Justice WHITE, with whom Justice BLACKMUN joins, concurring in the judgment.

Petitioner contends that the method by which the Senate convicted him on two articles of impeachment violates Art. I, § 3, cl. 6, of the Constitution, which mandates that the Senate "try" impeachments. The Court is of the view that the Constitution forbids us even to consider his contention. I find no such prohibition and would therefore reach the merits of the claim. I concur in the judgment because the Senate fulfilled its constitutional obligation to "try" petitioner.

I

It should be said at the outset that, as a practical matter, it will likely make little difference whether the Court's or my view controls this case. This is so because the Senate has very wide discretion in specifying impeachment trial procedures and because it is extremely unlikely that the Senate would abuse its discretion and insist on a procedure that could not be deemed a trial by reasonable judges. Even taking a wholly practical approach, I would prefer not to announce an unreviewable discretion in the Senate to ignore completely the constitutional direction to "try" impeachment cases. When asked at oral argument whether that direction would be satisfied if, after a House vote to impeach, the Senate, without any procedure whatsoever, unanimously found the accused guilty of being "a bad guy," counsel for the United States answered that the Government's theory "leads me to answer that question yes." Especially in light of this advice from the Solicitor General, I would not issue an invitation to the Senate to find an excuse, in the name of other pressing business, to be dismissive of its critical role in the impeachment process.

Practicalities aside, however, since the meaning of a constitutional provision is at issue, my disagreement with the Court should be stated.

II

The majority states that the question raised in this case meets two of the criteria for political questions set out in *Baker v. Carr*. It concludes first that there is a textually demonstrable constitutional commitment of the issue to a coordinate political department. It also finds that the question cannot be resolved for a lack of judicially discoverable and manageable standards.

Of course the issue in the political question doctrine is *not* whether the constitutional text commits exclusive responsibility for a particular governmental function to one of the political branches. There are numerous instances of this sort of textual commitment, *e.g.,* Art. I, § 8, and it is not thought that disputes implicating these provisions are nonjusticiable. Rather, the issue is whether the Constitution has given one of the political branches final responsibility for interpreting the scope and nature of such a power.

Although *Baker* directs the Court to search for a textually demonstrable constitutional commitment of such responsibility, there are few, if any, explicit and unequivocal instances in the Constitution of this sort of textual commitment. Conferral on Congress of the power to "Judge" qualifications of its Members by Art. I, § 5, may, for example, preclude judicial review of whether a prospective member in fact meets those qualifications. The courts therefore are usually left to infer the presence of a political question from the text and structure of the Constitution. In drawing the inference that the Constitution has committed final interpretive authority to one of the political branches, courts are sometimes aided by textual evidence that the Judiciary was not meant to exercise judicial review—a coordinate inquiry expressed in *Baker*'s "lack of judicially discoverable and manageable standards" criterion.

A

The majority finds a clear textual commitment in the Constitution's use of the word "sole" in the phrase "[t]he Senate shall have the sole Power to try all Impeachments." It attributes "considerable significance" to the fact that this term appears in only one other passage in the Constitution. The Framers' sparing use of "sole" is thought to indicate that its employment in the Impeachment Trial Clause demonstrates a concern to give the Senate exclusive interpretive authority over the Clause.

. . . . Even if the Impeachment Trial Clause is read without regard to its Companion clause, the Court's willingness to abandon its obligation to review the constitutionality of legislative acts merely on the strength of the word "sole" is perplexing. Consider, by comparison, the treatment of Art. I, § 1, which grants "All legislative powers" to the House and Senate. As used in that context "all" is nearly synonymous with "sole"—both connote entire and exclusive authority. Yet the Court has never thought it would unduly interfere with the operation of the Legislative Branch to entertain difficult and important questions as to the extent of the legislative power. Quite the opposite, we have stated that the proper interpretation of the Clause falls within the province of the Judiciary. Addressing the constitutionality of the legislative veto, for example, the Court found it necessary and proper to interpret Art. I, § 1, as one of the explicit and unambiguous provisions of the Constitution that prescribe and define the respective functions of the Congress and of the Executive in the legislative process.

The majority also claims support in the history and early interpretations of the Impeachment Clauses, noting the various arguments in support of the current system made at the Constitutional Convention and expressed powerfully by Hamilton in The Federalist Nos. 65 and 66. In light of these materials there can be little doubt that the Framers came to the view at the Convention that the trial of officials' public misdeeds should be conducted by representatives of the people; that the fledgling Judiciary lacked the wherewithal to adjudicate political intrigues; that the Judiciary ought not to try both impeachments and subsequent criminal cases emanating from them; and that the impeachment power must reside in the Legislative Branch to provide a check on the largely unaccountable Judiciary.

The majority's review of the historical record thus explains why the power to try impeachments properly resides with the Senate. It does not explain, however, the sweeping statement that the Judiciary was "not chosen to have any role in impeachments." Not a single word in the historical materials cited by the majority addresses judicial review of the Impeachment Trial Clause. And a glance at the arguments surrounding the Impeachment Clauses negates the majority's attempt to infer nonjusticiability from the Framers' arguments in support of the Senate's power to try impeachments.

What the relevant history mainly reveals is deep ambivalence among many of the Framers over the very institution of impeachment, which, by its nature, is not easily reconciled with our system of checks and balances. As they clearly recognized, the branch of the Federal Government which is possessed of the authority to try impeachments, by having final say over the membership of each branch, holds a potentially unanswerable power over the others. In addition, that branch, insofar as it is called upon to try not only members of other branches, but also its own, will have the advantage of being the judge of its own members' causes. . . .

Viewed against this history, the discord between the majority's position and the basic principles of checks and balances underlying the Constitution's separation of powers is clear. In essence, the majority suggests that the Framers' conferred upon Congress a potential tool of legislative dominance yet at the same time rendered Congress's exercise of that power one of the very few areas of legislative authority immune from any judicial review. While the majority rejects petitioner's justiciability argument as espousing a view "inconsistent with the Framers' insistence that our system be one of checks and balances," it is the Court's finding of nonjusticiability that truly upsets the Framers' careful design. In a truly balanced system, impeachments tried by the Senate would serve as a means of controlling the largely unaccountable Judiciary, even as judicial review would ensure that the Senate adhered to a minimal set of procedural standards in conducting impeachment trials.

B

The majority also contends that the term "try" does not present a judicially manageable standard. It notes that in 1787, as today, the word "try" may refer to an inquiry in the nature of a judicial proceeding, or, more generally, to experimentation or investigation. In light of the term's multiple senses, the Court finds itself unable to conclude that the Framers used the word "try" as "an implied limitation on the method by which the Senate might proceed in trying impeachments." Also according to the majority, comparison to the other more specific requirements listed in the Impeachment Trial Clause—that the senators must proceed under oath and vote by two-thirds to convict, and that the Chief Justice must preside over an impeachment trial of the President—indicates that the word "try" was not meant by the Framers to constitute a limitation on the Senate's conduct and further reveals the term's unmanageability.

It is apparently on this basis that the majority distinguishes *Powell v. McCormack*. In *Powell*, the House of Representatives argued that the grant to Congress of the power to "Judge" the qualifications of its members in Art. I, § 5, precluded the Court from reviewing the House's decision that Powell was not fit for membership. We held to the contrary, noting that, although the Constitution leaves the power to "Judge" in the hands of Congress, it also enumerates, in Art. I, § 2, the "qualifications" whose presence or absence Congress must adjudge. It is precisely the business of the courts, we concluded, to determine the nature and extent of these constitutionally specified qualifications. The majority finds this case different from *Powell* only on the grounds that, whereas the qualifications of Art. I, § 2, are readily susceptible to judicial interpretation, the term "try" does not provide an identifiable textual limit on the authority which is committed to the Senate.

This argument comes in two variants. The first, which asserts that one simply cannot ascertain the sense of "try" which the Framers employed and hence cannot undertake judicial review, is clearly untenable. To begin with, one would intuitively expect that, in defining the power of a political body to conduct an inquiry into official wrongdoing, the Framers used "try" in its legal sense. That intuition is borne out by reflection on the alternatives. The third Clause of Art. I, § 3, cannot seriously be read to mean that the Senate shall "attempt" or "experiment with" impeachments. It is equally implausible to say that the Senate is charged with "investigating" impeachments given that this description would substantially overlap with the House of Representatives's "sole" power to draw up articles of impeachment. That these alternatives are not realistic possibilities is finally evidenced by the use of "tried" in the third sentence of the Impeachment Trial Clause ("[w]hen the President of the United States is tried . . ."), and by Art. III, § 2, cl. 3 ("[t]he Trial of all Crimes, except in Cases of Impeachment . . .").

The other variant of the majority position focuses not on which sense of "try" is employed in the Impeachment Trial Clause, but on whether the legal sense of that term creates a judicially manageable standard. The majority concludes that the term provides no identifiable textual limit. Yet, as the Government itself conceded at oral argument, the term "try" is hardly so elusive as the majority would have it. Were the Senate, for example, to adopt the practice of automatically entering a judgment of conviction whenever articles of impeachment were delivered from the House, it is quite clear that the Senate will have failed to "try" impeachments. Indeed in this respect, "try" presents no greater, and perhaps fewer, interpretive difficulties than some other constitutional standards that have been found amenable to familiar techniques of judicial construction, including, for example, "Commerce . . . among the several States," Art. I, § 8, cl. 3, and "due process of law," Amdt. 5.[3]

³ The majority's *in terrorem* argument against justiciability—that judicial review of impeachments might cause national disruption and that the courts would be unable to fashion effective relief—merits only brief attention. In the typical instance, court review of impeachments would no more render the political system dysfunctional than has this litigation. Moreover, the same capacity for disruption was noted and rejected as a basis for not hearing *Powell.* The relief granted for unconstitutional impeachment trials would presumably be similar to the relief granted to other unfairly tried public employee-litigants. Finally, as applied to the special case of the President, the majority's argument merely points out that, were the Senate to convict the President without any kind of a trial, a constitutional crisis might well result. It hardly follows that the Court ought to refrain from upholding the Constitution in all impeachment cases. Nor does it follow that, in cases of Presidential impeachment, the Justices ought to abandon their constitutional responsibilities because the Senate has precipitated a crisis.

III

The majority's conclusion that "try" is incapable of meaningful judicial construction is not without irony. One might think that if any class of concepts would fall within the definitional abilities of the Judiciary, it would be that class having to do with procedural justice. Examination of the remaining question—whether proceedings in accordance with Senate Rule XI are compatible with the Impeachment Trial Clause—confirms this intuition.

Petitioner bears the rather substantial burden of demonstrating that, simply by employing the word "try," the Constitution prohibits the Senate from relying on a fact-finding committee. It is clear that the Framers were familiar with English impeachment practice and with that of the States employing a variant of the English model at the time of the Constitutional Convention. Hence there is little doubt that the term "try" as used in Art. I, § 3, cl. 6, meant that the Senate should conduct its proceedings in a manner somewhat resembling a judicial proceeding. Indeed, it is safe to assume that Senate trials were to follow the practice in England and the States, which contemplated a formal hearing on the charges, at which the accused would be represented by counsel, evidence would be presented, and the accused would have the opportunity to be heard. . . .

In short, textual and historical evidence reveals that the Impeachment Trial Clause was not meant to bind the hands of the Senate beyond establishing a set of minimal procedures. Without identifying the exact contours of these procedures, it is sufficient to say that the Senate's use of a factfinding committee under Rule XI is entirely compatible with the Constitution's command that the Senate "try all impeachments." Petitioner's challenge to his conviction must therefore fail.

IV

Petitioner has not asked the Court to conduct his impeachment trial; he has asked instead that it determine whether his impeachment was tried by the Senate. The majority refuses to reach this determination out of a laudable desire to respect the authority of the Legislature. Regrettably, this concern is manifested in a manner that does needless violence to the Constitution. The deference that is owed can be found in the Constitution itself, which provides the Senate ample discretion to determine how best to try impeachments.

Justice SOUTER, concurring in the judgment.

I agree with the Court that this case presents a nonjusticiable political question. Because my analysis differs somewhat from the Court's, however, I concur in its judgment by this separate opinion.

. . . . Whatever considerations feature most prominently in a particular case, the political question doctrine is essentially a function of the separation of powers, existing to restrain courts from inappropriate interference in the business of the other branches of Government, and deriving in large part from prudential concerns about the respect we owe the political departments. Not all interference is inappropriate or disrespectful, however, and application of the doctrine ultimately turns, as Learned Hand put it, on "how importunately the occasion demands an answer."

This occasion does not demand an answer. The Impeachment Trial Clause commits to the Senate "the sole Power to try all Impeachments" . . . . It seems fair to conclude that the Clause contemplates that the Senate may determine, within broad boundaries, such subsidiary issues as the procedures for receipt and consideration of evidence necessary to satisfy its duty to "try" impeachments. Other significant considerations confirm a conclusion that this case presents a nonjusticiable political question: the unusual need for unquestioning adherence to a political decision already made, as well as the potentiality of embarrassment from multifarious pronouncements by various departments on one question. As the Court observes, judicial review of an impeachment trial would under the best of circumstances entail significant disruption of government.

One can, nevertheless, envision different and unusual circumstances that might justify a more searching review of impeachment proceedings. If the Senate were to act in a manner seriously threatening the integrity of its results, convicting, say, upon a coin toss, or upon a summary determination that an officer of the United States was simply "a bad guy," judicial interference might well be appropriate. In such circumstances, the Senate's action might be so far beyond the scope of its constitutional authority, and the consequent impact on the Republic so great, as to merit a judicial response despite the prudential concerns that would ordinarily counsel silence. The political question doctrine, a tool for maintenance of governmental order, will not be so applied as to promote only disorder.

Zivotofsky v. Clinton (2012)

Chief Justice ROBERTS delivered the opinion of the Court.

Congress enacted a statute providing that Americans born in Jerusalem may elect to have "Israel" listed as the place of birth on their passports. The State Department declined to follow that law, citing its longstanding policy of not taking a position on the political status of Jerusalem. When sued by an American who invoked the statute, the Secretary of State argued that the courts lacked authority to decide the case because it presented a political question. The Court of Appeals so held.

We disagree. The courts are fully capable of determining whether this statute may be given effect, or instead must be struck down in light of authority conferred on the Executive by the Constitution. . . .

In general, the Judiciary has a responsibility to decide cases properly before it, even those it would gladly avoid. Our precedents have identified a narrow exception to that rule, known as the "political question" doctrine. We have explained that a controversy involves a political question . . . where there is a textually demonstrable constitutional commitment of the issue to a coordinate political department; or a lack of judicially discoverable and manageable standards for resolving it. *Nixon v. United States* (quoting *Baker v. Carr*). In such a case, we have held that a court lacks the authority to decide the dispute before it.

The lower courts ruled that this case involves a political question because deciding Zivotofsky's claim would force the Judicial Branch to interfere with the President's exercise of constitutional power committed to him alone. The District Court understood Zivotofsky to ask the courts to decide the political status of Jerusalem. This misunderstands the issue presented. Zivotofsky does not ask the courts to determine whether Jerusalem is the capital of Israel. He instead seeks to determine whether he may vindicate his statutory right to choose to have Israel recorded on his passport as his place of birth. . . . The federal courts are not being asked to supplant a foreign policy decision of the political branches with the courts' own unmoored determination of what United States policy toward Jerusalem should be. Instead, Zivotofsky requests that the courts enforce a specific statutory right. To resolve his claim, the Judiciary must decide if Zivotofsky's interpretation of the statute is correct, and whether the statute is constitutional. This is a familiar judicial exercise.

Moreover, because the parties do not dispute the interpretation of [the statute], the only real question for the courts is whether the statute is constitutional. At least since *Marbury v. Madison*, we have recognized that when an Act of Congress is alleged to conflict with the Constitution, it is emphatically the province and duty of the judicial department to say what the law is. That duty will sometimes involve the resolution of litigation challenging the constitutional authority of one of the three branches, but courts cannot avoid their responsibility merely because the issues have political implications.

In this case, determining the constitutionality of [the statute] involves deciding whether the statute impermissibly intrudes upon Presidential powers under the Constitution. If so, the law must be invalidated and Zivotofsky's case should be dismissed for failure to state a claim. If, on the other hand, the statute does not trench on the President's powers, then the Secretary must be ordered to issue Zivotofsky a passport that complies with [law]. Either way, the political question doctrine is not implicated. . . .

The Secretary contends that there is a textually demonstrable constitutional commitment to the President of the sole power to recognize foreign sovereigns and, as a corollary, to determine whether an American born in Jerusalem may choose to have Israel listed as his place of birth on his passport. Perhaps. But there is, of course, no exclusive commitment to the Executive of the power to determine the constitutionality of a statute. The Judicial Branch appropriately exercises that authority, including in a case such as this, where the question is whether Congress or the Executive is aggrandizing its power at the expense of another branch.

Our precedents have also found the political question doctrine implicated when there is a lack of judicially discoverable and manageable standards for resolving the question before the court. *Nixon* (quoting *Baker*). Framing the issue as the lower courts did, in terms of whether the Judiciary may decide the political status of Jerusalem, certainly raises those concerns. They dissipate, however, when the issue is recognized to be the more focused one of the constitutionality of [the statute]. . . . Recitation of these arguments—which sound in familiar principles of constitutional interpretation—is enough to establish that this case does not turn on standards that defy judicial application. Resolution of Zivotofksy's claim demands careful examination of the textual, structural, and historical evidence put forward by the parties regarding the nature of the statute and of the passport and recognition powers. This is what courts do. The political question doctrine poses no bar to judicial review of this case.

It is so ordered.

Justice SOTOMAYOR, with whom Justice BREYER joins concurring in part . . . .

As this case illustrates, the proper application of *Baker*'s six factors has generated substantial confusion in the lower courts. I concur in the Court's conclusion that this case does not present a political question. I write separately, however, because I understand the inquiry required by the political question doctrine to be more demanding than that suggested by the Court.

The political question doctrine speaks to an amalgam of circumstances in which courts properly examine whether a particular suit is justiciable—that is, whether the dispute is appropriate for resolution by courts. The doctrine is essentially a function of the separation of powers, which recognizes the limits that Article III imposes upon courts and accords appropriate respect to the other branches' exercise of their own constitutional powers.

In *Baker*, this Court identified six circumstances in which an issue might present a political question: (1) a textually demonstrable constitutional commitment of the issue to a coordinate political department; (2) a lack of judicially discoverable and manageable standards for resolving it; (3) the impossibility of deciding without an initial policy determination of a kind clearly for nonjudicial discretion; (4) the impossibility of a court's undertaking independent resolution without expressing lack of the respect due coordinate branches of government; (5) an unusual need for unquestioning adherence to a political decision already made; or (6) the potentiality of embarrassment from multifarious pronouncements by various departments on one question. *Baker* established that unless one of these formulations is inextricable from the case at bar, there should be no dismissal for nonjusticiability. But *Baker* left unanswered when the presence of one or more factors warrants dismissal, as well as the interrelationship of the six factors and the relative importance of each in determining whether a case is suitable for adjudication.

In my view, the *Baker* factors reflect three distinct justifications for withholding judgment on the merits of a dispute. When a case would require a court to decide an issue whose resolution is textually committed to a coordinate political department, as envisioned by *Baker*'s first factor, abstention is warranted because the court lacks authority to resolve that issue. In such cases, the Constitution itself requires that another branch resolve the question presented.

The second and third *Baker* factors reflect circumstances in which a dispute calls for decisionmaking beyond courts' competence. . . . That traditional role involves the application of some manageable and cognizable standard within the competence of the Judiciary to ascertain and employ to the facts of a concrete case. When a court is given no standard by which to adjudicate a dispute, or cannot resolve a dispute in the absence of a yet-unmade policy determination charged to a political branch, resolution of the suit is beyond the judicial role envisioned by Article III. This is not to say, of course, that courts are incapable of interpreting or applying somewhat ambiguous standards using familiar tools of statutory or constitutional interpretation. But where an issue leaves courts truly rudderless, there can be no doubt of the validity of a court's decision to abstain from judgment.

The final three *Baker* factors address circumstances in which prudence may counsel against a court's resolution of an issue presented. Courts should be particularly cautious before forgoing adjudication of a dispute on the basis that judicial intervention risks embarrassment from multifarious pronouncements by various departments on one question, would express a lack of the respect due coordinate branches of government, or because there exists an unusual need for unquestioning adherence to a political decision already made. We have repeatedly rejected the view that these thresholds are met whenever a court is called upon to resolve the constitutionality or propriety of the act of another branch of Government. A court may not refuse to adjudicate a dispute merely because a decision may have significant political overtones or affect the conduct of this Nation's foreign relations. Nor may courts decline to resolve a controversy within their traditional competence and proper jurisdiction simply because the question is difficult, the consequences weighty, or the potential real for conflict with the policy preferences of the political branches. . . .

Rare occasions implicating *Baker*'s final factors, however, may present an unusual case unfit for judicial disposition. Because of the respect due to a coequal and independent department, for instance, courts properly resist calls to question the good faith with which another branch attests to the authenticity of its internal acts. Likewise, we have long acknowledged that courts are particularly ill suited to intervening in exigent disputes necessitating unusual need for attributing finality to the action of the political departments, or creating acute risk of embarrassment of our government abroad, or grave disturbance at home. Finally, it may be appropriate for courts to stay their hand in cases implicating delicate questions concerning the distribution of political authority between coordinate branches until a dispute is ripe, intractable, and incapable of resolution by the political process. . . .

When such unusual cases arise, abstention accommodates considerations inherent in the separation of powers and the limitations envisioned by Article III, which conferred authority to federal courts against a common-law backdrop that recognized the propriety of abstention in exceptional cases. The political questions envisioned by *Baker*'s final categories find common ground, therefore, with many longstanding doctrines under which considerations of justiciability or comity lead courts to abstain from deciding questions whose initial resolution is better suited to another time, or another forum.

To be sure, it will be the rare case in which *Baker*'s final factors alone render a case nonjusticiable. But our long historical tradition recognizes that such exceptional cases arise, and due regard for the separation of powers and the judicial role envisioned by Article III confirms that abstention may be an appropriate response.

Rucho v. Common Cause (2019)

Chief Justice ROBERTS delivered the opinion of the Court.

Voters and other plaintiffs in North Carolina and Maryland challenged their States' congressional districting maps as unconstitutional partisan gerrymanders. The North Carolina plaintiffs complained that the State's districting plan discriminated against Democrats; the Maryland plaintiffs complained that their State's plan discriminated against Republicans. The plaintiffs alleged that the gerrymandering violated the First Amendment, the Equal Protection Clause of the Fourteenth Amendment, the Elections Clause, and Article I, § 2, of the Constitution. The District Courts in both cases ruled in favor of the plaintiffs, and the defendants appealed directly to this Court. These cases require us to consider once again whether claims of excessive partisanship in districting are "justiciable"—that is, properly suited for resolution by the federal courts. . . .

I
A

The first case involves a challenge to the congressional redistricting plan enacted by the Republican-controlled North Carolina General Assembly in 2016. The Republican legislators leading the redistricting effort instructed their mapmaker to use political data to draw a map that would produce a congressional delegation of ten Republicans and three Democrats. As one of the two Republicans chairing the redistricting committee stated, "I think electing Republicans is better than electing Democrats. So I drew this map to help foster what I think is better for the country." He further explained that the map was drawn with the aim of electing ten Republicans and three Democrats because he did not believe it would be possible to draw a map with 11 Republicans and 2 Democrats. One Democratic state senator objected that entrenching the 10-3 advantage for Republicans was not "fair, reasonable, [or] balanced" because, as recently as 2012, "Democratic congressional candidates had received more votes on a statewide basis than Republican candidates." The General Assembly was not swayed by that objection and approved the 2016 Plan by a party-line vote.

In November 2016, North Carolina conducted congressional elections using the 2016 Plan, and Republican candidates won 10 of the 13 congressional districts. In the 2018 elections, Republican candidates won nine congressional districts, while Democratic candidates won three. The Republican candidate narrowly prevailed in the remaining district, but the State Board of Elections called a new election after allegations of fraud.

This litigation began in August 2016, when the North Carolina Democratic Party, Common Cause (a nonprofit organization), and 14 individual North Carolina voters sued the two lawmakers who had led the redistricting effort and other state defendants in Federal District Court. Shortly thereafter, the League of Women Voters of North Carolina and a dozen additional North Carolina voters filed a similar complaint. The two cases were consolidated.

The plaintiffs challenged the 2016 Plan on multiple constitutional grounds. First, they alleged that the Plan violated the Equal Protection Clause of the Fourteenth Amendment by intentionally diluting the electoral strength of Democratic voters. Second, they claimed that the Plan violated their First Amendment rights by retaliating against supporters of Democratic candidates on the basis of their political beliefs. Third, they asserted that the Plan usurped the right of "the People" to elect their preferred candidates for Congress, in violation of the requirement in Article I, § 2, of the Constitution that Members of the House of Representatives be chosen "by the People of the several States." Finally, they alleged that the Plan violated the Elections Clause by exceeding the State's delegated authority to prescribe the "Times, Places and Manner of holding Elections" for Members of Congress.

After a four-day trial, the three-judge District Court unanimously concluded that the 2016 Plan violated the Equal Protection Clause and Article I of the Constitution. The court further held, with Judge Osteen dissenting, that the Plan violated the First Amendment. The defendants appealed directly to this Court under 28 U.S.C. § 1253. . . .

[W]e remanded the present case for further consideration by the District Court. On remand, the District Court again struck down the 2016 Plan. It found standing and concluded that the case was appropriate for judicial resolution. On the merits, the court found that "the General Assembly's predominant intent was to discriminate against voters who supported or were likely to support non-Republican candidates," and to "entrench Republican candidates" through widespread cracking and packing of Democratic voters. The court rejected the defendants' arguments that the distribution of Republican and Democratic voters throughout North Carolina and the interest in protecting incumbents neutrally explained the 2016 Plan's discriminatory effects. In the end, the District Court held that 12 of the 13 districts constituted partisan gerrymanders that violated the Equal Protection Clause.

The court also agreed with the plaintiffs that the 2016 Plan discriminated against them because of their political speech and association, in violation of the First Amendment. Judge Osteen dissented with respect to that ruling. Finally, the District Court concluded that the 2016 Plan violated the Elections Clause and Article I, § 2. The District Court enjoined the State from using the 2016 Plan in any election after the November 2018 general election. The defendants again appealed to this Court . . . .

B

The second case before us is *Lamone* v. *Benisek*. In 2011, the Maryland Legislature—dominated by Democrats—undertook to redraw the lines of that State's eight congressional districts. The Governor at the time, Democrat Martin O'Malley, led the process. He appointed a redistricting committee to help redraw the map, and asked Congressman Steny Hoyer, who has described himself as a "serial gerrymanderer," to advise the committee. The Governor later testified that his aim was to use the redistricting process to change the overall composition of Maryland's congressional delegation to 7 Democrats and 1 Republican by flipping one district. A decision was made to go for the Sixth, which had been held by a Republican for nearly two decades. To achieve the required equal population among districts, only about 10,000 residents needed to be removed from that district. The 2011 Plan accomplished that by moving roughly 360,000 voters out of the Sixth District and moving 350,000 new voters in. Overall, the Plan reduced the number of registered Republicans in the Sixth District by about 66,000 and increased the number of registered Democrats by about 24,000. The map was adopted by a party-line vote. It was used in the 2012 election and succeeded in flipping the Sixth District. A Democrat has held the seat ever since.

In November 2013, three Maryland voters filed this lawsuit. They alleged that the 2011 Plan violated the First Amendment, the Elections Clause, and Article I, § 2, of the Constitution. After considerable procedural skirmishing and litigation over preliminary relief, the District Court entered summary judgment for the plaintiffs. It concluded that the plaintiffs' claims were justiciable, and that the Plan violated the First Amendment by diminishing their ability to elect their candidate of choice because of their party affiliation and voting history, and by burdening their associational rights. On the latter point, the court relied upon findings that Republicans in the Sixth District were burdened in fundraising, attracting volunteers, campaigning, and generating interest in voting in an atmosphere of general confusion and apathy. The District Court permanently enjoined the State from using the 2011 Plan and ordered it to promptly adopt a new plan for the 2020 election. The defendants appealed directly to this Court under 28 U. S. C. § 1253. . . .

II
A

Article III of the Constitution limits federal courts to deciding "Cases" and "Controversies." We have understood that limitation to mean that federal courts can address only questions historically viewed as capable of resolution through the judicial process. In these cases we are asked to decide an important question of constitutional law. But before we do so, we must find that the question is presented in a "case" or "controversy" that is, in James Madison's words, "of a Judiciary Nature."

Chief Justice Marshall famously wrote that it is "the province and duty of the judicial department to say what the law is." *Marbury* v. *Madison* (1803). Sometimes, however, the law is that the judicial department has no business entertaining the claim of unlawfulness—because the question is entrusted to one of the political branches or involves no judicially enforceable rights. In such a case the claim is said to present a "political question" and to be nonjusticiable—outside the courts' competence and therefore beyond the courts' jurisdiction. *Baker* v. *Carr* (1962). Among the political question cases the Court has identified are those that lack judicially discoverable and manageable standards for resolving them. . . . The question here is whether there is an appropriate role for the Federal Judiciary in remedying the problem of partisan gerrymandering—whether such claims are claims of *legal* right, resolvable according to *legal* principles, or political questions that must find their resolution elsewhere.

B

Partisan gerrymandering is nothing new. Nor is frustration with it. The practice was known in the Colonies prior to Independence, and the Framers were familiar with it at the time of the drafting and ratification of the Constitution. During the very first congressional elections, George Washington and his Federalist allies accused Patrick Henry of trying to gerrymander Virginia's districts against their candidates—in particular James Madison, who ultimately prevailed over fellow future President James Monroe.

In 1812, Governor of Massachusetts and future Vice President Elbridge Gerry notoriously approved congressional districts that the legislature had drawn to aid the Democratic-Republican Party. The moniker "gerrymander" was born when an outraged Federalist newspaper observed that one of the misshapen districts resembled a salamander. By 1840, the gerrymander was a recognized force in party politics and was generally attempted in all legislation enacted for the formation of election districts. It was generally conceded that each party would attempt to gain power which was not proportionate to its numerical strength.

The Framers addressed the election of Representatives to Congress in the Elections Clause. Art. I, § 4, cl. 1. That provision assigns to state legislatures the power to prescribe the "Times, Places and Manner of holding Elections" for Members of Congress, while giving Congress the power to "make or alter" any such regulations. Whether to give that supervisory authority to the National Government was debated at the Constitutional Convention. When those opposed to such congressional oversight moved to strike the relevant language, Madison came to its defense:

> [T]he State Legislatures will sometimes fail or refuse to consult the common interest at the expense of their local conveniency or prejudices. . . . Whenever the State

Legislatures had a favorite measure to carry, they would take care so to mould their regulations as to favor the candidates they wished to succeed.

During the subsequent fight for ratification, the provision remained a subject of debate. Antifederalists predicted that Congress's power under the Elections Clause would allow Congress to make itself "omnipotent," setting the "time" of elections as never or the "place" in difficult to reach corners of the State. Federalists responded that, among other justifications, the revisionary power was necessary to counter state legislatures set on undermining fair representation, including through malapportionment. The Federalists were, for example, concerned that newly developing population centers would be deprived of their proper electoral weight, as some cities had been in Great Britain.

Congress has regularly exercised its Elections Clause power, including to address partisan gerrymandering. The Apportionment Act of 1842, which required single-member districts for the first time, specified that those districts be "composed of contiguous territory," in an attempt to forbid the practice of the gerrymander. Later statutes added requirements of compactness and equality of population. Only the single member district requirement remains in place today. Congress also used its Elections Clause power in 1870, enacting the first comprehensive federal statute dealing with elections as a way to enforce the Fifteenth Amendment. Starting in the 1950s, Congress enacted a series of laws to protect the right to vote through measures such as the suspension of literacy tests and the prohibition of English-only elections.

Appellants suggest that, through the Elections Clause, the Framers set aside electoral issues such as the one before us as questions that only Congress can resolve. We do not agree. In two areas—one-person, one-vote and racial gerrymandering—our cases have held that there is a role for the courts with respect to at least some issues that could arise from a State's drawing of congressional districts.

But the history is not irrelevant. The Framers were aware of electoral districting problems and considered what to do about them. They settled on a characteristic approach, assigning the issue to the state legislatures, expressly checked and balanced by the Federal Congress. As Alexander Hamilton explained, "it will . . . not be denied that a discretionary power over elections ought to exist somewhere. It will, I presume, be as readily conceded that there were only three ways in which this power could have been reasonably modified and disposed: that it must either have been lodged wholly in the national legislature, or wholly in the State legislatures, or primarily in the latter, and ultimately in the former." At no point was there a suggestion that the federal courts had a role to play. Nor was there any indication that the Framers had ever heard of courts doing such a thing.

C

Courts have nevertheless been called upon to resolve a variety of questions surrounding districting. . . . In the leading case of *Baker* v. *Carr*, ... [the Court] identified various considerations relevant to determining whether a claim is a nonjusticiable political question, including whether there is a lack of judicially discoverable and manageable standards for resolving it. The Court concluded that the claim of population inequality among districts did not fall into that category, because such a claim could be decided under basic equal protection principles. . . . Another line of challenges to districting plans has focused on race. Laws that explicitly discriminate on the basis of race, as well as those that are race neutral on their face but are unexplainable on grounds other than race, are of course presumptively invalid. The Court applied those principles to electoral boundaries in *Gomillion* v. *Lightfoot*, concluding that a challenge to an "uncouth twenty-eight sided" municipal boundary line that excluded black voters from city elections stated a constitutional claim. . . .

Partisan gerrymandering claims have proved far more difficult to adjudicate. The basic reason is that, while it is illegal for a jurisdiction to depart from the one-person, one-vote rule, or to engage in racial discrimination in districting, a jurisdiction may engage in constitutional political gerrymandering. To hold that legislators cannot take partisan interests into account when drawing district lines would essentially countermand the Framers' decision to entrust districting to political entities. The central problem is not determining whether a jurisdiction has engaged in partisan gerrymandering. It is determining when political gerrymandering has gone too far. . . .

III
A

In considering whether partisan gerrymandering claims are justiciable, we are mindful of Justice Kennedy's counsel in *Vieth*: Any standard for resolving such claims must be grounded in a "limited and precise rationale" and be "clear, manageable, and politically neutral." An important reason for those careful constraints is that . . . the opportunity to control the drawing of electoral boundaries through the legislative process of apportionment is a critical and traditional part of politics in the United States. An expansive standard requiring the correction of all election district lines drawn for partisan reasons would commit federal and state courts to unprecedented intervention in the American political process.

As noted, the question is one of degree: How to provide a standard for deciding how much partisan dominance is too much. And it is vital in such circumstances that the Court act only in accord with especially clear standards: With uncertain limits, intervening courts—even when proceeding with best intentions—would risk assuming political, not legal, responsibility for a process that often produces ill will and distrust. If federal courts are to inject themselves into the most heated partisan issues by adjudicating partisan gerrymandering claims, they must be armed with a standard that can reliably differentiate unconstitutional from constitutional political gerrymandering.

B

Partisan gerrymandering claims rest on an instinct that groups with a certain level of political support should enjoy a commensurate level of political power and influence. Explicitly or implicitly, a districting map is alleged to be unconstitutional because it makes it too difficult for one party to translate statewide support into seats in the legislature. But such a claim is based on a norm that does not exist in our electoral system—statewide elections for representatives along party lines.

Partisan gerrymandering claims invariably sound in a desire for proportional representation. As Justice O'Connor put it, such claims are based on a conviction that the greater the departure from proportionality, the more suspect an apportionment plan becomes. Our cases, however, clearly foreclose any claim that the Constitution requires proportional representation or that legislatures in reapportioning must draw district lines to come as near as possible to allocating seats to the contending parties in proportion to what their anticipated statewide vote will be. . . .

Unable to claim that the Constitution requires proportional representation outright, plaintiffs inevitably ask the courts to make their own political judgment about how much representation particular political parties *deserve*—based on the votes of their supporters—and to rearrange the challenged districts to achieve that end. But federal courts are not equipped to apportion political power as a matter of fairness, nor is there any basis for concluding that they were authorized to do so. As Justice Scalia put it for the plurality in *Vieth*:

> Fairness' does not seem to us a judicially manageable standard. . . . Some criterion more solid and more demonstrably met than that seems to us necessary to enable the state legislatures to discern the limits of their districting discretion, to meaningfully constrain the discretion of the courts, and to win public acceptance for the courts' intrusion into a process that is the very foundation of democratic decisionmaking.

The initial difficulty in settling on a "clear, manageable and politically neutral" test for fairness is that it is not even clear what fairness looks like in this context. There is a large measure of "unfairness" in any winner-take-all system. Fairness may mean a greater number of competitive districts. Such a claim seeks to undo packing and cracking so that supporters of the disadvantaged party have a better shot at electing their preferred candidates. But making as many districts as possible more competitive could be a recipe for disaster for the disadvantaged party. As Justice White has pointed out, if all or most of the districts are competitive, even a narrow statewide preference for either party would produce an overwhelming majority for the winning party in the state legislature.

On the other hand, perhaps the ultimate objective of a "fairer" share of seats in the congressional delegation is most readily achieved by yielding to the gravitational pull of proportionality and engaging in cracking and packing, to ensure each party its "appropriate" share of "safe" seats. Such an approach, however, comes at the expense of competitive districts and of individuals in districts allocated to the opposing party.

Or perhaps fairness should be measured by adherence to "traditional" districting criteria, such as maintaining political subdivisions, keeping communities of interest together, and protecting incumbents. But protecting incumbents, for example, enshrines a particular partisan distribution. And the natural political geography of a State—such as the fact that urban electoral districts are often dominated by one political party—can itself lead to inherently packed districts. As Justice Kennedy has explained, traditional criteria such as compactness and contiguity cannot promise political neutrality when used as the basis for relief. Instead, it seems, a decision under these standards would unavoidably have significant political effect, whether intended or not.

Deciding among just these different visions of fairness (you can imagine many others) poses basic questions that are political, not legal. There are no legal standards discernible in the Constitution for making such judgments, let alone limited and precise standards that are clear, manageable, and politically neutral. Any judicial decision on what is "fair" in this context would be an "unmoored determination" of the sort characteristic of a political question beyond the competence of the federal courts. *Zivotofsky* v. *Clinton* (2012).

And it is only after determining how to define fairness that you can even begin to answer the determinative question: How much is too much? At what point does permissible partisanship become unconstitutional? If compliance with traditional districting criteria is the fairness touchstone, for example, how much deviation from those criteria is constitutionally acceptable and how should mapdrawers prioritize competing criteria? Should a court "reverse gerrymander" other parts of a State to counteract "natural" gerrymandering caused, for example, by the urban concentration of one party? If a districting plan protected half of the incumbents but redistricted the rest into head to head races, would that be constitutional? A court would have to rank the relative importance of those traditional criteria and weigh how much deviation from each to allow.

If a court instead focused on the respective number of seats in the legislature, it would have to decide the ideal number of seats for each party and determine at what point deviation from that balance went too far. If a 5-3 allocation corresponds most closely to statewide vote totals, is a 6-2 allocation permissible, given that legislatures have the authority to engage in a certain degree of partisan gerrymandering? Which seats should be packed and which cracked? Or if the goal is as many competitive districts as possible, how close does the split need to be for the district to be considered competitive? Presumably not all districts could qualify, so how to choose? Even assuming the court knew which version of fairness to be looking for, there are no discernible and manageable standards for deciding whether there has been a violation. The questions are unguided and ill-suited to the development of judicial standards, and results from one gerrymandering case to the next would likely be disparate and inconsistent.

Appellees contend that if we can adjudicate one-person, one-vote claims, we can also assess partisan gerrymandering claims. But the one-person, one-vote rule is relatively easy to administer as a matter of math. The same cannot be said of partisan gerrymandering claims, because the Constitution supplies no objective measure for assessing whether a districting map treats a political party fairly. It hardly follows from the principle that each person must have an equal say in the election of representatives that a person is entitled to have his political party achieve representation in some way commensurate to its share of statewide support.

More fundamentally, "vote dilution" in the one-person, one-vote cases refers to the idea that each vote must carry equal weight. In other words, each representative must be accountable to (approximately) the same number of constituents. That requirement does not extend to political parties. It does not mean that each party must be influential in proportion to its number of supporters. . . .

Nor do our racial gerrymandering cases provide an appropriate standard for assessing partisan gerrymandering. Nothing in our case law compels the conclusion that racial and political gerrymanders are subject to precisely the same constitutional scrutiny. In fact, our country's long and persistent history of racial discrimination in voting—as well as our Fourteenth Amendment jurisprudence, which always has reserved the strictest scrutiny for discrimination on the basis of race—would seem to compel the opposite conclusion. Unlike partisan gerrymandering claims, a racial gerrymandering claim does not ask for a fair share of political power and influence, with all the justiciability conundrums that entails. It asks instead for the elimination of a racial classification. A partisan gerrymandering claim cannot ask for the elimination of partisanship.

IV

Appellees and the dissent propose a number of "tests" for evaluating partisan gerrymandering claims, but none meets the need for a limited and precise standard that is judicially discernible and manageable. And none provides a solid grounding for judges to take the extraordinary step of reallocating power and influence between political parties.

A

The *Common Cause* District Court concluded that all but one of the districts in North Carolina's 2016 Plan violated the Equal Protection Clause by intentionally diluting the voting strength of Democrats. In reaching that result the court first required the plaintiffs to prove that a legislative mapdrawer's predominant purpose in drawing the lines of a particular district was to subordinate adherents of one political party and entrench a rival party in power. The District Court next required a showing that the dilution of the votes of supporters of a disfavored party in a particular district—by virtue of cracking or packing—is likely to persist in subsequent elections such that an elected representative from the favored party in the district will not feel a need to be responsive to constituents who support the disfavored party. Finally, after a prima facie showing of partisan vote dilution, the District Court shifted the burden to the defendants to prove that the discriminatory effects are "attributable to a legitimate state interest or other neutral explanation."

The District Court's "predominant intent" prong is borrowed from the racial gerrymandering context. In racial gerrymandering cases, we rely on a "predominant intent" inquiry to determine whether race was, in fact, the reason particular district boundaries were drawn the way they were. If district lines were drawn for the purpose of separating racial groups, then they are subject to strict scrutiny because race-based decisionmaking is inherently suspect. But determining that lines were drawn on the basis of partisanship does not indicate that the districting was improper. A permissible intent—securing partisan advantage—does not become constitutionally impermissible, like racial discrimination, when that permissible intent "predominates."

The District Court tried to limit the reach of its test by requiring plaintiffs to show, in addition to predominant partisan intent, that vote dilution "is likely to persist" to such a degree that the elected representative will feel free to ignore the concerns of the supporters of the minority party. But to allow district courts to strike down apportionment plans on the basis of their prognostications as to the outcome of future elections invites findings on matters as to which neither judges nor anyone else can have any confidence. And the test adopted by the *Common Cause* court requires a far more nuanced prediction than simply who would prevail in future political contests. Judges must forecast with unspecified certainty whether a prospective winner will have a margin of victory sufficient to permit him to ignore the supporters of his defeated opponent (whoever that may turn out to be). Judges not only have to pick the winner—they have to beat the point spread.

The appellees assure us that the persistence of a party's advantage may be shown through sensitivity testing: probing how a plan would perform under other plausible electoral conditions. Experience proves that accurately predicting electoral outcomes is not so simple, either because the plans are based on flawed assumptions about voter preferences and behavior or because demographics and priorities change over time. In our two leading partisan gerrymandering cases themselves, the predictions of durability proved to be dramatically wrong. In 1981, Republicans controlled both houses of the Indiana Legislature as well as the governorship. Democrats challenged the state legislature districting map enacted by the Republicans. This Court in *Bandemer* rejected that challenge, and just months later the Democrats increased their share of House seats in the 1986 elections. Two years later the House was split 50–50 between Democrats and Republicans, and the Democrats took control of the chamber in 1990. Democrats also challenged the Pennsylvania congressional districting plan at issue in *Vieth*. Two years after that challenge failed, they gained four seats in the delegation, going from a 12–7 minority to an 11–8 majority. At the next election, they flipped another Republican seat.

Even the most sophisticated districting maps cannot reliably account for some of the reasons voters prefer one candidate over another, or why their preferences may change. Voters elect individual candidates in individual districts, and their selections depend on the issues that matter to them, the quality of the candidates, the tone of the candidates' campaigns, the performance of an incumbent, national events or local issues that drive voter turnout, and other considerations. Many voters split their tickets. Others never register with a political party, and vote for candidates from both major parties at different points during their lifetimes. For all of those reasons, asking judges to predict how a particular districting map will perform in future elections risks basing constitutional holdings on unstable ground outside judicial expertise.

It is hard to see what the District Court's third prong—providing the defendant an opportunity to show that the discriminatory effects were due to a "legitimate redistricting objective"—adds to the inquiry. The first prong already requires the plaintiff to prove that partisan advantage predominates. Asking whether a legitimate purpose other than partisanship was the motivation for a particular districting map just restates the question.

B

The District Courts also found partisan gerrymandering claims justiciable under the First Amendment, coalescing around a basic three-part test: proof of intent to burden individuals based on their voting history or party affiliation; an actual burden on political speech or associational rights; and a causal link between the invidious intent and actual burden. Both District Courts concluded that the districting plans at issue violated the plaintiffs' First Amendment right to association. The District Court in North Carolina relied on testimony that, after the 2016 Plan was put in place, the plaintiffs faced difficulty raising money, attracting candidates, and mobilizing voters to support the political causes and issues such Plaintiffs sought to advance. Similarly, the District Court in Maryland examined testimony that revealed a lack of enthusiasm, indifference to voting, a sense of disenfranchisement, a sense of disconnection, and confusion, and concluded that Republicans in the Sixth District were burdened in fundraising, attracting volunteers, campaigning, and generating interest in voting.

To begin, there are no restrictions on speech, association, or any other First Amendment activities in the districting plans at issue. The plaintiffs are free to engage in those activities no matter what the effect of a plan may be on their district.

The plaintiffs' argument is that partisanship in districting should be regarded as simple discrimination against supporters of the opposing party on the basis of political viewpoint. Under that theory, any level of partisanship in districting would constitute an infringement of their First Amendment rights. But as the Court has explained, it would be idle to contend that any political consideration taken into account in fashioning a reapportionment plan is sufficient to invalidate it. The First Amendment test simply describes the act of districting for partisan advantage. It provides no standard for determining when partisan activity goes too far.

As for actual burden, the slight anecdotal evidence found sufficient by the District Courts in these cases shows that this too is not a serious standard for separating constitutional from unconstitutional partisan gerrymandering. The District Courts relied on testimony about difficulty drumming up volunteers and enthusiasm. How much of a decline in voter engagement is enough to constitute a First Amendment burden? How many door knocks must go unanswered? How many petitions unsigned? How many calls for volunteers unheeded? The *Common Cause* District Court held that a partisan gerrymander places an unconstitutional burden on speech if it has more than a *de minimis* chilling effect or adverse impact on any First Amendment activity. The court went on to rule that there would be an adverse effect even if the speech of the plaintiffs was not *in fact* chilled; it was enough that the districting plan makes it easier for supporters of Republican candidates to translate their votes into seats, thereby enhancing their relative voice.

These cases involve blatant examples of partisanship driving districting decisions. But the First Amendment analysis below offers no "clear" and "manageable" way of distinguishing permissible from impermissible partisan motivation. The *Common Cause* court embraced that conclusion, observing that a judicially manageable framework for evaluating partisan gerrymandering claims need not distinguish an acceptable level of partisan gerrymandering from excessive partisan gerrymandering because the Constitution does not authorize state redistricting bodies to engage in such partisan gerrymandering. The decisions below prove the prediction of the *Vieth* plurality that a First Amendment claim, if it were sustained, would render unlawful *all* consideration of political affiliation in districting, contrary to our established precedent.

C

The dissent proposes using a State's own districting criteria as a neutral baseline from which to measure how extreme a partisan gerrymander is. The dissent would have us line up all the possible maps drawn using those criteria according to the partisan distribution they would produce. Distance from the "median" map would indicate whether a particular districting plan harms supporters of one party to an unconstitutional extent.

As an initial matter, it does not make sense to use criteria that will vary from State to State and year to year as the baseline for determining whether a gerrymander violates the Federal Constitution. The degree of partisan advantage that the Constitution tolerates should not turn on criteria offered by the gerrymanderers themselves. It is easy to imagine how different criteria could move the median map toward different partisan distributions. As a result, the same map could be constitutional or not depending solely on what the mapmakers said they set out to do. That possibility illustrates that the dissent's proposed constitutional test is indeterminate and arbitrary.

Even if we were to accept the dissent's proposed baseline, it would return us to the original unanswerable question (How much political motivation and effect is too much?). Would twenty percent away from the median map be okay? Forty percent? Sixty percent? Why or why not? (We appreciate that the dissent finds all the unanswerable questions annoying, but it seems a useful way to make the point.) The dissent's answer says it all: "This much is too much." That is not even trying to articulate a standard or rule.

The dissent argues that there are other instances in law where matters of degree are left to the courts. True enough. But those instances typically involve constitutional or statutory provisions or common law confining and guiding the exercise of judicial discretion. For example, the dissent cites the need to determine substantial anticompetitive effects in antitrust law. That language, however, grew out of the Sherman Act, understood from the beginning to have its origin in the common law and to be familiar in the law of this country prior to and at the time of the adoption of the Act. Judges began with a significant body of law about what constituted a legal violation. In other cases, the pertinent statutory terms draw meaning from related provisions or statutory context. Here, on the other hand, the Constitution provides no basis whatever to guide the exercise of judicial discretion. Common experience gives content to terms such as "substantial risk" or "substantial harm," but the same cannot be said of substantial deviation from a median map. There is no way to tell whether the prohibited deviation from that map should kick in at 25 percent or 75 percent or some other point. The only provision in the Constitution that specifically addresses the matter assigns it to the political branches.

D

The North Carolina District Court further concluded that the 2016 Plan violated the Elections Clause and Article I, § 2. We are unconvinced by that novel approach.

Article I, § 2, provides that "[t]he House of Representatives shall be composed of Members chosen every second Year by the People of the several States." The Elections Clause provides that "[t]he Times, Places and Manner of holding Elections for Senators and Representatives, shall be prescribed in each State by the Legislature thereof; but the Congress may at any time by Law make or alter such Regulations, except as to the Places of chusing Senators." Art. I, § 4, cl. 1.

The District Court concluded that the 2016 Plan exceeded the North Carolina General Assembly's Elections Clause authority because, among other reasons, the Elections Clause did not empower State legislatures to disfavor the interests of supporters of a particular candidate or party in drawing congressional districts. The court further held that partisan gerrymandering infringes the right of "the People" to select their representatives. Before the District Court's decision, no court had reached a similar conclusion. In fact, the plurality in *Vieth* concluded—without objection from any other Justice—that neither § 2 nor § 4 of Article I provides a judicially enforceable limit on the political considerations that the States and Congress may take into account when districting.

The District Court nevertheless asserted that partisan gerrymanders violate the core principle of our republican government preserved in Art. I, § 2, namely, that the voters should choose their representatives, not the other way around. That seems like an objection more properly grounded in the Guarantee Clause of Article IV, § 4, which "guarantee[s] to every State in

[the] Union a Republican Form of Government." This Court has several times concluded, however, that the Guarantee Clause does not provide the basis for a justiciable claim.

V

Excessive partisanship in districting leads to results that reasonably seem unjust. But the fact that such gerrymandering is incompatible with democratic principles does not mean that the solution lies with the federal judiciary. We conclude that partisan gerrymandering claims present political questions beyond the reach of the federal courts. Federal judges have no license to reallocate political power between the two major political parties, with no plausible grant of authority in the Constitution, and no legal standards to limit and direct their decisions. Judicial action must be governed by *standard*, by *rule*, and must be principled, rational, and based upon reasoned distinctions found in the Constitution or laws. Judicial review of partisan gerrymandering does not meet those basic requirements.

Today the dissent essentially embraces the argument that the Court unanimously rejected in *Gill*: "this Court *can* address the problem of partisan gerrymandering because it *must*." That is not the test of our authority under the Constitution; that document instead confines the federal courts to a properly judicial role.

What the appellees and dissent seek is an unprecedented expansion of judicial power. We have never struck down a partisan gerrymander as unconstitutional—despite various requests over the past 45 years. The expansion of judicial authority would not be into just any area of controversy, but into one of the most intensely partisan aspects of American political life. That intervention would be unlimited in scope and duration—it would recur over and over again around the country with each new round of districting, for state as well as federal representatives. Consideration of the impact of today's ruling on democratic principles cannot ignore the effect of the unelected and politically unaccountable branch of the Federal Government assuming such an extraordinary and unprecedented role.

Our conclusion does not condone excessive partisan gerrymandering. Nor does our conclusion condemn complaints about districting to echo into a void. The States, for example, are actively addressing the issue on a number of fronts. In 2015, the Supreme Court of Florida struck down that State's congressional districting plan as a violation of the Fair Districts Amendment to the Florida Constitution. The dissent wonders why we can't do the same. The answer is that there is no "Fair Districts Amendment" to the Federal Constitution. Provisions in state statutes and state constitutions can provide standards and guidance for state courts to apply. (We do not understand how the dissent can maintain that a provision saying that no districting plan "shall be drawn with the intent to favor or disfavor a political party" provides little guidance on the question.) Indeed, numerous other States are restricting partisan considerations in districting through legislation. One way they are doing so is by placing power to draw electoral districts in the hands of independent commissions. For example, in November 2018, voters in Colorado and Michigan approved constitutional amendments creating multimember commissions that will be responsible in whole or in part for creating and approving district maps for congressional and state legislative districts. Missouri is trying a different tack. Voters there overwhelmingly approved the creation of a new position—state demographer—to draw state legislative district lines.

Other States have mandated at least some of the traditional districting criteria for their mapmakers. Some have outright prohibited partisan favoritism in redistricting.

As noted, the Framers gave Congress the power to do something about partisan gerrymandering in the Elections Clause. The first bill introduced in the 116th Congress would require States to create 15-member independent commissions to draw congressional districts and would establish certain redistricting criteria, including protection for communities of interest, and ban partisan gerrymandering.

Dozens of other bills have been introduced to limit reliance on political considerations in redistricting. In 2010, H.R. 6250 would have required States to follow standards of compactness, contiguity, and respect for political subdivisions in redistricting. It also would have prohibited the establishment of congressional districts with the major purpose of diluting the voting strength of any person, or group, including any political party, except when necessary to comply with the Voting Rights Act of 1965.

Another example is the Fairness and Independence in Redistricting Act, which was introduced in 2005 and has been reintroduced in every Congress since. That bill would require every State to establish an independent commission to adopt redistricting plans. The bill also set forth criteria for the independent commissions to use, such as compactness, contiguity, and population equality. It would prohibit consideration of voting history, political party affiliation, or incumbent Representative's residence.

We express no view on any of these pending proposals. We simply note that the avenue for reform established by the Framers, and used by Congress in the past, remains open.

* * *

No one can accuse this Court of having a crabbed view of the reach of its competence. But we have no commission to allocate political power and influence in the absence of a constitutional directive or legal standards to guide us in the exercise of such authority. "It is emphatically the province and duty of the judicial department to say what the law is." In this rare circumstance, that means our duty is to say "this is not law."

The judgments of the United States District Court for the Middle District of North Carolina and the United States District Court for the District of Maryland are vacated, and the cases are remanded with instructions to dismiss for lack of jurisdiction. It is so ordered.

Justice KAGAN, with whom Justice GINSBURG, Justice BREYER, and Justice SOTOMAYOR join, dissenting.

For the first time ever, this Court refuses to remedy a constitutional violation because it thinks the task beyond judicial capabilities.

And not just any constitutional violation. The partisan gerrymanders in these cases deprived citizens of the most fundamental of their constitutional rights: the rights to participate equally in the political process, to join with others to advance political beliefs, and to choose their political representatives. In so doing, the partisan gerrymanders here debased and dishonored our democracy, turning upside-down the core American idea that all governmental power derives from the people. These gerrymanders enabled politicians to entrench themselves in office as against voters' preferences. They promoted partisanship above respect for the popular will. They encouraged a politics of polarization and dysfunction. If left unchecked, gerrymanders like the ones here may irreparably damage our system of government.

And checking them is *not* beyond the courts. The majority's abdication comes just when courts across the country, including those below, have coalesced around manageable judicial standards to resolve partisan gerrymandering claims. Those standards satisfy the majority's own benchmarks. They do not require—indeed, they do not permit—courts to rely on their own ideas of electoral fairness, whether proportional representation or any other. And they limit courts to correcting only egregious gerrymanders, so judges do not become omnipresent players in the political process. But yes, the standards used here do allow—as well they should—judicial intervention in the worst-of-the-worst cases of democratic subversion, causing blatant constitutional harms. In other words, they allow courts to undo partisan gerrymanders of the kind we face today from North Carolina and Maryland. In giving such gerrymanders a pass from judicial review, the majority goes tragically wrong.

I

. . . . "Governments," the Declaration of Independence states, "deriv[e] their just Powers from the Consent of the Governed." The Constitution begins: "We the People of the United

States." The Gettysburg Address (almost) ends: "[G]overnment of the people, by the people, for the people." If there is a single idea that made our Nation (and that our Nation commended to the world), it is this one: The people are sovereign. The "power," James Madison wrote, "is in the people over the Government, and not in the Government over the people."

Free and fair and periodic elections are the key to that vision. The people get to choose their representatives. And then they get to decide, at regular intervals, whether to keep them. . . .

And partisan gerrymandering can make it meaningless. At its most extreme—as in North Carolina and Maryland—the practice amounts to "rigging elections." By drawing districts to maximize the power of some voters and minimize the power of others, a party in office at the right time can entrench itself there for a decade or more, no matter what the voters would prefer. Just ask the people of North Carolina and Maryland. The core principle of republican government, this Court has recognized, is that the voters should choose their representatives, not the other way around. Partisan gerrymandering turns it the other way around. By that mechanism, politicians can cherry-pick voters to ensure their reelection. And the power becomes, as Madison put it, "in the Government over the people."

The majority disputes none of this. I think it important to underscore that fact: The majority disputes none of what I have said (or will say) about how gerrymanders undermine democracy. Indeed, the majority concedes (really, how could it not?) that gerrymandering is "incompatible with democratic principles." And therefore what? That recognition would seem to demand a response. The majority offers two ideas that might qualify as such. One is that the political process can deal with the problem—a proposition so dubious on its face that I feel secure in delaying my answer for some time.

The other is that political gerrymanders have always been with us. . . . That complacency has no cause. Yes, partisan gerrymandering goes back to the Republic's earliest days. (As does vociferous opposition to it.) But big data and modern technology—of just the kind that the mapmakers in North Carolina and Maryland used—make today's gerrymandering altogether different from the crude linedrawing of the past. Old-time efforts, based on little more than guesses, sometimes led to so-called dummymanders—gerrymanders that went spectacularly wrong. Not likely in today's world. Mapmakers now have access to more granular data about party preference and voting behavior than ever before. County-level voting data has given way to precinct-level or city-block-level data; and increasingly, mapmakers avail themselves of data sets providing wide-ranging information about even individual voters. Just as important, advancements in computing technology have enabled mapmakers to put that information to use with unprecedented efficiency and precision. While bygone mapmakers may have drafted three or four alternative districting plans, today's mapmakers can generate thousands of possibilities at the touch of a key—and then choose the one giving their party maximum advantage (usually while still meeting traditional districting requirements). The effect is to make gerrymanders far more effective and durable than before, insulating politicians against all but the most titanic shifts in the political tides. These are not your grandfather's—let alone the Framers'—gerrymanders. . . .

And gerrymanders will only get worse (or depending on your perspective, better) as time goes on—as data becomes ever more fine-grained and data analysis techniques continue to improve. What was possible with paper and pen—or even with Windows 95—doesn't hold a candle (or an LED bulb?) to what will become possible with developments like machine learning. And someplace along this road, "we the people" become sovereign no longer.

C

Partisan gerrymandering of the kind before us not only subverts democracy (as if that weren't bad enough). It violates individuals' constitutional rights as well. That statement is not the lonesome cry of a dissenting Justice. This Court has recognized extreme partisan gerrymandering as such a violation for many years.

Partisan gerrymandering operates through vote dilution—the devaluation of one citizen's vote as compared to others. A mapmaker draws district lines to "pack" and "crack" voters likely to support the disfavored party. He packs supermajorities of those voters into a relatively few districts, in numbers far greater than needed for their preferred candidates to prevail. Then he cracks the rest across many more districts, spreading them so thin that their candidates will not be able to win. Whether the person is packed or cracked, his vote carries less weight—has less consequence—than it would under a neutrally drawn (non-partisan) map. In short, the mapmaker has made some votes count for less, because they are likely to go for the other party.

That practice implicates the Fourteenth Amendment's Equal Protection Clause. The Fourteenth Amendment, we long ago recognized, guarantees the opportunity for equal participation by all voters in the election of legislators. And that opportunity can be denied by a debasement or dilution of the weight of a citizen's vote just as effectively as by wholly prohibiting the free exercise of the franchise. Based on that principle, this Court in its one-person-one-vote decisions prohibited creating districts with significantly different populations. A State could not, we explained, thus dilute the weight of votes because of place of residence. The constitutional injury in a partisan gerrymandering case is much the same, except that the dilution is based on party affiliation. In such a case, too, the districters have set out to reduce the weight of certain citizens' votes, and thereby deprive them of their capacity to fully and effectively participate in the political process. As Justice Kennedy (in a controlling opinion) once hypothesized: If districters declared that they were drawing a map so as most to burden the votes of Party X's supporters, it would violate the Equal Protection Clause. For (in the language of the one-person-one-vote decisions) it would infringe those voters' rights to equal electoral participation.

And partisan gerrymandering implicates the First Amendment too. That Amendment gives its greatest protection to political beliefs, speech, and association. Yet partisan gerrymanders subject certain voters to "disfavored treatment"—again, counting their votes for less—precisely because of their voting history and their expression of political views. And added to that strictly personal harm is an associational one. Representative democracy is unimaginable without the ability of citizens to band together in [support of] candidates who espouse their political views. By diluting the votes of certain citizens, the State frustrates their efforts to translate those affiliations into political effectiveness. In both those ways, partisan gerrymanders of the kind we confront here undermine the protections of democracy embodied in the First Amendment.

Though different Justices have described the constitutional harm in diverse ways, nearly all have agreed on this much: Extreme partisan gerrymandering (as happened in North Carolina and Maryland) violates the Constitution. Once again, the majority never disagrees; it appears to accept the principle that each person must have an equal say in the election of representatives. And indeed, without this settled and shared understanding that cases like these inflict constitutional injury, the question of whether there are judicially manageable standards for resolving them would never come up.

II

So the only way to understand the majority's opinion is as follows: In the face of grievous harm to democratic governance and flagrant infringements on individuals' rights—in the face of escalating partisan manipulation whose compatibility with this Nation's values and law no one defends—the majority declines to provide any remedy. For the first time in this Nation's history, the majority declares that it can do nothing about an acknowledged constitutional violation because it has searched high and low and cannot find a workable legal standard to apply.

The majority gives two reasons for thinking that the adjudication of partisan gerrymandering claims is beyond judicial capabilities. First and foremost, the majority says, it cannot find a neutral baseline—one not based on contestable notions of political fairness—from which to measure injury. . . . I'll give the majority this one—and important—thing: It identifies some dangers everyone should want to avoid. Judges should not be apportioning political power based on their own vision of electoral fairness, whether proportional representation or any other. And judges should not be striking down maps left, right, and center, on the view that every smidgen of politics is a smidgen too much. Respect for state legislative processes—and restraint in the exercise of judicial authority—counsels intervention in only egregious cases.

But in throwing up its hands, the majority misses something under its nose: What it says can't be done *has* been done. Over the past several years, federal courts across the country—including, but not exclusively, in the decisions below—have largely converged on a standard for adjudicating partisan gerrymandering claims (striking down both Democratic and Republican districting plans in the process). And that standard does what the majority says is impossible. The standard does not use any judge-made conception of electoral fairness—either proportional representation or any other; instead, it takes as its baseline a State's *own* criteria of fairness, apart from partisan gain. And by requiring plaintiffs to make difficult showings relating to both purpose and effects, the standard invalidates the most extreme, but only the most extreme, partisan gerrymanders. . . . .

A

Start with the standard the lower courts used. . . . Both courts focused on the harm of vote dilution, though the North Carolina court mostly grounded its analysis in the Fourteenth Amendment and the Maryland court in the First. And both courts (like others around the country) used basically the same three-part test to decide whether the plaintiffs had made out a vote dilution claim. As many legal standards do, that test has three parts: (1) intent; (2) effects; and (3) causation. First, the plaintiffs challenging a districting plan must prove that state officials' "predominant purpose" in drawing a district's lines was to entrench their party in power by diluting the votes of citizens favoring its rival. Second, the plaintiffs must establish that the lines drawn in fact have the intended effect by "substantially" diluting their votes. And third, if the plaintiffs make those showings, the State must come up with a legitimate, non-partisan justification to save its map. If you are a lawyer, you know that this test looks utterly ordinary. It is the sort of thing courts work with every day. . . .

The majority's response to the District Courts' purpose analysis is discomfiting. The majority does not contest the lower courts' findings; how could it? Instead, the majority says that state officials' intent to entrench their party in power is perfectly "permissible," even when it is the predominant factor in drawing district lines. But that is wrong. True enough, that the intent to inject "political considerations" into districting may not raise any constitutional concerns. . . . But when political actors have a specific and predominant intent to entrench themselves in power by manipulating district lines, that goes too far. Consider again Justice Kennedy's hypothetical of mapmakers who set out to maximally burden (*i.e.*, make count for as little as possible) the votes going to a rival party. Does the majority really think that goal is permissible? But why even bother with hypotheticals? Just consider the purposes here. It cannot be permissible and thus irrelevant, as the majority claims, that state officials have as their purpose the kind of grotesquely gerrymandered map that, according to all this Court has ever said, violates the Constitution.

On to the second step of the analysis, where the plaintiffs must prove that the districting plan substantially dilutes their votes. . . . The approach—which also has recently been used in Michigan and Ohio litigation—begins by using advanced computing technology to randomly generate a large collection of districting plans that incorporate the State's physical and political geography and meet its declared districting criteria, *except for* partisan gain. For each of those maps, the method then uses actual precinct-level votes from past elections to determine a partisan outcome (*i.e.*, the number of Democratic and Republican seats that map produces). Suppose we now have 1,000 maps, each with a partisan outcome attached to it. We can line up those maps on a continuum—the most favorable to Republicans on one end, the most favorable to Democrats on the other.[3] We can then find the median outcome—that is, the outcome smack dab in the center—in a world with no partisan manipulation. And we can see where the State's actual plan falls on the spectrum—at or near the median or way out on one of the tails? The further out on the tail, the more extreme the partisan distortion and the more significant the vote dilution.

> [3] As I'll discuss later, this distribution of outcomes provides what the majority says does not exist—a neutral comparator for the State's own plan. It essentially answers the question: In a State with these geographic features and this distribution of voters and this set of districting criteria—but without partisan manipulation—what would happen?

Using that approach, the North Carolina plaintiffs offered a boatload of alternative districting plans—all showing that the State's map was an out-out-out-outlier. One expert produced 3,000 maps, adhering in the way described above to the districting criteria that the North Carolina redistricting committee had used, other than partisan advantage. . . . The results were, shall we say, striking. Every single one of the 3,000 maps would have produced at least one more Democratic House Member than the State's actual map, and 77% would have elected three or four more. A second expert obtained essentially the same results with maps conforming to more generic districting criteria (*e.g.,* compactness and contiguity of districts). Over 99% of that expert's 24,518 simulations would have led to the election of at least one more Democrat, and over 70% would have led to two or three more. Based on those and other findings, the District Court determined that the North Carolina plan substantially dilutes the plaintiffs' votes.

Because the Maryland gerrymander involved just one district, the evidence in that case was far simpler—but no less powerful for that. You've heard some of the numbers before. The 2010 census required only a minimal change in the Sixth District's population—the subtraction of about 10,000 residents from more than 700,000. But instead of making a correspondingly minimal adjustment, Democratic officials reconfigured the entire district. They moved 360,000 residents out and another 350,000 in, while splitting some counties for the first time in almost two centuries. The upshot was a district with 66,000 fewer Republican voters and 24,000 more Democratic ones. In the old Sixth, 47% of registered voters were Republicans and only 36% Democrats. But in the new Sixth, 44% of registered voters were Democrats and only 33% Republicans. That reversal of the district's partisan composition translated into four consecutive Democratic victories, including in a wave election year for Republicans (2014). In what was once a party stronghold, Republicans now have little or no chance to elect their preferred candidate. The District Court thus found that the gerrymandered Maryland map substantially dilutes Republicans' votes.

The majority claims all these findings are mere "prognostications" about the future, in which no one "can have any confidence." But the courts below did not gaze into crystal balls, as the majority tries to suggest. Their findings about these gerrymanders' effects on voters— both in the past and predictably in the future—were evidence-based, data-based, statistics-based. Knowledge-based, one might say. The courts did what anyone would want a decisionmaker to do when so much hangs in the balance. They looked hard at the facts, and they went where the facts led them. They availed themselves of all the information that mapmakers (like Hofeller and Hawkins) and politicians (like Lewis and O'Malley) work so hard to amass and then use to make every districting decision. They refused to content themselves with unsupported and out-of-date musings about the unpredictability of the American voter. They did not bet America's future—as today the majority does—on the idea that maps constructed with so much expertise and care to make electoral outcomes impervious to voting would somehow or other come apart. They looked at the evidence—at the facts about how these districts operated—and they could reach only one conclusion. By substantially diluting the votes of citizens favoring their rivals, the politicians of one party had succeeded in entrenching themselves in office. They had beat democracy.

B

. . . . The majority's sole response misses the point. According to the majority, it does not make sense to use a State's own (non-partisan) districting criteria as the baseline from which to measure partisan gerrymandering because those criteria will vary from State to State and year to year. But that is a virtue, not a vice—a feature, not a bug. Using the criteria the State itself has chosen at the relevant time prevents any judicial predilections from affecting the analysis—exactly what the majority claims it wants. At the same time, using those criteria enables a court to measure just what it should: the extent to which the pursuit of partisan advantage—by these legislators at this moment—has distorted the State's districting decisions. . . . So once again, the majority's analysis falters because it equates the demand to eliminate partisan gerrymandering with a demand for a single partisan distribution—the one reflecting proportional representation. But those two demands are different, and only the former is at issue here.

The majority's "how much is too much" critique fares no better than its neutrality argument. How about the following for a first-cut answer: This much is too much. By any measure, a map that produces a greater partisan skew than any of 3,000 randomly generated maps (all with the State's political geography and districting criteria built in) reflects "too much" partisanship. Think about what I just said: The absolute worst of 3,001 possible maps. The *only one* that could produce a 10–3 partisan split even as Republicans got a bare majority of the statewide vote. And again: How much is too much? This much is too much: A map that without any evident non-partisan districting reason (to the contrary) shifted the composition of a district from 47% Republicans and 36% Democrats to 33% Republicans and 42% Democrats. A map that in 2011 was responsible for the largest partisan swing of a congressional district in the country. Even the majority acknowledges that these cases involve blatant examples of partisanship driving districting decisions. If the majority had done nothing else, it could have set the line here. How much is too much? At the least, any gerrymanders as bad as these. . . .

Nor is there any reason to doubt, as the majority does, the competence of courts to determine whether a district map "substantially" dilutes the votes of a rival party's supporters from the everything-but-partisanship baseline described above. . . . As this Court recently noted, the law is full of instances where a judge's decision rests on estimating rightly some matter of degree—including the "substantial[ity]" of risk or harm [under the Sherman Act]. The majority is wrong to think that these laws typically (let alone uniformly) further confine and guide judicial decisionmaking. They do not, either in themselves or through statutory context. To the extent additional guidance has developed over the years (as under the Sherman Act), courts themselves have been its author—as they could be in this context too. And contrary to the majority's suggestion, courts all the time make judgments about the substantiality of harm without reducing them to particular percentages. If courts are no longer competent to do so, they will have to relinquish, well, substantial portions of their docket. . . .

III

This Court has long understood that it has a special responsibility to remedy violations of constitutional rights resulting from politicians' districting decisions. Over 50 years ago, we committed to providing judicial review in that sphere, recognizing as we established the one-person-one-vote rule that our oath and our office require no less. Of course, our oath and our office require us to vindicate all constitutional rights. But the need for judicial review is at its most urgent in cases like these. For here, politicians' incentives conflict with voters' interests, leaving citizens without any political remedy for their constitutional harms. Those harms arise because politicians want to stay in office. No one can look to them for effective relief.

The majority disagrees, concluding its opinion with a paean to congressional bills limiting partisan gerrymanders. "Dozens of [those] bills have been introduced," the majority says. One was "introduced in 2005 and has been reintroduced in every Congress since." And might be reintroduced until the end of time. Because what all these *bills* have in common is that they are not *laws*. The politicians who benefit from partisan gerrymandering are unlikely to change partisan gerrymandering. And because those politicians maintain themselves in office through partisan gerrymandering, the chances for legislative reform are slight.

No worries, the majority says; it has another idea. The majority notes that voters themselves have recently approved ballot initiatives to put power over districting in the hands of independent commissions or other non-partisan actors. . . . Fewer than half the States offer voters an opportunity to put initiatives to direct vote; in all the rest (including North Carolina and Maryland), voters are dependent on legislators to make electoral changes (which for all the reasons already given, they are unlikely to do). And even when voters have a mechanism they can work themselves, legislators often fight their efforts tooth and nail. Look at Missouri. There, the majority touts a voter-approved proposal to turn districting over to a state demographer. But before the demographer had drawn a single line, Members of the state legislature had introduced a bill to start undoing the change. *See* Mo. H. J. Res. 48, 100th Gen. Assembly, 1st Reg. Sess. (2019). I'd put better odds on that bill's passage than on all the congressional proposals the majority cites.

The majority's most perplexing "solution" is to look to state courts. . . . But what do those courts know that this Court does not? If they can develop and apply neutral and manageable standards to identify unconstitutional gerrymanders, why couldn't we?[6]

[6] Contrary to the majority's suggestion, state courts do not typically have more specific "standards and guidance" to apply than federal courts have. The Pennsylvania Supreme Court based its gerrymandering decision on a constitutional clause providing only that "elections shall be free and equal" and no one shall "interfere to prevent the free exercise of the right of suffrage." And even the Florida "Free Districts Amendment," which the majority touts, says nothing more than that no districting plan

"shall be drawn with the intent to favor or disfavor a political party." If the majority wants the kind of guidance that will keep courts from intervening too far in the political sphere, that Amendment does not provide it: The standard is in fact a good deal less exacting than the one the District Courts below applied. In any event, only a few States have a constitutional provision like Florida's, so the majority's state-court solution does not go far.

We could have, and we should have. The gerrymanders here—and they are typical of many—violated the constitutional rights of many hundreds of thousands of American citizens. Those voters (Republicans in the one case, Democrats in the other) did not have an equal opportunity to participate in the political process. Their votes counted for far less than they should have because of their partisan affiliation. When faced with such constitutional wrongs, courts must intervene: "It is emphatically the province and duty of the judicial department to say what the law is." *Marbury* v. *Madison* (1803). That is what the courts below did. Their decisions are worth a read. They (and others that have recently remedied similar violations) are detailed, thorough, painstaking. They evaluated with immense care the factual evidence and legal arguments the parties presented. They used neutral and manageable and strict standards. They had not a shred of politics about them. Contra the majority, this *was* law. . . .

Of all times to abandon the Court's duty to declare the law, this was not the one. The practices challenged in these cases imperil our system of government. Part of the Court's role in that system is to defend its foundations. None is more important than free and fair elections. With respect but deep sadness, I dissent.

Federal-Question Jurisdiction

Introduction

The Constitution states that federal courts have Article III jurisdiction over "cases . . . arising under" federal law. The scope of this constitutional grant (also called "federal-question jurisdiction") and the policies underlying it are part of this topic. Because Congress controls the jurisdiction of the lower federal courts, the lower federal courts' jurisdiction under this grant must be authorized by statute, so another part of this topic is the scope and policy behind the statutory grant of "arising under" jurisdiction. As you read the constitutional text, statutory text, and caselaw interpretation, consider the following questions:

- When does a "case" "aris[e] under" federal law, especially if the case includes state claims?

- Are the constitutional and statutory grants different? Should they be?

- What policies animate the grants of "arising under" jurisdiction?

- What counterpolicies to "arising under" jurisdiction exist?

- Is the Court's interpretation of the statutory grant clear and workable?

- What parts of this doctrine affect federalism or separation-of-powers values?

United States Constitution

Article III, section 2. The judicial power shall extend to all cases, in law and equity, arising under this Constitution, the laws of the United States, and treaties made, or which shall be made, under their authority . . . .

Osborn v. Bank of the United States (1824)

Opinion by Mr. Chief Justice MARSHALL.

Appeal from the Circuit Court of Ohio.

[Ohio passed a law on Feb. 8, 1819, that purported to tax all bank offices in the state, including offices of the Bank of the United States, $50,000 dollars per office. The Auditor of Ohio, Ralph Osborn, asserted that he would tax the Bank of the United States under the Ohio Act despite *M'Culloch v. Maryland*, in which the Supreme Court had held that the Constitution prohibited states from taxing the bank. The bank then sued Osborn for injunctive relief in federal court and won an injunction against Osborn. Osborn then appointed a staff member, J.L. Harper, to collect the tax. Harper then went to the Bank of the United States and collected $100,000 in taxes. The bank then sued Osborn, Harper, and others for restoration of the unlawfully taken tax under a state-law cause of action.] . . .

The cause came on to be heard upon these answers . . . against Osborn and Harper, and the Court pronounced a decree directing them to restore to the Bank the sum of 100,000 dollars, with interest on 19,830 dollars . . . . The cause was then brought, by appeal, to this Court. . . . The appellants contest the jurisdiction of the Court on two grounds:

> 1st. That the act of Congress has not given it.
> 2d. That, under the constitution, Congress cannot give it.

1. The first part of the objection depends entirely on the language of the act. The words are, that the Bank shall be "made able and capable in law," "to sue and be used, plead and be impleaded, answer and be answered, defend and be defended, in all State Courts having competent jurisdiction, and in any Circuit Court of the United States."

These words seem to the Court to admit of but one interpretation. They cannot be made plainer by explanation. They give, expressly, the right "to sue and be sued," "in every Circuit Court of the United States," and it would be difficult to substitute other terms which would be more direct and appropriate for the purpose. . . . The act of incorporation, then, confers jurisdiction on the Circuit Courts of the United States, if Congress can confer it.

2. We will now consider the constitutionality of the clause in the act of incorporation, which authorizes the Bank to sue in the federal Courts.

In support of this clause, it is said, that the legislative, executive, and judicial powers, of every well-constructed government, are co-extensive with each other; that is, they are potentially co-extensive. The executive department may constitutionally execute every law which the Legislature may constitutionally make, and the judicial department may receive from the Legislature the power of construing every such law. All governments which are not extremely defective in their organization, must possess, within themselves, the means of expounding, as well as enforcing, their own laws. If we examine the constitution of the United States, we find that its framers kept this great political principle in view. The 2d article vests the whole executive power in the President; and the 3d article declares, "that the judicial power shall extend to all cases in law and equity arising under this constitution, the laws of the United States, and treaties made, or which shall be made, under their authority."

This clause enables the judicial department to receive jurisdiction to the full extent of the constitution, laws, and treaties of the United States, when any question respecting them shall assume such a form that the judicial power is capable of acting on it. That power is capable of acting only when the subject is submitted to it by a party who asserts his rights in the form prescribed by law. It then becomes a case, and the constitution declares that the judicial power shall extend to all cases arising under the constitution, laws, and treaties of the United States.

The suit of *The Bank of the United States v. Osborn*, is a case, and the question is, whether it arises under a law of the United States?

The appellants contend, that it does not, because several questions may arise in it, which depend on the general principles of the law, not on any act of Congress.

If this were sufficient to withdraw a case from the jurisdiction of the federal Courts, almost every case, although involving the construction of a law, would be withdrawn; and a clause in the constitution, relating to a subject of vital importance to the government, and expressed in the most comprehensive terms, would be construed to mean almost nothing. There is scarcely any case, every part of which depends on the constitution, laws, or treaties of the United States. The questions, whether the fact alleged as the foundation of the action, be real or fictitious; whether the conduct of the plaintiff has been such as to entitle him to maintain his action; whether his right is barred; whether he has received satisfaction, or has in any manner released his claims, are questions, some or all of which may occur in almost every case; and if their existence be sufficient to arrest the jurisdiction of the Court, words which seem intended to be as extensive as the constitution, laws, and treaties of the Union, which seem designed to give the Courts of the government the construction of all its acts, so far as they affect the rights of individuals, would be reduced to almost nothing. . . .

We think, then, that when a question to which the judicial power of the Union is extended by the constitution, forms an ingredient of the original cause, it is in the power of Congress to give the Circuit Courts jurisdiction of that cause, although other questions of fact or of law may be involved in it.

The case of the Bank is, we think, a very strong case of this description. The charter of incorporation not only creates it, but gives it every faculty which it possesses. The power to acquire rights of any description, to transact business of any description, to make contracts of any description, to sue on those contracts, is given and measured by its charter, and that charter is a law of the United States. This being can acquire no right, make no contract, bring no suit, which is not authorized by a law of the United States. It is not only itself the mere creature of a law, but all its actions and all its rights are dependent on the same law. Can a being, thus constituted, have a case which does not arise literally, as well as substantially, under the law?

When a Bank sues, the first question which presents itself, and which lies at the foundation of the cause, is, has this legal entity a right to sue? Has it a right to come, not into this Court particularly, but into any Court? This depends on a law of the United States. The next question is, has this being a right to make this particular contract? If this question be decided in the negative, the cause is determined against the plaintiff; and this question, too, depends entirely on a law of the United States. These are important questions, and they exist in every possible case. The right to sue, if decided once, is decided forever; but the power of Congress was exercised antecedently to the first decision on that right, and if it was constitutional then, it cannot cease to be so, because the particular question is decided. It may be revived at the will of the party, and most probably would be renewed, were the tribunal to be changed. But the question respecting the right to make a particular contract, or to acquire a particular property, or to sue on account of a particular injury, belongs to every particular case, and may be renewed in every case. The question forms an original ingredient in every cause. Whether it be in fact relied on or not, in the defense, it is still a part of the cause, and may be relied. on. The right of the plaintiff to sue cannot depend on the defense which the defendant may choose to set up. His right to sue is anterior to that defense, and must depend on the state of things when the action is brought. The questions which the case involves, then, must determine its character, whether those questions be made in the cause or not.

The appellants say that the case arises on the contract; but the validity of the contract depends on a law of the United States, and the plaintiff is compelled, in every case, to show its validity. The case arises emphatically under the law. The act of Congress is its foundation. The contract could never have been made, but under the authority of that act. The act itself is the first ingredient in the case, is its origin, is that from which every other part arises. That other questions may also arise, as the execution of the contract, or its performance, cannot change the case, or give it any other origin than the charter of incorporation. The action still originates in, and is sustained by, that charter. . . .

[I]f the act of Congress was a simple act of incorporation, and contained nothing more, [arguments to the contrary] might be entitled to great consideration. But the act does not stop with incorporating the Bank. It proceeds to bestow upon the being it has made, all the faculties and capacities which that being possesses. Every act of the Bank grows out of this law, and is tested by it. To use the language of the constitution, every act of the Bank arises out of this law.

A naturalized citizen is indeed made a citizen under an act of Congress, but the act does not proceed to give, to regulate, or to prescribe his capacities. He becomes a member of the society, possessing all the rights of a native citizen, and standing, in the view of the constitution, on the footing of a native. The constitution does not authorize Congress to enlarge or abridge those rights. The simple power of the national Legislature is to prescribe a uniform rule of naturalization, and the exercise of this power exhausts it, so far as respects the individual. The constitution then takes him up, and, among other rights, extends to him the capacity of suing in the Courts of the United States, precisely under the same circumstances under which a native might sue. He is distinguishable in nothing from a native citizen, except so far as the constitution makes the distinction. The law makes none.

There is, then, no resemblance between the act incorporating the Bank and the general naturalization law.

Upon the best consideration we have been able to bestow on this subject, we are of opinion, that the clause in the act of incorporation enabling the Bank to sue in the Courts of the United States is consistent with the constitution, and to be obeyed in all Courts. . . .

The decree of the Circuit Court for the district of Ohio is affirmed . . . .

Mr. Justice JOHNSON, dissenting.

. . . . I cannot persuade myself that the constitution sanctions the vesting of the right of action in this Bank, in cases in which the privilege is exclusively personal, or in any case, merely on the ground that a question might *possibly* be raised in it, involving the constitution, or constitutionality of a law, of the United States.

When laws were heretofore passed for raising a revenue by a duty on stamped paper, the tax was quietly acquiesced in, notwithstanding it entrenched so closely on the unquestionable power of the States over the law of contracts; but had the same law which declared void contracts not written upon stamped paper, declared, that every person holding such paper should be entitled to bring his action "in any Circuit Court" of the United States, it is confidently believed that there could have been but one opinion on the constitutionality of such a provision. The whole jurisdiction over contracts, might thus have been taken from the State Courts, and conferred upon those of the United States. Nor would the evil have rested there; by a similar exercise of power, imposing a stamp on deeds generally, jurisdiction over the territory of the State, whoever might be parties, even between citizens of the same State—jurisdiction of suits instituted for the recovery of legacies or distributive portions of intestates' estates—jurisdiction, in fact, over almost every possible case, might be transferred to the Courts of the United States. Wills may be required to be executed on stamped paper; taxes may be, and have been, imposed upon legacies and distributions; and, in all such cases, there is not only a possibility, but a probability, that a question may arise, involving the constitutionality, construction, &c. of a law of the United States. If the circumstance, that the questions which the case involves, are to determine its character, whether those questions be made in the case or not, then every case here alluded to, may as well be transferred to the jurisdiction of the United States, as those to which this Bank is a party.

. . . . [U]ntil a question involving the construction or administration of the laws of the United States did actually arise, the *casus federis* was not presented, on which the constitution authorized the government to take to itself the jurisdiction of the cause. That until such a question actually arose, until such a case was actually presented, *non constat*, but the cause depended upon general principles, exclusively cognizable in the State Courts; that neither the letter nor the spirit of the constitution sanctioned the assumption of jurisdiction on the part of the United States at any previous stage. . . .

Verlinden v. Central Bank of Nigeria (1983)

We granted certiorari to consider whether the Foreign Sovereign Immunities Act of 1976, by authorizing a foreign plaintiff to sue a foreign state in a United States District Court on a non-federal cause of action, violates Article III of the Constitution. . . .

On April 21, 1975, the Federal Republic of Nigeria and petitioner Verlinden B.V., a Dutch corporation with its principal offices in Amsterdam, entered into a contract providing for the purchase of 240,000 metric tons of cement by Nigeria. The parties agreed that the contract would be governed by the laws of the Netherlands and that disputes would be resolved by arbitration before the International Chamber of Commerce, Paris, France.

The contract provided that the Nigerian government was to establish an irrevocable, confirmed letter of credit for the total purchase price through Slavenburg's Bank in Amsterdam. According to petitioner's amended complaint, however, respondent Central Bank of Nigeria, an instrumentality of Nigeria, improperly established an unconfirmed letter of credit payable through Morgan Guaranty Trust Company in New York.

In August 1975, Verlinden subcontracted with a Liechtenstein corporation, Interbuco, to purchase the cement needed to fulfill the contract. Meanwhile, the ports of Nigeria had become clogged with hundreds of ships carrying cement, sent by numerous other cement suppliers with whom Nigeria also had entered contracts. In mid-September, Central Bank unilaterally directed its correspondent banks, including Morgan Guaranty, to adopt a series of amendments to all letters of credit issued in connection with the cement contracts. Central Bank also directly notified the suppliers that payment would be made only for those shipments approved by Central Bank two months before their arrival in Nigerian waters.

Verlinden then sued Central Bank in United States District Court for the Southern District of New York, alleging that Central Bank's actions constituted an anticipatory breach of the letter of credit. Verlinden alleged jurisdiction under § 2 of the Foreign Sovereign Immunities Act.[4] . . .

> [4] Section 2 provides: "(a) The district courts shall have original jurisdiction without regard to amount in controversy of any nonjury civil action against a foreign state as defined in section 1603(a) of this title as to any claim for relief in personam with respect to which the foreign state is not entitled to immunity . . . ."

In 1976, Congress passed the Foreign Sovereign Immunities Act in order to free the Government from . . . case-by-case diplomatic pressures, to clarify the governing standards, and to assure litigants that decisions are made on purely legal grounds and under procedures that insure due process. To accomplish these objectives, the Act contains a comprehensive set of legal standards governing claims of immunity in every civil action against a foreign state or its political subdivisions, agencies or instrumentalities.

For the most part, the Act codifies, as a matter of federal law, the restrictive theory of sovereign immunity. A foreign state is normally immune from the jurisdiction of federal and state courts, subject to a set of exceptions . . . . Those exceptions include actions in which the foreign state has explicitly or impliedly waived its immunity and actions based upon commercial activities of the foreign sovereign carried on in the United States or causing a direct effect in the United States. When one of these or the other specified exceptions applies, the foreign state shall be liable in the same manner and to the same extent as a private individual under like circumstances. The Act expressly provides that its standards control in "the courts of the United States and of the States," and thus clearly contemplates that such suits may be brought in either federal or state courts. . . .

We now turn to the core question presented by this case: whether Congress exceeded the scope of Article III of the Constitution by granting federal courts subject matter jurisdiction over certain civil actions by foreign plaintiffs against foreign sovereigns where the rule of decision may be provided by state law. . . .

The controlling decision on the scope of Article III "arising under" jurisdiction is Chief Justice Marshall's opinion for the Court in *Osborn*. In *Osborn,* the Court upheld the constitutionality of a statute that granted the Bank of the United States the right to sue in federal court on causes of action based upon state law. There, the Court concluded that the judicial department may receive the power of construing every law that the Legislature may constitutionally make. The rule was laid down that: "It is a sufficient foundation for jurisdiction that the title or right set up by the party may be defeated by one construction of the constitution or laws of the United States and sustained by the opposite construction."

Osborn thus reflects a broad conception of "arising under" jurisdiction, according to which Congress may confer on the federal courts jurisdiction over any case or controversy that might call for the application of federal law. . . . [A] suit against a foreign state under this Act necessarily raises questions of substantive federal law at the very outset, and hence clearly "arises under" federal law, as that term is used in Article III.

By reason of its authority over foreign commerce and foreign relations, Congress has the undisputed power to decide, as a matter of federal law, whether and under what circumstances foreign nations should be amenable to suit in the United States. Actions against foreign sovereigns in our courts raise sensitive issues concerning the foreign relations of the United States, and the primacy of federal concerns is evident.

To promote these federal interests, Congress exercised its Article I powers by enacting a statute comprehensively regulating the amenability of foreign nations to suit in the United States. The statute must be applied by the District Courts in every action against a foreign sovereign, since subject matter jurisdiction in any such action depends on the existence of one of the specified exceptions to foreign sovereign immunity. At the threshold of every action in a District Court against a foreign state, therefore, the court must satisfy itself that one of the exceptions applies—and in doing so it must apply the detailed federal law standards set forth in the Act. Accordingly, an action against a foreign sovereign arises under federal law, for purposes of Article III jurisdiction. . . .

[I]n enacting the Foreign Sovereign Immunities Act, Congress expressly exercised its power to regulate foreign commerce, along with other specified Article I powers. . . . The Act thus does not merely concern access to the federal courts. Rather, it governs the types of actions for which foreign sovereigns may be held liable in a court in the United States, federal or state. The Act codifies the standards governing foreign sovereign immunity as an aspect of substantive federal law, and applying those standards will generally require interpretation of numerous points of federal law. Finally, if a court determines that none of the exceptions to sovereign immunity applies, the plaintiff will be barred from raising his claim in any court in the United States—manifestly, the title or right set up by the party, may be defeated by one construction of the laws of the United States, and sustained by the opposite construction. That the inquiry into foreign sovereign immunity is labeled under the Act as a matter of jurisdiction does not affect the constitutionality of Congress's action in granting federal courts jurisdiction over cases calling for application of this comprehensive regulatory statute.

Congress, pursuant to its unquestioned Article I powers, has enacted a broad statutory framework governing assertions of foreign sovereign immunity. In so doing, Congress deliberately sought to channel cases against foreign sovereigns away from the state courts and into federal courts, thereby reducing the potential for a multiplicity of conflicting results among the courts of the 50 states. The resulting jurisdictional grant is within the bounds of Article III, since every action against a foreign sovereign necessarily involves application of a body of substantive federal law, and accordingly "arises under" federal law, within the meaning of Article III. . . .

United States Code

28 U.S.C. § 1331. The district courts shall have original jurisdiction of all civil actions arising under the Constitution, laws, or treaties of the United States.

Louisville & Nashville Railroad v. Mottley (1908)

The appellees (husband and wife), being residents and citizens of Kentucky, brought this suit in equity in the circuit court of the United States for the western district of Kentucky against the appellant, a railroad company and a citizen of the same state. The object of the suit was to compel the specific performance of the following contract:

Louisville, Ky., Oct. 2d, 1871.

The Louisville & Nashville Railroad Company, in consideration that E. L. Mottley and wife, Annie E. Mottley, have this day released company from all damages or claims for damages for injuries received by them on the 7th of September, 1871, in consequence of a collision of trains on the railroad of said company at Randolph's Station, Jefferson County, Kentucky, hereby agrees to issue free passes on said railroad and branches now existing or to exist, to said E. L. & Annie E. Mottley for the remainder of the present year, and thereafter to renew said passes annually during the lives of said Mottley and wife or either of them.

The bill alleged that in September, 1871, plaintiffs, while passengers upon the defendant railroad, were injured by the defendant's negligence, and released their respective claims for damages in consideration of the agreement for transportation during their lives, expressed in the contract.

It is alleged that the contract was performed by the defendant up to January 1, 1907, when the defendant declined to renew the passes. The bill then alleges that the refusal to comply with the contract was based solely upon that part of the act of Congress of June 29, 1906, which forbids the giving of free passes or free transportation. The bill further alleges: First, that the act of Congress referred to does not prohibit the giving of passes under the circumstances of this case; and, second, that, if the law is to be construed as prohibiting such passes, it is in conflict with the 5th Amendment of the Constitution, because it deprives the plaintiffs of their property without due process of law. The defendant demurred to the bill. The judge of the circuit court overruled the demurrer, entered a decree for the relief prayed for, and the defendant appealed directly to this court.

Two questions of law were raised by the demurrer to the bill, were brought here by appeal, and have been argued before us. They are, first, whether that part of the act of Congress of June 29, 1906, which forbids the giving of free passes or the collection of any different compensation for transportation of passengers than that specified in the tariff filed, makes it unlawful to perform a contract for transportation of persons who, in good faith, before the passage of the act, had accepted such contract in satisfaction of a valid cause of action against the railroad; and, second, whether the statute, if it should be construed to render such a contract unlawful, is in violation of the 5th Amendment of the Constitution of the United States. We do not deem it necessary, however, to consider either of these questions, because, in our opinion, the court below was without jurisdiction of the cause. Neither party has questioned that jurisdiction, but it is the duty of this court to see to it that the jurisdiction of the circuit court, which is defined and limited by statute, is not exceeded. This duty we have frequently performed of our own motion.

There was no diversity of citizenship, and it is not and cannot be suggested that there was any ground of jurisdiction, except that the case was a "suit . . . arising under the Constitution or laws of the United States." It is the settled interpretation of these words, as used in this statute conferring jurisdiction, that a suit arises under the Constitution and laws of the United States only when the plaintiff's statement of his own cause of action shows that it is based upon those laws or that Constitution. It is not enough that the plaintiff alleges some anticipated defense to his cause of action, and asserts that the defense is invalidated by some provision of the Constitution of the United States. Although such allegations show that very likely, in the course of the litigation, a question under the Constitution would arise, they do not show that the suit, that is, the plaintiff's original cause of action, arises under the Constitution. . . .

The application of this rule to the case at bar is decisive against the jurisdiction of the circuit court. It is ordered that the judgment be reversed and the case remitted to the circuit court with instructions to dismiss the suit for want of jurisdiction.

Grable & Sons Metal Products v. Darue Engineering & Manufacturing (2005)

Justice SOUTER delivered the opinion of the Court.

The question is whether want of a federal cause of action to try claims of title to land obtained at a federal tax sale precludes removal to federal court of a state action with non-diverse parties raising a disputed issue of federal title law. We answer no, and hold that the national interest in providing a federal forum for federal tax litigation is sufficiently substantial to support the exercise of federal question jurisdiction over the disputed issue on removal, which would not distort any division of labor between the state and federal courts, provided or assumed by Congress.

I

In 1994, the Internal Revenue Service seized Michigan real property belonging to petitioner Grable & Sons Metal Products, Inc., to satisfy Grable's federal tax delinquency. Title 26 U.S.C. § 6335 required the IRS to give notice of the seizure, and there is no dispute that Grable received actual notice by certified mail before the IRS sold the property to respondent Darue Engineering & Manufacturing. Although Grable also received notice of the sale itself, it did not exercise its statutory right to redeem the property within 180 days of the sale, and after that period had passed, the Government gave Darue a quitclaim deed.

Five years later, Grable brought a quiet title action in state court, claiming that Darue's record title was invalid because the IRS had failed to notify Grable of its seizure of the property in the exact manner required by § 6335(a), which provides that written notice must be "given by the Secretary to the owner of the property [or] left at his usual place of abode or business." Grable said that the statute required personal service, not service by certified mail.

Darue removed the case to Federal District Court as presenting a federal question, because the claim of title depended on the interpretation of the notice statute in the federal tax law. The District Court declined to remand the case at Grable's behest after finding that the claim does pose a significant question of federal law, and ruling that Grable's lack of a federal right of action to enforce its claim against Darue did not bar the exercise of federal jurisdiction. On the merits, the court granted summary judgment to Darue, holding that although § 6335 by its terms required personal service, substantial compliance with the statute was enough.

The Court of Appeals for the Sixth Circuit affirmed. On the jurisdictional question, the panel thought it sufficed that the title claim raised an issue of federal law that had to be resolved, and implicated a substantial federal interest (in construing federal tax law). The court went on to affirm the District Court's judgment on the merits. We granted certiorari on the jurisdictional question alone . . . . We now affirm.

II

Darue was entitled to remove the quiet title action if Grable could have brought it in federal district court originally, 28 U.S.C. § 1441(a), as a civil action "arising under the Constitution, laws, or treaties of the United States," § 1331. This provision for federal-question jurisdiction is invoked by and large by plaintiffs pleading a cause of action created by federal law (*e.g.*, claims under 42 U.S.C. § 1983). There is, however, another longstanding, if less frequently encountered, variety of federal "arising under" jurisdiction, this Court having recognized for nearly 100 years that in certain cases federal question jurisdiction will lie over state-law claims that implicate significant federal issues. The doctrine captures the commonsense notion that a federal court ought to be able to hear claims recognized under state law that nonetheless turn on substantial questions of federal law, and thus justify resort to the experience, solicitude, and hope of uniformity that a federal forum offers on federal issues.

The classic example is *Smith v. Kansas City Title*, a suit by a shareholder claiming that the defendant corporation could not lawfully buy certain bonds of the National Government because their issuance was unconstitutional. Although Missouri law provided the cause of action, the Court recognized federal-question jurisdiction because the principal issue in the case was the federal constitutionality of the bond issue. *Smith* thus held, in a somewhat generous statement of the scope of the doctrine, that a state-law claim could give rise to federal-question jurisdiction so long as it "appears from the complaint that the right to relief depends upon the construction or application of federal law."

. . . . It has in fact become a constant refrain in such cases that federal jurisdiction demands not only a contested federal issue, but a substantial one, indicating a serious federal interest in claiming the advantages thought to be inherent in a federal forum.

But even when the state action discloses a contested and substantial federal question, the exercise of federal jurisdiction is subject to a possible veto. For the federal issue will ultimately qualify for a federal forum only if federal jurisdiction is consistent with congressional judgment about the sound division of labor between state and federal courts governing the application of § 1331. . . . Because arising-under jurisdiction to hear a state-law claim always raises the possibility of upsetting the state-federal line drawn (or at least assumed) by Congress, the presence of a disputed federal issue and the ostensible importance of a federal forum are never necessarily dispositive; there must always be an assessment of any disruptive portent in exercising federal jurisdiction.

These considerations have kept us from stating a single, precise, all-embracing test for jurisdiction over federal issues embedded in state-law claims between nondiverse parties. We have not kept them out simply because they appeared in state raiment, as Justice Holmes would have done, but neither have we treated "federal issue" as a password opening federal courts to any state action embracing a point of federal law. Instead, the question is, does a state-law claim necessarily raise a stated federal issue, actually disputed and substantial, which a federal forum may entertain without disturbing any congressionally approved balance of federal and state judicial responsibilities.

III
A

This case warrants federal jurisdiction. Grable's state complaint must specify "the facts establishing the superiority of its claim," and Grable has premised its superior title claim on a failure by the IRS to give it adequate notice, as defined by federal law. Whether Grable was given notice within the meaning of the federal statute is thus an essential element of its quiet title claim, and the meaning of the federal statute is actually in dispute; it appears to be the only legal or factual issue contested in the case. The meaning of the federal tax provision is an important issue of federal law that sensibly belongs in a federal court. The Government has a strong interest in the prompt and certain collection of delinquent taxes, and the ability of the IRS to satisfy its claims from the property of delinquents requires clear terms of notice to allow buyers like Darue to satisfy themselves that the Service has touched the bases necessary for good title. The Government thus has a direct interest in the availability of a federal forum to vindicate its own administrative action, and buyers (as well as tax delinquents) may find it valuable to come before judges used to federal tax matters. Finally, because it will be the rare state title case that raises a contested matter of federal law, federal jurisdiction to resolve genuine disagreement over federal tax title provisions will portend only a microscopic effect on the federal-state division of labor. . . .

B

Merrell Dow Pharmaceuticals v. Thompson, on which Grable rests its position, is not to the contrary. *Merrell Dow* considered a state tort claim resting in part on the allegation that the defendant drug company had violated a federal misbranding prohibition, and was thus presumptively negligent under Ohio law. The Court assumed that federal law would have to be applied to resolve the claim, but after closely examining the strength of the federal interest at stake and the implications of opening the federal forum, held federal jurisdiction unavailable. Congress had not provided a private federal cause of action for violation of the federal branding requirement, and the Court found it would flout, or at least undermine, congressional intent to conclude that federal courts might nevertheless exercise federal-question jurisdiction and provide remedies for violations of that federal statute solely because the violation is said to be a "proximate cause" under state law.

Because federal law provides for no quiet title action that could be brought against Darue, Grable argues that there can be no federal jurisdiction here, stressing some broad language in *Merrell Dow* (including the passage just quoted) that on its face supports Grable's position. But an opinion is to be read as a whole, and *Merrell Dow* cannot be read whole as overturning decades of precedent, as it would have done by effectively adopting the Holmes dissent in *Smith* and converting a federal cause of action from a sufficient condition for federal-question jurisdiction into a necessary one.

In the first place, *Merrell Dow* disclaimed the adoption of any bright-line rule, as when the Court reiterated that in exploring the outer reaches of § 1331, determinations about federal jurisdiction require sensitive judgments about congressional intent, judicial power, and the federal system. The opinion included a lengthy footnote explaining that questions of jurisdiction over state-law claims require careful judgments about the nature of the federal interest at stake. And as a final indication that it did not mean to make a federal right of action mandatory, it expressly approved the exercise of jurisdiction sustained in *Smith,* despite the want of any federal cause of action available to *Smith*'s shareholder plaintiff. *Merrell Dow* then, did not toss out, but specifically retained the contextual enquiry that had been *Smith*'s hallmark for over 60 years. . . .

Accordingly, *Merrell Dow* should be read in its entirety as treating the absence of a federal private right of action as evidence relevant to, but not dispositive of, the sensitive judgments about congressional intent that § 1331 requires. The absence of any federal cause of action affected *Merrell Dow*'s result two ways. The Court saw the fact as worth some consideration in the assessment of substantiality. But its primary importance emerged when the Court treated the combination of no federal cause of action and no preemption of state remedies for misbranding as an important clue to Congress's conception of the scope of jurisdiction to be exercised under § 1331. The Court saw the missing cause of action not as a missing federal door key, always required, but as a missing welcome mat, required in the circumstances, when exercising federal jurisdiction over a state misbranding action would have attracted a horde of original filings and removal cases raising other state claims with embedded federal issues. For if the federal labeling standard without a federal cause of action could get a state claim into federal court, so could any other federal standard without a federal cause of action. And that would have meant a tremendous number of cases.

One only needed to consider the treatment of federal violations generally in garden variety state tort law. The violation of federal statutes and regulations is commonly given negligence per se effect in state tort proceedings. A general rule of exercising federal jurisdiction over state claims resting on federal mislabeling and other statutory violations would thus have heralded a potentially enormous shift of traditionally state cases into federal courts. Expressing concern over the increased volume of federal litigation, and noting the importance of adhering to legislative intent, *Merrell Dow* thought it improbable that the Congress, having made no provision for a federal cause of action, would have meant to welcome any state-law tort case implicating federal law solely because the violation of the federal statute is said to create a rebuttable presumption of negligence under state law. In this situation, no welcome mat meant keep out. *Merrell Dow*'s analysis thus fits within the framework of examining the importance of having a federal forum for the issue, and the consistency of such a forum with Congress's intended division of labor between state and federal courts.

As already indicated, however, a comparable analysis yields a different jurisdictional conclusion in this case. Although Congress also indicated ambivalence in this case by providing no private right of action to Grable, it is the rare state quiet title action that involves contested issues of federal law. Consequently, jurisdiction over actions like Grable's would not materially affect, or threaten to affect, the normal currents of litigation. Given the absence of threatening structural consequences and the clear interest the Government, its buyers, and its delinquents have in the availability of a federal forum, there is no good reason to shirk from federal jurisdiction over the dispositive and contested federal issue at the heart of the state-law title claim.

The judgment of the Court of Appeals, upholding federal jurisdiction over Grable's quiet title action, is affirmed.

Justice THOMAS, concurring.

. . . . In this case, no one has asked us to overrule those precedents and adopt the rule Justice Holmes set forth in *American Well Works*, limiting § 1331 jurisdiction to cases in which federal law creates the cause of action pleaded on the face of the plaintiff's complaint. In an appropriate case, and perhaps with the benefit of better evidence as to the original meaning of § 1331's text, I would be willing to consider that course.

Jurisdictional rules should be clear. Whatever the virtues of the *Smith* standard, it is anything but clear. Whatever the vices of the *American Well Works* rule, it is clear. Moreover, it accounts for the vast majority of cases that come within § 1331 under our current case law. Accordingly, I would be willing in appropriate circumstances to reconsider our interpretation of § 1331.

Gunn v. Minton (2013)

Federal courts have exclusive jurisdiction over cases "arising under any Act of Congress relating to patents." 28 U.S.C. § 1338(a). The question presented is whether a state law claim alleging legal malpractice in the handling of a patent case must be brought in federal court.

I

In the early 1990s, respondent Vernon Minton developed a computer program and telecommunications network designed to facilitate securities trading. In March 1995, he leased the system—known as the Texas Computer Exchange Network, or TEXCEN—to R.M. Stark & Co., a securities brokerage. A little over a year later, he applied for a patent for an interactive securities trading system that was based substantially on TEXCEN. The U.S. Patent and Trademark Office issued the patent in January 2000.

Patent in hand, Minton filed a patent infringement suit in Federal District Court against the National Association of Securities Dealers, Inc. (NASD) and the NASDAQ Stock Market, Inc. He was represented by Jerry Gunn and the other petitioners. NASD and NASDAQ moved for summary judgment on the ground that Minton's patent was invalid under the "on sale" bar. That provision specifies that an inventor is not entitled to a patent if "the invention was . . . on sale in [the United States], more than one year prior to the date of the application," and Minton had leased TEXCEN to Stark more than one year prior to filing his patent application. Rejecting Minton's argument that there were differences between TEXCEN and the patented system that precluded application of the on-sale bar, the District Court granted the summary judgment motion and declared Minton's patent invalid.

Minton then filed a motion for reconsideration in the District Court, arguing for the first time that the lease agreement with Stark was part of ongoing testing of TEXCEN and therefore fell within the "experimental use" exception to the on-sale bar. [The motion was denied, and] Minton appealed to the U.S. Court of Appeals for the Federal Circuit. That court affirmed, concluding that the District Court had appropriately held Minton's experimental-use argument waived.

Minton, convinced that his attorneys' failure to raise the experimental-use argument earlier had cost him the lawsuit and led to invalidation of his patent, brought this malpractice action in Texas state court. His former lawyers defended on the ground that the lease to Stark was not, in fact, for an experimental use, and that therefore Minton's patent infringement claims would have failed even if the experimental-use argument had been timely raised. The trial court agreed, holding that Minton had put forward "less than a scintilla of proof" that the lease had been for an experimental purpose. It accordingly granted summary judgment to Gunn and the other lawyer defendants.

On appeal, Minton raised a new argument: Because his legal malpractice claim was based on an alleged error in a patent case, it "aris[es] under" federal patent law for purposes of 28 U.S.C. § 1338(a). And because, under § 1338(a), "[n]o State court shall have jurisdiction over any claim for relief arising under any Act of Congress relating to patents," the Texas court—where Minton had originally brought his malpractice claim—lacked subject matter jurisdiction to decide the case. Accordingly, Minton argued, the trial court's order should be vacated and the case dismissed, leaving Minton free to start over in the Federal District Court.

A divided panel of the Court of Appeals of Texas rejected Minton's argument. . . . The Supreme Court of Texas reversed . . . . We granted certiorari.

II

Federal courts are courts of limited jurisdiction, possessing only that power authorized by Constitution and statute. There is no dispute that the Constitution permits Congress to extend federal court jurisdiction to a case such as this one, see *Osborn v. Bank of United States*; the question is whether Congress has done so.

As relevant here, Congress has authorized the federal district courts to exercise original jurisdiction in "all civil actions arising under the Constitution, laws, or treaties of the United States," 28 U.S.C. § 1331, and, more particularly, over "any civil action arising under any Act of Congress relating to patents," § 1338(a). Adhering to the demands of linguistic consistency, we have interpreted the phrase "arising under" in both sections identically, applying our § 1331 and § 1338(a) precedents interchangeably. For cases falling within the patent-specific arising under jurisdiction of § 1338(a), however, Congress has not only provided for federal jurisdiction but also eliminated state jurisdiction, decreeing that "[n]o State court shall have jurisdiction over any claim for relief arising under any Act of Congress relating to patents." To determine whether jurisdiction was proper in the Texas courts, therefore, we must determine whether it would have been proper in a federal district court— whether, that is, the case "aris[es] under any Act of Congress relating to patents."

For statutory purposes, a case can "arise under" federal law in two ways. Most directly, a case arises under federal law when federal law creates the cause of action asserted. As a rule of inclusion, this "creation" test admits of only extremely rare exceptions and accounts for the vast bulk of suits that arise under federal law. Minton's original patent infringement suit against NASD and NASDAQ, for example, arose under federal law in this manner because it was authorized by 35 U.S.C. §§ 271, 281.

But even where a claim finds its origins in state rather than federal law—as Minton's legal malpractice claim indisputably does—we have identified a special and small category of cases in which arising under jurisdiction still lies. In outlining the contours of this slim category, we do not paint on a blank canvas. Unfortunately, the canvas looks like one that Jackson Pollock got to first.

In an effort to bring some order to this unruly doctrine several Terms ago, we condensed our prior cases into the following inquiry: Does the state-law claim necessarily raise a stated federal issue, actually disputed and substantial, which a federal forum may entertain without disturbing any congressionally approved balance of federal and state judicial responsibilities? *Grable*. That is, federal jurisdiction over a state law claim will lie if a federal issue is: (1) necessarily raised, (2) actually disputed, (3) substantial, and (4) capable of resolution in federal court without disrupting the federal-state balance approved by Congress. Where all four of these requirements are met, we held, jurisdiction is proper because there is a serious federal interest in claiming the advantages thought to be inherent in a federal forum, which can be vindicated without disrupting Congress's intended division of labor between state and federal courts.

III

Applying *Grable*'s inquiry here, it is clear that Minton's legal malpractice claim does not arise under federal patent law. Indeed, for the reasons we discuss, we are comfortable concluding that state legal malpractice claims based on underlying patent matters will rarely, if ever, arise under federal patent law for purposes of § 1338(a). Although such cases may necessarily raise disputed questions of patent law, those cases are by their nature unlikely to have the sort of significance for the federal system necessary to establish jurisdiction.

A

To begin, we acknowledge that resolution of a federal patent question is "necessary" to Minton's case. Under Texas law, a plaintiff alleging legal malpractice must establish four elements: (1) that the defendant attorney owed the plaintiff a duty; (2) that the attorney breached that duty; (3) that the breach was the proximate cause of the plaintiff's injury; and (4) that damages occurred. In cases like this one, in which the attorney's alleged error came in failing to make a particular argument, the causation element requires a "case within a case" analysis of whether, had the argument been made, the outcome of the earlier litigation would have been different. To prevail on his legal malpractice claim, therefore, Minton must show that he would have prevailed in his federal patent infringement case if only petitioners had timely made an experimental-use argument on his behalf. That will necessarily require application of patent law to the facts of Minton's case.

B

The federal issue is also "actually disputed" here—indeed, on the merits, it is the central point of dispute. Minton argues that the experimental-use exception properly applied to his lease to Stark, saving his patent from the on-sale bar; petitioners argue that it did not. This is just the sort of dispute respecting the effect of federal law that *Grable* envisioned.

C

Minton's argument founders on *Grable*'s next requirement, however, for the federal issue in this case is not substantial in the relevant sense. In reaching the opposite conclusion, the Supreme Court of Texas focused on the importance of the issue to the plaintiff's case and to the parties before it. As our past cases show, however, it is not enough that the federal issue be significant to the particular parties in the immediate suit; that will *always* be true when the state claim "necessarily raise[s]" a disputed federal issue, as *Grable* separately requires. The substantiality inquiry under *Grable* looks instead to the importance of the issue to the federal system as a whole.

In *Grable* itself, for example, the Internal Revenue Service had seized property from the plaintiff and sold it to satisfy the plaintiff's federal tax delinquency. Five years later, the plaintiff filed a state law quiet title action against the third party that had purchased the property, alleging that the IRS had failed to comply with certain federally imposed notice requirements, so that the seizure and sale were invalid. In holding that the case arose under federal law, we primarily focused not on the interests of the litigants themselves, but rather on the broader significance of the notice question for the Federal Government. We emphasized the Government's strong interest in being able to recover delinquent taxes through seizure and sale of property, which in turn "require[d] clear terms of notice to allow buyers . . . to satisfy themselves that the Service has touched the bases necessary for good title." The Government's direct interest in the availability of a federal forum to vindicate its own administrative action made the question an important issue of federal law that sensibly belonged in a federal court.

A second illustration of the sort of substantiality we require comes from *Smith v. Kansas City Title*, which *Grable* described as the classic example of a state claim arising under federal law. In *Smith*, the plaintiff argued that the defendant bank could not purchase certain bonds issued by the Federal Government because the Government had acted unconstitutionally in issuing them. We held that the case arose under federal law, because the decision depends upon the determination of the constitutional validity of an act of Congress which is directly drawn in question. Again, the relevant point was not the importance of the question to the parties alone but rather the importance more generally of a determination that the Government securities were issued under an unconstitutional law, and hence of no validity.

Here, the federal issue carries no such significance. Because of the backward-looking nature of a legal malpractice claim, the question is posed in a merely hypothetical sense: *If* Minton's lawyers had raised a timely experimental-use argument, would the result in the patent infringement proceeding have been different? No matter how the state courts resolve that hypothetical "case within a case," it will not change the real-world result of the prior federal patent litigation. Minton's patent will remain invalid.

Nor will allowing state courts to resolve these cases undermine the development of a uniform body of patent law. Congress ensured such uniformity by vesting exclusive jurisdiction over actual patent cases in the federal district courts and exclusive appellate jurisdiction in the Federal Circuit. In resolving the nonhypothetical patent questions those cases present, the federal courts are of course not bound by state court case-within-a-case patent rulings. In any event, the state court case-within-a-case inquiry asks what would have happened in the prior federal proceeding if a particular argument had been made. In answering that question, state courts can be expected to hew closely to the pertinent federal precedents. It is those precedents, after all, that would have applied had the argument been made.

As for more novel questions of patent law that may arise for the first time in a state court "case within a case," they will at some point be decided by a federal court in the context of an actual patent case, with review in the Federal Circuit. If the question arises frequently, it will soon be resolved within the federal system, laying to rest any contrary state court precedent; if it does not arise frequently, it is unlikely to implicate substantial federal interests. The present case is poles apart from *Grable*, in which a state court's resolution of the federal question would be controlling in numerous other cases. . . .

Nor can we accept the suggestion that the federal courts' greater familiarity with patent law means that legal malpractice cases like this one belong in federal court. . . . [T]he possibility that a state court will incorrectly resolve a state claim is not, by itself, enough to trigger the federal courts' exclusive patent jurisdiction, even if the potential error finds its root in a misunderstanding of patent law.

There is no doubt that resolution of a patent issue in the context of a state legal malpractice action can be vitally important to the particular parties in that case. But something more, demonstrating that the question is significant to the federal system as a whole, is needed. That is missing here.

D

It follows from the foregoing that *Grable*'s fourth requirement is also not met. That requirement is concerned with the appropriate balance of federal and state judicial responsibilities. We have already explained the absence of a substantial federal issue within the meaning of *Grable*. The States, on the other hand, have a special responsibility for maintaining standards among members of the licensed professions. Their interest in regulating lawyers is especially great since lawyers are essential to the primary governmental function of administering justice, and have historically been officers of the courts. We have no reason to suppose that Congress—in establishing exclusive federal jurisdiction over patent cases—meant to bar from state courts state legal malpractice claims simply because they require resolution of a hypothetical patent issue.

* * *

As we recognized a century ago, the Federal courts have exclusive jurisdiction of all cases arising under the patent laws, but not of all questions in which a patent may be the subject-matter of the controversy. In this case, although the state courts must answer a question of patent law to resolve Minton's legal malpractice claim, their answer will have no broader effects. It will not stand as binding precedent for any future patent claim; it will not even affect the validity of Minton's patent. Accordingly, there is no serious federal interest in claiming the advantages thought to be inherent in a federal forum. Section 1338(a) does not deprive the state courts of subject matter jurisdiction.

The judgment of the Supreme Court of Texas is reversed . . . .

Diversity Jurisdiction

Introduction

The Constitution extends the judicial power of the federal courts to "controversies . . . between citizens of different states" and between citizens of states and foreign citizens. Congress extended this grant of "diversity jurisdiction" to the lower courts in the first Judiciary Act of 1789 and has currently codified it in 28 U.S.C. § 1332. Consider the following questions about diversity jurisdiction:

- What policies animate the constitutional and statutory grants of diversity jurisdiction? Do those policies still justify its scope today?

- How (and why) are the constitutional and statutory grants different?

- How does diversity jurisdiction implicate federalism values?

- Do the legal tests for diversity jurisdiction effectuate its underlying policies? Are the legal tests clear and easy to apply?

- What reforms of the scope of diversity jurisdiction might you propose?

United States Constitution

Article III, section 2. The judicial power shall extend . . . to controversies . . . between citizens of different states. . . , and between a state, or the citizens thereof, and foreign states, citizens or subjects.

United States Code

28 U.S.C. § 1332.

(a) The district courts shall have original jurisdiction of all civil actions where the matter in controversy exceeds the sum or value of $75,000, exclusive of interest and costs, and is between—

(1) citizens of different States;
(2) citizens of a State and citizens or subjects of a foreign state, except that the district courts shall not have original jurisdiction under this subsection of an action between citizens of a State and citizens or subjects of a foreign state who are lawfully admitted for permanent residence in the United States and are domiciled in the same State; [and]
(3) citizens of different States and in which citizens or subjects of a foreign state are additional parties . . . .

(c) For the purposes of this section . . . a corporation shall be deemed to be a citizen of every State and foreign state by which it has been incorporated and of the State or foreign state where it has its principal place of business . . . .

Mas v. Perry (5th Cir. 1974)

This case presents questions pertaining to federal diversity jurisdiction under 28 U.S.C. § 1332, which, pursuant to article III, section II of the Constitution, provides for original jurisdiction in federal district courts of all civil actions that are between, inter alia, citizens of different States or citizens of a State and citizens of foreign states and in which the amount in controversy is more than $10,000.

Appellees Jean Paul Mas, a citizen of France, and Judy Mas were married at her home in Jackson, Mississippi. Prior to their marriage, Mr. and Mrs. Mas were graduate assistants, pursuing coursework as well as performing teaching duties, for approximately nine months and one year, respectively, at Louisiana State University in Baton Rouge, Louisiana. Shortly after their marriage, they returned to Baton Rouge to resume their duties as graduate assistants at LSU. They remained in Baton Rouge for approximately two more years, after which they moved to Park Ridge, Illinois. At the time of the trial in this case, it was their intention to return to Baton Rouge While Mr. Mas finished his studies for the degree of Doctor of Philosophy. Mr. and Mrs. Mas were undecided as to where they would reside after that.

Upon their return to Baton Rouge after their marriage, appellees rented an apartment from appellant Oliver H. Perry, a citizen of Louisiana. This appeal arises from a final judgment entered on a jury verdict awarding $5,000 to Mr. Mas and $15,000 to Mrs. Mas for damages incurred by them as a result of the discovery that their bedroom and bathroom contained "two-way" mirrors and that they had been watched through them by the appellant during three of the first four months of their marriage.

At the close of the appellees' case at trial, appellant made an oral motion to dismiss for lack of jurisdiction. The motion was denied by the district court. Before this Court, appellant challenges the final judgment below solely on jurisdictional grounds, contending that appellees failed to prove diversity of citizenship among the parties and that the requisite jurisdictional amount is lacking with respect to Mr. Mas. Finding no merit to these contentions, we affirm. Under section 1332(a)(2), the federal judicial power extends to the claim of Mr. Mas, a citizen of France, against the appellant, a citizen of Louisiana. Since we conclude that Mrs. Mas is a citizen of Mississippi for diversity purposes, the district court also properly had jurisdiction under section 1332(a)(1) of her claim.

It has long been the general rule that complete diversity of parties is required in order that diversity jurisdiction obtain; that is, no party on one side may be a citizen of the same State as any party on the other side. *Strawbridge v. Curtiss*. This determination of one's State Citizenship for diversity purposes is controlled by federal law, not by the law of any State.

As is the case in other areas of federal jurisdiction, the diverse citizenship among adverse parties must be present at the time the complaint is filed. Jurisdiction is unaffected by subsequent changes in the citizenship of the parties. The burden of pleading the diverse citizenship is upon the party invoking federal jurisdiction, and if the diversity jurisdiction is properly challenged, that party also bears the burden of proof.

To be a citizen of a State within the meaning of section 1332, a natural person must be both a citizen of the United States and a domiciliary of that State. For diversity purposes, citizenship means domicile; mere residence in the State is not sufficient.

A person's domicile is the place of his true, fixed, and permanent home and principal establishment, and to which he has the intention of returning whenever he is absent therefrom. A change of domicile may be effected only by a combination of two elements: (a) taking up residence in a different domicile with (b) the intention to remain there.

It is clear that at the time of her marriage, Mrs. Mas was a domiciliary of the State of Mississippi. . . . Mrs. Mas's Mississippi domicile was disturbed neither by her year in Louisiana prior to her marriage nor as a result of the time she and her husband spent at LSU after their marriage, since for both periods she was a graduate assistant at LSU. Though she testified that after her marriage she had no intention of returning to her parents' home in Mississippi, Mrs. Mas did not effect a change of domicile since she and Mr. Mas were in Louisiana only as students and lacked the requisite intention to remain there. Until she acquires a new domicile, she remains a domiciliary, and thus a citizen, of Mississippi.[2]

[2] The original complaint in this case was filed within several days of Mr. and Mrs. Mas's realization that they had been watched through the mirrors, quite some time before they moved to Park Ridge, Illinois. Because the district court's jurisdiction is not affected by actions of the parties subsequent to the commencement of the suit, the testimony concerning Mr. and Mrs. Mas's moves after that time is not determinative of the issue of diverse citizenship, though it is of interest insofar as it supports their lack of intent to remain permanently in Louisiana.

Appellant also contends that Mr. Mas's claim should have been dismissed for failure to establish the requisite jurisdictional amount for diversity cases of more than $10,000. In their complaint Mr. and Mrs. Mas alleged that they had each been damaged in the amount of $100,000. As we have noted, Mr. Mas ultimately recovered $5,000.

It is well settled that the amount in controversy is determined by the amount claimed by the plaintiff in good faith. Federal jurisdiction is not lost because a judgment of less than the jurisdictional amount is awarded. That Mr. Mas recovered only $5,000 is, therefore, not compelling. As the Supreme Court stated in *St. Paul Mercury Indemnity v. Red Cab Co.*:

> The sum claimed by the plaintiff controls if the claim is apparently made in good faith. It must appear to a legal certainty that the claim is really for less than the jurisdictional amount to justify dismissal. The inability of the plaintiff to recover an amount adequate to give the court jurisdiction does not show his bad faith or oust the jurisdiction . . . .

Having heard the evidence presented at the trial, the district court concluded that the appellees properly met the requirements of section 1332 with respect to jurisdictional amount. Upon examination of the record in this case, we are also satisfied that the requisite amount was in controversy. . . .

Hertz Corp. v. Friend (2010)

The federal diversity jurisdiction statute provides that "a corporation shall be deemed to be a citizen of any State by which it has been incorporated *and of the State where it has its principal place of business.*" 28 U.S.C. § 1332(c)(1) (emphasis added). We seek here to resolve different interpretations that the Circuits have given this phrase. In doing so, we place primary weight upon the need for judicial administration of a jurisdictional statute to remain as simple as possible. And we conclude that the phrase "principal place of business" refers to the place where the corporation's high level officers direct, control, and coordinate the corporation's activities. Lower federal courts have often metaphorically called that place the corporation's "nerve center." We believe that the "nerve center" will typically be found at a corporation's headquarters.

I

In September 2007, respondents Melinda Friend and John Nhieu, two California citizens, sued petitioner, the Hertz Corporation, in a California state court. They sought damages for what they claimed were violations of California's wage and hour laws. And they requested relief on behalf of a potential class composed of California citizens who had allegedly suffered similar harms.

Hertz filed a notice seeking removal to a federal court. Hertz claimed that the plaintiffs and the defendant were citizens of different States. Hence, the federal court possessed diversity-of-citizenship jurisdiction. Friend and Nhieu, however, claimed that the Hertz Corporation was a California citizen, like themselves, and that, hence, diversity jurisdiction was lacking.

To support its position, Hertz submitted a declaration by an employee relations manager that sought to show that Hertz's "principal place of business" was in New Jersey, not in California. The declaration stated, among other things, that Hertz operated facilities in 44 States; and that California—which had about 12% of the Nation's population—accounted for 273 of Hertz's 1,606 car rental locations; about 2,300 of its 11,230 full-time employees; about $811 million of its $4.371 billion in annual revenue; and about 3.8 million of its approximately 21 million annual transactions, *i.e.*, rentals. The declaration also stated that the leadership of Hertz and its domestic subsidiaries is located at Hertz's "corporate headquarters" in Park Ridge, New Jersey; that its core executive and administrative functions are carried out there and to a lesser extent in Oklahoma City, Oklahoma; and that its major administrative operations are found at those two locations.

The District Court of the Northern District of California accepted Hertz's statement of the facts as undisputed. But it concluded that, given those facts, Hertz was a citizen of California.

In reaching this conclusion, the court applied Ninth Circuit precedent, which instructs courts to identify a corporation's "principal place of business" by first determining the amount of a corporation's business activity State by State. If the amount of activity is "significantly larger" or "substantially predominates" in one State, then that State is the corporation's "principal place of business." If there is no such State, then the "principal place of business" is the corporation's "nerve center," *i.e.*, the place where the majority of its executive and administrative functions are performed.

Applying this test, the District Court found that . . . . Hertz's "principal place of business" was California, and diversity jurisdiction was thus lacking. The District Court consequently remanded the case to the state courts. Hertz appealed the District Court's remand order. The Ninth Circuit affirmed . . . .

III

We begin our "principal place of business" discussion with a brief review of relevant history. The Constitution provides that the "judicial Power shall extend" to "Controversies . . . between Citizens of different States." Art. III, § 2. This language, however, does not automatically confer diversity jurisdiction upon the federal courts. Rather, it authorizes Congress to do so and, in doing so, to determine the scope of the federal courts' jurisdiction within constitutional limits.

Congress first authorized federal courts to exercise diversity jurisdiction in 1789 when, in the First Judiciary Act, Congress granted federal courts authority to hear suits "between a citizen of the State where the suit is brought, and a citizen of another State." The statute said nothing about corporations. . . . [To fill this gap], for diversity purposes, the federal courts considered a corporation to be a citizen of the State of its incorporation.

In 1928, this Court made clear that the "state of incorporation" rule was virtually absolute. It held that a corporation closely identified with State A could proceed in a federal court located in that State as long as the corporation had filed its incorporation papers in State B, perhaps a State where the corporation did no business at all. Subsequently, many in Congress and those who testified before it pointed out that this interpretation was at odds with diversity jurisdiction's basic rationale, namely, opening the federal courts' doors to those who might otherwise suffer from local prejudice against out-of-state parties. Through its choice of the State of incorporation, a corporation could manipulate federal-court jurisdiction, for example, opening the federal courts' doors in a State where it conducted nearly all its business by filing incorporation papers elsewhere. . . .

Subsequently, in 1958, Congress both codified the courts' traditional place of incorporation test and also enacted into law . . . "principal place of business" language. A corporation was to be deemed a citizen of any State by which it has been incorporated and of the State where it has its principal place of business.

IV

The phrase "principal place of business" has proved more difficult to apply than its originators likely expected. . . . If a corporation's headquarters and executive offices were in the same State in which it did most of its business, the test seemed straightforward. The "principal place of business" was located in that State. But suppose those corporate headquarters, including executive offices, are in one State, while the corporation's plants or other centers of business activity are located in other States? In 1959, a distinguished federal district judge, Edward Weinfeld, relied on the Second Circuit's interpretation of the Bankruptcy Act to answer this question in part:

> Where a corporation is engaged in far-flung and varied activities which are carried on in different states, its principal place of business is the nerve center from which it radiates out to its constituent parts and from which its officers direct, control and coordinate all activities without regard to locale, in the furtherance of the corporate objective. . . .

Numerous Circuits have since followed this rule, applying the "nerve center" test for corporations with "far-flung" business activities.

[Thi]s analysis, however, did not go far enough. For it did not answer what courts should do when the operations of the corporation are not "far-flung" but rather limited to only a few States. When faced with this question, various courts have focused more heavily on where a corporation's actual business activities are located.

Perhaps because corporations come in many different forms, involve many different kinds of business activities, and locate offices and plants for different reasons in different ways in different regions, a general "business activities" approach has proved unusually difficult to apply. Courts must decide which factors are more important than others: for example, plant location, sales or servicing centers; transactions, payrolls, or revenue generation.

The number of factors grew as courts explicitly combined aspects of the "nerve center" and "business activity" tests to look to a corporation's "total activities," sometimes to try to determine what treatises have described as the corporation's "center of gravity." A major treatise confirms this growing complexity, listing, Circuit by Circuit, cases that highlight different factors or emphasize similar factors differently, and reporting that the federal courts of appeals have employed various tests—tests which tend to overlap and which are sometimes described in language that is imprecise. Not surprisingly, different Circuits (and sometimes different courts within a single Circuit) have applied these highly general multifactor tests in different ways.

This complexity may reflect an unmediated judicial effort to apply the statutory phrase "principal place of business" in light of the general purpose of diversity jurisdiction, *i.e.,* an effort to find the State where a corporation is least likely to suffer out-of-state prejudice when it is sued in a local court. But, if so, that task seems doomed to failure. After all, the relevant purposive concern—prejudice against an out-of-state party—will often depend upon factors that courts cannot easily measure, for example, a corporation's image, its history, and its advertising, while the factors that courts can more easily measure, for example, its office or plant location, its sales, its employment, or the nature of the goods or services it supplies, will sometimes bear no more than a distant relation to the likelihood of prejudice. At the same time, this approach is at war with administrative simplicity. And it has failed to achieve a nationally uniform interpretation of federal law, an unfortunate consequence in a federal legal system.

V

A

In an effort to find a single, more uniform interpretation of the statutory phrase, we have reviewed the Courts of Appeals's divergent and increasingly complex interpretations. Having done so, we now return to, and expand, Judge Weinfeld's approach, as applied in the Seventh Circuit. We conclude that "principal place of business" is best read as referring to the place where a corporation's officers direct, control, and coordinate the corporation's activities. It is the place that Courts of Appeals have called the corporation's "nerve center." And in practice it should normally be the place where the corporation maintains its headquarters—provided that the headquarters is the actual center of direction, control, and coordination, *i.e.,* the "nerve center," and not simply an office where the corporation holds its board meetings (for example, attended by directors and officers who have traveled there for the occasion).

[The following] considerations, taken together, convince us that this approach, while imperfect, is superior to other possibilities. First, the statute's language supports the approach. The statute's text deems a corporation a citizen of the "State where it has its principal place of business." 28 U.S.C. § 1332(c)(1). The word "place" is in the singular, not the plural. The word "principal" requires us to pick out the "main, prominent" or "leading" place. And the fact that the word "place" follows the words "State where" means that the "place" is a place *within* a State. It is not the State itself.

A corporation's "nerve center," usually its main headquarters, is a single place. The public often (though not always) considers it the corporation's main place of business. And it is a place within a State. By contrast, the application of a more general business activities test has led some courts, as in the present case, to look, not at a particular place within a State, but incorrectly at the State itself, measuring the total amount of business activities that the corporation conducts there and determining whether they are "significantly larger" than in the next-ranking State. . . .

Second, administrative simplicity is a major virtue in a jurisdictional statute. Complex jurisdictional tests complicate a case, eating up time and money as the parties litigate, not the merits of their claims, but which court is the right court to decide those claims. Complex tests produce appeals and reversals, encourage gamesmanship, and, again, diminish the likelihood that results and settlements will reflect a claim's legal and factual merits. Judicial resources too are at stake. Courts have an independent obligation to determine whether subject-matter jurisdiction exists, even when no party challenges it. So courts benefit from straightforward rules under which they can readily assure themselves of their power to hear a case.

Simple jurisdictional rules also promote greater predictability. Predictability is valuable to corporations making business and investment decisions. Predictability also benefits plaintiffs deciding whether to file suit in a state or federal court.

A "nerve center" approach, which ordinarily equates that "center" with a corporation's headquarters, is simple to apply *comparatively speaking*. The metaphor of a corporate "brain," while not precise, suggests a single location. By contrast, a corporation's general business activities more often lack a single principal place where they take place. That is to say, the corporation may have several plants, many sales locations, and employees located in many different places. If so, it will not be as easy to determine which of these different business locales is the "principal" or most important "place." . . .

B

We recognize that there may be no perfect test that satisfies all administrative and purposive criteria. We recognize as well that, under the "nerve center" test we adopt today, there will be hard cases. For example, in this era of telecommuting, some corporations may divide their command and coordinating functions among officers who work at several different locations, perhaps communicating over the Internet. That said, our test nonetheless points courts in a single direction, toward the center of overall direction, control, and coordination. Courts do not have to try to weigh corporate functions, assets, or revenues different in kind, one from the other. Our approach provides a sensible test that is relatively easier to apply, not a test that will, in all instances, automatically generate a result.

We also recognize that the use of a "nerve center" test may in some cases produce results that seem to cut against the basic rationale for 28 U.S.C. § 1332. For example, if the bulk of a company's business activities visible to the public take place in New Jersey, while its top officers direct those activities just across the river in New York, the "principal place of business" is New York. One could argue that members of the public in New Jersey would be *less* likely to be prejudiced against the corporation than persons in New York—yet the corporation will still be entitled to remove a New Jersey state case to federal court. And note too that the same corporation would be unable to remove a New York state case to federal court, despite the New York public's presumed prejudice against the corporation.

We understand that such seeming anomalies will arise. However, in view of the necessity of having a clearer rule, we must accept them. Accepting occasionally counterintuitive results is the price the legal system must pay to avoid overly complex jurisdictional administration while producing the benefits that accompany a more uniform legal system. . . .

VI

Petitioner's unchallenged declaration suggests that Hertz's center of direction, control, and coordination, its "nerve center," and its corporate headquarters are one and the same, and they are located in New Jersey, not in California. Because respondents should have a fair opportunity to litigate their case in light of our holding, however, we vacate the Ninth Circuit's judgment and remand the case for further proceedings consistent with this opinion.

Americold Realty Trust v. ConAgra Foods (2016)

Federal law permits federal courts to resolve certain nonfederal controversies between "citizens" of different States. This rule is easy enough to apply to humans, but can become metaphysical when applied to legal entities. This case asks how to determine the citizenship of a "real estate investment trust," an inanimate creature of Maryland law. We answer: While humans and corporations can assert their own citizenship, other entities take the citizenship of their members.

I

This action began as a typical state-law controversy, one involving a contract dispute and an underground food-storage warehouse fire. A group of corporations whose food perished in that 1991 fire continues to seek compensation from the warehouse's owner, now known as Americold Realty Trust. After the corporations filed their latest suit in Kansas court, Americold removed the suit to the Federal District Court for the District of Kansas. The District Court accepted jurisdiction and resolved the dispute in favor of Americold.

On appeal, however, the Tenth Circuit asked for supplemental briefing on whether the District Court's exercise of jurisdiction was appropriate. The parties responded that the District Court possessed jurisdiction because the suit involved "citizens of different States."

The Tenth Circuit disagreed. The court considered the corporate plaintiffs citizens of the States where they were chartered and had their principal places of business: Delaware, Nebraska, and Illinois. The court applied a different test to determine Americold's citizenship because Americold is a "real estate investment trust," not a corporation. Distilling this Court's precedent, the Tenth Circuit reasoned that the citizenship of any non-corporate artificial entity is determined by considering all of the entity's members, which include, at minimum, its shareholders. As there was no record of the citizenship of Americold's shareholders, the court concluded that the parties failed to demonstrate that the plaintiffs were citizens of different States than the defendants.

We granted certiorari to resolve confusion among the Courts of Appeals regarding the citizenship of unincorporated entities. We now affirm.

II

Exercising its powers under Article III, the First Congress granted federal courts jurisdiction over controversies between a "citizen" of one State and "a citizen of another State." For a long time, however, Congress failed to explain how to determine the citizenship of a nonbreathing entity like a business association. In the early 19th century, this Court took that silence literally, ruling that only a human could be a citizen for jurisdictional purposes. If a "mere legal entity" like a corporation were sued, the relevant citizens were its "members," or the real persons who come into court in the entity's name.

This Court later carved a limited exception for corporations, holding that a corporation itself could be considered a citizen of its State of incorporation. Congress etched this exception into the U.S. Code, adding that a corporation should also be considered a citizen of the State where it has its principal place of business. But Congress never expanded this grant of citizenship to include artificial entities other than corporations, such as joint-stock companies or limited partnerships. For these unincorporated entities, we too have adhered to our oft-repeated rule that diversity jurisdiction in a suit by or against the entity depends on the citizenship of all its members.

Despite our oft-repetition of the rule linking unincorporated entities with their "members," we have never expressly defined the term. But we have equated an association's members with its owners or the several persons composing such association. Applying this principle with reference to specific States' laws, we have identified the members of a joint-stock company as its shareholders, the members of a partnership as its partners, the members of a union as the workers affiliated with it, and so on.

This case asks us to determine the citizenship of Americold Realty Trust, a real estate investment trust organized under Maryland law. As Americold is not a corporation, it possesses its members' citizenship. Nothing in the record designates who Americold's members are. But Maryland law provides an answer.

In Maryland, a real estate investment trust is an unincorporated business trust or association in which property is held and managed "for the benefit and profit of any person who may become a shareholder." As with joint-stock companies or partnerships, shareholders have ownership interests and votes in the trust by virtue of their shares of beneficial interest. These shareholders appear to be in the same position as the shareholders of a joint-stock company or the partners of a limited partnership—both of whom we viewed as members of their relevant entities. We therefore conclude that for purposes of diversity jurisdiction, Americold's members include its shareholders.

III

Americold disputes this conclusion. It cites a case called *Navarro Savings Association v. Lee* to argue that anything called a "trust" possesses the citizenship of its trustees alone, not its shareholder beneficiaries as well. As we have reminded litigants before, however, *Navarro* had nothing to do with the citizenship of a "trust." Rather, *Navarro* reaffirmed a separate rule that when a trustee files a lawsuit in *her* name, her jurisdictional citizenship is the State to which she belongs—as is true of any natural person. This rule coexists with our discussion above that when an artificial entity is sued in *its* name, it takes the citizenship of each of its members.

That said, Americold's confusion regarding the citizenship of a trust is understandable and widely shared. The confusion can be explained, perhaps, by tradition. Traditionally, a trust was not considered a distinct legal entity, but a fiduciary relationship between multiple people. Such a relationship was not a thing that could be haled into court; legal proceedings involving a trust were brought by or against the trustees in their own name. And when a trustee files a lawsuit or is sued in her own name, her citizenship is all that matters for diversity purposes. For a traditional trust, therefore, there is no need to determine its membership, as would be true if the trust, as an entity, were sued.

Many States, however, have applied the "trust" label to a variety of unincorporated entities that have little in common with this traditional template. Maryland, for example, treats a real estate investment trust as a separate legal entity that itself can sue or be sued. So long as such an entity is unincorporated, we apply our "oft-repeated rule" that it possesses the citizenship of all its members. But neither this rule nor *Navarro* limits an entity's membership to its trustees just because the entity happens to call itself a trust.

We therefore decline to apply the same rule to an unincorporated entity sued in its organizational name that applies to a human trustee sued in her personal name. We also decline an *amicus*'s invitation to apply the same rule to an unincorporated entity that applies to a corporation—namely, to consider it a citizen only of its State of establishment and its principal place of business. When we last examined the doctrinal wall between corporate and unincorporated entities in 1990, we saw no reason to tear it down. Then as now we reaffirm that it is up to Congress if it wishes to incorporate other entities into 28 U.S.C. § 1332(c)'s special jurisdictional rule.

Hoffman v. Vulcan Materials (M.D.N.C. 1998)

This matter comes before the Court on plaintiffs' motion to remand the case back to state court. . . .

Facts, Procedural History, and Contentions of the Parties

On February 9, 1998, plaintiffs, who are homeowners, filed a complaint in state court in Richmond County, North Carolina. They alleged that defendant committed nuisance and trespass against them through its operation of a quarry near their homes. The quarrying process allegedly creates excessive dust, flying rocks, noise, and blasting shocks. As a consequence, plaintiffs contended that their health, peace of mind, land, and homes have been damaged. In accordance with state law, plaintiffs listed their damages only as "in excess of $10,000." They each sought an amount in excess of $10,000 for damage to their homes and property from the blasting shocks, an amount in excess of $10,000 for the trespass and nuisance created by the dust and rocks which land on their property, and an amount in excess of $10,000 in punitive damages. They also asked for an injunction to prevent defendant's continuing trespass and nuisance.

Subsequently, defendant removed the case to this Court pursuant to 28 U.S.C. § 1441, contending that the case met the requirements for diversity jurisdiction as set out in 28 U.S.C. § 1332. Plaintiffs countered by seeking remand back to state court. They do not dispute that the parties are of diverse citizenship as required by 28 U.S.C. § 1332(a). However, they argue that defendant fails to show the jurisdictional amount of $75,000 because, on the face of the complaint, they only seek damages of *in excess* of $30,000 each.

Defendant argues that in determining the jurisdictional amount, the Court may look beyond the dollar amount of damages sought by plaintiffs and may consider as well the amount which plaintiffs' injunction request, if granted, would cost defendant. In support of its assertion, defendant has supplied an affidavit from Rodney Hobbs, an Area Production Manager for defendant. He states that closing the quarry near plaintiffs' homes would deprive defendant of at least $4,862,000 per year in pretax earnings, that each lost hour of daily production would amount to an annual economic impact of more than $979,000, and that any restriction which measurably reduced defendant's output would have an annual economic impact on defendant in excess of $75,000. Plaintiffs reply that the Court should determine the amount in controversy only from plaintiffs' perspective and not consider the economic impact on defendant.

Discussion

The law used to determine jurisdictional amount in diversity cases is quite clear, up to a point. Federal courts "have original jurisdiction of all civil actions where the matter in controversy exceeds the sum or value of $75,000, exclusive of interest and costs, and is between citizens of different states." 28 U.S.C. § 1332(a). In addition, any matter which may have been originally brought in federal court, but is filed in a state court, may be removed by the defendant to federal district court. 28 U.S.C. § 1441.

In either a case originally filed in, or one removed to, federal court, the party seeking to invoke the jurisdiction of the federal courts has the burden of proving its existence by showing that it does not appear to a legal certainty that its claim is for less than the jurisdictional amount.

Accordingly, in a removal case, the defendant, rather than the plaintiff, has the burden of proving that the jurisdictional requirements for removal are met. For a removal, this means defendant must prove to a "legal certainty" that plaintiffs' claim exceeds $75,000. . . . The amount in controversy is normally determined from the face of the pleadings. In this case, no specific amount is alleged in the complaint. Therefore, it will not aid in determining whether the action meets the jurisdictional amount in controversy. This is because, under North Carolina pleading rules, in negligence actions, claims in excess of $10,000 may only so state. That is how plaintiffs plead their demand for judgment.

When federal jurisdiction is not plain from the face of a plaintiff's complaint, the defendant must offer evidence in support of its claim that the controversy satisfies the federal jurisdictional amount. The court makes its determination on the basis of the existing record. This means pleadings, affidavits or other matters in the record.

In the instant case, plaintiffs' complaint only shows that the damages for each plaintiff exceeds $30,000. Defendant did not file a motion under Rule 8 of the North Carolina Rules of Civil Procedure in order to ascertain the exact amount in controversy as to each plaintiff. It, therefore, becomes incumbent on defendant to point to some evidence in the record or to submit independent evidence which would show that the plaintiffs' damage claims exceed $75,000. Defendant fails to do this. Instead, it submitted a supplemental brief, to which plaintiffs object, requesting that the Court combine all punitive damage demands and attribute the total demand to each plaintiff. However, defendant has failed to suggest an amount for the punitive damage award. Moreover, because punitive damages are discretionary, the Court would need substantial evidence before it would be willing to place a valuation on that kind of damage award. Consequently, the Court finds that defendant has failed to meet its burden of proof as to the amount of damages sought by plaintiffs. However, this does not end the matter because not only have plaintiffs sought money damages, but they also seek injunctive and declaratory relief.

In an action such as this one where plaintiffs seek injunctive or declaratory relief, the amount in controversy is measured by the value of the object of the litigation. . . . There is basic agreement among the courts concerning *what* must be valued. The seemingly never ending source of confusion concerns *how* to value it. The Supreme Court itself has never made one clear, definitive statement on how to go about placing a monetary value on the "object of the litigation." Consequently, lower courts, when faced with the myriad of fact patterns which arise in diversity cases, have formulated a number of different valuation rules, each with indirect support from various Supreme Court opinions.

One such rule is known as the "plaintiff-viewpoint" rule. Courts applying this rule look only to the benefit to be gained by the plaintiff in order to find the amount in controversy. The main criticism of the plaintiff-viewpoint rule is that it is an imperfect way to realize the purpose behind the jurisdictional amount limit, which is to keep trivial cases out of the federal courts. Unfortunately, the rule achieves this goal by also keeping out cases where great sums of money are involved on the part of the defendant, but not the plaintiff. . . .

An alternative rule, known as the either-viewpoint rule, has been adopted by a number of circuits and appears to be the more recent trend. . . . [and is based on an opinion in which] the Court determined that in a diversity litigation the value of the matter in controversy is measured not by the monetary result of determining the principle involved, but by its pecuniary consequence to those involved in the litigation.

. . . . Fourth Circuit law, which controls this case, appears to be somewhat unsettled. . . .

The above review satisfies the Court that neither Supreme Court nor Fourth Circuit law commands it to follow the plaintiff-viewpoint rule, the either-viewpoint rule, or any "viewpoint" rule. Indeed, it would appear that adoption of "viewpoint" valuation has led to some distraction and a great deal of confusion. The Supreme Court's cases do not mention "viewpoint" value. Rather they state that the amount in controversy is measured by the value of the object of the litigation and that, generally, the value is measured by pecuniary consequences to those involved in the litigation. Any rule constructed for valuing the amount in controversy must take into account that diversity cases, like their appellation, present federal courts with endlessly diverse sets of facts and demands for relief beyond simple money judgments.

In order to take into account both the factual variances and the numerous types of relief, the Court feels it best to move away from "viewpoint" terminology and instead recognize that any one case may be legitimately valued in a number of different ways, no one of which may be said to inherently represent true value in every case. By "value" the Court understands that its duty is to find the economic worth of the object in controversy. In a free market situation, any one object may have a different value to different individuals based on need, taste, etc. Nevertheless, appraisers and auditors often give opinions based on value to hypothetical willing sellers and buyers. Likewise, in a lawsuit seeking declaratory and injunctive relief, the relief will have both a cost and benefit to the parties, depending on whether relief is granted or denied. No one economic analysis will be right for all cases.

For example, in cases where injunctions or declaratory judgments are requested, the value of the relief could be determined by considering how much it would cost the plaintiff to purchase the given relief and how much the defendant would be willing to pay the plaintiff to be rid of the injunction. One federal court of appeals has suggested such an approach. . . . If the object of the injunction does not normally have economic value, a court may allow consideration of defendant's clerical and ministerial costs of compliance. . . .

A flexible approach better reflects the Supreme Court's mandate to consider the pecuniary consequence to those involved in the litigation. It fulfills without favoritism to either side the original purpose of jurisdictional amounts by only keeping minor cases out of federal court. This broader approach to valuation will allow the court to make better reasoned decisions by demanding a better evidentiary record. Defendants will no longer need to make gross speculations concerning the value to plaintiff of the injunction. They can set their own value based on their knowledge of their own affairs and back the assertions with facts and reasoned opinions. The Court will be in a position to demand and get higher quality offers of proof.

Turning now to the case before the Court, the amount in controversy must be greater than $75,000 in order for the Court to have jurisdiction. The plaintiffs have each requested in excess of $30,000 in damages in addition to an injunction. Therefore, if defendant can show that the injunction is worth more than $45,000 to any one plaintiff, then plaintiffs' motion to remand must be denied.

Plaintiffs have requested the injunction in order to protect their properties and their peace of mind. Plaintiffs have not put any information into the record concerning the value of their properties and the effect on property values of defendant's continued operations. Nor can the value of the injunction be determined based on plaintiffs' peace of mind. This is too subjective without more facts. That does not end the matter because defendant has offered evidence of the value of the injunction to itself.

Defendant runs a large-scale quarry. It has presented an affidavit showing a number of different ways of valuing the harm to it of any meaningful curtailing of its operations. The affidavit states:

(a) If the Rockingham Quarry were closed completely, Vulcan would lose at least $4,862,000.00 per year in pretax earnings, which is based upon conservative production and sales volumes for this facility.

(b) If the Rockingham Quarry operations were restricted by the hours of operation, the annual economic impact to Vulcan for each hour of lost production per day would exceed $979,000.

(c) The economic impact of any other restriction on the operation of the Rockingham Quarry would depend upon the nature of the restriction(s), but it is safe to predict that any restriction that causes a measurable reduction in the amount of crushed stone produced by this quarry would have an annual economic impact to Vulcan far in excess of $75,000.00.

Defendant also cites the loss of jobs to employees and harm to companies purchasing its materials. This does not constitute value to the defendant, except perhaps indirectly. The losses cited if quarry operations were curtailed is better evidence of the value of the injunction to defendant. And, because the defendant will sustain this loss even if only one plaintiff were to obtain the injunction, this is a case where plaintiffs have an undivided interest in the injunction so the loss will be attributed to each plaintiff.

Plaintiffs have not disputed the figures. If the quarry were closed, the jurisdictional amount is clearly met merely on an income valuation. Alternatively, even if the value of lost production per hour actually represents lost sales, not net income, it seems clear that a restriction in quarrying of one hour per day over some reasonable time period will still have a value to defendant of over $45,000. Therefore, defendant has met its burden of proof and has shown that, between the money damages and the value of the injunction, the $75,000 amount in controversy requirement is met in this case. Because the necessary amount is present, the Court has jurisdiction over the matter and plaintiffs' motion to remand must be denied.

Lumberman's Mutual Casualty Co. v. Elbert (1954)

Mr. Justice FRANKFURTER, concurring.

Not deeming it appropriate now to question [prior precedent], I join the Court's opinion. But our holding results in such a glaring perversion of the purpose to which the original grant of diversity jurisdiction was directed that it ought not to go without comment, as further proof of the mounting mischief inflicted on the federal judicial system by the unjustifiable continuance of diversity jurisdiction.

The stuff of diversity jurisdiction is state litigation. The availability of federal tribunals for controversies concerning matters which in themselves are outside federal power and exclusively within state authority is the essence of a jurisdiction solely resting on the fact that a plaintiff and a defendant are citizens of different States. The power of Congress to confer such jurisdiction was based on the desire of the Framers to assure out-of-state litigants courts free from susceptibility to potential local bias. That the supposed justification for this fear was not rooted in weighty experience is attested by the fact that so ardent a nationalist as Marshall gave that proposal of the Philadelphia Convention only tepid support in the Virginia Convention. But in any event, whatever "fears and apprehensions" were entertained by the Framers and ratifiers, there was fear that parochial prejudice by the citizens of one State toward those of another, as well as toward aliens, would lead to unjust treatment of citizens of other States and foreign countries.

Such was the reason for enabling a citizen of one State to press a claim or stand on a defense, wholly state-created, against a citizen of another in a federal court of the latter's State. The abuses to which this opportunity was put when, more than a hundred years ago, corporations began their transforming influence on American economic and social life are familiar history. . . .The short of the matter is that by resorting to the federal courts the out-of-state corporation sought to gain, and much too frequently did, an advantage as against the local citizen. Instead of protecting out-of-state litigants against discrimination by state courts, the effect of diversity jurisdiction was discrimination against citizens of the State in favor of litigants from without the State.

Diversity jurisdiction aroused opposition from its very inception, but the modern manifestation of these evils through corporate litigation gathered increasing hostility and led to repeated congressional attempts at restriction and eventually of abolition. The proliferation of the doctrine of *Swift v. Tyson* brought into lurid light the discriminatory distortions to which diversity jurisdiction could be subverted by judicial sanction of professional astuteness. . . . But by overruling the doctrine of *Swift*, despite its century-old credentials, this Court uprooted the most noxious weeds that had grown around diversity jurisdiction.

What with the increasing permeation of national feeling and the mobility of modern life, little excuse is left for diversity jurisdiction, now that *Erie* has put a stop to the unwarranted freedom of federal courts to fashion rules of local law in defiance of local law.

A legal device like that of federal diversity jurisdiction, which is inherently, as I believe it to be, not founded in reason, offers constant temptation to new abuses. This case is an instance. Here we have not an out-of-state litigant resorting to a federal court to be sure of obtaining for himself the same treatment which state courts mete out to their own citizens. Here we have a Louisiana citizen resorting to the federal court in Louisiana in order to avoid consequences of the Louisiana law by which every Louisiana citizen is bound when suing another Louisiana citizen. If Florence R. Elbert, the present plaintiff, had to sue the owner of the offending automobile which caused her injury, or if she were suing an insurance company chartered by Louisiana, she would have no choice but to go, like every other Louisiana plaintiff who sues a fellow citizen of Louisiana, to a Louisiana state court and receive the law as administered by the Louisiana courts. But by the fortuitous circumstance that this Louisiana litigant could sue directly an out-of-state insurance company, she can avoid her amenability to Louisiana law. In concrete terms, she can cash in on the law governing jury trials in the federal courts, with its restrictive appellate review of jury verdicts, and escape the rooted jurisprudence of Louisiana law in reviewing jury verdicts. There is, to be sure, a kind of irony for corporate defendants to discover that two can play at the game of working, to use a colloquial term, the perverse potentialities of diversity jurisdiction. But it is not the less unreason and no greater fairness for a citizen of the forum to gain a discriminatory advantage over fellow citizens of his State, than it is for an out-of-state citizen to secure more than the same treatment given local citizens, by going to a federal court for the adjudication of state-created rights.

This case, however, stirs anew an issue that cuts deeper than the natural selfishness of litigants to exploit the law's weaknesses. My concern is with the bearing of diversity jurisdiction on the effective functioning of the federal judiciary. . . . Diversity cases have long constituted a considerable portion of all civil cases filed in the federal courts. For the last ten years the proportion of diversity cases has greatly increased, so that it is safe to say that diversity cases are now taking at least half of the time that the District Courts are devoting to civil cases. (This is the conclusion of the Division of Procedural Studies and Statistics of the Administrative Office of the United States Courts.) The rise in motor-vehicle registration from 32 million in 1940 to 56 million in 1953 has inevitably been reflected in increasing resort to diversity jurisdiction in ordinary negligence suits. The consequences that this entails for the whole federal judicial system—for increase in the business of the District Courts means increase in the business of the Courts of Appeals and a swelling of the petitions for certiorari here—cannot be met by a steady increase in the number of federal judges. The business of courts, particularly of the federal courts, is drastically unlike the business of factories. The function and role of the federal courts and the nature of their judicial process involve impalpable factors, subtle but far-reaching, which cannot be satisfied by enlarging the judicial plant. . . . In the farthest reaches of the problem a steady increase in judges does not alleviate; in my judgment, it is bound to depreciate the quality of the federal judiciary and thereby adversely to affect the whole system.

Since diversity jurisdiction is increasingly the biggest source of the civil business of the District Courts, the continuance of that jurisdiction will necessarily involve inflation of the number of the district judges. This in turn will result, by its own Gresham's law, in a depreciation of the judicial currency and the consequent impairment of the prestige and of the efficacy of the federal courts. Madison believed that Congress would return to the state courts judicial power entrusted to the federal courts "when they find the tribunals of the states established on a good footing." Can it fairly be said that state tribunals are not now established on a sufficiently "good footing" to adjudicate state litigation that arises between citizens of different States, including the artificial corporate citizens, when they are the only resort for the much larger volume of the same type of litigation between their own citizens? Can the state tribunals not yet be trusted to mete out justice to nonresident litigants; should resident litigants not be compelled to trust their own state tribunals? In any event, is it sound public policy to withdraw from the incentives and energies for reforming state tribunals, where such reform is needed, the interests of influential groups who through diversity litigation are now enabled to avoid state courts?

Supplemental Jurisdiction

Introduction

It may happen that *part* of a case qualifies for statutory federal jurisdiction but other parts do not. If so, then three common options present themselves: (1) the whole case must or could be heard in federal court, (2) the whole case must be heard in state court, and (3) the federal part could be heard in federal court while the nonfederal part must be heard in state court. (A fourth option—the parts cannot be separated and the whole case cannot be heard anywhere— is intolerable except in highly unusual situations.)

Option (3) might be the best option if the parts are unrelated enough that segregation does not cause a great loss of efficiency or fairness. If the parts are so related that efficiency dictates that they should be heard together, then options (1) or (2) seem best, and the choice between them will depend upon how important the need for a federal forum over the federal part is.

The choices between these options is reflected in the doctrine of "supplemental jurisdiction." Before Congress codified the doctrine by statute, the courts developed the doctrine under the names "ancillary jurisdiction" and "pendent jurisdiction." With this background, consider the following questions as you read the materials in this topic:

- What constitutional and statutory sources authorize supplemental jurisdiction?

- What values underlie supplemental jurisdiction? Do the contours of supplemental jurisdiction further those values?

- Which branch—Congress or the Court—is better at formulating jurisdictional rules?

United Mine Workers v. Gibbs (1966)

Respondent Paul Gibbs was awarded compensatory and punitive damages in this action against petitioner United Mine Workers of America (NMW) for alleged violations of § 303 of the Labor Management Relations Act and of the common law of Tennessee. The case grew out of the rivalry between the United Mine Workers and the Southern Labor Union over representation of workers in the southern Appalachian coal fields. Tennessee Consolidated Coal Company, not a party here, laid off 100 miners of the UMW's Local 5881 when it closed one of its mines in southern Tennessee during the spring of 1960. Late that summer, Grundy Company, a wholly owned subsidiary of Consolidated, hired respondent as mine superintendent to attempt to open a new mine on Consolidated's property at nearby Gray's Creek through use of members of the Southern Labor Union. As part of the arrangement, Grundy also gave respondent a contract to haul the mine's coal to the nearest railroad loading point.

On August 15 and 16, 1960, armed members of Local 5881 forcibly prevented the opening of the mine, threatening respondent and beating an organizer for the rival union. The members of the local believed Consolidated had promised them the jobs at the new mine; they insisted that if anyone would do the work, they would. At this time, no representative of the UMW, their international union, was present. George Gilbert, the UMW's field representative for the area including Local 5881, was away at Middlesboro, Kentucky, attending an Executive Board meeting when the members of the local discovered Grundy's plan; he did not return to the area until late in the day of August 16. There was uncontradicted testimony that he first learned of the violence while at the meeting, and returned with explicit instructions from his international union superiors to establish a limited picket line, to prevent any further violence, and to see to it that the strike did not spread to neighboring mines. There was no further violence at the mine site; a picket line was maintained there for nine months; and no further attempts were made to open the mine during that period.

Respondent lost his job as superintendent, and never entered into performance of his haulage contract. He testified that he soon began to lose other trucking contracts and mine leases he held in nearby areas. Claiming these effects to be the result of a concerted union plan against him, he sought recovery not against Local 5881 or its members, but only against petitioner, the international union. The suit was brought in the United States District Court for the Eastern District of Tennessee, and jurisdiction was premised on allegations of secondary boycotts under § 303. The state law claim, for which jurisdiction was based upon the doctrine of pendent jurisdiction, asserted an unlawful conspiracy and an unlawful boycott aimed at him and Grundy to maliciously, wantonly and willfully interfere with his contract of employment and with his contract of haulage.

The trial judge refused to submit to the jury the claims of pressure intended to cause mining firms other than Grundy to cease doing business with Gibbs; he found those claims unsupported by the evidence. The jury's verdict was that the UMW had violated both § 303 and state law. Gibbs was awarded $60,000 as damages under the employment contract and $14,500 under the haulage contract; he was also awarded $100,000 punitive damages. On motion, the trial court set aside the award of damages with respect to the haulage contract on the ground that damage was unproved. It also held that union pressure on Grundy to discharge respondent as supervisor would constitute only a primary dispute with Grundy, as respondent's employer, and hence was not cognizable as a claim under § 303. Interference with the employment relationship was cognizable as a state claim, however, and a remitted award was sustained on the state law claim. . . .

A threshold question is whether the District Court properly entertained jurisdiction of the claim based on Tennessee law. . . . Pendent jurisdiction, in the sense of judicial power, exists whenever there is a claim "arising under [the] Constitution, the Laws of the United States, and Treaties made, or which shall be made, under their Authority," U.S. Const., Art. III, § 2, and the relationship between that claim and the state claim permits the conclusion that the entire action before the court comprises but one constitutional "case." The federal claim must have substance sufficient to confer subject matter jurisdiction on the court. The state and federal claims must derive from a common nucleus of operative fact. But if, considered without regard to their federal or state character, a plaintiff's claims are such that he would ordinarily be expected to try them all in one judicial proceeding, then, assuming substantiality of the federal issues, there is power in federal courts to hear the whole.

That power need not be exercised in every case in which it is found to exist. It has consistently been recognized that pendent jurisdiction is a doctrine of discretion, not of plaintiff's right. Its justification lies in considerations of judicial economy, convenience and fairness to litigants; if these are not present a federal court should hesitate to exercise jurisdiction over state claims, even though bound to apply state law to them. Needless decisions of state law should be avoided both as a matter of comity and to promote justice between the parties, by procuring for them a surer-footed reading of applicable law. Certainly, if the federal claims are dismissed before trial, even though not insubstantial in a jurisdictional sense, the state claims should be dismissed as well. Similarly, if it appears that the state issues substantially predominate, whether in terms of proof, of the scope of the issues raised, or of the comprehensiveness of the remedy sought, the state claims may be dismissed without prejudice and left for resolution to state tribunals. There may, on the other hand, be situations in which the state claim is so closely tied to questions of federal policy that the argument for exercise of pendent jurisdiction is particularly strong. In the present case, for example, the allowable scope of the state claim implicates the federal doctrine of pre-emption; while this interrelationship does not create statutory federal question jurisdiction, its existence is relevant to the exercise of discretion. Finally, there may be reasons independent of jurisdictional considerations, such as the likelihood of jury confusion in treating divergent legal theories of relief, that would justify separating state and federal claims for trial. If so, jurisdiction should ordinarily be refused.

The question of power will ordinarily be resolved on the pleadings. But the issue whether pendent jurisdiction has been properly assumed is one which remains open throughout the litigation. Pretrial procedures or even the trial itself may reveal a substantial hegemony of state law claims, or likelihood of jury confusion, which could not have been anticipated at the pleading stage. Although it will of course be appropriate to take account in this circumstance of the already completed course of the litigation, dismissal of the state claim might even then be merited. For example, it may appear that the plaintiff was well aware of the nature of his proofs and the relative importance of his claims; recognition of a federal court's wide latitude to decide ancillary questions of state law does not imply that it must tolerate a litigant's effort to impose upon it what is in effect only a state law case. Once it appears that a state claim constitutes the real body of a case, to which the federal claim is only an appendage, the state claim may fairly be dismissed.

We are not prepared to say that in the present case the District Court exceeded its discretion in proceeding to judgment on the state claim. We may assume for purposes of decision that the District Court was correct in its holding that the claim of pressure on Grundy to terminate the employment contract was outside the purview of § 303. Even so, the § 303 claims based on secondary pressures on Grundy relative to the haulage contract and on other coal operators generally were substantial. Although § 303 limited recovery to compensatory damages based on secondary pressures, and state law allowed both compensatory and punitive damages, and allowed such damages as to both secondary and primary activity, the state and federal claims arose from the same nucleus of operative fact and reflected alternative remedies. Indeed, the verdict sheet sent in to the jury authorized only one award of damages, so that recovery could not be given separately on the federal and state claims.

It is true that the § 303 claims ultimately failed and that the only recovery allowed respondent was on the state claim. We cannot confidently say, however, that the federal issues were so remote or played such a minor role at the trial that in effect the state claim only was tried. Although the District Court dismissed as unproved the § 303 claims that petitioner's secondary activities included attempts to induce coal operators other than Grundy to cease doing business with respondent, the court submitted the § 303 claims relating to Grundy to the jury. The jury returned verdicts against petitioner on those § 303 claims, and it was only on petitioner's motion for a directed verdict and a judgment n.o.v. that the verdicts on those claims were set aside. The District Judge considered the claim as to the haulage contract proved as to liability, and held it failed only for lack of proof of damages. Although there was some risk of confusing the jury in joining the state and federal claims—especially since, as will be developed, differing standards of proof of UMW involvement applied—the possibility of confusion could be lessened by employing a special verdict form, as the District Court did. Moreover, the question whether the permissible scope of the state claim was limited by the doctrine of pre-emption afforded a special reason for the exercise of pendent jurisdiction; the federal courts are particularly appropriate bodies for the application of pre-emption principles. We thus conclude that although it may be that the District Court might, in its sound discretion, have dismissed the state claim, the circumstances show no error in refusing to do so. . . .

Owen Equipment & Erection Co. v. Kroger (1978)

In an action in which federal jurisdiction is based on diversity of citizenship, may the plaintiff assert a claim against a third-party defendant when there is no independent basis for federal jurisdiction over that claim? The Court of Appeals for the Eighth Circuit held in this case that such a claim is within the ancillary jurisdiction of the federal courts. We granted certiorari because this decision conflicts with several recent decisions of other Courts of Appeals.

I

On January 18, 1972, James Kroger was electrocuted when the boom of a steel crane next to which he was walking came too close to a high-tension electric power line. The respondent (his widow, who is the administratrix of his estate) filed a wrongful-death action in the United States District Court for the District of Nebraska against the Omaha Public Power District (OPPD). Her complaint alleged that OPPD's negligent construction, maintenance, and operation of the power line had caused Kroger's death. Federal jurisdiction was based on diversity of citizenship, since the respondent was a citizen of Iowa and OPPD was a Nebraska corporation.

OPPD then filed a third-party complaint pursuant to Fed. Rule Civ. Proc. 14(a) against the petitioner, Owen Equipment and Erection Co. (Owen), alleging that the crane was owned and operated by Owen, and that Owen's negligence had been the proximate cause of Kroger's death. OPPD later moved for summary judgment on the respondent's complaint against it. While this motion was pending, the respondent was granted leave to file an amended complaint naming Owen as an additional defendant. Thereafter, the District Court granted OPPD's motion for summary judgment in an unreported opinion. The case thus went to trial between the respondent and the petitioner alone.

The respondent's amended complaint alleged that Owen was a Nebraska corporation with its principal place of business in Nebraska. Owen's answer admitted that it was a corporation organized and existing under the laws of the State of Nebraska, and denied every other allegation of the complaint. On the third day of trial, however, it was disclosed that the petitioner's principal place of business was in Iowa, not Nebraska,[5] and that the petitioner and the respondent were thus both citizens of Iowa. The petitioner then moved to dismiss the complaint for lack of jurisdiction. The District Court reserved decision on the motion, and the jury thereafter returned a verdict in favor of the respondent. In an unreported opinion issued after the trial, the District Court denied the petitioner's motion to dismiss the complaint.

[5] The problem apparently was one of geography. Although the Missouri River generally marks the boundary between Iowa and Nebraska, Carter Lake, Iowa, where the accident occurred and where Owen had its main office, lies west of the river, adjacent to Omaha, Neb. Apparently the river once avulsed at one of its bends, cutting Carter Lake off from the rest of Iowa.

The judgment was affirmed on appeal. . . .

II

It is undisputed that there was no independent basis of federal jurisdiction over the respondent's state-law tort action against the petitioner, since both are citizens of Iowa. And although Fed. Rule Civ. Proc. 14(a) permits a plaintiff to assert a claim against a third-party defendant, it does not purport to say whether or not such a claim requires an independent basis of federal jurisdiction. Indeed, it could not determine that question, since it is axiomatic that the Federal Rules of Civil Procedure do not create or withdraw federal jurisdiction.

In affirming the District Court's judgment, the Court of Appeals relied upon the doctrine of ancillary jurisdiction, whose contours it believed were defined by this Court's holding in *Gibbs*. The *Gibbs* case differed from this one in that it involved pendent jurisdiction, which concerns the resolution of a plaintiff's federal- and state-law claims against a single defendant in one action. By contrast, in this case there was no claim based upon substantive federal law, but rather state-law tort claims against two different defendants. Nonetheless, the Court of Appeals was correct in perceiving that *Gibbs* and this case are two species of the same generic problem: Under what circumstances may a federal court hear and decide a state-law claim arising between citizens of the same State? But we believe that the Court of Appeals failed to understand the scope of the doctrine of the *Gibbs* case.

The plaintiff in *Gibbs* alleged that the defendant union had violated the common law of Tennessee as well as the federal prohibition of secondary boycotts. This Court held that, although the parties were not of diverse citizenship, the District Court properly entertained the state-law claim as pendent to the federal claim. . . .

It is apparent that *Gibbs* delineated the constitutional limits of federal judicial power. But even if it be assumed that the District Court in the present case had constitutional power to decide the respondent's lawsuit against the petitioner, it does not follow that the decision of the Court of Appeals was correct. Constitutional power is merely the first hurdle that must be overcome in determining that a federal court has jurisdiction over a particular controversy.

For the jurisdiction of the federal courts is limited not only by the provisions of Art. III of the Constitution, but also by Acts of Congress.

. . . . [A] finding that federal and nonfederal claims arise from a "common nucleus of operative fact," the test of *Gibbs*, does not end the inquiry into whether a federal court has power to hear the nonfederal claims along with the federal ones. Beyond this constitutional minimum, there must be an examination of the posture in which the nonfederal claim is asserted and of the specific statute that confers jurisdiction over the federal claim, in order to determine whether Congress in that statute has . . . expressly or by implication negated the exercise of jurisdiction over the particular nonfederal claim.

III

The relevant statute in this case, 28 U.S.C. § 1332(a)(1), confers upon federal courts jurisdiction over "civil actions where the matter in controversy exceeds the sum or value of $10,000 . . . and is between . . . citizens of different States." This statute and its predecessors have consistently been held to require complete diversity of citizenship. That is, diversity jurisdiction does not exist unless *each* defendant is a citizen of a different State from *each* plaintiff. Over the years Congress has repeatedly re-enacted or amended the statute conferring diversity jurisdiction, leaving intact this rule of complete diversity. Whatever may have been the original purposes of diversity-of-citizenship jurisdiction, this subsequent history clearly demonstrates a congressional mandate that diversity jurisdiction is not to be available when any plaintiff is a citizen of the same State as any defendant.

Thus it is clear that the respondent could not originally have brought suit in federal court naming Owen and OPPD as codefendants, since citizens of Iowa would have been on both sides of the litigation. Yet the identical lawsuit resulted when she amended her complaint. Complete diversity was destroyed just as surely as if she had sued Owen initially. In either situation, in the plain language of the statute, the "matter in controversy" could not be "between . . . citizens of different States."

It is a fundamental precept that federal courts are courts of limited jurisdiction. The limits upon federal jurisdiction, whether imposed by the Constitution or by Congress, must be neither disregarded nor evaded. Yet under the reasoning of the Court of Appeals in this case, a plaintiff could defeat the statutory requirement of complete diversity by the simple expedient of suing only those defendants who were of diverse citizenship and waiting for them to implead nondiverse defendants. If, as the Court of Appeals thought, a "common nucleus of operative fact" were the only requirement for ancillary jurisdiction in a diversity case, there would be no principled reason why the respondent in this case could not have joined her cause of action against Owen in her original complaint as ancillary to her claim against OPPD. Congress's requirement of complete diversity would thus have been evaded completely.

It is true, as the Court of Appeals noted, that the exercise of ancillary jurisdiction over nonfederal claims has often been upheld in situations involving impleader, cross-claims or counterclaims. But in determining whether jurisdiction over a nonfederal claim exists, the context in which the nonfederal claim is asserted is crucial. And the claim here arises in a setting quite different from the kinds of nonfederal claims that have been viewed in other cases as falling within the ancillary jurisdiction of the federal courts.

It is not unreasonable to assume that, in generally requiring complete diversity, Congress did not intend to confine the jurisdiction of federal courts so inflexibly that they are unable to protect legal rights or effectively to resolve an entire, logically entwined lawsuit. Those practical needs are the basis of the doctrine of ancillary jurisdiction. But neither the convenience of litigants nor considerations of judicial economy can suffice to justify extension of the doctrine of ancillary jurisdiction to a plaintiff's cause of action against a citizen of the same State in a diversity case. Congress has established the basic rule that diversity jurisdiction exists under 28 U.S.C. § 1332 only when there is complete diversity of citizenship. The policy of the statute calls for its strict construction. To allow the requirement of complete diversity to be circumvented as it was in this case would simply flout the congressional command.

Accordingly, the judgment of the Court of Appeals is reversed.

United States Code

28 U.S.C. § 1367.

(a) Except as provided . . . otherwise by Federal statute, in any civil action of which the district courts have original jurisdiction, the district courts shall have supplemental jurisdiction over all other claims that are so related to claims in the action within such original jurisdiction that they form part of the same case or controversy under Article III of the United States Constitution. Such supplemental jurisdiction shall include claims that involve the joinder or intervention of additional parties.

(b) In any civil action of which the district courts have original jurisdiction founded solely on section 1332 of this title, the district courts shall not have supplemental jurisdiction under subsection (a) over claims by plaintiffs against persons made parties under Rule 14, 19, 20, or 24 of the Federal Rules of Civil Procedure, or over claims by persons proposed to be joined as plaintiffs under Rule 19 of such rules, or seeking to intervene as plaintiffs under Rule 24 of such rules, when exercising supplemental jurisdiction over such claims would be inconsistent with the jurisdictional requirements of section 1332.

(c) The district courts may decline to exercise supplemental jurisdiction over a claim under subsection (a) if—

(1) the claim raises a novel or complex issue of State law,
(2) the claim substantially predominates over the claim or claims over which the district court has original jurisdiction,
(3) the district court has dismissed all claims over which it has original jurisdiction, or
(4) in exceptional circumstances, there are other compelling reasons for declining jurisdiction.

Exxon Mobile v. Allapattah Services (2005)

Justice KENNEDY delivered the opinion of the Court.

These consolidated cases present the question whether a federal court in a diversity action may exercise supplemental jurisdiction over additional plaintiffs whose claims do not satisfy the minimum amount-in-controversy requirement, provided the claims are part of the same case or controversy as the claims of plaintiffs who do allege a sufficient amount in controversy. Our decision turns on the correct interpretation of 28 U.S.C. § 1367. The question has divided the Courts of Appeals, and we granted certiorari to resolve the conflict.

We hold that, where the other elements of jurisdiction are present and at least one named plaintiff in the action satisfies the amount-in-controversy requirement, § 1367 does authorize supplemental jurisdiction over the claims of other plaintiffs in the same Article III case or controversy, even if those claims are for less than the jurisdictional amount specified in the statute setting forth the requirements for diversity jurisdiction. . . .

In 1991, about 10,000 Exxon dealers filed a class-action suit against the Exxon Corporation in the United States District Court for the Northern District of Florida. The dealers alleged an intentional and systematic scheme by Exxon under which they were overcharged for fuel purchased from Exxon. The plaintiffs invoked the District Court's § 1332(a) diversity jurisdiction. After a unanimous jury verdict in favor of the plaintiffs, the District Court certified the case for interlocutory review, asking whether it had properly exercised § 1367 supplemental jurisdiction over the claims of class members who did not meet the jurisdictional minimum amount in controversy. . . .

The district courts of the United States, as we have said many times, are courts of limited jurisdiction. They possess only that power authorized by Constitution and statute. In order to provide a federal forum for plaintiffs who seek to vindicate federal rights, Congress has conferred on the district courts original jurisdiction in federal-question cases—civil actions that arise under the Constitution, laws, or treaties of the United States. In order to provide a neutral forum for what have come to be known as diversity cases, Congress also has granted district courts original jurisdiction in civil actions between citizens of different States, between U.S. citizens and foreign citizens, or by foreign states against U.S. citizens. To ensure that diversity jurisdiction does not flood the federal courts with minor disputes, § 1332(a) requires that the matter in controversy in a diversity case exceed a specified amount, currently $75,000.

Although the district courts may not exercise jurisdiction absent a statutory basis, it is well established—in certain classes of cases—that, once a court has original jurisdiction over some claims in the action, it may exercise supplemental jurisdiction over additional claims that are part of the same case or controversy. The leading modern case for this principle is *Mine Workers v. Gibbs* . . . .

As we later noted, the decision allowing jurisdiction over pendent state claims in *Gibbs* did not mention, let alone come to grips with, the text of the jurisdictional statutes and the bedrock principle that federal courts have no jurisdiction without statutory authorization. We nonetheless reaffirmed and rationalized *Gibbs* and its progeny by inferring from it the interpretive principle that, in cases involving supplemental jurisdiction over additional claims between parties properly in federal court, the jurisdictional statutes should be read broadly, on the assumption that in this context Congress intended to authorize courts to exercise their full Article III power to dispose of an entire action before the court which comprises but one constitutional "case."

We have not, however, applied *Gibbs*'s expansive interpretive approach to other aspects of the jurisdictional statutes. For instance, we have consistently interpreted § 1332 as requiring complete diversity: In a case with multiple plaintiffs and multiple defendants, the presence in the action of a single plaintiff from the same State as a single defendant deprives the district court of original diversity jurisdiction over the entire action. The complete diversity requirement is not mandated by the Constitution, or by the plain text of § 1332(a). The Court, nonetheless, has adhered to the complete diversity rule in light of the purpose of the diversity requirement, which is to provide a federal forum for important disputes where state courts might favor, or be perceived as favoring, home-state litigants. The presence of parties from the same State on both sides of a case dispels this concern, eliminating a principal reason for conferring § 1332 jurisdiction over any of the claims in the action. The specific purpose of the complete diversity rule explains both why we have not adopted *Gibbs*'s expansive interpretive approach to this aspect of the jurisdictional statute and why *Gibbs* does not undermine the complete diversity rule. In order for a federal court to invoke supplemental jurisdiction under *Gibbs*, it must first have original jurisdiction over at least one claim in the action. Incomplete diversity destroys original jurisdiction with respect to all claims, so there is nothing to which supplemental jurisdiction can adhere.

In contrast to the diversity requirement, most of the other statutory prerequisites for federal jurisdiction, including the federal-question and amount-in-controversy requirements, can be analyzed claim by claim. True, it does not follow by necessity from this that a district court has authority to exercise supplemental jurisdiction over all claims provided there is original jurisdiction over just one. Before the enactment of § 1367, the Court declined in contexts other than the pendent-claim instance to follow *Gibbs*'s expansive approach to interpretation of the jurisdictional statutes. The Court took a more restrictive view of the proper interpretation of these statutes in so-called pendent-party cases involving supplemental jurisdiction over claims involving additional parties—plaintiffs or defendants—where the district courts would lack original jurisdiction over claims by each of the parties standing alone.

As the jurisdictional statutes existed in 1989, then, here is how matters stood: First, the diversity requirement required complete diversity; absent complete diversity, the district court lacked original jurisdiction over all of the claims in the action. Second, if the district court had original jurisdiction over at least one claim, the jurisdictional statutes implicitly authorized supplemental jurisdiction over all other claims between the same parties arising out of the same Article III case or controversy. Third, even when the district court had original jurisdiction over one or more claims between particular parties, the jurisdictional statutes did not authorize supplemental jurisdiction over additional claims involving other parties. . . .

. . . . Section 1367(a) is a broad grant of supplemental jurisdiction over other claims within the same case or controversy, as long as the action is one in which the district courts would have original jurisdiction. The last sentence of § 1367(a) makes it clear that the grant of supplemental jurisdiction extends to claims involving joinder or intervention of additional parties. The single question before us, therefore, is whether a diversity case in which the claims of some plaintiffs satisfy the amount-in-controversy requirement, but the claims of others plaintiffs do not, presents a "civil action of which the district courts have original jurisdiction." If the answer is yes, § 1367(a) confers supplemental jurisdiction over all claims, including those that do not independently satisfy the amount-in-controversy requirement, if the claims are part of the same Article III case or controversy. If the answer is no, § 1367(a) is inapplicable and . . . the district court has no statutory basis for exercising supplemental jurisdiction over the additional claims.

We now conclude the answer must be yes. When the well-pleaded complaint contains at least one claim that satisfies the amount-in-controversy requirement, and there are no other relevant jurisdictional defects, the district court, beyond all question, has original jurisdiction over that claim. The presence of other claims in the complaint, over which the district court may lack original jurisdiction, is of no moment. If the court has original jurisdiction over a single claim in the complaint, it has original jurisdiction over a "civil action" within the meaning of § 1367(a), even if the civil action over which it has jurisdiction comprises fewer claims than were included in the complaint. Once the court determines it has original jurisdiction over the civil action, it can turn to the question whether it has a constitutional and statutory basis for exercising supplemental jurisdiction over the other claims in the action. . . .

We cannot accept the view, urged by some of the parties, commentators, and Courts of Appeals, that a district court lacks original jurisdiction over a civil action unless the court has original jurisdiction over every claim in the complaint. As we understand this position, it requires assuming either that all claims in the complaint must stand or fall as a single, indivisible "civil action" as a matter of definitional necessity—what we will refer to as the "indivisibility theory"—or else that the inclusion of a claim or party falling outside the district court's original jurisdiction somehow contaminates every other claim in the complaint, depriving the court of original jurisdiction over any of these claims—what we will refer to as the "contamination theory."

The indivisibility theory is easily dismissed, as it is inconsistent with the whole notion of supplemental jurisdiction. If a district court must have original jurisdiction over every claim in the complaint in order to have "original jurisdiction" over a "civil action," then in *Gibbs* there was no civil action of which the district court could assume original jurisdiction under § 1331, and so no basis for exercising supplemental jurisdiction over any of the claims. . . .

We also find it unconvincing to say that the definitional indivisibility theory applies in the context of diversity cases but not in the context of federal-question cases. The broad and general language of the statute does not permit this result. The contention is premised on the notion that the phrase "original jurisdiction of all civil actions" means different things in § 1331 and § 1332. It is implausible, however, to say that the identical phrase means one thing (original jurisdiction in all actions where at least one claim in the complaint meets the following requirements) in § 1331 and something else (original jurisdiction in all actions where every claim in the complaint meets the following requirements) in § 1332.

The contamination theory, as we have noted, can make some sense in the special context of the complete diversity requirement because the presence of nondiverse parties on both sides of a lawsuit eliminates the justification for providing a federal forum. The theory, however, makes little sense with respect to the amount-in-controversy requirement, which is meant to ensure that a dispute is sufficiently important to warrant federal-court attention. The presence of a single nondiverse party may eliminate the fear of bias with respect to all claims, but the presence of a claim that falls short of the minimum amount in controversy does nothing to reduce the importance of the claims that do meet this requirement.

It is fallacious to suppose, simply from the proposition that § 1332 imposes both the diversity requirement and the amount-in-controversy requirement, that the contamination theory germane to the former is also relevant to the latter. There is no inherent logical connection between the amount-in-controversy requirement and § 1332 diversity jurisdiction. After all, federal-question jurisdiction once had an amount-in-controversy requirement as well. If such a requirement were revived under § 1331, it is clear beyond peradventure that § 1367(a) provides supplemental jurisdiction over federal-question cases where some, but not all, of the federal-law claims involve a sufficient amount in controversy. . . .

The judgment of the Court of Appeals for the Eleventh Circuit is affirmed. . . .

. . . . Justice GINSBURG, with whom Justice STEVENS, Justice O'CONNOR, and Justice BREYER join, dissenting.

. . . . The Court adopts a plausibly broad reading of § 1367, a measure that is hardly a model of the careful drafter's art. There is another plausible reading, however, one less disruptive of our jurisprudence regarding supplemental jurisdiction. If one reads § 1367(a) to instruct, as the statute's text suggests, that the district court must first have "original jurisdiction" over a "civil action" before supplemental jurisdiction can attach, then [precedents] are preserved, and supplemental jurisdiction does not open the way for joinder of plaintiffs, or inclusion of class members, who do not independently meet the amount-in-controversy requirement. For the reasons that follow, I conclude that this narrower construction is the better reading of § 1367. . . .

Section 1367, by its terms, operates only in civil actions "of which the district courts have original jurisdiction." The "original jurisdiction" relevant here is diversity-of-citizenship jurisdiction, conferred by § 1332. The character of that jurisdiction is the essential backdrop for comprehension of § 1367. . . .

. . . Section 1367(a) addresses "civil action[s] of which the district courts have original jurisdiction," a formulation that, in diversity cases, is sensibly read to incorporate the rules on joinder and aggregation tightly tied to § 1332 at the time of § 1367's enactment. On this reading, a complaint must first meet that "original jurisdiction" measurement. If it does not, no supplemental jurisdiction is authorized. If it does, § 1367(a) authorizes "supplemental jurisdiction" over related claims. In other words, § 1367(a) would preserve undiminished, as part and parcel of § 1332 "original jurisdiction" determinations, both the "complete diversity" rule and the decisions restricting aggregation to arrive at the amount in controversy. Section 1367(b)'s office, then, would be to prevent the erosion of the complete diversity and amount-in-controversy requirements that might otherwise result from an expansive application of what was once termed the doctrine of ancillary jurisdiction. In contrast to the Court's construction of § 1367, which draws a sharp line between the diversity and amount-in-controversy components of § 1332, the interpretation presented here does not sever the two jurisdictional requirements. . . .

What is the utility of § 1367(b) under my reading of § 1367(a)? Section 1367(a) allows parties other than the plaintiff to assert *reactive* claims once entertained under the heading ancillary jurisdiction. As earlier observed, § 1367(b) stops plaintiffs from circumventing § 1332's jurisdictional requirements by using another's claim as a hook to add a claim that the plaintiff could not have brought in the first instance. . . . Section 1367(b), then, is corroborative of § 1367(a)'s coverage of claims formerly called ancillary, but provides exceptions to assure that accommodation of added claims would not fundamentally alter the jurisdictional requirements of section 1332. . . .

Erie

Introduction

The *Erie* doctrine can be thought of as a choice-of-law doctrine. When state and federal law purport to answer the same legal questions presented for adjudication, which should the court apply? The *Erie* doctrine can also be thought of as a doctrine of federal judicial power: may federal courts create federal common law to displace state common law?

Different problems arise for questions involving a conflict between state law and a codified federal rule of court, such as one of the Federal Rules of Civil Procedure. *Hanna*—not *Erie*—resolves those conflicts.

These doctrines raise several questions:

- What is the source of the *Erie* doctrine? Federalism? Separation of powers? Policy?

- Are the policy underpinnings of *Erie* and *Hanna* persuasive?

- Are *Erie* and *Hanna* workable doctrines?

United States Code

28 U.S.C. § 1652. The laws of the several states, except where the Constitution or treaties of the United States or Acts of Congress otherwise require or provide, shall be regarded as rules of decision in civil actions in the courts of the United States, in cases where they apply.

Swift v. Tyson (1842)

[Tyson issued bill of exchange—a promise to pay—as payment for some land in Maine sold by two speculators named Norton and Keith. Norton and Keith then gave Tyson's bill of exchange to Swift as payment for a preexisting debt owed to Swift. Swift then sought payment on the bill from Tyson, but it turned out that the speculators were frauds and never transferred any land title to Tyson. Tyson, having never received land, repudiated the bill. Swift was a *bona fide* purchaser, meaning he was an innocent party who had no knowledge of the fraud, and he was out his cash. So Swift then sued Tyson on the bill in the Southern District of New York.] . . .

There is no doubt that a *bona fide* holder of a negotiable instrument for a valuable consideration, without any notice of facts which impeach its validity as between the antecedent parties, if he takes it under an indorsement made before the same becomes due, holds the title unaffected by these facts and may recover thereon, although, as between the antecedent parties, the transaction may be without any legal validity. This is a doctrine so long and so well established, and so essential to the security of negotiable paper, that it is laid up among the fundamentals of the law, and requires no authority or reasoning to be now brought in its support. . . .

In the present case, the plaintiff is a *bona fide* holder, without notice, for what the law deems a good and valid consideration, that is, for a preexisting debt; and the only real question in the cause is whether, under the circumstances of the present case, such a pre-existing debt constitutes a valuable consideration in the sense of the general rule applicable to negotiable instruments. We say, under the circumstances of the present case, for the acceptance having been made in New York, the argument on behalf of the defendant is that the contract is to be treated as a New York contract, and therefore to be governed by the laws of New York, as expounded by its courts, as well upon general principles, as by the express provisions of the 34th section of the judiciary act of 1789, ch. 20. And then it is further contended, that by the law of New York, as thus expounded by its courts, a pre-existing debt does not constitute, in the sense of the general rule, a valuable consideration applicable to negotiable instruments.

[It appears that New York courts have issued divergent opinions as to whether a pre-existing debt can be valuable consideration for purposes of the *bona fide* purchaser rule.] . . . . But admitting the doctrine to be fully settled in New York, it remains to be considered whether it is obligatory upon this court, if it differs from the principles established in the general commercial law. It is observable that the courts of New York do not found their decisions upon this point upon any local statute, or positive, fixed or ancient local usage; but they deduce the doctrine from the general principles of commercial law.

It is, however, contended, that the 34th section of the judiciary act of 1789, ch. 20, furnishes a rule obligatory upon this court to follow the decisions of the state tribunals in all cases to which they apply. That section provides "that the laws of the several states, except where the constitution, treaties or statutes of the United States shall otherwise require or provide, shall be regarded as rules of decision, in trials at common law, in the courts of the United States, in cases where they apply." In order to maintain the argument, it is essential, therefore, to hold that the word "laws" in this section includes within the scope of its meaning the decisions of the local tribunals.

In the ordinary use of language, it will hardly be contended that the decisions of courts constitute laws. They are, at most, only evidence of what the laws are, and are not, of themselves, laws. They are often re-examined, reversed and qualified by the courts themselves, whenever they are found to be either defective, or ill-founded, or otherwise incorrect. The laws of a state are more usually understood to mean the rules and enactments promulgated by the legislative authority thereof, or long-established local customs having the force of laws. In all the various cases, which have hitherto come before us for decision, this court have uniformly supposed, that the true interpretation of the 34th section limited its application to state laws, strictly local, that is to say, to the positive statutes of the state, and the construction thereof adopted by the local tribunals, and to rights and titles to things having a permanent locality, such as the rights and titles to real estate, and other matters immovable and intra-territorial in their nature and character. It never has been supposed by us that the section did apply, or was designed to apply, to questions of a more general nature, not at all dependent upon local statutes or local usages of a fixed and permanent operation, as, for example, to the construction of ordinary contracts or other written instruments, and especially to questions of general commercial law, where the state tribunals are called upon to perform the like functions as ourselves, that is, to ascertain upon general reasoning and legal analogies what is the true exposition of the contract or instrument, or what is the just rule furnished by the principles of commercial law to govern the case. And we have not now the slightest difficulty in holding that this section, upon its true intendment and construction, is strictly limited to local statutes and local usages of the character before stated and does not extend to contracts and other instruments of a commercial nature, the true interpretation and effect whereof are to be sought not in the decisions of the local tribunals, but in the general principles and doctrines of commercial jurisprudence. Undoubtedly, the decisions of the local tribunals upon such subjects are entitled to, and will receive, the most deliberate attention and respect of this court; but they cannot furnish positive rules, or conclusive authority, by which our own judgments are to be bound up and governed. . . .

It becomes necessary for us, therefore, upon the present occasion, to express our own opinion of the true result of the commercial law upon the question now before us. And we have no hesitation in saying that a pre-existing debt does constitute a valuable consideration, in the sense of the general rule already stated, as applicable to negotiable instruments. . . . It is for the benefit and convenience of the commercial world, to give as wide an extent as practicable to the credit and circulation of negotiable paper, that it may pass not only as security for new purchases and advances, made upon the transfer thereof, but also in payment of, and as security for, pre-existing debts. The creditor is thereby enabled to realize or to secure his debt, and thus may safely give a prolonged credit, or forbear from taking any legal steps to enforce his rights. The debtor also has the advantage of making his negotiable securities of equivalent value to cash. But establish the opposite conclusion, that negotiable paper cannot be applied in payment of, or as security for, pre-existing debts, without letting in all the equities between the original and antecedent parties, and the value and circulation of such securities must be essentially diminished, and the debtor driven to the embarrassment of making a sale thereof, often at a ruinous discount, to some third person, and then, by circuity, to apply the proceeds to the payment of his debts. What indeed, upon such a doctrine, would become of that large class of cases, where new notes are given by the same or by other parties by way of renewal or security to banks in lieu of old securities discounted by them, which have arrived at maturity? Probably more than one-half of all bank transactions in our country, as well as those of other countries, are of this nature. The doctrine would strike a fatal blow at all discounts of negotiable securities for pre-existing debts.

This question has been several times before this court, and it has been uniformly held that it makes no difference whatsoever, as to the rights of the holder, whether the debt for which the negotiable instrument is transferred to him is a pre-existing debt or is contracted at the time of the transfer. In each case, he equally gives credit to the instrument. . . . [Thus, Swift is entitled to rely on the *bona fide* purchaser doctrine.]

Erie Railroad v. Tompkins (1938)

The question for decision is whether the oft-challenged doctrine of *Swift v. Tyson* shall now be disapproved.

Tompkins, a citizen of Pennsylvania, was injured on a dark night by a passing freight train of the Erie Railroad Company while walking along its right of way at Hughestown in that state. He claimed that the accident occurred through negligence in the operation or maintenance of the train; that he was rightfully on the premises as licensee because on a commonly used beaten footpath which ran for a short distance alongside the tracks; and that he was struck by something which looked like a door projecting from one of the moving cars. To enforce that claim he brought an action in the federal court for Southern New York, which had jurisdiction because the company is a corporation of that state. It denied liability, and the case was tried by a jury.

The Erie insisted that its duty to Tompkins was no greater than that owed to a trespasser. It contended, among other things, that its duty to Tompkins, and hence its liability, should be determined in accordance with the Pennsylvania law; that under the law of Pennsylvania, as declared by its highest court, persons who use pathways along the railroad right of way—that is, a longitudinal pathway as distinguished from a crossing—are to be deemed trespassers; and that the railroad is not liable for injuries to undiscovered trespassers resulting from its negligence, unless it be wanton or willful. Tompkins denied that any such rule had been established by the decisions of the Pennsylvania courts and contended that, since there was no statute of the state on the subject, the railroad's duty and liability is to be determined in federal courts as a matter of general law.

The trial judge refused to rule that the applicable law precluded recovery. The jury brought in a verdict of $30,000, and the judgment entered thereon was affirmed by the Circuit Court of Appeals, which held that it was unnecessary to consider whether the law of Pennsylvania was as contended, because the question was one not of local, but of general, law, and that upon questions of general law the federal courts are free, in absence of a local statute, to exercise their independent judgment as to what the law is; and it is well settled that the question of the responsibility of a railroad for injuries caused by its servants is one of general law. Where the public has made open and notorious use of a railroad right of way for a long period of time and without objection, the company owes to persons on such permissive pathway a duty of care in the operation of its trains. It is likewise generally recognized law that a jury may find that negligence exists toward a pedestrian using a permissive path on the railroad right of way if he is hit by some object projecting from the side of the train.

The Erie had contended that application of the Pennsylvania rule was required, among other things, by section 34 of the Federal Judiciary Act of September 24, 1789, which provides: "The laws of the several States, except where the Constitution, treaties, or statutes of the United States otherwise require or provide, shall be regarded as rules of decision in trials at common law, in the courts of the United States, in cases where they apply."

Because of the importance of the question whether the federal court was free to disregard the alleged rule of the Pennsylvania common law, we granted certiorari.

First. *Swift* held that federal courts exercising jurisdiction on the ground of diversity of citizenship need not, in matters of general jurisprudence, apply the unwritten law of the state as declared by its highest court; that they are free to exercise an independent judgment as to what the common law of the state is—or should be . . . .

Criticism of the doctrine became widespread after the decision of *Black & White Taxicab & Transfer Co. v. Brown & Yellow Taxicab & Transfer Co.* There, Brown & Yellow, a Kentucky corporation owned by Kentuckians, and the Louisville & Nashville Railroad, also a Kentucky corporation, wished that the former should have the exclusive privilege of soliciting passenger and baggage transportation at the Bowling Green, Ky., Railroad station; and that the Black & White, a competing Kentucky corporation, should be prevented from interfering with that privilege. Knowing that such a contract would be void under the common law of Kentucky, it was arranged that the Brown & Yellow reincorporate under the law of Tennessee, and that the contract with the railroad should be executed there. The suit was then brought by the Tennessee corporation in the federal court for Western Kentucky to enjoin competition by the Black & White; an injunction issued by the District Court was sustained by the Court of Appeals; and this Court, citing many decisions in which the doctrine of *Swift v. Tyson* had been applied, affirmed the decree.

Second. Experience in applying the doctrine of *Swift v. Tyson*, had revealed its defects, political and social, and the benefits expected to flow from the rule did not accrue. Persistence of state courts in their own opinions on questions of common law prevented uniformity, and the impossibility of discovering a satisfactory line of demarcation between the province of general law and that of local law developed a new well of uncertainties.

On the other hand, the mischievous results of the doctrine had become apparent. Diversity of citizenship jurisdiction was conferred in order to prevent apprehended discrimination in state courts against those not citizens of the state. *Swift v. Tyson* introduced grave discrimination by noncitizens against citizens. It made rights enjoyed under the unwritten "general law" vary according to whether enforcement was sought in the state or in the federal court, and the privilege of selecting the court in which the right should be determined was conferred upon the noncitizen. Thus, the doctrine rendered impossible equal protection of the law. In attempting to promote uniformity of law throughout the United States, the doctrine had prevented uniformity in the administration of the law of the state.

The discrimination resulting became in practice far-reaching. This resulted in part from the broad province accorded to the so-called "general law" as to which federal courts exercised an independent judgment. In addition to questions of purely commercial law, "general law" was held to include the obligations under contracts entered into and to be performed within the state; the extent to which a carrier operating within a state may stipulate for exemption from liability for his own negligence or that of his employee; the liability for torts committed within the state upon persons resident or property located there, even where the question of liability depended upon the scope of a property right conferred by the state; and the right to exemplary or punitive damages. Furthermore, state decisions construing local deeds, mineral conveyances, and even devises of real estate, were disregarded.

In part the discrimination resulted from the wide range of persons held entitled to avail themselves of the federal rule by resort to the diversity of citizenship jurisdiction. Through this jurisdiction individual citizens willing to remove from their own state and become citizens of another might avail themselves of the federal rule. And, without even change of residence, a corporate citizen of the state could avail itself of the federal rule by reincorporating under the laws of another state, as was done in the *Taxicab* case.

The injustice and confusion incident to the doctrine of *Swift v. Tyson* have been repeatedly urged as reasons for abolishing or limiting diversity of citizenship jurisdiction. Other legislative relief has been proposed. If only a question of statutory construction were involved, we should not be prepared to abandon a doctrine so widely applied throughout nearly a century. But the unconstitutionality of the course pursued has now been made clear, and compels us to do so.

Third. Except in matters governed by the Federal Constitution or by acts of Congress, the law to be applied in any case is the law of the state. And whether the law of the state shall be declared by its Legislature in a statute or by its highest court in a decision is not a matter of federal concern. There is no federal general common law. Congress has no power to declare substantive rules of common law applicable in a state whether they be local in their nature or "general," be they commercial law or a part of the law of torts. And no clause in the Constitution purports to confer such a power upon the federal courts. . . .

The fallacy underlying the rule declared in *Swift v. Tyson* is made clear by Mr. Justice Holmes. The doctrine rests upon the assumption that there is a transcendental body of law outside of any particular State but obligatory within it unless and until changed by statute, that federal courts have the power to use their judgment as to what the rules of common law are; and that in the federal courts the parties are entitled to an independent judgment on matters of general law: "But law in the sense in which courts speak of it today does not exist without some definite authority behind it. The common law so far as it is enforced in a State, whether called common law or not, is not the common law generally but the law of that State existing by the authority of that State without regard to what it may have been in England or anywhere else. . . . The authority and only authority is the State, and if that be so, the voice adopted by the State as its own (whether it be of its Legislature or of its Supreme Court) should utter the last word."

Thus the doctrine of *Swift v. Tyson* is, as Mr. Justice Holmes said, an unconstitutional assumption of powers by the Courts of the United States which no lapse of time or respectable array of opinion should make us hesitate to correct. In disapproving that doctrine we do not hold unconstitutional section 34 of the Federal Judiciary Act of 1789 or any other act of Congress. We merely declare that in applying the doctrine this Court and the lower courts have invaded rights which in our opinion are reserved by the Constitution to the several states.

Fourth. The defendant contended that by the common law of Pennsylvania . . . , the only duty owed to the plaintiff was to refrain from willful or wanton injury. The plaintiff denied that such is the Pennsylvania law. In support of their respective contentions, the parties discussed and cited many decisions of the Supreme Court of the state. The Circuit Court of Appeals ruled that the question of liability is one of general law; and on that ground declined to decide the issue of state law. As we hold this was error, the judgment is reversed and the case remanded to it for further proceedings in conformity with our opinion.

United States Code

28 U.S.C. § 2072.

(a) The Supreme Court shall have the power to prescribe general rules of practice and procedure and rules of evidence for cases in the United States district courts (including proceedings before magistrate judges thereof) and courts of appeals.

(b) Such rules shall not abridge, enlarge or modify any substantive right. . . .

(c) Such rules may define when a ruling of a district court is final for the purposes of appeal under section 1291 of this title.

Hanna v. Plumer (1965)

The question to be decided is whether, in a civil action where the jurisdiction of the United States district court is based upon diversity of citizenship between the parties, service of process shall be made in the manner prescribed by state law or that set forth in Rule 4(d)(1) of the Federal Rules of Civil Procedure.

On February 6, 1963, petitioner, a citizen of Ohio, filed her complaint in the District Court for the District of Massachusetts, claiming damages in excess of $10,000 for personal injuries resulting from an automobile accident in South Carolina, allegedly caused by the negligence of one Louise Plumer Osgood, a Massachusetts citizen deceased at the time of the filing of the complaint. Respondent, Mrs. Osgood's executor and also a Massachusetts citizen, was named as defendant. On February 8, service was made by leaving copies of the summons and the complaint with respondent's wife at his residence, concededly in compliance with Rule 4(d)(1), which provides:

> The summons and complaint shall be served together. The plaintiff shall furnish the person making service with such copies as are necessary. Service shall be made as follows: (1) Upon an individual other than an infant or an incompetent person, by delivering a copy of the summons and of the complaint to him personally or by leaving copies thereof at his dwelling house or usual place of abode with some person of suitable age and discretion then residing therein . . . .

Respondent filed his answer on February 26, alleging, inter alia, that the action could not be maintained because it had been brought contrary to and in violation of the provisions of Massachusetts General Laws Chapter 197, Section 9. That section provides:

> Except as provided in this chapter, an executor or administrator shall not be held to answer to an action by a creditor of the deceased which is not commenced within one year from the time of his giving bond for the performance of his trust, or to such an action which is commenced within said year unless before the expiration thereof the writ in such action has been served by delivery in hand upon such executor or administrator or service thereof accepted by him or a notice stating the name of the estate, the name and address of the creditor, the amount of the claim and the court in which the action has been brought has been filed in the proper registry of probate. . .
> .

On October 17, 1963, the District Court granted respondent's motion for summary judgment, in support of its conclusion that the adequacy of the service was to be measured by § 9, with which, the court held, petitioner had not complied. On appeal, petitioner admitted noncompliance with § 9, but argued that Rule 4(d)(1) defines the method by which service of process is to be effected in diversity actions. The Court of Appeals for the First Circuit . . . unanimously affirmed. Because of the threat to the goal of uniformity of federal procedure posed by the decision below, we granted certiorari.

We conclude that the adoption of Rule 4(d)(1), designed to control service of process in diversity actions, neither exceeded the congressional mandate embodied in the Rules Enabling Act nor transgressed constitutional bounds, and that the Rule is therefore the standard against which the District Court should have measured the adequacy of the service. Accordingly, we reverse the decision of the Court of Appeals.

. . . . Under the cases construing the scope of the Enabling Act, Rule 4(d)(1) clearly passes muster. Prescribing the manner in which a defendant is to be notified that a suit has been instituted against him, it relates to the "practice and procedure of the district courts." . . . Thus were there no conflicting state procedure, Rule 4(d)(1) would clearly control. However, respondent, focusing on the contrary Massachusetts rule, calls to the Court's attention another line of cases, a line which—like the Federal Rules—had its birth in 1938. *Erie* held that federal courts sitting in diversity cases, when deciding questions of "substantive" law, are bound by state court decisions as well as state statutes. The broad command of *Erie* was therefore identical to that of the Enabling Act: federal courts are to apply state substantive law and federal procedural law. However, as subsequent cases sharpened the distinction between substance and procedure, the line of cases following *Erie* diverged markedly from the line construing the Enabling Act. . . .

Respondent . . . suggests that the Erie doctrine acts as a check on the Federal Rules of Civil Procedure, that despite the clear command of Rule 4(d)(1), *Erie* and its progeny demand the application of the Massachusetts rule. . . .

In the first place, it is doubtful that, even if there were no Federal Rule making it clear that in-hand service is not required in diversity actions, the *Erie* rule would have obligated the District Court to follow the Massachusetts procedure. . . . [C]hoices between state and federal law are to be made not by application of any automatic, litmus paper criterion, but rather by reference to the policies underlying the *Erie* rule.

The *Erie* rule is rooted in part in a realization that it would be unfair for the character of result of a litigation materially to differ because the suit had been brought in a federal court. . . . The decision was also in part a reaction to the practice of forum shopping which had grown up in response to the rule of *Swift*. . . . The "outcome-determinative" test [that had arisen in *York*, a case decided after *Erie*, which proposed that *Erie* directed that state law apply whenever a conflict between state and federal law would determine the ultimate outcome in a case] therefore cannot be read without reference to the twin aims of the *Erie* rule: discouragement of forum-shopping and avoidance of inequitable administration of the laws.

The difference between the conclusion that the Massachusetts rule is applicable, and the conclusion that it is not, is of course at this point "outcome-determinative" in the sense that if we hold the state rule to apply, respondent prevails, whereas if we hold that Rule 4(d)(1) governs, the litigation will continue. But in this sense every procedural variation is "outcome-determinative." For example, having brought suit in a federal court, a plaintiff cannot then insist on the right to file subsequent pleadings in accord with the time limits applicable in state courts, even though enforcement of the federal timetable will, if he continues to insist that he must meet only the state time limit, result in determination of the controversy against him. So it is here. Though choice of the federal or state rule will at this point have a marked effect upon the outcome of the litigation, the difference between the two rules would be of scant, if any, relevance to the choice of a forum. Petitioner, in choosing her forum, was not presented with a situation where application of the state rule would wholly bar recovery; rather, adherence to the state rule would have resulted only in altering the way in which process was served. Moreover, it is difficult to argue that permitting service of defendant's wife to take the place of in-hand service of defendant himself alters the mode of enforcement of state-created rights in a fashion sufficiently substantial to raise the sort of equal protection problems to which the *Erie* opinion alluded.

There is, however, a more fundamental flaw in respondent's syllogism: the incorrect assumption that the rule of *Erie* constitutes the appropriate test of the validity and therefore the applicability of a Federal Rule of Civil Procedure. The *Erie* rule has never been invoked to void a Federal Rule. It is true that there have been cases where this Court has held applicable a state rule in the face of an argument that the situation was governed by one of the Federal Rules. *See Ragan.* But the holding of each such case was not that *Erie* commanded displacement of a Federal Rule by an inconsistent state rule, but rather that the scope of the Federal Rule was not as broad as the losing party urged, and therefore, there being no Federal Rule which covered the point in dispute, *Erie* commanded the enforcement of state law. Here, of course, the clash is unavoidable; Rule 4(d)(1) says—implicitly, but with unmistakable clarity—that in-hand service is not required in federal courts.

At the same time, in cases adjudicating the validity of Federal Rules, we have not applied . . . refinements of *Erie*, but have to this day continued to decide questions concerning the scope of the Enabling Act and the constitutionality of specific Federal Rules . . . . Nor has the development of two separate lines of cases been inadvertent. . . . It is true that both the Enabling Act and the *Erie* rule say, roughly, that federal courts are to apply state "substantive" law and federal "procedural" law, but from that it need not follow that the tests are identical. For they were designed to control very different sorts of decisions. When a situation is covered by one of the Federal Rules, the question facing the court is a far cry from the typical, relatively unguided Erie Choice: the court has been instructed to apply the Federal Rule, and can refuse to do so only if the Advisory Committee, this Court, and Congress erred in their prima facie judgment that the Rule in question transgresses neither the terms of the Enabling Act nor constitutional restrictions.

We are reminded by the *Erie* opinion that neither Congress nor the federal courts can, under the guise of formulating rules of decision for federal courts, fashion rules which are not supported by a grant of federal authority contained in Article I or some other section of the Constitution; in such areas state law must govern because there can be no other law. But the opinion in *Erie*, which involved no Federal Rule and dealt with a question which was "substantive" in every traditional sense (whether the railroad owed a duty of care to Tompkins as a trespasser or a licensee), surely neither said nor implied that measures like Rule 4(d)(1) are unconstitutional. For the constitutional provision for a federal court system (augmented by the Necessary and Proper Clause) carries with it congressional power to make rules governing the practice and pleading in those courts, which in turn includes a power to regulate matters which, though falling within the uncertain area between substance and procedure, are rationally capable of classification as either. . . .

Erie and its offspring cast no doubt on the long-recognized power of Congress to prescribe housekeeping rules for federal courts even though some of those rules will inevitably differ from comparable state rules. . . . Thus, though a court, in measuring a Federal Rule against the standards contained in the Enabling Act and the Constitution, need not wholly blind itself to the degree to which the Rule makes the character and result of the federal litigation stray from the course it would follow in state courts, it cannot be forgotten that the *Erie* rule, and the guidelines suggested [by the outcome-determinative test], were created to serve another purpose altogether. To hold that a Federal Rule of Civil Procedure must cease to function whenever it alters the mode of enforcing state-created rights would be to disembowel either the Constitution's grant of power over federal procedure or Congress's attempt to exercise that power in the Enabling Act. Rule 4(d)(1) is valid and controls the instant case.

Reversed.

Walker v. Armco Steel (1980)

This case presents the issue whether in a diversity action the federal court should follow state law or, alternatively, Rule 3 of the Federal Rules of Civil Procedure in determining when an action is commenced for the purpose of tolling the state statute of limitations.

I

According to the allegations of the complaint, petitioner, a carpenter, was injured on August 22, 1975, in Oklahoma City, Okla., while pounding a Sheffield nail into a cement wall. Respondent was the manufacturer of the nail. Petitioner claimed that the nail contained a defect which caused its head to shatter and strike him in the right eye, resulting in permanent injuries. The defect was allegedly caused by respondent's negligence in manufacture and design.

Petitioner is a resident of Oklahoma, and respondent is a foreign corporation having its principal place of business in a State other than Oklahoma. Since there was diversity of citizenship, petitioner brought suit in the United States District Court for the Western District of Oklahoma. The complaint was filed on August 19, 1977. Although summons was issued that same day, service of process was not made on respondent's authorized service agent until December 1, 1977. On January 5, 1978, respondent filed a motion to dismiss the complaint on the ground that the action was barred by the applicable Oklahoma statute of limitations. Although the complaint had been filed within the 2-year statute of limitations, state law does not deem the action "commenced" for purposes of the statute of limitations until service of the summons on the defendant. If the complaint is filed within the limitations period, however, the action is deemed to have commenced from that date of filing if the plaintiff serves the defendant within 60 days, even though that service may occur outside the limitations period. In this case, service was not effectuated until long after this 60-day period had expired. Petitioner in his reply brief to the motion to dismiss admitted that his case would be foreclosed in state court, but he argued that Rule 3 of the Federal Rules of Civil Procedure governs the manner in which an action is commenced in federal court for all purposes, including the tolling of the state statute of limitations.

The District Court dismissed the complaint as barred by the Oklahoma statute of limitations. . . . The United States Court of Appeals for the Tenth Circuit affirmed. . . .

II

. . . . In *Ragan*, the plaintiff had filed his complaint in federal court on September 4, 1945, pursuant to Rule 3 of the Federal Rules of Civil Procedure. The accident from which the claim arose had occurred on October 1, 1943. Service was made on the defendant on December 28, 1945. The applicable statute of limitations supplied by Kansas law was two years. Kansas had an additional statute which provided: "An action shall be deemed commenced within the meaning of [the statute of limitations], as to each defendant, at the date of the summons which is served on him . . . . An attempt to commence an action shall be deemed equivalent to the commencement thereof within the meaning of this article when the party faithfully, properly and diligently endeavors to procure a service; but such attempt must be followed by the first publication or service of the summons within sixty days." The defendant moved for summary judgment on the ground that the Kansas statute of limitations barred the action since service had not been made within either the 2-year period or the 60-day period. It was conceded that had the case been brought in Kansas state court it would have been barred. Nonetheless, the District Court held that the statute had been tolled by the filing of the complaint. The Court of Appeals reversed because the requirement of service of summons within the statutory period was an integral part of that state's statute of limitations.

We affirmed, relying on *Erie* and *York*: "We cannot give [the cause of action] longer life in the federal court than it would have had in the state court without adding something to the cause of action. We may not do that consistently with *Erie R. Co. v. Tompkins*." We rejected the argument that Rule 3 of the Federal Rules of Civil Procedure governed the manner in which an action was commenced in federal court for purposes of tolling the state statute of limitations. Instead, we held that the service of summons statute controlled because it was an integral part of the state statute of limitations, and under *York* that statute of limitations was part of the state-law cause of action.

Ragan was not our last pronouncement in this difficult area, however. In 1965 we decided *Hanna*, holding that in a civil action where federal jurisdiction was based upon diversity of citizenship, Rule 4(d)(1) of the Federal Rules of Civil Procedure, rather than state law, governed the manner in which process was served. . . . The Court noted that in the absence of a conflicting state procedure, the Federal Rule would plainly control. We stated that the "outcome-determination" test of *Erie* and *York* had to be read with reference to the "twin aims" of *Erie*: discouragement of forum-shopping and avoidance of inequitable administration of the laws. We determined that the choice between the state in-hand service rule and the Federal Rule would be of scant, if any, relevance to the choice of a forum, for the plaintiff was not presented with a situation where application of the state rule would wholly bar recovery; rather, adherence to the state rule would have resulted only in altering the way in which process was served. This factor served to distinguish that case from *York* and *Ragan*.

The Court in *Hanna*, however, pointed out "a more fundamental flaw" in the defendant's argument in that case. The Court concluded that the *Erie* doctrine was simply not the appropriate test of the validity and applicability of one of the Federal Rules of Civil Procedure:

> The *Erie* rule has never been invoked to void a Federal Rule. It is true that there have been cases where this Court had held applicable a state rule in the face of an argument that the situation was governed by one of the Federal Rules. But the holding of each such case was not that *Erie* commanded displacement of a Federal Rule by an inconsistent state rule, but rather that the scope of the Federal Rule was not as broad as the losing party urged, and therefore, there being no Federal Rule which covered the point in dispute, *Erie* commanded the enforcement of state law.

The Court cited *Ragan* as one of the examples of this proposition. The Court explained that where the Federal Rule was clearly applicable, as in *Hanna*, the test was whether the Rule was within the scope of the Rules Enabling Act, 28 U.S.C. § 2072, and if so, within a constitutional grant of power such as the Necessary and Proper Clause of Art. I.

III

The present case is indistinguishable from *Ragan*. The statutes in both cases require service of process to toll the statute of limitations, and in fact the predecessor to the Oklahoma statute in this case was derived from the predecessor to the Kansas statute in *Ragan*. Here, as in *Ragan*, the complaint was filed in federal court under diversity jurisdiction within the 2-year statute of limitations, but service of process did not occur until after the 2-year period and the 60-day service period had run. In both cases the suit would concededly have been barred in the applicable state court, and in both instances the state service statute was held to be an integral part of the statute of limitations by the lower court more familiar than we with state law. Accordingly, as the Court of Appeals held below, the instant action is barred by the statute of limitations unless *Ragan* is no longer good law.

Petitioner argues that the analysis and holding of *Ragan* did not survive our decision in *Hanna*. Petitioner's position is that Okla. Stat., Tit. 12, § 97 (1971), is in direct conflict with the Federal Rule. Under *Hanna*, petitioner contends, the appropriate question is whether Rule 3 is within the scope of the Rules Enabling Act and, if so, within the constitutional power of Congress. In petitioner's view, the Federal Rule is to be applied unless it violates one of those two restrictions. This argument ignores both the force of *stare decisis* and the specific limitations that we carefully placed on the *Hanna* analysis.

We note at the outset that the doctrine of *stare decisis* weighs heavily against petitioner in this case. Petitioner seeks to have us overrule our decision in *Ragan*. *Stare decisis* does not mandate that earlier decisions be enshrined forever, of course, but it does counsel that we use caution in rejecting established law. In this case, the reasons petitioner asserts for overruling *Ragan* are the same factors which we concluded in *Hanna* did not undermine the validity of *Ragan*. A litigant who in effect asks us to reconsider not one but two prior decisions bears a heavy burden of supporting such a change in our jurisprudence. Petitioner here has not met that burden.

This Court in *Hanna* distinguished *Ragan* rather than overruled it, and for good reason. Application of the *Hanna* analysis is premised on a direct collision between the Federal Rule and the state law. In *Hanna* itself the clash between Rule 4(d)(1) and the state in-hand service requirement was unavoidable. The first question must therefore be whether the scope of the Federal Rule in fact is sufficiently broad to control the issue before the Court. It is only if that question is answered affirmatively that the *Hanna* analysis applies.

As has already been noted, we recognized in *Hanna* that the present case is an instance where the scope of the Federal Rule is not as broad as the losing party urges, and therefore, there being no Federal Rule which covers the point in dispute, *Erie* commands the enforcement of state law. Rule 3 simply states that "[a] civil action is commenced by filing a complaint with the court." There is no indication that the Rule was intended to toll a state statute of limitations,[10] much less that it purported to displace state tolling rules for purposes of state statutes of limitations.

> [10] Rule 3 simply provides that an action is commenced by filing the complaint and has as its primary purpose the measuring of time periods that begin running from the date of commencement; the rule does not state that filing tolls the statute of limitations.

In our view, in diversity actions[11] Rule 3 governs the date from which various timing requirements of the Federal Rules begin to run, but does not affect state statutes of limitations.

> [11] The Court suggested in *Ragan* that in suits to enforce rights under a federal statute Rule 3 means that filing of the complaint tolls the applicable statute of limitations. We do not here address the role of Rule 3 as a tolling provision for a statute of limitations, whether set by federal law or borrowed from state law, if the cause of action is based on federal law.

In contrast to Rule 3, the Oklahoma statute is a statement of a substantive decision by that State that actual service on, and accordingly actual notice by, the defendant is an integral part of the several policies served by the statute of limitations. The statute of limitations establishes a deadline after which the defendant may legitimately have peace of mind; it also recognizes that after a certain period of time it is unfair to require the defendant to attempt to piece together his defense to an old claim. A requirement of actual service promotes both of those functions of the statute. It is these policy aspects which make the service requirement an integral part of the statute of limitations both in this case and in *Ragan*. As such, the service rule must be considered part and parcel of the statute of limitations. Rule 3 does not replace such policy determinations found in state law. Rule 3 and Okla. Stat., Tit. 12, § 97 (1971), can exist side by side, therefore, each controlling its own intended sphere of coverage without conflict.

Since there is no direct conflict between the Federal Rule and the state law, the *Hanna* analysis does not apply. Instead, the policies behind *Erie* and *Ragan* control the issue whether, in the absence of a federal rule directly on point, state service requirements which are an integral part of the state statute of limitations should control in an action based on state law which is filed in federal court under diversity jurisdiction. The reasons for the application of such a state service requirement in a diversity action in the absence of a conflicting federal rule are well explained in *Erie* and *Ragan* and need not be repeated here. It is sufficient to note that although in this case failure to apply the state service law might not create any problem of forum shopping, the result would be an inequitable administration of the law. There is simply no reason why, in the absence of a controlling federal rule, an action based on state law which concededly would be barred in the state courts by the state statute of limitations should proceed through litigation to judgment in federal court solely because of the fortuity that there is diversity of citizenship between the litigants. The policies underlying diversity jurisdiction do not support such a distinction between state and federal plaintiffs, and *Erie* and its progeny do not permit it.

The judgment of the Court of Appeals is *Affirmed.*

Shady Grove Orthopedic v. Allstate Insurance (2010)

Justice SCALIA announced the judgment of the Court and delivered the opinion of the Court with respect to Parts I and II–A, an opinion with respect to Parts II–B and II–D, in which THE CHIEF JUSTICE, Justice THOMAS, and Justice SOTOMAYOR join, and an opinion with respect to Part II–C, in which THE CHIEF JUSTICE and Justice THOMAS join.

New York law prohibits class actions in suits seeking penalties or statutory minimum damages.[1]

> [1] N.Y. Civ. Prac. Law Ann. § 901 (West 2006) provides: "(a) One or more members of a class may sue or be sued as representative parties on behalf of all if [requirements are met]. (b) Unless [specifically authorized], an action to recover a penalty, or minimum measure of recovery created or imposed by statute may not be maintained as a class action."

We consider whether this precludes a federal district court sitting in diversity from entertaining a class action under Federal Rule of Civil Procedure 23.[2]

> [2] Rule 23(a) provides: "(a) Prerequisites. One or more members of a class may sue or be sued as representative parties on behalf of all members only if [requirements are met]. (b) A class action may be maintained if Rule 23(a) is satisfied and if [the suit falls into one of three described categories].

I

The petitioner's complaint alleged the following: Shady Grove Orthopedic Associates provided medical care to Sonia E. Galvez for injuries she suffered in an automobile accident. As partial payment for that care, Galvez assigned to Shady Grove her rights to insurance benefits under a policy issued in New York by Allstate Insurance. Shady Grove tendered a claim for the assigned benefits to Allstate, which under New York law had 30 days to pay the claim or deny it. Allstate apparently paid, but not on time, and it refused to pay the statutory interest that accrued on the overdue benefits (at two percent per month).

Shady Grove filed this diversity suit in the Eastern District of New York to recover the unpaid statutory interest. Alleging that Allstate routinely refuses to pay interest on overdue benefits, Shady Grove sought relief on behalf of itself and a class of all others to whom Allstate owes interest. The District Court dismissed the suit for lack of jurisdiction. It reasoned that N.Y. Civ. Prac. Law Ann. § 901(b), which precludes a suit to recover a "penalty" from proceeding as a class action, applies in diversity suits in federal court, despite Federal Rule of Civil Procedure 23. Concluding that statutory interest is a "penalty" under New York law, it held that § 901(b) prohibited the proposed class action. And, since Shady Grove conceded that its individual claim (worth roughly $500) fell far short of the amount-in-controversy requirement for individual suits under 28 U.S.C. § 1332(a), the suit did not belong in federal court. The Second Circuit affirmed. . . . We granted certiorari.

II

The framework for our decision is familiar. We must first determine whether Rule 23 answers the question in dispute. If it does, it governs—New York's law notwithstanding— unless it exceeds statutory authorization or Congress's rulemaking power. We do not wade into *Erie*'s murky waters unless the federal rule is inapplicable or invalid.

A

The question in dispute is whether Shady Grove's suit may proceed as a class action. Rule 23 provides an answer. It states that "[a] class action may be maintained" if two conditions are met: The suit must satisfy the criteria set forth in subdivision (a) (*i.e.,* numerosity, commonality, typicality, and adequacy of representation), and it also must fit into one of the three categories described in subdivision (b). By its terms this creates a categorical rule entitling a plaintiff whose suit meets the specified criteria to pursue his claim as a class action. (The Federal Rules regularly use "may" to confer categorical permission, as do federal statutes that establish procedural entitlements.) Thus, Rule 23 provides a one-size-fits-all formula for deciding the class-action question. Because § 901(b) attempts to answer the same question—*i.e.,* it states that Shady Grove's suit "may *not* be maintained as a class action" (emphasis added) because of the relief it seeks—it cannot apply in diversity suits unless Rule 23 is ultra vires.

The Second Circuit believed that § 901(b) and Rule 23 do not conflict because they address different issues. Rule 23, it said, concerns only the criteria for determining whether a given class can and should be certified; section 901(b), on the other hand, addresses an antecedent question: whether the particular type of claim is eligible for class treatment in the first place—a question on which Rule 23 is silent. Allstate embraces this analysis.

We disagree. To begin with, the line between eligibility and certifiability is entirely artificial. Both are preconditions for maintaining a class action. Allstate suggests that eligibility must depend on the "particular cause of action" asserted, instead of some other attribute of the suit. But that is not so. Congress could, for example, provide that only claims involving more than a certain number of plaintiffs are "eligible" for class treatment in federal court. In other words, relabeling Rule 23(a)'s prerequisites "eligibility criteria" would obviate Allstate's objection—a sure sign that its eligibility-certifiability distinction is made-to-order.

There is no reason, in any event, to read Rule 23 as addressing only whether claims made eligible for class treatment by some *other* law should be certified as class actions. Allstate asserts that Rule 23 neither explicitly nor implicitly empowers a federal court to certify a class in each and every case where the Rule's criteria are met. But that is *exactly* what Rule 23 does: It says that if the prescribed preconditions are satisfied "[a] class action *may be maintained* " (emphasis added)—not "*a class action may be permitted.*" Courts do not maintain actions; litigants do. The discretion suggested by Rule 23's "may" is discretion residing in the plaintiff: He may bring his claim in a class action if he wishes. . . .

The dissent argues that § 901(b) has nothing to do with whether Shady Grove may maintain its suit as a class action, but affects only the *remedy* it may obtain if it wins. Whereas Rule 23 governs procedural aspects of class litigation by prescribing the considerations relevant to class certification and postcertification proceedings, § 901(b) addresses only the size of a monetary award a class plaintiff may pursue. Accordingly, the dissent says, Rule 23 and New York's law may coexist in peace.

We need not decide whether a state law that limits the remedies available in an existing class action would conflict with Rule 23; that is not what § 901(b) does. By its terms, the provision precludes a plaintiff from "maintain[ing]" a class action seeking statutory penalties. Unlike a law that sets a ceiling on damages (or puts other remedies out of reach) in properly filed class actions, § 901(b) says nothing about what remedies a court may award; it prevents the class actions it covers from coming into existence at all.[4] Consequently, a court bound by § 901(b) could not certify a class action seeking both statutory penalties and other remedies even if it announces in advance that it will refuse to award the penalties in the event the plaintiffs prevail; to do so would violate the statute's clear prohibition on "maintain[ing]" such suits as class actions.

> [4] Contrary to the dissent's implication, we express no view as to whether state laws that set a ceiling on damages recoverable in a single suit are pre-empted. Whether or not those laws conflict with Rule 23, § 901(b) does conflict because it addresses not the remedy, but the procedural right to maintain a class action. As Allstate and the dissent note, several federal statutes also limit the recovery available in class actions. But Congress has plenary power to override the Federal Rules, so its enactments, unlike those of the States, prevail even in case of a conflict.

The dissent asserts that a plaintiff can avoid § 901(b)'s barrier by omitting from his complaint (or removing) a request for statutory penalties. Even assuming all statutory penalties are waivable, the fact that a complaint omitting them could be brought as a class action would not at all prove that § 901(b) is addressed only to remedies. If the state law instead banned class actions for fraud claims, a would-be class-action plaintiff could drop the fraud counts from his complaint and proceed with the remainder in a class action. Yet that would not mean the law provides no remedy for fraud; the ban would affect only the procedural means by which the remedy may be pursued. In short, although the dissent correctly abandons Allstate's eligibility-certifiability distinction, the alternative it offers fares no better.

The dissent all but admits that the literal terms of § 901(b) address the same subject as Rule 23—*i.e.,* whether a class action may be maintained—but insists the provision's *purpose* is to restrict only remedies. Unlike Rule 23, designed to further procedural fairness and efficiency, § 901(b) (we are told) responds to an entirely different concern: the fear that allowing statutory damages to be awarded on a class-wide basis would produce overkill. . . . But even accepting the dissent's account of the Legislature's objective at face value, it cannot override the statute's clear text. Even if its aim is to restrict the remedy a plaintiff can obtain, § 901(b) achieves that end by limiting a plaintiff's power to maintain a class action. The manner in which the law could have been written, has no bearing; what matters is the law the Legislature *did* enact. We cannot rewrite that to reflect our perception of legislative purpose.[6]

[6] Our decision in *Walker*, discussed by the dissent, is not to the contrary. There we held that Rule 3 (which provides that a federal civil action is "commenced" by filing a complaint in federal court) did not displace a state law providing that "an action shall be deemed commenced, *within the meaning of this article [the statute of limitations],* as to each defendant, at the date of the summons which is served on him." Rule 3, we explained, governs the date from which various timing requirements of the Federal Rules begin to run, but does not affect state statutes of limitations or tolling rules, which it did not purport to displace. The texts were therefore not in conflict. While our opinion observed that the State's actual-service rule was (in the State's judgment) an integral part of the several policies served by the statute of limitations, nothing in our decision suggested that a federal court may resolve an obvious conflict between the texts of state and federal rules by resorting to the state law's ostensible objectives.

. . . . But while the dissent does indeed artificially narrow the scope of § 901(b) by finding that it pursues only substantive policies, that is not the central difficulty of the dissent's position. The central difficulty is that even artificial narrowing cannot render § 901(b) compatible with Rule 23. *Whatever* the policies they pursue, they flatly contradict each other.

Allstate asserts (and the dissent implies) that we can (and must) *interpret* Rule 23 in a manner that avoids overstepping its authorizing statute. If the Rule were susceptible of two meanings—one that would violate § 2072(b) and another that would not—we would agree. But it is not. Rule 23 unambiguously authorizes *any* plaintiff, in *any* federal civil proceeding, to maintain a class action if the Rule's prerequisites are met. We cannot contort its text, even to avert a collision with state law that might render it invalid.[8] What the dissent's approach achieves is not the avoiding of a conflict between Rule 23 and § 901(b), but rather the invalidation of Rule 23 (pursuant to § 2072(b) of the Rules Enabling Act) to the extent that it conflicts with the substantive policies of § 901. There is no other way to reach the dissent's destination. We must therefore confront head-on whether Rule 23 falls within the statutory authorization.

[8] The cases chronicled by the dissent each involved a Federal Rule that we concluded could fairly be read not to control the issue addressed by the pertinent state law, thus avoiding a direct collision between federal and state law. But here, as in *Hanna*, a collision is unavoidable.

B

Erie involved the constitutional power of federal courts to supplant state law with judge-made rules. In that context, it made no difference whether the rule was technically one of substance or procedure; the touchstone was whether it significantly affects the result of a litigation. That is not the test for either the constitutionality or the statutory validity of a Federal Rule of Procedure. Congress has undoubted power to supplant state law, and undoubted power to prescribe rules for the courts it has created, so long as those rules regulate matters rationally capable of classification as procedure. In the Rules Enabling Act, Congress authorized this Court to promulgate rules of procedure subject to its review, 28 U.S.C. § 2072(a), but with the limitation that those rules "shall not abridge, enlarge or modify any substantive right," § 2072(b).

We have long held that this limitation means that the Rule must really regulate procedure—the judicial process for enforcing rights and duties recognized by substantive law and for justly administering remedy and redress for disregard or infraction of them. The test is not whether the rule affects a litigant's substantive rights; most procedural rules do. What matters is what the rule itself regulates: If it governs only the manner and the means by which the litigants' rights are enforced, it is valid; if it alters the rules of decision by which the court will adjudicate those rights, it is not.

Applying that test, we have rejected every statutory challenge to a Federal Rule that has come before us. We have found to be in compliance with § 2072(b) rules prescribing methods for serving process, and requiring litigants whose mental or physical condition is in dispute to submit to examinations. Likewise, we have upheld rules authorizing imposition of sanctions upon those who file frivolous appeals or who sign court papers without a reasonable inquiry into the facts asserted. Each of these rules had some practical effect on the parties' rights, but each undeniably regulated only the process for enforcing those rights; none altered the rights themselves, the available remedies, or the rules of decision by which the court adjudicated either.

Applying that criterion, we think it obvious that rules allowing multiple claims (and claims by or against multiple parties) to be litigated together are also valid. Such rules neither change plaintiffs' separate entitlements to relief nor abridge defendants' rights; they alter only how the claims are processed. For the same reason, Rule 23—at least insofar as it allows willing plaintiffs to join their separate claims against the same defendants in a class action—falls within § 2072(b)'s authorization. A class action, no less than traditional joinder (of which it is a species), merely enables a federal court to adjudicate claims of multiple parties at once, instead of in separate suits. And like traditional joinder, it leaves the parties' legal rights and duties intact and the rules of decision unchanged.

Allstate contends that the authorization of class actions is not substantively neutral: Allowing Shady Grove to sue on behalf of a class transforms the dispute over a five *hundred* dollar penalty into a dispute over a five *million* dollar penalty. Allstate's aggregate liability, however, does not depend on whether the suit proceeds as a class action. Each of the 1,000–plus members of the putative class could (as Allstate acknowledges) bring a freestanding suit asserting his individual claim. It is undoubtedly true that some plaintiffs who would not bring individual suits for the relatively small sums involved will choose to join a class action. That has no bearing, however, on Allstate's or the plaintiffs' legal rights. The likelihood that some (even many) plaintiffs will be induced to sue by the availability of a class action is just the sort of incidental effect we have long held does not violate § 2072(b).

Allstate argues that Rule 23 violates § 2072(b) because the state law it displaces, § 901(b), creates a right that the Federal Rule abridges—namely, a substantive right not to be subjected to aggregated class-action liability in a single suit. To begin with, we doubt that that is so. Nothing in the text of § 901(b) (which is to be found in New York's procedural code) confines it to claims under New York law; and of course New York has no power to alter substantive rights and duties created by other sovereigns. As we have said, the *consequence* of excluding certain class actions may be to cap the damages a defendant can face in a single suit, but the law itself alters only procedure. In that respect, § 901(b) is no different from a state law forbidding simple joinder.

As a fallback argument, Allstate argues that even if § 901(b) is a procedural provision, it was enacted for *substantive reasons.* Its end was not to improve the conduct of the litigation process itself but to alter the outcome of that process. The fundamental difficulty with both these arguments is that the substantive nature of New York's law, or its substantive purpose, *makes no difference.* A Federal Rule of Procedure is not valid in some jurisdictions and invalid in others—or valid in some cases and invalid in others—depending upon whether its effect is to frustrate a state substantive law (or a state procedural law enacted for substantive purposes). . . .

In sum, it is not the substantive or procedural nature or purpose of the affected state law that matters, but the substantive or procedural nature of the Federal Rule. . . . [T]he validity of a Federal Rule depends entirely upon whether it regulates procedure. If it does, it is authorized by § 2072 and is valid in all jurisdictions, with respect to all claims, regardless of its incidental effect upon state-created rights. . . .

D

We must acknowledge the reality that keeping the federal-court door open to class actions that cannot proceed in state court will produce forum shopping. That is unacceptable when it comes as the consequence of judge-made rules created to fill supposed gaps in positive federal law. For where neither the Constitution, a treaty, nor a statute provides the rule of decision or authorizes a federal court to supply one, state law must govern because there can be no other law. But divergence from state law, with the attendant consequence of forum shopping, is the inevitable (indeed, one might say the intended) result of a uniform system of federal procedure. Congress itself has created the possibility that the same case may follow a different course if filed in federal instead of state court. The short of the matter is that a Federal Rule governing procedure is valid whether or not it alters the outcome of the case in a way that induces forum shopping. To hold otherwise would be to disembowel either the Constitution's grant of power over federal procedure or Congress's exercise of it.

* * *

The judgment of the Court of Appeals is reversed, and the case is remanded for further proceedings.

Justice STEVENS [concurred in the judgment to reverse and joined Parts I and II-A of the Court's opinion but would have held Rule 23 invalid under the Rules Enabling Act]. . . .

Justice GINSBURG, with whom Justice KENNEDY, Justice BREYER, and Justice ALITO join, dissenting.

The Court today approves Shady Grove's attempt to transform a $500 case into a $5,000,000 award, although the State creating the right to recover has proscribed this alchemy. If Shady Grove had filed suit in New York state court, the 2% interest payment authorized by New York Ins. Law Ann. § 5106(a) as a penalty for overdue benefits would, by Shady Grove's own measure, amount to no more than $500. By instead filing in federal court based on the parties' diverse citizenship and requesting class certification, Shady Grove hopes to recover, for the class, statutory damages of more than $5,000,000. The New York Legislature has barred this remedy, instructing that, unless specifically permitted, "an action to recover a penalty, or minimum measure of recovery created or imposed by statute may not be maintained as a class action." The Court nevertheless holds that Federal Rule of Civil Procedure 23, which prescribes procedures for the conduct of class actions in federal courts, preempts the application of § 901(b) in diversity suits.

The Court reads Rule 23 relentlessly to override New York's restriction on the availability of statutory damages. Our decisions, however, caution us to ask, before undermining state legislation: Is this conflict really necessary? Had the Court engaged in that inquiry, it would not have read Rule 23 to collide with New York's legitimate interest in keeping certain monetary awards reasonably bounded. I would continue to interpret Federal Rules with awareness of, and sensitivity to, important state regulatory policies. Because today's judgment radically departs from that course, I dissent.

I

. . . . In our prior decisions in point, many of them not mentioned in the Court's opinion, we have avoided immoderate interpretations of the Federal Rules that would trench on state prerogatives without serving any countervailing federal interest. Application of the *Hanna* analysis, we have said, is premised on a direct collision between the Federal Rule and the state law. *See Walker*. To displace state law, a Federal Rule, when fairly construed, must be sufficiently broad so as to control the issue before the court, thereby leaving *no room* for the operation of that law.

In pre-*Hanna* decisions, the Court vigilantly read the Federal Rules to avoid conflict with state laws. . . . In all of these cases, the Court stated in *Hanna*, the scope of the Federal Rule was not as broad as the losing party urged, and therefore, there being no Federal Rule which covered the point in dispute, *Erie* commanded the enforcement of state law. In *Hanna* itself, the Court found the clash unavoidable; the petitioner had effected service of process as prescribed by Federal Rule 4(d)(1), but that how-to method did not satisfy the special Massachusetts law applicable to service on an executor or administrator. Even as it rejected the Massachusetts prescription in favor of the federal procedure, however, the majority in Hanna recognized that federal rules must be interpreted by the courts applying them, and that the process of interpretation can and should reflect an awareness of legitimate state interests.

Following *Hanna*, we continued to interpret the federal rules to avoid conflict with important state regulatory policies. In *Walker*, the Court took up the question whether *Ragan* should be overruled; we held, once again, that Federal Rule 3 does not directly conflict with state rules governing the time when an action commences for purposes of tolling a limitations period. Rule 3, we said, addresses only the date from which various timing requirements of the Federal Rules begin to run and does not purport to displace state tolling rules. Significant state policy interests would be frustrated, we observed, were we to read Rule 3 as superseding the state rule, which required actual service on the defendant to stop the clock on the statute of limitations. . . .

In sum, both before and after *Hanna*, the above-described decisions show, federal courts have been cautioned by this Court to interpret the Federal Rules with sensitivity to important state interests and a will to avoid conflict with important state regulatory policies. The Court veers away from that approach . . . in favor of a mechanical reading of Federal Rules, insensitive to state interests and productive of discord. . . .

Shady Grove contends—and the Court today agrees—that Rule 23 unavoidably preempts New York's prohibition on the recovery of statutory damages in class actions. The Federal Rule, the Court emphasizes, states that Shady Grove's suit "may be" maintained as a class action, which conflicts with § 901(b)'s instruction that it "may not" so proceed. . . . The Court, I am convinced, finds conflict where none is necessary. . . . Rule 23 prescribes the considerations relevant to class certification and postcertification proceedings—but it does not command that a particular remedy be available when a party sues in a representative capacity. Section 901(b), in contrast, trains on that latter issue. Sensibly read, Rule 23 governs procedural aspects of class litigation, but allows state law to control the size of a monetary award a class plaintiff may pursue.

In other words, Rule 23 describes a method of enforcing a claim for relief, while § 901(b) defines the dimensions of the claim itself. In this regard, it is immaterial that § 901(b) bars statutory penalties in wholesale, rather than retail, fashion. The New York Legislature could have embedded the limitation in every provision creating a cause of action for which a penalty is authorized; § 901(b) operates as shorthand to the same effect. It is as much a part of the delineation of the claim for relief as it would be were it included claim by claim in the New York Code.

The Court single-mindedly focuses on whether a suit "may" or "may not" be maintained as a class action. Putting the question that way, the Court does not home in on the reason *why*. Rule 23 authorizes class treatment for suits satisfying its prerequisites because the class mechanism generally affords a fair and efficient way to aggregate claims for adjudication. Section 901(b) responds to an entirely different concern; it does not allow class members to recover statutory damages because the New York Legislature considered the result of adjudicating such claims en masse to be exorbitant. The fair and efficient *conduct* of class litigation is the legitimate concern of Rule 23; the *remedy* for an infraction of state law, however, is the legitimate concern of the State's lawmakers and not of the federal rulemakers.

Suppose, for example, that a State, wishing to cap damages in class actions at $1,000,000, enacted a statute providing that "a suit to recover more than $1,000,000 may not be maintained as a class action." Under the Court's reasoning—which attributes dispositive significance to the words "may not be maintained"—Rule 23 would preempt this provision, nevermind that Congress, by authorizing the promulgation of rules of procedure for federal courts, surely did not intend to displace state-created ceilings on damages. The Court suggests that the analysis might differ if the statute limited the remedies available in an existing class action, such that Rule 23 might not conflict with a state statute prescribing that no more than $1,000,000 may be recovered in a class action. There is no real difference in the purpose and intended effect of these two hypothetical statutes. . . .

The absence of an inevitable collision between Rule 23 and § 901(b) becomes evident once it is comprehended that a federal court sitting in diversity can accord due respect to both state and federal prescriptions. Plaintiffs seeking to vindicate claims for which the State has provided a statutory penalty may pursue relief through a class action if they forgo statutory damages and instead seek actual damages or injunctive or declaratory relief; any putative class member who objects can opt out and pursue actual damages, if available, and the statutory penalty in an individual action. In this manner, the Second Circuit explained, Rule 23's procedural requirements for class actions can be applied along with the substantive requirement of CPLR 901(b). In sum, while phrased as responsive to the question whether certain class actions may begin, § 901(b) is unmistakably aimed at controlling how those actions must end. On that remedial issue, Rule 23 is silent. . . .

By finding a conflict without considering whether Rule 23 rationally should be read to avoid any collision, the Court unwisely and unnecessarily retreats from the federalism principles undergirding *Erie*. . . .

II

Because I perceive no unavoidable conflict between Rule 23 and § 901(b), I would decide this case by inquiring whether application of the state rule would have so important an effect upon the fortunes of one or both of the litigants that failure to apply it would be likely to cause a plaintiff to choose the federal court.

. . . . By barring the recovery of statutory damages in a class action, § 901(b) controls a defendant's maximum liability in a suit seeking such a remedy. The remedial provision could have been written as an explicit cap: "In any class action seeking statutory damages, relief is limited to the amount the named plaintiff would have recovered in an individual suit." That New York's Legislature used other words to express the very same meaning should be inconsequential.

We have long recognized the impropriety of displacing, in a diversity action, state-law limitations on state-created remedies. . . . I would therefore hold that the New York Legislature's limitation on the recovery of statutory damages applies in this case, and would affirm the Second Circuit's judgment.

Federal Common Law

Introduction

Although *Erie* declared the absence of "general federal common law," federal common law does exist, especially in areas preempted by federal statutory or constitutional law. Sometimes, the challenge to federal common law is the presence of state law, as in the mode of *Swift v. Tyson*. Other times, the challenge to federal common law is the absence of congressional authorization. The following questions should guide your reading:

- When is federal common law appropriate?

- What difficulties do courts have in fashioning federal common law? What policies or principles should guide their decisionmaking?

- When should federal courts borrow state-law principles when fashioning standards for federal common law?

- Which branch—Congress or the courts—should have priority in fashioning constitutional remedies? Why?

Clearfield Trust v. United States (1943)

On April 28, 1936, a check was drawn on the Treasurer of the United States through the Federal Reserve Bank of Philadelphia to the order of Clair A. Barner in the amount of $24.20. It was dated at Harrisburg, Pennsylvania and was drawn for services rendered by Barner to the Works Progress Administration. The check was placed in the mail addressed to Barner at his address in Mackeyville, Pa. Barner never received the check. Some unknown person obtained it in a mysterious manner and presented it to the J. C. Penney Co. store in Clearfield, Pa., representing that he was the payee and identifying himself to the satisfaction of the employees of J. C. Penney. He endorsed the check in the name of Barner and transferred it to J. C. Penney in exchange for cash and merchandise. Barner never authorized the endorsement nor participated in the proceeds of the check. J. C. Penney endorsed the check over to the Clearfield Trust Co. which accepted it as agent for the purpose of collection and endorsed it as follows: "Pay to the order of Federal Reserve Bank of Philadelphia, Prior Endorsements Guaranteed." Clearfield Trust collected the check from the United States through the Federal Reserve Bank of Philadelphia and paid the full amount thereof to J. C. Penney. Neither Clearfield Trust nor J. C. Penney had any knowledge or suspicion of the forgery. Each acted in good faith. On or before May 10, Barner advised the timekeeper and the foreman of the W.P.A. project on which he was employed that he had not received the check in question. This information was duly communicated to other agents of the United States and on Nov. 30, Barner executed an affidavit alleging that the endorsement of his name on the check was a forgery. No notice was given Clearfield Trust or J. C. Penney of the forgery until Jan. 12, at which time Clearfield Trust was notified. The first notice received by Clearfield Trust that the United States was asking reimbursement was on Aug. 31.

This suit was instituted in 1939 by the United States against the Clearfield Trust, the jurisdiction of the federal District Court [based on a statute providing for jurisdiction when the U.S. is a party]. The cause of action was based on the express guaranty of prior endorsements made by Clearfield Trust. J. C. Penney intervened as a defendant. . . . The District Court held that the rights of the parties were to be determined by the law of Pennsylvania and that since the United States unreasonably delayed in giving notice of the forgery to the Clearfield Trust, it was barred from recovery under [Pennsylvania law]. It accordingly dismissed the complaint. On appeal the Circuit Court of Appeals reversed. . . .

We agree with the Circuit Court of Appeals that the rule of *Erie* does not apply to this action. The rights and duties of the United States on commercial paper which it issues are governed by federal rather than local law. When the United States disburses its funds or pays its debts, it is exercising a constitutional function or power. This check was issued for services performed under the Federal Emergency Relief Act of 1935. The authority to issue the check had its origin in the Constitution and the statutes of the United States and was in no way dependent on the laws of Pennsylvania or of any other state. The duties imposed upon the United States and the rights acquired by it as a result of the issuance find their roots in the same federal sources. In absence of an applicable Act of Congress it is for the federal courts to fashion the governing rule of law according to their own standards. . . .

In our choice of the applicable federal rule we have occasionally selected state law. But reasons which may make state law at times the appropriate federal rule are singularly inappropriate here. The issuance of commercial paper by the United States is on a vast scale and transactions in that paper from issuance to payment will commonly occur in several states. The application of state law, even without the conflict of laws rules of the forum, would subject the rights and duties of the United States to exceptional uncertainty. It would lead to great diversity in results by making identical transactions subject to the vagaries of the laws of the several states. The desirability of a uniform rule is plain. And while the federal law merchant developed for about a century under the regime of *Swift v. Tyson* represented general commercial law rather than a choice of a federal rule designed to protect a federal right, it nevertheless stands as a convenient source of reference for fashioning federal rules applicable to these federal questions.

. . . . If it is shown that the drawee on learning of the forgery did not give prompt notice of it and that damage resulted, recovery by the drawee is barred. The fact that the drawee is the United States and the laches those of its employees are not material. The United States as drawee of commercial paper stands in no different light than any other drawee. As stated in *U.S. v. National Exchange Bank*, "The United States does business on business terms." It is not excepted from the general rules governing the rights and duties of drawees by the largeness of its dealings and its having to employ agents to do what if done by a principal in person would leave no room for doubt. But the damage occasioned by the delay must be established and not left to conjecture. Cases . . . place the burden on the drawee of giving prompt notice of the forgery—injury to the defendant being presumed by the mere fact of delay. But we do not think that he who accepts a forged signature of a payee deserves that preferred treatment. It is his neglect or error in accepting the forger's signature which occasions the loss. He should be allowed to shift that loss to the drawee only on a clear showing that the drawee's delay in notifying him of the forgery caused him damage. No such damage has been shown by Clearfield Trust who so far as appears can still recover from J. C. Penney. The only showing on the part of the latter is contained in the stipulation to the effect that if a check cashed for a customer is returned unpaid or for reclamation a short time after the date on which it is cashed, the employees can often locate the person who cashed it. It is further stipulated that when J. C. Penney was notified of the forgery in the present case none of its employees was able to remember anything about the transaction or check in question. The inference is that the more prompt the notice the more likely the detection of the forger. But that falls short of a showing that the delay caused a manifest loss. It is but another way of saying that mere delay is enough. Affirmed.

De Sylva v. Ballantine (1956)

The present Copyright Act provides for a second 28-year copyright after the expiration of the original 28-year term, if application for renewal is made within one year before the expiration of the original term. This right to renew the copyright appears in § 24 of the Act:

> [I]n the case of any other copyrighted work, the author of such work, if still living, or the widow, widower, or children of the author, if the author be not living, . . . shall be entitled to a renewal and extension of the copyright in such work for a further term of twenty-eight years when application for such renewal and extension shall have been made to the copyright office and duly registered therein within one year prior to the expiration of the original term of copyright.

In this case, an author who secured original copyright on numerous musical compositions died before the time to apply for renewals arose. He was survived by his widow and one illegitimate child, who are both still living. The question this case presents is whether that child is entitled to share in the copyrights which come up for renewal during the widow's lifetime.

Respondent, the child's mother, brought this action on the child's behalf against the widow, who is the petitioner here, seeking a declaratory judgment that the child has an interest in the copyrights already renewed by the widow and those that will become renewable during her lifetime, and for an accounting of profits from such copyrights as have been already renewed. The District Court, holding that the child was within the meaning of the term "children" as used in the statute but that the renewal rights belonged exclusively to the widow, gave judgment for the widow. Agreeing with the District Court on the first point, the Court of Appeals reversed, holding that on the author's death both widow and child shared in the renewal copyrights. Because of the great importance of these questions in the administration of the Copyright Act, we granted certiorari.

. . . . We come, then, to the question of whether an illegitimate child is included within the term "children" as used in § 24. The scope of a federal right is, of course, a federal question, but that does not mean that its content is not to be determined by state, rather than federal law. This is especially true where a statute deals with a familial relationship; there is no federal law of domestic relations, which is primarily a matter of state concern.

If we look at the other persons who, under this section of the Copyright Act, are entitled to renew the copyright after the author's death, it is apparent that this is the general scheme of the statute. To decide who is the widow or widower of a deceased author, or who are his executors or next of kin, requires a reference to the law of the State which created those legal relationships. The word "children," although it to some extent describes a purely physical relationship, also describes a legal status not unlike the others. To determine whether a child has been legally adopted, for example, requires a reference to state law. We think it proper, therefore, to draw on the ready-made body of state law to define the word "children" in § 24. This does not mean that a State would be entitled to use the word "children" in a way entirely strange to those familiar with its ordinary usage, but at least to the extent that there are permissible variations in the ordinary concept of "children" we deem state law controlling.

This raises two questions: first, to what State do we look, and second, given a particular State, what part of that State's law defines the relationship. The answer to the first question, in this case, is not difficult, since it appears from the record that the only State concerned is California, and both parties have argued the case on that assumption. The second question, however, is less clear. An illegitimate child who is acknowledged by his father, by a writing signed in the presence of a witness, is entitled under [California law] to inherit his father's estate as well as his mother's. . . .

Considering the purposes of § 24 of the Copyright Act, we think it sufficient that the status of the child is that described by [California law]. The evident purpose of § 24 is to provide for the family of the author after his death. Since the author cannot assign his family's renewal rights, § 24 takes the form of a compulsory bequest of the copyright to the designated persons. This is really a question of the descent of property, and we think the controlling question under state law should be whether the child would be an heir of the author. It is clear that under [California law] the child is, at least to that extent, included within the term "children."

. . . . For the foregoing reasons, the judgment of the Court of Appeals is affirmed.

Semtek International v. Lockheed Martin (2001)

This case presents the question whether the claim-preclusive effect of a federal judgment dismissing a diversity action on statute-of-limitations grounds is determined by the law of the State in which the federal court sits.

Petitioner filed a complaint against respondent in California state court, alleging inducement of breach of contract and various business torts. Respondent removed the case to the United States District Court for the Central District of California on the basis of diversity of citizenship and successfully moved to dismiss petitioner's claims as barred by California's 2-year statute of limitations. In its order of dismissal, the District Court, adopting language suggested by respondent, dismissed petitioner's claims "in [their] entirety on the merits and with prejudice." Without contesting the District Court's designation of its dismissal as "on the merits," petitioner appealed to the Court of Appeals for the Ninth Circuit, which affirmed the District Court's order.

Petitioner also brought suit against respondent in the State Circuit Court for Baltimore City, Maryland, alleging the same causes of action, which were not time barred under Maryland's 3-year statute of limitations. Respondent sought injunctive relief against this action from the California federal court under the All Writs Act and removed the action to the United States District Court for the District of Maryland on federal-question grounds (diversity grounds were not available because Lockheed is a Maryland citizen). The California federal court denied the relief requested, and the Maryland federal court remanded the case to state court because the federal question arose only by way of defense. Following a hearing, the Maryland state court granted respondent's motion to dismiss on the ground of res judicata. Petitioner then returned to the California federal court and the Ninth Circuit, unsuccessfully moving both courts to amend the former's earlier order so as to indicate that the dismissal was not "on the merits." Petitioner also appealed the Maryland trial court's order of dismissal to the Maryland Court of Special Appeals. The Court of Special Appeals affirmed, holding that, regardless of whether California would have accorded claim-preclusive effect to a statute-of-limitations dismissal by one of its own courts, the dismissal by the California federal court barred the complaint filed in Maryland, since the res judicata effect of federal diversity judgments is prescribed by federal law, under which the earlier dismissal was on the merits and claim preclusive. After the Maryland Court of Appeals declined to review the case, we granted certiorari.

. . . . Neither the Full Faith and Credit Clause, nor the full faith and credit statute, addresses the question. By their terms they govern the effects to be given only to state-court judgments (and, in the case of the statute, to judgments by courts of territories and possessions). And no other federal textual provision, neither of the Constitution nor of any statute, addresses the claim-preclusive effect of a judgment in a federal diversity action.

It is also true, however, that no federal textual provision addresses the claim-preclusive effect of a federal-court judgment in a federal-question case, yet we have long held that States cannot give those judgments merely whatever effect they would give their own judgments, but must accord them the effect that this Court prescribes. The reasoning of that line of cases suggests, moreover, that even when States are allowed to give federal judgments (notably, judgments in diversity cases) no more than the effect accorded to state judgments, that disposition is by direction of *this* Court, which has the last word on the claim-preclusive effect of *all* federal judgments . . . . In short, federal common law governs the claim-preclusive effect of a dismissal by a federal court sitting in diversity.

It is left to us, then, to determine the appropriate federal rule. . . . Since state, rather than federal, substantive law is at issue there is no need for a uniform federal rule. And indeed, nationwide uniformity in the substance of the matter is better served by having the same claim-preclusive rule (the state rule) apply whether the dismissal has been ordered by a state or a federal court. This is, it seems to us, a classic case for adopting, as the federally prescribed rule of decision, the law that would be applied by state courts in the State in which the federal diversity court sits. As we have alluded to above, any other rule would produce the sort of forum-shopping and inequitable administration of the laws that *Erie* seeks to avoid, since filing in, or removing to, federal court would be encouraged by the divergent effects that the litigants would anticipate from likely grounds of dismissal.

This federal reference to state law will not obtain, of course, in situations in which the state law is incompatible with federal interests. If, for example, state law did not accord claim-preclusive effect to dismissals for willful violation of discovery orders, federal courts' interest in the integrity of their own processes might justify a contrary federal rule. No such conflict with potential federal interests exists in the present case. Dismissal of this state cause of action was decreed by the California federal court only because the California statute of limitations so required; and there is no conceivable federal interest in giving that time bar more effect in other courts than the California courts themselves would impose.

Because the claim-preclusive effect of the California federal court's dismissal "upon the merits" of petitioner's action on statute-of-limitations grounds is governed by a federal rule that in turn incorporates California's law of claim preclusion (the content of which we do not pass upon today), the Maryland Court of Special Appeals erred in holding that the dismissal necessarily precluded the bringing of this action in the Maryland courts. The judgment is reversed, and the case remanded for further proceedings not inconsistent with this opinion.

Bivens v. Six Unknown Named Agents (1971)

Mr. Justice BRENNAN delivered the opinion of the Court.

The Fourth Amendment provides that: "The right of the people to be secure in their persons, houses, papers, and effects, against unreasonable searches and seizures, shall not be violated. . . ."

[W]e [previously] reserved the question whether violation of that command by a federal agent acting under color of his authority gives rise to a cause of action for damages consequent upon his unconstitutional conduct. Today we hold that it does.

This case has its origin in an arrest and search carried out on the morning of November 26, 1965. Petitioner's complaint alleged that on that day respondents, agents of the Federal Bureau of Narcotics acting under claim of federal authority, entered his apartment and arrested him for alleged narcotics violations. The agents manacled petitioner in front of his wife and children, and threatened to arrest the entire family. They searched the apartment from stem to stern. Thereafter, petitioner was taken to the federal courthouse in Brooklyn, where he was interrogated, booked, and subjected to a visual strip search.

On July 7, 1967, petitioner brought suit in Federal District Court. In addition to the allegations above, his complaint asserted that the arrest and search were effected without a warrant, and that unreasonable force was employed in making the arrest; fairly read, it alleges as well that the arrest was made without probable cause. Petitioner claimed to have suffered great humiliation, embarrassment, and mental suffering as a result of the agents' unlawful conduct, and sought $15,000 damages from each of them. The District Court, on respondents' motion, dismissed the complaint on the ground, inter alia, that it failed to state a cause of action. . . . The Court of Appeals, one judge concurring specially, affirmed on that basis. We granted certiorari. We reverse.

I

Respondents do not argue that petitioner should be entirely without remedy for an unconstitutional invasion of his rights by federal agents. In respondents' view, however, the rights that petitioner asserts—primarily rights of privacy—are creations of state and not of federal law. Accordingly, they argue, petitioner may obtain money damages to redress invasion of these rights only by an action in tort, under state law, in the state courts. In this scheme the Fourth Amendment would serve merely to limit the extent to which the agents could defend the state law tort suit by asserting that their actions were a valid exercise of federal power: if the agents were shown to have violated the Fourth Amendment, such a defense would be lost to them and they would stand before the state law merely as private individuals. Candidly admitting that it is the policy of the Department of Justice to remove all such suits from the state to the federal courts for decision, respondents nevertheless urge that we uphold dismissal of petitioner's complaint in federal court, and remit him to filing an action in the state courts in order that the case may properly be removed to the federal court for decision on the basis of state law.

We think that respondents' thesis rests upon an unduly restrictive view of the Fourth Amendment's protection against unreasonable searches and seizures by federal agents, a view that has consistently been rejected by this Court. Respondents seek to treat the relationship between a citizen and a federal agent unconstitutionally exercising his authority as no different from the relationship between two private citizens. In so doing, they ignore the fact that power, once granted, does not disappear like a magic gift when it is wrongfully used. An agent acting—albeit unconstitutionally—in the name of the United States possesses a far greater capacity for harm than an individual trespasser exercising no authority other than his own. Accordingly, as our cases make clear, the Fourth Amendment operates as a limitation upon the exercise of federal power regardless of whether the State in whose jurisdiction that power is exercised would prohibit or penalize the identical act if engaged in by a private citizen. It guarantees to citizens of the United States the absolute right to be free from unreasonable searches and seizures carried out by virtue of federal authority. And where federally protected rights have been invaded, it has been the rule from the beginning that courts will be alert to adjust their remedies so as to grant the necessary relief.

First. Our cases have long since rejected the notion that the Fourth Amendment proscribes only such conduct as would, if engaged in by private persons, be condemned by state law. . . . In light of these cases, respondents' argument that the Fourth Amendment serves only as a limitation on federal defenses to a state law claim, and not as an independent limitation upon the exercise of federal power, must be rejected.

Second. The interests protected by state laws regulating trespass and the invasion of privacy, and those protected by the Fourth Amendment's guarantee against unreasonable searches and seizures, may be inconsistent or even hostile. Thus, we may bar the door against an unwelcome private intruder, or call the police if he persists in seeking entrance. The availability of such alternative means for the protection of privacy may lead the State to restrict imposition of liability for any consequent trespass. A private citizen, asserting no authority other than his own, will not normally be liable in trespass if he demands, and is granted, admission to another's house. But one who demands admission under a claim of federal authority stands in a far different position. The mere invocation of federal power by a federal law enforcement official will normally render futile any attempt to resist an unlawful entry or arrest by resort to the local police; and a claim of authority to enter is likely to unlock the door as well. In such cases there is no safety for the citizen, except in the protection of the judicial tribunals, for rights which have been invaded by the officers of the government, professing to act in its name. There remains to him but the alternative of resistance, which may amount to crime. Nor is it adequate to answer that state law may take into account the different status of one clothed with the authority of the Federal Government. For just as state law may not authorize federal agents to violate the Fourth Amendment, neither may state law undertake to limit the extent to which federal authority can be exercised. The inevitable consequence of this dual limitation on state power is that the federal question becomes not merely a possible defense to the state law action, but an independent claim both necessary and sufficient to make out the plaintiff's cause of action.

Third. That damages may be obtained for injuries consequent upon a violation of the Fourth Amendment by federal officials should hardly seem a surprising proposition. Historically, damages have been regarded as the ordinary remedy for an invasion of personal interests in liberty. Of course, the Fourth Amendment does not in so many words provide for its enforcement by an award of money damages for the consequences of its violation. But it is well settled that where legal rights have been invaded, and a federal statute provides for a general right to sue for such invasion, federal courts may use any available remedy to make good the wrong done. The present case involves no special factors counseling hesitation in the absence of affirmative action by Congress. We are not dealing with a question of federal fiscal policy . . . . Nor are we asked in this case to impose liability upon a congressional employee for actions contrary to no constitutional prohibition, but merely said to be in excess of the authority delegated to him by the Congress.

Finally, we cannot accept respondents' formulation of the question as whether the availability of money damages is necessary to enforce the Fourth Amendment. For we have here no explicit congressional declaration that persons injured by a federal officer's violation of the Fourth Amendment may not recover money damages from the agents, but must instead be remitted to another remedy, equally effective in the view of Congress. The question is merely whether petitioner, if he can demonstrate an injury consequent upon the violation by federal agents of his Fourth Amendment rights, is entitled to redress his injury through a particular remedial mechanism normally available in the federal courts. "The very essence of civil liberty certainly consists in the right of every individual to claim the protection of the laws, whenever he receives an injury." *Marbury v. Madison.* Having concluded that petitioner's complaint states a cause of action under the Fourth Amendment, we hold that petitioner is entitled to recover money damages for any injuries he has suffered as a result of the agents' violation of the Amendment. . . .

Judgment reversed and case remanded. . . .

Mr. Chief Justice BURGER, dissenting.

I dissent from today's holding which judicially creates a damage remedy not provided for by the Constitution and not enacted by Congress. We would more surely preserve the important values of the doctrine of separation of powers—and perhaps get a better result—by recommending a solution to the Congress as the branch of government in which the Constitution has vested the legislative power. Legislation is the business of the Congress, and it has the facilities and competence for that task—as we do not. . . .

Mr. Justice BLACK, dissenting.

. . . . There can be no doubt that Congress could create a federal cause of action for damages for an unreasonable search in violation of the Fourth Amendment. Although Congress has created such a federal cause of action against state officials acting under color of state law,[*] it has never created such a cause of action against federal officials. If it wanted to do so, Congress could, of course, create a remedy against federal officials who violate the Fourth Amendment in the performance of their duties. But the point of this case and the fatal weakness in the Court's judgment is that neither Congress nor the State of New York has enacted legislation creating such a right of action. For us to do so is, in my judgment, an exercise of power that the Constitution does not give us.

> [*] "Every person who, under color of any statute, ordinance, regulation, custom, or usage, of any State or Territory, subjects, or causes to be subjected, any citizen of the United States or other person within the jurisdiction thereof to the deprivation of any rights, privileges, or immunities secured by the Constitution and laws, shall be liable to the party injured in an action at law, suit in equity, or other proper proceeding for redress." 42 U.S.C. § 1983.

Even if we had the legislative power to create a remedy, there are many reasons why we should decline to create a cause of action where none has existed since the formation of our Government. The courts of the United States as well as those of the States are choked with lawsuits. The number of cases on the docket of this Court have reached an unprecedented volume in recent years. A majority of these cases are brought by citizens with substantial complaints—persons who are physically or economically injured by torts or frauds or governmental infringement of their rights; persons who have been unjustly deprived of their liberty or their property; and persons who have not yet received the equal opportunity in education, employment, and pursuit of happiness that was the dream of our forefathers. Unfortunately, there have also been a growing number of frivolous lawsuits, particularly actions for damages against law enforcement officers whose conduct has been judicially sanctioned by state trial and appellate courts and in many instances even by this Court. My fellow Justices on this Court and our brethren throughout the federal judiciary know only too well the time-consuming task of conscientiously poring over hundreds of thousands of pages of factual allegations of misconduct by police, judicial, and corrections officials. Of course, there are instances of legitimate grievances, but legislators might well desire to devote judicial resources to other problems of a more serious nature. . . .

All of these considerations make imperative careful study and weighing of the arguments both for and against the creation of such a remedy under the Fourth Amendment. I would have great difficulty for myself in resolving the competing policies, goals, and priorities in the use of resources, if I thought it were my job to resolve those questions. But that is not my task. The task of evaluating the pros and cons of creating judicial remedies for particular wrongs is a matter for Congress and the legislatures of the States. Congress has not provided that any federal court can entertain a suit against a federal officer for violations of Fourth Amendment rights occurring in the performance of his duties. A strong inference can be drawn from creation of such actions against state officials that Congress does not desire to permit such suits against federal officials. Should the time come when Congress desires such lawsuits, it has before it a model of valid legislation, § 1983, to create a damage remedy against federal officers. Cases could be cited to support the legal proposition which I assert, but it seems to me to be a matter of common understanding that the business of the judiciary is to interpret the laws and not to make them.

Mr. Justice BLACKMUN, dissenting.

I, too, dissent. . . . I also feel that the judicial legislation, which the Court by its opinion today concededly is effectuating, opens the door for another avalanche of new federal cases. Whenever a suspect imagines, or chooses to assert, that a Fourth Amendment right has been violated, he will now immediately sue the federal officer in federal court. This will tend to stultify proper law enforcement and to make the day's labor for the honest and conscientious officer even more onerous and more critical. Why the Court moves in this direction at this time of our history, I do not know. The Fourth Amendment was adopted in 1791, and in all the intervening years neither the Congress nor the Court has seen fit to take this step. I had thought that for the truly aggrieved person other quite adequate remedies have always been available. If not, it is the Congress and not this Court that should act.

Carlson v. Green (1980)

Mr. Justice BRENNAN delivered the opinion of the Court.

Respondent brought this suit in the District Court for the Southern District of Indiana on behalf of the estate of her deceased son, Joseph Jones, Jr., alleging that he suffered personal injuries from which he died because the petitioners, federal prison officials, violated his due process, equal protection, and Eighth Amendment rights. Asserting jurisdiction under 28 U.S.C. § 1331(a), she claimed compensatory and punitive damages for the constitutional violations. Two questions are presented for decision: (1) Is a remedy available directly under the Constitution, given that respondent's allegations could also support a suit against the United States under the Federal Tort Claims Act? And (2) if so, is survival of the cause of action governed by federal common law or by state statutes?

I

The District Court held that [the plaintiff] pleaded a violation of the Eighth Amendment's proscription against infliction of cruel and unusual punishment, giving rise to a cause of action for damages under *Bivens*. The court recognized that the decedent could have maintained this action if he had survived, but dismissed the complaint because in its view the damages remedy as a matter of federal law was limited to that provided by Indiana's survivorship and wrongful-death laws and, as the court construed those laws, the damages available to Jones's estate failed to meet § 1331(a)'s $10,000 jurisdictional-amount requirement. The Court of Appeals for the Seventh Circuit agreed that an Eighth Amendment violation was pleaded under *Estelle* and that a cause of action was stated under *Bivens*, but reversed the holding that § 1331(a)'s jurisdictional-amount requirement was not met. Rather, the Court of Appeals held that § 1331(a) was satisfied because whenever the relevant state survival statute would abate a *Bivens*-type action brought against defendants whose conduct results in death, the federal common law allows survival of the action. The court reasoned that the Indiana law, if applied, would subvert the policy of allowing complete vindication of constitutional rights by making it more advantageous for a tortfeasor to kill rather than to injure. We granted certiorari. We affirm.

II

Bivens established that the victims of a constitutional violation by a federal agent have a right to recover damages against the official in federal court despite the absence of any statute conferring such a right. Such a cause of action may be defeated in a particular case, however, in two situations. The first is when defendants demonstrate special factors counselling hesitation in the absence of affirmative action by Congress. The second is when defendants show that Congress has provided an alternative remedy which it explicitly declared to be a *substitute* for recovery directly under the Constitution and viewed as equally effective.

Neither situation obtains in this case. First, the case involves no special factors counselling hesitation in the absence of affirmative action by Congress. Petitioners do not enjoy such independent status in our constitutional scheme as to suggest that judicially created remedies against them might be inappropriate. Moreover, even if requiring them to defend respondent's suit might inhibit their efforts to perform their official duties, the qualified immunity accorded them under [our decisions] provides adequate protection.

Second, we have here no explicit congressional declaration that persons injured by federal officers' violations of the Eighth Amendment may not recover money damages from the agents but must be remitted to another remedy, equally effective in the view of Congress. Petitioners point to nothing in the Federal Tort Claims Act (FTCA) or its legislative history to show that Congress meant to pre-empt a *Bivens* remedy or to create an equally effective remedy for constitutional violations. FTCA was enacted long before *Bivens* was decided, but when Congress amended FTCA in 1974 to create a cause of action against the United States for intentional torts committed by federal law enforcement officers, the congressional comments accompanying that amendment made it crystal clear that Congress views FTCA and *Bivens* as parallel, complementary causes of action . . . . This conclusion is buttressed by the significant fact that Congress follows the practice of explicitly stating when it means to make FTCA an exclusive remedy. Furthermore, Congress has not taken action on other bills that would expand the exclusivity of FTCA.

Four additional factors, each suggesting that the *Bivens* remedy is more effective than the FTCA remedy, also support our conclusion that Congress did not intend to limit respondent to an FTCA action. First, the *Bivens* remedy, in addition to compensating victims, serves a deterrent purpose. Because the *Bivens* remedy is recoverable against individuals, it is a more effective deterrent than the FTCA remedy against the United States. It is almost axiomatic that the threat of damages has a deterrent effect, surely particularly so when the individual official faces personal financial liability.

Petitioners argue that FTCA liability is a more effective deterrent because the individual employees responsible for the Government's liability would risk loss of employment and because the Government would be forced to promulgate corrective policies. That argument suggests, however, that the superiors would not take the same actions when an employee is found personally liable for violation of a citizen's constitutional rights. The more reasonable assumption is that responsible superiors are motivated not only by concern for the public fisc but also by concern for the Government's integrity.

Second, our decisions, although not expressly addressing and deciding the question, indicate that punitive damages may be awarded in a *Bivens* suit. Punitive damages are a particular remedial mechanism normally available in the federal courts, and are especially appropriate to redress the violation by a Government official of a citizen's constitutional rights. Moreover, punitive damages are available in a proper § 1983 action, and . . . the constitutional design would be stood on its head if federal officials did not face at least the same liability as state officials guilty of the same constitutional transgression. But punitive damages in an FTCA suit are statutorily prohibited. Thus FTCA is that much less effective than a *Bivens* action as a deterrent to unconstitutional acts.

Third, a plaintiff cannot opt for a jury in an FTCA action, as he may in a *Bivens* suit. Petitioners argue that this is an irrelevant difference because juries have been biased against *Bivens* claimants. Significantly, however, they do not assert that judges trying the claims as FTCA actions would have been more receptive, and they cannot explain why the plaintiff should not retain the choice.

Fourth, an action under FTCA exists only if the State in which the alleged misconduct occurred would permit a cause of action for that misconduct to go forward. Yet it is obvious that the liability of federal officials for violations of citizens' constitutional rights should be governed by uniform rules. The question whether respondent's action for violations by federal officials of federal constitutional rights should be left to the vagaries of the laws of the several States admits of only a negative answer in the absence of a contrary congressional resolution.

Plainly FTCA is not a sufficient protector of the citizens' constitutional rights, and without a clear congressional mandate we cannot hold that Congress relegated respondent exclusively to the FTCA remedy.

III

Bivens actions are a creation of federal law and, therefore, the question whether respondent's action survived Jones' death is a question of federal law. Petitioners, however, would have us fashion a federal rule of survivorship that incorporates the survivorship laws of the forum State, at least where the state law is not inconsistent with federal law. Respondent argues, on the other hand, that only a uniform federal rule of survivorship is compatible with the goal of deterring federal officials from infringing federal constitutional rights in the manner alleged in respondent's complaint. We agree with respondent. Whatever difficulty we might have resolving the question were the federal involvement less clear, we hold that only a uniform federal rule of survivorship will suffice to redress the constitutional deprivation here alleged and to protect against repetition of such conduct. . . . *Affirmed.*

Mr. Chief Justice BURGER, dissenting.

Although I would be prepared to join an opinion giving effect to *Bivens*—which I thought wrongly decided—I cannot join today's unwarranted expansion of that decision. The Federal Tort Claims Act provides an adequate remedy for prisoners' claims of medical mistreatment. For me, that is the end of the matter. . . .

Until today, I had thought that *Bivens* was limited to those circumstances in which a civil rights plaintiff had no other effective remedy. Now it would seem that implication of a *Bivens*-type remedy is permissible even though a victim of unlawful official action may be fully recompensed under an existing statutory scheme. I have difficulty believing that the Court has thought through, and intends the natural consequences of, this novel test; I cannot escape the conclusion that in future cases the Court will be obliged to retreat from the language of today's decision.

Mr. Justice REHNQUIST, dissenting.

The Court today adopts a formalistic procedural approach for inferring private damages remedies from constitutional provisions that in my view still further highlights the wrong turn this Court took in *Bivens* . . . . In my view, it is an exercise of power that the Constitution does not give us for this Court to infer a private civil damages remedy from the Eighth Amendment or any other constitutional provision. The creation of such remedies is a task that is more appropriately viewed as falling within the legislative sphere of authority.

I

. . . . Despite the lack of a textual constitutional foundation or any precedential or other historical support, *Bivens* inferred a constitutional damages remedy from the Fourth Amendment, authorizing a party whose constitutional rights had been infringed by a federal officer to recover damages from that officer. . . . And the Court today further adds to the growing list of Amendments from which a civil damages remedy may be inferred. In so doing, the Court appears to be fashioning for itself a legislative role resembling that once thought to be the domain of Congress, when the latter created a damages remedy for individuals whose constitutional rights had been violated by state officials, § 1983 . . . .

In my view the authority of federal courts to fashion remedies based on the common law of damages for constitutional violations likewise falls within the legislative domain, and does not exist where not conferred by Congress. The determination by federal courts of the scope of such a remedy involves the creation of a body of common law analogous to that repudiated in *Erie* . . . . This determination raises such questions as the types of damages recoverable, the injuries compensable, the degree of intent required for recovery, and the extent to which official immunity will be available as a defense. And the creation of such a remedy by federal courts has the effect of diverting judicial resources from areas that Congress has explicitly provided for by statute. It thereby may impair the ability of federal courts to comply with judicial priorities established by Congress. . . .

In my view, absent a clear indication from Congress, federal courts lack the authority to grant damages relief for constitutional violations. Although Congress surely may direct federal courts to grant relief in *Bivens*-type actions, it is enough that it has not done so. . . .

II

. . . . The Court not only fails to explain why the *Bivens* remedy is effective in the promotion of deterrence, but also does not provide any reason for believing that other sanctions on federal employees—such as a threat of deductions in pay, reprimand, suspension, or firing—will be ineffective in promoting the desired level of deterrence, or that Congress did not consider the marginal increase in deterrence here to be outweighed by other considerations. And while it may be generally true that the extent to which a sanction is imposed directly on a wrongdoer will have an impact on the effectiveness of a deterrent remedy, there are also a number of other factors that must be taken into account—such as the amount of damages necessary to offset the benefits of the objectionable conduct, the risk that the wrongdoer might escape liability, the clarity with which the objectionable conduct is defined, and the perceptions of the individual who is a potential wrongdoer. In a *Bivens* action, however, there is no relationship whatsoever between the damages awarded and the benefits from infringing the individual's rights because the damages award focuses solely on the loss to the plaintiff. The damages in such an action do not take into account the risk that the wrongdoer will escape liability altogether. In addition, it is often not clear what conduct violates the Constitution. In many cases the uncertainty as to what constitutes a constitutional violation will impair the deterrent impact of a *Bivens* remedy. Finally, the perceptions of the potential wrongdoer as to the above considerations may also detract from the deterrent effect of a *Bivens* action. The Court makes no attempt to assess these factors or to examine them in relation to an FTCA action. In my view, its assertion that the *Bivens* remedy is a more effective deterrent than the FTCA remedy, and that this is a reason for concluding that Congress intended *Bivens* actions to exist concurrently with FTCA actions, remains an unsupported assertion.

In addition, there are important policy considerations at stake here that Congress may decide outweigh the interest in deterrence promoted by personal liability of federal officials. Indeed, the fear of personal liability may dampen the ardor of all but the most resolute, or the most irresponsible, in the unflinching discharge of their duties. And, as one commentator has observed: "Despite the small odds an employee will actually be held liable in a civil suit, morale within the federal services has suffered as employees have been dragged through drawn-out lawsuits, many of which are frivolous."

The Court next argues that Congress did not intend that FTCA to displace the *Bivens* remedy because it did not provide for punitive damages in the FTCA. . . . Even if punitive damages were appropriate in a *Bivens* action, such damages are typically determined by reference to factors such as the character of the wrong, the amount necessary to "punish" the defendant, etc., and the jury has a great deal of discretion in deciding both whether such damages should be awarded and the amount of the punitive award. The determination whether this or some other remedy—such as a fixed fine, a threat of being reprimanded, suspended, or fired, or simply compensatory damages—provides the desired level of deterrence is one for Congress. This Court should defer to Congress even when Congress has not explicitly stated that its remedy is a substitute for a *Bivens* action.

The third factor relied on by the Court to support its conclusion that Congress did not intend the FTCA to serve as a substitute for a *Bivens* action is that a plaintiff cannot opt for a jury in a FTCA action while he can in a *Bivens* suit. The Court, however, offers no reason why a judge is preferable to a jury, or vice versa, in this context. Rather, the Court merely notes that petitioners cannot explain why plaintiffs should not retain the choice between a judge and jury. I do not think the fact that Congress failed to specify that the FTCA was a substitute for a *Bivens* action supports the conclusion that Congress viewed the plaintiff's ability to choose between a judge and a jury as a reason for retaining a *Bivens* action in addition to an action under the FTCA.

Finally, I do not think it is obvious, as the Court states, that liability of federal officials for violations of constitutional rights should be governed by uniform rules absent an explicit statement by Congress indicating a contrary intention. The importance of federalism in our constitutional system has been recognized both by this Court and by Congress, and in accommodating the values of federalism with other constitutional principles and congressional statutes, this Court has often deferred to state rules. As observed by Mr. Justice Powell, federal courts routinely refer to state law to fill the procedural gaps in national remedial schemes. Indeed, the Rules of Decision Act would seem ordinarily to require it. . . .

Correctional Services Corp. v. Malesko (2001)

Chief Justice REHNQUIST delivered the opinion of the Court.

We decide here whether the implied damages action first recognized in *Bivens* should be extended to allow recovery against a private corporation operating a halfway house under contract with the Bureau of Prisons. We decline to so extend *Bivens*.

Petitioner Correctional Services Corporation (CSC), under contract with the federal Bureau of Prisons (BOP), operates Community Corrections Centers and other facilities that house federal prisoners and detainees. Since the late 1980's, CSC has operated Le Marquis Community Correctional Center (Le Marquis), a halfway house located in New York City. Respondent John E. Malesko is a former federal inmate who, having been convicted of federal securities fraud in December 1992, was sentenced to a term of 18 months' imprisonment under the supervision of the BOP. During his imprisonment, respondent was diagnosed with a heart condition and treated with prescription medication. Respondent's condition limited his ability to engage in physical activity, such as climbing stairs.

In February 1993, the BOP transferred respondent to Le Marquis where he was to serve the remainder of his sentence. Respondent was assigned to living quarters on the fifth floor. On or about March 1, 1994, CSC instituted a policy at Le Marquis requiring inmates residing below the sixth floor to use the staircase rather than the elevator to travel from the first-floor lobby to their rooms. There is no dispute that respondent was exempted from this policy on account of his heart condition. Respondent alleges that on March 28, 1994, however, Jorge Urena, an employee of CSC, forbade him to use the elevator to reach his fifth-floor bedroom. Respondent protested that he was specially permitted elevator access, but Urena was adamant. Respondent then climbed the stairs, suffered a heart attack, and fell, injuring his left ear.

Three years after this incident occurred, respondent filed a *pro se* action against CSC and unnamed CSC employees in the United States District Court for the Southern District of New York. Two years later, now acting with counsel, respondent filed an amended complaint which named Urena as 1 of the 10 John Doe defendants. The amended complaint alleged that CSC, Urena, and unnamed defendants were negligent in failing to obtain requisite medication for respondent's condition and were further negligent by refusing respondent the use of the elevator. It further alleged that respondent injured his left ear and aggravated a pre-existing condition as a result of the negligence of the Defendants. Respondent demanded judgment in the sum of $1 million in compensatory damages, $3 million in anticipated future damages, and punitive damages for such sum as the Court and/or jury may determine.

The District Court . . . dismissed respondent's cause of action in its entirety. . . . The Court of Appeals for the Second Circuit [reversed as to the *Bivens* claims against CSC and] . . . . reasoned that private entities like CSC should be held liable under *Bivens* to accomplish the important *Bivens* goal of providing a remedy for constitutional violations. We granted certiorari and now reverse.

In *Bivens*, we recognized for the first time an implied private action for damages against federal officers alleged to have violated a citizen's constitutional rights. Respondent now asks that we extend this limited holding to confer a right of action for damages against private entities acting under color of federal law. He contends that the Court must recognize a federal remedy at law wherever there has been an alleged constitutional deprivation, no matter that the victim of the alleged deprivation might have alternative remedies elsewhere, and that the proposed remedy would not significantly deter the principal wrongdoer, an individual private employee. We have heretofore refused to imply new substantive liabilities under such circumstances, and we decline to do so here.

Our authority to imply a new constitutional tort, not expressly authorized by statute, is anchored in our general jurisdiction to decide all cases "arising under the Constitution, laws, or treaties of the United States." We first exercised this authority in *Bivens*, where we held that a victim of a Fourth Amendment violation by federal officers may bring suit for money damages against the officers in federal court. *Bivens* acknowledged that Congress had never provided for a private right of action against federal officers, and that the Fourth Amendment does not in so many words provide for its enforcement by award of money damages for the consequences of its violation. Nonetheless, relying largely on earlier decisions implying private damages actions into federal statutes, and finding "no special factors counseling hesitation in the absence of affirmative action by Congress," we found an implied damages remedy available under the Fourth Amendment. . . .

Since *Carlson* we have consistently refused to extend *Bivens* liability to any new context or new category of defendants. . . . Most recently, in *FDIC v. Meyer*, we unanimously declined an invitation to extend *Bivens* to permit suit against a federal agency, even though the agency—because Congress had waived sovereign immunity—was otherwise amenable to suit. Our opinion emphasized that the purpose of *Bivens* is to deter *the officer*, not the agency. We reasoned that if given the choice, plaintiffs would sue a federal agency instead of an individual who could assert qualified immunity as an affirmative defense. To the extent aggrieved parties had less incentive to bring a damages claim against individuals, the deterrent effects of the *Bivens* remedy would be lost. Accordingly, to allow a *Bivens* claim against federal agencies would mean the evisceration of the *Bivens* remedy, rather than its extension. We noted further that "special factors" counseled hesitation in light of the potentially enormous financial burden that agency liability would entail. . . .

[T]he claim urged by respondent is fundamentally different from anything recognized in *Bivens* or subsequent cases. In 30 years of *Bivens* jurisprudence we have extended its holding only twice, to provide an otherwise nonexistent cause of action against *individual officers* alleged to have acted unconstitutionally, or to provide a cause of action for a plaintiff who lacked *any alternative remedy* for harms caused by an individual officer's unconstitutional conduct. Where such circumstances are not present, we have consistently rejected invitations to extend *Bivens*, often for reasons that foreclose its extension here.

The purpose of *Bivens* is to deter individual federal officers from committing constitutional violations. *Meyer* made clear that the threat of litigation and liability will adequately deter federal officers for *Bivens* purposes no matter that they may enjoy qualified immunity, are indemnified by the employing agency or entity, or are acting pursuant to an entity's policy. *Meyer* also made clear that the threat of suit against an individual's employer was not the kind of deterrence contemplated by *Bivens*. This case is, in every meaningful sense, the same. For if a corporate defendant is available for suit, claimants will focus their collection efforts on it, and not the individual directly responsible for the alleged injury. On the logic of *Meyer*, inferring a constitutional tort remedy against a private entity like CSC is therefore foreclosed.

Respondent claims that even under *Meyer*'s deterrence rationale, implying a suit against private corporations acting under color of federal law is still necessary to advance the core deterrence purpose of *Bivens*. He argues that because corporations respond to market pressures and make decisions without regard to constitutional obligations, requiring payment for the constitutional harms they commit is the best way to discourage future harms. That may be so, but it has no relevance to *Bivens*, which is concerned solely with deterring the unconstitutional acts of individual officers. If deterring the conduct of a policymaking entity was the purpose of *Bivens*, then *Meyer* would have implied a damages remedy against the Federal Deposit Insurance Corporation; it was after all an agency policy that led to *Meyer's* constitutional deprivation. But *Bivens* from its inception has been based not on that premise, but on the deterrence of individual officers who commit unconstitutional acts.

There is no reason for us to consider extending *Bivens* beyond this core premise here. To begin with, *no federal prisoners* enjoy respondent's contemplated remedy. If a federal prisoner in a BOP facility alleges a constitutional deprivation, he may bring a *Bivens* claim against the offending individual officer, subject to the defense of qualified immunity. The prisoner may not bring a *Bivens* claim against the officer's employer, the United States, or the BOP. With respect to the alleged constitutional deprivation, his only remedy lies against the individual, a remedy *Meyer* found sufficient, and which respondent did not timely pursue. Whether it makes sense to impose asymmetrical liability costs on private prison facilities alone is a question for Congress, not us, to decide.

Nor are we confronted with a situation in which claimants in respondent's shoes lack effective remedies. It was conceded at oral argument that alternative remedies are at least as great, and in many respects greater, than anything that could be had under *Bivens*. For example, federal prisoners in private facilities enjoy a parallel tort remedy that is unavailable to prisoners housed in Government facilities. . . . [Further,] the heightened "deliberate indifference" standard of Eighth Amendment liability would make it considerably more difficult for respondent to prevail than on a theory of ordinary negligence. . . .

Inmates in respondent's position also have full access to remedial mechanisms established by the BOP, including suits in federal court for injunctive relief and grievances filed through the BOP's Administrative Remedy Program. This program provides yet another means through which allegedly unconstitutional actions and policies can be brought to the attention of the BOP and prevented from recurring. And unlike the *Bivens* remedy, which we have never considered a proper vehicle for altering an entity's policy, injunctive relief has long been recognized as the proper means for preventing entities from acting unconstitutionally.

In sum, respondent is not a plaintiff in search of a remedy as in *Bivens* . . . . Nor does he seek a cause of action against an individual officer, otherwise lacking, as in *Carlson*. Respondent instead seeks a marked extension of *Bivens*, to contexts that would not advance *Bivens*'s core purpose of deterring individual officers from engaging in unconstitutional wrongdoing. The caution toward extending *Bivens* remedies into any new context, a caution consistently and repeatedly recognized for three decades, forecloses such an extension here.

The judgment of the Court of Appeals is reversed.

Justice STEVENS, with whom Justice SOUTER, Justice GINSBURG, and Justice BREYER join, dissenting.

In *Bivens*, the Court affirmatively answered the question . . . whether a violation of the Fourth Amendment by *a federal agent* acting under color of his authority gives rise to a cause of action for damages consequent upon his unconstitutional conduct. Nearly a decade later, in *Carlson v. Green*, we held that a violation of the Eighth Amendment by federal prison officials gave rise to a *Bivens* remedy despite the fact that the plaintiffs also had a remedy against the United States under the Federal Tort Claims Act (FTCA). We stated: "*Bivens* established that the victims of a constitutional violation by *a federal agent* have a right to recover damages against the official in federal court despite the absence of any statute conferring such a right."

In subsequent cases, we have decided that a *Bivens* remedy is not available for every conceivable constitutional violation. We have never, however, qualified our holding that Eighth Amendment violations are actionable under *Bivens*. Nor have we ever suggested that a category of federal agents can commit Eighth Amendment violations with impunity.

The parties before us have assumed that respondent's complaint has alleged a violation of the Eighth Amendment. The violation was committed by a federal agent—a private corporation employed by the Bureau of Prisons to perform functions that would otherwise be performed by individual employees of the Federal Government. Thus, the question presented by this case is whether the Court should create an exception to the straightforward application of *Bivens* and not whether it should extend our cases beyond their "core premise." . . .

Meyer, which concluded that federal agencies are not suable under *Bivens*, does not lead to the outcome reached by the Court today. In that case, we did not discuss private corporate agents, nor suggest that such agents should be viewed differently from human ones. Rather, in *Meyer*, we drew a distinction between "federal agents" and "an agency of the Federal Government." Indeed, our repeated references to the Federal Deposit Insurance Corporation's (FDIC) status as a "federal agency" emphasized the FDIC's affinity to the federal sovereign. We expressed concern that damages sought directly from federal agencies, such as the FDIC, would create a potentially enormous financial burden for the Federal Government. And it must be kept in mind that *Meyer* involved the FDIC's waiver of sovereign immunity, which, had the Court in *Meyer* recognized a cause of action, would have permitted the very sort of lawsuit that *Bivens* presumed impossible: a direct action against the Government.

. . . . Because *Meyer* does not dispose of this case, the Court claims that the rationales underlying *Bivens*—namely, lack of alternative remedies and deterrence—are not present in cases in which suit is brought against a private corporation serving as a federal agent. However, common sense, buttressed by all of the reasons that supported the holding in *Bivens*, leads to the conclusion that corporate agents should not be treated more favorably than human agents.

First, the Court argues that respondent enjoys alternative remedies against the corporate agent that distinguish this case from *Bivens*. In doing so, the Court characterizes *Bivens* and its progeny as cases in which plaintiffs lacked "*any alternative remedy.*" In *Bivens,* however, even though the plaintiff's suit against the Federal Government under state tort law may have been barred by sovereign immunity, a suit against the officer himself under state tort law was theoretically possible. Moreover, as the Court recognized in *Carlson, Bivens* plaintiffs also have remedies available under the FTCA. Thus, the Court is incorrect to portray *Bivens* plaintiffs as lacking any other avenue of relief, and to imply as a result that respondent in this case had a substantially wider array of non-*Bivens* remedies at his disposal than do other *Bivens* plaintiffs. If alternative remedies provide a sufficient justification for closing the federal forum here, where the defendant is a private corporation, the claims against the individual defendants in *Carlson*, in light of the FTCA alternative, should have been rejected as well.

It is ironic that the Court relies so heavily for its holding on this assumption that alternative effective remedies—primarily negligence actions in state court—are available to respondent. Like Justice Harlan, I think it entirely proper that these injuries be compensable according to uniform rules of federal law, especially in light of the very large element of federal law which must in any event control the scope of official defenses to liability. And aside from undermining uniformity, the Court's reliance on state tort law will jeopardize the protection of the full scope of federal constitutional rights. State law might have comparable causes of action for tort claims like the Eighth Amendment violation alleged here, but other unconstitutional actions by prison employees, such as violations of the Equal Protection or Due Process Clauses, may find no parallel causes of action in state tort law. Even though respondent here may have been able to sue for some degree of relief under state law because his Eighth Amendment claim could have been pleaded as negligence, future plaintiffs with constitutional claims less like traditional torts will not necessarily be so situated.

Second, the Court claims that the deterrence goals of *Bivens* would not be served by permitting liability here. It cannot be seriously maintained, however, that tort remedies against corporate employers have less deterrent value than actions against their employees. As the Court has previously noted, the organizational structure of private prisons is one subject to the ordinary competitive pressures that normally help private firms adjust their behavior in response to the incentives that tort suits provide—pressures not necessarily present in government departments. Thus, the private corporate entity at issue here is readily distinguishable from the federal agency in *Meyer*. Indeed, a tragic consequence of today's decision is the clear incentive it gives to corporate managers of privately operated custodial institutions to adopt cost-saving policies that jeopardize the constitutional rights of the tens of thousands of inmates in their custody.[9]

[9] As *amici* for respondent explain, private prisons are exempt from much of the oversight and public accountability faced by the Bureau of Prisons, a federal entity. Indeed, because a private prison corporation's first loyalty is to its stockholders, rather than the public interest, it is no surprise that cost-cutting measures jeopardizing prisoners' rights are more likely in private facilities than in public ones.

The Court raises a concern with imposing asymmetrical liability costs on private prison facilities and further claims that because federal prisoners in Government-run institutions can only sue officers, it would be unfair to permit federal prisoners in private institutions to sue an officer's employer. Permitting liability in the present case, however, would *produce* symmetry: both private and public prisoners would be unable to sue the principal (*i.e.*, the Government), but would be able to sue the primary federal agent (*i.e.*, the Government official or the corporation). Indeed, it is the *Court*'s decision that creates asymmetry—between federal and state prisoners housed in private correctional facilities. Under 42 U.S.C. § 1983, a state prisoner may sue a private prison for deprivation of constitutional rights, yet the Court denies such a remedy to that prisoner's federal counterpart. . . .

I respectfully dissent.

Hernández v. Mesa (2020)

Justice ALITO delivered the opinion of the Court.

. . . . Sergio Adrián Hernández Güereca, a 15-year-old Mexican national, was with a group of friends in a concrete culvert that separates El Paso, Texas, from Ciudad Juarez, Mexico. . . . . Border Patrol Agent Jesus Mesa, Jr., detained one of Hernández's friends who had run onto the U.S. side of the culvert. After Hernández, who was also on the U.S. side, ran back across the culvert onto Mexican soil, Agent Mesa fired two shots at Hernández; one struck and killed him on the other side of the border.

Petitioners and Agent Mesa disagree about what Hernández and his friends were doing at the time of shooting. According to petitioners, they were simply playing a game, running across the culvert, touching the fence on the U.S. side, and then running back across the border. According to Agent Mesa, Hernández and his friends were involved in an illegal border crossing attempt, and they pelted him with rocks.

The shooting quickly became an international incident, with the United States and Mexico disagreeing about how the matter should be handled. On the U.S. side, the Department of Justice conducted an investigation. When it finished, the Department, while expressing regret over Hernández's death, concluded that Agent Mesa had not violated Customs and Border Patrol policy or training, and it declined to bring charges or take other action against him. Mexico was not and is not satisfied with the U.S. investigation. It requested that Agent Mesa be extradited to face criminal charges in a Mexican court, a request that the United States has denied.

Petitioners, Hernández's parents, were also dissatisfied and therefore brought suit for damages in the United States District Court for the Western District of Texas. Among other claims, they sought recovery of damages under *Bivens*, alleging that Mesa violated Hernández's Fourth and Fifth Amendment rights. The District Court granted Mesa's motion to dismiss, and the Court of Appeals for the Fifth Circuit sitting en banc has twice affirmed this dismissal. . . . We granted certiorari and now affirm.

II

In *Bivens*, the Court broke new ground by holding that a person claiming to be the victim of an unlawful arrest and search could bring a Fourth Amendment claim for damages against the responsible agents even though no federal statute authorized such a claim. The Court subsequently extended *Bivens* to cover . . . a federal prisoner's Eighth Amendment claim for failure to provide adequate medical treatment. After those decisions, however, the Court changed course.

Bivens . . . and *Carlson* were the products of an era when the Court routinely inferred causes of action that were not explicit in the text of the provision that was allegedly violated. . . . *Bivens* extended this practice to claims based on the Constitution itself.

In later years, we came to appreciate more fully the tension between this practice and the Constitution's separation of legislative and judicial power. The Constitution grants legislative power to Congress; this Court and the lower federal courts, by contrast, have only judicial Power. But when a court recognizes an implied claim for damages on the ground that doing so furthers the purpose of the law, the court risks arrogating legislative power. . . . [A] lawmaking body that enacts a provision that creates a right or prohibits specified conduct may not wish to pursue the provision's purpose to the extent of authorizing private suits for damages. For this reason, finding that a damages remedy is implied by a provision that makes no reference to that remedy may upset the careful balance of interests struck by the lawmakers.

In constitutional cases, we . . . . have recognized that Congress is best positioned to evaluate whether, and the extent to which, monetary and other liabilities should be imposed upon individual officers and employees of the Federal Government based on constitutional torts. We [recently] stated that expansion of *Bivens* is a disfavored judicial activity . . . . And for almost 40 years, we have consistently rebuffed requests to add to the claims allowed under *Bivens*.

When asked to extend *Bivens*, we engage in a two-step inquiry. We first inquire whether the request involves a claim that arises in a "new context" or involves a "new category of defendants." And our understanding of a "new context" is broad. We regard a context as "new" if it is different in a meaningful way from previous *Bivens* cases decided by this Court.

When we find that a claim arises in a new context, we proceed to the second step and ask whether there are any special factors that counsel hesitation about granting the extension. If there are—that is, if we have reason to pause before applying *Bivens* in a new context or to a new class of defendants—we reject the request.

We . . . have explained that central to this analysis are separation-of-powers principles. We thus consider the risk of interfering with the authority of the other branches, and we ask whether there are sound reasons to think Congress might doubt the efficacy or necessity of a damages remedy, and whether the Judiciary is well suited, absent congressional action or instruction, to consider and weigh the costs and benefits of allowing a damages action to proceed.

III

The *Bivens* claims in this case assuredly arise in a new context. Petitioners contend that their Fourth and Fifth Amendment claims do not involve a new context because *Bivens* and [another case decided just after *Bivens* called] *Davis* involved claims under those same two amendments, but that argument rests on a basic misunderstanding of what our cases mean by a new context. A claim may arise in a new context even if it is based on the same constitutional provision as a claim in a case in which a damages remedy was previously recognized. *See Malesko*. And once we look beyond the constitutional provisions . . . , it is glaringly obvious that petitioners' claims involve a new context, *i.e.*, one that is meaningfully different. *Bivens* concerned an allegedly unconstitutional arrest and search carried out in New York City, *Davis* concerned alleged sex discrimination on Capitol Hill. There is a world of difference between those claims and petitioners' cross-border shooting claims, where the risk of disruptive intrusion by the Judiciary into the functioning of other branches is significant.

Because petitioners assert claims that arise in a new context, we must proceed to the next step and ask whether there are factors that counsel hesitation. As we will explain, there are multiple, related factors that raise warning flags.

The first is the potential effect on foreign relations. The political branches, not the Judiciary, have the responsibility and institutional capacity to weigh foreign-policy concerns. . . . A cross-border shooting is by definition an international incident; it involves an event that occurs simultaneously in two countries and affects both countries' interests. Such an incident may lead to a disagreement between those countries, as happened in this case. . . . It is not our task to arbitrate between them. . . .

. . . . [A second factor is national security.] The responsibility for attempting to prevent the illegal entry of dangerous persons and goods rests primarily with the U.S. Customs and Border Protection Agency, and one of its main responsibilities is to detect, respond to, and interdict terrorists, drug smugglers and traffickers, human smugglers and traffickers, and other persons who may undermine the security of the United States. While Border Patrol agents often work miles from the border, some, like Agent Mesa, are stationed right at the border and have the responsibility of attempting to prevent illegal entry. For these reasons, the conduct of agents positioned at the border has a clear and strong connection to national security, as the Fifth Circuit understood.

Petitioners protest that shooting people who are just walking down a street in Mexico does not involve national security, but that misses the point. The question is not whether national security requires such conduct—of course, it does not—but whether the Judiciary should alter the framework established by the political branches for addressing cases in which it is alleged that lethal force was unlawfully employed by an agent at the border. We have declined to extend *Bivens* where doing so would interfere with the system of military discipline created by statute and regulation, and a similar consideration is applicable here. Since regulating the conduct of agents at the border unquestionably has national security implications, the risk of undermining border security provides reason to hesitate before extending *Bivens* into this field.

Our reluctance to take that step is reinforced by our survey of what Congress has done in statutes addressing related matters. . . . Congress has repeatedly declined to authorize the award of damages for injury inflicted outside our borders. . . . When Congress has enacted statutes creating a damages remedy for persons injured by United States Government officers, it has taken care to preclude claims for injuries that occurred abroad. Instead, when Congress has provided compensation for injuries suffered by aliens outside the United States, it has done so by empowering Executive Branch officials to make payments under circumstances found to be appropriate. . . . This pattern of congressional action—refraining from authorizing damages actions for injury inflicted abroad by Government officers, while providing alternative avenues for compensation in some situations—gives us further reason to hesitate about extending *Bivens* in this case.

In sum, this case features multiple factors that counsel hesitation about extending *Bivens,* but they can all be condensed to one concern—respect for the separation of powers. Foreign policy and national security decisions are delicate, complex, and involve large elements of prophecy for which the Judiciary has neither aptitude, facilities, nor responsibility. To avoid upsetting the delicate web of international relations, we typically presume that even congressionally crafted causes of action do not apply outside our borders. These concerns are only heightened when judges are asked to fashion constitutional remedies. Congress, which has authority in the field of foreign affairs, has chosen not to create liability in similar statutes, leaving the resolution of extraterritorial claims brought by foreign nationals to executive officials and the diplomatic process. . . .

When evaluating whether to extend *Bivens,* the most important question is who should decide whether to provide for a damages remedy, Congress or the courts? The correct answer most often will be Congress. That is undoubtedly the answer here.

* * *

The judgment of the United States Court of Appeals for the Fifth Circuit is affirmed. It is so ordered.

Justice THOMAS, with whom Justice GORSUCH joins, concurring.

The Court correctly applies our precedents to conclude that the implied cause of action created in *Bivens* should not be extended to cross-border shootings. I therefore join its opinion.

I write separately because, in my view, the time has come to consider discarding the *Bivens* doctrine altogether. The foundation for *Bivens*—the practice of creating implied causes of action in the statutory context—has already been abandoned. And the Court has consistently refused to extend the *Bivens* doctrine for nearly 40 years, even going so far as to suggest that *Bivens* and its progeny were wrongly decided. *Stare decisis* provides no veneer of respectability to our continued application of these demonstrably incorrect precedents. To ensure that we are not perpetuating a usurpation of the legislative power, we should reevaluate our continued recognition of even a limited form of the *Bivens* doctrine. . . .

Federal courts lack the authority to engage in the distinctly legislative task of creating causes of action for damages to enforce federal positive law. We have clearly recognized as much in the statutory context. I see no reason for us to take a different approach if the right asserted to recover damages derives from the Constitution, rather than from a federal statute. Either way, we are exercising legislative power vested in Congress.

This usurpation of legislative power is all the more troubling because Congress has demonstrated that it knows how to create a cause of action to recover damages for constitutional violations when it wishes to do so. In 42 U. S. C. § 1983, Congress provided a cause of action that allows persons to recover damages for certain deprivations of constitutional rights by *state officers*. Congress has chosen not to provide such a cause of action against *federal officers*. In fact, it has pre-empted the state tort suits that traditionally served as the mechanism by which damages were recovered from federal officers.

* * *

The analysis underlying *Bivens* cannot be defended. We have cabined the doctrine's scope, undermined its foundation, and limited its precedential value. It is time to correct this Court's error and abandon the doctrine altogether.

Justice GINSBURG, with whom Justices BREYER, SOTOMAYOR, and KAGAN join, dissenting.

. . . . Rogue U. S. officer conduct falls within a familiar, not a "new," *Bivens* setting. Even if the setting could be characterized as "new," plaintiffs lack recourse to alternative remedies, and no "special factors" counsel against a *Bivens* remedy. Neither U.S. foreign policy nor national security is in fact endangered by the litigation. Moreover, concerns attending the application of our law to conduct occurring abroad are not involved, for plaintiffs seek the application of U.S. law to conduct occurring inside our borders. I would therefore hold that the plaintiffs' complaint crosses the *Bivens* threshold. . . .

Plaintiffs' *Bivens* action arises in a setting kin to *Bivens* itself: Mesa, plaintiffs allege, acted in disregard of instructions governing his conduct and of Hernández's constitutional rights. [This Court has] acknowledged the "fixed principle" that plaintiffs may bring *Bivens* suits against federal law enforcement officers for seizures that violate the Fourth Amendment. Using lethal force against a person who poses no immediate threat to the officer and no threat to others surely qualifies as an unreasonable seizure. The complaint states that Mesa engaged in that very conduct; it alleged, specifically, that Hernández was unarmed and posed no threat to Mesa or others. For these reasons, as Mesa acknowledged at oral argument, Hernández's parents could have maintained a *Bivens* action had the bullet hit Hernández while he was running up or down the United States side of the embankment.

The only salient difference here: the fortuity that the bullet happened to strike Hernández on the Mexican side of the embankment. But Hernández's location at the precise moment the bullet landed should not matter one whit. After all, the purpose of *Bivens* is to deter the *officer*. And primary conduct constrained by the Fourth Amendment is an *officer*'s unjustified resort to excessive force. Mesa's allegedly unwarranted deployment of deadly force occurred on United States soil. It scarcely makes sense for a remedy trained on deterring rogue officer conduct to turn upon a happenstance subsequent to the conduct—a bullet landing in one half of a culvert, not the other. . . .

Even accepting, *arguendo*, that the setting in this case could be characterized as "new," there is still no good reason why Hernández's parents should face a closed courtroom door. As in *Bivens*, plaintiffs lack recourse to alternative remedies. And not one of the "special factors" the Court identifies weigh any differently based on where a bullet happens to land. . . .

The special factors featured by the Court relate, in the main, to foreign policy and national security. But, as suggested earlier, no policies or policymakers are challenged in this case. Plaintiffs target the rogue actions of a rank-and-file law enforcement officer acting in violation of rules controlling his office. . . .

The Court nevertheless asserts that the instant suit has a potential effect on foreign relations because it invites courts to arbitrate between the United States and Mexico. Plaintiffs, however, have brought a civil damages action, no different from one a federal court would entertain had the fatal shot hit Hernández before he reached the Mexican side of the border. True, cross-border shootings spark bilateral discussion, but so too does a range of smuggling and other border-related issues that courts routinely address concurrently with whatever diplomacy may also be addressing them. The Government has identified no deleterious effect on diplomatic negotiations in any case after the Ninth Circuit held that the mother of a boy killed in a cross-border shooting could institute a *Bivens* action. Moreover, the Court, in this case, cannot escape a potential effect on foreign relations by declining to recognize a *Bivens* action. As the Mexican Government alerted the Court: "Refusal to consider Hernández's parents' claim on the merits is what has the potential to negatively affect international relations." . . .

The Court also asserts, as cause for hesitation, "the risk of undermining border security." But the Court speaks with generality of the national-security involvement of Border Patrol officers. It does not home in on how a *Bivens* suit for an unjustified killing would in fact undermine security at the border. . . . National-security concerns must not become a talisman used to ward off inconvenient claims—a label used to cover a multitude of sins. Instructions regulating Border Patrol agents tell them to guard against deploying unjustified deadly force. Given that instruction, I do not grasp how allowing a *Bivens* action here would intrude upon the political branches' national-security prerogatives.

Congress, although well aware of the Court's opinion in *Bivens*, has not endeavored to dislodge the decision. . . . I resist the conclusion that "nothing" is the answer required in this case. I would reverse the Fifth Circuit's judgment and hold that plaintiffs can sue Mesa in federal court for violating their son's Fourth and Fifth Amendment rights.

Abstention

Introduction

Federal jurisdictional statutes are broadly worded. Accordingly, some cases come to federal court with issues that nevertheless should be heard or decided in the first instance by other tribunals, such as state courts or administrative agencies. Reasons why vary but include the specialized expertise of those alternative tribunals or the respect for federalism values. In such instances, a federal court will "abstain" from hearing the case or the issue. Abstention can take the form of a stay, in which the federal court will retain jurisdiction but exercise discretion to discontinue proceedings until some other tribunal has rendered a decision. Abstention might also take the form of a dismissal or remand so that the other tribunal can heard the case without a pending federal proceeding. Note that some doctrines addressed in this section, including exhaustion and certification, are akin to abstention but often are categorized as independent doctrines.

Congress has, at times, codified abstention in jurisdictional statutes. For example, in the supplemental-jurisdiction statute, Congress granted federal district courts discretion to keep or retain claims over which district courts exercised supplemental jurisdiction based on some statutory factors.

But what happens when circumstances seem to justify abstention but Congress has not statutorily provided for abstention? The answer is that the Supreme Court has created abstention rules through its opinions. As you read them, consider the following:

- What policies animate the various abstention doctrines? Are they generalizable or specific to each species of abstention?

- What authority do federal courts have to abstain from jurisdiction generally authorized by Congress?

- Are the abstention doctrines workable? Who is better—Congress or the Court—at setting nuanced jurisdictional boundaries?

- How does the Court control the scope of abstention doctrines? Are those controls effective?

Patsy v. Board of Regents (1982)

Justice MARSHALL delivered the opinion of the Court.

This case presents the question whether exhaustion of state administrative remedies is a prerequisite to an action under 42 U.S.C. § 1983. Petitioner Georgia Patsy filed this action, alleging that her employer, Florida International University (FIU), had denied her employment opportunities solely on the basis of her race and sex. By a divided vote, the United States Court of Appeals for the Fifth Circuit found that petitioner was required to exhaust "adequate and appropriate" administrative remedies, and remanded the case to the District Court to consider the adequacy of the administrative procedures. We granted certiorari and reverse the decision of the Court of Appeals.

I

Petitioner alleges that even though she is well qualified and has received uniformly excellent performance evaluations from her supervisors, she has been rejected for more than 13 positions at FIU. She further claims that FIU has unlawfully filled positions through intentional discrimination on the basis of race and sex. She seeks declaratory and injunctive relief or, in the alternative, damages.

The United States District Court for the Southern District of Florida granted respondent Board of Regents' motion to dismiss because petitioner had not exhausted available administrative remedies. On appeal, a panel of the Court of Appeals reversed, and remanded the case for further proceedings. The full court then granted respondent's petition for rehearing and vacated the panel decision.

The Court of Appeals reviewed numerous opinions of this Court holding that exhaustion of administrative remedies was not required, and concluded that these cases did not preclude the application of a flexible exhaustion rule. After canvassing the policy arguments in favor of an exhaustion requirement, the Court of Appeals decided that a § 1983 plaintiff could be required to exhaust administrative remedies if the following minimum conditions are met: (1) an orderly system of review or appeal is provided by statute or agency rule; (2) the agency can grant relief more or less commensurate with the claim; (3) relief is available within a reasonable period of time; (4) the procedures are fair, are not unduly burdensome, and are not used to harass or discourage those with legitimate claims; and (5) interim relief is available, in appropriate cases, to prevent irreparable injury and to preserve the plaintiff's rights during the administrative process. Where these minimum standards are met, a court must further consider the particular administrative scheme, the nature of the plaintiff's interest, and the values served by the exhaustion doctrine in order to determine whether exhaustion should be required. The Court of Appeals remanded the case to the District Court to determine whether exhaustion would be appropriate in this case.

II

We have on numerous occasions rejected the argument that a § 1983 action should be dismissed where the plaintiff has not exhausted state administrative remedies. Respondent may be correct in arguing that several of these decisions could have been based on traditional exceptions to the exhaustion doctrine. Nevertheless, this Court has stated categorically that exhaustion is not a prerequisite to an action under § 1983, and we have not deviated from that position . . . . Therefore, we do not address the question presented in this case as one of first impression.

III

. . . . Respondent and the Court of Appeals argue that exhaustion of administrative remedies should be required because it would further various policies. They argue that an exhaustion requirement would lessen the perceived burden that § 1983 actions impose on federal courts;[13] would further the goal of comity and improve federal-state relations by postponing federal-court review until after the state administrative agency had passed on the issue; and would enable the agency, which presumably has expertise in the area at issue, to enlighten the federal court's ultimate decision.

> [13] Of course, this burden alone is not sufficient to justify a judicial decision to alter congressionally imposed jurisdiction. In any event, it is by no means clear that judicial discretion to impose an exhaustion requirement in § 1983 actions would lessen the caseload of the federal courts, at least in the short run.

As we noted earlier, policy considerations alone cannot justify judicially imposed exhaustion unless exhaustion is consistent with congressional intent. Furthermore, as the debates over incorporating the exhaustion requirement in § 1997e demonstrate, the relevant policy considerations do not invariably point in one direction, and there is vehement disagreement over the validity of the assumptions underlying many of them.[15] The very difficulty of these policy considerations, and Congress's superior institutional competence to pursue this debate, suggest that legislative not judicial solutions are preferable.

> [15] For example, there is serious disagreement over whether judicial or administrative procedures offer § 1983 plaintiffs the swiftest, least costly, and most reliable remedy. Similarly, there is debate over whether the specialization of federal courts in constitutional law is more important than the specialization of administrative

agencies in their areas of expertise, and over whether the symbolic and institutional function of federal courts in defining, legitimizing, and enforcing constitutional claims outweighs the educational function that state and local agencies can serve. Finally, it is uncertain whether the present "free market" system, under which litigants are free to pursue administrative remedies if they truly appear to be cheaper, more efficient, and more effective, is more likely to induce the creation of adequate remedies . . . .

Beyond the policy issues that must be resolved in deciding *whether* to require exhaustion, there are equally difficult questions concerning the design and scope of an exhaustion requirement. These questions include how to define those categories of § 1983 claims in which exhaustion might be desirable; how to unify and centralize the standards for judging the kinds of administrative procedures that should be exhausted; what tolling requirements and time limitations should be adopted; what is the res judicata and collateral estoppel effect of particular administrative determinations; what consequences should attach to the failure to comply with procedural requirements of administrative proceedings; and whether federal courts could grant necessary interim injunctive relief and hold the action pending exhaustion, or proceed to judgment without requiring exhaustion even though exhaustion might otherwise be required, where the relevant administrative agency is either powerless or not inclined to grant such interim relief. These and similar questions might be answered swiftly and surely by legislation, but would create costly, remedy-delaying, and court-burdening litigation if answered incrementally by the judiciary in the context of diverse constitutional claims relating to thousands of different state agencies.

The very variety of claims, claimants, and state agencies involved in § 1983 cases argues for congressional consideration of the myriad of policy considerations, and may explain why Congress, in deciding whether to require exhaustion in certain § 1983 actions brought by adult prisoners, carved out such a narrow, detailed exception to the no-exhaustion rule. After full debate and consideration of the various policy arguments, Congress adopted § 1997e, taking the largest class of § 1983 actions and constructing an exhaustion requirement that differs substantially from the . . . standard urged by respondent and adopted by the Court of Appeals. It is not for us to say whether Congress will or should create a similar scheme for other categories of § 1983 claims or whether Congress will or should adopt an altogether different exhaustion requirement for nonprisoner § 1983 claims.

IV

Based on the legislative histories of both § 1983 and § 1997e, we conclude that exhaustion of state administrative remedies should not be required as a prerequisite to bringing an action pursuant to § 1983. We decline to overturn our prior decisions holding that such exhaustion is not required. The decision of the Court of Appeals is reversed, and the case is remanded for proceedings consistent with this opinion.

Justice WHITE, concurring in part.

. . . . As the Court acknowledges, the policy arguments cut in both directions. The Court concludes that the very difficulty of these policy considerations, and Congress's superior institutional competence suggest that legislative not judicial decisions are preferable. To be sure, exhaustion is a statutory issue and the dispositive word on the matter belongs to Congress. It does not follow, however, that, were the issue not foreclosed by earlier decisions, we would be institutionally incompetent to formulate an exhaustion rule. The lack of an exhaustion requirement in § 1983 actions is itself an exception to the general rule, judicially formulated, that exhaustion of administrative remedies is required in a civil action. Unlike other statutory questions, exhaustion is a rule of judicial administration, and unless Congress directs otherwise, rightfully subject to crafting by judges. Our resolution of this case as governed by *stare decisis*, reinforced by the legislative history of § 1983, should not be taken as undercutting the general exhaustion principle of long standing. . . .

Justice POWELL, with whom THE CHIEF JUSTICE joins as to Part II, dissenting.

. . . . The requirement that a § 1983 plaintiff exhaust adequate state administrative remedies was the accepted rule of law until quite recently. The rule rests on sound considerations. It does not defeat federal-court jurisdiction, it merely defers it. It permits the States to correct violations through their own procedures, and it encourages the establishment of such procedures. It is consistent with the principles of comity that apply whenever federal courts are asked to review state action or supersede state proceedings. *See Younger v. Harris.*

Moreover, and highly relevant to the effective functioning of the overburdened federal court system, the rule conserves and supplements scarce judicial resources. In 1961, . . . only 270 civil rights actions were begun in the federal district courts. In 1981, over 30,000 such suits were commenced. The result of this unprecedented increase in civil rights litigation is a heavy burden on the federal courts to the detriment of all federal-court litigants, including others who assert that their constitutional rights have been infringed.

. . . . The requirement that plaintiffs exhaust available and adequate administrative remedies—subject to well-developed exceptions—is firmly established in virtually every area of the law. This is dictated in § 1983 actions by common sense, as well as by comity and federalism, where adequate state administrative remedies are available. . . . I would affirm the Court of Appeals.

Railroad Commission of Texas v. Pullman (1941)

In those sections of Texas where the local passenger traffic is slight, trains carry but one sleeping car. These trains, unlike trains having two or more sleepers, are without a Pullman conductor; the sleeper is in charge of a porter who is subject to the train conductor's control. As is well known, porters on Pullmans are colored and conductors are white. Addressing itself to this situation, the Texas Railroad Commission after due hearing ordered that no sleeping car shall be operated on any line of railroad in the State of Texas unless such cars are continuously in the charge of an employee having the rank and position of Pullman conductor.

Thereupon, the Pullman Company and the railroads affected brought this action in a federal district court to enjoin the Commission's order. Pullman porters were permitted to intervene as complainants, and Pullman conductors entered the litigation in support of the order. Three judges having been convened, the court enjoined enforcement of the order. From this decree, the case came here directly.

The Pullman Company and the railroads assailed the order as unauthorized by Texas law as well as violative of the Equal Protection, the Due Process and the Commerce Clauses of the Constitution. The intervening porters adopted these objections but mainly objected to the order as a discrimination against Negroes in violation of the Fourteenth Amendment.

The complaint of the Pullman porters undoubtedly tendered a substantial constitutional issue. It is more than substantial. It touches a sensitive area of social policy upon which the federal courts ought not to enter unless no alternative to its adjudication is open. Such constitutional adjudication plainly can be avoided if a definitive ruling on the state issue would terminate the controversy. It is therefore our duty to turn to a consideration of questions under Texas law.

The Commission found justification for its order in a Texas statute which we quote in the margin.[1] It is common ground that if the order is within the Commission's authority its subject matter must be included in the Commission's power to prevent unjust discrimination and to prevent any and all other abuses in the conduct of railroads. Whether arrangements pertaining to the staffs of Pullman cars are covered by the Texas concept of "discrimination" is far from clear. What practices of the railroads may be deemed to be "abuses" subject to the Commission's correction is equally doubtful. Reading the Texas statutes and the Texas decisions as outsiders without special competence in Texas law, we would have little confidence in our independent judgment regarding the application of that law to the present situation. The lower court did deny that the Texas statutes sustained the Commission's assertion of power. And this represents the view of an able and experienced circuit judge of the circuit which includes Texas and of two capable district judges trained in Texas law. Had we or they no choice in the matter but to decide what is the law of the state, we should hesitate long before rejecting their forecast of Texas law. But no matter how seasoned the judgment of the district court may be, it cannot escape being a forecast rather than a determination. The last word on the meaning of Article 6445 of the Texas Civil Statutes, and therefore the last word on the statutory authority of the Railroad Commission in this case, belongs neither to us nor to the district court but to the supreme court of Texas. In this situation a federal court of equity is asked to decide an issue by making a tentative answer which may be displaced tomorrow by a state adjudication. The reign of law is hardly promoted if an unnecessary ruling of a federal court is thus supplanted by a controlling decision of a state court. The resources of equity are equal to an adjustment that will avoid the waste of a tentative decision as well as the friction of a premature constitutional adjudication.

[1] Vernon's Anno. Texas Civil Statutes, Article 6445: "Power and authority are hereby conferred upon the Railroad Commission of Texas over all railroads, and suburban, belt and terminal railroads, and over all public wharves, docks, piers, elevators, warehouses, sheds, tracks and other property used in connection therewith in this State, and over all persons, associations and corporations, private or municipal, owning or operating such railroad, wharf, dock, pier, elevator, warehouse, shed, track or other property to fix, and it is hereby made the duty of the said Commission to adopt all necessary rates, charges and regulations, to govern and regulate such railroads, persons, associations and corporations, and to correct abuses and prevent unjust discrimination in the rates, charges and tolls of such railroads, persons, associations and corporations, and to fix division of rates, charges and regulations between railroads and other utilities and common carriers where a division is proper and correct, and to prevent any and all other abuses in the conduct of their business and to do and perform such other duties and details in connection therewith as may be provided by law."

An appeal to the chancellor, as we had occasion to recall only the other day, is an appeal to the exercise of the sound discretion, which guides the determination of courts of equity. The history of equity jurisdiction is the history of regard for public consequences in employing the extraordinary remedy of the injunction. There have been as many and as variegated applications of this supple principle as the situations that have brought it into play. Few public interests have a higher claim upon the discretion of a federal chancellor than the avoidance of needless friction with state policies, whether the policy relates to the enforcement of the criminal law, or the administration of a specialized scheme for liquidating embarrassed business enterprises, or the final authority of a state court to interpret doubtful regulatory laws of the state. These cases reflect a doctrine of abstention appropriate to our federal system whereby the federal courts, exercising a wise discretion, restrain their authority because of scrupulous regard for the rightful independence of the state governments and for the smooth working of the federal judiciary. This use of equitable powers is a contribution of the courts in furthering the harmonious relation between state and federal authority without the need of rigorous congressional restriction of those powers.

Regard for these important considerations of policy in the administration of federal equity jurisdiction is decisive here. If there was no warrant in state law for the Commission's assumption of authority there is an end of the litigation; the constitutional issue does not arise. The law of Texas appears to furnish easy and ample means for determining the Commission's authority. Article 6453 of the Texas Civil Statutes gives a review of such an order in the state courts. Or, if there are difficulties in the way of this procedure of which we have not been apprised, the issue of state law may be settled by appropriate action on the part of the State to enforce obedience to the order. In the absence of any showing that these obvious methods for securing a definitive ruling in the state courts cannot be pursued with full protection of the constitutional claim, the district court should exercise its wise discretion by staying its hands.

We therefore remand the cause to the district court, with directions to retain the bill pending a determination of proceedings, to be brought with reasonable promptness, in the state court in conformity with this opinion.

Burford v. Sun Oil (1943)

Mr. Justice BLACK delivered the opinion of the Court.

In this proceeding brought in a federal district court, the Sun Oil Co. attacked the validity of an order of the Texas Railroad Commission granting the petitioner Burford a permit to drill four wells on a small plot of land in the East Texas oil field. Jurisdiction of the federal court was invoked because of the diversity of citizenship of the parties, and because of the Companies' contention that the order denied them due process of law. . . . [T]he Circuit Court of Appeals in its decision correctly viewed this as a simple proceeding in equity to enjoin the enforcement of the Commission's order.

Although a federal equity court does have jurisdiction of a particular proceeding, it may, in its sound discretion, whether its jurisdiction is invoked on the ground of diversity of citizenship or otherwise, refuse to enforce or protect legal rights, the exercise of which may be prejudicial to the public interest; for it is in the public interest that federal courts of equity should exercise their discretionary power with proper regard for the rightful independence of state governments in carrying out their domestic policy. While many other questions are argued, we find it necessary to decide only one: Assuming that the federal district court had jurisdiction, should it, as a matter of sound equitable discretion, have declined to exercise that jurisdiction here?

The order under consideration is part of the general regulatory system devised for the conservation of oil and gas in Texas, an aspect of as thorny a problem as has challenged the ingenuity and wisdom of legislatures. The East Texas field, in which the Burford tract is located, is one of the largest in the United States. It is approximately forty miles long and between five and nine miles wide, and over 26,000 wells have been drilled in it. . . . The practice of attempting to drain oil from under the surface holdings of others leads to offset wells and other wasteful practices; and this problem is increased by the fact that the surface rights are split up into many small tracts. There are approximately nine hundred operators in the East Texas field alone.

For these, and many other reasons based on geologic realities, each oil and gas field must be regulated as a unit for conservation purposes. The federal government, for the present at least, has chosen to leave the principal regulatory responsibility with the states, but does supplement state control. While there is no question of the constitutional power of the State to take appropriate action to protect the industry and protect the public interest, the State's attempts to control the flow of oil and at the same time protect the interest of the many operators have from time to time been entangled in geological-legal problems of novel nature.

Texas interests in this matter are more than that very large one of conserving gas and oil, two of our most important natural resources. It must also weigh the impact of the industry on the whole economy of the state and must consider its revenue, much of which is drawn from taxes on the industry and from mineral lands preserved for the benefit of its educational and eleemosynary institutions. To prevent past, present, and imminent evils in the production of natural gas, a statute was enacted for the protection of public and private interests against such evils by prohibiting waste and compelling ratable production. The primary task of attempting adjustment of these diverse interests is delegated to the Railroad Commission which Texas has vested with broad discretion in administering the law.

The Commission, in cooperation with other oil producing states, has accepted State oil production quotas and has undertaken to translate the amount to be produced for the State as a whole into a specific amount for each field and for each well. These judgments are made with due regard for the factors of full utilization of the oil supply, market demand, and protection of the individual operators, as well as protection of the public interest. As an essential aspect of the control program, the State also regulates the spacing of wells. The legislature has disavowed a purpose of requiring that the separately owned properties in any pool (should) be unitized under one management, control or ownership and the Commission must thus work out the difficult spacing problem with due regard for whatever rights Texas recognizes in the separate owners to a share of the common reservoir. At the same time it must restrain waste, whether by excessive production or by the unwise dissipation of the gas and other geologic factors that cause the oil to flow.

Since 1919 the Commission has attempted to solve this problem by its Rule 37. The rule provides for certain minimum spacing between wells, but also allows exceptions where necessary to prevent waste or to prevent the confiscation of property. The prevention of confiscation is based on the premises that, insofar as these privileges are compatible with the prevention of waste and the achievement of conservation, each surface owner should be permitted to withdraw the oil under his surface area, and that no one else can fairly be permitted to drain his oil away. Hence the Commission may protect his interest either by adjusting his amount of production upward, or by permitting him to drill additional wells. By this method each person will be entitled to recover a quantity of oil and gas substantially equivalent in amount to the recoverable oil and gas under his land.

Additional wells may be required to prevent waste as has been noticed, where geologic circumstances require immediate drilling: The term "waste," as used in oil and gas Rule 37, undoubtedly means the ultimate loss of oil. If a substantial amount of oil will be saved by the drilling of a well that otherwise would ultimately be lost, the permit to drill such well may be justified under one of the exceptions provided in Rule 37 to prevent waste.

The delusive simplicity with which these principles of exception to Rule 37 can be stated should not obscure the actual nonlegal complexities involved in their application. While the surface holder may, subject to qualifications noted, be entitled under current Texas law to the oil under his land, there can be no absolute certainty as to how much oil actually is present, and since the waste and confiscation problems are as a matter of physical necessity so closely interrelated, decision of one of the questions necessarily involves recognition of the other. The sheer quantity of exception cases makes their disposition of great public importance. It is estimated that over two-thirds of the wells in the East Texas field exist as exceptions to the rule, and since each exception may provoke a conflict among the interested parties, the volume of litigation arising from the administration of the rule is considerable. The instant case arises from just such an exception. It is not peculiar that the state should be represented here by its Attorney General, for cases like this, involving "confiscation," are not mere isolated disputes between private parties. Aside from the general principles which may evolve from these proceedings, the physical facts are such that an additional permit may affect pressure on a well miles away. The standards applied by the Commission in a given case necessarily affect the entire state conservation system. Of far more importance than any other private interest is the fact that the over-all plan of regulation, as well as each of its case by case manifestations, is of vital interest to the general public which must be assured that the speculative interests of individual tract owners will be put aside when necessary to prevent the irretrievable loss of oil in other parts of the field. The Commission in applying the statutory standards of course considers the Rule 37 cases as a part of the entire conservation program with implications to the whole economy of the state.

With full knowledge of the importance of the decisions of the Railroad Commission both to the State and to the oil operators, the Texas legislature has established a system of thorough judicial review by its own State courts. The Commission orders may be appealed to a State district court in Travis County, and are reviewed by a branch of the Court of Civil Appeals and by the State Supreme Court. While the constitutional power of the Commission to enforce Rule 37 or to make exceptions to it is seldom seriously challenged, the validity of particular orders from the standpoint of statutory interpretation may present a serious problem, and a substantial number of such cases have been disposed of by the Texas courts which alone have the power to give definite answers to the questions of State law posed in these proceedings.

In describing the relation of the Texas court to the Commission no useful purpose will be served by attempting to label the court's position as legislative, or judicial—suffice it to say that the Texas courts are working partners with the Railroad Commission in the business of creating a regulatory system for the oil industry. The Commission is charged with principal responsibility for fact finding and for policy making and the courts expressly disclaim the administrative responsibility, but on the other hand, the orders of the Commission are tested for reasonableness by trial de novo before the court, and the Court may on occasion make a careful analysis of all the facts of the case in reversing a Commission order. The court has fully as much power as the Commission to determine particular cases, since after trial de novo it can either restrain the leaseholder from proceeding to drill, or, if the case is appropriate, can restrain the Commission from interfering with the leaseholder. The court may even formulate new standards for the Commission's administrative practice and suggest that the Commission adopt them. . . .

To prevent the confusion of multiple review of the same general issues, the legislature provided for concentration of all direct review of the Commission's orders in the State district courts of Travis County. . . . Time and experience, say the Texas courts, have shown the wisdom of this rule. Concentration of judicial supervision of Railroad Commission orders permits the state courts, like the Railroad Commission itself, to acquire a specialized knowledge which is useful in shaping the policy of regulation of the ever-changing demands in this field. At the present time, less than ten per cent of these cases come before the federal district court.

The very confusion which the Texas legislature and Supreme Court feared might result from review by many state courts of the Railroad Commission's orders has resulted from the exercise of federal equity jurisdiction. As a practical matter, the federal courts can make small contribution to the well organized system of regulation and review which the Texas statutes provide. Texas courts can give fully as great relief, including temporary restraining orders, as the federal courts. Delay, misunderstanding of local law, and needless federal conflict with the State policy, are the inevitable product of this double system of review. The most striking example of misunderstanding has come where the federal court has flatly disagreed with the position later taken by a State court as to State law. . . .

These federal court decisions on state law have created a constant task for the Texas Governor, the Texas legislature, and the Railroad Commission. The Governor of Texas, as has been noted above, felt called upon to forge his oil program in the light of the remotest inferences of federal court opinions. In one instance he thought it necessary to declare martial law. Special sessions of the legislature have been occupied with consideration of federal court decisions. Legislation passed under the circumstances of the strain and doubt created by these decisions was necessarily unsatisfactory. The Railroad Commission has had to adjust itself to the permutations of the law as seen by the federal courts. The most recent example was in connection with the Rowan and Nichols case in which the Commission felt compelled to adopt a new proration scheme to comply with the demands of a federal court decision which was reversed when it came to this Court.

As has been noted the federal court cases have dealt primarily with the interpretation of state law, some of it state law fairly remote from oil and gas problems. The instant case raised a number of problems of no general significance on which a federal court can only try to ascertain state law. For example, we are asked to determine whether a previous Travis county district court decision makes this case res judicata and whether another case pending in Travis county deprived the Commission of jurisdiction to consider Burford's application. The existence of these problems throughout the oil regulatory field creates a further possibility of serious delay which can injury the conservation program, for under our decision in *Pullman*, it may be necessary to stay federal action pending authoritative determination of the difficult state questions. . . .

Insofar as we have discretion to do so, we should leave these problems of Texas law to the State court where each may be handled as one more item in a continuous series of adjustments. These questions of regulation of the industry by the State administrative agency, whether involving gas or oil prorationing programs or Rule 37 cases, so clearly involves basic problems of Texas policy that equitable discretion should be exercised to give the Texas courts the first opportunity to consider them. . . . The state provides a unified method for the formation of policy and determination of cases by the Commission and by the state courts. The judicial review of the Commission's decisions in the state courts is expeditious and adequate. Conflicts in the interpretation of state law, dangerous to the success of state policies, are almost certain to result from the intervention of the lower federal courts. On the other hand, if the state procedure is followed from the Commission to the State Supreme Court, ultimate review of the federal questions is fully preserved here. Under such circumstances, a sound respect for the independence of state action requires the federal equity court to stay its hand.

The decision of the Circuit Court of Appeals is reversed and the judgment of the District Court dismissing the complaint is affirmed for the reasons here stated.

Mr. Justice DOUGLAS, concurring.

I agree with the opinion of the Court and join in it. But there are observations in the dissenting opinion which impel me to add a few words. If the issues in this case were framed as the dissenting opinion frames them, I would agree that we should reach the merits and not direct a dismissal of the complaint. But the opinion of the Court as I read it does not hold or even fairly imply that "the enforcement of state rights created by state legislation and affecting state policies is limited to the state courts." Any such holding would result in a drastic inroad on diversity jurisdiction—a limitation which I agree might be desirable but which Congress not this Court should make. The holding in these cases, however, goes to no such length.

This decision is but an application of the principle . . . that federal courts of equity should exercise their discretionary power with proper regard for the rightful independence of state governments in carrying out their domestic policy. . . . The Texas statute which governs suits to set aside these orders of the Railroad Commission has been construed by the Texas courts to give to the supervising courts a large measure of control over the administrative process. That control is much greater, for example, than the control exercised by federal Circuit Courts of Appeal over the orders of such agencies as the National Labor Relations Board. The opinion of the Court calls the Railroad Commission and the Texas courts "working partners." But as its review of Texas decisions shows the courts may at times be the senior and dominant member of that partnership if they perform the functions which Texas law places on them. The courts do not sit merely to enforce rights based on orders of the state administrative agency. They sit in judgment on that agency. That to me is the crux of the matter. If the federal courts undertook to sit in review, so to speak, of this state administrative agency, they would in effect actively participate in the fashioning of the state's domestic policy. That interference would be a continuing one, as the opinion of the Court points out. Moreover, divided authority would result. Divided authority breeds friction . . . .

Mr. Justice FRANKFURTER, dissenting.

. . . . I believe it to be wholly accurate to say that throughout our history it has never been questioned that a right created by state law and enforceable in the state courts can also be enforced in the federal courts where the parties to the controversy are citizens of different states. The reasons which led Congress to grant such jurisdiction to the federal courts are familiar. It was believed that, consciously or otherwise, the courts of a state may favor their own citizens. Bias against outsiders may become embedded in a judgment of a state court and yet not be sufficiently apparent to be made the basis of a federal claim. To avoid possible discriminations of this sort, so the theory goes, a citizen of a state other than that in which he is suing or being sued ought to be able to go into a wholly impartial tribunal, namely, the federal court sitting in that state. Thus, the basic premise of federal jurisdiction based upon diversity of the parties' citizenship is that the federal courts should afford remedies which are coextensive with rights created by state law and enforceable in state courts.

That is the theory of diversity jurisdiction. Whether it is a sound theory, whether diversity jurisdiction is necessary or desirable in order to avoid possible unfairness by state courts, state judges and juries, against outsiders, whether the federal courts ought to be relieved of the burden of diversity litigation—these are matters which are not my concern as a judge. They are the concern of those whose business it is to legislate, not mine. I speak as one who has long favored the entire abolition of diversity jurisdiction. But I must decide this case as a judge and not as a legislative reformer. . . .

[*Pullman* is] merely illustrative of one phase of the basic constitutional doctrine that substantial constitutional issues should be adjudicated only when no alternatives are open. A definitive ruling by the state courts upon the questions of construction of the state statutes might have terminated the controvers[y] . . . and thus eliminated serious constitutional questions. Under such circumstances it was an affirmation and not a denial of federal jurisdiction in each of those cases for the district court to hold the bill pending a seasonable determination of the local issues in a proceeding to be brought in the state courts. . . .

Clearly, therefore, the scope of judicial review in a Rule 37 case, as declared by the Supreme Court of Texas, is precisely as well defined, for example, as the scope of judicial review by the federal courts of orders of the Interstate Commerce Commission or the National Labor Relations Board. That the scope of review may be different does not make the standards of review any less definite or less susceptible of application by a court. I think there can be no doubt that under the Constitution and laws of Texas, as construed by the decisions of the state courts, such courts exercise a judicial power in these cases precisely similar to that wielded by the federal courts under Article III. Can it be said, therefore, that in considering the validity of an exception allowed by the Texas Railroad Commission under Rule 37, the federal judges sitting in that state are engaged in duties which are foreign to their experience and abilities? Judges who sit in judgment upon the legality of orders made by the Interstate Commerce Commission are certainly not incompetent to apply the narrowly defined standards of law established by Texas for review of the orders of its Railroad Commission. . . .

And so, the case really reduces itself to this: in the actual application of the standards governing judicial review of Commission orders allowing exceptions under Rule 37—standards which today have been authoritatively and precisely defined—a different result may be obtained if suit is brought in the federal rather than the state courts. . . . It is the essence of diversity jurisdiction that federal judges and juries should pass on asserted claims because the result might be different if they were decided by a state court. . . . The Congressional premise of diversity jurisdiction is that the possibility of unfairness against outside litigants is to be avoided by providing the neutral forum of a federal court. The Court today is in effect withdrawing this grant of jurisdiction in order to avoid possible unfairness against state interests in the federal courts. That which Congress created to assure impartiality of adjudication is now destroyed to prevent what is deemed to be hostility and bias in adjudication.

Of course, the usual considerations governing the exercise of equity jurisdiction are equally applicable to suits in the federal courts where jurisdiction depends upon the diversity of the parties' citizenship. The chancellor certainly must balance the equities before granting relief; he should stay his hand where another court seized of the controversy can do justice to the claims of the parties; he may refuse equitable relief where the asserted right is doubtful because of the substantive law which he must find as declared by the state. But it . . . . is not for us to say that litigation affecting state laws and state policies ought to be tried only in the state courts. Congress has chosen to confer diversity jurisdiction upon the federal courts. It is not for us to reject that which Congress has made the law of the land simply because of our independent conviction that such legislation is unwise. . . .

The opinion of the Court cuts deep into our judicial fabric. The duty of the judiciary is to exercise the jurisdiction which Congress has conferred. What the Court is doing today I might wholeheartedly approve if it were done by Congress. But I cannot justify translation of the circumstance of my membership on this Court into an opportunity of writing my private view of legislative policy into law and thereby effacing a far greater area of diversity jurisdiction than Senator Norris, as chairman of the Senate Judiciary Committee, was ever able to persuade Congress itself to do.

Mr. Justice ROBERTS and Mr. Justice REED join in this dissent. The CHIEF JUSTICE expresses no views as to the desirability, as a matter of legislative policy, of retaining the diversity jurisdiction. In all other respects he concurs in the opinion of Mr. Justice FRANKFURTER.

Quackenbush v. Allstate (1996)

Justice O'CONNOR delivered the opinion of the Court.

In this case, we consider whether . . . the abstention doctrine first recognized in *Burford v. Sun Oil Co.* can be applied in a common-law suit for damages.

I

Petitioner, the Insurance Commissioner for the State of California, was appointed trustee over the assets of the Mission Insurance Company and its affiliates (Mission companies) in 1987, after those companies were ordered into liquidation by a California court. In an effort to gather the assets of the defunct Mission companies, the Commissioner filed the instant action against respondent Allstate Insurance Company in state court, seeking contract and tort damages for Allstate's alleged breach of certain reinsurance agreements, as well as a general declaration of Allstate's obligations under those agreements.

Allstate removed the action to federal court on diversity grounds and filed a motion to compel arbitration under the Federal Arbitration Act. The Commissioner sought remand to state court, arguing that the District Court should abstain from hearing the case under *Burford* because its resolution might interfere with California's regulation of the Mission insolvency. Specifically, the Commissioner indicated that Allstate would be asserting its right to set off its own contract claims against the Commissioner's recovery under the contract, that the viability of these setoff claims was a hotly disputed question of state law, and that this question was currently pending before the state courts in another case arising out of the Mission insolvency.

The District Court observed that California has an overriding interest in regulating insurance insolvencies and liquidations in a uniform and orderly manner, and that in this case this important state interest could be undermined by inconsistent rulings from the federal and state courts. Based on these observations, and its determination that the setoff question should be resolved in state court, the District Court concluded this case was an appropriate one for the exercise of *Burford* abstention. The District Court did not stay its hand pending the California courts' resolution of the setoff issue, but instead remanded the entire case to state court. The District Court entered this remand order without ruling on Allstate's motion to compel arbitration.

. . . . [T]he Court of Appeals for the Ninth Circuit vacated the District Court's decision and ordered the case sent to arbitration. The Ninth Circuit concluded that federal courts can abstain from hearing a case under *Burford* only when the relief being sought is equitable in nature, and therefore held that abstention was inappropriate in this case because the Commissioner purported to be seeking only legal relief. . . . We granted certiorari . . . and now affirm on grounds different from those provided by the Ninth Circuit. . . .

III

A

We have often acknowledged that federal courts have a strict duty to exercise the jurisdiction that is conferred upon them by Congress. This duty is not, however, absolute. Indeed, we have held that federal courts may decline to exercise their jurisdiction, in otherwise "exceptional circumstances," where denying a federal forum would clearly serve an important countervailing interest, for example, where abstention is warranted by considerations of proper constitutional adjudication, regard for federal-state relations, or wise judicial administration. *Colorado River*.

We have thus held that federal courts have the power to refrain from hearing cases that would interfere with a pending state criminal proceeding, *see Younger v. Harris*, or with certain types of state civil proceedings; cases in which the resolution of a federal constitutional question might be obviated if the state courts were given the opportunity to interpret ambiguous state law, *see Pullman*; cases raising issues intimately involved with the States' sovereign prerogative, the proper adjudication of which might be impaired by unsettled questions of state law; cases whose resolution by a federal court might unnecessarily interfere with a state system for the collection of taxes; and cases which are duplicative of a pending state proceeding, *see Colorado River*.

Our longstanding application of these doctrines reflects the common-law background against which the statutes conferring jurisdiction were enacted. And, as the Ninth Circuit correctly indicated it has long been established that a federal court has the authority to decline to exercise its jurisdiction when it is asked to employ its historic powers as a court of equity. This tradition informs our understanding of the jurisdiction Congress has conferred upon the federal courts, and explains the development of our abstention doctrines. In *Pullman*, for example, we explained the principle underlying our abstention doctrines as follows: "The history of equity jurisdiction is the history of regard for public consequences in employing the extraordinary remedy of the injunction. Few public interests have a higher claim upon the discretion of a federal chancellor than the avoidance of needless friction with state policies. . . . This use of equitable powers is a contribution of the courts in furthering the harmonious relation between state and federal authority without the need of rigorous congressional restriction of those powers."

Though we have thus located the power to abstain in the historic discretion exercised by federal courts sitting in equity, we have not treated abstention as a technical rule of equity procedure. Rather, we have recognized that the authority of a federal court to abstain from exercising its jurisdiction extends to all cases in which the court has discretion to grant or deny relief. Nevertheless, we have not previously addressed whether the principles underlying our abstention cases would support the remand or dismissal of a common-law action for damages. . . . [And] we have applied abstention principles to actions at law only to permit a federal court to enter a stay order that *postpones* adjudication of the dispute, not to dismiss the federal suit altogether.

Our [precedents] illustrate the distinction we have drawn between abstention-based remand orders or dismissals and abstention-based decisions merely to stay adjudication of a federal suit. In *Thibodaux*, a city in Louisiana brought an eminent domain proceeding in state court, seeking to condemn for public use certain property owned by a Florida corporation. After the corporation removed the action to federal court on diversity grounds, the Federal District Court decided on its own motion to stay the case, pending a state court's determination whether the city could exercise the power of eminent domain under state law. The case did not arise within the equity jurisdiction of the federal courts, because the suit sought compensation for a taking, and the District Court lacked discretion to deny relief on the corporation's claim. Nonetheless, the issues in the suit were intimately involved with the State's sovereign prerogative. We concluded that the considerations that prevailed in conventional equity suits for avoiding the hazards of serious disruption by federal courts of state government or needless friction between state and federal authorities are similarly appropriate in a state eminent domain proceeding brought in, or removed to, a federal court. And based on that conclusion, we affirmed the District Court's order staying the case. . . .

We were careful to note in *Thibodaux* that the District Court had only *stayed* the federal suit pending adjudication of the dispute in state court. Unlike the outright dismissal or remand of a federal suit, we held, an order merely staying the action does not constitute abnegation of judicial duty. On the contrary, it is a wise and productive discharge of it. There is only postponement of decision for its best fruition. We have thus held that in cases where the relief being sought is equitable in nature or otherwise discretionary, federal courts not only have the power to stay the action based on abstention principles, but can also, in otherwise appropriate circumstances, decline to exercise jurisdiction altogether by either dismissing the suit or remanding it to state court. By contrast, while we have held that federal courts may stay actions for damages based on abstention principles, we have not held that those principles support the outright dismissal or remand of damages actions. . . .

The fact that we have applied the *forum non conveniens* doctrine [to allow federal courts to dismiss, rather than stay, damages actions] does not change our analysis in this case, where we deal with the scope of the *Burford* abstention doctrine. To be sure, the abstention doctrines and the doctrine of *forum non conveniens* proceed from a similar premise: In rare circumstances, federal courts can relinquish their jurisdiction in favor of another forum. But our abstention doctrine is of a distinct historical pedigree, and the traditional considerations behind dismissal for *forum non conveniens* differ markedly from those informing the decision to abstain. Federal courts abstain out of deference to the paramount interests of another sovereign, and the concern is with principles of comity and federalism. Dismissal for *forum non conveniens*, by contrast, has historically reflected a far broader range of considerations, most notably the convenience to the parties and the practical difficulties that can attend the adjudication of a dispute in a certain locality.

B

With these background principles in mind, we consider the contours of the *Burford* doctrine. The principal issue presented in *Burford* was the "reasonableness" of an order issued by the Texas Railroad Commission, which granted a permit to drill four oil wells on a small plot of land in the East Texas oil field. Due to the potentially overlapping claims of the many parties who might have an interest in a common pool of oil and the need for uniform regulation of the oil industry, Texas endowed the Railroad Commission with exclusive regulatory authority in the area. Texas also placed the authority to review the Commission's orders in a single set of state courts, to prevent the confusion of multiple review and to permit an experienced cadre of state judges to obtain specialized knowledge in the field. Though Texas had thus demonstrated its interest in maintaining uniform review of the Commission's orders, the federal courts had, in the years preceding *Burford*, become increasingly involved in reviewing the reasonableness of the Commission's orders, both under a constitutional standard imposed under the Due Process Clause, and under state law, which established a similar standard.

Viewing the case as a simple proceeding in equity to enjoin the enforcement of the Commissioner's order, we framed the question presented in terms of the power of a federal court of equity to abstain from exercising its jurisdiction . . . . Having thus posed the question in terms of the District Court's discretion, as a court sitting in equity, to decline jurisdiction, we approved the District Court's dismissal of the complaint on a number of grounds that were unique to that case. We noted, for instance, the difficulty of the regulatory issues presented, stating that the order under consideration is part of the general regulatory system devised for the conservation of oil and gas in Texas, an aspect of as thorny a problem as has challenged the ingenuity and wisdom of legislatures. We also stressed the demonstrated need for uniform regulation in the area, citing the unified procedures Texas had established to prevent the confusion of multiple review, and the important state interests this uniform system of review was designed to serve Most importantly, we also described the detrimental impact of ongoing federal court review of the Commission's orders, which review had already led to contradictory adjudications by the state and federal courts.

We ultimately concluded in *Burford* that dismissal was appropriate because the availability of an alternative, federal forum threatened to frustrate the purpose of the complex administrative system that Texas had established. . . .

In *NOPSI*, our most recent exposition of the *Burford* doctrine, we again located the power to dismiss based on abstention principles in the discretionary power of a federal court sitting in equity, and we again illustrated the narrow range of circumstances in which *Burford* can justify the dismissal of a federal action. The issue in *NOPSI* was preemption. A New Orleans utility that had been saddled by a decision of the Federal Energy Regulatory Commission (FERC) with part of the cost of building and operating a nuclear reactor sought approval of a rate increase from the Council of the City of New Orleans. The council denied the rate increase on the grounds that a public hearing was necessary to explore the legality and prudency of the expenses allocated to the utility under the FERC decision, and the utility brought suit in federal court, seeking an injunction against enforcement of the council's order and a declaration that the utility was entitled to a rate increase. The utility claimed that federal law required the Council to allow it to recover, through an increase in retail rates, its FERC-allocated share of the cost of the reactor. The federal preemption question was the only issue raised in the case; there were no state law claims.

In reversing the District Court's decision to dismiss under *Burford*, we recognized the federal courts' discretion in determining whether to grant certain types of relief, and we indicated . . . that *Burford* permits a federal court sitting in equity to dismiss a case only in extraordinary circumstances. We thus indicated that *Burford* allows a federal court to dismiss a case only if it presents difficult questions of state law bearing on policy problems of substantial public import whose importance transcends the result in the case then at bar, or if its adjudication in a federal forum would be disruptive of state efforts to establish a coherent policy with respect to a matter of substantial public concern.

We ultimately held that *Burford* did not provide proper grounds for an abstention-based dismissal in *NOPSI* because the case did not involve a state-law claim, nor even an assertion that the federal claims were in any way entangled in a skein of state law that must be untangled before the federal case can proceed, and because there was no serious threat of conflict between the adjudication of the federal claim presented in the case and the State's interest in ensuring uniformity in ratemaking decisions . . . .

These cases do not provide a formulaic test for determining when dismissal under *Burford* is appropriate, but they do demonstrate that the power to dismiss under the *Burford* doctrine, as with other abstention doctrines, derives from the discretion historically enjoyed by courts of equity. They further demonstrate that exercise of this discretion must reflect principles of federalism and comity. Ultimately, what is at stake is a federal court's decision, based on a careful consideration of the federal interests in retaining jurisdiction over the dispute and the competing concern for the independence of state action, that the State's interests are paramount and that a dispute would best be adjudicated in a state forum. This equitable decision balances the strong federal interest in having certain classes of cases, and certain federal rights, adjudicated in federal court, against the State's interests in maintaining uniformity in the treatment of an 'essentially local problem, and retaining local control over difficult questions of state law bearing on policy problems of substantial public import. This balance only rarely favors abstention, and the power to dismiss recognized in *Burford* represents an extraordinary and narrow exception to the duty of the District Court to adjudicate a controversy properly before it.

C

We turn, finally, to the application of *Burford* in this case. As in *NOPSI*, the federal interests in this case are pronounced, as Allstate's motion to compel arbitration under the Federal Arbitration Act (FAA) implicates a substantial federal concern for the enforcement of arbitration agreements. With regard to the state interests, however, the case appears at first blush to present nothing more than a run-of-the-mill contract dispute. The Commissioner seeks damages from Allstate for Allstate's failure to perform its obligations under a reinsurance agreement. What differentiates this case from other diversity actions seeking damages for breach of contract, if anything, is the impact federal adjudication of the dispute might have on the ongoing liquidation proceedings in state court: The Commissioner claims that any recovery by Allstate on its setoff claims would amount to an illegal "preference" under state law. This question appears now to have been conclusively answered by the California Supreme Court, although at the time the District Court ruled this question was still hotly contested.

The Ninth Circuit concluded that the District Court's remand order was inappropriate because *Burford* abstention does not apply to suits seeking solely legal relief. Addressing our abstention cases, the Ninth Circuit held that the federal courts' power to abstain in certain cases is located in the unique powers of equitable courts, and that it derives from equity courts' discretionary power to grant or withhold relief. The Ninth Circuit's reversal of the District Court's abstention-based remand order in this case therefore reflects the application of a *per se* rule: The power of federal courts to abstain from exercising their jurisdiction, at least in *Burford* abstention cases, is founded upon a discretion they possess only in equitable cases.

To the extent the Ninth Circuit held only that a federal court cannot, under *Burford*, dismiss or remand an action when the relief sought is not discretionary, its judgment is consistent with our abstention cases. We have explained the power to dismiss or remand a case under the abstention doctrines in terms of the discretion federal courts have traditionally exercised in deciding whether to provide equitable or discretionary relief, and the Commissioner appears to have conceded that the relief being sought in this case is neither equitable nor otherwise committed to the discretion of the court. In those cases in which we have applied traditional abstention principles to damages actions, we have only permitted a federal court to withhold action until the state proceedings have concluded; that is, we have permitted federal courts applying abstention principles in damages actions to enter a stay, but we have not permitted them to dismiss the action altogether.

The *per se* rule described by the Ninth Circuit is, however, more rigid than our precedents require. We have not strictly limited abstention to equitable cases, but rather have extended the doctrine to all cases in which a federal court is asked to provide some form of discretionary relief. Moreover, as demonstrated by our decision in *Thibodaux*, we have not held that abstention principles are completely inapplicable in damages actions. *Burford* might support a federal court's decision to postpone adjudication of a damages action pending the resolution by the state courts of a disputed question of state law. For example, given the situation the District Court faced in this case, a stay order might have been appropriate: The setoff issue was being decided by the state courts at the time the District Court ruled, and in the interest of avoiding inconsistent adjudications on that point, the District Court might have been justified in entering a stay to await the outcome of the state court litigation.

Like the Ninth Circuit, we review only the remand order which was entered, and find it unnecessary to determine whether a more limited abstention-based stay order would have been warranted on the facts of this case. [We do not] find it necessary to inquire fully as to whether this case presents the sort of "exceptional circumstance" in which *Burford* abstention or other grounds for yielding federal jurisdiction might be appropriate. Under our precedents, federal courts have the power to dismiss or remand cases based on abstention principles only where the relief being sought is equitable or otherwise discretionary. Because this was a damages action, we conclude that the District Court's remand order was an unwarranted application of the *Burford* doctrine. The judgment is affirmed.

Justice SCALIA, concurring.

Justice Kennedy, while joining the opinion of the Court, says that he would not rule out the possibility that a federal court might dismiss a suit for damages in a case where a serious affront to the interests of federalism could be averted in no other way. I would not have joined today's opinion if I believed it left such discretionary dismissal available. . . .

Justice Kennedy's projected horrible of a serious affront to the interests of federalism cannot possibly materialize under the Court's holding. There *is* no serious affront to the interests of federalism when Congress lawfully decides to preempt state action—which is what our cases hold (and today's opinion affirms) Congress does whenever it instructs federal courts to assert jurisdiction over matters as to which relief is not discretionary.

If the Court today felt empowered to decide for itself when congressionally decreed jurisdiction constitutes a serious affront and when it does not, the opinion would have read much differently. Most pertinently, it would not have found it *unnecessary* to inquire fully as to whether this case presents the sort of "exceptional circumstance" in which *Burford* abstention or other grounds for yielding federal jurisdiction might be appropriate. There were certainly grounds for such an inquiry if we thought it relevant. The then unsettled but since resolved question of California law to which Justice Kennedy refers, was only part of the basis for the District Court's decision to remand to state court; the court also pointed more generally to what it thought was the State's overriding interest in regulating insurance insolvencies and liquidations in a uniform and orderly manner. As the Court's opinion says, it is not necessary to inquire fully into that matter because this was a damages action.

Justice KENNEDY, concurring.

. . . . [W]e have not considered a case in which dismissal of a suit for damages by extension of the doctrine of *Burford* was held to be authorized and necessary. As the Court explains, no doubt the preferred course in such circumstances is to resolve any serious potential for federal intrusion by staying the suit while retaining jurisdiction. We ought not rule out, though, the possibility that a federal court might dismiss a suit for damages in a case where a serious affront to the interests of federalism could be averted in no other way. We need not reach that question here.

Abstention doctrines are a significant contribution to the theory of federalism and to the preservation of the federal system in practice. They allow federal courts to give appropriate and necessary recognition to the role and authority of the States. The duty to take these considerations into account must inform the exercise of federal jurisdiction. Principles of equity thus are not the sole foundation for abstention rules; obligations of comity, and respect for the appropriate balance between state and federal interests, are an important part of the justification and authority for abstention as well. The traditional role of discretion in the exercise of equity jurisdiction makes abstention easiest to justify in cases where equitable relief is sought, but abstention, including dismissal, is a possibility that may yet be addressed in a suit for damages, if fundamental concerns of federalism require us to face the issue. With these observations, I join the opinion of the Court.

Lehman Brothers v. Stein (1974)

Mr. Justice DOUGLAS delivered the opinion of the Court.

These cases are here on petitions for certiorari and raise one identical question. These are suits brought in the District Court for the Southern District of New York. Lum's, one of the respondents in the Lehman Bros. petition, is a Florida corporation with headquarters in Miami. Each of the three petitions, which we consolidated for oral argument, involves shareholders' derivative suits naming Lum's and others as defendants; and the basis of federal jurisdiction is diversity of citizenship, about which there is no dispute.

The complaints allege that Chasen, president of Lum's, called Simon, a representative of Lehman Bros., and told him about disappointing projections of Lum's earnings, estimates that were confidential, not public. Simon is said to have told an employee of IDS about them. On the next day, it is alleged that the IDS defendants sold 83,000 shares of Lum's on the New York Stock Exchange for about $17.50 per share. Later that day the exchanges halted trading in Lum's stock and on the next trading day it opened at $14 per share, the public being told that the projected earnings would be substantially lower than anticipated. The theory of the complaints was that Chasen was a fiduciary but used the inside information along with others for profit and that Chasen and his group are liable to Lum's for their unlawful profits.

Lehman and Simon defended on the ground that the IDS sale was not made through them and that neither one benefited from the sales. Nonetheless plaintiffs claimed that Chasen and the other defendants were liable . . . . on the theory that inside information of an officer or director of a corporation is an asset of the corporation which had been acquired by the insiders as fiduciaries of the company and misappropriated in violation of trust. The District Court looked to the choice-of-law rules of the State of New York and held that the law of the State of incorporation governs the existence and extent of corporate fiduciary obligations, as well as the liability for violation of them. Diamond did, indeed, so indicate.

The District Court in examining Florida law concluded that, although the highest court in Florida has not considered the question, several district courts of appeal indicate that a complaint which fails to allege both wrongful acts and damage to the corporation must be dismissed. The District Court went on the consider whether if Florida followed the Diamond rationale, defendants would be liable. It concluded that the present complaints to beyond Diamond, as Chasen, the only fiduciary of Lum's involved in the suits, never sold any of his holdings on the basis of inside information. The other defendants were not fiduciaries of Lum's. The District Court accordingly dismissed the complaints.

The Court of Appeals by a divided vote reversed the District Court. While the Court of Appeals held that Florida law was controlling, it found none that was decisive. So it then turned to the law of other jurisdictions, particularly that of New York, to see if Florida "would probably" interpret Diamond to make it applicable here. [Using those laws, t]he Court of Appeals concluded that the defendants had engaged with Chasen to misuse corporate property, viewing the case as the Florida court would probably view it. . . .

The dissenter on the Court of Appeals urged that that court certify the state-law question to the Florida Supreme Court as is provided [by Florida law]. That path is open to this Court and to any court of appeals of the United States. We have, indeed, used it before as have courts of appeals.

. . . . We do not suggest that where there is doubt as to local law and where the certification procedure is available, resort to it is obligatory. It does, of course, in the long run save time, energy, and resources and helps build a cooperative judicial federalism. Its use in a given case rests in the sound discretion of the federal court.

Here resort to it would seem particularly appropriate in view of the novelty of the question and the great unsettlement of Florida law, Florida being a distant State. When federal judges in New York attempt to predict uncertain Florida law, they act, as we have referred to ourselves on this Court in matters of state law, as "outsiders" lacking the common exposure to local law which comes from sitting in the jurisdiction. . . .

The judgment of the Court of Appeals is vacated and the cases are remanded so that that court may reconsider whether the controlling issue of Florida law should be certified to the Florida Supreme Court . . . .

Mr. Justice REHNQUIST, concurring.

. . . . While certification may engender less delay and create fewer additional expenses for litigants than would abstention, it entails more delay and expense than would an ordinary decision of the state question on the merits by the federal court. The Supreme Court of Florida has promulgated an appellate rule, which provides that upon certification by a federal court to that court, the parties shall file briefs there according to a specified briefing schedule, that oral argument may be granted upon application, and that the parties shall pay the costs of the certification. Thus while the certification procedure is more likely to produce the correct determination of state law, additional time and money are required to achieve such a determination. . . .

Colorado River Water Conservation District v. United States (1976)

Mr. Justice BRENNAN delivered the opinion of the Court.

The McCarran Amendment provides that "consent is hereby given to join the United States as a defendant in any suit (1) for the adjudication of rights to the use of water of a river system or other source, or (2) for the administration of such rights, where it appears that the United States is the owner of or is in the process of acquiring water rights by appropriation under State law, by purchase, by exchange, or otherwise, and the United States is a necessary party to such suit." The questions presented by this case concern the effect of the McCarran Amendment upon the jurisdiction of the federal district courts under 28 U.S.C. § 1345 over suits for determination of water rights brought by the United States as trustee for certain Indian tribes and as owner of various non-Indian Government claims.

I

It is probable that no problem of the Southwest section of the Nation is more critical than that of scarcity of water. As southwestern populations have grown, conflicting claims to this scarce resource have increased. To meet these claims, several Southwestern States have established elaborate procedures for allocation of water and adjudication of conflicting claims to that resource. In 1969, Colorado enacted its Water Rights Determination and Administration Act in an effort to revamp its legal procedures for determining claims to water within the State.

Under the Colorado Act, the State is divided into seven Water Divisions, each Division encompassing one or more entire drainage basins for the larger rivers in Colorado. Adjudication of water claims within each Division occurs on a continuous basis. Each month, Water Referees in each Division rule on applications for water rights filed within the preceding five months or refer those applications to the Water Judge of their Division. Every six months, the Water Judge passes on referred applications and contested decisions by Referees. A State Engineer and engineers for each Division are responsible for the administration and distribution of the waters of the State according to the determinations in each Division.

Colorado applies the doctrine of prior appropriation in establishing rights to the use of water. Under that doctrine, one acquires a right to water by diverting it from its natural source and applying it to some beneficial use. Continued beneficial use of the water is required in order to maintain the right. In periods of shortage, priority among confirmed rights is determined according to the date of initial diversion.

The reserved rights of the United States extend to Indian reservations and other federal lands, such as national parks and forests. The reserved rights claimed by the United States in this case affect waters within Colorado Water Division No. 7. On November 14, 1972, the Government instituted this suit in the United States District Court for the District of Colorado, invoking the court's jurisdiction under 28 U.S.C. § 1345. The District Court is located in Denver, some 300 miles from Division 7. The suit, against some 1,000 water users, sought declaration of the Government's rights to waters in certain rivers and their tributaries located in Division 7. In the suit, the Government asserted reserved rights on its own behalf and on behalf of certain Indian tribes, as well as rights based on state law. It sought appointment of a water master to administer any waters decreed to the United States. Prior to institution of this suit, the Government had pursued adjudication of non-Indian reserved rights and other water claims based on state law in Water Divisions 4, 5, and 6, and the Government continues to participate fully in those Divisions.

Shortly after the federal suit was commenced, one of the defendants in that suit filed an application in the state court for Division 7, seeking an order directing service of process on the United States in order to make it a party to proceedings in Division 7 for the purpose of adjudicating all of the Government's claims, both state and federal. On January 3, 1973, the United States was served pursuant to authority of the McCarran Amendment. Several defendants and intervenors in the federal proceeding then filed a motion in the District Court to dismiss on the ground that under the Amendment, the court was without jurisdiction to determine federal water rights. Without deciding the jurisdictional question, the District Court, on June 21, 1973, granted the motion in an unreported oral opinion stating that the doctrine of abstention required deference to the proceedings in Division 7. On appeal, the Court of Appeals for the Tenth Circuit reversed, holding that the suit of the United States was within district-court jurisdiction under 28 U.S.C. § 1345, and that abstention was inappropriate. We granted certiorari to consider the important questions of whether the McCarran Amendment terminated jurisdiction of federal courts to adjudicate federal water rights and whether, if that jurisdiction was not terminated, the District Court's dismissal in this case was nevertheless appropriate. We reverse.

II

[The Court first determined that the district court had jurisdiction under § 1345.]

III

We turn next to the question whether this suit nevertheless was properly dismissed in view of the concurrent state proceedings in Division 7. . . .

Abstention from the exercise of federal jurisdiction is the exception, not the rule. The doctrine of abstention, under which a District Court may decline to exercise or postpone the exercise of its jurisdiction, is an extraordinary and narrow exception to the duty of a District Court to adjudicate a controversy properly before it. Abdication of the obligation to decide cases can be justified under this doctrine only in the exceptional circumstances where the order to the parties to repair to the state court would clearly serve an important countervailing interest. It was never a doctrine of equity that a federal court should exercise its judicial discretion to dismiss a suit merely because a State court could entertain it. Our decisions have confined the circumstances appropriate for abstention to three general categories.

(a) Abstention is appropriate in cases presenting a federal constitutional issue which might be mooted or presented in a different posture by a state court determination of pertinent state law. This case, however, presents no federal constitutional issue for decision.

(b) Abstention is also appropriate where there have been presented difficult questions of state law bearing on policy problems of substantial public import whose importance transcends the result in the case then at bar. . . . In some cases, however, the state question itself need not be determinative of state policy. It is enough that exercise of federal review of the question in a case and in similar cases would be disruptive of state efforts to establish a coherent policy with respect to a matter of substantial public concern. In *Burford v. Sun Oil Co.*, for example, the Court held that a suit seeking review of the reasonableness under Texas state law of a state commission's permit to drill oil wells should have been dismissed by the District Court. The reasonableness of the permit in that case was not of transcendent importance, but review of reasonableness by the federal courts in that and future cases, where the State had established its own elaborate review system for dealing with the geological complexities of oil and gas fields, would have had an impermissibly disruptive effect on state policy for the management of those fields.

The present case clearly does not fall within this second category of abstention. While state claims are involved in the case, the state law to be applied appears to be settled. No questions bearing on state policy are presented for decision. Nor will decision of the state claims impair efforts to implement state policy as in Burford. To be sure, the federal claims that are involved in the case go to the establishment of water rights which may conflict with similar rights based on state law. But the mere potential for conflict in the results of adjudications, does not, without more, warrant staying exercise of federal jurisdiction. The potential conflict here, involving state claims and federal claims, would not be such as to impair impermissibly the State's effort to effect its policy respecting the allocation of state waters. Nor would exercise of federal jurisdiction here interrupt any such efforts by restraining the exercise of authority vested in state officers.

(c) Finally, abstention is appropriate where, absent bad faith, harassment, or a patently invalid state statute, federal jurisdiction has been invoked for the purpose of restraining state criminal proceedings, *see Younger v. Harris*, state nuisance proceedings antecedent to a criminal prosecution, which are directed at obtaining the closure of places exhibiting obscene films, or collection of state taxes. Like the previous two categories, this category also does not include this case. We deal here neither with a criminal proceeding, nor such a nuisance proceeding, nor a tax collection. We also do not deal with an attempt to restrain such actions or to seek a declaratory judgment as to the validity of a state criminal law under which criminal proceedings are pending in a state court.

C

Although this case falls within none of the abstention categories, there are principles unrelated to considerations of proper constitutional adjudication and regard for federal-state relations which govern in situations involving the contemporaneous exercise of concurrent jurisdictions, either by federal courts or by state and federal courts. These principles rest on considerations of wise judicial administration, giving regard to conservation of judicial resources and comprehensive disposition of litigation. Generally, as between state and federal courts, the rule is that the pendency of an action in the state court is no bar to proceedings concerning the same matter in the Federal court having jurisdiction. As between federal district courts, however, though no precise rule has evolved, the general principle is to avoid duplicative litigation. This difference in general approach between state-federal concurrent jurisdiction and wholly federal concurrent jurisdiction stems from the virtually unflagging obligation of the federal courts to exercise the jurisdiction given them. Given this obligation, and the absence of weightier considerations of constitutional adjudication and state-federal relations, the circumstances permitting the dismissal of a federal suit due to the presence of a concurrent state proceeding for reasons of wise judicial administration are considerably more limited than the circumstances appropriate for abstention. The former circumstances, though exceptional, do nevertheless exist.

It has been held, for example, that the court first assuming jurisdiction over property may exercise that jurisdiction to the exclusion of other courts. This has been true even where the Government was a claimant in existing state proceedings and then sought to invoke district-court jurisdiction under the jurisdictional provision antecedent to 28 U.S.C. § 1345. In assessing the appropriateness of dismissal in the event of an exercise of concurrent jurisdiction, a federal court may also consider such factors as the inconvenience of the federal forum; the desirability of avoiding piecemeal litigation; and the order in which jurisdiction was obtained by the concurrent forums. No one factor is necessarily determinative; a carefully considered judgment taking into account both the obligation to exercise jurisdiction and the combination of factors counselling against that exercise is required. Only the clearest of justifications will warrant dismissal.

Turning to the present case, a number of factors clearly counsel against concurrent federal proceedings. The most important of these is the McCarran Amendment itself. The clear federal policy evinced by that legislation is the avoidance of piecemeal adjudication of water rights in a river system. This policy is akin to that underlying the rule requiring that jurisdiction be yielded to the court first acquiring control of property, for the concern in such instances is with avoiding the generation of additional litigation through permitting inconsistent dispositions of property. This concern is heightened with respect to water rights, the relationships among which are highly interdependent. Indeed, we have recognized that actions seeking the allocation of water essentially involve the disposition of property and are best conducted in unified proceedings. The consent to jurisdiction given by the McCarran Amendment bespeaks a policy that recognizes the availability of comprehensive state systems for adjudication of water rights as the means for achieving these goals.

As has already been observed, the Colorado Water Rights Determination and Administration Act established such a system for the adjudication and management of rights to the use of the State's waters. As the Government concedes . . . , the Act established a single continuous proceeding for water rights adjudication which antedated the suit in District Court. That proceeding reaches all claims, perhaps month by month but inclusively in the totality. Additionally, the responsibility of managing the State's waters, to the end that they be allocated in accordance with adjudicated water rights, is given to the State Engineer.

Beyond the congressional policy expressed by the McCarran Amendment and consistent with furtherance of that policy, we also find significant (a) the apparent absence of any proceedings in the District Court, other than the filing of the complaint, prior to the motion to dismiss, (b) the extensive involvement of state water rights occasioned by this suit naming 1,000 defendants, (c) the 300-mile distance between the District Court in Denver and the court in Division 7, and (d) the existing participation by the Government in Division 4, 5, and 6 proceedings. We emphasize, however, that we do not overlook the heavy obligation to exercise jurisdiction. We need not decide, for example, whether, despite the McCarran Amendment, dismissal would be warranted if more extensive proceedings had occurred in the District Court prior to dismissal, if the involvement of state water rights were less extensive than it is here, or if the state proceeding were in some respect inadequate to resolve the federal claims. But the opposing factors here, particularly the policy underlying the McCarran Amendment, justify the District Court's dismissal in this particular case.

The judgment of the Court of Appeals is reversed and the judgment of the District Court dismissing the complaint is affirmed for the reasons here stated.

Mr. Justice STEWART, with whom Mr. Justice BLACKMUN and Mr. Justice STEVENS concur, dissenting.

The Court says that the United States District Court for the District of Colorado clearly had jurisdiction over this lawsuit. I agree. The Court further says that the McCarran Amendment in no way diminished the District Court's jurisdiction. I agree. The Court also says that federal courts have a "virtually unflagging obligation . . . to exercise the jurisdiction given them." I agree. And finally, the Court says that nothing in the abstention doctrine in any of its forms justified the District Court's dismissal of the Government's complaint. I agree. These views would seem to lead ineluctably to the conclusion that the District Court was wrong in dismissing the complaint. Yet the Court holds that the order of dismissal was "appropriate." With that conclusion I must respectfully disagree. . . .

The Court's principal reason for deciding to close the doors of the federal courthouse to the United States in this case seems to stem from the view that its decision will avoid piecemeal adjudication of water rights.[6] To the extent that this view is based on the special considerations governing in rem proceedings, it is without precedential basis, as the decisions discussed above demonstrate. To the extent that the Court's view is based on the realistic practicalities of this case, it is simply wrong, because the relegation of the Government to the state courts will not avoid piecemeal litigation.

> [6] The Court lists four other policy reasons for the "appropriateness" of the District Court's dismissal of this lawsuit. All of those reasons are insubstantial. First, the fact that no significant proceedings had yet taken place in the federal court at the time of the dismissal means no more than that the federal court was prompt in granting the defendants' motion to dismiss. At that time, of course, no proceedings involving the Government's claims had taken place in the state court either. Second, the geographic distance of the federal court from the rivers in question is hardly a significant factor in this age of rapid and easy transportation. Since the basic issues here involve the determination of the amount of water the Government intended to reserve rather than the amount it actually appropriated on a given date, there is little likelihood that live testimony by water district residents would be necessary. In any event, the Federal District Court in Colorado is authorized to sit at Durango, the headquarters of Water Division 7. Third, the Government's willingness to participate in some of the state proceedings certainly does not mean that it had no right to bring this action, unless the Court has today unearthed a new kind of waiver. Finally, the fact that there were many defendants in the federal suit is hardly relevant. It only indicates that the federal court had all the necessary parties before it in order to issue a decree finally settling the Government's claims. Indeed, the presence of all interested parties in the federal court made the lawsuit [a] unified proceeding . . . .

The Colorado courts are currently engaged in two types of proceedings under the State's water-rights law. First, they are processing new claims to water based on recent appropriations. Second, they are integrating these new awards of water rights with all past decisions awarding such rights into one all-inclusive tabulation for each water source. The claims of the United States that are involved in this case have not been adjudicated in the past. Yet they do not involve recent appropriations of water. In fact, these claims are wholly dissimilar to normal state water claims, because they are not based on actual beneficial use of water but rather on an intention formed at the time the federal land use was established to reserve a certain amount of water to support the federal reservations. The state court will, therefore, have to conduct separate proceedings to determine these claims. And only after the state court adjudicates the claims will they be incorporated into the water source tabulations. If this suit were allowed to proceed in federal court the same procedures would be followed, and the federal court decree would be incorporated into the state tabulation, as other federal court decrees have been incorporated in the past. Thus, the same process will occur regardless of which forum considers these claims. Whether the virtually identical separate proceedings take place in a federal court or a state court, the adjudication of the claims will be neither more nor less "piecemeal." Essentially the same process will be followed in each instance.

As the Court says, it is the virtual "unflagging obligation" of a federal court to exercise the jurisdiction that has been conferred upon it. Obedience to that obligation is particularly "appropriate" in this case, for at least two reasons.

First, the issues involved are issues of federal law. A federal court is more likely than a state court to be familiar with federal water law and to have had experience in interpreting the relevant federal statutes, regulations, and Indian treaties. Moreover, if tried in a federal court, these issues of federal law will be reviewable in a federal appellate court, whereas federal judicial review of the state courts' resolution of issues of federal law will be possible only on review by this Court in the exercise of its certiorari jurisdiction.

Second, some of the federal claims in this lawsuit relate to water reserved for Indian reservations. It is not necessary to determine that there is no state-court jurisdiction of these claims to support the proposition that a federal court is a more appropriate forum than a state court for determination of questions of life-and-death importance to Indians. This Court has long recognized that the policy of leaving Indians free from state jurisdiction and control is deeply rooted in the Nation's history.

The Court says that only the clearest of justifications will warrant dismissal of a lawsuit within the jurisdiction of a federal court. In my opinion there was no justification at all for the District Court's order of dismissal in this case. I would affirm the judgment of the Court of Appeals.

Younger v. Harris (1971)

Appellee, John Harris, Jr., was indicted in a California state court, charged with violation of the California Penal Code §§ 11400 and 11401, known as the California Criminal Syndicalism Act, set out below.[1]

> [1] s 11400. Definition
> "Criminal syndicalism" as used in this article means any doctrine or precept advocating, teaching or aiding and abetting the commission of crime, sabotage (which word is hereby defined as meaning willful and malicious physical damage or injury to physical property), or unlawful acts of force and violence or unlawful methods of terrorism as a means of accomplishing a change in industrial ownership or control, or effecting any political change.
> s 11401. Offense; punishment
> Any person who:
> 1. By spoken or written words or personal conduct advocates, teaches or aids and abets criminal syndicalism or the duty, necessity or propriety of committing crime, sabotage, violence or any unlawful method of terrorism as a means of accomplishing a change in industrial ownership or control, or effecting any political change; or
> 2. Willfully and deliberately by spoken or written words justifies or attempts to justify criminal syndicalism or the commission or attempt to commit crime, sabotage, violence or unlawful methods of terrorism with intent to approve, advocate or further the doctrine of criminal syndicalism; or
> 3. Prints, publishes, edits, issues or circulates or publicly displays any book, paper, pamphlet, document, poster or written or printed matter in any other form, containing or carrying written or printed advocacy, teaching, or aid and abetment of, or advising, criminal syndicalism; or
> 4. Organizes or assists in organizing, or is or knowingly becomes a member of, any organization, society, group or assemblage of persons organized or assembled to advocate, teach or aid and abet criminal syndicalism; or
> 5. Willfully by personal act or conduct, practices or commits any act advised, advocated, taught or aided and abetted by the doctrine or precept of criminal syndicalism, with intent to accomplish a change in industrial ownership or control, or effecting any political change;
> Is guilty of a felony and punishable by imprisonment in the state prison not less than one nor more than 14 years.

He then filed a complaint in the Federal District Court, asking that court to enjoin the appellant, Younger, the District Attorney of Los Angeles County, from prosecuting him, and alleging that the prosecution and even the presence of the Act inhibited him in the exercise of his rights of free speech and press, rights guaranteed him by the First and Fourteenth Amendments. Appellees Jim Dan and Diane Hirsch intervened as plaintiffs in the suit, claiming that the prosecution of Harris would inhibit them as members of the Progressive Labor Party from peacefully advocating the program of their party, which was to replace capitalism with socialism and to abolish the profit system of production in this country. Appellee Farrell Broslawsky, an instructor in history at Los Angeles Valley College, also intervened claiming that the prosecution of Harris made him uncertain as to whether he could teach about the doctrines of Karl Marx or read from the Communist Manifesto as part of his classwork. All claimed that unless the United States court restrained the state prosecution of Harris each would suffer immediate and irreparable injury.

A three-judge Federal District Court, convened pursuant to 28 U.S.C. § 2284, held that it had jurisdiction and power to restrain the District Attorney from prosecuting, held that the State's Criminal Syndicalism Act was void for vagueness and overbreadth in violation of the First and Fourteenth Amendments, and accordingly restrained the District Attorney from further prosecution of the currently pending action against plaintiff Harris for alleged violation of the Act.

The case is before us on appeal by the State's District Attorney Younger, pursuant to 28 U.S.C. § 1253. . . . [W]e have concluded that the judgment of the District Court, enjoining appellant Younger from prosecuting under these California statutes, must be reversed as a violation of the national policy forbidding federal courts to stay or enjoin pending state court proceedings except under special circumstances. We express no view about the circumstances under which federal courts may act when there is no prosecution pending in state courts at the time the federal proceeding is begun.

I

Appellee Harris has been indicted, and was actually being prosecuted by California for a violation of its Criminal Syndicalism Act at the time this suit was filed. He thus has an acute, live controversy with the State and its prosecutor. But none of the other parties plaintiff in the District Court, Dan, Hirsch, or Broslawsky, has such a controversy. None has been indicted, arrested, or even threatened by the prosecutor. . . . Whatever right Harris, who is being prosecuted under the state syndicalism law may have, Dan, Hirsch, and Broslawsky cannot share it with him. If these three had alleged that they would be prosecuted for the conduct they planned to engage in, and if the District Court had found this allegation to be true—either on the admission of the State's district attorney or on any other evidence—then a genuine controversy might be said to exist. But here appellees Dan, Hirsch, and Broslawsky do not claim that they have ever been threatened with prosecution, that a prosecution is likely, or even that a prosecution is remotely possible. They claim the right to bring this suit solely because, in the language of their complaint, they "feel inhibited." We do not think this allegation even if true, is sufficient to bring the equitable jurisdiction of the federal courts into play to enjoin a pending state prosecution. A federal lawsuit to stop a prosecution in a state court is a serious matter. And persons having no fears of state prosecution except those that are imaginary or speculative, are not to be accepted as appropriate plaintiffs in such cases. *See Golden v. Zwickler*. Since Harris is actually being prosecuted under the challenged laws, however, we proceed with him as a proper party.

II

Since the beginning of this country's history Congress has, subject to few exceptions, manifested a desire to permit state courts to try state cases free from interference by federal courts. . . . The precise reasons for this longstanding public policy against federal court interference with state court proceedings have never been specifically identified but the primary sources of the policy are plain.

One is the basic doctrine of equity jurisprudence that courts of equity should not act, and particularly should not act to restrain a criminal prosecution, when the moving party has an adequate remedy at law and will not suffer irreparable injury if denied equitable relief. The doctrine may originally have grown out of circumstances peculiar to the English judicial system and not applicable in this country, but its fundamental purpose of restraining equity jurisdiction within narrow limits is equally important under our Constitution, in order to prevent erosion of the role of the jury and avoid a duplication of legal proceedings and legal sanctions where a single suit would be adequate to protect the rights asserted.

This underlying reason for restraining courts of equity from interfering with criminal prosecutions is reinforced by an even more vital consideration, the notion of "comity," that is, a proper respect for state functions, a recognition of the fact that the entire country is made up of a Union of separate state governments, and a continuance of the belief that the National Government will fare best if the States and their institutions are left free to perform their separate functions in their separate ways. This, perhaps for lack of a better and clearer way to describe it, is referred to by many as "Our Federalism," and one familiar with the profound debates that ushered our Federal Constitution into existence is bound to respect those who remain loyal to the ideals and dreams of "Our Federalism." The concept does not mean blind deference to "States' Rights" any more than it means centralization of control over every important issue in our National Government and its courts. The Framers rejected both these courses. What the concept does represent is a system in which there is sensitivity to the legitimate interests of both State and National Governments, and in which the National Government, anxious though it may be to vindicate and protect federal rights and federal interests, always endeavors to do so in ways that will not unduly interfere with the legitimate activities of the States. It should never be forgotten that this slogan, "Our Federalism," born in the early struggling days of our Union of States, occupies a highly important place in our Nation's history and its future.

This brief discussion should be enough to suggest some of the reasons why it has been perfectly natural for our cases to repeat time and time again that the normal thing to do when federal courts are asked to enjoin pending proceedings in state courts is not to issue such injunctions. . . .

In all of these cases the Court stressed the importance of showing irreparable injury, the traditional prerequisite to obtaining an injunction. In addition, however, the Court also made clear that in view of the fundamental policy against federal interference with state criminal prosecutions, even irreparable injury is insufficient unless it is both great and immediate. Certain types of injury, in particular, the cost, anxiety, and inconvenience of having to defend against a single criminal prosecution, could not by themselves be considered "irreparable" in the special legal sense of that term. Instead, the threat to the plaintiff's federally protected rights must be one that cannot be eliminated by his defense against a single criminal prosecution. . . .

It is against the background of these principles that we must judge the propriety of an injunction under the circumstances of the present case. Here a proceeding was already pending in the state court, affording Harris an opportunity to raise his constitutional claims. There is no suggestion that this single prosecution against Harris is brought in bad faith or is only one of a series of repeated prosecutions to which he will be subjected. In other words, the injury that Harris faces is solely that incidental to every criminal proceeding brought lawfully and in good faith, and therefore under the settled doctrine we have already described he is not entitled to equitable relief even if such statutes are unconstitutional.

. . . . It is undoubtedly true . . . that a criminal prosecution under a statute regulating expression usually involves imponderables and contingencies that themselves may inhibit the full exercise of First Amendment freedoms. But this sort of "chilling effect," . . . should not by itself justify federal intervention. In the first place, the chilling effect cannot be satisfactorily eliminated by federal injunctive relief . . . . [because it may] not effectively eliminate uncertainty as to the coverage of the state statute and leaves most citizens with virtually the same doubts as before regarding the danger that their conduct might eventually be subjected to criminal sanctions. The chilling effect can, of course, be eliminated by an injunction that would prohibit any prosecution whatever for conduct occurring prior to a satisfactory rewriting of the statute. But the States would then be stripped of all power to prosecute even the socially dangerous and constitutionally unprotected conduct that had been covered by the statute, until a new statute could be passed by the state legislature and approved by the federal courts in potentially lengthy trial and appellate proceedings. Thus, . . . the Court [has] carefully reaffirmed the principle that even in the direct prosecution in the State's own courts, a valid narrowing construction can be applied to conduct occurring prior to the date when the narrowing construction was made, in the absence of fair warning problems.

Moreover, the existence of a "chilling effect," even in the area of First Amendment rights, has never been considered a sufficient basis, in and of itself, for prohibiting state action. Where a statute does not directly abridge free speech, but—while regulating a subject within the State's power—tends to have the incidental effect of inhibiting First Amendment rights, it is well settled that the statute can be upheld if the effect on speech is minor in relation to the need for control of the conduct and the lack of alternative means for doing so. Just as the incidental "chilling effect" of such statutes does not automatically render them unconstitutional, so the chilling effect that admittedly can result from the very existence of certain laws on the statute books does not in itself justify prohibiting the State from carrying out the important and necessary task of enforcing these laws against socially harmful conduct that the State believes in good faith to be punishable under its laws and the Constitution. . . .

There may, of course, be extraordinary circumstances in which the necessary irreparable injury can be shown even in the absence of the usual prerequisites of bad faith and harassment. . . . Other unusual situations calling for federal intervention might also arise, but there is no point in our attempting now to specify what they might be. It is sufficient for purposes of the present case to hold, as we do, that the possible unconstitutionality of a statute "on its face" does not in itself justify an injunction against good-faith attempts to enforce it, and that appellee Harris has failed to make any showing of bad faith, harassment, or any other unusual circumstance that would call for equitable relief. . . .

The judgment of the District Court is reversed, and the case is remanded for further proceedings not inconsistent with this opinion.

Samuels v. Mackell (1971)

The appellants in these two cases were all indicted in a New York state court on charges of criminal anarchy, in violation of . . . the New York Penal Law. They later filed these actions in federal district court, alleging (1) that the anarchy statute was void for vagueness in violation of due process, and an abridgment of free speech, press, and assembly, in violation of the First and Fourteenth Amendments; (2) that the anarchy statute had been pre-empted by federal law; and (3) that the New York laws under which the grand jury had been drawn violated the Due Process and Equal Protection Clauses of the Fourteenth Amendment because they disqualified from jury service any member of the community who did not own real or personal property of the value of at least $250, and because the laws furnished no definite standards for determining how jurors were to be selected. Appellants charged that trial of these indictments in state courts would harass them, and cause them to suffer irreparable damages, and they therefore prayed that the state courts should be enjoined from further proceedings. In the alternative, appellants asked the District Court to enter a declaratory judgment to the effect that the challenged state laws were unconstitutional and void on the same grounds. The three-judge court, convened pursuant to 28 U.S.C. § 2284, held that the New York criminal anarchy law was constitutional as it had been construed by the New York courts and held that the complaints should therefore be dismissed.

In . . . *Younger v. Harris*, we today decided on facts very similar to the facts in these cases that a United States District Court could not issue an injunction to stay proceedings pending in a state criminal court at the time the federal suit was begun. This was because it did not appear from the record that the plaintiffs would suffer immediate irreparable injury . . . . Since in the present case there is likewise no sufficient showing in the record that the plaintiffs have suffered or would suffer irreparable injury, our decision in the *Younger* case is dispositive of the prayers for injunctions here. The plaintiffs in the present cases also included in their complaints an alternative prayer for a declaratory judgment, but for the reasons indicated below, we hold that this alternative prayer does not require a different result, and that under the circumstances of these cases, the plaintiffs were not entitled to federal relief, declaratory or injunctive. Accordingly we affirm the judgment of the District Court, although not for the reasons given in that court's opinion.

In our opinion in the *Younger* case, we set out in detail the historical and practical basis for the settled doctrine of equity that a federal court should not enjoin a state criminal prosecution begun prior to the institution of the federal suit except in very unusual situations, where necessary to prevent immediate irreparable injury. The question presented here is whether under ordinary circumstances the same considerations that require the withholding of injunctive relief will make declaratory relief equally inappropriate. . . .

Although the declaratory judgment sought by the plaintiffs [i]s a statutory remedy rather than a traditional form of equitable relief, . . . a suit for declaratory judgment [i]s nevertheless essentially an equitable cause of action, and [i]s analogous to the equity jurisdiction in suits quia timet or for a decree quieting title. In addition, the legislative history of the Federal Declaratory Judgment Act of 1934 show[s] that Congress had explicitly contemplated that the courts would decide to grant or withhold declaratory relief on the basis of traditional equitable principles. . . .

[D]eeply rooted and long-settled principles of equity have narrowly restricted the scope for federal intervention, and ordinarily a declaratory judgment will result in precisely the same interference with and disruption of state proceedings that the longstanding policy limiting injunctions was designed to avoid. This is true for at least two reasons. In the first place, the Declaratory Judgment Act provides that after a declaratory judgment is issued the district court may enforce it by granting "further necessary or proper relief," and therefore a declaratory judgment issued while state proceedings are pending might serve as the basis for a subsequent injunction against those proceedings to protect or effectuate the declaratory judgment, and thus result in a clearly improper interference with the state proceedings. Secondly, even if the declaratory judgment is not used as a basis for actually issuing an injunction, the declaratory relief alone has virtually the same practical impact as a formal injunction would. . . . Is the declaration contemplated here to be res judicata, so that the state court cannot hear evidence and decide any matter for itself? If so, the federal court has virtually lifted the case out of the State court before it could be heard.

. . . . We therefore hold that, in cases where the state criminal prosecution was begun prior to the federal suit, the same equitable principles relevant to the propriety of an injunction must be taken into consideration by federal district courts in determining whether to issue a declaratory judgment, and that where an injunction would be impermissible under these principles, declaratory relief should ordinarily be denied as well.

We do not mean to suggest that a declaratory judgment should never be issued in cases of this type if it has been concluded that injunctive relief would be improper. There may be unusual circumstances in which an injunction might be withheld because, despite a plaintiff's strong claim for relief under the established standards, the injunctive remedy seemed particularly intrusive or offensive; in such a situation, a declaratory judgment might be appropriate and might not be contrary to the basic equitable doctrines governing the availability of relief. Ordinarily, however, the practical effect of the two forms of relief will be virtually identical, and the basic policy against federal interference with pending state criminal prosecutions will be frustrated as much by a declaratory judgment as it would be by an injunction. . . .

We affirm the judgment dismissing the complaint, but solely on the ground that, in the appropriate exercise of the court's discretion, relief by way of declaratory judgment should have been denied without consideration of the merits. We, of course, express no views on the propriety of declaratory relief when no state proceeding is pending at the time the federal suit is begun.

Steffel v. Thompson (1974)

When a state criminal proceeding under a disputed state criminal statute is pending against a federal plaintiff at the time his federal complaint is filed, *Younger* and *Samuels* held, respectively, that, unless bad-faith enforcement or other special circumstances are demonstrated, principles of equity, comity, and federalism preclude issuance of a federal injunction restraining enforcement of the criminal statute and, in all but unusual circumstances, a declaratory judgment upon the constitutionality of the statute. This case presents the important question reserved in *Samuels v. Mackell*, whether declaratory relief is precluded when a state prosecution has been threatened, but is not pending, and a showing of bad-faith enforcement or other special circumstances has not been made.

Petitioner, and others, filed a complaint in the District Court for the Northern District of Georgia, invoking 42 U.S.C. § 1983, and its jurisdictional implementation, 28 U.S.C. § 1343. The complaint requested a declaratory judgment . . . that [Georgia's criminal-trespass law] was being applied in violation of petitioner's First and Fourteenth Amendment rights, and an injunction restraining respondents—the Solicitor of the Civil and Criminal Court of DeKalb County, the chief of the DeKalb County Police, the owner of the North DeKalb Shopping Center, and the manager of that shopping center—from enforcing the statute so as to interfere with petitioner's constitutionally protected activities.

The parties stipulated to the relevant facts: On October 8, 1970, while petitioner and other individuals were distributing handbills protesting American involvement in Vietnam on an exterior sidewalk of the North DeKalb Shopping Center, shopping center employees asked them to stop handbilling and leave. They declined to do so, and police officers were summoned. The officers told them that they would be arrested if they did not stop handbilling. The group then left to avoid arrest. Two days later petitioner and a companion returned to the shopping center and again began handbilling. The manager of the center called the police, and petitioner and his companion were once again told that failure to stop their handbilling would result in their arrests. Petitioner left to avoid arrest. His companion stayed, however, continued handbilling, and was arrested and subsequently arraigned on a charge of criminal trespass . . . . Petitioner alleged in his complaint that, although he desired to return to the shopping center to distribute handbills, he had not done so because of his concern that he, too, would be arrested . . . ; the parties stipulated that, if petitioner returned and refused upon request to stop handbilling, a warrant would be sworn out and he might be arrested and charged with a violation of the Georgia statute.

After hearing, the District Court denied all relief and dismissed the action . . . . The Court of Appeals for the Fifth Circuit, one judge concurring in the result, affirmed the District Court's judgment refusing declaratory relief. . . . We granted certiorari and now reverse.

I

At the threshold we must consider whether petitioner presents an "actual controversy," a requirement imposed by Art. III of the Constitution and the express terms of the Federal Declaratory Judgment act, 28 U.S.C. § 2201.

Unlike three of the appellees in *Younger*, petitioner has alleged threats of prosecution that cannot be characterized as imaginary or speculative. He has been twice warned to stop handbilling that he claims is constitutionally protected and has been told by the police that if he again handbills at the shopping center and disobeys a warning to stop he will likely be prosecuted. The prosecution of petitioner's handbilling companion is ample demonstration that petitioner's concern with arrest has not been chimerical. In these circumstances, it is not necessary that petitioner first expose himself to actual arrest or prosecution to be entitled to challenge a statute that he claims deters the exercise of his constitutional rights. Moreover, petitioner's challenge is to those specific provisions of state law which have provided the basis for threats of criminal prosecution against him.

Nonetheless, there remains a question as to the continuing existence of a live and acute controversy that must be resolved on the remand we order today. In *Golden v. Zwickler*, the appellee sought a declaratory judgment that a state criminal statute prohibiting the distribution of anonymous election-campaign literature was unconstitutional. The appellee's complaint had expressed a desire to distribute handbills during the forthcoming re-election campaign of a Congressman, but it was later learned that the Congressman had retired from the House of Representatives to become a New York Supreme Court Justice. In that circumstance, we found no extant controversy, since the record revealed that appellee's sole target of distribution had been the Congressman and there was no immediate prospect of the Congressman's again becoming a candidate for public office. Here, petitioner's complaint indicates that his handbilling activities were directed against the war in Vietnam and the United States, foreign policy in Southeast Asia. Since we cannot ignore the recent developments reducing the Nation's involvement in that part of the world, it will be for the District Court on remand to determine if subsequent events have so altered petitioner's desire to engage in handbilling at the shopping center that it can no longer be said that this case presents a substantial controversy, between parties having adverse legal interests, of sufficient immediacy and reality to warrant the issuance of a declaratory judgment.

II

We now turn to the question of whether the District Court and the Court of Appeals correctly found petitioner's request for declaratory relief inappropriate.

Sensitive to principles of equity, comity, and federalism, we recognized in *Younger* that federal courts should ordinarily refrain from enjoining ongoing state criminal prosecutions. We were cognizant that a pending state proceeding, in all but unusual cases, would provide the federal plaintiff with the necessary vehicle for vindicating his constitutional rights, and, in that circumstance, the restraining of an ongoing prosecution would entail an unseemly failure to give effect to the principle that state courts have the solemn responsibility, equally with the federal courts to guard, enforce, and protect every right granted or secured by the constitution of the United States. In *Samuels*, the Court also found that the same principles ordinarily would be flouted by issuance of a federal declaratory judgment when a state proceeding was pending, since the intrusive effect of declaratory relief will result in precisely the same interference with and disruption of state proceedings that the long-standing policy limiting injunctions was designed to avoid. We therefore held in *Samuels* that, in cases where the state criminal prosecution was begun prior to the federal suit, the same equitable principles relevant to the propriety of an injunction must be taken into consideration by federal district courts in determining whether to issue a declaratory judgment.

Neither *Younger* nor *Samuels*, however, decided the question whether federal intervention might be permissible in the absence of a pending state prosecution. In *Younger*, the Court said: "We express no view about the circumstances under which federal courts may act when there is no prosecution pending in state courts at the time the federal proceeding is begun." Similarly, in *Samuels*, the Court stated: "We, of course, express no views on the propriety of declaratory relief when no state proceeding is pending at the time the federal suit is begun."

These reservations anticipated the Court's recognition that the relevant principles of equity, comity, and federalism have little force in the absence of a pending state proceeding. When no state criminal proceeding is pending at the time the federal complaint is filed, federal intervention does not result in duplicative legal proceedings or disruption of the state criminal justice system; nor can federal intervention, in that circumstance, be interpreted as reflecting negatively upon the state court's ability to enforce constitutional principles. In addition, while a pending state prosecution provides the federal plaintiff with a concrete opportunity to vindicate his constitutional rights, a refusal on the part of the federal courts to intervene when no state proceeding is pending may place the hapless plaintiff between the Scylla of intentionally flouting state law and the Charybdis of forgoing what he believes to be constitutionally protected activity in order to avoid becoming enmeshed in a criminal proceeding.

When no state proceeding is pending and thus considerations of equity, comity, and federalism have little vitality, the propriety of granting federal declaratory relief may properly be considered independently of a request for injunctive relief. Here, the Court of Appeals held that, because injunctive relief would not be appropriate since petitioner failed to demonstrate irreparable injury—a traditional prerequisite to injunctive relief—it followed that declaratory relief was also inappropriate. Even if the Court of Appeals correctly viewed injunctive relief as inappropriate—a question we need not reach today since petitioner has abandoned his request for that remedy—the court erred in treating the requests for injunctive and declaratory relief as a single issue. When no state prosecution is pending and the only question is whether declaratory relief is appropriate, . . . the congressional scheme that makes the federal courts the primary guardians of constitutional rights, and the express congressional authorization of declaratory relief, afforded because it is a less harsh and abrasive remedy than the injunction, become the factors of primary significance.

The subject matter jurisdiction of the lower federal courts was greatly expanded in the wake of the Civil War. A pervasive sense of nationalism led to enactment of the Civil Rights Act of 1871, empowering the lower federal courts to determine the constitutionality of actions, taken by persons under color of state law, allegedly depriving other individuals of rights guaranteed by the Constitution and federal law. Four years later, in the Judiciary Act of March 3, 1875, Congress conferred upon the lower federal courts, for but the second time in their nearly century-old history, general federal-question jurisdiction subject only to a jurisdictional-amount requirement, see 28 U.S.C. § 1331. With this latter enactment, the lower federal courts ceased to be restricted tribunals of fair dealing between citizens of different states and became the primary and powerful reliance for vindicating every right given by the Constitution, the laws, and treaties of the United States. These two statutes, together with the Court's decision in *Ex parte Young*—holding that state officials who threaten to enforce an unconstitutional state statute may be enjoined by a federal court of equity and that a federal court may, in appropriate circumstances, enjoin future state criminal prosecutions under the unconstitutional Act—have established the modern framework for federal protection of constitutional rights from state interference.

A storm of controversy raged in the wake of *Ex parte Young*, focusing principally on the power of a single federal judge to grant ex parte interlocutory injunctions against the enforcement of state statutes. . . . [In response,] Congress in 1934 enacted the Declaratory Judgment Act. That Congress plainly intended declaratory relief to act as an alternative to the strong medicine of the injunction and to be utilized to test the constitutionality of state criminal statutes in cases where injunctive relief would be unavailable is amply evidenced by the legislative history of the Act . . . .

The different considerations entering into a decision whether to grant declaratory relief have their origins in the preceding historical summary. First, as Congress recognized in 1934, a declaratory judgment will have a less intrusive effect on the administration of state criminal laws. . . . Where the highest court of a State has had an opportunity to give a statute regulating expression a narrowing or clarifying construction but has failed to do so, and later a federal court declares the statute unconstitutionally vague or overbroad, it may well be open to a state prosecutor, after the federal court decision, to bring a prosecution under the statute if he reasonably believes that the defendant's conduct is not constitutionally protected and that the state courts may give the statute a construction so as to yield a constitutionally valid conviction. Even where a declaration of unconstitutionality is not reviewed by this Court, the declaration may still be able to cut down the deterrent effect of an unconstitutional state statute. The persuasive force of the court's opinion and judgment may lead state prosecutors, courts, and legislators to reconsider their respective responsibilities toward the statute. Enforcement policies or judicial construction may be changed, or the legislature may repeal the statute and start anew. What is clear, however, is that even though a declaratory judgment has the force and effect of a final judgment, it is a much milder form of relief than an injunction. Though it may be persuasive, it is not ultimately coercive; noncompliance with it may be inappropriate, but is not contempt.

Second, engrafting upon the Declaratory Judgment Act a requirement that all of the traditional equitable prerequisites to the issuance of an injunction be satisfied before the issuance of a declaratory judgment is considered would defy Congress's intent to make declaratory relief available in cases where an injunction would be inappropriate. . . .

The only occasions where this Court has disregarded these different considerations and found that a preclusion of injunctive relief inevitably led to a denial of declaratory relief have been cases in which principles of federalism militated altogether against federal intervention in a class of adjudications. In the instant case, principles of federalism not only do not preclude federal intervention, they compel it. Requiring the federal courts totally to step aside when no state criminal prosecution is pending against the federal plaintiff would turn federalism on its head. When federal claims are premised on 42 U.S.C. § 1983 and 28 U.S.C. § 1343(3)—as they are here—we have not required exhaustion of state judicial or administrative remedies, recognizing the paramount role Congress has assigned to the federal courts to protect constitutional rights. But exhaustion of state remedies is precisely what would be required if both federal injunctive and declaratory relief were unavailable in a case where no state prosecution had been commenced.

III

. . . . We therefore hold that, regardless of whether injunctive relief may be appropriate, federal declaratory relief is not precluded when no state prosecution is pending and a federal plaintiff demonstrates a genuine threat of enforcement of a disputed state criminal statute, whether an attack is made on the constitutionality of the statute on its face or as applied. The judgment of the Court of Appeals is reversed, and the case is remanded for further proceedings consistent with this opinion.

Huffman v. Pursue (1975)

Mr. Justice REHNQUIST delivered the opinion of the Court.

This case requires that we decide whether our decision in *Younger v. Harris* bars a federal district court from intervening in a state civil proceeding such as this, when the proceeding is based on a state statute believed by the district court to be unconstitutional. . . . [We] conclude that in the circumstances presented here the principles of *Younger* are applicable even though the state proceeding is civil in nature.

I

Appellants are the sheriff and prosecuting attorney of Allen County, Ohio. This case arises from their efforts to close the Cinema I Theatre, in Lima, Ohio. Under the management of both its current tenant, appellee Pursue, Ltd., and appellee's predecessor, William Dakota, the Cinema I has specialized in the display of films which may fairly be characterized as pornographic, and which in numerous instances have been adjudged obscene after adversary hearings.

Appellants sought to invoke the Ohio public nuisance statute against appellee. [It] provides that a place which exhibits obscene films is a nuisance [and] requires closure for up to a year of any place determined to be a nuisance. The statute also provides for preliminary injunctions pending final determination of status as a nuisance, for sale of all personal property used in conducting the nuisance, and for release from a closure order upon satisfaction of certain conditions (including a showing that the nuisance will not be reestablished).

Appellants instituted a nuisance proceeding in the Court of Common Pleas of Allen County against appellee's predecessor, William Dakota. During the course of the somewhat involved legal proceedings which followed, the Court of Common Pleas reviewed 16 movies which had been shown at the theater. The court rendered a judgment that Dakota had engaged in a course of conduct of displaying obscene movies at the Cinema I, and that the theater was therefore to be closed for any purpose for a period of one year unless sooner released by Order of the Court pursuant to defendant-owners fulfilling the requirements provided in Section 3767.04 of the Revised Code of Ohio. The judgment also provided for the seizure and sale of personal property used in the theater's operations.

Appellee, Pursue, Ltd., had succeeded to William Dakota's leasehold interest in the Cinema I prior to entry of the state-court judgment. Rather than appealing that judgment within the Ohio court system, it immediately filed suit in the United States District Court for the

Northern District of Ohio. The complaint was based on 42 U.S.C. § 1983 and alleged that appellants' use of Ohio's nuisance statute constituted a deprivation of constitutional rights under the color of state law. It sought injunctive relief and a declaratory judgment that the statute was unconstitutional and unenforceable. Since the complaint was directed against the constitutionality of a state statute, a three-judge court was convened. The District Court concluded that while the statute was not vague, it did constitute an overly broad prior restraint on First Amendment rights insofar as it permanently or temporarily prevented the showing of films which had not been adjudged obscene in prior adversary hearings. Fashioning its remedy to match the perceived constitutional defect, the court permanently enjoined the execution of that portion of the state court's judgment that closed the Cinema I to films which had not been adjudged obscene. The judgment and opinion of the District Court give no indication that it considered whether it should have stayed its hand in deference to the principles of federalism which find expression in *Younger*.

On this appeal, appellants raise the *Younger* problem, as well as a variety of constitutional and statutory issues. We need consider only the applicability of *Younger*. . . .

III

The seriousness of federal judicial interference with state civil functions has long been recognized by this Court. We have consistently required that when federal courts are confronted with requests for such relief, they should abide by standards of restraint that go well beyond those of private equity jurisprudence. . . . [I]nterference with a state judicial proceeding prevents the state not only from effectuating its substantive policies, but also from continuing to perform the separate function of providing a forum competent to vindicate any constitutional objections interposed against those policies. Such interference also results in duplicative legal proceedings, and can readily be interpreted "as reflecting negatively upon the state courts' ability to enforce constitutional principles."

The component of *Younger* which rests upon the threat to our federal system is thus applicable to a civil proceeding such as this quite as much as it is to a criminal proceeding. *Younger* however, also rests upon the traditional reluctance of courts of equity, even within a unitary system, to interfere with a criminal prosecution. Strictly speaking, this element of *Younger* is not available to mandate federal restraint in civil cases. But whatever may be the weight attached to this factor in civil litigation involving private parties, we deal here with a state proceeding which in important respects is more akin to a criminal prosecution than are most civil cases. The State is a party to the Court of Common Pleas proceeding, and the proceeding is both in aid of and closely related to criminal statutes which prohibit the dissemination of obscene materials. Thus, an offense to the State's interest in the nuisance litigation is likely to be every bit as great as it would be were this a criminal proceeding.

Similarly, while in this case the District Court's injunction has not directly disrupted Ohio's criminal justice system, it has disrupted that State's efforts to protect the very interests which underlie its criminal laws and to obtain compliance with precisely the standards which are embodied in its criminal laws. . . .

VI

Younger, and its civil counterpart which we apply today, do of course allow intervention in those cases where the District Court properly finds that the state proceeding is motivated by a desire to harass or is conducted in bad faith, or where the challenged statute is "flagrantly and patently violative of express constitutional prohibitions in every clause, sentence and paragraph, and in whether manner and against whomever an effort might be made to apply it." As we have noted, the District Court in this case did not rule on the *Younger* issue, and thus apparently has not considered whether its intervention was justified by one of these narrow exceptions. . . . We therefore think that this case is appropriate for remand so that the District Court may consider whether irreparable injury can be shown . . . and if so, whether that injury is of such a nature that the District Court may assume jurisdiction under an exception to the policy against federal judicial interference with state court proceedings of this kind.

The judgment of the District Court is vacated and the cause is remanded for further proceedings consistent with this opinion.

Mr. Justice BRENNAN, with whom Mr. Justice DOUGLAS and Mr. Justice MARSHALL join, dissenting.

I dissent. The treatment of the state civil proceeding as one in aid of and closely related to criminal statutes is obviously only the first step toward extending to state civil proceedings generally the holding of *Younger* that federal courts should not interfere with pending state criminal proceedings except under extraordinary circumstances. Similarly, today's holding that the plaintiff in an action under 42 U.S.C. § 1983 may not maintain it without first exhausting state appellate procedures for review of an adverse state trial court decision is but an obvious first step toward discard of heretofore settled law that such actions may be maintained without first exhausting state judicial remedies. . . .

The line of decisions culminating in *Younger* reflects this Court's longstanding recognition that equitable interference by federal courts with pending state prosecutions is incompatible in our federal system with the paramount role of the States in the definition of crimes and the enforcement of criminal laws. Federal-court noninterference with state prosecution of crimes protects against the most sensitive source of friction between States and Nation.

The tradition, however, has been quite the opposite as respects federal injunctive interference with pending state civil proceedings. . . . The extension also threatens serious prejudice to the potential federal-court plaintiff not present when the pending state proceeding is a criminal prosecution. That prosecution does not come into existence until completion of steps designed to safeguard him against spurious prosecution—arrest, charge, information, or indictment. In contrast, the civil proceeding, as in this case, comes into existence merely upon the filing of a complaint, whether or not well founded. To deny by fiat of this Court the potential federal plaintiff a federal forum in that circumstance is obviously to arm his adversary (here the public authorities) with an easily wielded weapon to strip him of a forum and a remedy that federal statutes were enacted to assure him. The Court does not escape this consequence by characterizing the state civil proceeding involved here as in aid of and closely related to criminal statutes. The nuisance action was brought into being by the mere filing of the complaint in state court, and the untoward consequences for the federal plaintiff were thereby set in train without regard to the connection, if any, of the proceeding to the State's criminal laws.

Even if the extension of *Younger* to pending state civil proceedings can be appropriate in any case, and I do not think it can be,[2] it is plainly improper in the case of an action by a federal plaintiff, as in this case, grounded upon § 1983. That statute serves a particular congressional objective long recognized and enforced by the Court. Today's extension will defeat that objective. . . . That Act, and the Judiciary Act of 1875, which granted the federal courts general federal-question jurisdiction, completely altered Congress's pre-Civil War policy of relying on state courts to vindicate rights arising under the Constitution and federal laws. These statutes constituted the lower federal courts the primary and powerful reliance for vindicating every right given by the Constitution, the laws, and treaties of the United States. The fact, standing alone, that state courts also must protect federal rights can never justify a refusal of federal courts to exercise that jurisdiction. This is true notwithstanding the possibility of review by this Court of state decisions for, even when available by appeal rather than only by discretionary writ of certiorari that possibility is an inadequate substitute for the initial District Court determination . . . to which the litigant is entitled in the federal courts. . . . I therefore dissent . . . .

[2] Abstention where authoritative resolution by state courts of ambiguities in a state statute is sufficiently likely to avoid or significantly modify federal questions raised by the statute is another matter. Abstention is justified in such cases primarily by the policy of avoidance of premature constitutional adjudication. The federal plaintiff is

therefore not dismissed from federal court as he is in *Younger* cases. On the contrary, he may reserve his federal questions for decision by the federal district court and not submit them to the state courts. Accordingly, retention by the federal court of jurisdiction of the federal complaint pending state-court decision, not dismissal of the complaint, is the correct practice.

Pennzoil v. Texaco (1987)

Justice POWELL delivered the opinion of the Court.

The principal issue in this case is whether a federal district court lawfully may enjoin a plaintiff who has prevailed in a trial in state court from executing the judgment in its favor pending appeal of that judgment to a state appellate court.

I

Getty Oil Co. and appellant Pennzoil Co. negotiated an agreement under which Pennzoil was to purchase about three-sevenths of Getty's outstanding shares for $110 a share. Appellee Texaco Inc. eventually purchased the shares for $128 a share. On February 8, 1984, Pennzoil filed a complaint against Texaco in the Harris County District Court, a state court located in Houston, Texas, the site of Pennzoil's corporate headquarters. The complaint alleged that Texaco tortiously had induced Getty to breach a contract to sell its shares to Pennzoil; Pennzoil sought actual damages of $7.53 billion and punitive damages in the same amount. On November 19, 1985, a jury returned a verdict in favor of Pennzoil, finding actual damages of $7.53 billion and punitive damages of $3 billion. The parties anticipated that the judgment, including prejudgment interest, would exceed $11 billion.

Although the parties disagree about the details, it was clear that the expected judgment would give Pennzoil significant rights under Texas law. By recording an abstract of a judgment in the real property records of any of the 254 counties in Texas, a judgment creditor can secure a lien on all of a judgment debtor's real property located in that county. If a judgment creditor wishes to have the judgment enforced by state officials so that it can take possession of any of the debtor's assets, it may secure a writ of execution from the clerk of the court that issued the judgment. . . . But the judgment debtor may suspend the execution of the judgment by filing a good and sufficient bond to be approved by the clerk. For a money judgment, the amount of the bond shall be at least the amount of the judgment, interest, and costs.

Even before the trial court entered judgment, the jury's verdict cast a serious cloud on Texaco's financial situation. The amount of the bond required by Rule 364(b) would have been more than $13 billion. It is clear that Texaco would not have been able to post such a bond. Accordingly, the business and financial community concluded that Pennzoil would be able, under the lien and bond provisions of Texas law, to commence enforcement of any judgment entered on the verdict before Texaco's appeals had been resolved. The effects on Texaco were substantial: the price of its stock dropped markedly; it had difficulty obtaining credit; the rating of its bonds was lowered; and its trade creditors refused to sell it crude oil on customary terms.

Texaco did not argue to the trial court that the judgment, or execution of the judgment, conflicted with federal law. Rather, on December 10, 1985—before the Texas court entered judgment—Texaco filed this action in the United States District Court for the Southern District of New York in White Plains, New York, the site of Texaco's corporate headquarters. Texaco alleged that the Texas proceedings violated rights secured to Texaco by the Constitution and various federal statutes. It asked the District Court to enjoin Pennzoil from taking any action to enforce the judgment. Pennzoil's response, and basic position, was that the District Court could not hear the case . . . . under the doctrine of *Younger v. Harris* . . . .

The District Court rejected all of these arguments. . . . [and] issued a preliminary injunction. On appeal, the Court of Appeals for the Second Circuit affirmed. . . . Pennzoil filed a jurisdictional statement in this Court. We noted probable jurisdiction under 28 U.S.C. § 1254(2). We reverse.

II

The courts below should have abstained under the principles of federalism enunciated in *Younger*. Both the District Court and the Court of Appeals failed to recognize the significant interests harmed by their unprecedented intrusion into the Texas judicial system. Similarly, neither of those courts applied the appropriate standard in determining whether adequate relief was available in the Texas courts.

A

The first ground for the *Younger* decision was the basic doctrine of equity jurisprudence that courts of equity should not act, and particularly should not act to restrain a criminal prosecution, when the moving party has an adequate remedy at law. The Court also offered a second explanation for its decision:

> This underlying reason . . . is reinforced by an even more vital consideration, the notion of "comity," that is, a proper respect for state functions, a recognition of the fact that the entire country is made up of a Union of separate state governments, and a continuance of the belief that the National Government will fare best if the States and their institutions are left free to perform their separate functions in their separate ways. . . . The concept does not mean blind deference to 'States' Rights' any more than it means centralization of control over every important issue in our National Government and its courts. The Framers rejected both these courses. What the concept does represent is a system in which there is sensitivity to the legitimate interests of both State and National Governments, and in which the National

Government, anxious though it may be to vindicate and protect federal rights and federal interests, always endeavors to do so in ways that will not unduly interfere with the legitimate activities of the States.

This concern mandates application of *Younger* abstention not only when the pending state proceedings are criminal, but also when certain civil proceedings are pending, if the State's interests in the proceeding are so important that exercise of the federal judicial power would disregard the comity between the States and the National Government.

Another important reason for abstention is to avoid unwarranted determination of federal constitutional questions. When federal courts interpret state statutes in a way that raises federal constitutional questions, a constitutional determination is predicated on a reading of the statute that is not binding on state courts and may be discredited at any time—thus essentially rendering the federal-court decision advisory and the litigation underlying it meaningless.[9] This concern has special significance in this case. Because Texaco chose not to present to the Texas courts the constitutional claims asserted in this case, it is impossible to be certain that the governing Texas statutes and procedural rules actually raise these claims. Moreover, the Texas Constitution contains an "open courts" provision, Art. I, § 13, that appears to address Texaco's claims more specifically than the Due Process Clause of the Fourteenth Amendment. Thus, when this case was filed in federal court, it was entirely possible that the Texas courts would have resolved this case on state statutory or constitutional grounds, without reaching the federal constitutional questions Texaco raises in this case. As we have noted, *Younger* abstention in situations like this offers the opportunity for narrowing constructions that might obviate the constitutional problem and intelligently mediate federal constitutional concerns and state interests.

[9] In some cases, the probability that any federal adjudication would be effectively advisory is so great that this concern alone is sufficient to justify abstention, even if there are no pending state proceedings in which the question could be raised. *See Railroad Comm'n of Texas v. Pullman Co.* Because appellant has not argued in this Court that *Pullman* abstention is proper, we decline to address Justice Blackmun's conclusion that *Pullman* abstention is the appropriate disposition of this case. We merely note that considerations similar to those that mandate *Pullman* abstention are relevant to a court's decision whether to abstain under *Younger*. The various types of abstention are not rigid pigeonholes into which federal courts must try to fit cases. Rather, they reflect a complex of considerations designed to soften the tensions inherent in a system that contemplates parallel judicial processes.

Texaco's principal argument against *Younger* abstention is that exercise of the District Court's power did not implicate a "vital" or "important" state interest. This argument reflects a misreading of our precedents. This Court repeatedly has recognized that the States have important interests in administering certain aspects of their judicial systems. . . . Not only would federal injunctions in such cases interfere with the execution of state judgments, but they would do so on grounds that challenge the very process by which those judgments were obtained. So long as those challenges relate to pending state proceedings, proper respect for the ability of state courts to resolve federal questions presented in state-court litigation mandates that the federal court stay its hand.

B

Texaco also argues that *Younger* abstention was inappropriate because no Texas court could have heard Texaco's constitutional claims within the limited time available to Texaco. But the burden on this point rests on the federal plaintiff to show that state procedural law barred presentation of its claims.

Moreover, denigrations of the procedural protections afforded by Texas law hardly come from Texaco with good grace, as it apparently made no effort under Texas law to secure the relief sought in this case. Article VI of the United States Constitution declares that "the Judges in every State shall be bound" by the Federal Constitution, laws, and treaties. We cannot assume that state judges will interpret ambiguities in state procedural law to bar presentation of federal claims. Accordingly, when a litigant has not attempted to present his federal claims in related state-court proceedings, a federal court should assume that state procedures will afford an adequate remedy, in the absence of unambiguous authority to the contrary. . . . Accordingly, Texaco has failed to meet its burden on this point.

In sum, the lower courts should have deferred on principles of comity to the pending state proceedings. They erred in accepting Texaco's assertions as to the inadequacies of Texas procedure to provide effective relief. It is true that this case presents an unusual fact situation, never before addressed by the Texas courts, and that Texaco urgently desired prompt relief. But we cannot say that those courts, when this suit was filed, would have been any less inclined than a federal court to address and decide the federal constitutional claims. Because Texaco apparently did not give the Texas courts an opportunity to adjudicate its constitutional claims, and because Texaco cannot demonstrate that the Texas courts were not then open to adjudicate its claims, there is no basis for concluding that the Texas law and procedures were so deficient that *Younger* abstention is inappropriate. Accordingly, we conclude that the District Court should have abstained. . . .

Justice BRENNAN, with whom Justice MARSHALL joins, concurring in the judgment.

. . . . I adhere to my view that *Younger* is, in general, inapplicable to civil proceedings, especially when a plaintiff brings a § 1983 action alleging violation of federal constitutional rights. The State's interest in this case is negligible. The State of Texas—not a party in this appeal—expressly represented to the Court of Appeals that it "has no interest in the outcome of the state-court adjudication underlying this cause," except in its fair adjudication. The . . . . interest in enforcing the bond and lien requirement is privately held by Pennzoil, not by the State of Texas. The Court of Appeals correctly stated that this "is a suit between two private parties stemming from the defendant's alleged tortious interference with the plaintiff's contract with a third private party." Pennzoil was free to waive the bond and lien requirements under Texas law, without asking the State of Texas for permission. Since Texas law directs state officials to do Pennzoil's bidding in executing the judgment, it is the decision of Pennzoil, not that of the state judiciary, to utilize state agents to undertake the collection process, and the state officials can act only upon Pennzoil's unilateral determination. The State's decision to grant private parties unilateral power to invoke, or not invoke, the State's bond and lien provisions demonstrates that the State has no independent interest in the enforcement of those provisions. . . . [Brennan then found the state procedures constitutional on the merits and thus concurred.]

Justice BLACKMUN, concurring in the judgment.

. . . . In my view, to rule [that *Younger* applies here] would expand the *Younger* doctrine to an unprecedented extent and would effectively allow the invocation of *Younger* abstention whenever any state proceeding is ongoing, no matter how attenuated the State's interests are in that proceeding and no matter what abuses the federal plaintiff might be sustaining. . . .

I conclude instead that this case presents an example of the narrowly limited special circumstances, where the District Court should have abstained under the principles announced in *Railroad Comm'n of Texas v. Pullman Co.* Although the *Pullman* issue was not pressed before us, it was considered by the Court of Appeals and rejected. In particular, the court determined that there was nothing unclear or uncertain about the Texas lien and bond provisions and that abstention was not demanded when there was only a mere possibility that the Texas courts would find such provisions unconstitutional. I disagree. If the extensive briefing by the parties on the numerous Texas statutes and constitutional provisions at issue here suggests anything, it is that on the unique facts of *this* case unsettled questions of state law must be resolved before a substantial federal constitutional question can be decided. The possibility of such a state-law resolution of this dispute seems to me still to exist.

Sprint v. Jacobs (2013)

This case involves two proceedings, one pending in state court, the other in federal court. Each seeks review of an Iowa Utilities Board (IUB or Board) order. And each presents the question whether Windstream Iowa Communications, Inc. (Windstream), a local telecommunications carrier, may impose on Sprint Communications, Inc. (Sprint), intrastate access charges for telephone calls transported via the Internet. Federal-court jurisdiction over controversies of this kind was confirmed . . . . Invoking *Younger v. Harris*, the U.S. District Court for the Southern District of Iowa abstained from adjudicating Sprint's complaint in deference to the parallel state-court proceeding, and the Court of Appeals for the Eighth Circuit affirmed the District Court's abstention decision.

We reverse the judgment of the Court of Appeals. In the main, federal courts are obliged to decide cases within the scope of federal jurisdiction. Abstention is not in order simply because a pending state-court proceeding involves the same subject matter. This Court has recognized, however, certain instances in which the prospect of undue interference with state proceedings counsels against federal relief.

Younger exemplifies one class of cases in which federal-court abstention is required: When there is a parallel, pending state criminal proceeding, federal courts must refrain from enjoining the state prosecution. This Court has extended *Younger* abstention to particular state civil proceedings that are akin to criminal prosecutions, *see Huffman*, or that implicate a State's interest in enforcing the orders and judgments of its courts, *see Pennzoil*. We have cautioned, however, that federal courts ordinarily should entertain and resolve on the merits an action within the scope of a jurisdictional grant, and should not refuse to decide a case in deference to the States.

Circumstances fitting within the *Younger* doctrine, we have stressed, are "exceptional"; they include . . . state criminal prosecutions, civil enforcement proceedings, and civil proceedings involving certain orders that are uniquely in furtherance of the state courts' ability to perform their judicial functions. Because this case presents none of the circumstances the Court has ranked as "exceptional," the general rule governs: The pendency of an action in a state court is no bar to proceedings concerning the same matter in the Federal court having jurisdiction.

I

Sprint, a national telecommunications service provider, has long paid intercarrier access fees to the Iowa communications company Windstream (formerly Iowa Telecom) for certain long distance calls placed by Sprint customers to Windstream's in-state customers. In 2009, however, Sprint decided to withhold payment for a subset of those calls, classified as Voice over Internet Protocol (VoIP), after concluding that the Telecommunications Act of 1996 preempted intrastate regulation of VoIP traffic. In response, Windstream threatened to block all calls to and from Sprint customers.

Sprint filed a complaint against Windstream with the IUB asking the Board to enjoin Windstream from discontinuing service to Sprint. In Sprint's view, Iowa law entitled it to withhold payment while it contested the access charges and prohibited Windstream from carrying out its disconnection threat. In answer to Sprint's complaint, Windstream retracted its threat to discontinue serving Sprint, and Sprint moved, successfully, to withdraw its complaint. Because the conflict between Sprint and Windstream over VoIP calls was "likely to recur," however, the IUB decided to continue the proceedings to resolve the underlying legal question, *i.e.,* whether VoIP calls are subject to intrastate regulation. The question retained by the IUB, Sprint argued, was governed by federal law, and was not within the IUB's adjudicative jurisdiction. The IUB disagreed, ruling that the intrastate fees applied to VoIP calls.

Seeking to overturn the Board's ruling, Sprint commenced two lawsuits. First, Sprint sued the members of the IUB (respondents here) in their official capacities in the United States District Court for the Southern District of Iowa. In its federal-court complaint, Sprint sought a declaration that the Telecommunications Act of 1996 preempted the IUB's decision; as relief, Sprint requested an injunction against enforcement of the IUB's order. Second, Sprint petitioned for review of the IUB's order in Iowa state court. The state petition reiterated the preemption argument Sprint made in its federal-court complaint; in addition, Sprint asserted state law and procedural due process claims. Because Eighth Circuit precedent effectively required a plaintiff to exhaust state remedies before proceeding to federal court, Sprint urges that it filed the state suit as a protective measure. Failing to do so, Sprint explains, risked losing the opportunity to obtain any review, federal or state, should the federal court decide to abstain after the expiration of the Iowa statute of limitations.

As Sprint anticipated, the IUB filed a motion asking the Federal District Court to abstain in light of the state suit, citing *Younger v. Harris.* The District Court granted the IUB's motion and dismissed the suit. The IUB's decision, and the pending state-court review of it, the District Court said, composed one "uninterruptible process" implicating important state interests. On that ground, the court ruled, *Younger* abstention was in order.

For the most part, the Eighth Circuit agreed with the District Court's judgment. The Court of Appeals rejected the argument, accepted by several of its sister courts, that *Younger* abstention is appropriate only when the parallel state proceedings are "coercive," rather than "remedial," in nature. Instead, the Eighth Circuit read this Court's precedent to require *Younger* abstention whenever an ongoing state judicial proceeding implicates important state interests, and the state proceedings provide adequate opportunity to raise federal challenges. Those criteria were satisfied here, the appeals court held, because the ongoing state-court review of the IUB's decision concerned Iowa's important state interest in regulating and enforcing its intrastate utility rates. . . . We granted certiorari . . . .

II

. . . . Federal courts, it was early and famously said, have "no more right to decline the exercise of jurisdiction which is given, than to usurp that which is not given." *Cohens v. Virginia.* Jurisdiction existing, this Court has cautioned, a federal court's "obligation" to hear and decide a case is "virtually unflagging." *Colorado River Water Conservation Dist. v. United States.* Parallel state-court proceedings do not detract from that obligation.

In *Younger*, we recognized a far-from-novel exception to this general rule. . . . We have since applied *Younger* to bar federal relief in certain civil actions. *Huffman v. Pursue* is the pathmarking decision. There, Ohio officials brought a civil action in state court to abate the showing of obscene movies in Pursue's theater. Because the State was a party and the proceeding was in aid of and closely related to the State's criminal statutes, the Court held *Younger* abstention appropriate.

More recently, in *NOPSI*, the Court had occasion to review and restate our *Younger* jurisprudence. *NOPSI* addressed and rejected an argument that a federal court should refuse to exercise jurisdiction to review a state council's ratemaking decision. Only exceptional circumstances, we reaffirmed, justify a federal court's refusal to decide a case in deference to the States. Those "exceptional circumstances" exist, the Court determined after surveying prior decisions, in three types of proceedings. First, *Younger* precluded federal intrusion into ongoing state criminal prosecutions. Second, certain civil enforcement proceedings warranted abstention. Finally, federal courts refrained from interfering with pending civil proceedings involving certain orders uniquely in furtherance of the state courts' ability to perform their judicial functions. We have not applied *Younger* outside these three "exceptional" categories, and today hold, in accord with *NOPSI*, that they define *Younger's* scope.

. . . . The IUB proceeding, we conclude, does not fall within any of the three exceptional categories described in *NOPSI* and therefore does not trigger *Younger* abstention. The first and third categories plainly do not accommodate the IUB's proceeding. That proceeding was civil, not criminal in character, and it did not touch on a state court's ability to perform its judicial function.

Nor does the IUB's order rank as an act of civil enforcement of the kind to which *Younger* has been extended. Our decisions applying *Younger* to instances of civil enforcement have generally concerned state proceedings akin to a criminal prosecution in important respects. Such enforcement actions are characteristically initiated to sanction the federal plaintiff, *i.e.*, the party challenging the state action, for some wrongful act. In cases of this genre, a state actor is routinely a party to the state proceeding and often initiates the action. Investigations are commonly involved, often culminating in the filing of a formal complaint or charges.

The IUB proceeding does not resemble the state enforcement actions this Court has found appropriate for *Younger* abstention. It is not akin to a criminal prosecution. Nor was it initiated by the State in its sovereign capacity. A private corporation, Sprint, initiated the action. No state authority conducted an investigation into Sprint's activities, and no state actor lodged a formal complaint against Sprint.

In its brief, the IUB emphasizes Sprint's decision to withdraw the complaint that commenced proceedings before the Board. At that point, the IUB argues, Sprint was no longer a willing participant, and the proceedings became, essentially, a civil enforcement action. The IUB's adjudicative authority, however, was invoked to settle a civil dispute between two private parties, not to sanction Sprint for commission of a wrongful act. Although Sprint withdrew its complaint, administrative efficiency, not misconduct by Sprint, prompted the IUB to answer the underlying federal question. By determining the intercarrier compensation regime applicable to VoIP calls, the IUB sought to avoid renewed litigation of the parties' dispute. Because the underlying legal question remained unsettled, the Board observed, the controversy was likely to recur. Nothing here suggests that the IUB proceeding was more akin to a criminal prosecution than are most civil cases.

In holding that abstention was the proper course, the Eighth Circuit [would apply *Younger*] whenever three conditions are met: There is (1) an ongoing state judicial proceeding, which (2) implicates important state interests, and (3) provides an adequate opportunity to raise [federal] challenges. . . . [That] extraordinary breadth. . . . would extend *Younger* to virtually all parallel state and federal proceedings, at least where a party could identify a plausibly important state interest. That result is irreconcilable with our dominant instruction that, even in the presence of parallel state proceedings, abstention from the exercise of federal jurisdiction is the exception, not the rule. In short, to guide other federal courts, we today clarify and affirm that *Younger* extends to the three "exceptional circumstances" identified in *NOPSI*, but no further.

For the reasons stated, the judgment of the United States Court of Appeals for the Eighth Circuit is *Reversed.*

Substance-Based Exceptions to Jurisdiction

Introduction

Congress can, as it has with the supplemental-jurisdiction statute, expressly grant federal courts discretion to decline jurisdiction. In the absence of express authorization, federal courts can use abstention doctrines—judicially created exceptions to jurisdiction generally conferred by Congress. Alternatively, federal courts might *infer* discretion from congressional statute, even when that discretion is not expressly stated. The following cases discuss two kinds of implied statutory exceptions to jurisdiction: the domestic-relations exception and the probate exception. As you read them, consider the following questions:

- What motivates—both substantively and legislatively—the Court's inference of exceptions in these areas? What is problematic about those inferences?

- Are the justifications for inferring statutory exceptions more or less satisfying than the justifications for abstention?

- What, if anything, is special about these subject-matter areas? Are there others that might justify judicial inferences of exceptions in other areas?

- How successful are the Court's attempts to cabin the exceptions?

Ankenbrandt v. Richards (1992)

Justice WHITE delivered the opinion of the Court.

This case presents the issue whether the federal courts have jurisdiction or should abstain in a case involving alleged torts committed by the former husband of petitioner and his female companion against petitioner's children, when the sole basis for federal jurisdiction is the diversity-of-citizenship provision of 28 U.S.C. § 1332.

I

Petitioner Carol Ankenbrandt, a citizen of Missouri, brought this lawsuit on September 26, 1989, on behalf of her daughters L.R. and S.R. against respondents Jon A. Richards and Debra Kesler, citizens of Louisiana, in the United States District Court for the Eastern District of Louisiana. Alleging federal jurisdiction based on the diversity-of-citizenship provision of § 1332, Ankenbrandt's complaint sought monetary damages for alleged sexual and physical abuse of the children committed by Richards and Kesler. Richards is the divorced father of the children and Kesler his female companion. On December 10, 1990, the District Court granted respondents' motion to dismiss this lawsuit. Citing *In re Burrus* for the proposition that the whole subject of the domestic relations of husband and wife, parent and child, belongs to the laws of the States and not to the laws of the United States, the court concluded that this case fell within what has become known as the "domestic relations" exception to diversity jurisdiction, and that it lacked jurisdiction over the case. . . . The Court of Appeals affirmed in an unpublished opinion. . . .

We granted certiorari limited to the following questions: (1) Is there a domestic relations exception to federal jurisdiction? (2) If so, does it permit a district court to abstain from exercising diversity jurisdiction over a tort action for damages? . . .

II

The domestic relations exception upon which the courts below relied to decline jurisdiction has been invoked often by the lower federal courts. The seeming authority for doing so originally stemmed from the announcement in *Barber v. Barber* that the federal courts have no jurisdiction over suits for divorce or the allowance of alimony. In that case, the Court heard a suit in equity brought by a wife (by her next friend) in Federal District Court pursuant to diversity jurisdiction against her former husband. She sought to enforce a decree from a New York state court, which had granted a divorce and awarded her alimony. The former husband thereupon moved to Wisconsin to place himself beyond the New York courts' jurisdiction so that the divorce decree there could not be enforced against him; he then sued for divorce in a Wisconsin court, representing to that court that his wife had abandoned him and failing to disclose the existence of the New York decree. In a suit brought by the former wife in Wisconsin Federal District Court, the former husband alleged that the court lacked jurisdiction. The court accepted jurisdiction and gave judgment for the divorced wife.

On appeal, it was argued that the District Court lacked jurisdiction on two grounds: first, that there was no diversity of citizenship because although divorced, the wife's citizenship necessarily remained that of her former husband; and second, that the whole subject of divorce and alimony, including a suit to enforce an alimony decree, was exclusively ecclesiastical at the time of the adoption of the Constitution and that the Constitution therefore placed the whole subject of divorce and alimony beyond the jurisdiction of the United States courts. Over the dissent of three Justices, the Court rejected both arguments. After an exhaustive survey of the authorities, the Court concluded that a divorced wife could acquire a citizenship separate from that of her former husband and that a suit to enforce an alimony decree rested within the federal courts' equity jurisdiction. The Court reached these conclusions after summarily dismissing the former husband's contention that the case involved a subject matter outside the federal courts' jurisdiction. In so stating, however, the Court also announced the following limitation on federal jurisdiction: "Our first remark is— and we wish it to be remembered—that this is not a suit asking the court for the allowance of alimony. That has been done by a court of competent jurisdiction. The court in Wisconsin was asked to interfere to prevent that decree from being defeated by fraud. We disclaim altogether any jurisdiction in the courts of the United States upon the subject of divorce, or for the allowance of alimony, either as an original proceeding in chancery or as an incident to divorce *a vinculo,* or to one from bed and board."

As a general matter, the dissenters agreed with these statements, but took issue with the Court's holding that the instant action to enforce an alimony decree was within the equity jurisdiction of the federal courts.

The statements disclaiming jurisdiction over divorce and alimony decree suits, though technically dicta, formed the basis for excluding "domestic relations" cases from the jurisdiction of the lower federal courts, a jurisdictional limitation those courts have recognized ever since. The *Barber* Court, however, cited no authority and did not discuss the foundation for its announcement. Since that time, the Court has dealt only occasionally with the domestic relations limitation on federal-court jurisdiction, and it has never addressed the basis for such a limitation. Because we are unwilling to cast aside an understood rule that has been recognized for nearly a century and a half, we feel compelled to explain why we will continue to recognize this limitation on federal jurisdiction.

A

Counsel argued in *Barber* that the Constitution prohibited federal courts from exercising jurisdiction over domestic relations cases. An examination of Article III, *Barber* itself, and our cases since *Barber* make clear that the Constitution does not exclude domestic relations cases from the jurisdiction otherwise granted by statute to the federal courts.

Article III, § 2, of the Constitution . . . . delineates the absolute limits on the federal courts' jurisdiction. But in articulating three different terms to define jurisdiction—"Cases, in Law and Equity," "Cases," and "Controversies"—this provision contains no limitation on subjects of a domestic relations nature. Nor did *Barber* purport to ground the domestic relations exception in these constitutional limits on federal jurisdiction. The Court's discussion of federal judicial power to hear suits of a domestic relations nature contains no mention of the Constitution, and it is logical to presume that the Court based its statement limiting such power on narrower statutory, rather than broader constitutional, grounds.

. . . . We therefore have no difficulty concluding that when the *Barber* Court disclaimed altogether any jurisdiction in the courts of the United States upon the subject of divorce, it was not basing its statement on the Constitution.

B

That Article III, § 2, does not mandate the exclusion of domestic relations cases from federal-court jurisdiction, however, does not mean that such courts necessarily must retain and exercise jurisdiction over such cases. Other constitutional provisions explain why this is so. Article I, § 8, cl. 9, for example, authorizes Congress "[t]o constitute Tribunals inferior to the supreme Court" and Article III, § 1, states that "[t]he judicial Power of the United States, shall be vested in one supreme Court, and in such inferior Courts as the Congress may from time to time ordain and establish." The Court's cases state the rule that if inferior federal courts were created, Congress was not required to invest them with all the jurisdiction it was authorized to bestow under Art. III.

This position has held constant since at least 1845, when the Court stated that the judicial power of the United States is, except in enumerated instances, applicable exclusively to this Court dependent for its distribution and organization, and for the modes of its exercise, entirely upon the action of Congress, who possess the sole power of creating the tribunals inferior to the Supreme Court and of investing them with jurisdiction either limited, concurrent, or exclusive, and of withholding jurisdiction from them in the exact degrees and character which to Congress may seem proper for the public good. We thus turn our attention to the relevant jurisdictional statutes.

The Judiciary Act of 1789 provided that "the circuit courts shall have original cognizance, concurrent with the courts of the several States, of *all suits of a civil nature at common law or in equity, where the matter in dispute exceeds,* exclusive of costs, the sum or value of *five hundred dollars,* and . . . an alien is a party, or the suit is *between a citizen of the State where the suit is brought, and a citizen of another State.*" The defining phrase, "all suits of a civil nature at common law or in equity," remained a key element of statutory provisions demarcating the terms of diversity jurisdiction until 1948, when Congress amended the diversity jurisdiction provision to eliminate this phrase and replace in its stead the term "all civil actions."

. . . . We thus are content to rest our conclusion that a domestic relations exception exists as a matter of statutory construction not on the accuracy of the historical justifications on which it was seemingly based, but rather on Congress's apparent acceptance of this construction of the diversity jurisdiction provisions in the years prior to 1948, when the statute limited jurisdiction to suits of a civil nature at common law or in equity. . . . More than a century has elapsed since the *Barber* dictum without any intimation of Congressional dissatisfaction. Whatever Article III may or may not permit, we thus accept the *Barber* dictum as a correct interpretation of the Congressional grant. Considerations of *stare decisis* have particular strength in this context, where the legislative power is implicated, and Congress remains free to alter what we have done.

When Congress amended the diversity statute in 1948 to replace the law/equity distinction with the phrase "all civil actions," we presume Congress did so with full cognizance of the Court's nearly century-long interpretation of the prior statutes, which had construed the statutory diversity jurisdiction to contain an exception for certain domestic relations matters. . . . With respect to such a longstanding and well-known construction of the diversity statute, and where Congress made substantive changes to the statute in other respects, we presume, absent any indication that Congress intended to alter this exception.

III

In the more than 100 years since this Court laid the seeds for the development of the domestic relations exception, the lower federal courts have applied it in a variety of circumstances. Many of these applications go well beyond the circumscribed situations posed by *Barber* and its progeny. *Barber* itself disclaimed federal jurisdiction over a narrow range of domestic relations issues involving the granting of a divorce and a decree of alimony . . . .

The *Barber* Court thus did not intend to strip the federal courts of authority to hear cases arising from the domestic relations of persons unless they seek the granting or modification of a divorce or alimony decree. The holding of the case itself sanctioned the exercise of federal jurisdiction over the enforcement of an alimony decree that had been properly obtained in a state court of competent jurisdiction. . . . [T]he enforcement of such validly obtained orders does not regulate the domestic relations of society and produce an inquisitorial authority in which federal tribunals enter the habitations and even into the chambers and nurseries of private families, and inquire into and pronounce upon the morals and habits and affections or antipathies of the members of every household. . . .

Subsequently, this Court expanded the domestic relations exception to include decrees in child custody cases. In a child custody case brought pursuant to a writ of habeas corpus, for instance, the Court held void a writ issued by a Federal District Court to restore a child to the custody of the father. As to the right to the control and possession of this child, as it is contested by its father and its grandfather, it is one in regard to which neither the Congress of the United States nor any authority of the United States has any special jurisdiction.

. . . . We conclude, therefore, that the domestic relations exception, as articulated by this Court since *Barber,* divests the federal courts of power to issue divorce, alimony, and child custody decrees. Given the long passage of time without any expression of congressional dissatisfaction, we have no trouble today reaffirming the validity of the exception as it pertains to divorce and alimony decrees and child custody orders.

Not only is our conclusion rooted in respect for this long-held understanding, it is also supported by sound policy considerations. Issuance of decrees of this type not infrequently involves retention of jurisdiction by the court and deployment of social workers to monitor compliance. As a matter of judicial economy, state courts are more eminently suited to work of this type than are federal courts, which lack the close association with state and local government organizations dedicated to handling issues that arise out of conflicts over divorce, alimony, and child custody decrees. Moreover, as a matter of judicial expertise, it makes far more sense to retain the rule that federal courts lack power to issue these types of decrees because of the special proficiency developed by state tribunals over the past century and a half in handling issues that arise in the granting of such decrees.

By concluding, as we do, that the domestic relations exception encompasses only cases involving the issuance of a divorce, alimony, or child custody decree, we necessarily find that the Court of Appeals erred by affirming the District Court's invocation of this exception. This lawsuit in no way seeks such a decree; rather, it alleges that respondents Richards and Kesler committed torts against L.R. and S.R., Ankenbrandt's children by Richards. Federal subject-matter jurisdiction pursuant to § 1332 thus is proper in this case.

. . . . We thus conclude that the Court of Appeals erred by affirming the District Court's rulings to decline jurisdiction based on the domestic relations exception to diversity jurisdiction . . . . The exception has no place in a suit such as this one, in which a former spouse sues another on behalf of children alleged to have been abused. Because the allegations in this complaint do not request the District Court to issue a divorce, alimony, or child custody decree, we hold that the suit is appropriate for the exercise of § 1332 jurisdiction given the existence of diverse citizenship between petitioner and respondents and the pleading of the relevant amount in controversy. Accordingly, we reverse the decision of the Court of Appeals and remand the case for further proceedings consistent with this opinion.

Justice BLACKMUN, concurring in the judgment.

I agree with the Court that the District Court had jurisdiction over petitioner's claims in tort. Moreover, I agree that the federal courts should not entertain claims for divorce, alimony, and child custody. I am unable to agree, however, that the diversity statute contains any "exception" for domestic relations matters. The Court goes to remarkable lengths to craft an exception that is simply not in the statute and is not supported by the case law. In my view, the longstanding, unbroken practice of the federal courts in refusing to hear domestic relations cases is precedent at most for continued discretionary abstention rather than mandatory limits on federal jurisdiction. For these reasons I concur only in the Court's judgment.

I

The Court holds that the diversity statute contains an "exception" for cases seeking the issuance of a divorce, alimony, or child custody decree. Yet no such exception appears in the statute. The diversity statute is not ambiguous at all. It extends the jurisdiction of the district courts to "*all* civil actions" between diverse parties involving the requisite amount in controversy. 28 U.S.C. § 1332 (emphasis added).

This Court has recognized that in the absence of a clearly expressed intention to the contrary, the language of the statute itself is ordinarily conclusive. The Court apparently discovers in the history of the diversity statute and this Court's own case law a clearly expressed intention contrary to the words of the statute. . . .

I have great difficulty with the Court's approach. Starting at the most obvious point, I do not see how a language change that, if anything, expands the jurisdictional scope of the statute can be said to constitute evidence of approval of a prior narrow construction. Any inaction on the part of Congress in 1948 in failing expressly to mention domestic relations matters in the diversity statute reflects the fact, as is discussed below, that Congress likely had no idea until the Court's decision today that the diversity statute contained an exception for domestic relations matters. . . .

II

A

To reject the Court's construction of the diversity statute is not, however, necessarily to reject the federal courts' longstanding practice of declining to hear certain domestic relations cases. My point today is that no coherent jurisdictional explanation for this practice emerges from our line of such cases, and it is unreasonable to presume that Congress divined and accepted one from these cases. To be sure, this Court's old line of domestic relations cases disclaimed "jurisdiction" over domestic relations matters well before the growth and general acceptance in recent decades of modern doctrines of federal abstention that distinguish the refusal to exercise jurisdiction from disclaiming jurisdiction altogether. Nevertheless, the common concern reflected in these earlier cases is, in modern terms, abstentional—and not jurisdictional—in nature. These cases are premised not upon a concern for the historical limitation of equity jurisdiction of the English courts, but upon the virtually exclusive primacy at that time of the States in the regulation of domestic relations. As noted above, this Court justified its exercise of jurisdiction over actions for divorce and alimony not by any reference to the scope of equity jurisdiction but by reference to the absence of any interest of the States in appeals from courts in territories controlled by the National Government. . . . As the Court once stated: "The whole subject of the domestic relations of husband and wife, parent and child, belongs to the laws of the States and not to the laws of the United States."

Whether the interest of States remains a sufficient justification today for abstention is uncertain in view of the expansion in recent years of federal law in the domestic relations area. I am confident, nonetheless, that the unbroken and unchallenged practice of the federal courts since before the War Between the States of declining to hear certain domestic relations cases provides the very rare justification for continuing to do so. It is not without significance, moreover, that, because of this historical practice of the federal courts, the States have developed specialized courts and institutions in family matters, while Congress and the federal courts generally have not done so. Absent a contrary command of Congress, the federal courts properly should abstain, at least from diversity actions traditionally excluded from the federal courts, such as those seeking divorce, alimony, and child custody. . . .

B

Whether or not the domestic relations "exception" is properly grounded in principles of abstention or principles of jurisdiction, I do not believe this case falls within the exception. This case only peripherally involves the subject of domestic relations. "Domestic relations" actions are loosely classifiable into four categories. The first, or core, category involves declarations of status, *e.g.*, marriage, annulment, divorce, custody, and paternity. The second, or semicore, category involves declarations of rights or obligations arising from status (or former status), *e.g.*, alimony, child support, and division of property. The third category consists of secondary suits to enforce declarations of status, rights, or obligations. The final, catchall category covers the suits not directly involving status or obligations arising from status but that nonetheless generally relate to domestic relations matters, *e.g.*, tort suits between family or former family members for sexual abuse, battering, or intentional infliction of emotional distress. None of this Court's prior cases that consider the domestic relations "exception" involves the type of periphery domestic relations claim at issue here. . . .

Markham v. Allen (1946)

The question is whether a district court of the United States has jurisdiction of a suit brought by the Alien Property Custodian against an executor and resident heirs to determine the Custodian's asserted right to share in decedent's estate which is in course of probate administration in a state court.

On January 23, 1943, petitioner, the Alien Property Custodian, acting under § 5(b)(1)(B) of the Trading with the Enemy Act issued vesting order No. 762, by which he purported to vest in himself as Custodian all right, title and interest of German legatees in the estate of Alvina Wagner, who died testate, a resident of California, whose will was admitted to probate and whose estate is being administered in the Superior Court of California. Previously, on December 30, 1942, six of the other heirs-at-law of decedent, residing in the United States, filed a petition in the Superior Court of California for determination of heirship, asserting that under the provisions of California Statutes, the German legatees were ineligible as beneficiaries, and that the American heirs were therefore entitled to inherit decedent's estate. This proceeding is still pending.

On April 6, 1943, the Custodian brought the present suit in the district court for the northern district of California against the executor and the six California claimants, seeking a judgment determining that the resident claimants have no interest in the estate, and that the Custodian, by virtue of his vesting order, is entitled to the entire net estate of the decedent after payment of expenses of administration, debts, and taxes, and is the owner of specified real estate of decedent passing under the will. The complaint prayed that the executor be ordered to pay the entire net estate to the Custodian upon the allowance by the state court of the executor's final account. On motion of respondents to strike the complaint, and on petitioner's motion for judgment on the pleadings, the district court gave judgment for petitioner. The court held that it had jurisdiction to enforce the vesting order of petitioner; that its jurisdiction is derived from the Constitution and laws of the United States and is not subject to restriction or ouster by state legislation; and that the California Statute is invalid. The judgment declared that petitioner had acquired the interests of the German nationals in the estate of decedent; that none of respondents have any right, title or interest in the estate; and that petitioner is entitled to receive the net estate in distribution after payment of expenses of administration, debts and taxes.

Without passing upon the merits, the Court of Appeals for the Ninth Circuit reversed and ordered the cause dismissed, upon the ground that the district court was without jurisdiction of the subject matter of the action. The court thought that since the matter is within probate jurisdiction and that court is in possession of the property, its right to proceed to determine heirship cannot be interfered with by the federal court.

It is not denied that the present suit is a suit of a civil nature in equity, brought by an officer of the United States, authorized to sue, of which district courts are given jurisdiction by 28 U.S.C. § 41(1), of the Judicial Code. But respondents argue, as the Circuit Court of Appeals held, that as the district courts of the United States are without jurisdiction over probate matters, which the court of appeals thought are not "cases or controversies within the meaning of Art. III of the Constitution," and since the present suit to determine heirship of property being administered in a state probate court is an exercise of probate jurisdiction, the district court is without jurisdiction.

It is true that a federal court has no jurisdiction to probate a will or administer an estate, the reason being that the equity jurisdiction conferred by the Judiciary Act of 1789 did not extend to probate matters. But it has been established by a long series of decisions of this Court that federal courts of equity have jurisdiction to entertain suits in favor of creditors, legatees and heirs and other claimants against a decedent's estate to establish their claims so long as the federal court does not interfere with the probate proceedings or assume general jurisdiction of the probate or control of the property in the custody of the state court.

Similarly, while a federal court may not exercise its jurisdiction to disturb or affect the possession of property in the custody of a state court, it may exercise its jurisdiction to adjudicate rights in such property where the final judgment does not undertake to interfere with the state court's possession save to the extent that the state court is bound by the judgment to recognize the right adjudicated by the federal court.

Although in this case petitioner sought a judgment in the district court ordering defendant executor to pay over the entire net estate to the petitioner upon an allowance of the executor's final account, the judgment declared only that petitioner is entitled to receive the net estate of the late Alvina Wagner in distribution, after the payment of expenses of administration, debts, and taxes. The effect of the judgment was to leave undisturbed the orderly administration of decedent's estate in the state probate court and to decree petitioner's right in the property to be distributed after its administration. This, as our authorities demonstrate, is not an exercise of probate jurisdiction or an interference with property in the possession or custody of a state court.

. . . . The cause was therefore within the jurisdiction of the district court, which could appropriately proceed with the case, and the Court of Appeals erroneously ordered its dismissal. The judgment is reversed and the cause remanded to the Circuit Court of Appeals for further proceedings in conformity to this opinion.

Marshall v. Marshall (2006)

Justice GINSBURG delivered the opinion of the Court.

In *Cohens v. Virginia*, Chief Justice Marshall famously cautioned: "It is most true that this Court will not take jurisdiction if it should not: but it is equally true, that it must take jurisdiction, if it should. . . . We have no more right to decline the exercise of jurisdiction which is given, than to usurp that which is not given." Among longstanding limitations on federal jurisdiction otherwise properly exercised are the so-called "domestic relations" and "probate" exceptions. Neither is compelled by the text of the Constitution or federal statute. Both are judicially created doctrines stemming in large measure from misty understandings of English legal history. . . .

I

Petitioner, Vickie Lynn Marshall (Vickie), also known as Anna Nicole Smith, is the surviving widow of J. Howard Marshall II (J. Howard). Vickie and J. Howard met in October 1991. After a courtship lasting more than two years, they were married on June 27, 1994. J. Howard died on August 4, 1995. Although he lavished gifts and significant sums of money on Vickie during their courtship and marriage, J. Howard did not include anything for Vickie in his will. According to Vickie, J. Howard intended to provide for her financial security through a gift in the form of a "catch-all" trust.

Respondent, E. Pierce Marshall (Pierce), one of J. Howard's sons, was the ultimate beneficiary of J. Howard's estate plan, which consisted of a living trust and a "pourover" will. Under the terms of the will, all of J. Howard's assets not already included in the trust were to be transferred to the trust upon his death.

Competing claims regarding J. Howard's fortune ignited proceedings in both state and federal courts. In January 1996, while J. Howard's estate was subject to ongoing proceedings in Probate Court in Harris County, Texas, Vickie filed for bankruptcy under Chapter 11 of the Bankruptcy Code, in the United States Bankruptcy Court for the Central District of California. In June 1996, Pierce filed a proof of claim in the federal bankruptcy proceeding, alleging that Vickie had defamed him when, shortly after J. Howard's death, lawyers representing Vickie told members of the press that Pierce had engaged in forgery, fraud, and overreaching to gain control of his father's assets. Pierce sought a declaration that the debt he asserted in that claim was not dischargeable in bankruptcy. Vickie answered, asserting truth as a defense. She also filed counterclaims, among them a claim that Pierce had tortiously interfered with a gift she expected. Vickie alleged that Pierce prevented the transfer of his father's intended gift to her by, among other things: effectively imprisoning J. Howard against his wishes; surrounding him with hired guards for the purpose of preventing personal contact between him and Vickie; making misrepresentations to J. Howard; and transferring property against J. Howard's expressed wishes.

Vickie's tortious interference counterclaim turned her objection to Pierce's claim into an adversary proceeding. In that proceeding, the Bankruptcy Court granted summary judgment in favor of Vickie on Pierce's claim and, after a trial on the merits, entered judgment for Vickie on her tortious interference counterclaim. The Bankruptcy Court also held that both Vickie's objection to Pierce's claim and Vickie's counterclaim qualified as "core proceedings" under 28 U.S.C. § 157, which meant that the court had authority to enter a final judgment disposing of those claims. The court awarded Vickie compensatory damages of more than $449 million—less whatever she recovered in the ongoing probate action in Texas—as well as $25 million in punitive damages.

Pierce filed a post-trial motion to dismiss for lack of subject-matter jurisdiction, asserting that Vickie's tortious interference claim could be tried only in the Texas probate proceedings. The Bankruptcy Court held that the "probate exception" argument was waived because it was not timely raised. Relying on this Court's decision in *Markham*, the court observed that a federal court has jurisdiction to adjudicate rights in probate property, so long as its final judgment does not undertake to interfere with the state court's possession of the property.

Meanwhile, in the Texas Probate Court, Pierce sought a declaration that the living trust and his father's will were valid. Vickie, in turn, challenged the validity of the will and filed a tortious interference claim against Pierce, but voluntarily dismissed both claims once the Bankruptcy Court entered its judgment. Following a jury trial, the Probate Court declared the living trust and J. Howard's will valid.

Back in the federal forum, Pierce sought district-court review of the Bankruptcy Court's judgment. While rejecting the Bankruptcy Court's determination that Pierce had forfeited any argument based on the probate exception, the District Court held that the exception did not reach Vickie's claim. The Bankruptcy Court did not assert jurisdiction generally over the probate proceedings or take control over the estate's assets, the District Court observed, thus, the probate exception would bar federal jurisdiction over Vickie's counterclaim only if such jurisdiction would "interfere" with the probate proceedings. Federal jurisdiction would not "interfere" with the probate proceedings, the District Court concluded, because: (1) success on Vickie's counterclaim did not necessitate any declaration that J. Howard's will was invalid, and (2) under Texas law, probate courts do not have exclusive jurisdiction to entertain claims of the kind asserted in Vickie's counterclaim.

The District Court also held that Vickie's claim did not qualify as a core proceeding arising under title 11, or arising in a case under title 11. A bankruptcy court may exercise plenary power only over "core proceedings." In non-core matters, a bankruptcy court may not enter final judgment; it has authority to issue only proposed findings of fact and conclusions of law, which are reviewed *de novo* by the district court. Accordingly, the District Court treated the Bankruptcy Court's judgment as proposed, rather than final, and undertook a comprehensive, complete, and independent review of the Bankruptcy Court's determinations.

Adopting and supplementing the Bankruptcy Court's findings, the District Court determined that Pierce had tortiously interfered with Vickie's expectancy. Specifically, the District Court found that J. Howard directed his lawyers to prepare an *inter vivos* trust for Vickie consisting of half the appreciation of his assets from the date of their marriage. It further found that Pierce conspired to suppress or destroy the trust instrument and to strip J. Howard of his assets by backdating, altering, and otherwise falsifying documents, arranging for surveillance of J. Howard and Vickie, and presenting documents to J. Howard under false pretenses. Based on these findings, the District Court awarded Vickie some $44.3 million in compensatory damages. In addition, finding overwhelming evidence of Pierce's "willfulness, maliciousness, and fraud," the District Court awarded an equal amount in punitive damages.

The Court of Appeals for the Ninth Circuit reversed. The appeals court recognized that Vickie's claim does not involve the administration of an estate, the probate of a will, or any other purely probate matter. Nevertheless, the court held that the probate exception bars federal jurisdiction in this case. In the Ninth Circuit's view, a claim falls within the probate exception if it raises questions which would ordinarily be decided by a probate court in determining the validity of the decedent's estate planning instrument, whether those questions involve fraud, undue influence, or tortious interference with the testator's intent.

The Ninth Circuit was also of the view that state-court delineation of a probate court's exclusive adjudicatory authority could control federal subject-matter jurisdiction. In this regard, the Court of Appeals stated: "Where a state has relegated jurisdiction over probate matters to a special court and the state's trial courts of general jurisdiction do not have jurisdiction to hear probate matters, then federal courts also lack jurisdiction over probate matters." Noting that the Probate Court ruled it had exclusive jurisdiction over all of Vickie's claims, the Ninth Circuit held that ruling binding on the United States District Court.

We granted certiorari to resolve the apparent confusion among federal courts concerning the scope of the probate exception. Satisfied that the instant case does not fall within the ambit of the narrow exception recognized by our decisions, we reverse the Ninth Circuit's judgment. . . .

III

Federal jurisdiction in this case is premised on 28 U.S.C. § 1334, the statute vesting in federal district courts jurisdiction in bankruptcy cases and related proceedings. Decisions of this Court have recognized a "probate exception," kin to the domestic relations exception, to otherwise proper federal jurisdiction. *See Markham*. Like the domestic relations exception, the probate exception has been linked to language contained in the Judiciary Act of 1789.

Markham, the Court's most recent and pathmarking pronouncement on the probate exception, stated that the equity jurisdiction conferred by the Judiciary Act of 1789, which is that of the English Court of Chancery in 1789, did not extend to probate matters. As in *Ankenbrandt*, so in this case, we have no occasion to join the historical debate over the scope of English chancery jurisdiction in 1789, for Vickie Marshall's claim falls far outside the bounds of the probate exception described in *Markham*. We therefore need not consider in this case whether there exists any uncodified probate exception to federal bankruptcy jurisdiction under § 1334.

In *Markham*, the plaintiff Alien Property Custodian commenced suit in Federal District Court against an executor and resident heirs to determine the Custodian's asserted rights regarding a decedent's estate. Jurisdiction was predicated on § 24(1) of the Judicial Code, which provides for federal jurisdiction over suits brought by an officer of the United States. At the time the federal suit commenced, the estate was undergoing probate administration in a state court. The Custodian had issued an order vesting in himself all right, title, and interest of German legatees. He sought and gained in the District Court a judgment determining that the resident heirs had no interest in the estate, and that the Custodian, substituting himself for the German legatees, was entitled to the entire net estate, including specified real estate passing under the will.

Reversing the Ninth Circuit, which had ordered the case dismissed for want of federal subject-matter jurisdiction, this Court held that federal jurisdiction was properly invoked. The Court first stated: "It is true that a federal court has no jurisdiction to probate a will or administer an estate . . . . But it has been established by a long series of decisions of this Court that federal courts of equity have jurisdiction to entertain suits in favor of creditors, legatees and heirs and other claimants against a decedent's estate to establish their claims so long as the federal court does not interfere with the probate proceedings or assume general jurisdiction of the probate or control of the property in the custody of the state court."

Next, the Court described a probate exception of distinctly limited scope: "While a federal court may not exercise its jurisdiction to disturb or affect the possession of property in the custody of a state court, it may exercise its jurisdiction to adjudicate rights in such property where the final judgment does not undertake to interfere with the state court's possession save to the extent that the state court is bound by the judgment to recognize the right adjudicated by the federal court."

The first of the above-quoted passages from *Markham* is not a model of clear statement. The Court observed that federal courts have jurisdiction to entertain suits to determine the rights of creditors, legatees, heirs, and other claimants against a decedent's estate, "so long as the federal court does not *interfere with the probate proceedings*." Lower federal courts have puzzled over the meaning of the words "interfere with the probate proceedings," and some have read those words to block federal jurisdiction over a range of matters well beyond probate of a will or administration of a decedent's estate.

We read *Markham*'s enigmatic words, in sync with the second above-quoted passage, to proscribe disturbing or affecting the possession of property in the custody of a state court. True, that reading renders the first-quoted passage in part redundant, but redundancy in this context, we do not doubt, is preferable to incoherence. In short, we comprehend the "interference" language in *Markham* as essentially a reiteration of the general principle that, when one court is exercising *in rem* jurisdiction over a *res*, a second court will not assume *in rem* jurisdiction over the same *res*. Thus, the probate exception reserves to state probate courts the probate or annulment of a will and the administration of a decedent's estate; it also precludes federal courts from endeavoring to dispose of property that is in the custody of a state probate court. But it does not bar federal courts from adjudicating matters outside those confines and otherwise within federal jurisdiction.

As the Court of Appeals correctly observed, Vickie's claim does not involve the administration of an estate, the probate of a will, or any other purely probate matter. Provoked by Pierce's claim in the bankruptcy proceedings, Vickie's claim, like Carol Ankenbrandt's, alleges a widely recognized tort. Vickie seeks an *in personam* judgment against Pierce, not the probate or annulment of a will. Nor does she seek to reach a *res* in the custody of a state court.

Furthermore, no sound policy considerations militate in favor of extending the probate exception to cover the case at hand. Trial courts, both federal and state, often address conduct of the kind Vickie alleges. State probate courts possess no special proficiency in handling such issues. . . . .

For the reasons stated, the judgment of the Court of Appeals for the Ninth Circuit is reversed, and the case is remanded for further proceedings consistent with this opinion.

Justice STEVENS, concurring in part and concurring in the judgment.

The administration of decedents' estates typically is governed by rules of state law and conducted by state probate courts. Occasionally, however, disputes between interested parties arise, either in the probate proceeding itself or elsewhere, that qualify as cases or controversies that federal courts have jurisdiction to decide. In her opinion for the Court, Justice Ginsburg has cogently explained why this is such a case. I write separately to explain why I do not believe there is any "probate exception" that ousts a federal court of jurisdiction it otherwise possesses.

The familiar aphorism that hard cases make bad law should extend to easy cases as well. *Markham v. Allen*, like this case, was an easy case. In *Markham*, as here, it was unnecessary to question the historical or logical underpinnings of the probate exception to federal jurisdiction because, whatever the scope of the supposed exception, it did not extend to the case at hand. But *Markham*'s obiter dicta—dicta that the Court now describes as redundant if not incoherent—generated both confusion and abdication of the obligation Chief Justice Marshall so famously articulated, *see Cohens v. Virginia*. While the Court today rightly abandons much of that dicta, I would go further. . . .

Rather than preserving whatever vitality that the "exception" has retained as a result of the *Markham* dicta, I would provide the creature with a decent burial in a grave adjacent to the resting place of the *Rooker-Feldman* doctrine.

State Sovereign Immunity

Introduction

The United States formed from independent states accustomed both to the law of nations and to the laws of England. The states ratified the Constitution with some notions of sovereignty in mind, including the ancient doctrine of sovereign immunity, whereby the sovereign could not be sued in its own courts without its consent. The states, of course, also understood that they were ceding much of their sovereignty in the original Constitution (and even more through ratification of the Civil War Amendments). But the Eleventh Amendment, ratified shortly after the *Chisholm* decision of the Supreme Court, does codify some notion of state sovereign immunity. Whether and to what extent the doctrine of sovereign immunity protects the states today remain complicated and hazy questions. This topic presents the opportunity to explore a number of questions, including the following:

- What is the nature of state sovereignty? What features of sovereign immunity are compatible in the U.S. federal system?

- What are the practical justifications for immunity?

- What is the character of immunity: jurisdictional, prudential, constitutional?

- Which branch is best suited to protect state sovereignty in a federal system: Congress or the Supreme Court?

- How sensible are the contours of state sovereign immunity? What policies or legal sources justify them?

- What are the underlying tensions represented by state sovereign immunity and the doctrine of *Ex Parte Young*?

- What separation-of-powers implications does sovereign-immunity doctrine present?

United States Constitution

Article III, section 2. The judicial power shall extend to all cases, in law and equity, arising under this Constitution, the laws of the United States, and treaties made, or which shall be made, under their authority; . . . to controversies between two or more states;—between a state and citizens of another state;—between citizens of different states. . . , and between a state, or the citizens thereof, and foreign states, citizens or subjects.

Amendment XI. The Judicial power of the United States shall not be construed to extend to any suit in law or equity, commenced or prosecuted against one of the United States by Citizens of another State, or by Citizens or Subjects of any Foreign State.

Hans v. Louisiana (1890)

This is an action brought in the circuit court of the United States, in December 1884, against the state of Louisiana, by Hans, a citizen of that state, to recover the amount of certain coupons annexed to bonds of the state, issued under the provisions of an act of the legislature approved January 24, 1874. [The plaintiff alleged that the state's repudiation of the bond obligations transgressed Article 1, Section 10 of U.S. Constitution, which states that "[n]o State shall . . . pass . . . any law impairing the obligation of contracts."] . . .

A citation being issued directed to the state, and served upon the governor thereof, the attorney general of the state filed an exception, of which the following is a copy, to-wit: "Now comes defendant, by the attorney general, and excepts to plaintiff's suit, on the ground that this court is without jurisdiction *ratione personae*. Plaintiff cannot sue the state without its permission; the constitution and laws do not give this honorable court jurisdiction of a suit against the state; and its jurisdiction is respectfully declined. Wherefore respondent prays to be hence dismissed, with costs, and for general relief." By the judgment of the court this exception was sustained, and the suit was dismissed.

To this judgment the present writ of error is brought; and the question is presented whether a state can be sued in a circuit court of the United States by one of its own citizens upon a suggestion that the case is one that arises under the constitution or laws of the United States.

The ground taken is that under the constitution, as well as under the act of congress passed to carry it into effect, a case is within the jurisdiction of the federal courts, without regard to the character of the parties, if it arises under the constitution or laws of the United States, or, which is the same thing, if it necessarily involves a question under said constitution or laws. The language relied on is that clause of the third article of the constitution, which declares that "the judicial power of the United States shall extend to all cases in law and equity arising under this constitution, the laws of the United States, and treaties made, or which shall be made, under their authority;" and the corresponding clause of the act conferring jurisdiction upon the circuit court, which, as found in the act of March 3, 1875, is as follows, to-wit: "That the circuit courts of the United States shall have original cognizance, concurrent with the courts of the several states, of all suits of a civil nature, at common law or in equity, . . . arising under the constitution or laws of the United States, or treaties made, or which shall be made, under their authority." It is said that these jurisdictional clauses make no exception arising from the character of the parties, and therefore that a state can claim no exemption from suit, if the case is really one arising under the constitution, laws, or treaties of the United States. It is conceded that, where the jurisdiction depends alone upon the character of the parties, a controversy between a state and its own citizens is not embraced within it; but it is contended that, though jurisdiction does not exist on that ground, it nevertheless does exist if the case itself is one which necessarily involves a federal question; and, with regard to ordinary parties, this is undoubtedly true. The question now to be decided is whether it is true where one of the parties is a state, and is sued as a defendant by one of its own citizens.

That a state cannot be sued by a citizen of another state, or of a foreign state, on the mere ground that the case is one arising under the constitution or laws of the United States, is clearly established by the decisions of this court in several recent cases. Those were cases arising under the constitution of the United States, upon laws complained of as impairing the obligation of contracts . . . complained of in the present case. Relief was sought against state officers who professed to act in obedience to those laws. This court held that the suits were virtually against the states themselves, and were consequently violative of the eleventh amendment of the constitution, and could not be maintained. It was not denied that they presented cases arising under the constitution; but, notwithstanding that, they were held to be prohibited by the amendment referred to.

In the present case the plaintiff in error contends that he, being a citizen of Louisiana, is not embarrassed by the obstacle of the eleventh amendment, inasmuch as that amendment only prohibits suits against a state which are brought by the citizens of another state, or by citizens or subjects of a foreign state. It is true the amendment does so read, and, if there were no other reason or ground for abating his suit, it might be maintainable; and then we should have this anomalous result, that, in cases arising under the constitution or laws of the United States, a state may be sued in the federal courts by its own citizens, though it cannot be sued for a like cause of action by the citizens of other states, or of a foreign state; and may be thus sued in the federal courts, although not allowing itself to be sued in its own courts. If this is the necessary consequence of the language of the constitution and the law, the result is no less startling and unexpected than was the original decision of this court, that, under the language of the constitution and of the judiciary act of 1789, a state was liable to be sued by a citizen of another state or of a foreign country. That decision was made in the case of *Chisholm v. Georgia* and created such a shock of surprise throughout the country that, at the first meeting of congress thereafter, the eleventh amendment to the constitution was almost unanimously proposed, and was in due course adopted by the legislatures of the states. This amendment, expressing the will of the ultimate sovereignty of the whole country, superior to all legislatures and all courts, actually reversed the decision of the supreme court. It did not in terms prohibit suits by individuals against the states, but declared that the constitution should not be construed to import any power to authorize the bringing of such suits. The language of the amendment is that "the judicial power of the United States shall not be construed to extend to any suit, in law or equity, commenced or prosecuted against one of the United States by citizens of another state, or by citizens or subjects of any foreign state." The supreme court had construed the judicial power as extending to such a suit, and its decision was thus overruled. . . .

This view of the force and meaning of the amendment is important. It shows that, on this question of the suability of the states by individuals, the highest authority of this country was in accord rather with the minority than with the majority of the court in the decision of the case of *Chisholm v. Georgia*; and this fact lends additional interest to the able opinion of Mr. Justice Iredell on that occasion. The other justices were more swayed by a close observance of the letter of the constitution, without regard to former experience and usage; and because the letter said that the judicial power shall extend to controversies "between a state and citizens of another state" and "between a state and foreign states, citizens or subjects," they felt constrained to see in this language a power to enable the individual citizens of one state, or of a foreign state, to sue another state of the Union in the federal courts. Justice Iredell, on the contrary, contended that it was not the intention to create new and unheard of remedies, by subjecting sovereign states to actions at the suit of individuals (which he conclusively showed was never done before) but only, by proper legislation, to invest the federal courts with jurisdiction to hear and determine controversies and cases, between the parties designated, that were properly susceptible of litigation in courts.

Looking back from our present stand-point at the decision in *Chisholm v. Georgia*, we do not greatly wonder at the effect which it had upon the country. Any such power as that of authorizing the federal judiciary to entertain suits by individuals against the states had been expressly disclaimed, and even resented, by the great defenders of the constitution while it was on its trial before the American people. As some of their utterances are directly pertinent to the question now under consideration, we deem it proper to quote them.

The eighty-first number of the Federalist, written by Hamilton, has the following profound remarks: "It has been suggested that an assignment of the public securities of one state to the citizens of another would enable them to prosecute that state in the federal courts for the amount of those securities, a suggestion which the following considerations prove to be without foundation: It is inherent in the nature of sovereignty not to be amenable to the suit of an individual without its consent. This is the general sense and the general practice of mankind; and the exemption, as one of the attributes of sovereignty, is now enjoyed by the government of every state in the Union. Unless, therefore, there is a surrender of this immunity in the plan of the convention, it will remain with the states, and the danger intimated must be merely ideal. The circumstances which are necessary to produce an alienation of state sovereignty were discussed in considering the article of taxation, and need not be repeated here. A recurrence to the principles there established will satisfy us that there is no color to pretend that the state governments would, by the adoption of that plan, be divested of the privilege of paying their own debts in their own way, free from every constraint but that which flows from the obligations of good faith. The contracts between a nation and individuals are only binding on the conscience of the sovereign, and have no pretension to a compulsive force. They confer no right of action independent of the sovereign will. To what purpose would it be to authorize suits against states for the debts they owe? How could recoveries be enforced? It is evident that it could not be done without waging war against the contracting state; and to ascribe to the federal courts by mere implication, and in destruction of a pre-existing right of the state governments, a power which would involve such a consequence, would be altogether forced and unwarrantable."

. . . . But Hamilton was not alone in protesting against the construction put upon the constitution by its opponents. In the Virginia convention the same objections were raised by George Mason and Patrick Henry, and were met by Madison and Marshall as follows. Madison said: "Its jurisdiction [the federal jurisdiction] in controversies between a state and citizens of another state is much objected to, and perhaps without reason. It is not in the power of individuals to call any state into court. The only operation it can have is that, if a state should wish to bring a suit against a citizen, it must be brought before the federal court. This will give satisfaction to individuals, as it will prevent citizens on whom a state may have a claim being dissatisfied with the state courts. . . . It appears to me that this [clause] can have no operation but this: to give a citizen a right to be heard in the federal courts, and, if a state should condescend to be a party, this court may take cognizance of it." Marshall, in answer to the same objection, said: "With respect to disputes between a state and the citizens of another state, its jurisdiction has been decried with unusual vehemence. I hope that no gentleman will think that a state will be called at the bar of the federal court. . . . It is not rational to suppose that the sovereign power should be dragged before a court. The intent is to enable states to recover claims of individuals residing in other states. . . . But, say they, there will be partiality in it if a state cannot be a defendant; if an individual cannot proceed to obtain judgment against a state, though he may be sued by a state. It is necessary to be so, and cannot be avoided. I see a difficulty in making a state defendant which does not prevent its being plaintiff."

It seems to us that these views of those great advocates and defenders of the constitution were most sensible and just, and they apply equally to the present case as to that then under discussion. The letter is appealed to now, as it was then, as a ground for sustaining a suit brought by an individual against a state. The reason against it is as strong in this case as it was in that. It is an attempt to strain the constitution and the law to a construction never imagined or dreamed of. Can we suppose that, when the eleventh amendment was adopted, it was understood to be left open for citizens of a state to sue their own state in the federal courts, while the idea of suits by citizens of other states, or of foreign states, was indignantly repelled? Suppose that congress, when proposing the eleventh amendment, had appended to it a proviso that nothing therein contained should prevent a state from being sued by its own citizens in cases arising under the constitution or laws of the United States, can we imagine that it would have been adopted by the states? The supposition that it would is almost an absurdity on its face.

The truth is that the cognizance of suits and actions unknown to the law, and forbidden by the law, was not contemplated by the constitution when establishing the judicial power of the United States. . . . The suability of a state, without its consent, was a thing unknown to the law. This has been so often laid down and acknowledged by courts and jurists that it is hardly necessary to be formally asserted. . . .

Some reliance is placed by the plaintiff upon the observations of Chief Justice Marshall in *Cohens v. Virginia*. The chief justice was there considering the power of review exercisable by this court over the judgments of a state court, wherein it might be necessary to make the state itself a defendant in error. He showed that this power was absolutely necessary in order to enable the judiciary of the United States to take cognizance of all cases arising under the constitution and laws of the United States. He also showed that making a state a defendant in error was entirely different from suing a state in an original action in prosecution of a demand against it, and was not within the meaning of the eleventh amendment; that the prosecution of a writ of error against a state was not the prosecution of a suit in the sense of that amendment, which had reference to the prosecution by suit of claims against a state. . . . With regard to the question then before the court, it may be observed that writs of error to judgments in favor of the crown, or of the state, had been known to the law from time immemorial, and had never been considered as exceptions to the rule that an action does not lie against the sovereign. . . .

The judgment of the circuit court is affirmed.

South Dakota v. North Carolina (1904)

[North Carolina issued some bonds]. . . . Simon Schafer and Samuel M. Schafer, either individually or as partners, owned a large proportion of these outstanding bonds, having held them for about thirty years. In 1901 Simon Schafer gave ten of these bonds to the state of South Dakota. . . . [South Dakota filed suit in federal district court to enforce the bonds.] . . . . North Carolina in its answer denied both the jurisdiction of this court and the title of the plaintiff . . . .

Mr. Justice BREWER delivered the opinion of the court:

There can be no reasonable doubt of the validity of the bonds and mortgages in controversy. There is no challenge of the statutes by which they were authorized. . . . Neither can there be any question respecting the title of South Dakota to these bonds. They are not held by the state as representative of individual owners, for they were given outright and absolutely to the state. It is true that the gift may be considered a rare and unexpected one. Apparently the statute of South Dakota was passed in view of the expected gift, and probably the donor made the gift under a not unreasonable expectation that South Dakota would bring an action against North Carolina to enforce these bonds, and that such action might inure to his benefit as the owner of other like bonds. But the motive with which a gift is made, whether good or bad, does not affect its validity or the question of jurisdiction. . . .

The title of South Dakota is as perfect as though it had received these bonds directly from North Carolina. We have, therefore, before us the case of a state with an unquestionable title to bonds issued by another state, secured by a mortgage of railroad stock belonging to that state, coming into this court and invoking its jurisdiction to compel payment of those bonds and a subjection of the mortgaged property to the satisfaction of the debt.

Has this court jurisdiction of such a controversy, and to what extent may it grant relief? Obviously, that jurisdiction is not affected by the fact that the donor of these bonds could not invoke it. The payee of a foreign bill of exchange may not sue the drawer in the Federal court of a state of which both are citizens, but that does not oust the court of jurisdiction of an action by a subsequent holder if the latter be a citizen of another state. The question of jurisdiction is determined by the status of the present parties, and not by that of prior holders of the thing in controversy. Obviously, too, the subject-matter is one of judicial cognizance. If anything can be considered as justiciable it is a claim for money due on a written promise to pay; and if it be justiciable, does it matter how the plaintiff acquires title, providing it be honestly acquired? It would seem strangely inconsistent to take jurisdiction of an action by South Dakota against North Carolina on a promise to pay made by the latter directly to the former, and refuse jurisdiction of an action on a like promise made by the latter to an individual, and by him sold or donated to the former. . . .

Coming now to the right of South Dakota to maintain this suit against North Carolina, we remark that it is a controversy between two states; that by § 2, art. III., of the Constitution, this court is given original jurisdiction of "controversies between two or more states." . . .

The Constitution, as it originally stood, also gave to this court jurisdiction of controversies "between a state and citizens of another state." Under that clause *Chisholm* v. *Georgia* was decided, in which it was held that a citizen of one state might maintain in this court an action of assumpsit against another state. In consequence of that decision the 11th Amendment was adopted . . . . It will be perceived that this amendment only granted to a state immunity from suit by an individual, and did not affect the jurisdiction over controversies between two or more states. In respect to this it was said by Chief Justice Marshall in *Cohen* v. *Virginia*:

> It is a part of our history that, at the adoption of the Constitution, all the states were greatly indebted; and the apprehension that these debts might be prosecuted in the Federal courts formed a very serious objection to that instrument. Suits were instituted; and the court maintained its jurisdiction. The alarm was general; and, to quiet the apprehensions that were so extensively entertained, this amendment was proposed in Congress, and adopted by the state legislatures. That its motive was not to maintain the sovereignty of a state from the degradation supposed to attend a compulsory appearance before the tribunal of the nation may be inferred from the terms of the amendment. It does not comprehend controversies between two or more states, or between a state and a foreign state. The jurisdiction of the court still extends to these cases; and in these a state may still be sued. We must ascribe the amendment, then, to some other cause than the dignity of a state. There is no difficulty in finding this cause. Those who were inhibited from commencing a suit against a state, or from prosecuting one which might be commenced before the adoption of the amendment, were persons who might probably be its creditors. There was not much reason to fear that foreign or sister states would be creditors to any considerable amount, and there was reason to retain the jurisdiction of the court in those cases, because it might be essential to the preservation of peace. The amendment, therefore, extended to suits commenced or prosecuted by individuals, but not to those brought by states.

. . . . [T]he clear import of the decisions of this court from the beginning to the present time is in favor of its jurisdiction over an action brought by one state against another, to enforce a property right. . . . And surely if, as we have often held, this court has jurisdiction of an action by one state against another to recover a tract of land, there would seem to be no doubt of the jurisdiction of one to enforce the delivery of personal property. . . .

Mr. Justice WHITE, dissenting, with whom concurred Mr. Chief Justice FULLER, Mr. Justice McKENNA, and Mr. Justice DAY:

The decision in this cause seems to me to disregard an express and absolute prohibition of the Constitution. . . .

My mind cannot escape the conclusion that if, wherever an individual has a claim, whether in contract or tort, against a state, he may, by transferring it to another state, bring into play the judicial power of the United States to enforce such claim, then the prohibition contained in the 11th Amendment is a mere letter, without spirit and without force. This is said because no escape is seen from the conclusion if the application of the prohibition is to depend solely upon the willingness of the creditor of a state, whether citizen or alien, to transfer, and the docility or cupidity of another state in accepting such transfer, that the provision will have no efficacy whatever. And this becomes doubly cogent when the history of the 11th Amendment is considered, and the purpose of its adoption is borne in mind. . . .

As the purpose of the amendment was to prohibit the enforcement of individual claims against the several states by means of the judicial power of the United States, and as the amendment was subsequent to the grant of judicial power made by the Constitution, the amendment qualified the whole grant of judicial power to the extent necessary to render it impossible, by indirection, to escape the operation of the avowed purpose which the people of the United States expressed in adopting the amendment. How, as declared by Chief Justice Marshall, could the adoption of the amendment have quieted the apprehensions concerning the right to enforce private claims against the states, if the power was left open, after the amendment, to do so if only they were transferred to another state? It is also to be observed that the construction now given causes the judicial power of the United States to embrace claims not within even the reach of the ruling in *Chisholm v. Georgia*, for that case only decided that under the grant of power a citizen of one state might sue another state. But under the rule of construction now announced, not only claims held by citizens of other states and aliens, but those held by a citizen of the state, become capable of enforcement, if only the holders of such claims, after the state has refused to pay them, choose to sell or make gift thereof to another state, found willing to become a party to a plan to evade a constitutional provision inserted for the protection of all the states. . . .

United States v. Mississippi (1965)

The United States by the Attorney General brought this action in the United States District Court for the Southern District of Mississippi, Jackson Division, against the State of Mississippi, the three members of the Mississippi State Board of Election Commissioners, and six county Registrars of Voters. The complaint charged that the defendants and their agents had engaged and, unless restrained, would continue to engage in acts and practices hampering and destroying the right of Negro citizens of Mississippi to vote, in violation of 42 U.S.C. § 1971(a), and of the Fourteenth and Fifteenth Amendments and Article I of the United States Constitution. . . . [T]he State moved separately to dismiss on the ground that the United States had no power to make it a defendant in such a suit . . . . The District Court in an opinion by the late Circuit Judge Cameron, in which District Judge Cox joined, dismissed the complaint . . . .

The Eleventh Amendment in terms forbids suits against States only when "commenced or prosecuted . . . by Citizens of another State, or by Citizens or Subjects of any Foreign State." While this has been read to bar a suit by a State's own citizen as well, nothing in this or any other provision of the Constitution prevents or has ever been seriously supposed to prevent a State's being sued by the United States. The United States in the past has in many cases been allowed to file suits in this and other courts against States. In light of this history, it seems rather surprising that the District Court entertained seriously the argument that the United States could not constitutionally sue a State. . . . We hold that the State was properly made a defendant in this case. . . .

Reversed and remanded.

Principality of Monaco v. Mississippi (1934)

The Principality of Monaco asks leave to bring suit in this Court against the State of Mississippi upon bonds issued by the State and alleged to be the absolute property of the Principality.

. . . . In each count it was alleged that the bonds were transferred and delivered to the Principality at its legation in Paris, France, on or about September 27, 1933, as an absolute gift. Accompanying the declaration and made a part of it is a letter of the donors, dated September 26, 1933, stating that the bonds had been handed down from their respective families who purchased them at the time of their issue by the State of Mississippi; that the State had long since defaulted on the principal and interest of these bonds, the holders of which have waited for some 90 years in the hope that the State would meet its obligations and make payment; that the donors had been advised that there was no basis upon which they could maintain a suit against Mississippi on the bonds, but that such a suit could only be maintained by a foreign government or one of the United States; and that in these circumstances the donors were making an unconditional gift of the bonds to the Principality to be applied to the causes of any of its charities, to the furtherance of its internal development or to the benefit of its citizens in such manner as it may select.

The State of Mississippi, in its return to the rule to show cause why leave should not be granted, raises the following objections: . . . that the State of Mississippi has not consented and does not consent that she be sued by the Principality of Monaco and that without such consent the State cannot be sued . . . . In reply to these objections, the Principality asserts that she is a foreign State recognized as such by the Government of the United States; that the consent of the State of Mississippi is not necessary to give the Court jurisdiction . . . .

The Principality relies upon the provisions of section 2 of article 3 of the Constitution of the United States that the judicial power shall extend to controversies "between a State, or the Citizens thereof, and foreign States, Citizens or Subjects" (clause 1), and that in cases "in which a State shall be Party" this Court shall have original jurisdiction (clause 2). The absence of qualification requiring the consent of the State in the case of a suit by a foreign State is asserted to be controlling. And the point is stressed that the Eleventh Amendment of the Constitution, providing that the judicial power shall not be construed to extend to any suit against one of the United States "by Citizens of another State, or by Citizens or subjects of any Foreign State," contains no reference to a suit brought by a foreign State.

The argument drawn from the lack of an express requirement of consent to be sued is inconclusive. Thus there is no express provision that the United States may not be sued in the absence of consent. Clause 1 of section 2 of article 3 extends the judicial power "to

Controversies to which the United States shall be a Party." Literally, this includes such controversies, whether the United States be party plaintiff or defendant. But by reason of the established doctrine of the immunity of the sovereign from suit except upon consent, the provision of clause 1 of section 2 of article 3 does not authorize the maintenance of suits against the United States. And while clause 2 of section 2 of article 3 gives this Court original jurisdiction in those cases in which "a State shall be Party," this Court has no jurisdiction of a suit by a State against the United States in the absence of consent. Clause 2 merely distributes the jurisdiction conferred by clause 1, and deals with cases in which resort may be had to the original jurisdiction of this Court in the exercise of the judicial power as previously given.

Similarly, neither the literal sweep of the words of clause 1 of section 2 of article 3, nor the absence of restriction in the letter of the Eleventh Amendment, permits the conclusion that in all controversies of the sort described in clause 1, and omitted from the words of the Eleventh Amendment, a State may be sued without her consent. Thus clause 1 specifically provides that the judicial power shall extend "to all Cases, in Law and Equity, arising under this Constitution, the Laws of the United States, and Treaties made, or which shall be made, under their Authority." But, although a case may arise under the Constitution and laws of the United States, the judicial power does not extend to it if the suit is sought to be prosecuted against a State without her consent, by one of her own citizens. The requirement of consent is necessarily implied. The State has the same immunity in case of a suit brought by a corporation created by act of Congress. Yet in neither case is the suit within the express prohibition of the Eleventh Amendment. Again, the Eleventh Amendment mentions only suits "in law or equity"; it does not refer to suits in admiralty. But this Court has held that the Amendment does not leave open a suit against a state in the admiralty jurisdiction by individuals, whether its own citizens or not.

Manifestly, we cannot rest with a mere literal application of the words of section 2 of article 3, or assume that the letter of the Eleventh Amendment exhausts the restrictions upon suits against nonconsenting States. Behind the words of the constitutional provisions are postulates which limit and control. There is the essential postulate that the controversies, as contemplated, shall be found to be of a justiciable character. There is also the postulate that States of the Union, still possessing attributes of sovereignty,[] shall be immune from suits, without their consent, save where there has been "a surrender of this immunity in the plan of the convention." *The Federalist* No. 81. The question is whether the plan of the Constitution involves the surrender of immunity when the suit is brought against a State, without her consent, by a foreign State.

The debates in the Constitutional Convention do not disclose a discussion of this question. But Madison, in the Virginia Convention, answering objections to the ratification of the

Constitution, clearly stated his view as to the purpose and effect of the provision conferring jurisdiction over controversies between States of the Union and foreign States. That purpose was suitably to provide for adjudication in such cases if consent should be given but not otherwise.[] Madison said: "The next case provides for disputes between a foreign state and one of our states, should such a case ever arise; and between a citizen and a foreign citizen or subject. I do not conceive that any controversy can ever be decided, in these courts, between an American state and a foreign state, without the consent of the parties. If they consent, provision is here made."

Marshall, in the same Convention, expressed a similar view. Replying to an objection as to the admissibility of a suit by a foreign state, Marshall said: "He objects, in the next place, to its jurisdiction in controversies between a state and a foreign state. Suppose, says he, in such a suit, a foreign state is cast; will she be bound by the decision? If a foreign state brought a suit against the commonwealth of Virginia, would she not be barred from the claim if the federal judiciary thought it unjust? The previous consent of the parties is necessary; and, as the federal judiciary will decide, each party will acquiesce."

Hamilton, in *The Federalist*, No. 81, made the following emphatic statement of the general principle of immunity:

> It is inherent in the nature of sovereignty not to be amenable to the suit of an individual without its consent. This is the general sense and the general practice of mankind; and the exemption, as one of the attributes of sovereignty, is now enjoyed by the government of every State in the Union. Unless, therefore, there is a surrender of this immunity in the plan of the convention, it will remain with the States, and the danger intimated must be merely ideal. The circumstances which are necessary to produce an alienation of State sovereignty were discussed in considering the article of taxation and need not be repeated here. A recurrence to the principles there established will satisfy us that there is no color to pretend that the State governments would by the adoption of that plan be divested of the privilege of paying their own debts in their own way, free from every constraint but that which flows from the obligations of good faith. The contracts between a nation and individuals are only binding on the conscience of the sovereign, and have no pretensions to a compulsive force. They confer no right of action independent of the sovereign will. To what purpose would it be to authorize suits against States for the debts they owe? How could recoveries be enforced? It is evident it could not be done without waging was against the contracting State; and to ascribe to the federal courts by mere implication, and in destruction of a pre-existing right of the State governments, a power which would involve such a consequence would be altogether forced and unwarrantable.

It is true that, despite these cogent statements of the views which prevailed when the Constitution was ratified, the Court held, in *Chisholm v. Georgia*, over the vigorous dissent of Mr. Justice Iredell, that a State was liable to suit by a citizen of another State or of a foreign country. But this decision created such a shock of surprise that the Eleventh Amendment was at once proposed and adopted. As the Amendment did not in terms apply to a suit against a State by its own citizen, the Court had occasion, when that question was presented in *Hans v. Louisiana* (a case alleged to arise under the Constitution of the United States), to give elaborate consideration to the application of the general principle of the immunity of States from suits brought against them without their consent. . . .

South Dakota v. North Carolina was a suit by one State against another State and did not present the question of the maintenance either of a suit by individuals against a State or by a foreign State against a State. As a suit by one State against another State, it involved a distinct and essential principle of the constitutional plan which provided means for the judicial settlement of controversies between States of the Union, a principle which necessarily operates regardless of the consent of the defendant State. . . .

The question of that immunity, in the light of the provisions of clause 1 of section 2 of article 3 of the Constitution, is thus presented in several distinct classes of cases, that is, in those brought against a State (a) by another State of the Union; (b) by the United States; (c) by the citizens of another State or by the citizens or subjects of a foreign State; (d) by citizens of the same State or by federal corporations; and (e) by foreign States. Each of these classes has its characteristic aspect, from the standpoint of the effect, upon sovereign immunity from suits, which has been produced by the constitutional scheme.

1. The establishment of a permanent tribunal with adequate authority to determine controversies between the States, in place of an inadequate scheme of arbitration, was essential to the peace of the Union. With respect to such controversies, the States by the adoption of the Constitution, acting in their highest sovereign capacity, in the convention of the people, waived their exemption from judicial power. The jurisdiction of this Court over the parties in such cases was thus established by their own consent and delegated authority as a necessary feature of the formation of a more perfect Union.

2. Upon a similar basis rests the jurisdiction of this Court of a suit by the United States against a State, albeit without the consent of the latter. While that jurisdiction is not conferred by the Constitution in express words, it is inherent in the constitutional plan. Without such a provision, as this Court said in *United States v. Texas*, the permanence of the Union might be endangered.

3. To suits against a State, without her consent, brought by citizens of another State or by citizens or subjects of a foreign State, the Eleventh Amendment erected an absolute bar. Superseding the decision in *Chisholm v. Georgia*, the Amendment established in effective operation the principle asserted by Madison, Hamilton, and Marshall in expounding the Constitution and advocating its ratification. The entire judicial power granted by the Constitution does not embrace authority to entertain such suits in the absence of the State's consent.

4. Protected by the same fundamental principle, the States, in the absence of consent, are immune from suits brought against them by their own citizens or by federal corporations, although such suits are not within the explicit prohibitions of the Eleventh Amendment. *Hans v. Louisiana.*

5. We are of the opinion that the same principle applies to suits against a State by a foreign State. . . . We think that Madison correctly interpreted clause 1 of section 2 of article 3 of the Constitution as making provision for jurisdiction of a suit against a State by a foreign State in the event of the State's consent but not otherwise. In such a case, the grounds of coercive jurisdiction which are present in suits to determine controversies between States of the Union, or in suits brought by the United States against a State, are not present. The foreign State lies outside the structure of the Union. The waiver or consent, on the part of a State, which inheres in the acceptance of the constitutional plan, runs to the other States who have likewise accepted that plan, and to the United States as the sovereign which the Constitution creates. We perceive no ground upon which it can be said that any waiver or consent by a State of the Union has run in favor of a foreign State. As to suits brought by a foreign State, we think that the States of the Union retain the same immunity that they enjoy with respect to suits by individuals whether citizens of the United States or citizens or subjects of a foreign State. The foreign State enjoys a similar sovereign immunity and without her consent may not be sued by a State of the Union.

. . . . We conclude that the Principality of Monaco, with respect to the right to maintain the proposed suit, is in no better case than the donors of the bonds, and that the application for leave to sue must be denied.

Rule discharged, and leave denied.

Blatchford v. Native Village of Noatak (1991)

Justice SCALIA delivered the opinion of the Court.

. . . . In 1980, Alaska enacted a revenue-sharing statute that provided annual payments of $25,000 to each Native village government located in a community without a state-chartered municipal corporation. The State's attorney general believed the statute to be unconstitutional. In his view, Native village governments were racially exclusive groups or racially exclusive organizations whose status turned exclusively on the racial ancestry of their members; therefore, the attorney general believed, funding these groups would violate the equal protection clause of Alaska's Constitution. Acting on the attorney general's advice, the Commissioner of Alaska's Department of Community and Regional Affairs (petitioner here), enlarged the program to include all unincorporated communities, whether administered by Native governments or not. Shortly thereafter, the legislature increased funding under the program to match its increased scope. Funding, however, never reached the full $25,000 initially allocated to each unincorporated Native community. . . . [R]espondents filed this suit, challenging the commissioner's action on federal equal protection grounds, and seeking an order requiring the commissioner to pay them the money that they would have received had the commissioner not enlarged the program. The District Court . . . dismissed the suit as violating the Eleventh Amendment. The Court of Appeals for the Ninth Circuit reversed . . . .

In arguing that sovereign immunity does not restrict suit by Indian tribes, respondents submit, first, that sovereign immunity only restricts suits by *individuals* against sovereigns, not by *sovereigns* against sovereigns, and as we have recognized, Indian tribes are sovereigns. Respondents' conception of the nature of sovereign immunity finds some support both in the apparent understanding of the Founders and in dicta of our own opinions.[1]

> [1] As Alexander Hamilton said: "It is inherent in the nature of sovereignty, not to be amenable to the suit of an *individual* without its consent." James Madison expressed a similar understanding at the Virginia Convention ("It is not in the power of *individuals* to call any state into court"), as did Chief Justice Marshall ("[A]n *individual* cannot proceed to obtain judgment against a state, though he may be sued by a state") . . . .

But whatever the reach or meaning of these early statements, the notion that traditional principles of sovereign immunity only restrict suits by individuals was rejected in *Principality of Monaco*. . . . Our clear assumption in *Monaco* was that sovereign immunity extends against both individuals and sovereigns, so that there must be found inherent in the plan of the convention a surrender by the States of immunity as to either. Because we perceived in the plan no ground upon which it can be said that any waiver or consent by a State of the Union has run in favor of a foreign State, we concluded that foreign states were still subject to the immunity of the States.

We pursue the same inquiry in the present case, and thus confront respondents' second contention: that the States waived their immunity against Indian tribes when they adopted the Constitution. Just as in *Monaco* with regard to foreign sovereigns, so also here with regard to Indian tribes, there is no compelling evidence that the Founders thought such a surrender inherent in the constitutional compact. We have hitherto found a surrender of immunity against particular litigants in only two contexts: suits by sister States, and suits by the United States. . . .

Respondents argue that Indian tribes are more like States than foreign sovereigns. That is true in some respects: They are, for example, domestic. The relevant difference between States and foreign sovereigns, however, is not domesticity, but the role of each in the convention within which the surrender of immunity was for the former, but not for the latter, implicit. What makes the States' surrender of immunity from suit by sister States plausible is the mutuality of that concession. There is no such mutuality with either foreign sovereigns or Indian tribes. We have repeatedly held that Indian tribes enjoy immunity against suits by States, as it would be absurd to suggest that the tribes surrendered immunity in a convention to which they were not even parties. But if the convention could not surrender *the tribes'* immunity for the benefit of the *States*, we do not believe that it surrendered the States' immunity for the benefit of the tribes. . . . The judgment of the Court of Appeals is reversed, and the case is remanded for further proceedings consistent with this opinion. . . .

Justice BLACKMUN, with whom Justice MARSHALL and Justice STEVENS join, dissenting.

. . . . As some of us previously have stated, I do not believe the Eleventh Amendment is implicated by a suit such as this one, in which litigants seek to vindicate federal rights against a State. In my view, the Amendment has no application outside the context of State/citizen and State/alien diversity suits. . . . Accordingly, I would affirm the judgment of the Court of Appeals. . . .

Lapides v. Board of Regents (2002)

The Eleventh Amendment grants a State immunity from suit in federal court by citizens of other States and by its own citizens as well. The question before us is whether the State's act of removing a lawsuit from state court to federal court waives this immunity. We hold that it does.

I

Paul Lapides, a professor employed by the Georgia state university system, brought this lawsuit in a Georgia state court. He sued respondents, the Board of Regents of the University System of Georgia (hereinafter Georgia or State) and university officials acting in both their personal capacities and as agents of the State. Lapides's lawsuit alleged that university officials placed allegations of sexual harassment in his personnel files. And Lapides claimed that their doing so violated both Georgia law and federal law.

All defendants joined in removing the case to Federal District Court, where they sought dismissal. Those individuals whom Lapides had sued in their personal capacities argued that the doctrine of qualified immunity barred Lapides's federal-law claims against them. And the District Court agreed. The State, while conceding that a state statute had waived sovereign immunity from state-law suits in state court, argued that, by virtue of the Eleventh Amendment, it remained immune from suit in federal court. But the District Court did not agree. Rather, in its view, by removing the case from state to federal court, the State had waived its Eleventh Amendment immunity.

The State appealed the District Court's Eleventh Amendment ruling. And the Court of Appeals for the Eleventh Circuit reversed. In its view, state law was, at the least, unclear as to whether the State's attorney general possessed the legal authority to waive the State's Eleventh Amendment immunity. And, that being so, the State retained the legal right to assert its immunity, even after removal.

Lapides sought certiorari. We agreed to decide whether a state waives its Eleventh Amendment immunity by its affirmative litigation conduct when it removes a case to federal court.

II

. . . . A State remains free to waive its Eleventh Amendment immunity from suit in a federal court. And the question before us now is whether a State waives that immunity when it removes a case from state court to federal court.

It would seem anomalous or inconsistent for a State both (1) to invoke federal jurisdiction, thereby contending that the "Judicial power of the United States" extends to the case at hand, and (2) to claim Eleventh Amendment immunity, thereby denying that the "Judicial power of the United States" extends to the case at hand. And a Constitution that permitted States to follow their litigation interests by freely asserting both claims in the same case could generate seriously unfair results. Thus, it is not surprising that more than a century ago this Court indicated that a State's voluntary appearance in federal court amounted to a waiver of its Eleventh Amendment immunity. The Court subsequently held, in the context of a bankruptcy claim, that a State waives any immunity respecting the adjudication of a claim that it voluntarily files in federal court. And the Court has made clear in general that where a State *voluntarily* becomes a party to a cause and submits its rights for judicial determination, it will be bound thereby and cannot escape the result of its own voluntary act by invoking the prohibitions of the Eleventh Amendment. The Court has long accepted this statement of the law as valid, often citing with approval the cases embodying that principle.

In this case, the State was brought involuntarily into the case as a defendant in the original state-court proceedings. But the State then voluntarily agreed to remove the case to federal court. In doing so, it voluntarily invoked the federal court's jurisdiction. And unless we are to abandon the general principle just stated, or unless there is something special about removal or about this case, the general legal principle requiring waiver ought to apply.

. . . . Georgia argues that state law, while authorizing its attorney general to represent the state in all civil actions tried in any court, does not authorize the attorney general to waive the State's Eleventh Amendment immunity. Georgia adds that . . . . [this Court has] sustained an Eleventh Amendment defense raised for the first time after a State had litigated a claim brought against it in federal court. That is to say, in [prior cases] a State regained immunity by showing the attorney general's lack of statutory authority to waive—even after the State litigated and lost a case brought against it in federal court. Why, then, asks Georgia, can it not regain immunity in the same way, even after it removed its case to federal court?

The short answer to this question is that this case involves a State that *voluntarily* invoked the jurisdiction of the federal court, while [other cases] involved a State that a private plaintiff had *involuntarily* made a defendant in federal court. This Court consistently has found a waiver when a State's attorney general, authorized (as here) to bring a case in federal court, has voluntarily invoked that court's jurisdiction. And the Eleventh Amendment waiver rules are different when a State's federal-court participation is involuntary.

But there is a more important answer. . . . [W]hether a particular set of state laws, rules, or activities amounts to a waiver of the State's Eleventh Amendment immunity is a question of federal law. A rule of federal law that finds waiver through a state attorney general's invocation of federal-court jurisdiction avoids inconsistency and unfairness. A rule of federal law that . . . denies waiver despite the state attorney general's state-authorized litigating decision, does the opposite. . . .

Finally, Georgia says that our conclusion will prove confusing, for States will have to guess what conduct might be deemed a waiver in order to avoid accidental waivers. But we believe the rule is a clear one, easily applied by both federal courts and the States themselves. It says that removal is a form of voluntary invocation of a federal court's jurisdiction sufficient to waive the State's otherwise valid objection to litigation of a matter (here of state law) in a federal forum.

We conclude that the State's action joining the removing of this case to federal court waived its Eleventh Amendment immunity—though, as we have said, the District Court may well find that this case, now raising only state-law issues, should nonetheless be remanded to the state courts for determination.

For these reasons, the judgment of the Court of Appeals is reversed.

Northern Insurance Co. of New York v. Chatham County (2006)

Petitioner Northern Insurance Company of New York (Northern) filed suit against respondent Chatham County, Georgia, in the United States District Court for the Southern District of Georgia, seeking damages resulting from an alleged tort committed by employees of the County. The District Court granted the County's motion for summary judgment on the ground that the suit was barred by sovereign immunity. Relying on Circuit precedent, the Court of Appeals for the Eleventh Circuit affirmed. We granted certiorari to consider whether an entity that does not qualify as an arm of the State for Eleventh Amendment purposes can nonetheless assert sovereign immunity as a defense to an admiralty suit.

The County owns, operates, and maintains the Causton Bluff Bridge, a drawbridge over the Wilmington River. On October 6, 2002, James Ludwig requested that the bridge be raised to allow his boat to pass. The bridge malfunctioned, a portion falling and colliding with Mr. Ludwig's boat. As a result of the collision, Mr. Ludwig and his wife incurred damages in excess of $130,000.

The Ludwigs submitted a claim for those damages to their insurer, Northern, which paid in accordance with the terms of their insurance policy. Northern then sought to recover its costs by filing suit in admiralty against the County in the District Court. The County sought summary judgment, arguing that Northern's claims were barred by sovereign immunity. The County conceded that Eleventh Amendment immunity did not extend to counties, but nonetheless contended that it was immune under the universal rule of state immunity from suit without the state's consent. The District Court conclude[d] that sovereign immunity extends to counties and municipalities that, as here, exercise power delegated from the State. The Eleventh Circuit . . . affirmed. . . .

This Court's cases have recognized that the immunity of States from suit is a fundamental aspect of the sovereignty which the States enjoyed before the ratification of the Constitution, and which they retain today except as altered by the plan of the Convention or certain constitutional Amendments. Consistent with this recognition, which no party asks us to reexamine today, we have observed that the phrase "Eleventh Amendment immunity" is convenient shorthand but something of a misnomer, for the sovereign immunity of the States neither derives from, nor is limited by, the terms of the Eleventh Amendment.

A consequence of this Court's recognition of preratification sovereignty as the source of immunity from suit is that only States and arms of the State possess immunity from suits authorized by federal law. Accordingly, this Court has repeatedly refused to extend sovereign immunity to counties. This is true even when, as respondent alleges here, such entities exercise a slice of state power. . . . [R]eversed.

Ex Parte Young (1908)

An original application was made to this court for leave to file a petition for writs of habeas corpus and certiorari in behalf of Edward T. Young, petitioner, as attorney general of the state of Minnesota. Leave was granted and a rule entered directing the United States marshal for the district of Minnesota, third division, who held the petitioner in his custody, to show cause why such petition should not be granted.

The marshal, upon the return of the order to show cause, justified his detention on the petitioner by virtue of an order of the circuit court of the United States for the district of Minnesota, which adjudged the petitioner guilty of contempt of that court, and directed that he be fined the sum of $100, and that he should dismiss the mandamus proceedings brought by him in the name and in behalf of the state, in the circuit court of the state, and that he should stand committed to the custody of the marshal until that order was obeyed. The case involves the validity of the order of the circuit court committing him for contempt.

The facts are these: The legislature of the state of Minnesota duly created a railroad and warehouse commission, and that commission, on the 6th of September 1906, made an order fixing the rates for the various railroad companies for the carriage of merchandise between stations in that state of the kind and classes specified in what is known as the "Western Classification." [In a series of acts, the state imposed additional requirements on railroads.] . . .

[T]he day before the act was to take effect, nine suits in equity were commenced in the circuit court of the United States for the district of Minnesota, third division, each suit being brought by stockholders of the particular railroad mentioned in the bill, and in each case the defendants named were the railroad company of which the complainants were, respectively, stockholders, and the members of the railroad and warehouse commission, and the attorney general of the state, Edward T. Young, and individual defendants, representing the shippers of freight upon the railroad.

. . . . [T]he objects and purposes of the suit were to enjoin the railway company from [complying with the Minnesota laws] and also to enjoin the other defendants from attempting to enforce such provisions, or from instituting any action or proceeding against the defendant railway company, its officers, etc., on account of any violation thereof, for the reason that the said acts and orders were and each of them was violative of the Constitution of the United States. . . . A temporary restraining order was made by the circuit court, which . . . . restrained Edward T. Young, attorney general, from taking any steps against the railroads to enforce the remedies or penalties specified in the act[s].

Copies of the bill and the restraining order were served, among others, upon the defendant Mr. Edward T. Young, attorney general, who appeared specially and only for the purpose of moving to dismiss the bill as to him, on the ground that the court had no jurisdiction over him as attorney general; and he averred that the state of Minnesota had not consented, and did not consent, to the commencement of this suit against him as attorney general of the state, which suit was in truth and effect a suit against the said state of Minnesota, contrary to the 11th Amendment of the Constitution of the United States. . . . Thereupon, on the 23d of September 1907, the court, after a hearing of all parties and taking proofs in regard to the issues involved, ordered a temporary injunction to issue against . . . . the defendant Young, as attorney general of the state of Minnesota, pending the final hearing of the cause, from taking or instituting any action or proceeding to enforce the penalties and remedies specified in the act above mentioned, or to compel obedience to that act, or compliance therewith, or any part thereof. . . .

The day after the granting of this preliminary injunction the attorney general, in violation of such injunction, filed a petition for an alternative writ of mandamus in one of the courts of the state, and obtained an order from that court September 24, 1907, directing the alternative writ to issue as prayed for in the petition. The writ was thereafter issued and served upon the Northern Pacific Railway Company, commanding the company [to comply with the state laws under penalty of state enforcement.]

Upon an affidavit showing these facts the United States circuit court ordered Mr. Young to show cause why he should not be punished as for a contempt for his misconduct in violating the temporary injunction issued by that court in the case therein pending.

Upon the return of this order the attorney general filed his answer, in which he set up the same objections which he had made to the jurisdiction of the court in his motion to dismiss the bill, and in his demurrer; he disclaimed any intention to treat the court with disrespect in the commencement of the proceedings referred to, but believing that the decision of the court in the action, holding that it had jurisdiction to enjoin him, as attorney general, from performing his discretionary official duties, was in conflict with the 11th Amendment of the Constitution of the United States, as the same has been interpreted and applied by the United States Supreme Court, he believed it to be his duty, as such attorney general, to commence the mandamus proceedings for and in behalf of the state, and it was in this belief that the proceedings were commenced solely for the purpose of enforcing the law of the state of Minnesota. The order adjudging him in contempt was then made. . . .

We recognize and appreciate to the fullest extent the very great importance of this case, not only to the parties now before the court, but also to the great mass of the citizens of this country, all of whom are interested in the practical working of the courts of justice throughout the land, both Federal and state, and in the proper exercise of the jurisdiction of the Federal courts, as limited and controlled by the Federal Constitution and the laws of Congress. That there has been room for difference of opinion with regard to such limitations the reported cases in this court bear conclusive testimony. It cannot be stated that the case before us is entirely free from any possible doubt, nor that intelligent men may not differ as to the correct answer to the question we are called upon to decide. The question of jurisdiction, whether of the circuit court or of this court, is frequently a delicate matter to deal with, and it is especially so in this case, where the material and most important objection to the jurisdiction of the circuit court is the assertion that the suit is, in effect, against one of the states of the Union. It is a question, however, which we are called upon, and which it is our duty to decide. . . .

Jurisdiction is given to the circuit court in suits involving the requisite amount, arising under the Constitution or laws of the United States, and the question really to be determined under this objection is whether the acts of the legislature and the orders of the railroad commission, if enforced, would take property without due process of law; and although that question might incidentally involve a question of fact, its solution, nevertheless, is one which raises a Federal question. . . . Another Federal question is the alleged unconstitutionality of these acts because of the enormous penalties denounced for their violation, which prevent the railway company, as alleged, or any of its servants or employees, from resorting to the courts for the purpose of determining the validity of such acts. . . . Still another Federal question is urged, growing out of the assertion that the laws are, by their necessary effect, an interference with and a regulation of interstate commerce, the grounds for which assertion it is not now necessary to enlarge upon. The question is not, at any rate, frivolous. We conclude that the circuit court had jurisdiction in the case before it, because it involved the decision of Federal questions arising under the Constitution of the United States. . . .

[The Court first found the state laws unconstitutional.] . . . We have, therefore, upon this record, the case of an unconstitutional act of the state legislature and an intention by the attorney general of the state to endeavor to enforce its provisions, to the injury of the company, in compelling it, at great expense, to defend legal proceedings of a complicated and unusual character, and involving questions of vast importance to all employees and officers of the company, as well as to the company itself. The question that arises is whether there is a remedy that the parties interested may resort to, by going into a Federal court of equity, in a case involving a violation of the Federal Constitution, and obtaining a judicial investigation of the problem, and, pending its solution, obtain freedom from suits, civil or criminal, by a temporary injunction, and, if the question be finally decided favorably to the contention of the company, a permanent injunction restraining all such actions or proceedings.

This inquiry necessitates an examination of the most material and important objection made to the jurisdiction of the circuit court, the objection being that the suit is, in effect, one against the state of Minnesota, and that the injunction issued against the attorney general illegally prohibits state action, either criminal or civil, to enforce obedience to the statutes of the state. This objection is to be considered with reference to the 11th and 14th Amendments. The 11th Amendment prohibits the commencement or prosecution of any suit against one of the United States by citizens of another state or citizens or subjects of any foreign state. The 14th Amendment provides that no state shall deprive any person of life, liberty, or property without due process of law, nor shall it deny to any person within its jurisdiction the equal protection of the laws. . . .

[I]ndividuals who, as officers of the state, are clothed with some duty in regard to the enforcement of the laws of the state, and who threaten and are about to commence proceedings, either of a civil or criminal nature, to enforce against parties affected an unconstitutional act, violating the Federal Constitution, may be enjoined by a Federal court of equity from such action. . . .

The act to be enforced is alleged to be unconstitutional; and if it be so, the use of the name of the state to enforce an unconstitutional act to the injury of complainants is a proceeding without the authority of, and one which does not affect, the state in its sovereign or governmental capacity. It is simply an illegal act upon the part of a state official in attempting, by the use of the name of the state, to enforce a legislative enactment which is void because unconstitutional. If the act which the state attorney general seeks to enforce be a violation of the Federal Constitution, the officer, in proceeding under such enactment, comes into conflict with the superior authority of that Constitution, and he is in that case stripped of his official or representative character and is subjected in his person to the consequences of his individual conduct. The state has no power to impart to him any immunity from responsibility to the supreme authority of the United States. It would be an injury to complainant to harass it with a multiplicity of suits or litigation generally in an endeavor to enforce penalties under an unconstitutional enactment, and to prevent it ought to be within the jurisdiction of a court of equity. If the question of unconstitutionality, with reference, at least, to the Federal Constitution, be first raised in a Federal court, that court . . . has the right to decide it, to the exclusion of all other courts. . . .

It is proper to add that the right to enjoin an individual, even though a state official, from commencing suits under circumstances already stated, does not include the power to restrain a court from acting in any case brought before it, either of a civil or criminal nature, nor does it include power to prevent any investigation or action by a grand jury. The latter body is part of the machinery of a criminal court, and an injunction against a state court would be a violation of the whole scheme of our government. . . . The rule to show cause is discharged and the petition for writs of habeas corpus and certiorari is dismissed.

Edelman v. Jordan (1974)

Respondent John Jordan filed a complaint in the United States District Court for the Northern District of Illinois, individually and as a representative of a class, seeking declaratory and injunctive relief against two former directors of the Illinois Department of Public Aid, the director of the Cook County Department of Public Aid, and the comptroller of Cook County. Respondent alleged that these state officials were administering the federal-state programs of Aid to the Aged, Blind, or Disabled (AABD) in a manner inconsistent with various federal regulations and with the Fourteenth Amendment to the Constitution.

AABD is one of the categorical aid programs administered by the Illinois Department of Public Aid pursuant to the Illinois Public Aid Code. Under the Social Security Act, the program is funded by the State and the Federal Governments. The Department of Health, Education, and Welfare (HEW), which administers these payments for the Federal Government, issued regulations prescribing maximum permissible time standards within which States participating in the program had to process AABD applications. Those regulations, originally issued in 1968, required, at the time of the institution of this suit, that eligibility determinations must be made by the States within 30 days of receipt of applications for aid to the aged and blind, and within 45 days of receipt of applications for aid to the disabled. For those persons found eligible, the assistance check was required to be received by them within the applicable time period.

During the period in which the federal regulations went into effect, Illinois public aid officials were administering the benefits pursuant to their own regulations as provided in the Categorical Assistance Manual of the Illinois Department of Public Aid. Respondent's complaint charged that the Illinois defendants, operating under those regulations, were improperly authorizing grants to commence only with the month in which an application was approved and not including prior eligibility months for which an applicant was entitled to aid under federal law. The complaint also alleged that the Illinois defendants were not processing the applications within the applicable time requirements of the federal regulations; specifically, respondent alleged that his own application for disability benefits was not acted on by the Illinois Department of Public Aid for almost four months. Such actions of the Illinois officials were alleged to violate federal law and deny the equal protection of the laws. Respondent's prayer requested declaratory and injunctive relief, and specifically requested "a permanent injunction enjoining the defendants to award to the entire class of plaintiffs all AABD benefits wrongfully withheld."

In its judgment of March 15, 1972, the District Court declared § 4004 of the Illinois Manual to be invalid insofar as it was inconsistent with the federal regulations . . . , and granted a permanent injunction requiring compliance with the federal time limits for processing and paying AABD applicants. The District Court, in paragraph 5 of its judgment, also ordered the state officials to release and remit AABD benefits wrongfully withheld to all applicants for AABD in the State of Illinois who applied between July 1, 1968 (the date of the federal regulations) and April 16, 197(1) (the date of the preliminary injunction issued by the District Court) and were determined eligible.

On appeal to the United States Court of Appeals for the Seventh Circuit, the Illinois officials contended, inter alia, that the Eleventh Amendment barred the award of retroactive benefits . . . . The Court of Appeals rejected these contentions and affirmed the judgment of the District Court. . . . Because we believe the Court of Appeals erred in its disposition of the Eleventh Amendment claim, we reverse that portion of the Court of Appeals decision which affirmed the District Court's order that retroactive benefits be paid by the Illinois state officials.

The historical basis of the Eleventh Amendment has been oft stated, and it represents one of the more dramatic examples of this Court's effort to derive meaning from the document given to the Nation by the Framers nearly 200 years ago. . . . While the Amendment by its terms does not bar suits against a State by its own citizens, this Court has consistently held that an unconsenting State is immune from suits brought in federal courts by her own citizens as well as by citizens of another State. It is also well established that even though a State is not named a party to the action, the suit may nonetheless be barred by the Eleventh Amendment . . . . When the action is in essence one for the recovery of money from the state, the state is the real, substantial party in interest and is entitled to invoke its sovereign immunity from suit even though individual officials are nominal defendants.

Thus the rule has evolved that a suit by private parties seeking to impose a liability which must be paid from public funds in the state treasury is barred by the Eleventh Amendment. . . . Petitioner concedes that *Ex parte Young* is no bar to that part of the District Court's judgment that prospectively enjoined petitioner's predecessors from failing to process applications within the time limits established by the federal regulations. Petitioner argues, however, that *Ex parte Young* does not extend so far as to permit a suit which seeks the award of an accrued monetary liability which must be met from the general revenues of a State, absent consent or waiver by the State of its Eleventh Amendment immunity, and that therefore the award of retroactive benefits by the District Court was improper.

Ex parte Young was a watershed case in which this Court held that the Eleventh Amendment did not bar an action in the federal courts seeking to enjoin the Attorney General of Minnesota from enforcing a statute claimed to violate the Fourteenth Amendment of the United States Constitution. This holding has permitted the Civil War Amendments to the Constitution to serve as a sword, rather than merely as a shield, for those whom they were designed to protect. But the relief awarded in *Ex parte Young* was prospective only; the Attorney General of Minnesota was enjoined to conform his future conduct of that office to the requirement of the Fourteenth Amendment. Such relief is analogous to that awarded by the District Court in the prospective portion of its order under review in this case.

But the retroactive position of the District Court's order here, which requires the payment of a very substantial amount of money which that court held should have been paid, but was not, stands on quite a different footing. These funds will obviously not be paid out of the pocket of petitioner Edelman. . . . . The funds to satisfy the award in this case must inevitably come from the general revenues of the State of Illinois, and thus the award resembles far more closely the monetary award against the State itself than it does the prospective injunctive relief awarded in *Ex parte Young*.

The Court of Appeals, in upholding the award in this case, held that it was permissible because it was in the form of equitable restitution instead of damages, and therefore capable of being tailored in such a way as to minimize disruptions of the state program of categorical assistance. But we must judge the award actually made in this case, and not one which might have been differently tailored in a different case, and we must judge it in the context of the important constitutional principle embodied in the Eleventh Amendment.[11] . . . .

> [11] It may be true, as stated by our Brother Douglas in dissent, that most welfare decisions by federal courts have a financial impact on the States. But we cannot agree that such a financial impact is the same where a federal court applies *Ex parte Young* to grant prospective declaratory and injunctive relief, as opposed to an order of retroactive payments as was made in the instant case. It is not necessarily true that whether the decree is prospective only or requires payments for the weeks or months wrongfully skipped over by the state officials, the nature of the impact on the state treasury is precisely the same. This argument neglects the fact that where the State has a definable allocation to be used in the payment of public aid benefits, and pursues a certain course of action such as the processing of applications within certain time periods as did Illinois here, the subsequent ordering by a federal court of retroactive payments to correct delays in such processing will invariably mean there is less money available for payments for the continuing obligations of the public aid system. . . .

As in most areas of the law, the difference between the type of relief barred by the Eleventh Amendment and that permitted under *Ex parte Young* will not in many instances be that between day and night. The injunction issued in *Ex parte Young* was not totally without effect on the State's revenues, since the state law which the Attorney General was enjoined from enforcing provided substantial monetary penalties against railroads which did not conform to its provisions. . . . But the fiscal consequences to state treasuries in these cases were the necessary result of compliance with decrees which by their terms were prospective in nature. State officials, in order to shape their official conduct to the mandate of the Court's decrees, would more likely have to spend money from the state treasury than if they had been left free to pursue their previous course of conduct. Such an ancillary effect on the state treasury is a permissible and often an inevitable consequence of the principle announced in *Ex parte Young*.

But that portion of the District Court's decree which petitioner challenges on Eleventh Amendment grounds goes much further than any of the cases cited. It requires payment of state funds, not as a necessary consequence of compliance in the future with a substantive federal-question determination, but as a form of compensation to those whose applications were processed on the slower time schedule at a time when petitioner was under no court-imposed obligation to conform to a different standard. While the Court of Appeals described this retroactive award of monetary relief as a form of "equitable restitution," it is in practical effect indistinguishable in many aspects from an award of damages against the State. It will to a virtual certainty be paid from state funds, and not from the pockets of the individual state officials who were the defendants in the action. It is measured in terms of a monetary loss resulting from a past breach of a legal duty on the part of the defendant state officials. . . .

Respondent urges that since the various Illinois officials sued in the District Court failed to raise the Eleventh Amendment as a defense to the relief sought by respondent, petitioner is therefore barred from raising the Eleventh Amendment defense in the Court of Appeals or in this Court. The Court of Appeals apparently felt the defense was properly presented, and dealt with it on the merits. We approve of this resolution, since it has been well settled . . . that the Eleventh Amendment defense sufficiently partakes of the nature of a jurisdictional bar so that it need not be raised in the trial court:

For the foregoing reasons we decide that the Court of Appeals was wrong in holding that the Eleventh Amendment did not constitute a bar to that portion of the District Court decree which ordered retroactive payment of benefits found to have been wrongfully withheld. The judgment of the Court of Appeals is therefore reversed and the cause remanded for further proceedings consistent with this opinion.

Mr. Justice DOUGLAS, dissenting.

. . . . As the complaint in the instant case alleges violations by officials of Illinois of the Equal Protections Clause of the Fourteenth Amendment, it seems that the case is governed by *Ex parte Young* so far as injunctive relief is concerned. The main thrust of the argument is that the instant case asks for relief which if granted would affect the treasury of the State.

Most welfare decisions by federal courts have a financial impact on the States. Under the existing federal-state cooperative system, a state desiring to participate, submits a state plan to HEW for approval; once HEW approves the plan the State is locked into the cooperative scheme until it withdraws . . . . The welfare cases coming here have involved ultimately the financial responsibility of the State to beneficiaries claiming they were deprived of federal rights. . . . In no case when the responsibility of the State is increased to meet the lawful demand of the beneficiary, is there any levy on state funds. Whether the decree is prospective only or requires payments for the weeks or months wrongfully skipped over by the state officials, the nature of the impact on the state treasury is precisely the same. . . .

It is said however, that the Eleventh Amendment is concerned, not with immunity of States from suit, but with the jurisdiction of the federal courts to entertain the suit. The Eleventh Amendment does not speak of jurisdiction; it withholds the "judicial power" of federal courts "to any suit in law or equity . . . against one of the United States." If that "judicial power," or "jurisdiction" if one prefers that concept, may not be exercised even in "any suit in . . . equity" then *Ex parte Young* should be overruled. But there is none eager to take the step. Where a State has consented to join a federal-state cooperative project, it is realistic to conclude that the State has agreed to assume its obligations under that legislation. There is nothing in the Eleventh Amendment to suggest a difference between suits at law and suits in equity, for it treats the two without distinction. If common sense has any role to play in constitutional adjudication, once there is a waiver of immunity it must be true that it is complete so far as effective operation of the state-federal joint welfare program is concerned. . . .

I would affirm the judgment of the Court of Appeals.

Pennhurst State School & Hospital v. Halderman (1984)

Justice POWELL delivered the opinion of the Court.

This case presents the question whether a federal court may award injunctive relief against state officials on the basis of state law.

I

This litigation, here for the second time, concerns the conditions of care at petitioner Pennhurst State School and Hospital, a Pennsylvania institution for the care of the mentally retarded. . . .

This suit originally was brought in 1974 by respondent Terri Lee Halderman, a resident of Pennhurst, in the District Court for the Eastern District of Pennsylvania. Ultimately, plaintiffs included a class consisting of all persons who were or might become residents of Pennhurst; the Pennsylvania Association for Retarded Citizens (PARC); and the United States. Defendants were Pennhurst and various Pennhurst officials; the Pennsylvania Department of Public Welfare and several of its officials; and various county commissioners, county mental retardation administrators, and other officials of five Pennsylvania counties surrounding Pennhurst. Respondents' amended complaint charged that conditions at Pennhurst violated the class members' rights under the Eighth and Fourteenth Amendments; § 504 of the Rehabilitation Act of 1973; the Developmentally Disabled Assistance and Bill of Rights Act; and the Pennsylvania Mental Health and Mental Retardation Act of 1966 (the "MH/MR Act"). Both damages and injunctive relief were sought.

In 1977, following a lengthy trial, the District Court rendered its decision. As noted in our prior opinion, the court's findings were undisputed: "Conditions at Pennhurst are not only dangerous, with the residents often physically abused or drugged by staff members, but also inadequate for the 'habilitation' of the retarded. Indeed, the court found that the physical, intellectual, and emotional skills of some residents have deteriorated at Pennhurst." The District Court held that these conditions violated each resident's right to minimally adequate habilitation under the Due Process Clause and the MH/MR Act, freedom from harm under the Eighth and Fourteenth Amendments, and nondiscriminatory habilitation under the Equal Protection Clause and § 504 of the Rehabilitation Act. Furthermore, the court found that due process demands that if a state undertakes the habilitation of a retarded person, it must do so in the *least restrictive setting* consistent with that individual's habilitative needs. After concluding that the large size of Pennhurst prevented it from providing the necessary habilitation in the least restrictive environment, the court ordered that immediate steps be taken to remove the retarded residents from Pennhurst. Petitioners were ordered "to provide suitable community living arrangements" for the class members, and the court appointed a Special Master "with the power and duty to plan, organize, direct, supervise and monitor the implementation of this and any further Orders of the Court."

The Court of Appeals for the Third Circuit affirmed most of the District Court's judgment. It agreed that respondents had a right to habilitation in the least restrictive environment, but it grounded this right solely on the bill of rights provision in the Developmentally Disabled Assistance and Bill of Rights Act. The court did not consider the constitutional issues or § 504 of the Rehabilitation Act, and while it affirmed the District Court's holding that the MH/MR Act provides a right to adequate habilitation, the court did not decide whether that state right encompassed a right to treatment in the least restrictive setting.

On the question of remedy, the Court of Appeals affirmed except as to the District Court's order that Pennhurst be closed. The court observed that some patients would be unable to adjust to life outside an institution, and it determined that none of the legal provisions relied on by plaintiffs precluded institutionalization. It therefore remanded for individual determinations by the District Court, or by the Special Master, as to the appropriateness of an improved Pennhurst for each such patient, guided by a presumption in favor of placing individuals in community living arrangements.

On remand the District Court established detailed procedures for determining the proper residential placement for each patient. A team consisting of the patient, his parents or guardian, and his case manager must establish an individual habilitation plan providing for habilitation of the patient in a designated community living arrangement. The plan is subject to review by the Special Master. A second master, called the Hearing Master, is available to conduct hearings, upon request by the resident, his parents or his advocate, on the question whether the services of Pennhurst would be more beneficial to the resident than the community living arrangement provided in the resident's plan. The Hearing Master then determines where the patient should reside, subject to possible review by the District Court.

This Court reversed the judgment of the Court of Appeals, finding that [the relevant sections of the Developmentally Disabled Assistance and Bill of Rights Act] did not create any substantive rights. We remanded the case to the Court of Appeals to determine if the remedial order could be supported on the basis of state law, the Constitution, or § 504 of the Rehabilitation Act. We also remanded for consideration of whether any relief was available under other provisions of the Developmentally Disabled Assistance and Bill of Rights Act.

On remand the Court of Appeals affirmed its prior judgment in its entirety. It determined that in a recent decision the Supreme Court of Pennsylvania had spoken definitively in holding that the MH/MR Act required the State to adopt the least restrictive environment approach for the care of the mentally retarded. The Court of Appeals concluded that this state statute fully supported its prior judgment, and therefore did not reach the remaining issues of federal law. It also rejected petitioners' argument that the Eleventh Amendment barred a federal court from considering this pendent state-law claim. The court noted that the Amendment did not bar a federal court from granting prospective injunctive relief against state officials on the basis of federal claims, and concluded that the same result obtained with respect to a pendent state-law claim. . . .

We granted certiorari, and now reverse and remand.

II

Petitioners [challenge] the judgment of the Court of Appeals [on the grounds that] the Eleventh Amendment prohibited the District Court from ordering state officials to conform their conduct to state law . . . . [W]e find the Eleventh Amendment challenge dispositive.

A

. . . . [T]he principle of sovereign immunity is a constitutional limitation on the federal judicial power established in Art. III. A sovereign's immunity may be waived, and the Court consistently has held that a State may consent to suit against it in federal court. We have insisted, however, that the State's consent be unequivocally expressed. Similarly, although Congress has power with respect to the rights protected by the Fourteenth Amendment to abrogate the Eleventh Amendment immunity, we have required an unequivocal expression of congressional intent to overturn the constitutionally guaranteed immunity of the several States. Our reluctance to infer that a State's immunity from suit in the federal courts has been negated stems from recognition of the vital role of the doctrine of sovereign immunity in our federal system. A State's constitutional interest in immunity encompasses not merely *whether* it may be sued, but *where* it may be sued. As Justice Marshall well has noted, because of the problems of federalism inherent in making one sovereign appear against its will in the courts of the other, a restriction upon the exercise of the federal judicial power has long been considered to be appropriate in a case such as this. Accordingly, in deciding this case we must be guided by the principles of federalism that inform Eleventh Amendment doctrine.

B

This Court's decisions thus establish that an unconsenting State is immune from suits brought in federal courts by her own citizens as well as by citizens of another state. There may be a question, however, whether a particular suit in fact is a suit against a State. It is clear, of course, that in the absence of consent a suit in which the State or one of its agencies or departments is named as the defendant is proscribed by the Eleventh Amendment. This jurisdictional bar applies regardless of the nature of the relief sought.

When the suit is brought only against state officials, a question arises as to whether that suit is a suit against the State itself. Although prior decisions of this Court have not been entirely consistent on this issue, certain principles are well established. The Eleventh Amendment bars a suit against state officials when the state is the real, substantial party in interest. Thus, the general rule is that relief sought nominally against an officer is in fact against the sovereign if the decree would operate against the latter.[11] And, as when the State itself is named as the defendant, a suit against state officials that is in fact a suit against a State is barred regardless of whether it seeks damages or injunctive relief.

> [11] The general rule is that a suit is against the sovereign if the judgment sought would expend itself on the public treasury or domain, or interfere with the public administration, or if the effect of the judgment would be to restrain the Government from acting, or to compel it to act. . . .

The Court has recognized an important exception to this general rule: a suit challenging the constitutionality of a state official's action is not one against the State. This was the holding in *Ex parte Young*, in which a federal court enjoined the Attorney General of the State of Minnesota from bringing suit to enforce a state statute that allegedly violated the Fourteenth Amendment. This Court held that the Eleventh Amendment did not prohibit issuance of this injunction. The theory of the case was that an unconstitutional enactment is "void" and therefore does not impart to the officer any immunity from responsibility to the supreme authority of the United States. Since the State could not authorize the action, the officer was stripped of his official or representative character and was subjected to the consequences of his official conduct.

While the rule permitting suits alleging conduct contrary to the supreme authority of the United States has survived, the theory of *Young* has not been provided an expansive interpretation. Thus, in *Edelman v. Jordan*, the Court emphasized that the Eleventh Amendment bars some forms of injunctive relief against state officials for violation of federal law. In particular, *Edelman* held that when a plaintiff sues a state official alleging a violation of federal law, the federal court may award an injunction that governs the official's future conduct, but not one that awards retroactive monetary relief. Under the theory of *Young*, such a suit would not be one against the State since the federal-law allegation would strip the state officer of his official authority. Nevertheless, retroactive relief was barred by the Eleventh Amendment.

III

With these principles in mind, we now turn to the question whether the claim that petitioners violated *state law* in carrying out their official duties at Pennhurst is one against the State and therefore barred by the Eleventh Amendment. Respondents advance two principal arguments in support of the judgment below. First, they contend that under the doctrine of *Edelman v. Jordan*, the suit is not against the State because the courts below ordered only prospective injunctive relief. Second, they assert that the state-law claim properly was decided under the doctrine of pendent jurisdiction. Respondents rely on decisions of this Court awarding relief against state officials on the basis of a pendent state-law claim.

A

We first address the contention that respondents' state-law claim is not barred by the Eleventh Amendment because it seeks only prospective relief as defined in *Edelman*. The Court of Appeals held that if the judgment below rested on federal law, it could be entered against petitioner state officials under the doctrine established in *Edelman* and *Young* even though the prospective financial burden was substantial and ongoing. The court assumed, and respondents assert, that this reasoning applies as well when the official acts in violation of state law. This argument misconstrues the basis of the doctrine established in *Young* and *Edelman*.

As discussed above, the injunction in *Young* was justified, notwithstanding the obvious impact on the State itself, on the view that sovereign immunity does not apply because an official who acts unconstitutionally is stripped of his official or representative character. This rationale, of course, created the well-recognized irony that an official's unconstitutional conduct constitutes state action under the Fourteenth Amendment but not the Eleventh Amendment. Nonetheless, the *Young* doctrine has been accepted as necessary to permit the federal courts to vindicate federal rights and hold state officials responsible to the supreme authority of the United States. As Justice Brennan has observed, "*Ex parte Young* was the culmination of efforts by this Court to harmonize the principles of the Eleventh Amendment with the effective supremacy of rights and powers secured elsewhere in the Constitution." Our decisions repeatedly have emphasized that the *Young* doctrine rests on the need to promote the vindication of federal rights.

The Court also has recognized, however, that the need to promote the supremacy of federal law must be accommodated to the constitutional immunity of the States. This is the significance of . . . . *Edelman*'s distinction between prospective and retroactive relief [that] fulfills the underlying purpose of *Ex parte Young* while at the same time preserving to an important degree the constitutional immunity of the States.

This need to reconcile competing interests is wholly absent, however, when a plaintiff alleges that a state official has violated *state* law. In such a case the entire basis for the doctrine of *Young* and *Edelman* disappears. A federal court's grant of relief against state officials on the basis of state law, whether prospective or retroactive, does not vindicate the supreme authority of federal law. On the contrary, it is difficult to think of a greater intrusion on state sovereignty than when a federal court instructs state officials on how to conform their conduct to state law. Such a result conflicts directly with the principles of federalism that underlie the Eleventh Amendment. We conclude that *Young* and *Edelman* are inapplicable in a suit against state officials on the basis of state law.

B

The contrary view of Justice Stevens's dissent rests on fiction, is wrong on the law, and, most important, would emasculate the Eleventh Amendment. Under his view, an allegation that official conduct is contrary to a state statute would suffice to override the State's protection under that Amendment. The theory is that such conduct is contrary to the official's "instructions," and thus *ultra vires* his authority. Accordingly, official action based on a reasonable interpretation of any statute might, if the interpretation turned out to be erroneous, provide the basis for injunctive relief against the actors in their official capacities. In this case, where officials of a major state department, clearly acting within the scope of their authority, were found not to have improved conditions in a state institution adequately under state law, the dissent's result would be that the State itself has forfeited its constitutionally provided immunity.

The theory is out of touch with reality. The dissent does not dispute that the general criterion for determining when a suit is in fact against the sovereign is the *effect* of the relief sought. According to the dissent, the relief sought and ordered here—which in effect was that a major state institution be closed and smaller state institutions be created and expansively funded— did not operate against the State. This view would make the law a pretense. No other court or judge in the ten-year history of this litigation has advanced this theory. And the dissent's underlying view that the named defendants here were acting beyond and contrary to their authority cannot be reconciled with reality—or with the record. The District Court in this case held that the individual defendants acted in the utmost good faith *within the sphere of their official responsibilities*, and therefore were entitled to immunity from damages. The named defendants had nothing to gain personally from their conduct; they were not found to have acted willfully or even negligently. The court expressly noted that the individual defendants apparently took every means available to them to reduce the incidents of abuse and injury, but were constantly faced with staff shortages. It also found that the individual defendants are dedicated professionals in the field of retardation who were given very little with which to accomplish the habilitation of the retarded at Pennhurst. As a result, all the relief ordered by the courts below was institutional and official in character. To the extent there was a violation of state law in this case, it is a case of the State itself not fulfilling its legislative promises.[17]

[17] The dissent appears to be confused about our argument here. It is of course true, as the dissent says, that the finding below that petitioners acted in good faith and therefore were immune from damages does not affect whether an injunction might be issued against them by a court possessed of jurisdiction. The point is that the courts below did not have jurisdiction because the relief ordered so plainly ran against the State. No one questions that the petitioners in operating Pennhurst were acting in their official capacity. Nor can it be questioned that the judgments under review commanded action that could be taken by petitioners only in their official capacity—and, of course, *only* if the State provided the necessary funding. It is evident that the dissent would vest in federal courts authority, acting solely under *state law*, to ignore the sovereignty of the States that the Eleventh Amendment was adopted to protect. Article III confers no jurisdiction on this Court to strip an explicit Amendment of the Constitution of its substantive meaning. Contrary to the dissent's view, an injunction based on federal law stands on very different footing, particularly in light of the Civil War Amendments. As we have explained, in such cases this Court is vested with the constitutional duty to vindicate the supreme authority of the United States. There is no corresponding mandate to enforce state law.

. . . . The crucial element of the dissent's theory was . . . . that a sovereign, like any other principal, cannot authorize its agent to violate the law, so that when the agent does so he cannot be acting for the sovereign. . .[25]

[25] . . . . The dissent attempts to distinguish *Edelman* on the ground that the retroactive relief there, unlike injunctive relief, does not run only against the agent. To say that injunctive relief against State officials acting in their official capacity does not run against the State is to resort to the fictions that characterize the dissent's theories. Unlike the English sovereign perhaps, an American State can act only through its officials. It is true that the Court in *Edelman* recognized that retroactive relief often, or at least sometimes, has a greater impact on the State treasury than does injunctive relief, but there was no suggestion that damages alone were thought to run against the State while injunctive relief did not. We have noted that the authority-stripping theory of *Young* is a fiction that has been narrowly construed. In this light, it may well be wondered what principled basis there is to the *ultra vires* doctrine . . . . That doctrine excepts from the Eleventh Amendment bar suits against officers acting in their official capacities but without any statutory authority, even though the relief would operate against the State. At bottom, the doctrine is based on the fiction of the

Young opinion. The dissent's method is merely to take this fiction to its extreme. While the dissent's result may be logical, in the sense that it is difficult to draw principled lines short of that end, its view would virtually eliminate the constitutional doctrine of sovereign immunity. It is a result from which the Court [has] wisely recoiled. We do so again today. For present purposes, however, we do no more than question the continued vitality of the *ultra vires* doctrine in the Eleventh Amendment context. We hold only that to the extent the doctrine is consistent with the analysis of this opinion, it is a very narrow exception . . . .

. . . . Under the dissent's view of the *ultra vires* doctrine, the Eleventh Amendment would have force only in the rare case in which a plaintiff foolishly attempts to sue the State in its own name, or where he cannot produce some state statute that has been violated to his asserted injury. Thus, the *ultra vires* doctrine, a narrow and questionable exception, would swallow the general rule that a suit is against the State if the relief will run against it. That result gives the dissent no pause presumably because of its view that the Eleventh Amendment and sovereign immunity undoubtedly run counter to modern democratic notions of the moral responsibility of the State. Moreover, the argument substantially misses the point with respect to Eleventh Amendment sovereign immunity. As Justice Marshall has observed, the Eleventh Amendment's restriction on the federal judicial power is based in large part on the problems of federalism inherent in making one sovereign appear against its will in the courts of the other. The dissent totally rejects the Eleventh Amendment's basis in federalism.

C

The reasoning of our recent decisions on sovereign immunity thus leads to the conclusion that a federal suit against state officials on the basis of state law contravenes the Eleventh Amendment when—as here—the relief sought and ordered has an impact directly on the State itself. In reaching a contrary conclusion, the Court of Appeals relied principally on a separate line of cases dealing with pendent jurisdiction. The crucial point for the Court of Appeals was that this Court has granted relief against state officials on the basis of a pendent state-law claim. We therefore must consider the relationship between pendent jurisdiction and the Eleventh Amendment. . . .

The Eleventh Amendment is an explicit limitation on the judicial power of the United States. It deprives a federal court of power to decide certain claims against States that otherwise would be within the scope of Art. III's grant of jurisdiction. For example, if a lawsuit against state officials under 42 U.S.C. § 1983 alleges a constitutional claim, the federal court is barred from awarding damages against the state treasury even though the claim arises under the Constitution. Similarly, if a § 1983 action alleging a constitutional claim is brought directly against a State, the Eleventh Amendment bars a federal court from granting any relief on that claim. The Amendment thus is a specific constitutional bar against hearing even *federal* claims that otherwise would be within the jurisdiction of the federal courts.

This constitutional bar applies to pendent claims as well. As noted above, pendent jurisdiction is a . . . doctrine of expediency and efficiency derived from the general Art. III language conferring power to hear all "cases" arising under federal law or between diverse parties. The Eleventh Amendment should not be construed to apply with less force to this . . . form of jurisdiction . . . . The history of the adoption and development of the Amendment confirms that it is an independent limitation on all exercises of Art. III power: the entire judicial power granted by the Constitution does not embrace authority to entertain suit brought by private parties against a State without consent given. If we were to hold otherwise, a federal court could award damages against a State on the basis of a pendent claim. Our decision in *Edelman v. Jordan* makes clear that pendent jurisdiction does not permit such an evasion of the immunity guaranteed by the Eleventh Amendment. . . .

In sum, . . . neither pendent jurisdiction nor any other basis of jurisdiction may override the Eleventh Amendment. A federal court must examine each claim in a case to see if the court's jurisdiction over that claim is barred by the Eleventh Amendment. We concluded above that a claim that state officials violated state law in carrying out their official responsibilities is a claim against the State that is protected by the Eleventh Amendment. We now hold that this principle applies as well to state-law claims brought into federal court under pendent jurisdiction.

D

Respondents urge that application of the Eleventh Amendment to pendent state-law claims will have a disruptive effect on litigation against state officials. They argue that the considerations of judicial economy, convenience, and fairness to litigants that underlie pendent jurisdiction counsel against a result that may cause litigants to split causes of action between state and federal courts. They also contend that the policy of avoiding unnecessary constitutional decisions will be contravened if plaintiffs choose to forgo their state-law claims and sue only in federal court or, alternatively, that the policy of *Ex parte Young* will be hindered if plaintiffs choose to forgo their right to a federal forum and bring all of their claims in state court.

It may be that applying the Eleventh Amendment to pendent claims results in federal claims being brought in state court, or in bifurcation of claims. That is not uncommon in this area. Under *Edelman*, a suit against state officials for retroactive monetary relief, whether based on federal or state law, must be brought in state court. Challenges to the validity of state tax systems under § 1983 also must be brought in state court. Under the abstention doctrine, unclear issues of state law commonly are split off and referred to the state courts. In any case, the answer to respondents' assertions is that such considerations of policy cannot override the constitutional limitation on the authority of the federal judiciary to adjudicate suits against a State. . . .

The judgment of the Court of Appeals is reversed, and the case remanded for further proceedings consistent with this opinion.

Justice STEVENS, with whom Justice BRENNAN, Justice MARSHALL, and Justice BLACKMUN join, dissenting.

. . . . The pivotal consideration in *Young* was that it was not conduct of the sovereign that was at issue. The rule that unlawful acts of an officer should not be attributed to the sovereign has deep roots in the history of sovereign immunity and makes *Young* reconcilable with the principles of sovereign immunity found in the Eleventh Amendment, rather than merely an unprincipled accommodation between federal and state interests that ignores the principles contained in the Eleventh Amendment.

This rule plainly applies to conduct of state officers in violation of state law. *Young* states that the significance of the charge of unconstitutional conduct is that it renders the state official's conduct simply an illegal act, and hence the officer is not entitled to the sovereign's immunity. Since a state officer's conduct in violation of state law is certainly no less illegal than his violation of federal law, in either case the official, by committing an illegal act, is stripped of his official or representative character. . . .

These cases are based on the simple idea that an illegal act strips the official of his state-law shield, thereby depriving the official of the sovereign's immunity. The majority criticizes this approach as being "out of touch with reality" because it ignores the practical impact of an injunction on the State though directed at its officers. Yet that criticism cannot account for *Young*, since an injunction has the same effect on the State whether it is based on federal or state law. Indeed, the majority recognizes that injunctions approved by *Young* have an obvious impact on the State itself. In the final analysis the distinction between the State and its officers, realistic or not, is one firmly embedded in the doctrine of sovereign immunity. It is that doctrine and not any theory of federal supremacy which the Framers placed in the Eleventh Amendment and which this Court therefore has a duty to respect.

It follows that the basis for the *Young* rule is present when the officer sued has violated the law of the sovereign; in all such cases the conduct is of a type that would not be permitted by the sovereign and hence is not attributable to the sovereign under traditional sovereign immunity principles. In such a case, the sovereign's interest lies with those who seek to enforce its laws, rather than those who have violated them. . . .

The majority's position that the Eleventh Amendment does not permit federal courts to enjoin conduct that the sovereign State itself seeks to prohibit thus is inconsistent with both the doctrine of sovereign immunity and the underlying respect for the integrity of State policy which the Eleventh Amendment protects. The issuance of injunctive relief which enforces state laws and policies, if anything, enhances federal courts' respect for the sovereign prerogatives of the States. The majority's approach, which requires federal courts to ignore questions of state law and to rest their decisions on federal bases, will create more rather than less friction between the States and the federal judiciary. . . .

Petitioners readily concede, both in their brief and at oral argument, that the Eleventh Amendment does not bar a suit against state officers who have acted *ultra vires.* The majority makes a similar concession. Yet both ignore the fact that the cases . . . set out a two-step analysis for *ultra vires* conduct—conduct that is completely beyond the scope of the officer's authority, or conduct that the sovereign has forbidden. . . . This omission is understandable, since petitioners' conduct in this case clearly falls into the category of conduct the sovereign has specifically forbidden by statute. Petitioners were told by Pennsylvania how to run Pennhurst, and there is no dispute that they disobeyed their instructions. . . .

In sum, a century and a half of this Court's Eleventh Amendment jurisprudence has established the following. A suit alleging that the official had acted within his authority but in a manner contrary to state statutes was not barred because the Eleventh Amendment prohibits suits against States; it does not bar suits against state officials for actions not permitted by the State under its own law. The sovereign could not and would not authorize its officers to violate its own law; hence an action against a state officer seeking redress for conduct not permitted by state law is a suit against the officer, not the sovereign. *Ex parte Young* concluded in as explicit a fashion as possible that unconstitutional action by state officials is not action by the State even if it purports to be authorized by state law, *because the federal Constitution strikes down the state law shield.* In the tort cases, if the plaintiff proves his case, there is by definition no state-law defense to shield the defendant. Similarly, *when the state officer violates a state statute, the sovereign has by definition erected no shield against liability.* These precedents make clear that there is no foundation for the contention that the majority embraces—that *Ex parte Young* authorizes injunctive relief against state officials only on the basis of federal law. To the contrary, *Young* is as clear as a bell: the Eleventh Amendment does not apply where there is no state-law shield. That simple principle should control this case.

IV

. . . . [T]he rule the majority creates today serves none of the interests of the State. The majority prevents federal courts from implementing State policies through equitable enforcement of State law. Instead, federal courts are required to resolve cases on federal grounds that no State authority can undo. Leaving violations of state law unredressed and ensuring that the decisions of federal courts may never be reexamined by the States hardly comports with the respect for States as sovereign entities commanded by the Eleventh Amendment.

V

One basic fact underlies this case: far from immunizing petitioners' conduct, the State of Pennsylvania prohibited it. Respondents do not complain about the conduct of the State of Pennsylvania—it is Pennsylvania's commands which they seek to enforce. Respondents seek only to have Pennhurst run the way Pennsylvania envisioned that it be run. Until today, the Court understood that the Eleventh Amendment does not shield the conduct of state officers which has been prohibited by their sovereign. . . .

I respectfully dissent.

Idaho v. Couer d'Alene Tribe of Idaho (1997)

Justice KENNEDY announced the judgment of the Court and delivered the opinion of the Court . . . .

In the northern region of Idaho, close by the Coeur d'Alene Mountains which are part of Bitterroot Range, lies tranquil Lake Coeur d'Alene. . . . To the south of the lake lies the more populated part of the Coeur d'Alene Reservation. Whether the Coeur d'Alene Tribe's ownership extends to the banks and submerged lands of the lake and various of [its] rivers and streams, or instead ownership is vested in the State of Idaho, is the underlying dispute. We are limited here, however, to the important, preliminary question whether the Eleventh Amendment bars a federal court from hearing the Tribe's claim.

I

Alleging ownership in the submerged lands and bed of Lake Coeur d'Alene and of the various navigable rivers and streams that form part of its water system, the Coeur d'Alene Tribe, a federally recognized Tribe, together with various individual Tribe members, sued in federal court. . . . The suit named the State of Idaho, various state agencies, and numerous state officials in their individual capacities. In addition to its title claims, the Tribe further sought a declaratory judgment to establish its entitlement to the exclusive use and occupancy and the right to quiet enjoyment of the submerged lands as well as a declaration of the invalidity of all Idaho statutes, ordinances, regulations, customs, or usages which purport to regulate, authorize, use, or affect in any way the submerged lands. Finally, it sought a preliminary and permanent injunction prohibiting defendants from regulating, permitting, or taking any action in violation of the Tribe's rights of exclusive use and occupancy, quiet enjoyment, and other ownership interest in the submerged lands along with an award for costs and attorney's fees and such other relief as the court deemed appropriate. . . .

[While affirming the district court's dismissal of most claims based on the Eleventh Amendment,] the Court of Appeals found the *Ex parte Young* doctrine applicable and allowed the claims for declaratory and injunctive relief against the officials to proceed insofar as they sought to preclude continuing violations of federal law. . . .

II
A

. . . . When suit is commenced against state officials, even if they are named and served as individuals, the State itself will have a continuing interest in the litigation whenever state policies or procedures are at stake. This commonsense observation of the State's real interest when its officers are named as individuals has not escaped notice or comment from this Court, either before or after *Young*. Indeed, the suit in *Young*, which sought to enjoin the state attorney general from enforcing state law, implicated substantial state interests. We agree with these observations.

To interpret *Young* to permit a federal-court action to proceed in every case where prospective declaratory and injunctive relief is sought against an officer, named in his individual capacity, would be to adhere to an empty formalism and to undermine the principle, reaffirmed just last Term in *Seminole Tribe*, that Eleventh Amendment immunity represents a real limitation on a federal court's federal-question jurisdiction. The real interests served by the Eleventh Amendment are not to be sacrificed to elementary mechanics of captions and pleading. Application of the *Young* exception must reflect a proper understanding of its role in our federal system and respect for state courts instead of a reflexive reliance on an obvious fiction. . . .

III

We now turn to consider whether the Tribe may avoid the Eleventh Amendment bar and avail itself of the *Young* exception. Although the difference between the type of relief barred by the Eleventh Amendment and that permitted under *Ex parte Young* will not in many instances be that between day and night, this suit, we decide, falls on the Eleventh Amendment side of the line, and Idaho's sovereign immunity controls. . . .

An allegation of an ongoing violation of federal law where the requested relief is prospective is ordinarily sufficient to invoke the *Young* fiction. However, this case is unusual in that the Tribe's suit is the functional equivalent of a quiet title action which implicates special sovereignty interests. . . . It is common ground between the parties, at this stage of the litigation, that the Tribe could not maintain a quiet title suit against Idaho in federal court, absent the State's consent. The Eleventh Amendment would bar it. Despite this prohibition, the declaratory and injunctive relief the Tribe seeks is close to the functional equivalent of quiet title in that substantially all benefits of ownership and control would shift from the State to the Tribe. This is especially troubling when coupled with the far-reaching and invasive relief the Tribe seeks, relief with consequences going well beyond the typical stakes in a real property quiet title action. The suit seeks, in effect, a determination that the lands in question are not even within the regulatory jurisdiction of the State. The requested injunctive relief would bar the State's principal officers from exercising their governmental powers and authority over the disputed lands and waters. The suit would diminish, even extinguish, the State's control over a vast reach of lands and waters long deemed by the State to be an integral part of its territory. To pass this off as a judgment causing little or no offense to

Idaho's sovereign authority and its standing in the Union would be to ignore the realities of the relief the Tribe demands. . . .

It is apparent, then, that if the Tribe were to prevail, Idaho's sovereign interest in its lands and waters would be affected in a degree fully as intrusive as almost any conceivable retroactive levy upon funds in its Treasury. Under these particular and special circumstances, we find the *Young* exception inapplicable. The dignity and status of its statehood allow Idaho to rely on its Eleventh Amendment immunity and to insist upon responding to these claims in its own courts, which are open to hear and determine the case.

The judgment of the Court of Appeals is reversed in part, and the case is remanded for proceedings consistent with this opinion.

It is so ordered.

Justice O'CONNOR, with whom Justice SCALIA and Justice THOMAS join, concurring in part and concurring in the judgment.

. . . . This case is unlike a typical *Young* action in two important respects. First, as the Tribe concedes, the suit is the functional equivalent of an action to quiet its title to the bed of Lake Coeur d'Alene. It asks a federal court to declare that the lands are for the exclusive use, occupancy, and enjoyment of the Tribe and to invalidate all statutes and ordinances purporting to regulate the lands. The Tribe could not maintain a quiet title action in federal court without the State's consent, and for good reason: A federal court cannot summon a State before it in a private action seeking to divest the State of a property interest. Second, the Tribe does not merely seek to possess land that would otherwise remain subject to state regulation, or to bring the State's regulatory scheme into compliance with federal law. Rather, the Tribe seeks to eliminate altogether the State's regulatory power over the submerged lands at issue—to establish not only that the State has no right to possess the property, but also that the property is not within Idaho's sovereign jurisdiction at all. We have repeatedly emphasized the importance of submerged lands to state sovereignty. Control of such lands is critical to a State's ability to regulate use of its navigable waters. . . .

The *Young* doctrine rests on the premise that a suit against a state official to enjoin an ongoing violation of federal law is not a suit against the State. Where a plaintiff seeks to divest the State of all regulatory power over submerged lands—in effect, to invoke a federal court's jurisdiction to quiet title to sovereign lands—it simply cannot be said that the suit is not a suit against the State. I would not narrow our *Young* doctrine, but I would not extend it to reach this case. Accordingly, I join Parts I, II–A, and III of the Court's opinion.

Justice SOUTER, with whom Justice STEVENS, Justice GINSBURG, and Justice BREYER join, dissenting.

Congress has implemented the Constitution's grant of federal-question jurisdiction by authorizing federal courts to enforce rights arising under the Constitution and federal law. The federal courts have an obligation to exercise that jurisdiction, and in doing so have applied the doctrine of *Ex parte Young*, that in the absence of some congressional limitation a federal court may entertain an individual's suit to enjoin a state officer from official action that violates federal law. The Coeur d'Alene Tribe claims that officers of the State of Idaho are acting to regulate land that belongs to the Tribe under federal law, and the Tribe prays for declaratory and injunctive relief to halt the regulation as an ongoing violation of that law. The Tribe's suit falls squarely within the *Young* doctrine, and the District Court had an obligation to hear it.

The response of today's Court, however, is to deny that obligation . . . . because the Tribe's suit is said to be indistinguishable from one to quiet title to the submerged lands and could leave the State not only without possession of the lands but without present opportunity to regulate them under state law. The Tribe's suit, however, is no more (or less) against the State than any of the claims brought in our prior cases applying *Young*, and the State's regulatory authority would be no more imposed upon than the State's authority in *Young* itself. . . .

I respectfully dissent. . . . [A]n officer suit implicating title is no more or less the "functional equivalent" of an action against the government than any other *Young* suit. States are functionally barred from imposing a railroad rate found unconstitutional when enforced by a state officer; States are functionally barred from withholding welfare benefits when their officers have violated federal law on timely payment; States are functionally barred from locking up prisoners whom their wardens are told to release. There is nothing unique about the consequences of an officer suit involving title, and if the Court's reasoning were good in a title case it would be good in any *Young* case. . . .

Seminole Tribe of Florida v. Florida (1996)

Chief Justice REHNQUIST delivered the opinion of the Court.

The Indian Gaming Regulatory Act provides that an Indian tribe may conduct certain gaming activities only in conformance with a valid compact between the tribe and the State in which the gaming activities are located. The Act, passed by Congress under the Indian Commerce Clause, imposes upon the States a duty to negotiate in good faith with an Indian tribe toward the formation of a compact, and authorizes a tribe to bring suit in federal court against a State in order to compel performance of that duty. We hold that notwithstanding Congress's clear intent to abrogate the States' sovereign immunity, the Indian Commerce Clause does not grant Congress that power, and therefore [the Act] cannot grant jurisdiction over a State that does not consent to be sued. We further hold that the doctrine of *Ex parte Young* may not be used to enforce [the Act] against a state official.

I

Congress passed the Indian Gaming Regulatory Act in 1988 in order to provide a statutory basis for the operation and regulation of gaming by Indian tribes. The Act divides gaming on Indian lands into three classes—I, II, and III—and provides a different regulatory scheme for each class. Class III gaming—the type with which we are here concerned—. . . includes such things as slot machines, casino games, banking card games, dog racing, and lotteries. It is the most heavily regulated of the three classes. The Act provides that class III gaming is lawful only where it is: (1) authorized by an ordinance or resolution that (a) is adopted by the governing body of the Indian tribe, (b) satisfies certain statutorily prescribed requirements, and (c) is approved by the National Indian Gaming Commission; (2) located in a State that permits such gaming for any purpose by any person, organization, or entity; and (3) "conducted in conformance with a Tribal–State compact entered into by the Indian tribe and the State under paragraph (3) that is in effect."

The "paragraph (3)" . . . . describes the process by which a State and an Indian tribe begin negotiations toward a Tribal-State compact:

> (A) Any Indian tribe having jurisdiction over the Indian lands upon which a class III gaming activity is being conducted, or is to be conducted, shall request the State in which such lands are located to enter into negotiations for the purpose of entering into a Tribal–State compact governing the conduct of gaming activities. Upon receiving such a request, the State shall negotiate with the Indian tribe in good faith to enter into such a compact.

The State's obligation to "negotiate with the Indian tribe in good faith" is made judicially enforceable by [the statute]:

(A) The United States district courts shall have jurisdiction over—
(i) any cause of action initiated by an Indian tribe arising from the failure of a State to enter into negotiations with the Indian tribe for the purpose of entering into a Tribal–State compact under paragraph (3) or to conduct such negotiations in good faith. . . .
(B)(i) An Indian tribe may initiate a cause of action described in subparagraph (A)(i) only after the close of the 180–day period beginning on the date on which the Indian tribe requested the State to enter into negotiations under paragraph (3)(A).

[The statutory provisions] describe an elaborate remedial scheme designed to ensure the formation of a Tribal-State compact. A tribe that brings an action . . . must show that no Tribal-State compact has been entered and that the State failed to respond in good faith to the tribe's request to negotiate; at that point, the burden then shifts to the State to prove that it did in fact negotiate in good faith. If the district court concludes that the State has failed to negotiate in good faith toward the formation of a Tribal-State compact, then it shall order the State and Indian Tribe to conclude such a compact within a 60-day period. If no compact has been concluded 60 days after the court's order, then the Indian tribe and the State shall each submit to a mediator appointed by the court a proposed compact that represents their last best offer for a compact. The mediator chooses from between the two proposed compacts the one which best comports with the terms of the Act and any other applicable Federal law and with the findings and order of the court, and submits it to the State and the Indian tribe. If the State consents to the proposed compact within 60 days of its submission by the mediator, then the proposed compact is treated as a Tribal-State compact entered into under paragraph (3). If, however, the State does not consent within that 60-day period, then the Act provides that the mediator shall notify the Secretary of the Interior and that the Secretary shall prescribe procedures under which class III gaming may be conducted on the Indian lands over which the Indian tribe has jurisdiction.

In September 1991, the Seminole Tribe of Florida, petitioner, sued the State of Florida and its Governor, Lawton Chiles, respondents. . . . [P]etitioner alleged that respondents had refused to enter into any negotiation for inclusion of certain gaming activities in a tribal-state compact, thereby violating the requirement of good faith negotiation contained in [the statute]. Respondents moved to dismiss the complaint, arguing that the suit violated the State's sovereign immunity from suit in federal court. The District Court denied respondents' motion, and respondents took an interlocutory appeal of that decision.

The Court of Appeals for the Eleventh Circuit reversed the decision of the District Court, holding that the Eleventh Amendment barred petitioner's suit against respondents. . . . The court further held that *Ex parte Young* does not permit an Indian tribe to force good-faith negotiations by suing the Governor of a State. Finding that it lacked subject-matter jurisdiction, the Eleventh Circuit remanded to the District Court with directions to dismiss petitioner's suit.

Petitioner sought our review of the Eleventh Circuit's decision, and we granted certiorari . . . . [We] affirm the Eleventh Circuit's dismissal of petitioner's suit. . . .

Although the text of the Amendment would appear to restrict only the Article III diversity jurisdiction of the federal courts, we have understood the Eleventh Amendment to stand not so much for what it says, but for the presupposition which it confirms. That presupposition, first observed over a century ago in *Hans v. Louisiana*, has two parts: first, that each State is a sovereign entity in our federal system; and second, that it is inherent in the nature of sovereignty not to be amenable to the suit of an individual without its consent. For over a century we have reaffirmed that federal jurisdiction over suits against unconsenting States was not contemplated by the Constitution when establishing the judicial power of the United States.

Here, petitioner has sued the State of Florida and it is undisputed that Florida has not consented to the suit. Petitioner nevertheless contends that its suit is not barred by state sovereign immunity. First, it argues that Congress through the Act abrogated the States' sovereign immunity. Alternatively, petitioner maintains that its suit against the Governor may go forward under *Ex parte Young*. We consider each of those arguments in turn.

II

Petitioner argues that Congress through the Act abrogated the States' immunity from suit. In order to determine whether Congress has abrogated the States' sovereign immunity, we ask two questions: first, whether Congress has unequivocally expressed its intent to abrogate the immunity, and second, whether Congress has acted pursuant to a valid exercise of power.

A

Congress's intent to abrogate the States' immunity from suit must be obvious from a clear legislative statement. This rule arises from a recognition of the important role played by the Eleventh Amendment and the broader principles that it reflects. . . . Here, we agree with the parties, with the Eleventh Circuit in the decision below, and with virtually every other court that has confronted the question that Congress has . . . provided an unmistakably clear statement of its intent to abrogate. . . .

B

Having concluded that Congress clearly intended to abrogate the States' sovereign immunity . . . , we turn now to consider whether the Act was passed pursuant to a valid exercise of power. . . . In *Pennsylvania v. Union Gas Co.*, a plurality of the Court found that the Interstate Commerce Clause granted Congress the power to abrogate state sovereign immunity, stating that the power to regulate interstate commerce would be incomplete without the authority to render States liable in damages. Justice White added the fifth vote necessary to the result in that case, but wrote separately in order to express that he did not agree with much of the plurality's reasoning.

. . . . We agree with petitioner that the plurality opinion in *Union Gas* allows no principled distinction in favor of the States to be drawn between the Indian Commerce Clause and the Interstate Commerce Clause. [Thus, *Union Gas* controls this case.] Respondents argue, however, that . . . . *Union Gas* should be reconsidered and overruled. . . .

The Court in *Union Gas* reached a result without an expressed rationale agreed upon by a majority of the Court. . . . The plurality's rationale also deviated sharply from our established federalism jurisprudence and essentially eviscerated our decision in *Hans*. . . . Never before the decision in *Union Gas* had we suggested that the bounds of Article III could be expanded by Congress operating pursuant to any constitutional provision other than the Fourteenth Amendment. Indeed, it had seemed fundamental that Congress could not expand the jurisdiction of the federal courts beyond the bounds of Article III. . . .

The plurality's extended reliance upon our decision in *Fitzpatrick v. Bitzer*, that Congress could under the Fourteenth Amendment abrogate the States' sovereign immunity was also, we believe, misplaced. *Fitzpatrick* was based upon a rationale wholly inapplicable to the Interstate Commerce Clause, viz., that the Fourteenth Amendment, adopted well after the adoption of the Eleventh Amendment and the ratification of the Constitution, operated to alter the pre-existing balance between state and federal power achieved by Article III and the Eleventh Amendment. As the dissent in *Union Gas* made clear, *Fitzpatrick* cannot be read to justify limitation of the principle embodied in the Eleventh Amendment through appeal to antecedent provisions of the Constitution.

In the five years since it was decided, *Union Gas* has proved to be a solitary departure from established law. Reconsidering the decision in *Union Gas*, we conclude that none of the policies underlying *stare decisis* requires our continuing adherence to its holding. . . . We feel bound to conclude that *Union Gas* was wrongly decided and that it should be, and now is, overruled.

For over a century, we have grounded our decisions in the oft-repeated understanding of state sovereign immunity as an essential part of the Eleventh Amendment. . . . [W]e cannot rest with a mere literal application of the words of § 2 of Article III, or assume that the letter of the Eleventh Amendment exhausts the restrictions upon suits against non-consenting States. Behind the words of the constitutional provisions are postulates which limit and control. There is the essential postulate that the controversies, as contemplated, shall be found to be of a justiciable character. There is also the postulate that States of the Union, still possessing attributes of sovereignty, shall be immune from suits, without their consent, save where there has been a surrender of this immunity in the plan of the convention.

It is true that we have not had occasion previously to apply established Eleventh Amendment principles to the question whether Congress has the power to abrogate state sovereign immunity (save in *Union Gas*). But consideration of that question must proceed with fidelity to this century-old doctrine.

The dissent, to the contrary, disregards our case law in favor of a theory cobbled together from law review articles and its own version of historical events. The dissent cites not a single decision since *Hans* (other than *Union Gas*) that supports its view of state sovereign immunity, instead relying upon the now-discredited decision in *Chisholm v. Georgia*. Its undocumented and highly speculative extralegal explanation of the decision in *Hans* is a disservice to the Court's traditional method of adjudication.

The dissent mischaracterizes the *Hans* opinion. That decision found its roots not solely in the common law of England, but in the much more fundamental jurisprudence in all civilized nations. . . . The dissent's lengthy analysis of the text of the Eleventh Amendment is directed at a straw man—we long have recognized that blind reliance upon the text of the Eleventh Amendment is to strain the Constitution and the law to a construction never imagined or dreamed of. The text dealt in terms only with the problem presented by the decision in *Chisholm*; in light of the fact that the federal courts did not have federal question jurisdiction at the time the Amendment was passed (and would not have it until 1875), it seems unlikely that much thought was given to the prospect of federal-question jurisdiction over the States.

In putting forward a new theory of state sovereign immunity, the dissent develops its own vision of the political system created by the Framers, concluding with the statement that the Framers' principal objectives in rejecting English theories of unitary sovereignty would have been impeded if a new concept of sovereign immunity had taken its place in federal-question cases, and would have been substantially thwarted if that new immunity had been held untouchable by any congressional effort to abrogate it.[14] This sweeping statement ignores the fact that the Nation survived for nearly two centuries without the question of the existence of such power ever being presented to this Court. And Congress itself waited nearly a century before even conferring federal-question jurisdiction on the lower federal courts.

[14] This argument wholly disregards other methods of ensuring the States' compliance with federal law: The Federal Government can bring suit in federal court against a State; an individual can bring suit against a state officer in order to ensure that the officer's conduct is in compliance with federal law; and this Court is empowered to review a question of federal law arising from a state-court decision where a State has consented to suit.

In overruling *Union Gas* today, we reconfirm that the background principle of state sovereign immunity embodied in the Eleventh Amendment is not so ephemeral as to dissipate when the subject of the suit is an area, like the regulation of Indian commerce, that is under the exclusive control of the Federal Government. Even when the Constitution vests in Congress complete law-making authority over a particular area, the Eleventh Amendment prevents congressional authorization of suits by private parties against unconsenting States. The Eleventh Amendment restricts the judicial power under Article III, and Article I cannot be used to circumvent the constitutional limitations placed upon federal jurisdiction. Petitioner's suit against the State of Florida must be dismissed for a lack of jurisdiction.

III

Petitioner argues that we may exercise jurisdiction over its suit . . . against the Governor notwithstanding the jurisdictional bar of the Eleventh Amendment. Petitioner notes that since our decision in *Ex parte Young*, we often have found federal jurisdiction over a suit against a state official when that suit seeks only prospective injunctive relief in order to end a continuing violation of federal law. The situation presented here, however, is sufficiently different from that giving rise to the traditional *Ex parte Young* action so as to preclude the availability of that doctrine. . . .

Where Congress has created a remedial scheme for the enforcement of a particular federal right, we have, in suits against federal officers, refused to supplement that scheme with one created by the judiciary. *See Malesko*. Here, of course, the question is not whether a remedy should be created, but instead is whether the Eleventh Amendment bar should be lifted, as it was in *Ex parte Young*, in order to allow a suit against a state officer. Nevertheless, we think that the same general principle applies: Therefore, where Congress has prescribed a detailed remedial scheme for the enforcement against a State of a statutorily created right, a court should hesitate before casting aside those limitations and permitting an action against a state officer based upon *Ex parte Young.*

Here, . . . the intricate procedures set forth in [the statute] show that Congress intended therein not only to define, but also to limit significantly, the duty imposed . . . . For example, where the court finds that the State has failed to negotiate in good faith, the only remedy prescribed is an order directing the State and the Indian tribe to conclude a compact within 60 days. And if the parties disregard the court's order and fail to conclude a compact within the 60-day period, the only sanction is that each party then must submit a proposed compact to a mediator who selects the one which best embodies the terms of the Act. Finally, if the State fails to accept the compact selected by the mediator, the only sanction against it is that the mediator shall notify the Secretary of the Interior who then must prescribe regulations governing class III gaming on the tribal lands at issue. By contrast with this quite modest set of sanctions, an action brought against a state official under *Ex parte Young* would expose that official to the full remedial powers of a federal court, including, presumably, contempt sanctions. . . . [I]t is difficult to see why an Indian tribe would suffer through the intricate scheme of [the statute] when more complete and more immediate relief would be available under *Ex parte Young.*[17]

[17] Contrary to the claims of the dissent, we do not hold that Congress *cannot* authorize federal jurisdiction under *Ex parte Young* over a cause of action with a limited remedial scheme. We find only that Congress did not intend that result in the Indian Gaming Regulatory Act. . . .

Here, of course, we have found that Congress does not have authority under the Constitution to make the State suable in federal court . . . . Nevertheless, the fact that Congress chose to impose upon the State a liability that is significantly more limited than would be the liability imposed upon the state officer under *Ex parte Young* strongly indicates that Congress had no wish to create the latter . . . . Nor are we free to rewrite the statutory scheme in order to approximate what we think Congress might have wanted had it known that [the statute] was beyond its authority. If that effort is to be made, it should be made by Congress, and not by the federal courts. We hold that *Ex parte Young* is inapplicable to petitioner's suit against the Governor of Florida, and therefore that suit is barred by the Eleventh Amendment and must be dismissed for a lack of jurisdiction. . . . The Eleventh Circuit's dismissal of petitioner's suit is hereby affirmed.

Justice STEVENS, dissenting.

. . . . The majority's opinion does not simply preclude Congress from establishing the rather curious statutory scheme under which Indian tribes may seek the aid of a federal court to secure a State's good-faith negotiations over gaming regulations. Rather, it prevents Congress from providing a federal forum for a broad range of actions against States, from those sounding in copyright and patent law, to those concerning bankruptcy, environmental law, and the regulation of our vast national economy.

There may be room for debate over whether, in light of the Eleventh Amendment, Congress has the power to ensure that such a cause of action may be enforced in federal court by a citizen of another State or a foreign citizen. There can be no serious debate, however, over whether Congress has the power to ensure that such a cause of action may be brought by a citizen of the State being sued. Congress's authority in that regard is clear. . . . Except insofar as it has been incorporated into the text of the Eleventh Amendment, the doctrine [of sovereign immunity] is entirely the product of judge-made law. Three features of its English ancestry make it particularly unsuitable for incorporation into the law of this democratic Nation.

First, the assumption that it could be supported by a belief that "the King can do no wrong" has always been absurd; the bloody path trod by English monarchs both before and after they reached the throne demonstrated the fictional character of any such assumption. Even if the fiction had been acceptable in Britain, the recitation in the Declaration of Independence of the wrongs committed by George III made that proposition unacceptable on this side of the Atlantic.

Second, centuries ago the belief that the monarch served by divine right made it appropriate to assume that redress for wrongs committed by the sovereign should be the exclusive province of still higher authority. While such a justification for a rule that immunized the sovereign from suit in a secular tribunal might have been acceptable in a jurisdiction where a particular faith is endorsed by the government, it should give rise to skepticism concerning the legitimacy of comparable rules in a society where a constitutional wall separates the State from the Church.

Third, in a society where noble birth can justify preferential treatment, it might have been unseemly to allow a commoner to hale the monarch into court. Justice Wilson explained how foreign such a justification is to this Nation's principles. Moreover, Chief Justice Marshall early on laid to rest the view that the purpose of the Eleventh Amendment was to protect a State's dignity. *See Cohens v. Virginia*. . . . That, of course, is an embarrassingly insufficient rationale for the rule. . . .

In this country the sovereignty of the individual States is subordinate both to the citizenry of each State and to the supreme law of the federal sovereign. . . . In my view, neither the majority's opinion today, nor any earlier opinion by any Member of the Court, has identified any acceptable reason for concluding that the absence of a State's consent to be sued in federal court should affect the power of Congress to authorize federal courts to remedy violations of federal law by States or their officials in actions not covered by the Eleventh Amendment's explicit text.

While I am persuaded that there is no justification for permanently enshrining the judge-made law of sovereign immunity, I recognize that federalism concerns—and even the interest in protecting the solvency of the States that was at work in *Chisholm* and *Hans*—may well justify a grant of immunity from federal litigation in certain classes of cases. Such a grant, however, should be the product of a reasoned decision by the policymaking branch of our Government. For this Court to conclude that timeworn shibboleths iterated and reiterated by judges should take precedence over the deliberations of the Congress of the United States is simply irresponsible. . . . I respectfully dissent.

Justice SOUTER, with whom Justice GINSBURG and Justice BREYER join, dissenting.

. . . . The doctrine of sovereign immunity comprises two distinct rules, which are not always separately recognized. The one rule holds that the King or the Crown, as the font of law, is not bound by the law's provisions; the other provides that the King or Crown, as the font of justice, is not subject to suit in its own courts.[2] The one rule limits the reach of substantive law; the other, the jurisdiction of the courts. We are concerned here only with the latter rule, which took its common-law form in the high Middle Ages. At least as early as the thirteenth century, during the reign of Henry III (1216-1272), it was recognized that the king could not be sued in his own courts.

> [2] The first of these notions rests on the ancient maxim that the King can do no wrong. In any event, it is clear that the idea of the sovereign, or any part of it, being above the law in this sense has not survived in American law.

The significance of this doctrine in the nascent American law is less clear, however, than its early development and steady endurance in England might suggest. While some colonial governments may have enjoyed some such immunity, the scope (and even the existence) of this governmental immunity in pre-Revolutionary America remains disputed.

Whatever the scope of sovereign immunity might have been in the Colonies, however, or during the period of Confederation, the proposal to establish a National Government under the Constitution drafted in 1787 presented a prospect unknown to the common law prior to the American experience: the States would become parts of a system in which sovereignty over even domestic matters would be divided or parceled out between the States and the Nation, the latter to be invested with its own judicial power and the right to prevail against the States whenever their respective substantive laws might be in conflict. With this prospect in mind, the 1787 Constitution might have addressed state sovereign immunity by eliminating whatever sovereign immunity the States previously had, as to any matter subject to federal law or jurisdiction; by recognizing an analogue to the old immunity in the new context of federal jurisdiction, but subject to abrogation as to any matter within that jurisdiction; or by enshrining a doctrine of inviolable state sovereign immunity in the text, thereby giving it constitutional protection in the new federal jurisdiction.

The 1787 draft in fact said nothing on the subject, and it was this very silence that occasioned some, though apparently not widespread, dispute among the Framers and others over whether ratification of the Constitution would preclude a State sued in federal court from asserting sovereign immunity as it could have done on any matter of nonfederal law litigated in its own courts. . . .

The argument among the Framers and their friends about sovereign immunity in federal citizen-state diversity cases, in any event, was short lived and ended when this Court, in *Chisholm v. Georgia*, chose between the constitutional alternatives of abrogation and recognition of the immunity enjoyed at common law. The 4-to-1 majority adopted the reasonable (although not compelled) interpretation that the first of the two Citizen-State Diversity Clauses abrogated for purposes of federal jurisdiction any immunity the States might have enjoyed in their own courts, and Georgia was accordingly held subject to the judicial power in a common-law assumpsit action by a South Carolina citizen suing to collect a debt. . . .

The Eleventh Amendment, of course, repudiated *Chisholm* and clearly divested federal courts of some jurisdiction as to cases against state parties. . . . There are two plausible readings of this provision's text. Under the first, it simply repeals the Citizen-State Diversity Clauses of Article III for all cases in which the State appears as a defendant. Under the second, it strips the federal courts of jurisdiction in any case in which a state defendant is sued by a citizen not its own, even if jurisdiction might otherwise rest on the existence of a federal question in the suit. Neither reading of the Amendment, of course, furnishes authority for the Court's view in today's case, but we need to choose between the competing readings for the light that will be shed on the *Hans* doctrine and the legitimacy of inflating that doctrine to the point of constitutional immutability as the Court has chosen to do.

The history and structure of the Eleventh Amendment convincingly show that it reaches only to suits subject to federal jurisdiction exclusively under the Citizen-State Diversity Clauses. In precisely tracking the language in Article III providing for citizen-state diversity jurisdiction, the text of the Amendment does, after all, suggest to common sense that only the Diversity Clauses are being addressed. If the Framers had meant the Amendment to bar federal-question suits as well, they could not only have made their intentions clearer very easily, but could simply have adopted the first post-*Chisholm* proposal, introduced in the House of Representatives by Theodore Sedgwick of Massachusetts on instructions from the Legislature of that Commonwealth. Its provisions would have had exactly that expansive effect:

> No state shall be liable to be made a party defendant, in any of the judicial courts, established, or which shall be established under the authority of the United States, at the suit of any person or persons, whether a citizen or citizens, or a foreigner or foreigners, or of any body politic or corporate, whether within or without the United States.

With its references to suits by citizens as well as non-citizens, the Sedgwick amendment would necessarily have been applied beyond the Diversity Clauses, and for a reason that would have been wholly obvious to the people of the time. Sedgwick sought such a broad amendment because many of the States, including his own, owed debts subject to collection under the Treaty of Paris. Suits to collect such debts would arise under that Treaty and thus be subject to federal-question jurisdiction under Article III. Such a suit, indeed, was then already pending against Massachusetts, having been brought in this Court by Christopher Vassall, an erstwhile Bostonian whose move to England on the eve of revolutionary hostilities had presented his former neighbors with the irresistible temptation to confiscate his vacant mansion.

Congress took no action on Sedgwick's proposal, however, and the Amendment as ultimately adopted two years later could hardly have been meant to limit federal-question jurisdiction, or it would never have left the States open to federal-question suits by their own citizens. To be sure, the majority of state creditors were not citizens, but nothing in the Treaty would have prevented foreign creditors from selling their debt instruments (thereby assigning their claims) to citizens of the debtor State. If the Framers of the Eleventh Amendment had meant it to immunize States from federal-question suits like those that might be brought to enforce the Treaty of Paris, they would surely have drafted the Amendment differently.

It should accordingly come as no surprise that the weightiest commentary following the Amendment's adoption described it simply as constricting the scope of the Citizen-State Diversity Clauses. In *Cohens v. Virginia*, for instance, Chief Justice Marshall, writing for the

Court, emphasized that the Amendment had no effect on federal courts' jurisdiction grounded on the "arising under" provision of Article III and concluded that a case arising under the constitution or laws of the United States is cognizable in the Courts of the Union, whoever may be the parties to that case. The point of the Eleventh Amendment, according to *Cohens*, was to bar jurisdiction in suits at common law by Revolutionary War debt creditors, not to strip the government of the means of protecting, by the instrumentality of its courts, the constitution and laws from active violation. . . .

Because the plaintiffs in today's case are citizens of the State that they are suing, the Eleventh Amendment simply does not apply to them. We must therefore look elsewhere for the source of that immunity by which the Court says their suit is barred from a federal court.

The obvious place to look elsewhere, of course, is *Hans v. Louisiana*, and *Hans* was indeed a leap in the direction of today's holding, even though it does not take the Court all the way. The parties in *Hans* raised, and the Court in that case answered, only what I have called the second question, that is, whether the Constitution, without more, permits a State to plead sovereign immunity to bar the exercise of federal-question jurisdiction. Although the Court invoked a principle of sovereign immunity to cure what it took to be the Eleventh Amendment's anomaly of barring only those state suits brought by noncitizen plaintiffs, the *Hans* Court had no occasion to consider whether Congress could abrogate that background immunity by statute. . . .

The majority does not dispute the point that *Hans v. Louisiana* had no occasion to decide whether Congress could abrogate a State's immunity from federal-question suits. The Court insists, however, that the negative answer to that question that it finds in *Hans* and subsequent opinions is not mere *obiter dicta,* but rather the "well-established rationale upon which the Court based the results of its earlier decisions." The exact rationale to which the majority refers, unfortunately, is not easy to discern. . . . The "rationale" which the majority seeks to invoke is, I think, more nearly stated in its quotation from *Principality of Monaco*. There, the Court said that we cannot rest with a mere literal application of the words of § 2 of Article III, or assume that the letter of the Eleventh Amendment exhausts the restrictions upon suits against non-consenting States. This statement certainly is true to *Hans*, which clearly recognized a pre-existing principle of sovereign immunity, broader than the Eleventh Amendment itself, that will ordinarily bar federal-question suits against a nonconsenting State. That was the "rationale" which was sufficient to decide *Hans* and all of its progeny prior to *Union Gas*. But leaving aside the indefensibility of that rationale, which I will address further below, that was as far as it went.

The majority, however, would read the rationale of *Hans* and its line of subsequent cases as answering the further question whether the "postulate" of sovereign immunity that limits and controls the exercise of Article III jurisdiction is constitutional in stature and therefore unalterable by Congress. . . . If it is indeed true that private suits against States are not permitted under Article III (by virtue of the understanding represented by the Eleventh Amendment), then it is hard to see how a State's sovereign immunity may be waived any more than it may be abrogated by Congress. Likewise, the Court's broad theory of immunity runs doubly afoul of the appellate jurisdiction problem that I noted earlier in rejecting an interpretation of the Eleventh Amendment's text that would bar federal-question suits. . . .

There is and could be no dispute that the doctrine of sovereign immunity that *Hans* purported to apply had its origins in the familiar doctrine of the common law, derived from the laws and practices of our English ancestors. Although statutes came to affect its importance in the succeeding centuries, the doctrine was never reduced to codification, and Americans took their understanding of immunity doctrine from Blackstone. Here, as in the mother country, it remained a common-law rule.

This fact of the doctrine's common-law status in the period covering the founding and the later adoption of the Eleventh Amendment should have raised a warning flag to the *Hans* Court and it should do the same for the Court today. For although the Court has persistently assumed that the common law's presence in the minds of the early Framers must have functioned as a limitation on their understanding of the new Nation's constitutional powers, this turns out not to be so at all. . . . While the States had limited their reception of English common law to principles appropriate to American conditions, the 1787 draft Constitution contained no provision for adopting the common law at all. . . . Instead, the Framers chose to recognize only particular common-law concepts, such as the writ of habeas corpus, and the distinction between law and equity, by specific reference in the constitutional text. This approach reflected widespread agreement that ratification would not itself entail a general reception of the common law of England. . . .

Given the refusal to entertain any wholesale reception of common law, given the failure of the new Constitution to make any provision for adoption of common law as such, and given the protests already quoted that no general reception had occurred, the *Hans* Court and the Court today cannot reasonably argue that something like the old immunity doctrine somehow slipped in as a tacit but enforceable background principle. . . .

The considerations expressed so far, based on text, *Chisholm,* caution in common-law reception, and sovereignty theory, have pointed both to the mistakes inherent in *Hans* and, even more strongly, to the error of today's holding. Although for reasons of *stare decisis* I would not today disturb the century-old precedent, I surely would not extend its error by placing the common-law immunity it mistakenly recognized beyond the power of Congress to abrogate. . . .

The Court's holding that the States' *Hans* immunity may not be abrogated by Congress leads to the final question in this case, whether federal-question jurisdiction exists to order prospective relief enforcing IGRA against a state officer, respondent Chiles, who is said to be authorized to take the action required by the federal law. . . . The answer to this question is an easy yes, the officer is subject to suit under the rule in *Ex parte Young*, and the case could, and should, readily be decided on this point alone.

In *Ex parte Young*, this Court held that a federal court has jurisdiction in a suit against a state officer to enjoin official actions violating federal law, even though the State itself may be immune. . . . *Young* provided, as it does today, a sensible way to reconcile the Court's expansive view of immunity expressed in *Hans* with the principles embodied in the Supremacy Clause and Article III. . . . *Ex parte Young* [codified] the principle that state officers never have authority to violate the Constitution or federal law, so that any illegal action is stripped of state character and rendered an illegal individual act. Suits against these officials are consequently barred by neither the Eleventh Amendment nor *Hans* immunity. The officer's action is simply an illegal act upon the part of a state official in attempting by the use of the name of the State to enforce a legislative enactment which is void because unconstitutional. The State has no power to impart to him any immunity from responsibility to the supreme authority of the United States.

The decision in *Ex parte Young*, and the historic doctrine it embodies, thus plays a foundational role in American constitutionalism, and while the doctrine is sometimes called a "fiction," the long history of its felt necessity shows it to be something much more estimable, as we may see by considering the facts of the case. . . . *Ex parte Young* is nothing short of indispensable to the establishment of constitutional government and the rule of law.

A rule of such lineage, engendered by such necessity, should not be easily displaced, if indeed it is displaceable at all, for it marks the frontier of the enforceability of federal law against sometimes competing state policies. We have in fact never before inferred a congressional intent to eliminate this time-honored practice of enforcing federal law. That, of course, does not mean that the intent may never be inferred, and where, as here, the underlying right is one of statutory rather than constitutional dimension, I do not in theory reject the Court's assumption that Congress may bar enforcement by suit even against a state official. But because in practice, in the real world of congressional legislation, such an intent would be exceedingly odd, it would be equally odd for this Court to recognize an intent to block the customary application of *Ex parte Young* without applying the rule recognized in our previous cases, which have insisted on a clear statement before assuming a congressional purpose to affect the federal balance.

. . . . No clear statement of intent to displace the doctrine of *Ex parte Young* occurs in IGRA, and the Court is instead constrained to rest its effort to skirt *Young* on a series of suggestions thought to be apparent in Congress's provision of intricate procedures for enforcing a State's obligation under the Act. [This basis for displacing such an important feature of immunity jurisprudence is wholly insufficient.] . . .

Alden v. Maine (1999)

Justice KENNEDY delivered the opinion of the Court.

In 1992, petitioners, a group of probation officers, filed suit against their employer, the State of Maine, in the United States District Court for the District of Maine. The officers alleged the State had violated the overtime provisions of the Fair Labor Standards Act of 1938 (FLSA) and sought compensation and liquidated damages. While the suit was pending, this Court decided *Seminole Tribe v. Florida*, which made it clear that Congress lacks power under Article I to abrogate the States' sovereign immunity from suits commenced or prosecuted in the federal courts. Upon consideration of *Seminole Tribe*, the District Court dismissed petitioners' action, and the Court of Appeals affirmed. Petitioners then filed the same action in state court. The state trial court dismissed the suit on the basis of sovereign immunity, and the Maine Supreme Judicial Court affirmed. . . .

We hold that the powers delegated to Congress under Article I of the United States Constitution do not include the power to subject nonconsenting States to private suits for damages in state courts. We decide as well that the State of Maine has not consented to suits for overtime pay and liquidated damages under the FLSA. On these premises we affirm the judgment sustaining dismissal of the suit.

I

The Eleventh Amendment makes explicit reference to the States' immunity from suits "commenced or prosecuted against one of the United States by Citizens of another State, or by Citizens or Subjects of any Foreign State." We have, as a result, sometimes referred to the States' immunity from suit as "Eleventh Amendment immunity." The phrase is convenient shorthand but something of a misnomer, for the sovereign immunity of the States neither derives from, nor is limited by, the terms of the Eleventh Amendment. Rather, as the Constitution's structure, its history, and the authoritative interpretations by this Court make clear, the States' immunity from suit is a fundamental aspect of the sovereignty which the States enjoyed before the ratification of the Constitution, and which they retain today (either literally or by virtue of their admission into the Union upon an equal footing with the other States) except as altered by the plan of the Convention or certain constitutional Amendments.

Although the Constitution establishes a National Government with broad, often plenary authority over matters within its recognized competence, the founding document specifically recognizes the States as sovereign entities. Various textual provisions of the Constitution assume the States' continued existence and active participation in the fundamental processes of governance. The limited and enumerated powers granted to the Legislative, Executive, and Judicial Branches of the National Government, moreover, underscore the vital role reserved to the States by the constitutional design. Any doubt regarding the constitutional role of the States as sovereign entities is removed by the Tenth Amendment, which, like the other provisions of the Bill of Rights, was enacted to allay lingering concerns about the extent of the national power. The Amendment confirms the promise implicit in the original document: "The powers not delegated to the United States by the Constitution, nor prohibited by it to the States, are reserved to the States respectively, or to the people."

The federal system established by our Constitution preserves the sovereign status of the States in two ways. First, it reserves to them a substantial portion of the Nation's primary sovereignty, together with the dignity and essential attributes inhering in that status. The States form distinct and independent portions of the supremacy, no more subject, within their respective spheres, to the general authority than the general authority is subject to them, within its own sphere.

Second, even as to matters within the competence of the National Government, the constitutional design secures the founding generation's rejection of the concept of a central government that would act upon and through the States in favor of a system in which the State and Federal Governments would exercise concurrent authority over the people—who were, in Hamilton's words, the only proper objects of government. . . . The States thus retain a residuary and inviolable sovereignty. They are not relegated to the role of mere provinces or political corporations, but retain the dignity, though not the full authority, of sovereignty.

The generation that designed and adopted our federal system considered immunity from private suits central to sovereign dignity. . . . The text and history of the Eleventh Amendment . . . suggest that Congress acted not to change but to restore the original constitutional design. . . . By its terms, then, the Eleventh Amendment did not redefine the federal judicial power but instead overruled the Court . . . . Congress chose not to enact language codifying the traditional understanding of sovereign immunity but rather to address the specific provisions of the Constitution that had raised concerns during the ratification debates and formed the basis of the *Chisholm* decision. . . . [T]he Constitution was understood, in light of its history and structure, to preserve the States' traditional immunity from private suits. As the Amendment clarified the only provisions of the Constitution that anyone had suggested might support a contrary understanding, there was no reason to draft with a broader brush. . . .

[Thus,] sovereign immunity derives not from the Eleventh Amendment but from the structure of the original Constitution itself. The Eleventh Amendment confirmed, rather than established, sovereign immunity as a constitutional principle; it follows that the scope of the

States' immunity from suit is demarcated not by the text of the Amendment alone but by fundamental postulates implicit in the constitutional design. . . .

II

In this case we must determine whether Congress has the power, under Article I, to subject nonconsenting States to private suits in their own courts. As the foregoing discussion makes clear, the fact that the Eleventh Amendment by its terms limits only "[t]he Judicial power of the United States" does not resolve the question. To rest on the words of the Amendment alone would be to engage in the type of ahistorical literalism we have rejected in interpreting the scope of the States' sovereign immunity since the discredited decision in *Chisholm.*

While the constitutional principle of sovereign immunity does pose a bar to federal jurisdiction over suits against nonconsenting States, this is not the only structural basis of sovereign immunity implicit in the constitutional design. Rather, there is also the postulate that States of the Union, still possessing attributes of sovereignty, shall be immune from suits, without their consent, save where there has been a surrender of this immunity in the plan of the convention. This separate and distinct structural principle is not directly related to the scope of the judicial power established by Article III, but inheres in the system of federalism established by the Constitution. In exercising its Article I powers Congress may subject the States to private suits in their own courts only if there is compelling evidence that the States were required to surrender this power to Congress pursuant to the constitutional design.

. . . . [Our decisions have concluded] that neither the Supremacy Clause nor the enumerated powers of Congress confer authority to abrogate the States' immunity from suit in federal court. The logic of the decisions, however, does not turn on the forum in which the suits were prosecuted but extends to state-court suits as well.

The dissenting opinion seeks to reopen these precedents, contending that state sovereign immunity must derive either from the common law (in which case the dissent contends it is defeasible by statute) or from natural law (in which case the dissent believes it cannot bar a federal claim). As should be obvious to all, this is a false dichotomy. The text and the structure of the Constitution protect various rights and principles. Many of these, such as the right to trial by jury and the prohibition on unreasonable searches and seizures, derive from the common law. The common-law lineage of these rights does not mean they are defeasible by statute or remain mere common-law rights, however. They are, rather, constitutional rights, and form the fundamental law of the land.

Although the sovereign immunity of the States derives at least in part from the common-law tradition, the structure and history of the Constitution make clear that the immunity exists today by constitutional design. . . . We do not contend the Founders could not have stripped the States of sovereign immunity and granted Congress power to subject them to private suit but only that they did not do so. By the same token, the contours of sovereign immunity are determined by the Founders' understanding, not by the principles or limitations derived from natural law. . . .

Whether Congress has authority under Article I to abrogate a State's immunity from suit in its own courts is, then, a question of first impression. [And we find no] compelling evidence that this derogation of the States' sovereignty is inherent in the constitutional compact. . . .

III

The constitutional privilege of a State to assert its sovereign immunity in its own courts does not confer upon the State a concomitant right to disregard the Constitution or valid federal law. The States and their officers are bound by obligations imposed by the Constitution and by federal statutes that comport with the constitutional design. We are unwilling to assume the States will refuse to honor the Constitution or obey the binding laws of the United States. The good faith of the States thus provides an important assurance that "[t]his Constitution, and the Laws of the United States which shall be made in Pursuance thereof . . . shall be the supreme Law of the Land."

Sovereign immunity, moreover, does not bar all judicial review of state compliance with the Constitution and valid federal law. Rather, certain limits are implicit in the constitutional principle of state sovereign immunity.

The first of these limits is that sovereign immunity bars suits only in the absence of consent. Many States, on their own initiative, have enacted statutes consenting to a wide variety of suits. The rigors of sovereign immunity are thus mitigated by a sense of justice which has continually expanded by consent the suability of the sovereign. Nor, subject to constitutional limitations, does the Federal Government lack the authority or means to seek the States' voluntary consent to private suits.

The States have consented, moreover, to some suits pursuant to the plan of the Convention or to subsequent constitutional Amendments. In ratifying the Constitution, the States consented to suits brought by other States or by the Federal Government. A suit which is commenced and prosecuted against a State in the name of the United States by those who are entrusted with the constitutional duty to "take Care that the Laws be faithfully executed," differs in kind from the suit of an individual: While the Constitution contemplates suits among the members of the federal system as an alternative to extralegal measures, the fear of private suits against nonconsenting States was the central reason given by the Founders who chose to preserve the States' sovereign immunity. Suits brought by the United States itself require the exercise of political responsibility for each suit prosecuted against a State, a control which is absent from a broad delegation to private persons to sue nonconsenting States.

We have held also that in adopting the Fourteenth Amendment, the people required the States to surrender a portion of the sovereignty that had been preserved to them by the original Constitution, so that Congress may authorize private suits against nonconsenting States pursuant to its § 5 enforcement power. By imposing explicit limits on the powers of the States and granting Congress the power to enforce them, the Amendment fundamentally altered the balance of state and federal power struck by the Constitution. When Congress enacts appropriate legislation to enforce this Amendment, federal interests are paramount, and Congress may assert an authority over the States which would be otherwise unauthorized by the Constitution.

The second important limit to the principle of sovereign immunity is that it bars suits against States but not lesser entities. The immunity does not extend to suits prosecuted against a municipal corporation or other governmental entity which is not an arm of the State. Nor does sovereign immunity bar all suits against state officers. Some suits against state officers are barred by the rule that sovereign immunity is not limited to suits which name the State as a party if the suits are, in fact, against the State. The rule, however, does not bar certain actions against state officers for injunctive or declaratory relief. Even a suit for money damages may be prosecuted against a state officer in his individual capacity for unconstitutional or wrongful conduct fairly attributable to the officer himself, so long as the relief is sought not from the state treasury but from the officer personally.

The principle of sovereign immunity as reflected in our jurisprudence strikes the proper balance between the supremacy of federal law and the separate sovereignty of the States. Established rules provide ample means to correct ongoing violations of law and to vindicate the interests which animate the Supremacy Clause. That we have, during the first 210 years of our constitutional history, found it unnecessary to decide the question presented here suggests a federal power to subject nonconsenting States to private suits in their own courts is unnecessary to uphold the Constitution and valid federal statutes as the supreme law. . . .

The judgment of the Supreme Judicial Court of Maine is *Affirmed.*

Justice SOUTER, with whom Justice STEVENS, Justice GINSBURG, and Justice BREYER join, dissenting.

. . . . The Court rests its decision principally on the claim that immunity from suit was a fundamental aspect of the sovereignty which the States enjoyed before the ratification of the Constitution, an aspect which the Court understands to have survived the ratification . . . . [as] a structural basis in the Constitution's creation of a federal system. . . . That is, the Court believes that the federal constitutional structure itself necessitates recognition of some degree of state autonomy broad enough to include sovereign immunity from suit in a State's own courts, regardless of the federal source of the claim asserted against the State. If one were to read the Court's federal structure rationale in isolation from the preceding portions of the opinion, it would appear that the Court's position on state sovereign immunity might have been rested entirely on federalism alone. If it had been, however, I would still be in dissent, for the Court's argument that state-court sovereign immunity on federal questions is inherent in the very concept of federal structure is demonstrably mistaken. . . .

In America, the powers of sovereignty are divided between the government of the Union, and those of the States. They are each sovereign, with respect to the objects committed to it, and neither sovereign with respect to the objects committed to the other. Hence the flaw in the Court's appeal to federalism. The State of Maine is not sovereign with respect to the national objectives of the FLSA. It is not the authority that promulgated the FLSA, on which the right of action in this case depends. That authority is the United States acting through the Congress, whose legislative power under Article I of the Constitution to extend FLSA coverage to state employees has already been decided and is not contested here.

Nor can it be argued that because the State of Maine creates its own court system, it has authority to decide what sorts of claims may be entertained there, and thus in effect to control the right of action in this case. Maine has created state courts of general jurisdiction; once it has done so, the Supremacy Clause of the Constitution, which requires state courts to enforce federal law and state-court judges to be bound by it, requires the Maine courts to entertain this federal cause of action. . . . The Court's insistence that the federal structure bars Congress from making States susceptible to suit in their own courts is, then, plain mistake.

It is symptomatic of the weakness of the structural notion proffered by the Court that it seeks to buttress the argument by relying on "the dignity and respect afforded a State, which the immunity is designed to protect," and by invoking the many demands on a State's fisc. Apparently beguiled by Gilded Era language describing private suits against States as neither becoming nor convenient, the Court calls immunity from private suits central to sovereign dignity, and assumes that this "dignity" is a quality easily translated from the person of the King to the participatory abstraction of a republican State. The thoroughly anomalous character of this appeal to dignity is obvious from a reading of Blackstone's description of royal dignity, which he sets out as a premise of his discussion of sovereignty:

> First, then, of the royal dignity. Under every monarchical establishment, it is necessary to distinguish the prince from his subjects. The law therefore ascribes to the king certain attributes of a great and transcendent nature; by which the people are led to consider him in the light of a superior being, and to pay him that awful respect, which may enable him with greater ease to carry on the business of government. This is what I understand by the royal dignity, the several branches of which we will now proceed to examine.

It would be hard to imagine anything more inimical to the republican conception, which rests on the understanding of its citizens precisely that the government is not above them, but of them, its actions being governed by law just like their own. Whatever justification there may be for an American government's immunity from private suit, it is not dignity. . . .

It is true, of course, that the FLSA does authorize the Secretary of Labor to file suit seeking damages, but unless Congress plans a significant expansion of the National Government's litigating forces to provide a lawyer whenever private litigation is barred by today's decision and *Seminole Tribe*, the allusion to enforcement of private rights by the National Government is probably not much more than whimsy. Facing reality, Congress specifically found, as long ago as 1974, that the enforcement capability of the Secretary of Labor is not alone sufficient to provide redress in all or even a substantial portion of the situations where compliance is not forthcoming voluntarily. One hopes that such voluntary compliance will prove more popular than it has in Maine, for there is no reason today to suspect that enforcement by the Secretary of Labor alone would likely prove adequate to assure compliance with this federal law in the multifarious circumstances of some 4.7 million employees of the 50 States of the Union. . . .[43]

[43] . . . [D]espite the Court's professed unwillingness to assume the States will refuse to honor the Constitution and obey the binding laws of the United States, ... [and despite the State's representation] that Maine now pays employees like petitioners overtime as covered by the FLSA. . . , the State still has not paid damages to petitioners . . . .

Federal Maritime Commission v. South Carolina State Ports Authority (2002)

Justice THOMAS delivered the opinion of the Court.

This case presents the question whether state sovereign immunity precludes petitioner Federal Maritime Commission (FMC or Commission) from adjudicating a private party's complaint that a state-run port has violated the Shipping Act of 1984. We hold that state sovereign immunity bars such an adjudicative proceeding.

I

On five occasions, South Carolina Maritime Services, Inc. (Maritime Services), asked respondent South Carolina State Ports Authority (SCSPA) for permission to berth a cruise ship, the M/V *Tropic Sea*, at the SCSPA's port facilities in Charleston, South Carolina. Maritime Services intended to offer cruises on the M/V *Tropic Sea* originating from the Port of Charleston. Some of these cruises would stop in the Bahamas while others would merely travel in international waters before returning to Charleston with no intervening ports of call. On all of these trips, passengers would be permitted to participate in gambling activities while on board.

The SCSPA repeatedly denied Maritime Services' requests, contending that it had an established policy of denying berths in the Port of Charleston to vessels whose primary purpose was gambling. As a result, Maritime Services filed a complaint with the FMC, contending that the SCSPA's refusal to provide berthing space to the M/V *Tropic Sea* violated the Shipping Act. Maritime Services alleged in its complaint that the SCSPA had implemented its antigambling policy in a discriminatory fashion by providing berthing space in Charleston to two Carnival Cruise Lines vessels even though Carnival offered gambling activities on these ships. Maritime Services therefore complained that the SCSPA had unduly and unreasonably preferred Carnival over Maritime Services in violation of [federal law] and unreasonably refused to deal or negotiate with Maritime Services in violation of [federal law]. It further alleged that the SCSPA's unlawful actions had inflicted upon Maritime Services a loss of profits, loss of earnings, loss of sales, and loss of business opportunities.

To remedy its injuries, Maritime Services prayed that the FMC: (1) seek a temporary restraining order and preliminary injunction in the United States District Court for the District of South Carolina enjoining the SCSPA from utilizing its discriminatory practice to refuse to provide berthing space and passenger services to Maritime Services; (2) direct the SCSPA to pay reparations to Maritime Services as well as interest and reasonable attorneys' fees; (3) issue an order commanding, among other things, the SCSPA to cease and desist from violating the Shipping Act; and (4) award Maritime Services such other and further relief as is just and proper.

Consistent with the FMC's Rules of Practice and Procedure, Maritime Services' complaint was referred to an Administrative Law Judge (ALJ). The SCSPA then filed an answer, maintaining, *inter alia*, that it had adhered to its antigambling policy in a nondiscriminatory manner. It also filed a motion to dismiss, asserting, as relevant, that the SCSPA, as an arm of the State of South Carolina, was entitled to Eleventh Amendment immunity from Maritime Services' suit. The SCSPA argued that the Constitution prohibits Congress from passing a statute authorizing Maritime Services to file this Complaint before the Commission and, thereby, sue the State of South Carolina for damages and injunctive relief.

The ALJ agreed, concluding that recent decisions of this Court interpreting the 11th Amendment and State sovereign immunity from private suits required that Maritime Services' complaint be dismissed. . . . While Maritime Services did not appeal the ALJ's dismissal of its complaint, the FMC on its own motion decided to review the ALJ's ruling to consider whether state sovereign immunity from private suits extends to proceedings before the Commission. It concluded that the doctrine of state sovereign immunity is meant to cover proceedings before judicial tribunals, whether Federal or state, not executive branch administrative agencies like the Commission. As a result, the FMC held that sovereign immunity did not bar the Commission from adjudicating private complaints against state-run ports and reversed the ALJ's decision dismissing Maritime Services' complaint.

The SCSPA filed a petition for review, and the United States Court of Appeals for the Fourth Circuit reversed. . . . We granted the FMC's petition for certiorari and now affirm.

II

Dual sovereignty is a defining feature of our Nation's constitutional blueprint. States, upon ratification of the Constitution, did not consent to become mere appendages of the Federal Government. Rather, they entered the Union with their sovereignty intact. An integral component of that residuary and inviolable sovereignty retained by the States is their immunity from private suits. . . .

States, in ratifying the Constitution, did surrender a portion of their inherent immunity by consenting to suits brought by sister States or by the Federal Government. Nevertheless, the Convention did not disturb States' immunity from private suits, thus firmly enshrining this principle in our constitutional framework. . . . Instead of explicitly memorializing the full breadth of the sovereign immunity retained by the States when the Constitution was ratified, Congress chose in the text of the Eleventh Amendment only to address the specific provisions of the Constitution that had raised concerns during the ratification debates and formed the basis of the *Chisholm* decision. As a result, the Eleventh Amendment does not define the scope of the States' sovereign immunity; it is but one particular exemplification of that immunity.

III

We now consider whether the sovereign immunity enjoyed by States as part of our constitutional framework applies to adjudications conducted by the FMC. Petitioner FMC and respondent United States initially maintain that the Court of Appeals erred because sovereign immunity only shields States from exercises of "judicial power" and FMC adjudications are not judicial proceedings. As support for their position, they point to the text of the Eleventh Amendment and contend that the Amendment's reference to "judicial Power" and to "any suit in law or equity" clearly mark it as an immunity from judicial process.

For purposes of this case, we will assume, *arguendo*, that in adjudicating complaints filed by private parties under the Shipping Act, the FMC does not exercise the judicial power of the United States. Such an assumption, however, does not end our inquiry as this Court has repeatedly held that the sovereign immunity enjoyed by the States extends beyond the literal text of the Eleventh Amendment. Adhering to that well-reasoned precedent, we must determine whether the sovereign immunity embedded in our constitutional structure and retained by the States when they joined the Union extends to FMC adjudicative proceedings.

A

. . . . The Framers, who envisioned a limited Federal Government, could not have anticipated the vast growth of the administrative state. Because formalized administrative adjudications were all but unheard of in the late 18th century and early 19th century, the dearth of specific evidence indicating whether the Framers believed that the States' sovereign immunity would apply in such proceedings is unsurprising.

This Court, however, has applied a presumption—first explicitly stated in *Hans v. Louisiana*—that the Constitution was not intended to raise up any proceedings against the States that were anomalous and unheard of when the Constitution was adopted. We therefore attribute great significance to the fact that States were not subject to private suits in administrative adjudications at the time of the founding or for many years thereafter. For instance, while the United States asserts that state entities have long been subject to similar administrative enforcement proceedings, the earliest example it provides did not occur until 1918.

B

To decide whether the *Hans* presumption applies here, however, we must examine FMC adjudications to determine whether they are the type of proceedings from which the Framers would have thought the States possessed immunity when they agreed to enter the Union. . . .

Turning to FMC adjudications specifically, neither the Commission nor the United States disputes the Court of Appeals's characterization below that such a proceeding "walks, talks, and squawks very much like a lawsuit." Nor do they deny that the similarities . . . between administrative adjudications and trial court proceedings are present here.

A review of the FMC's Rules of Practice and Procedure confirms that FMC administrative proceedings bear a remarkably strong resemblance to civil litigation in federal courts. For example, the FMC's Rules governing pleadings are quite similar to those found in the Federal Rules of Civil Procedure. A case is commenced by the filing of a complaint. The defendant then must file an answer, generally within 20 days of the date of service of the complaint, and may also file a motion to dismiss. A defendant is also allowed to file counterclaims against the plaintiff. If a defendant fails to respond to a complaint, default judgment may be entered on behalf of the plaintiff. Intervention is also allowed.

Likewise, discovery in FMC adjudications largely mirrors discovery in federal civil litigation. In both types of proceedings, parties may conduct depositions, which are governed by similar requirements. Parties may also discover evidence by: (1) serving written interrogatories; (2) requesting that another party either produce documents, or allow entry on that party's property for the purpose of inspecting the property or designated objects thereon; and (3) submitting requests for admissions. And a party failing to obey discovery orders in either type of proceeding is subject to a variety of sanctions, including the entry of default judgment.

Not only are discovery procedures virtually indistinguishable, but the role of the ALJ, the impartial officer designated to hear a case, is similar to that of an Article III judge. An ALJ has the authority to arrange and give notice of hearing. At that hearing, he may

> prescribe the order in which evidence shall be presented; dispose of procedural requests or similar matters; hear and rule upon motions; administer oaths and affirmations; examine witnesses; direct witnesses to testify or produce evidence available to them which will aid in the determination of any question of fact in issue; rule upon offers of proof and dispose of any other matter that normally and properly arises in the course of proceedings.

The ALJ also fixes the time and manner of filing briefs, which contain findings of fact as well as legal argument. After the submission of these briefs, the ALJ issues a decision that includes a statement of findings and conclusions, as well as the reasons or basis therefor, upon all the material issues presented on the record, and the appropriate rule, order, section, relief, or denial thereof. Such relief may include an order directing the payment of reparations to an aggrieved party. The ALJ's ruling subsequently becomes the final decision of the FMC unless a party, by filing exceptions, appeals to the Commission or the Commission decides to review the ALJ's decision on its own initiative. In cases where a complainant obtains reparations, an ALJ may also require the losing party to pay the prevailing party's attorney's fees.

In short, the similarities between FMC proceedings and civil litigation are overwhelming. In fact, to the extent that situations arise in the course of FMC adjudications which are not covered by a specific Commission rule, the FMC's own Rules of Practice and Procedure specifically provide that "the Federal Rules of Civil Procedure will be followed to the extent that they are consistent with sound administrative practice."

C

The preeminent purpose of state sovereign immunity is to accord States the dignity that is consistent with their status as sovereign entities. The founding generation thought it neither becoming nor convenient that the several States of the Union, invested with that large residuum of sovereignty which had not been delegated to the United States, should be summoned as defendants to answer the complaints of private persons.

Given both this interest in protecting States' dignity and the strong similarities between FMC proceedings and civil litigation, we hold that state sovereign immunity bars the FMC from adjudicating complaints filed by a private party against a nonconsenting State. Simply put, if the Framers thought it an impermissible affront to a State's dignity to be required to answer the complaints of private parties in federal courts, we cannot imagine that they would have found it acceptable to compel a State to do exactly the same thing before the administrative tribunal of an agency, such as the FMC. The affront to a State's dignity does not lessen when an adjudication takes place in an administrative tribunal as opposed to an Article III court. In both instances, a State is required to defend itself in an adversarial proceeding against a private party before an impartial federal officer. Moreover, it would be quite strange to prohibit Congress from exercising its Article I powers to abrogate state sovereign immunity in Article III judicial proceedings but permit the use of those same Article I powers to create court-like administrative tribunals where sovereign immunity does not apply.

D

The United States suggests two reasons why we should distinguish FMC administrative adjudications from judicial proceedings for purposes of state sovereign immunity. Both of these arguments are unavailing.

1

The United States first contends that sovereign immunity should not apply to FMC adjudications because the Commission's orders are not self-executing. Whereas a court may enforce a judgment through the exercise of its contempt power, the FMC cannot enforce its own orders. Rather, the Commission's orders can only be enforced by a federal district court.

The United States presents a valid distinction between the authority possessed by the FMC and that of a court. For purposes of this case, however, it is a distinction without a meaningful difference. To the extent that the United States highlights this fact in order to suggest that a party alleged to have violated the Shipping Act is not coerced to participate in FMC proceedings, it is mistaken. The relevant statutory scheme makes it quite clear that, absent sovereign immunity, States would effectively be required to defend themselves against private parties in front of the FMC.

A State seeking to contest the merits of a complaint filed against it by a private party must defend itself in front of the FMC or substantially compromise its ability to defend itself at all. For example, once the FMC issues a nonreparation order, and either the Attorney General or the injured private party seeks enforcement of that order in a federal district court, the sanctioned party is *not* permitted to litigate the merits of its position in that court. Moreover, if a party fails to appear before the FMC, it may not then argue the merits of its position in an appeal of the Commission's determination . . . .

Should a party choose to ignore an order issued by the FMC, the Commission may impose monetary penalties for each day of noncompliance. The Commission may then request that the Attorney General of the United States seek to recover the amount assessed by the Commission in federal district court, and a State's sovereign immunity would not extend to that action, as it is one brought by the United States. Furthermore, once the FMC issues an order assessing a civil penalty, a sanctioned party may not later contest the merits of that order in an enforcement action brought by the Attorney General in federal district court.

Thus, any party, including a State, charged in a complaint by a private party with violating the Shipping Act is faced with the following options: appear before the Commission in a bid to persuade the FMC of the strength of its position or stand defenseless once enforcement of the Commission's nonreparation order or assessment of civil penalties is sought in federal district court. To conclude that this choice does not coerce a State to participate in an FMC adjudication would be to blind ourselves to reality.

The United States and Justice Breyer maintain that any such coercion to participate in FMC proceedings is permissible because the States have consented to actions brought by the Federal Government. The Attorney General's decision to bring an enforcement action against a State after the conclusion of the Commission's proceedings, however, does not retroactively convert an FMC adjudication initiated and pursued by a private party into one initiated and pursued by the Federal Government. The prosecution of a complaint filed by a private party with the FMC is plainly not controlled by the United States, but rather is controlled by that private party; the only duty assumed by the FMC, and hence the United States, in conjunction with a private complaint is to assess its merits in an impartial manner. Indeed, the FMC does not even have the discretion to refuse to adjudicate complaints brought by private parties. As a result, the United States plainly does not exercise political responsibility for such complaints, but instead has impermissibly effected a broad delegation to private persons to sue nonconsenting States.

2

The United States next suggests that sovereign immunity should not apply to FMC proceedings because they do not present the same threat to the financial integrity of States as do private judicial suits. The Government highlights the fact that, in contrast to a nonreparation order, for which the Attorney General may seek enforcement at the request of the Commission, a reparation order may be enforced in a United States district court only in an action brought by the private party to whom the award was made. The United States then points out that a State's sovereign immunity would extend to such a suit brought by a private party.

This argument, however, reflects a fundamental misunderstanding of the purposes of sovereign immunity. While state sovereign immunity serves the important function of shielding state treasuries and thus preserving the States' ability to govern in accordance with the will of their citizens, the doctrine's central purpose is to accord the States the respect owed them as joint sovereigns. It is for this reason, for instance, that sovereign immunity applies regardless of whether a private plaintiff's suit is for monetary damages or some other type of relief.

Sovereign immunity does not merely constitute a defense to monetary liability or even to all types of liability. Rather, it provides an immunity from suit. The statutory scheme, as interpreted by the United States, is thus no more permissible than if Congress had allowed private parties to sue States in federal court for violations of the Shipping Act but precluded a court from awarding them any relief. . . .

By guarding against encroachments by the Federal Government on fundamental aspects of state sovereignty, such as sovereign immunity, we strive to maintain the balance of power embodied in our Constitution and thus to reduce the risk of tyranny and abuse from either front. Although the Framers likely did not envision the intrusion on state sovereignty at issue in today's case, we are nonetheless confident that it is contrary to their constitutional design, and therefore affirm the judgment of the Court of Appeals.

It is so ordered.

Justice BREYER, with whom Justice STEVENS, Justice SOUTER, and Justice GINSBURG join, dissenting.

The Court holds that a private person cannot bring a complaint against a State to a federal administrative agency where the agency (1) will use an internal adjudicative process to decide if the complaint is well founded, and (2) if so, proceed to court to enforce the law. Where does the Constitution contain the principle of law that the Court enunciates? I cannot find the answer to this question in any text, in any tradition, or in any relevant purpose. In saying this, I do not simply reiterate the dissenting views set forth in many of the Court's recent sovereign immunity decisions. For even were I to believe that those decisions properly stated the law—which I do not—I still could not accept the Court's conclusion here.

. . . . The case before us presents a fairly typical example of a federal administrative agency's use of agency adjudication. Congress has enacted a statute, the Shipping Act of 1984, which, among other things, forbids marine terminal operators to discriminate against terminal users. The Act grants the Federal Maritime Commission the authority to administer the Act. The law grants the Commission the authority to enforce the Act in a variety of ways, for example, by making rules and by issuing or revoking licenses, and by conducting investigations and issuing reports. It also permits a private person to file a complaint, which the Commission is to consider. . . .

The upshot is that this case involves a typical Executive Branch agency exercising typical Executive Branch powers seeking to determine whether a particular person has violated federal law. The particular person in this instance is a state entity, the South Carolina State Ports Authority, and the agency is acting in response to the request of a private individual. But at first blush it is difficult to see why these special circumstances matter. After all, the Constitution created a Federal Government empowered to enact laws that would bind the

States and it empowered that Federal Government to enforce those laws against the States. It also left private individuals perfectly free to complain to the Federal Government about unlawful state activity, and it left the Federal Government free to take subsequent legal action. Where then can the Court find its constitutional principle—the principle that the Constitution forbids an Executive Branch agency to determine through ordinary adjudicative processes whether such a private complaint is justified? As I have said, I cannot find that principle anywhere in the Constitution.

. . . . In a typical instance, the private individual will file a complaint, the agency will adjudicate the complaint, and the agency will reach a decision. The State subsequently may take the matter to court in order to obtain judicial review of any adverse agency ruling, but, if it does so, its opponent in that court proceeding is *not* a private party, but the agency itself. (And unlike some other administrative schemes, the Commission would not be a party in name only.) Alternatively, the State may do nothing, in which case either the Commission or the Attorney General must seek a court order compelling the State to obey. The Commission, but not a private party, may assess a penalty against the State for noncompliance, and only a court acting at the Commission's request can compel compliance with a penalty order. In sum, no one can legally compel the State's obedience to the Shipping Act's requirements without a court order, and in no case would a court issue such an order (absent a State's voluntary waiver of sovereign immunity) absent the request of a federal agency or other federal instrumentality. . . .

Certainly, a private citizen's decision to file a complaint with the Commission can produce practical pressures upon the State to respond and eventually to comply with a Commission decision. By appearing before the Commission, the State will be able to obtain full judicial review of an adverse agency decision in a court of appeals (where it will face in opposition the Commission itself, not the private party). By appearing, the State will avoid any potential Commission-assessed monetary penalty. And by complying, it will avoid the adverse political, practical, and symbolic implications of being labeled a federal lawbreaker.

Practical pressures such as these, however, cannot sufficiently affront a State's dignity as to warrant constitutional sovereign immunity protections, for it is easy to imagine comparable instances of clearly lawful private citizen complaints to Government that place a State under far greater practical pressures to comply. No one doubts, for example, that a private citizen can complain to Congress, which may threaten (should the State fail to respond) to enact a new law that the State opposes. Nor does anyone deny that a private citizen, in complaining to a federal agency, may seek a rulemaking proceeding, which may lead the agency (should the State fail to respond) to enact a new agency rule that the State opposes. A private citizen may ask an agency formally to declare that a State is not in compliance with a statute or federal rule, even though from that formal declaration may flow a host of legal consequences adverse to a State's interests. And one can easily imagine a legal scheme in which a private individual files a complaint like the one before us, but asks an agency staff member to investigate the matter, which investigation would lead to an order similar to the order at issue here with similar legal and practical consequences. . . .

The Court cannot justify today's decision in terms of its practical consequences. The decision, while permitting an agency to bring enforcement actions against States, forbids it to use agency adjudication in order to help decide whether to do so. Consequently the agency must rely more heavily upon its own informal staff investigations in order to decide whether a citizen's complaint has merit. The natural result is less agency flexibility, a larger federal bureaucracy, less fair procedure, and potentially less effective law enforcement. And at least one of these consequences, the forced growth of unnecessary federal bureaucracy, undermines the very constitutional objectives the Court's decision claims to serve. . . .

Central Virginia Community College v. Katz (2006)

Justice STEVENS delivered the opinion of the Court.

Article I, § 8, cl. 4, of the Constitution provides that Congress shall have the power to establish "uniform Laws on the subject of Bankruptcies throughout the United States." . . . In this case we consider whether a proceeding initiated by a bankruptcy trustee to set aside preferential transfers by the debtor to state agencies is barred by sovereign immunity. . . . [W]e reject the sovereign immunity defense advanced by the state agencies.

I

Petitioners are Virginia institutions of higher education that are considered arms of the State entitled to sovereign immunity. Wallace's Bookstores did business with petitioners before it filed a petition for relief under chapter 11 of the Bankruptcy Code, in the United States Bankruptcy Court for the Eastern District of Kentucky. Respondent, Bernard Katz, is the court-appointed liquidating supervisor of the bankrupt estate. He has commenced proceedings in the Bankruptcy Court pursuant to §§ 547(b) and 550(a) to avoid and recover alleged preferential transfers to each of the petitioners made by the debtor when it was insolvent. Petitioners' motions to dismiss those proceedings on the basis of sovereign immunity were denied by the Bankruptcy Court. The denial was affirmed by the District Court and the Court of Appeals . . . .

Bankruptcy jurisdiction, at its core, is *in rem*. . . . [I]t does not implicate States' sovereignty to nearly the same degree as other kinds of jurisdiction. That was as true in the 18th century as it is today. Then, as now, the jurisdiction of courts adjudicating rights in the bankrupt estate included the power to issue compulsory orders to facilitate the administration and distribution of the res.

. . . . We acknowledge that statements in both the majority and the dissenting opinions in *Seminole Tribe* reflected an assumption that the holding in that case would apply to the Bankruptcy Clause. Careful study and reflection have convinced us, however, that that assumption was erroneous. For the reasons stated by Chief Justice Marshall in *Cohens v. Virginia*, we are not bound to follow our dicta in a prior case in which the point now at issue was not fully debated.

II

Critical features of every bankruptcy proceeding are the exercise of exclusive jurisdiction over all of the debtor's property, the equitable distribution of that property among the debtor's creditors, and the ultimate discharge that gives the debtor a "fresh start" by releasing him, her, or it from further liability for old debts. Under our longstanding precedent, States, whether or not they choose to participate in the proceeding, are bound by a bankruptcy court's discharge order no less than other creditors. Petitioners here . . . have conceded as much. . . .

III

Bankruptcy jurisdiction, as understood today and at the time of the framing, is principally *in rem* jurisdiction. In bankruptcy, the court's jurisdiction is premised on the debtor and his estate, and not on the creditors. As such, its exercise does not, in the usual case, interfere with state sovereignty even when States' interests are affected.

The text of Article I, § 8, cl. 4, of the Constitution, however, provides that Congress shall have the power to establish "uniform Laws on the subject of Bankruptcies throughout the United States." Although the interest in avoiding unjust imprisonment for debt and making federal discharges in bankruptcy enforceable in every State was a primary motivation for the adoption of that provision, its coverage encompasses the entire "subject of Bankruptcies." The power granted to Congress by that Clause is a unitary concept rather than an amalgam of discrete segments. . . .

[T]hose who crafted the Bankruptcy Clause would have understood it to give Congress the power to authorize courts to avoid preferential transfers and to recover the transferred property. Petitioners do not dispute that that authority has been a core aspect of the administration of bankrupt estates since at least the 18th century. And it, like the authority to issue writs of habeas corpus releasing debtors from state prisons, operates free and clear of the State's claim of sovereign immunity.

IV

Insofar as orders ancillary to the bankruptcy courts' *in rem* jurisdiction, like orders directing turnover of preferential transfers, implicate States' sovereign immunity from suit, the States agreed in the plan of the Convention not to assert that immunity. So much is evidenced not only by the history of the Bankruptcy Clause, which shows that the Framers' primary goal was to prevent competing sovereigns' interference with the debtor's discharge, but also by legislation considered and enacted in the immediate wake of the Constitution's ratification.

Congress considered proposed legislation establishing uniform federal bankruptcy laws in the first and each succeeding Congress until 1800, when the first Bankruptcy Act was passed. The Bankruptcy Act of 1800 was in many respects a copy of the English bankruptcy statute then in force. It was, like the English law, chiefly a measure designed to benefit creditors. . . . The American legislation differed slightly from the English, however. That difference reflects both the uniqueness of a system involving multiple sovereigns and the concerns that lay at the core of the Bankruptcy Clause itself. The English statute gave a judge sitting on a court where the debtor had obtained his discharge the power to order a sheriff, "Bailiff or Officer, Gaoler or Keeper of any Prison" to release the "Bankrupt out of Custody" if he were arrested subsequent to the discharge. The American version of this provision was worded differently; it specifically granted federal courts the authority to issue writs of habeas corpus effective to release debtors from state prisons.

This grant of habeas power is remarkable not least because it would be another 67 years, after ratification of the Fourteenth Amendment, before the writ would be made generally available to state prisoners. Moreover, the provision of the 1800 Act granting that power was considered and adopted during a period when state sovereign immunity could hardly have been more prominent among the Nation's concerns. *Chisholm v. Georgia*, the case that had so "shocked" the country in its lack of regard for state sovereign immunity, was decided in 1793. The ensuing five years that culminated in adoption of the Eleventh Amendment were rife with discussion of States' sovereignty and their amenability to suit. Yet there appears to be no record of any objection to the bankruptcy legislation or its grant of habeas power to federal courts based on an infringement of sovereign immunity.

This history strongly supports the view that the Bankruptcy Clause of Article I, the source of Congress's authority to effect this intrusion upon state sovereignty, simply did not contravene the norms this Court has understood the Eleventh Amendment to exemplify. Petitioners, ignoring this history, contend that nothing in the *words* of the Bankruptcy Clause evinces an intent on the part of the Framers to alter the "background principle" of state sovereign immunity. Specifically, they deny that the word "uniform" in the Clause implies anything about pre-existing immunities or Congress's power to interfere with those immunities. Whatever the merits of petitioners' argument, it misses the point; text aside, the Framers, in adopting the Bankruptcy Clause, plainly intended to give Congress the power to redress the rampant injustice resulting from States' refusal to respect one another's discharge orders. As demonstrated by the First Congress's immediate consideration and the Sixth Congress's enactment of a provision granting federal courts the authority to release debtors from state prisons, the power to enact bankruptcy legislation was understood to carry with it the power to subordinate state sovereignty, albeit within a limited sphere.

The ineluctable conclusion, then, is that States agreed in the plan of the Convention not to assert any sovereign immunity defense they might have had in proceedings brought pursuant to "Laws on the subject of Bankruptcies." The scope of this consent was limited; the jurisdiction exercised in bankruptcy proceedings was chiefly *in rem*—a narrow jurisdiction that does not implicate state sovereignty to nearly the same degree as other kinds of jurisdiction. But while the principal focus of the bankruptcy proceedings is and was always the res, some exercises of bankruptcy courts' powers—issuance of writs of habeas corpus included—unquestionably involved more than mere adjudication of rights in a res. In ratifying the Bankruptcy Clause, the States acquiesced in a subordination of whatever sovereign immunity they might otherwise have asserted in proceedings necessary to effectuate the *in rem* jurisdiction of the bankruptcy courts.

V

.... Congress may, at its option, either treat States in the same way as other creditors insofar as concerns "Laws on the subject of Bankruptcies" or exempt them from operation of such laws. Its power to do so arises from the Bankruptcy Clause itself; the relevant "abrogation" is the one effected in the plan of the Convention, not by statute.

The judgment of the Court of Appeals for the Sixth Circuit is affirmed.

Justice THOMAS, with whom THE CHIEF JUSTICE, Justice SCALIA, and Justice KENNEDY join, dissenting.

Under our Constitution, the States are not subject to suit by private parties for monetary relief absent their consent or a valid congressional abrogation, and it is settled doctrine that nothing in Article I of the Constitution establishes those preconditions. *Alden v. Maine.* Yet the majority today casts aside these long-established principles to hold that the States are subject to suit by a rather unlikely class of individuals—bankruptcy trustees seeking recovery of preferential transfers for a bankrupt debtor's estate. This conclusion cannot be justified by the text, structure, or history of our Constitution. In addition, today's ruling is impossible to square with this Court's settled state sovereign immunity jurisprudence ....

The majority maintains that the States' consent to suit can be ascertained from the history of the Bankruptcy Clause. But history confirms that the adoption of the Constitution merely established federal power to legislate in the area of bankruptcy law, and did not manifest an additional intention to waive the States' sovereign immunity against suit. Accordingly, I respectfully dissent.

I

The majority does not appear to question the established framework for examining the question of state sovereign immunity under our Constitution. ...

The majority finds a surrender of the States' immunity from suit in Article I of the Constitution, which authorizes Congress "[t]o establish . . . uniform Laws on the subject of Bankruptcies throughout the United States." But nothing in the text of the Bankruptcy Clause suggests an abrogation or limitation of the States' sovereign immunity. Indeed, as this Court has noted on numerous occasions, "[t]he Eleventh Amendment restricts the judicial power under Article III, and Article I cannot be used to circumvent the constitutional limitations placed upon federal jurisdiction." *Seminole Tribe*. It is settled doctrine that neither substantive federal law nor attempted congressional abrogation under Article I bars a State from raising a constitutional defense of sovereign immunity in federal court. And we have specifically applied this "settled doctrine" to bar abrogation of state sovereign immunity under various clauses within § 8 of Article I.

It is difficult to discern an intention to abrogate state sovereign immunity through the Bankruptcy Clause when no such intention has been found in any of the other clauses in Article I. Indeed, our cases are replete with acknowledgments that there is nothing special about the Bankruptcy Clause in this regard. Today's decision thus cannot be reconciled with our established sovereign immunity jurisprudence, which the majority does not purport to overturn. . . .

II

The majority supports its break from precedent by relying on historical evidence that purportedly reveals the Framers' intent to eliminate state sovereign immunity in bankruptcy proceedings. The Framers undoubtedly wanted to give Congress the authority to enact a national law of bankruptcy, as the text of the Bankruptcy Clause confirms. But the majority goes further, contending that the Framers found it intolerable that bankruptcy laws could vary from State to State, and demanded the enactment of a single, uniform national body of bankruptcy law. The majority then concludes that, to achieve a uniform national bankruptcy law, the Framers must have intended to waive the States' sovereign immunity against suit. Both claims are unwarranted.

A

In contending that the States waived their immunity from suit by adopting the Bankruptcy Clause, the majority conflates two distinct attributes of sovereignty: the authority of a sovereign to enact legislation regulating its own citizens, and sovereign immunity against suit by private citizens. Nothing in the history of the Bankruptcy Clause suggests that, by including that clause in Article I, the founding generation intended to waive the latter aspect of sovereignty. These two attributes of sovereignty often do not run together—and for purposes of enacting a uniform law of bankruptcy, they need not run together.

For example, Article I also empowers Congress to regulate interstate commerce and to protect copyrights and patents. These provisions, no less than the Bankruptcy Clause, were motivated by the Framers' desire for nationally uniform legislation. Thus, we have recognized that the need for uniformity in the construction of patent law is undoubtedly important. Nonetheless, we have refused, in addressing patent law, to give the need for uniformity the weight the majority today assigns it in the context of bankruptcy, instead recognizing that this need is a factor which belongs to the Article I patent-power calculus, rather than to any determination of whether a state plea of sovereign immunity deprives a patentee of property without due process of law.

Nor is the abrogation of state sovereign immunity from suit necessary to the enactment of nationally uniform bankruptcy laws. The sovereign immunity of the States against suit does not undermine the objective of a uniform national law of bankruptcy, any more than does any differential treatment between different categories of creditors. . . .

* * *

It would be one thing if the majority simply wanted to overrule *Seminole Tribe* altogether. That would be wrong, but at least the terms of our disagreement would be transparent. The majority's action today, by contrast, is difficult to comprehend. Nothing in the text, structure, or history of the Constitution indicates that the Bankruptcy Clause, in contrast to all of the other provisions of Article I, manifests the States' consent to be sued by private citizens.

I respectfully dissent.

Franchise Tax Board of California v. Hyatt (2019)

Justice THOMAS delivered the opinion of the Court.

This case, now before us for the third time, requires us to decide whether the Constitution permits a State to be sued by a private party without its consent in the courts of a different State. We hold that it does not and overrule our decision to the contrary in *Nevada* v. *Hall*, 440 U. S. 410 (1979).

I

In the early 1990s, respondent Gilbert Hyatt earned substantial income from a technology patent for a computer formed on a single integrated circuit chip. Although Hyatt's claim was later canceled, his royalties in the interim totaled millions of dollars. Prior to receiving the patent, Hyatt had been a long-time resident of California. But in 1991, Hyatt sold his house in California and rented an apartment, registered to vote, obtained insurance, opened a bank account, and acquired a driver's license in Nevada. When he filed his 1991 and 1992 tax returns, he claimed Nevada—which collects no personal income tax—as his primary place of residence.

Petitioner Franchise Tax Board of California (Board), the state agency responsible for assessing personal income tax, suspected that Hyatt's move was a sham. Thus, in 1993, the Board launched an audit to determine whether Hyatt underpaid his 1991 and 1992 state income taxes by misrepresenting his residency. In the course of the audit, employees of the Board traveled to Nevada to conduct interviews with Hyatt's estranged family members and shared his personal information with business contacts. In total, the Board sent more than 100 letters and demands for information to third parties. The Board ultimately concluded that Hyatt had not moved to Nevada until April 1992 and owed California more than $10 million in back taxes, interest, and penalties. Hyatt protested the audit before the Board, which upheld the audit after an 11-year administrative proceeding. The appeal of that decision remains pending before the California Office of Tax Appeals.

In 1998, Hyatt sued the Board in Nevada state court for torts he alleged the agency committed during the audit. . . . [T]he trial court conducted a 4-month jury trial that culminated in a verdict for Hyatt that, with prejudgment interest and costs, exceeded $490 million. On appeal, the Nevada Supreme Court rejected most of the damages awarded by the lower court . . . . [and] instructed the trial court to enter damages in accordance with the statutory cap [of $50,000] for Nevada agencies.

We granted . . . the Board's petition for certiorari [based on whether California was entitled to sovereign immunity from the suit in the first instance]. The sole question presented is whether *Nevada* v. *Hall* should be overruled.

II

Nevada v. *Hall* is contrary to our constitutional design and the understanding of sovereign immunity shared by the States that ratified the Constitution. *Stare decisis* does not compel continued adherence to this erroneous precedent. We therefore overrule *Hall* and hold that States retain their sovereign immunity from private suits brought in the courts of other States.

A

Hall held that the Constitution does not bar private suits against a State in the courts of another State. The opinion conceded that States were immune from such actions at the time of the founding, but it nonetheless concluded that nothing implicit in the Constitution requires States to adhere to the sovereign-immunity doctrine as it prevailed when the Constitution was adopted. Instead, the Court concluded that the Founders assumed that prevailing notions of comity would provide adequate protection against the unlikely prospect of an attempt by the courts of one State to assert jurisdiction over another. The Court's view rested primarily on the idea that the States maintained sovereign immunity vis-à-vis each other in the same way that foreign nations do, meaning that immunity is available only if the forum State voluntarily decides to respect the dignity of the defendant State as a matter of comity.

The *Hall* majority was unpersuaded that the Constitution implicitly altered the relationship between the States. In the Court's view, the ratification debates, the Eleventh Amendment, and our sovereign-immunity precedents did not bear on the question because they concerned questions of federal-court jurisdiction. The Court also found unpersuasive the fact that the Constitution delineates several limitations on States' authority, such as Article I powers granted exclusively to Congress and Article IV requirements imposed on States. Despite acknowledging that ours is not a union of 50 wholly independent sovereigns, *Hall* inferred from the lack of an express sovereign immunity granted to the States and from the Tenth Amendment that the States retained the power in their own courts to deny immunity to other States.

Chief Justice Burger, Justice Blackmun, and Justice Rehnquist dissented.

B

Hall's determination that the Constitution does not contemplate sovereign immunity for each State in a sister State's courts misreads the historical record and misapprehends the implicit ordering of relationships within the federal system necessary to make the Constitution a workable governing charter and to give each provision within that document the full effect intended by the Framers. As Chief Justice Marshall explained, the Founders did not state every postulate on which they formed our Republic—"we must never forget, that it is *a constitution* we are expounding." *McCulloch* v. *Maryland* (1819). And although the Constitution assumes that the States retain their sovereign immunity except as otherwise provided, it also fundamentally adjusts the States' relationship with each other and curtails their ability, as sovereigns, to decline to recognize each other's immunity.

1

After independence, the States considered themselves fully sovereign nations. . . . An integral component of the States' sovereignty was their immunity from private suits. This fundamental aspect of the States' inviolable sovereignty was well established and widely accepted at the founding. . . .

The Founders believed that both "common law sovereign immunity" and "law-of-nations sovereign immunity" prevented States from being amenable to process in any court without their consent. The common-law rule was that no suit or action can be brought against the king, even in civil matters, because no court can have jurisdiction over him. The law-of-nations rule followed from the perfect equality and absolute independence of sovereigns under that body of international law. . . .

The founding generation thus took as given that States could not be haled involuntarily before each other's courts. This understanding is perhaps best illustrated by preratification examples. In 1781, a creditor named Simon Nathan tried to recover a debt that Virginia allegedly owed him by attaching some of its property in Philadelphia. James Madison and other Virginia delegates to the Confederation Congress responded by sending a communique to Pennsylvania requesting that its executive branch have the action dismissed. As Madison framed it, the Commonwealth's property could not be attached by process issuing from a court of any other State in the Union. To permit otherwise would require Virginia to abandon its Sovereignty by descending to answer before the Tribunal of another Power. Pennsylvania Attorney General William Bradford intervened, urging the Court of Common Pleas to dismiss the action. According to Bradford, the suit violated international law because all sovereigns are in a state of equality and independence, exempt from each other's jurisdiction. All jurisdiction implies superiority over the party, Bradford argued, but there could be no superiority between the States, and thus no jurisdiction, because the States were perfectly equal and entirely independent. The court agreed and refused to grant Nathan the writ of attachment. . . .

In short, at the time of the founding, it was well settled that States were immune under both the common law and the law of nations. The Constitution's use of the term "States" reflects both of these kinds of traditional immunity. And the States retained these aspects of sovereignty, except as altered by the plan of the Convention or certain constitutional Amendments.

2

One constitutional provision that abrogated certain aspects of this traditional immunity was Article III, which provided a neutral federal forum in which the States agreed to be amenable to suits brought by other States. The establishment of a permanent tribunal with adequate authority to determine controversies between the States, in place of an inadequate scheme of arbitration, was essential to the peace of the Union. As James Madison explained during the Convention debates, there can be no impropriety in referring such disputes between coequal sovereigns to a superior tribunal.

The States, in ratifying the Constitution, similarly surrendered a portion of their immunity by consenting to suits brought against them by the United States in federal courts. While that jurisdiction is not conferred by the Constitution in express words, it is inherent in the constitutional plan. Given that all jurisdiction implies superiority of power, the only forums in which the States have consented to suits by one another and by the Federal Government are Article III courts.

The Antifederalists worried that Article III went even further by extending the federal judicial power over controversies between a State and Citizens of another State. They suggested that this provision implicitly waived the States' sovereign immunity against *private* suits in federal courts. But the leading advocates of the Constitution [Madison, Marshall, and Hamilton] assured the people in no uncertain terms that this reading was incorrect. . . .

Not long after the founding, however, the Antifederalists' fears were realized. In *Chisholm* v. *Georgia* (1793), the Court held that Article III allowed the very suits that the "Madison-Marshall-Hamilton triumvirate" insisted it did not. That decision precipitated an immediate "furor" and "uproar" across the country. Congress and the States accordingly acted swiftly to remedy the Court's blunder by drafting and ratifying the Eleventh Amendment.

The Eleventh Amendment confirmed that the Constitution was not meant to raise up any suits against the States that were anomalous and unheard of when the Constitution was adopted. Although the terms of that Amendment address only the specific provisions of the Constitution that had raised concerns during the ratification debates and formed the basis of the *Chisholm* decision, the natural inference from its speedy adoption is that the Constitution was understood, in light of its history and structure, to preserve the States' traditional immunity from private suits. We have often emphasized that the Amendment is rooted in a recognition that the States, although a union, maintain certain attributes of sovereignty, including sovereign immunity. In proposing the Amendment, Congress acted not to change but to restore the original constitutional design. The sovereign immunity of the States, we have said, neither derives from, nor is limited by, the terms of the Eleventh Amendment. . . .

3

Despite this historical evidence that interstate sovereign immunity is preserved in the constitutional design, Hyatt insists that such immunity exists only as a matter of comity and can be disregarded by the forum State. He reasons that, before the Constitution was ratified, the States had the power of fully independent nations to deny immunity to fellow sovereigns; thus, the States must retain that power today with respect to each other because nothing in the Constitution or formation of the Union altered that balance among the still-sovereign states. . . .

The problem with Hyatt's argument is that the Constitution affirmatively altered the relationships between the States, so that they no longer relate to each other solely as foreign sovereigns. Each State's equal dignity and sovereignty under the Constitution implies certain constitutional limitations on the sovereignty of all of its sister States. One such limitation is the inability of one State to hale another into its courts without the latter's consent. The Constitution does not merely allow States to afford each other immunity as a matter of comity; it embeds interstate sovereign immunity within the constitutional design. Numerous provisions reflect this reality.

To begin, Article I divests the States of the traditional diplomatic and military tools that foreign sovereigns possess. Specifically, the States can no longer prevent or remedy departures from customary international law because the Constitution deprives them of the independent power to lay imposts or duties on imports and exports, to enter into treaties or compacts, and to wage war.

Article IV also imposes duties on the States not required by international law. The Court's Full Faith and Credit Clause precedents, for example, demand that state-court judgments be accorded full effect in other States and preclude States from adopting any policy of hostility to the public Acts of other States. States must also afford citizens of each State "all Privileges and Immunities of Citizens in the several States" and honor extradition requests upon "Demand of the executive Authority of the State" from which the fugitive fled. Art. IV, § 2. Foreign sovereigns cannot demand these kinds of reciprocal responsibilities absent consent or compact. But the Constitution imposes them as part of its transformation of the States from a loose league of friendship into a perpetual Union based on the fundamental principle of *equal* sovereignty among the States.

The Constitution also reflects implicit alterations to the States' relationships with each other, confirming that they are no longer fully independent nations. For example, States may not supply rules of decision governing disputes implicating their conflicting rights. Thus, no State can apply its own law to interstate disputes over borders, water rights, or the interpretation of interstate compacts. The States would have had the raw power to apply their own law to such matters before they entered the Union, but the Constitution implicitly forbids that exercise of power because the interstate nature of the controversy makes it inappropriate for state law to control. Some subjects that were decided by pure political power before ratification now turn on federal rules of law.

Interstate sovereign immunity is similarly integral to the structure of the Constitution. Like a dispute over borders or water rights, a State's assertion of compulsory judicial process over another State involves a direct conflict between sovereigns. The Constitution implicitly strips States of any power they once had to refuse each other sovereign immunity, just as it denies them the power to resolve border disputes by political means. Interstate immunity, in other words, is implied as an essential component of federalism.

Hyatt argues that we should find no right to sovereign immunity in another State's courts because no constitutional provision explicitly grants that immunity. But this is precisely the type of ahistorical literalism that we have rejected when interpreting the scope of the States' sovereign immunity since the discredited decision in *Chisholm*. In light of our constitutional structure, the historical understanding of state immunity, and the swift enactment of the Eleventh Amendment after the Court departed from this understanding in *Chisholm*, it is not rational to suppose that the sovereign power should be dragged before a court. Indeed, the spirited historical debate over Article III courts and the immediate reaction to *Chisholm* make little sense if the Eleventh Amendment were the only source of sovereign immunity and private suits against the States could already be brought in partial, local tribunals. Nor would the Founders have objected so strenuously to a neutral federal forum for private suits against States if they were open to a State being sued in a different State's courts. Hyatt's view thus inverts the Founders' concerns about state-court parochialism.

Moreover, Hyatt's ahistorical literalism proves too much. There are many other constitutional doctrines that are not spelled out in the Constitution but are nevertheless implicit in its structure and supported by historical practice—including, for example, judicial review, intergovernmental tax immunity, executive privilege, executive immunity, and the President's removal power. Like these doctrines, the States' sovereign immunity is a historically rooted principle embedded in the text and structure of the Constitution. . . .

Nevada v. *Hall* is irreconcilable with our constitutional structure and with the historical evidence showing a widespread preratification understanding that States retained immunity from private suits, both in their own courts and in other courts. We therefore overrule that decision. Because the Board is thus immune from Hyatt's suit in Nevada's courts, the judgment of the Nevada Supreme Court is reversed, and the case is remanded for proceedings not inconsistent with this opinion.

Justice BREYER, with whom Justice GINSBURG, SOTOMAYOR, and KAGAN join, dissenting.

Can a private citizen sue one State in the courts of another? Normally the answer to this question is no, because the State where the suit is brought will choose to grant its sister States immunity. But the question here is whether the Federal Constitution *requires* each State to grant its sister States immunity, or whether the Constitution instead *permits* a State to grant or deny its sister States immunity as it chooses.

We answered that question 40 years ago in *Nevada* v. *Hall* (1979). The Court in *Hall* held that the Constitution took the permissive approach, leaving it up to each State to decide whether to grant or deny its sister States sovereign immunity. Today, the majority takes the contrary approach—the absolute approach—and overrules *Hall*. I can find no good reason to overrule *Hall*, however, and I consequently dissent. . . .

At the time of the founding, nations granted other nations sovereign immunity in their courts not as a matter of legal obligation but as a matter of choice, *i.e.*, of comity or grace or consent. Foreign sovereign immunity was a doctrine of implied consent by the territorial sovereign deriving from standards of public morality, fair dealing, reciprocal self-interest, and respect. Since customary international law made the matter one of choice, a nation could withdraw that sovereign immunity if it so chose. . . .

Drawing on the comparison to foreign nations, the Court in *Hall* emphasized that California had made a sovereign decision not to extend immunity to Nevada as a matter of comity.

Unless some constitutional rule required California to grant immunity that it had chosen to withhold, the Court had no power to disturb the judgment of the California courts. . . .

The Court in *Hall* next held that ratification of the Constitution did not alter principles of state sovereign immunity in any relevant respect. The Court concluded that express provisions of the Constitution—such as the Eleventh Amendment and the Full Faith and Credit Clause of Article IV—did not require States to accord each other sovereign immunity. And the Court held that nothing implicit in the Constitution treats States differently in respect to immunity than international law treats sovereign nations.

To the contrary, the Court in *Hall* observed that an express provision of the Constitution undermined the assertion that States were absolutely immune in each other's courts. Unlike suits brought against a State in the State's own courts, *Hall* noted, a suit against a State in the courts of a different State necessarily implicates the power and authority of both States. The defendant State has a sovereign interest in immunity from suit, while the forum State has a sovereign interest in defining the jurisdiction of its own courts. The Court in *Hall* therefore justified its decision in part by reference to the Tenth Amendment's reminder that powers not delegated to the Federal Government nor prohibited to the States are reserved to the States or to the people. Compelling States to grant immunity to their sister States would risk interfering with sovereign rights that the Tenth Amendment leaves to the States. . . .

The majority asserts that before ratification it was well settled that States were immune under both the common law and the law of nations. The majority thus maintains that States were exempt from suit in each other's courts.

But the question in *Hall* concerned the *basis* for that exemption. Did one sovereign have an absolute right to an exemption from the jurisdiction of the courts of another, or was that exemption a customary matter, a matter of consent that a sovereign might withdraw? As to that question, nothing in the majority's opinion casts doubt on *Hall*'s conclusion that States—like foreign nations—were accorded immunity as a matter of consent rather than absolute right. . . .

The majority next argues that the Constitution affirmatively altered the relationships between the States by giving them immunity that they did not possess when they were fully independent. The majority thus maintains that, whatever the nature of state immunity before ratification, the Constitution accorded States an absolute immunity that they did not previously possess.

The most obvious problem with this argument is that no provision of the Constitution gives States absolute immunity in each other's courts. The majority does not attempt to situate its newfound constitutional immunity in any provision of the Constitution itself. Instead, the majority maintains that a State's immunity in other States' courts is "implicit" in the Constitution, "embed[ded] . . . within the constitutional design," and reflected in "the plan of the Convention."

I agree with today's majority and the dissenters in *Hall* that the Constitution contains implicit guarantees as well as explicit ones. But, as I have previously noted, concepts like the "constitutional design" and "plan of the Convention" are highly abstract, making them difficult to apply"—at least absent support in considerations of history, of constitutional purpose, or of related consequence. Such concepts invite differing interpretations at least as much as do the Constitution's own broad liberty-protecting phrases such as "due process" and "liberty," and they suffer the additional disadvantage that they do not actually appear anywhere in the Constitution.

At any rate, I can find nothing in the "plan of the Convention" or elsewhere to suggest that the Constitution converted what had been the customary practice of extending immunity by consent into an absolute federal requirement that no State could withdraw. None of the majority's arguments indicates that the Constitution accomplished any such transformation. . . .

[W]here the Constitution alters the authority of States vis-à-vis other States, it tends to do so explicitly. The Import-Export Clause cited by the majority, for example, creates harmony among the States by preventing them from burdening commerce among themselves." The Full Faith and Credit Clause, also invoked by the majority, prohibits States from adopting a policy of hostility to the public Acts of another State. By contrast, the Constitution says nothing explicit about interstate sovereign immunity.

Nor does there seem to be any need to create implicit constitutional protections for States. As the history of this case shows, the Constitution's express provisions seem adequate to prohibit one State from treating its sister States unfairly—even if the State permits suits against its sister States in its courts. . . .

Why would the Framers, silently and without any evident reason, have transformed sovereign immunity from a permissive immunity predicated on comity and consent into an absolute immunity that States must accord one another? The Court in *Hall* could identify no such reason. Nor can I. . . .

I respectfully dissent.

United States Constitution

Amendment XIV.

Section 1. . . . No state shall make or enforce any law which shall abridge the privileges or immunities of citizens of the United States; nor shall any state deprive any person of life, liberty, or property, without due process of law; nor deny to any person within its jurisdiction the equal protection of the laws. . . .

Section 5. The Congress shall have power to enforce, by appropriate legislation, the provisions of this article.

Fitzpatrick v. Bitzer (1976)

In the 1972 Amendments to Title VII of the Civil Rights Act of 1964, Congress, acting under § 5 of the Fourteenth Amendment, authorized federal courts to award money damages in favor of a private individual against a state government found to have subjected that person to employment discrimination on the basis of "race, color, religion, sex, or national origin." The principal question presented by these cases is whether, as against the shield of sovereign immunity afforded the State by the Eleventh Amendment, Congress has the power to authorize Federal courts to enter such an award against the State as a means of enforcing the substantive guarantees of the Fourteenth Amendment. The Court of Appeals for the Second Circuit held that the effect of our decision in *Edelman* was to foreclose Congress's power. We granted certiorari to resolve this important constitutional question. We reverse.

I

Petitioners in No. 75-251 sued in the United States District Court for the District of Connecticut on behalf of all present and retired male employees of the State of Connecticut. Their amended complaint asserted, inter alia, that certain provisions in the State's statutory retirement benefit plan discriminated against them because of their sex, and therefore contravened Title VII. . . .

The District Court held that the Connecticut State Employees Retirement Act violated Title VII's prohibition against sex-based employment discrimination. It entered prospective injunctive relief in petitioners' favor against respondent state officials. Petitioners also sought an award of retroactive retirement benefits as compensation for losses caused by the State's discrimination, as well as a reasonable attorney's fee as part of the costs. But the District Court held that both would constitute recovery of money damages from the State's treasury, and were therefore precluded by the Eleventh Amendment and by this Court's decision in *Edelman*.

On petitioners' appeal, the Court of Appeals affirmed in part and reversed in part. . . . Notwithstanding this statutory authority, the Court of Appeals affirmed the District Court and held that under *Edelman* a private federal action for retroactive damages is not a constitutionally permissible method of enforcing Fourteenth Amendment rights. It reversed the District Court and remanded as to attorneys' fees, however, reasoning that such an award would have only an ancillary effect on the state treasury of the kind permitted under *Edelman*. . . .

II

.... As ratified by the States after the Civil War, [the Fourteenth] Amendment quite clearly contemplates limitations on [States'] authority.... The substantive provisions are by express terms directed at the States. Impressed upon them by those provisions are duties with respect to their treatment of private individuals. Standing behind the imperatives is Congress's power to "enforce" them "by appropriate legislation." [As we have stated]:

> The prohibitions of the Fourteenth Amendment are directed to the States, and they are to a degree restrictions of State power. It is these which Congress is empowered to enforce, and to enforce against State action, however put forth, whether that action be executive, legislative, or judicial. Such enforcement is no invasion of State sovereignty. No law can be, which the people of the States have, by the Constitution of the United States, empowered Congress to enact. It is said the selection of jurors for her courts and the administration of her laws belong to each State; that they are her rights. This is true in the general. But in exercising her rights, a State cannot disregard the limitations which the Federal Constitution has applied to her power. Her rights do not reach to that extent. Nor can she deny to the general government the right to exercise all its granted powers, though they may interfere with the full enjoyment of rights she would have if those powers had not been thus granted. Indeed, every addition of power to the general government involves a corresponding diminution of the governmental powers of the States. It is carved out of them. ... [T]he Constitution now expressly gives authority for congressional interference and compulsion in the cases embraced within the Fourteenth Amendment. It is but a limited authority, true, extending only to a single class of cases; but within its limits it is complete.

.... There can be no doubt that this line of cases has sanctioned intrusions by Congress, acting under the Civil War Amendments, into the judicial, executive, and legislative spheres of autonomy previously reserved to the States. The legislation considered in each case was grounded on the expansion of Congress's powers with the corresponding diminution of state sovereignty found to be intended by the Framers and made part of the Constitution upon the States' ratification of those Amendments ....

It is true that none of these previous cases presented the question of the relationship between the Eleventh Amendment and the enforcement power granted to Congress under § 5 of the Fourteenth Amendment. But we think that the Eleventh Amendment, and the principle of state sovereignty which it embodies, are necessarily limited by the enforcement provisions of § 5 of the Fourteenth Amendment. In that section Congress is expressly granted authority to enforce "by appropriate legislation" the substantive provisions of the Fourteenth

Amendment, which themselves embody significant limitations on state authority. When Congress acts pursuant to § 5, not only is it exercising legislative authority that is plenary within the terms of the constitutional grant, it is exercising that authority under one section of a constitutional Amendment whose other sections by their own terms embody limitations on state authority. We think that Congress may, in determining what is "appropriate legislation" for the purpose of enforcing the provisions of the Fourteenth Amendment, provide for private suits against States or state officials which are constitutionally impermissible in other contexts. . . .

Board of Trustees of the University of Alabama v. Garrett (2001)

Chief Justice REHNQUIST delivered the opinion of the Court.

We decide here whether employees of the State of Alabama may recover money damages by reason of the State's failure to comply with the provisions of Title I of the Americans with Disabilities Act of 1990. We hold that such suits are barred by the Eleventh Amendment.

The ADA prohibits certain employers, including the States, from discriminating against a qualified individual with a disability because of the disability of such individual in regard to job application procedures, the hiring, advancement, or discharge of employees, employee compensation, job training, and other terms, conditions, and privileges of employment. To this end, the Act requires employers to make reasonable accommodations to the known physical or mental limitations of an otherwise qualified individual with a disability who is an applicant or employee, unless the employer can demonstrate that the accommodation would impose an undue hardship on the operation of the employer's business.

The Act defines "disability" to include "(A) a physical or mental impairment that substantially limits one or more of the major life activities of such individual; (B) a record of such an impairment; or (C) being regarded as having such an impairment." A disabled individual is otherwise "qualified" if he or she, "with or without reasonable accommodation, can perform the essential functions of the employment position that such individual holds or desires."

Respondent Patricia Garrett, a registered nurse, was employed as the Director of Nursing, OB/Gyn/Neonatal Services, for the University of Alabama in Birmingham Hospital. In 1994, Garrett was diagnosed with breast cancer and subsequently underwent a lumpectomy, radiation treatment, and chemotherapy. Garrett's treatments required her to take substantial leave from work. Upon returning to work in July 1995, Garrett's supervisor informed Garrett that she would have to give up her Director position. Garrett then applied for and received a transfer to another, lower paying position as a nurse manager.

Respondent Milton Ash worked as a security officer for the Alabama Department of Youth Services (Department). Upon commencing this employment, Ash informed the Department that he suffered from chronic asthma and that his doctor recommended he avoid carbon monoxide and cigarette smoke, and Ash requested that the Department modify his duties to minimize his exposure to these substances. Ash was later diagnosed with sleep apnea and requested, again pursuant to his doctor's recommendation, that he be reassigned to daytime shifts to accommodate his condition. Ultimately, the Department granted none of the requested relief. Shortly after Ash filed a discrimination claim with the Equal Employment

Opportunity Commission, he noticed that his performance evaluations were lower than those he had received on previous occasions.

Garrett and Ash filed separate lawsuits in the District Court, both seeking money damages under the ADA. Petitioners moved for summary judgment, claiming that the ADA exceeds Congress's authority to abrogate the State's Eleventh Amendment immunity. In a single opinion disposing of both cases, the District Court agreed with petitioners' position and granted their motions for summary judgment. The cases were consolidated on appeal to the Eleventh Circuit. The Court of Appeals reversed, adhering to its intervening decision that the ADA validly abrogates the States' Eleventh Amendment immunity.

We granted certiorari to resolve a split among the Courts of Appeals on the question whether an individual may sue a State for money damages in federal court under the ADA.

I

. . . . Although by its terms the Amendment applies only to suits against a State by citizens of another State, our cases have extended the Amendment's applicability to suits by citizens against their own States. The ultimate guarantee of the Eleventh Amendment is that nonconsenting States may not be sued by private individuals in federal court.

We have recognized, however, that Congress may abrogate the States' Eleventh Amendment immunity when it both unequivocally intends to do so and acts pursuant to a valid grant of constitutional authority. The first of these requirements is not in dispute here. *See* 42 U.S.C. § 12202 ("A State shall not be immune under the eleventh amendment to the Constitution of the United States from an action in [a] Federal or State court of competent jurisdiction for a violation of this chapter."). The question, then, is whether Congress acted within its constitutional authority by subjecting the States to suits in federal court for money damages under the ADA.

Congress may not, of course, base its abrogation of the States' Eleventh Amendment immunity upon the powers enumerated in Article I. In *Fitzpatrick v. Bitzer*, however, we held that the Eleventh Amendment, and the principle of state sovereignty which it embodies, are necessarily limited by the enforcement provisions of § 5 of the Fourteenth Amendment. As a result, we concluded, Congress may subject nonconsenting States to suit in federal court when it does so pursuant to a valid exercise of its § 5 power. Our cases have adhered to this proposition. Accordingly, the ADA can apply to the States only to the extent that the statute is appropriate § 5 legislation.

. . . . Section 5 of the Fourteenth Amendment grants Congress the power to enforce the substantive guarantees contained in § 1 by enacting "appropriate legislation." Congress is not limited to mere legislative repetition of this Court's constitutional jurisprudence. Rather, Congress's power "to enforce" the Amendment includes the authority both to remedy and to deter violation of rights guaranteed thereunder by prohibiting a somewhat broader swath of conduct, including that which is not itself forbidden by the Amendment's text.

. . . [I]t is the responsibility of this Court, not Congress, to define the substance of constitutional guarantees. Accordingly, § 5 legislation reaching beyond the scope of § 1's actual guarantees must exhibit "congruence and proportionality" between the injury to be prevented or remedied and the means adopted to that end.

II

The first step in applying these now familiar principles is to identify with some precision the scope of the constitutional right at issue. Here, that inquiry requires us to examine the limitations § 1 of the Fourteenth Amendment places upon States' treatment of the disabled. . . .

States are not required by the Fourteenth Amendment to make special accommodations for the disabled, so long as their actions toward such individuals are rational. They could quite hardheadedly—and perhaps hardheartedly—hold to job-qualification requirements which do not make allowance for the disabled. If special accommodations for the disabled are to be required, they have to come from positive law and not through the Equal Protection Clause.

III

Once we have determined the metes and bounds of the constitutional right in question, we examine whether Congress identified a history and pattern of unconstitutional employment discrimination by the States against the disabled. Just as § 1 of the Fourteenth Amendment applies only to actions committed "under color of state law," Congress's § 5 authority is appropriately exercised only in response to state transgressions. The legislative record of the ADA, however, simply fails to show that Congress did in fact identify a pattern of irrational state discrimination in employment against the disabled.

Respondents contend that the inquiry as to unconstitutional discrimination should extend not only to States themselves, but to units of local governments, such as cities and counties. All of these, they say, are "state actors" for purposes of the Fourteenth Amendment. This is quite true, but the Eleventh Amendment does not extend its immunity to units of local government. These entities are subject to private claims for damages under the ADA without Congress's ever having to rely on § 5 of the Fourteenth Amendment to render them so. It would make no sense to consider constitutional violations on their part, as well as by the States themselves, when only the States are the beneficiaries of the Eleventh Amendment.

Congress made a general finding in the ADA that historically, society has tended to isolate and segregate individuals with disabilities, and, despite some improvements, such forms of discrimination against individuals with disabilities continue to be a serious and pervasive social problem. The record assembled by Congress includes many instances to support such a finding. But the great majority of these incidents do not deal with the activities of States.

Respondents in their brief cite half a dozen examples from the record that did involve States. . . .[6]

> [6] The record does show that some States, adopting the tenets of the eugenics movement of the early part of this century, required extreme measures such as sterilization of persons suffering from hereditary mental disease. These laws were upheld against constitutional attack 70 years ago in *Buck v. Bell*. But there is no indication that any State had persisted in requiring such harsh measures as of 1990 when the ADA was adopted.

Several of these incidents undoubtedly evidence an unwillingness on the part of state officials to make the sort of accommodations for the disabled required by the ADA. . . . [E]ven if it were to be determined that each incident upon fuller examination showed unconstitutional action on the part of the State, these incidents taken together fall far short of even suggesting the pattern of unconstitutional discrimination on which § 5 legislation must be based. Congress, in enacting the ADA, found that some 43,000,000 Americans have one or more physical or mental disabilities. In 1990, the States alone employed more than 4.5 million people. It is telling, we think, that given these large numbers, Congress assembled only such minimal evidence of unconstitutional state discrimination in employment against the disabled.

Justice Breyer maintains that Congress applied Title I of the ADA to the States in response to a host of incidents representing unconstitutional state discrimination in employment against persons with disabilities. A close review of the relevant materials, however, undercuts that conclusion. Justice Breyer's Appendix C consists not of legislative findings, but of unexamined, anecdotal accounts of adverse, disparate treatment by state officials. Of course, as we have already explained, adverse, disparate treatment often does not amount to a constitutional violation where rational-basis scrutiny applies. . . . And, had Congress truly understood this information as reflecting a pattern of unconstitutional behavior by the States, one would expect some mention of that conclusion in the Act's legislative findings. There is none. . . .

Even were it possible to squeeze out of these examples a pattern of unconstitutional discrimination by the States, the rights and remedies created by the ADA against the States would raise . . . concerns as to congruence and proportionality . . . . For example, whereas it would be entirely rational (and therefore constitutional) for a state employer to conserve scarce financial resources by hiring employees who are able to use existing facilities, the ADA requires employers to make existing facilities used by employees readily accessible to and usable by individuals with disabilities. . . .

Congress is the final authority as to desirable public policy, but in order to authorize private individuals to recover money damages against the States, there must be a pattern of discrimination by the States which violates the Fourteenth Amendment, and the remedy imposed by Congress must be congruent and proportional to the targeted violation. Those requirements are not met here, and to uphold the Act's application to the States would allow Congress to rewrite the Fourteenth Amendment law . . . .[9]

> [9] Our holding here that Congress did not validly abrogate the States' sovereign immunity from suit by private individuals for money damages under Title I does not mean that persons with disabilities have no federal recourse against discrimination. Title I of the ADA still prescribes standards applicable to the States. Those standards can be enforced by the United States in actions for money damages, as well as by private individuals in actions for injunctive relief under *Ex parte Young*. In addition, state laws protecting the rights of persons with disabilities in employment and other aspects of life provide independent avenues of redress.

Section 5 does not so broadly enlarge congressional authority. The judgment of the Court of Appeals is therefore *Reversed.*

Justice KENNEDY, with whom Justice O'CONNOR joins, concurring.

. . . . One of the undoubted achievements of statutes designed to assist those with impairments is that citizens have an incentive, flowing from a legal duty, to develop a better understanding, a more decent perspective, for accepting persons with impairments or disabilities into the larger society. The law works this way because the law can be a teacher. So I do not doubt that the Americans with Disabilities Act of 1990 will be a milestone on the path to a more decent, tolerant, progressive society.

It is a question of quite a different order, however, to say that the States in their official capacities, the States as governmental entities, must be held in violation of the Constitution on the assumption that they embody the misconceived or malicious perceptions of some of their citizens. It is a most serious charge to say a State has engaged in a pattern or practice designed to deny its citizens the equal protection of the laws, particularly where the accusation is based not on hostility but instead on the failure to act or the omission to remedy. States can, and do, stand apart from the citizenry. States act as neutral entities, ready to take instruction and to enact laws when their citizens so demand. The failure of a State to revise policies now seen as incorrect under a new understanding of proper policy does not always constitute the purposeful and intentional action required to make out a violation of the Equal Protection Clause.

For the reasons explained by the Court, an equal protection violation has not been shown with respect to the several States in this case. If the States had been transgressing the Fourteenth Amendment by their mistreatment or lack of concern for those with impairments, one would have expected to find in decisions of the courts of the States and also the courts of the United States extensive litigation and discussion of the constitutional violations. This confirming judicial documentation does not exist. That there is a new awareness, a new consciousness, a new commitment to better treatment of those disadvantaged by mental or physical impairments does not establish that an absence of state statutory correctives was a constitutional violation. . . .

Justice BREYER, with whom Justices STEVENS, SOUTER, and GINSBURG join, dissenting.

Reviewing the congressional record as if it were an administrative agency record, the Court holds the statutory provision before us unconstitutional. . . . Section 5, however, grants Congress the power to enforce, by appropriate legislation, the Fourteenth Amendment's equal protection guarantee. As the Court recognizes, state discrimination in employment against persons with disabilities might run afoul of the Equal Protection Clause where there is no rational relationship between the disparity of treatment and some legitimate governmental purpose. In my view, Congress reasonably could have concluded that the remedy before us constitutes an "appropriate" way to enforce this basic equal protection requirement. And that is all the Constitution requires.

I

The Court says that its primary problem with this statutory provision is one of legislative evidence. It says that Congress assembled only minimal evidence of unconstitutional state discrimination in employment. In fact, Congress compiled a vast legislative record documenting "massive, society-wide discrimination" against persons with disabilities. In addition to the information presented at 13 congressional hearings, and its own prior experience gathered over 40 years during which it contemplated and enacted considerable similar legislation, Congress created a special task force to assess the need for comprehensive legislation. That task force held hearings in every State, attended by more than 30,000 people, including thousands who had experienced discrimination first hand. The task force hearings, Congress's own hearings, and an analysis of census data, national polls, and other studies led Congress to conclude that people with disabilities, as a group, occupy an inferior status in our society, and are severely disadvantaged socially, vocationally, economically, and educationally. As to employment, Congress found that two-thirds of all disabled Americans between the age of 16 and 64 were not working at all, even though a large majority wanted to, and were able to, work productively. And Congress found that this discrimination flowed in significant part from stereotypic assumptions as well as purposeful unequal treatment.

The powerful evidence of discriminatory treatment throughout society in general, including discrimination by private persons and local governments, implicates state governments as well, for state agencies form part of that same larger society. There is no particular reason to believe that they are immune from the stereotypic assumptions and pattern of purposeful unequal treatment that Congress found prevalent. The Court claims that it makes no sense to take into consideration constitutional violations committed by local governments. But the substantive obligation that the Equal Protection Clause creates applies to state and local governmental entities alike. Local governments often work closely with, and under the supervision of, state officials, and in general, state and local government employers are similarly situated. . . .

In any event, there is no need to rest solely upon evidence of discrimination by local governments or general societal discrimination. There are roughly 300 examples of discrimination by state governments themselves in the legislative record. I fail to see how this evidence falls far short of even suggesting the pattern of unconstitutional discrimination on which § 5 legislation must be based. . . .

In reviewing § 5 legislation, we have never required the sort of extensive investigation of each piece of evidence that the Court appears to contemplate. Nor has the Court traditionally required Congress to make findings as to state discrimination, or to break down the record evidence, category by category.

. . . . A complete listing of the hundreds of examples of discrimination by state and local governments that were submitted to the task force is set forth in Appendix C. Congress could have reasonably believed that these examples represented signs of a widespread problem of unconstitutional discrimination.

II

The Court's failure to find sufficient evidentiary support may well rest upon its decision to hold Congress to a strict, judicially created evidentiary standard, particularly in respect to lack of justification. . . . Imposing this special "burden" upon Congress, the Court fails to find in the legislative record sufficient indication that Congress has negatived the presumption that state action is rationally related to a legitimate objective. The problem with the Court's approach is that neither the "burden of proof" that favors States nor any other rule of restraint applicable to *judges* applies to *Congress* when it exercises its § 5 power. . . .

I recognize nonetheless that this statute imposes a burden upon States in that it removes their Eleventh Amendment protection from suit, thereby subjecting them to potential monetary liability. Rules for interpreting § 5 that would provide States with special protection, however, run counter to the very object of the Fourteenth Amendment. By its terms, that Amendment prohibits *States* from denying their citizens equal protection of the laws. Hence principles of federalism that might otherwise be an obstacle to congressional authority are necessarily overridden by the power to enforce the Civil War Amendments by appropriate legislation. Those Amendments were specifically designed as an expansion of federal power and an intrusion on state sovereignty. And, ironically, the greater the obstacle the Eleventh Amendment poses to the creation by Congress of the kind of remedy at issue here—the decentralized remedy of private damages actions—the more Congress, seeking to cure important national problems, such as the problem of disability discrimination before us, will have to rely on more uniform remedies, such as federal standards and court injunctions, which are sometimes draconian and typically more intrusive. For these reasons, I doubt that today's decision serves any constitutionally based federalism interest. . . .

For the reasons stated, I respectfully dissent.

Tennessee v. Lane (2004)

Justice STEVENS delivered the opinion of the Court.

Title II of the Americans with Disabilities Act of 1990 (ADA or Act) provides that "no qualified individual with a disability shall, by reason of such disability, be excluded from participation in or be denied the benefits of the services, programs or activities of a public entity, or be subjected to discrimination by any such entity." The question presented in this case is whether Title II exceeds Congress's power under § 5 of the Fourteenth Amendment.

I

In August 1998, respondents George Lane and Beverly Jones filed this action against the State of Tennessee and a number of Tennessee counties, alleging past and ongoing violations of Title II. Respondents, both of whom are paraplegics who use wheelchairs for mobility, claimed that they were denied access to, and the services of, the state court system by reason of their disabilities. Lane alleged that he was compelled to appear to answer a set of criminal charges on the second floor of a county courthouse that had no elevator. At his first appearance, Lane crawled up two flights of stairs to get to the courtroom. When Lane returned to the courthouse for a hearing, he refused to crawl again or to be carried by officers to the courtroom; he consequently was arrested and jailed for failure to appear. Jones, a certified court reporter, alleged that she has not been able to gain access to a number of county courthouses, and, as a result, has lost both work and an opportunity to participate in the judicial process. Respondents sought damages and equitable relief.

The State moved to dismiss the suit on the ground that it was barred by the Eleventh Amendment. The District Court denied the motion without opinion, and the State appealed. The United States intervened to defend Title II's abrogation of the States' Eleventh Amendment immunity. . . . [A] panel of the Court of Appeals entered an order affirming the District Court's denial of the State's motion to dismiss in this case. . . . We granted certiorari and now affirm.

II

The ADA was passed by large majorities in both Houses of Congress after decades of deliberation and investigation into the need for comprehensive legislation to address discrimination against persons with disabilities. In the years immediately preceding the ADA's enactment, Congress held 13 hearings and created a special task force that gathered evidence from every State in the Union. The conclusions Congress drew from this evidence are set forth in the task force and Committee Reports, described in lengthy legislative hearings, and summarized in the preamble to the statute. Central among these conclusions was Congress's finding that

> individuals with disabilities are a discrete and insular minority who have been faced with restrictions and limitations, subjected to a history of purposeful unequal treatment, and relegated to a position of political powerlessness in our society, based on characteristics that are beyond the control of such individuals and resulting from stereotypic assumptions not truly indicative of the individual ability of such individuals to participate in, and contribute to, society.

Invoking the sweep of congressional authority, including the power to enforce the fourteenth amendment and to regulate commerce, the ADA is designed to provide a clear and comprehensive national mandate for the elimination of discrimination against individuals with disabilities. It forbids discrimination against persons with disabilities in three major areas of public life: employment, which is covered by Title I of the statute; public services, programs, and activities, which are the subject of Title II; and public accommodations, which are covered by Title III.

Title II prohibits any public entity from discriminating against "qualified" persons with disabilities in the provision or operation of public services, programs, or activities. The Act defines the term "public entity" to include state and local governments, as well as their agencies and instrumentalities. Persons with disabilities are "qualified" if they, "with or without reasonable modifications to rules, policies, or practices, the removal of architectural, communication, or transportation barriers, or the provision of auxiliary aids and services, mee[t] the essential eligibility requirements for the receipt of services or the participation in programs or activities provided by a public entity." Title II's enforcement provision incorporates by reference § 505 of the Rehabilitation Act of 1973, which authorizes private citizens to bring suits for money damages.

III

.... In *Fitzpatrick v. Bitzer*, we held that Congress can abrogate a State's sovereign immunity when it does so pursuant to a valid exercise of its power under § 5 of the Fourteenth Amendment to enforce the substantive guarantees of that Amendment. This enforcement power, as we have often acknowledged, is a broad power indeed. It includes the authority both to remedy and to deter violation of rights guaranteed by the Fourteenth Amendment by prohibiting a somewhat broader swath of conduct, including that which is not itself forbidden by the Amendment's text. We have thus repeatedly affirmed that Congress may enact so-called prophylactic legislation that proscribes facially constitutional conduct, in order to prevent and deter unconstitutional conduct. The most recent affirmation of the breadth of

Congress's § 5 power came in *Hibbs*, in which we considered whether a male state employee could recover money damages against the State for its failure to comply with the family-care leave provision of the Family and Medical Leave Act of 1993 (FMLA). We upheld the FMLA as a valid exercise of Congress's § 5 power to combat unconstitutional sex discrimination, even though there was no suggestion that the State's leave policy was adopted or applied with a discriminatory purpose that would render it unconstitutional . . . . When Congress seeks to remedy or prevent unconstitutional discrimination, § 5 authorizes it to enact prophylactic legislation proscribing practices that are discriminatory in effect, if not in intent, to carry out the basic objectives of the Equal Protection Clause.

Congress's § 5 power is not, however, unlimited. . . . Section 5 legislation is valid if it exhibits a congruence and proportionality between the injury to be prevented or remedied and the means adopted to that end. . . . Applying [this] test in *Garrett*, we concluded that Title I of the ADA was not a valid exercise of Congress's § 5 power to enforce the Fourteenth Amendment's prohibition on unconstitutional disability discrimination in public employment. . . . Congress's exercise of its prophylactic § 5 power was unsupported by a relevant history and pattern of constitutional violations. Although the dissent pointed out that Congress had before it a great deal of evidence of discrimination by the States against persons with disabilities, the Court's opinion noted that the "overwhelming majority" of that evidence related to the provision of public services and public accommodations, which areas are addressed in Titles II and III, rather than Title I. We also noted that neither the ADA's legislative findings nor its legislative history reflected a concern that the States had been engaging in a pattern of unconstitutional employment discrimination. We emphasized that the House and Senate Committee Reports on the ADA focused on discrimination in *employment in the private sector* and made no mention of discrimination in public employment. Finally, we concluded that Title I's broad remedial scheme was insufficiently targeted to remedy or prevent unconstitutional discrimination in public employment. Taken together, the historical record and the broad sweep of the statute suggested that Title I's true aim was not so much to enforce the Fourteenth Amendment's prohibitions against disability discrimination in public employment as it was to "rewrite" this Court's Fourteenth Amendment jurisprudence.

In view of the significant differences between Titles I and II, however, *Garrett* left open the question whether Title II is a valid exercise of Congress's § 5 enforcement power. It is to that question that we now turn.

IV

. . . . [C]lassifications based on disability violate [the Equal Protection Clause] if they lack a rational relationship to a legitimate governmental purpose. Title II, like Title I, seeks to enforce this prohibition on irrational disability discrimination. But it also seeks to enforce a variety of other basic constitutional guarantees, infringements of which are subject to more searching judicial review. These rights include some, like the right of access to the courts at issue in this case, that are protected by the Due Process Clause of the Fourteenth Amendment. The Due Process Clause and the Confrontation Clause of the Sixth Amendment, as applied to the States via the Fourteenth Amendment, both guarantee to a criminal defendant such as respondent Lane the right to be present at all stages of the trial where his absence might frustrate the fairness of the proceedings. The Due Process Clause also requires the States to afford certain civil litigants a meaningful opportunity to be heard by removing obstacles to their full participation in judicial proceedings. We have held that the Sixth Amendment guarantees to criminal defendants the right to trial by a jury composed of a fair cross section of the community, noting that the exclusion of identifiable segments playing major roles in the community cannot be squared with the constitutional concept of jury trial. And, finally, we have recognized that members of the public have a right of access to criminal proceedings secured by the First Amendment.

Whether Title II validly enforces these constitutional rights is a question that must be judged with reference to the historical experience which it reflects. While § 5 authorizes Congress to enact reasonably prophylactic remedial legislation, the appropriateness of the remedy depends on the gravity of the harm it seeks to prevent. . . . It is not difficult to perceive the harm that Title II is designed to address. Congress enacted Title II against a backdrop of pervasive unequal treatment in the administration of state services and programs, including systematic deprivations of fundamental rights. For example, as of 1979, most States categorically disqualified "idiots" from voting, without regard to individual capacity. . . . Similarly, a number of States have prohibited and continue to prohibit persons with disabilities from engaging in activities such as marrying and serving as jurors. The historical experience that Title II reflects is also documented in this Court's cases, which have identified unconstitutional treatment of disabled persons by state agencies in a variety of settings, including unjustified commitment, the abuse and neglect of persons committed to state mental health hospitals, and irrational discrimination in zoning decisions. The decisions of other courts, too, document a pattern of unequal treatment in the administration of a wide range of public services, programs, and activities, including the penal system, public education, and voting. Notably, these decisions also demonstrate a pattern of unconstitutional treatment in the administration of justice.

This pattern of disability discrimination persisted despite several federal and state legislative efforts to address it. In the deliberations that led up to the enactment of the ADA, Congress identified important shortcomings in existing laws that rendered them inadequate to address the pervasive problems of discrimination that people with disabilities are facing. It also uncovered further evidence of those shortcomings, in the form of hundreds of examples of unequal treatment of persons with disabilities by States and their political subdivisions. As the Court's opinion in *Garrett* observed, the "overwhelming majority" of these examples concerned discrimination in the administration of public programs and services.

With respect to the particular services at issue in this case, Congress learned that many individuals, in many States across the country, were being excluded from courthouses and court proceedings by reason of their disabilities. A report before Congress showed that some 76% of public services and programs housed in state-owned buildings were inaccessible to and unusable by persons with disabilities, even taking into account the possibility that the services and programs might be restructured or relocated to other parts of the buildings. Congress itself heard testimony from persons with disabilities who described the physical inaccessibility of local courthouses. And its appointed task force heard numerous examples of the exclusion of persons with disabilities from state judicial services and programs, including exclusion of persons with visual impairments and hearing impairments from jury service, failure of state and local governments to provide interpretive services for the hearing impaired, failure to permit the testimony of adults with developmental disabilities in abuse cases, and failure to make courtrooms accessible to witnesses with physical disabilities.

Given the sheer volume of evidence demonstrating the nature and extent of unconstitutional discrimination against persons with disabilities in the provision of public services, the dissent's contention that the record is insufficient to justify Congress's exercise of its prophylactic power is puzzling, to say the least. Just last Term in *Hibbs*, we approved the family-care leave provision of the FMLA as valid § 5 legislation based primarily on evidence of disparate provision of parenting leave, little of which concerned unconstitutional state conduct. . . . Title II is aimed at the enforcement of a variety of basic rights, including the right of access to the courts at issue in this case, that call for a standard of judicial review at least as searching, and in some cases more searching, than the standard that applies to sex-based classifications. And in any event, the record of constitutional violations in this case—including judicial findings of unconstitutional state action, and statistical, legislative, and anecdotal evidence of the widespread exclusion of persons with disabilities from the enjoyment of public services—far exceeds the record in *Hibbs*.

The conclusion that Congress drew from this body of evidence is set forth in the text of the ADA itself: "Discrimination against individuals with disabilities persists in such critical areas as education, transportation, communication, recreation, institutionalization, health services, voting, and *access to public services*." This finding, together with the extensive record of disability discrimination that underlies it, makes clear beyond peradventure that inadequate provision of public services and access to public facilities was an appropriate subject for prophylactic legislation.

V

The only question that remains is whether Title II is an appropriate response to this history and pattern of unequal treatment. At the outset, we must determine the scope of that inquiry. Title II—unlike RFRA, the Patent Remedy Act, and the other statutes we have reviewed for validity under § 5—reaches a wide array of official conduct in an effort to enforce an equally wide array of constitutional guarantees. Petitioner urges us both to examine the broad range of Title II's applications all at once, and to treat that breadth as a mark of the law's invalidity. According to petitioner, the fact that Title II applies not only to public education and voting-booth access but also to seating at state-owned hockey rinks indicates that Title II is not appropriately tailored to serve its objectives. But nothing in our case law requires us to consider Title II, with its wide variety of applications, as an undifferentiated whole. Whatever might be said about Title II's other applications, the question presented in this case is not whether Congress can validly subject the States to private suits for money damages for failing to provide reasonable access to hockey rinks, or even to voting booths, but whether Congress had the power under § 5 to enforce the constitutional right of access to the courts. Because we find that Title II unquestionably is valid § 5 legislation as it applies to the class of cases implicating the accessibility of judicial services, we need go no further.

Congress's chosen remedy for the pattern of exclusion and discrimination described above, Title II's requirement of program accessibility, is congruent and proportional to its object of enforcing the right of access to the courts. The unequal treatment of disabled persons in the administration of judicial services has a long history, and has persisted despite several legislative efforts to remedy the problem of disability discrimination. Faced with considerable evidence of the shortcomings of previous legislative responses, Congress was justified in concluding that this difficult and intractable problem warranted added prophylactic measures in response.

The remedy Congress chose is nevertheless a limited one. Recognizing that failure to accommodate persons with disabilities will often have the same practical effect as outright exclusion, Congress required the States to take reasonable measures to remove architectural and other barriers to accessibility. But Title II does not require States to employ any and all means to make judicial services accessible to persons with disabilities, and it does not require States to compromise their essential eligibility criteria for public programs. It requires only "reasonable modifications" that would not fundamentally alter the nature of the service provided, and only when the individual seeking modification is otherwise eligible for the service. As Title II's implementing regulations make clear, the reasonable modification requirement can be satisfied in a number of ways. In the case of facilities built or altered after 1992, the regulations require compliance with specific architectural accessibility standards. But in the case of older facilities, for which structural change is likely to be more difficult, a public entity may comply with Title II by adopting a variety of less costly measures, including relocating services to alternative, accessible sites and assigning aides to assist persons with disabilities in accessing services. Only if these measures are ineffective in achieving accessibility is the public entity required to make reasonable structural changes. And in no event is the entity required to undertake measures that would impose an undue financial or administrative burden, threaten historic preservation interests, or effect a fundamental alteration in the nature of the service.

This duty to accommodate is perfectly consistent with the well-established due process principle that, within the limits of practicability, a State must afford to all individuals a meaningful opportunity to be heard in its courts. . . . Judged against this backdrop, Title II's affirmative obligation to accommodate persons with disabilities in the administration of justice cannot be said to be so out of proportion to a supposed remedial or preventive object that it cannot be understood as responsive to, or designed to prevent, unconstitutional behavior. It is, rather, a reasonable prophylactic measure, reasonably targeted to a legitimate end.

For these reasons, we conclude that Title II, as it applies to the class of cases implicating the fundamental right of access to the courts, constitutes a valid exercise of Congress's § 5 authority to enforce the guarantees of the Fourteenth Amendment. The judgment of the Court of Appeals is therefore affirmed.

Chief Justice REHNQUIST, with whom Justice KENNEDY and Justice THOMAS join, dissenting.

. . . . In this case, the task of identifying the scope of the relevant constitutional protection is more difficult because Title II purports to enforce a panoply of constitutional rights of disabled persons: not only the equal protection right against irrational discrimination, but also certain rights protected by the Due Process Clause. However, because the Court ultimately upholds Title II as it applies to the class of cases implicating the fundamental right of access to the courts, the proper inquiry focuses on the scope of those due process rights. The Court cites four access-to-the-courts rights that Title II purportedly enforces: (1) the right of the criminal defendant to be present at all critical stages of the trial, (2) the right of litigants to have a "meaningful opportunity to be heard" in judicial proceedings, (3) the right of the criminal defendant to trial by a jury composed of a fair cross section of the community, and (4) the public right of access to criminal proceedings.

Having traced the metes and bounds of the constitutional rights at issue, the next step in the congruence-and-proportionality inquiry requires us to examine whether Congress identified a history and pattern of violations of these constitutional rights by the States with respect to the disabled. This step is crucial to determining whether Title II is a legitimate attempt to remedy or prevent actual constitutional violations by the States or an illegitimate attempt to rewrite the constitutional provisions it purports to enforce. Indeed, Congress's § 5 authority is appropriately exercised *only* in response to state transgressions. But the majority identifies nothing in the legislative record that shows Congress was responding to widespread violations of the due process rights of disabled persons.

Rather than limiting its discussion of constitutional violations to the due process rights on which it ultimately relies, the majority sets out on a wide-ranging account of societal discrimination against the disabled. This digression recounts historical discrimination against the disabled through institutionalization laws, restrictions on marriage, voting, and public education, conditions in mental hospitals, and various other forms of unequal treatment in the administration of public programs and services. Some of this evidence would be relevant if the Court were considering the constitutionality of the statute as a whole; but the Court rejects that approach in favor of a narrower as-applied inquiry. We discounted much the same type of outdated, generalized evidence in *Garrett* as unsupportive of Title I's ban on employment discrimination. The evidence here is likewise irrelevant to Title II's purported enforcement of due process access-to-the-courts rights.

Even if it were proper to consider this broader category of evidence, much of it does not concern *unconstitutional* action by the *States*. The bulk of the Court's evidence concerns discrimination by nonstate governments, rather than the States themselves. We have repeatedly held that such evidence is irrelevant to the inquiry whether Congress has validly abrogated Eleventh Amendment immunity, a privilege enjoyed only by the sovereign States. Moreover, the majority today cites the same congressional task force evidence we rejected in *Garrett*. As in *Garrett*, this unexamined, anecdotal evidence does not suffice. Most of the brief anecdotes do not involve States at all, and those that do are not sufficiently detailed to determine whether the instances of unequal treatment were irrational, and thus unconstitutional under our decision in *Cleburne*. Therefore, even outside the access to the courts context, the Court identifies few, if any, constitutional violations perpetrated by the States against disabled persons.

With respect to the due process access to the courts rights on which the Court ultimately relies, Congress's failure to identify a pattern of actual constitutional violations by the States is even more striking. Indeed, there is *nothing* in the legislative record or statutory findings to indicate that disabled persons were systematically denied the right to be present at criminal trials, denied the meaningful opportunity to be heard in civil cases, unconstitutionally excluded from jury service, or denied the right to attend criminal trials.[4]

[4] Certainly, respondents Lane and Jones were not denied these constitutional rights. The majority admits that Lane was able to attend the initial hearing of his criminal trial. Lane was arrested for failing to appear at his second hearing only after he refused assistance from officers dispatched by the court to help him to the courtroom. The court conducted a preliminary hearing in the first-floor library to accommodate Lane's disability and later offered to move all further proceedings in the case to a handicapped-accessible courthouse in a nearby town. In light of these facts, it can hardly be said that the State violated Lane's right to be present at his trial; indeed, it made affirmative attempts to secure that right. Respondent Jones, a disabled court reporter, does not seriously contend that she suffered a constitutional injury.

. . . . For the foregoing reasons, I respectfully dissent.

Justice SCALIA, dissenting.

. . . . I yield to the lessons of experience. The "congruence and proportionality" standard, like all such flabby tests, is a standing invitation to judicial arbitrariness and policy-driven decisionmaking. Worse still, it casts this Court in the role of Congress's taskmaster. Under it, the courts (and ultimately this Court) must regularly check Congress's homework to make sure that it has identified sufficient constitutional violations to make its remedy congruent and proportional. As a general matter, we are ill advised to adopt or adhere to constitutional rules that bring us into constant conflict with a coequal branch of Government. And when conflict is unavoidable, we should not come to do battle with the United States Congress armed only with a test ("congruence and proportionality") that has no demonstrable basis in the text of the Constitution and cannot objectively be shown to have been met or failed. As I wrote for the Court in an earlier case, low walls and vague distinctions will not be judicially defensible in the heat of interbranch conflict.

I would replace "congruence and proportionality" with another test—one that provides a clear, enforceable limitation supported by the text of § 5. Section 5 grants Congress the power "to *enforce*, by appropriate legislation," the other provisions of the Fourteenth Amendment. . . . [O]ne does not, within any normal meaning of the term, "enforce" a prohibition by issuing a still broader prohibition directed to the same end. One does not, for example, "enforce" a 55-mile-per-hour speed limit by imposing a 45-mile-per-hour speed limit—even though that is indeed directed to the same end of automotive safety and will undoubtedly result in many fewer violations of the 55-mile-per-hour limit. And one does not "enforce" the right of access to the courts at issue in this case by requiring that disabled persons be provided access to *all* of the services, programs, or activities furnished or conducted by the State. That is simply not what the power to enforce means—or ever meant. . . . Nothing in § 5 allows Congress to go *beyond* the provisions of the Fourteenth Amendment to proscribe, prevent, or remedy conduct that does not *itself* violate any provision of the Fourteenth Amendment. So-called prophylactic legislation is reinforcement rather than enforcement. . . .

[P]rincipally for reasons of *stare decisis*, I shall henceforth [allow prophylactic legislation] designed to remedy racial discrimination by the States. I would not, however, ... subject to "congruence and proportionality" analysis congressional action under § 5 that is *not* directed to racial discrimination. Rather, I shall give full effect to that action when it consists of "enforcement" of the provisions of the Fourteenth Amendment, within the broad but not unlimited meaning of that term I have described above. When it goes beyond enforcement to prophylaxis, however, I shall consider it ultra vires. The present legislation is plainly of the latter sort. . . .

Federal Review of State Decisions

Introduction

The Constitution grants the Supreme Court appellate jurisdiction but does not specify the tribunals it can review. Early on, Congress provided, and the Court upheld, appellate jurisdiction over state-court decisions. This review implications considerations of federalism and federal supremacy. It also expands the federal docket. In certain specific kinds of cases, Congress has provided the federal district courts with appellate power, but it has not assigned to the federal district courts general appellate review over state-court judgments. As you consider the regime of federal-court review of state-court decisions, consider the following:

- How have Congress and the Court balanced the need for the supremacy and uniformity of federal law with the independence and respect for state courts?

- What policies animate the balance struck, and is the balance workable?

- Why has Congress not provided the federal district courts with general appellate-review power over state courts?

- How do principles of preclusion factor into federal review?

United States Constitution

Article III, section 1. The judicial power of the United States, shall be vested in one Supreme Court, and in such inferior courts as the Congress may from time to time ordain and establish. . . .

Article III, section 2. . . . . [T]he Supreme Court shall have appellate jurisdiction, both as to law and fact, with such exceptions, and under such regulations as the Congress shall make.

United States Code

28 U.S.C. § 1257(a). Final judgments or decrees rendered by the highest court of a State in which a decision could be had, may be reviewed by the Supreme Court by writ of certiorari where the validity of a treaty or statute of the United States is drawn in question or where the validity of a statute of any State is drawn in question on the ground of its being repugnant to the Constitution, treaties, or laws of the United States, or where any title, right, privilege, or immunity is specially set up or claimed under the Constitution or the treaties or statutes of, or any commission held or authority exercised under, the United States.

28 U.S.C. § 1738. The records and judicial proceedings of any court of any . . . State, Territory or Possession, or copies thereof . . . . shall have the same full faith and credit in every court within the United States and its Territories and Possessions as they have by law or usage in the courts of such State, Territory or Possession from which they are taken.

Martin v. Hunter's Lessee (1816)

. . . . This is a writ of error from the court of appeals of Virginia, founded upon the refusal of that court to obey the mandate of this court, requiring the judgment rendered in this very cause, at February term, 1813, to be carried into due execution. The following is the judgment of the court of appeals rendered on the mandate: "The court is unanimously of opinion, that the appellate power of the supreme court of the United States does not extend to this court, under a sound construction of the constitution of the United States . . . ."

The questions involved in this judgment are of great importance and delicacy. Perhaps it is not too much to affirm, that, upon their right decision, rest some of the most solid principles which have hitherto been supposed to sustain and protect the constitution itself. The great respectability, too, of the court whose decisions we are called upon to review, and the entire deference which we entertain for the learning and ability of that court, add much to the difficulty of the task which has so unwelcomely fallen upon us. It is, however, a source of consolation, that we have had the assistance of most able and learned arguments to aid our inquiries; and that the opinion which is now to be pronounced has been weighed with every solicitude to come to a correct result, and matured after solemn deliberation. . . .

The third article of the constitution is that which must principally attract our attention. . . . The judicial power of the United States *shall be vested* (not may be vested) in one supreme court, and in such inferior courts as congress may, from time to time, ordain and establish. . . . If, then, it is a duty of congress to vest the judicial power of the United States, it is a duty to vest the *whole judicial power*. The language, if imperative as to one part, is imperative as to all. If it were otherwise, this anomaly would exist, that congress might successively refuse to vest the jurisdiction in any one class of cases enumerated in the constitution, and thereby defeat the jurisdiction as to all; for the constitution has not singled out any class on which congress are bound to act in preference to others. . . .

This leads us to the consideration of the great question as to the nature and extent of the appellate jurisdiction of the United States. We have already seen that appellate jurisdiction is given by the constitution to the supreme court in all cases where it has not original jurisdiction; subject, however, to such exceptions and regulations as congress may prescribe. It is, therefore, capable of embracing every case enumerated in the constitution, which is not exclusively to be decided by way of original jurisdiction. But the exercise of appellate jurisdiction is far from being limited by the terms of the constitution to the supreme court. There can be no doubt that congress may create a succession of inferior tribunals, in each of which it may vest appellate as well as original jurisdiction. . . .

As, then, by the terms of the constitution, the appellate jurisdiction is not limited as to the supreme court, and as to this court it may be exercised in all other cases than those of which it has original cognizance, what is there to restrain its exercise over state tribunals in the enumerated cases? The appellate power is not limited by the terms of the third article to any particular courts. The words are, "the judicial power (which includes appellate power) shall extend *to all cases*," &c., and "in all other cases before mentioned the supreme court shall have appellate jurisdiction." It is the *case*, then, and not *the court*, that gives the jurisdiction. If the judicial power extends to the case, it will be in vain to search in the letter of the constitution for any qualification as to the tribunal where it depends. . . .

If the constitution meant to limit the appellate jurisdiction to cases pending in the courts of the United States, it would necessarily follow that the jurisdiction of these courts would, in all the cases enumerated in the constitution, be exclusive of state tribunals. How otherwise could the jurisdiction extend to *all* cases arising under the constitution, laws, and treaties of the United States, or *to all cases* of admiralty and maritime jurisdiction? If some of these cases might be entertained by state tribunals, and no appellate jurisdiction as to them should exist, then the appellate power would not extend to *all*, but to *some*, cases. If state tribunals might exercise concurrent jurisdiction over all or some of the other classes of cases in the constitution without control, then the appellate jurisdiction of the United States might, as to such cases, have no real existence, contrary to the manifest intent of the constitution. Under such circumstances, to give effect to the judicial power, it must be construed to be exclusive; and this not only when the *casus foederis* should arise directly, but when it should arise, incidentally, in cases pending in state courts. This construction would abridge the jurisdiction of such court far more than has been ever contemplated in any act of congress.

On the other hand, if, as has been contended, a discretion be vested in congress to establish, or not to establish, inferior courts at their own pleasure, and congress should not establish such courts, the appellate jurisdiction of the supreme Court would have nothing to act upon, unless it could act upon cases pending in the state courts. Under such circumstances it must be held that the appellate power would extend to state courts; for the constitution is peremptory that it shall extend to certain enumerated cases, which cases could exist in no other courts. Any other construction, upon this supposition, would involve this strange contradiction, that a discretionary power vested in congress, and which they might rightfully omit to exercise, would defeat the absolute injunctions of the constitution in relation to the whole appellate power.

But it is plain that the framers of the constitution did contemplate that cases within the judicial cognizance of the United States not only might but would arise in the state courts, in the exercise of their ordinary jurisdiction. . . . It was foreseen that in the exercise of their ordinary jurisdiction, state courts would incidentally take cognizance of cases arising under the constitution, the laws, and treaties of the United States. Yet to all these cases the judicial power, by the very terms of the constitution, is to extend. It cannot extend by original jurisdiction if that was already rightfully and exclusively attached in the state courts, which (as has been already shown) may occur; it must, therefore, extend by appellate jurisdiction, or not at all. It would seem to follow that the appellate power of the United States must, in such cases, extend to state tribunals; and if in such cases, there is no reason why it should not equally attach upon all others within the purview of the constitution. . . .

It is further argued, that no great public mischief can result from a construction which shall limit the appellate power of the United States to cases in their own courts: first, because state judges are bound by an oath to support the constitution of the United States, and must be presumed to be men of learning and integrity . . . . As to the first reason—admitting that the judges of the state courts are, and always will be, of as much learning, integrity, and wisdom, as those of the courts of the United States, (which we very cheerfully admit), it does not aid the argument. . . . The constitution has presumed (whether rightly or wrongly we do not inquire) that state attachments, state prejudices, state jealousies, and state interests, might sometimes obstruct, or control, or be supposed to obstruct or control, the regular administration of justice. Hence, in controversies between states; between citizens of different states; between citizens claiming grants under different states; between a state and its citizens, or foreigners, and between citizens and foreigners, it enables the parties, under the authority of congress, to have the controversies heard, tried, and determined before the national tribunals. No other reason than that which has been stated can be assigned, why some, at least, of those cases should not have been left to the cognizance of the state courts. In respect to the other enumerated cases—the cases arising under the constitution, laws, and treaties of the United States, cases affecting ambassadors and other public ministers, and cases of admiralty and maritime jurisdiction—reasons of a higher and more extensive nature, touching the safety, peace, and sovereignty of the nation, might well justify a grant of exclusive jurisdiction.

This is not all. A motive of another kind, perfectly compatible with the most sincere respect for state tribunals, might induce the grant of appellate power over their decisions. That motive is the importance, and even necessity of *uniformity* of decisions throughout the whole United States, upon all subjects within the purview of the constitution. Judges of equal learning and integrity, in different states, might differently interpret a statute, or a treaty of the United States, or even the constitution itself: If there were no revising authority to control these jarring and discordant judgments, and harmonize them into uniformity, the laws, the treaties, and the constitution of the United States would be different in different states, and might, perhaps, never have precisely the same construction, obligation, or efficacy, in any two states. The public mischiefs that would attend such a state of things would be truly deplorable; and it cannot be believed that they could have escaped the enlightened convention which formed the constitution. What, indeed, might then have been only prophecy, has now become fact; and the appellate jurisdiction must continue to be the only adequate remedy for such evils.

There is an additional consideration, which is entitled to great weight. The constitution of the United States was designed for the common and equal benefit of all the people of the United States. The judicial power was granted for the same benign and salutary purposes. It was not to be exercised exclusively for the benefit of parties who might be plaintiffs, and would elect the national forum, but also for the protection of defendants who might be entitled to try their rights, or assert their privileges, before the same forum. . . .

On the whole, the court are of opinion that the appellate power of the United States does extend to cases pending in the state courts; and that the 25th section of the judiciary act, which authorizes the exercise of this jurisdiction in the specified cases, by a writ of error, is supported by the letter and spirit of the constitution. We find no clause in that instrument which limits this power; and we dare not interpose a limitation where the people have not been disposed to create one. . . .

It is the opinion of the whole court, that the judgment of the court of appeals of Virginia, rendered on the mandate in this cause, be reversed, and the judgment of the district court, held at Winchester, be, and the same is hereby affirmed.

Murdock v. City of Memphis (1874)

Mr. Justice MILLER delivered the opinion of the court.

. . . . When the case standing at the head of this opinion came on to be argued, it was insisted by counsel for defendants in error that none of the questions were involved in the case necessary to give jurisdiction to this court . . . and that if they were, there were other questions exclusively of State court cognizance which were sufficient to dispose of the case, and that, therefore, the writ of error should be dismissed.

Counsel for plaintiffs in error, on the other hand, argued that not only was there a question in the case decided against them which authorized the writ of error from this court under either act, but that this court having for this reason obtained jurisdiction of the case, should re-examine all the questions found in the record, though some of them might be questions of general common law or equity, or raised by State statutes, unaffected by any principle of Federal law, constitutional or otherwise. . . .

But we have not yet considered the most important part of the [jurisdictional] statute, namely, that which declares that it is only upon the existence of certain questions in the case that this court can entertain jurisdiction at all. Nor is the mere existence of such a question in the case sufficient to give jurisdiction—the question must have been *decided* in the State court. Nor is it sufficient that such a question was raised and was decided. It must have been decided in a certain way, that is, against the right set up under the Constitution, laws, treaties, or authority of the United States. The Federal question may have been erroneously decided. It may be quite apparent to this court that a wrong construction has been given to the Federal law, but if the right claimed under it by plaintiff in error has been conceded to him, this court cannot entertain jurisdiction of the case, so very careful is the statute . . . to narrow, to limit, and define the jurisdiction which this court exercises over the judgments of the State courts. Is it consistent with this extreme caution to suppose that Congress intended, when those cases came here, that this court should not only examine those questions, but all others found in the record?—questions of common law, of State statutes, of controverted facts, and conflicting evidence. Or is it the more reasonable inference that Congress intended that the cases should be brought here that *those questions* might be decided and *finally* decided by the court established by the Constitution of the Union, and the court which has always been supposed to be not only the most appropriate but the only proper tribunal for their final decision? No such reason nor any necessity exists for the decision by this court of other questions in those cases. The jurisdiction has been exercised for nearly a century without serious inconvenience to the due administration of justice. The State courts are the appropriate tribunals, as this court has repeatedly held, for the decision of questions arising under their local law, whether statutory or otherwise. And it is not lightly to be presumed that Congress acted upon a principle which implies a distrust of their integrity or of their ability to construe those laws correctly.

Let us look for a moment into the effect of the proposition contended for upon the cases as they come up for consideration in the conference-room. If it is found that no such question is raised or decided in the court below, then all will concede that it must be dismissed for want of jurisdiction. But if it is found that the Federal question was raised and was decided against the plaintiff in error, then the first duty of the court obviously is to determine whether it was correctly decided by the State court. Let us suppose that we find that the court below was right in its decision on that question. What, then, are we to do? Was it the intention of Congress to say that while you can only bring the case here on account of this question, yet when it is here, though it may turn out that the plaintiff in error was wrong on that question, and the judgment of the court below was right, though he has wrongfully dragged the defendant into this court by the allegation of an error which did not exist, and without which the case could not rightfully be here, he can still insist on an inquiry into all the other matters which were litigated in the case? This is neither reasonable nor just.

In such case both the nature of the jurisdiction conferred and the nature and fitness of things demand that, no error being found in the matter which authorized the re-examination, the judgment of the State court should be affirmed, and the case remitted to that court for its further enforcement.

The whole argument we are combating, however, goes upon the assumption that when it is found that the record shows that one of the questions mentioned has been decided against the claim of the plaintiff in error, this court has jurisdiction, and that jurisdiction extends to the whole case. If it extends to the whole case then the court must re-examine the whole case, and if it re-examines it must decide the whole case. It is difficult to escape the logic of the argument if the first premise be conceded. But it is here the error lies. We are of opinion that . . . the jurisdiction conferred is limited to the decision of the questions mentioned in the statute, and, as a necessary consequence of this, to the exercise of such powers as may be necessary to cause the judgment in that decision to be respected.

We will now advert to one or two considerations apart from the mere language of the statute, which seem to us to give additional force to this conclusion.

It has been many times decided by this court, on motions to dismiss this class of cases for want of jurisdiction, that if it appears from the record that the plaintiff in error raised and presented to the court by pleadings, prayer for instruction, or other appropriate method, one of the questions specified in the statute, and the court ruled against him, the jurisdiction of this court attached, and we must hear the case on its merits. Heretofore these merits have been held to be to determine whether the proposition of law involved in the specific Federal question were rightly decided, and if not, did the *case* of plaintiff in error, on the pleadings and evidence, come within the principle ruled by this court. This has always been held to be the exercise of the jurisdiction and re-examination of the case provided by the statute. But if when we once get jurisdiction, everything in the case is open to re-examination, it follows that every case tried in any State court, from that of a justice of the peace to the highest court of the State, may be brought to this court for final decision on all the points involved in it. . . .

It is impossible to believe that Congress intended this result, and equally impossible that they did not see that it would follow if they intended to open the cases that are brought here under this section to re-examination on all the points involved in them and necessary to a final judgment on the merits. . . .

It is not difficult to discover what the purpose of Congress in the passage of this law was. In a vast number of cases the rights of the people of the Union, as they are administered in the courts of the States, must depend upon the construction which those courts gave to the Constitution, treaties, and laws of the United States. The highest courts of the States were sufficiently numerous, even in 1789, to cause it to be feared that, with the purest motives, this construction given in different courts would be various and conflicting. It was desirable, however, that whatever conflict of opinion might exist in those courts on other subjects, the rights which depended on the Federal laws should be the same everywhere, and that their construction should be uniform. This could only be done by conferring upon the Supreme Court of the United States—the appellate tribunal established by the Constitution—the right to decide these questions finally and in a manner which would be conclusive on all other courts, State or National. This was the first purpose of the statute, and it does not require that, in a case involving a variety of questions, any other should be decided than those described in the act.

. . . . It was no doubt the purpose of Congress to secure to every litigant whose rights depended on any question of Federal law that that question should be decided for him by the highest Federal tribunal if he desired it, when the decisions of the State courts were against him on that question. That rights of this character, guaranteed to him by the Constitution and laws of the Union, should not be left to the exclusive and final control of the State courts.

There may be some plausibility in the argument that these rights cannot be protected in all cases unless the Supreme Court has final control of the whole case. But the experience of eighty-five years of the administration of the law under the opposite theory would seem to be a satisfactory answer to the argument. It is not to be presumed that the State courts, where the rule is clearly laid down to them on the Federal question, and its influence on the case fully seen, will disregard or overlook it, and this is all that the rights of the party claiming under it require. Besides, by the very terms of this statute, when the Supreme Court is of opinion that the question of Federal law is of such relative importance to the whole case that it should control the final judgment, that court is authorized to render such judgment and enforce it by its own process. It cannot, therefore, be maintained that it is in any case necessary for the security of the rights claimed under the Constitution, laws, or treaties of the United States that the Supreme Court should examine and decide other questions not of a Federal character. . . .

It is proper, in this first attempt to construe this important statute as amended, to say a few words on another point. What shall be done by this court when the question has been found to exist in the record, and to have been decided against the plaintiff in error, and *rightfully* decided, we have already seen, and it presents no difficulties.

But when it appears that the Federal question was decided erroneously against the plaintiff in error, we must then reverse the case undoubtedly, if there are no other issues decided in it than that. It often has occurred, however, and will occur again, that there are other points in the case than those of Federal cognizance, on which the judgment of the court below may stand; those points being of themselves sufficient to control the case.

Or it may be, that there are other issues in the case, but they are not of such controlling influence on the whole case that they are alone sufficient to support the judgment.

It may also be found that notwithstanding there are many other questions in the record of the case, the issue raised by the Federal question is such that its decision must dispose of the whole case.

In the two latter instances there can be no doubt that the judgment of the State court must be reversed, and under the new act this court can either render the final judgment or decree here, or remand the case to the State court for that purpose.

But in the other cases supposed, why should a judgment be reversed for an error in deciding the Federal question, if the same judgment must be rendered on the other points in the case? And why should this court reverse a judgment which is right on the whole record presented to us; or where the same judgment will be rendered by the court below, after they have corrected the error in the Federal question?

We have already laid down the rule that we are not authorized to examine these other questions for the purpose of deciding whether the State court ruled correctly on them or not.

We are of opinion that on these subjects not embraced in the class of questions stated in the statute, we must receive the decision of the State courts as conclusive.

But when we find that the State court had decided the Federal question erroneously, then to prevent a useless and profitless reversal, which can do the plaintiff in error no good, and can only embarrass and delay the defendant, we must so far look into the remainder of the record as to see whether the decision of the Federal question alone is sufficient to dispose of the case, or to require its reversal; or on the other hand, whether there exist other matters in the record actually decided by the State court which are sufficient to maintain the judgment of that court, notwithstanding the error in deciding the Federal question. In the latter case the court would not be justified in reversing the judgment of the State court.

But this examination into the points in the record other than the Federal question is not for the purpose of determining whether they were correctly or erroneously decided, but to ascertain if any such have been decided, and their sufficiency to maintain the final judgment, as decided by the State court.

Beyond this we are not at liberty to go, and we can only go this far to prevent the injustice of reversing a judgment which must in the end be reaffirmed, even in this court, if brought here again from the State court after it has corrected its error in the matter of Federal law.

Finally, we hold the following propositions on this subject as flowing from the statute as it now stands:

1. That it is essential to the jurisdiction of this court over the judgment of a State court, that it shall appear that one of the questions mentioned in the act must have been raised, and presented to the State court.

2. That it must have been decided by the State court, or that its decision was necessary to the judgment or decree, rendered in the case.

3. That the decision must have been against the right claimed or asserted by plaintiff in error under the Constitution, treaties, laws, or authority of the United States.

4. These things appearing, this court has jurisdiction and must examine the judgment so far as to enable it to decide whether this claim of right was correctly adjudicated by the State court.

5. If it finds that it was rightly decided, the judgment must be affirmed.

6. If it was erroneously decided against plaintiff in error, then this court must further inquire, whether there is any other matter or issue adjudged by the State court, which is sufficiently broad to maintain the judgment of that court, notwithstanding the error in deciding the issue raised by the Federal question. If this is found to be the case, the judgment must be affirmed without inquiring into the soundness of the decision on such other matter or issue.

7. But if it be found that the issue raised by the question of Federal law is of such controlling character that its correct decision is necessary to any final judgment in the case, or that there has been no decision by the State court of any other matter or issue which is sufficient to maintain the judgment of that court without regard to the Federal question, then this court will reverse the judgment of the State court, and will either render such judgment here as the State court should have rendered, or remand the case to that court, as the circumstances of the case may require.

Applying the principles here laid down to the case now before the court, we are of opinion that this court has jurisdiction, and that the judgment of the Supreme Court of Tennessee must be affirmed.

The suit was a bill in chancery brought by Murdock and others against the city of Memphis to have a decree establishing their right in certain real estate near that city. The United States having determined to build a navy yard at Memphis, about the year 1844, or previous thereto, the city of Memphis, on the 14th day of September of that year, conveyed to the United States the land in controversy by an ordinary deed of general warranty, expressing on its face the consideration of $20,000 paid, and designating no purpose for which the land was conveyed. After retaining possession of the land for about ten years without building a navy yard, the United States abandoned that purpose, and by an act approved August 5th, 1854, ceded the property to the city of Memphis by its corporate name for the use and benefit of said city.

The plaintiffs in error, by their bill, allege that the title was originally conveyed to the city of Memphis, in trust, for certain purposes, including that of having a navy yard built on it by the United States; that when the title reverted to the city by reason of the abandonment of the place as a navy yard by the United States, and the act of Congress aforesaid, the city received the title in trust for the original grantors, who are the plaintiffs, or who are represented by plaintiffs. A demurrer to the bill was filed. Also an answer denying the trust and pleading the statute of limitations. On the hearing the bill was dismissed, and this decree was affirmed by the Supreme Court of the State. The complainants, in their bill, and throughout the case, insisted that the effect of the act of 1854 was to vest the title in the mayor or aldermen of the city in trust for them.

It may be very true that it is not easy to see anything in the deed by which the United States received the title from the city, or the act by which they ceded it back, which raises such a trust, but the complainants claimed a right under this act of the United States, which was decided against them by the Supreme Court of Tennessee, and this claim gives jurisdiction of that question to this court.

But we need not consume many words to prove that neither by the deed of the city to the United States, which is an ordinary deed of bargain and sale for a valuable consideration, nor from anything found in the act of 1854, is there any such trust to be inferred. The act, so far from recognizing or implying any such trust, cedes the property to the mayor and aldermen *for the use of the city*. We are, therefore, of opinion that this, the only Federal question in the case, was rightly decided by the Supreme Court of Tennessee.

But conceding this to be true, the plaintiffs in error have argued that the court having jurisdiction of the case must now examine it upon all the questions which affect its merits; and they insist that the conveyance by which the city of Memphis received the title previous to the deed from the city to the government, and the circumstances attending the making of the former deed are such, that when the title reverted to the city, a trust was raised for the benefit of plaintiffs.

After what has been said in the previous part of this opinion, we need discuss this matter no further. The claim of right here set up is one to be determined by the general principles of equity jurisprudence, and is unaffected by anything found in the Constitution, laws, or treaties of the United States. Whether decided well or otherwise by the State court, we have no authority to inquire. According to the principles we have laid down as applicable to this class of cases, the judgment of the Supreme Court of Tennessee must be affirmed.

Mr. Justice CLIFFORD, with whom concurred Mr. Justice SWAYNE, dissenting:

I dissent from so much of the opinion of the court as denies the jurisdiction of this court to determine the whole case, where it appears that the record presents a Federal question and that the Federal question was erroneously decided to the prejudice of the plaintiff in error; as in that state of the record it is, in my judgment, the duty of this court, under the recent act of Congress, to decide the whole merits of the controversy, and to affirm or reverse the judgment of the State court. Tested by the new law it would seem that it must be so, as this court cannot in that state of the record dismiss the writ of error, nor can the court reverse the judgment without deciding every question which the record presents.

Where the Federal question is rightly decided the judgment of the State court may be affirmed, upon the ground that the jurisdiction does not attach to the other questions involved in the merits of the controversy; but where the Federal question is erroneously decided the whole merits must be decided by this court . . . .

Mr. Justice BRADLEY, dissenting:

. . . . I cannot concur in the conclusion that we can only decide the Federal question raised by the record. If we have jurisdiction at all, in my judgment we have jurisdiction of the *case*, and not merely of a *question* in it. . . . In my judgment, therefore, if the court had jurisdiction of the case, it was bound to consider not only the Federal question raised by the record, but the whole case. As the court, however, has decided otherwise, it is not proper that I should express any opinion on the merits.

Mr. Justice WHITE delivered the opinion of the Court.

The issue before us in this case is whether, consistently with the First and Fourteenth Amendments, a State may extend a cause of action for damages for invasion of privacy caused by the publication of the name of a deceased rape victim which was publicly revealed in connection with the prosecution of the crime.

I

In August 1971, appellee's 17-year-old daughter was the victim of a rape and did not survive the incident. Six youths were soon indicted for murder and rape. Although there was substantial press coverage of the crime and of subsequent developments, the identity of the victim was not disclosed pending trial, perhaps because of Ga. Code § 26-9901, which makes it a misdemeanor to publish or broadcast the name or identity of a rape victim. In April 1972, some eight months later, the six defendants appeared in court. Five pleaded guilty to rape or attempted rape, the charge of murder having been dropped. The guilty pleas were accepted by the court, and the trial of the defendant pleading not guilty was set for a later date.

In the course of the proceedings that day, appellant Wassell, a reporter covering the incident for his employer, learned the name of the victim from an examination of the indictments which were made available for his inspection in the courtroom. That the name of the victim appears in the indictments and that the indictments were public records available for inspection are not disputed. Later that day, Wassell broadcast over the facilities of station WSB-TV, a television station owned by appellant Cox Broadcasting Corp., a news report concerning the court proceedings. The report named the victim of the crime and was repeated the following day.

In May 1972, appellee brought an action for money damages against appellants, relying on § 26-9901 and claiming that his right to privacy had been invaded by the television broadcasts giving the name of his deceased daughter. Appellants admitted the broadcasts but claimed that they were privileged under both state law and the First and Fourteenth Amendments. The trial court, rejecting appellants' constitutional claims and holding that the Georgia statute gave a civil remedy to those injured by its violation, granted summary judgment to appellee as to liability, with the determination of damages to await trial by jury.

On appeal, the Georgia Supreme Court, in its initial opinion, held that the trial court had erred in construing § 26-9901 to extend a civil cause of action for invasion of privacy and thus found it unnecessary to consider the constitutionality of the statute. The court went on to rule, however, that the complaint stated a cause of action for the invasion of the appellee's right of privacy, or for the tort of public disclosure—a "common law tort exist[ing] in this jurisdiction without the help of the statute that the trial judge in this case relied on." Although the privacy invaded was not that of the deceased victim, the father was held to have stated a claim for invasion of his own privacy by reason of the publication of his daughter's name. The court explained, however, that liability did not follow as a matter of law and that summary judgment was improper; whether the public disclosure of the name actually invaded appellee's "zone of privacy," and if so, to what extent, were issues to be determined by the trier of fact. . . . [T]he court felt compelled to determine the constitutionality of the statute and sustained it as a legitimate limitation on the right of freedom of expression contained in the First Amendment. The court could discern no public interest or general concern about the identity of the victim of such a crime as will make the right to disclose the identity of the victim rise to the level of First Amendment protection.

We postponed decision as to our jurisdiction over this appeal to the hearing on the merits. We conclude that the Court has jurisdiction and reverse the judgment of the Georgia Supreme Court.

II

Appellants invoke the appellate jurisdiction of this Court under 28 U.S.C. § 1257(2) . . . . [We must consider] whether the decision from which this appeal has been taken is a "[f]inal judgment or decree." . . .

The Court has noted that considerations of English usage as well as those of judicial policy would justify an interpretation of the final-judgment rule to preclude review where anything further remains to be determined by a State court, no matter how dissociated from the only federal issue that has finally been adjudicated by the highest court of the State. But the Court there observed that the rule had not been administered in such a mechanical fashion and that there were circumstances in which there has been a departure from this requirement of finality for federal appellate jurisdiction.

These circumstances were said to be very few, but as the cases have unfolded, the Court has recurringly encountered situations in which the highest court of a State has finally determined the federal issue present in a particular case, but in which there are further proceedings in the lower state courts to come. There are now at least four categories of such cases in which the Court has treated the decision on the federal issue as a final judgment for the purposes of 28 U.S.C. § 1257 and has taken jurisdiction without awaiting the completion of the additional proceedings anticipated in the lower state courts. . . .

In the first category are those cases in which there are further proceedings—even entire trials—yet to occur in the state courts but where for one reason or another the federal issue is conclusive or the outcome of further proceedings preordained. In these circumstances, because the case is for all practical purposes concluded, the judgment of the state court on the federal issue is deemed final. . . . Second, there are cases . . . in which the federal issue, finally decided by the highest court in the State, will survive and require decision regardless of the outcome of future state-court proceedings. . . . In the third category are those situations where the federal claim has been finally decided, with further proceedings on the merits in the state courts to come, but in which later review of the federal issue cannot be had, whatever the ultimate outcome of the case. Thus, in these cases, if the party seeking interim review ultimately prevails on the merits, the federal issue will be mooted; if he were to lose on the merits, however, the governing state law would not permit him again to present his federal claims for review. . . . Lastly, there are those situations where the federal issue has been finally decided in the state courts with further proceedings pending in which the party seeking review here might prevail on the merits on nonfederal grounds, thus rendering unnecessary review of the federal issue by this Court, and where reversal of the state court on the federal issue would be preclusive of any further litigation on the relevant cause of action rather than merely controlling the nature and character of, or determining the admissibility of evidence in, the state proceedings still to come. In these circumstances, if a refusal immediately to review the state court decision might seriously erode federal policy, the Court has entertained and decided the federal issue, which itself has been finally determined by the state courts for purposes of the state litigation. . . .

In light of the prior cases, we conclude that we have jurisdiction to review the judgment of the Georgia Supreme Court rejecting the challenge under the First and Fourteenth Amendments to the state law authorizing damage suits against the press for publishing the name of a rape victim whose identity is revealed in the course of a public prosecution. The Georgia Supreme Court's judgment is plainly final on the federal issue and is not subject to further review in the state courts. Appellants will be liable for damages if the elements of the state cause of action are proved. They may prevail at trial on nonfederal grounds, it is true, but if the Georgia court erroneously upheld the statute, there should be no trial at all. Moreover, even if appellants prevailed at trial and made unnecessary further consideration of the constitutional question, there would remain in effect the unreviewed decision of the State Supreme Court that a civil action for publishing the name of a rape victim disclosed in a public judicial proceeding may go forward despite the First and Fourteenth Amendments. Delaying final decision of the First Amendment claim until after trial will leave unanswered an important question of freedom of the press under the First Amendment, an uneasy and unsettled constitutional posture that could only further harm the operation of a free press. On the other hand, if we now hold that the First and Fourteenth Amendments bar civil liability for broadcasting the victim's name, this litigation ends. Given these factors—that the litigation could be terminated by our decision on the merits and that a failure to decide the question now will leave the press in Georgia operating in the shadow of the civil and criminal sanctions of a rule of law and a statute the constitutionality of which is in serious doubt—we find that reaching the merits is consistent with the pragmatic approach that we have followed in the past in determining finality.

III

[On the merits, the Court held the statute to be in violation of the First Amendment.] . . .

Reversed.

Mr. Justice REHNQUIST, dissenting.

. . . . That comity and federalism are significant elements of § 1257 finality has been recognized by other members of the Court as well . . . . Indeed, we have in recent years emphasized and re-emphasized the importance of comity and federalism in dealing with a related problem, that of district court interference with ongoing state judicial proceedings. *See Younger v. Harris.* Because these concerns are important, and because they provide added force to § 1257's finality requirement, I believe that the Court has erred by simply importing the approach of cases in which the only concern is efficient judicial administration. . . .

But quite apart from the considerations of federalism which counsel against an expansive reading of our jurisdiction under § 1257, the Court's holding today enunciates a virtually formless exception to the finality requirement, one which differs in kind from those previously carved out. . . .

But the greatest difficulty with the test enunciated today is that it totally abandons the principle that constitutional issues are too important to be decided save when absolutely necessary, and are to be avoided if there are grounds for decision of lesser dimension. The long line of cases which established this rule makes clear that it is a principle primarily designed, not to benefit the lower courts, or state-federal relations, but rather to safeguard this Court's own process of constitutional adjudication. . . .

I would dismiss for want of jurisdiction.

Howell v. Mississippi (2005)

Petitioner Marlon Howell contends that the Mississippi courts violated his rights under the Eighth and Fourteenth Amendments to the United States Constitution by refusing to require a jury instruction about a lesser included offense in his capital case. He did not, however, raise this claim in the Supreme Court of Mississippi, which unsurprisingly did not address it. As a result, we dismiss the writ of certiorari as improvidently granted.

Petitioner was convicted and sentenced to death for killing Hugh David Pernell. . . . At trial, petitioner argued both that he was in another city at the time of the killing and that the evidence was insufficient to prove that Pernell was killed during an attempted robbery (which would deprive the State of an element of capital murder). As part of his nonalibi defense, petitioner sought to supplement the State's proposed jury instruction on capital murder with instructions on manslaughter and simple murder. The trial court refused the additional instructions. The jury found petitioner guilty of capital murder and separately concluded that he should be sentenced to death.

On appeal to the State Supreme Court, one of petitioner's 28 claims of error was the trial court's failure to give the defendant an instruction on the offense of simple murder or manslaughter. In that argument, petitioner cited three cases from the State Supreme Court about lesser-included-offense instructions, and the only opinion whose original language he quoted was a noncapital case. Petitioner argued that, because the jury could have found and returned the lesser included offense of simple murder or manslaughter, the failure to give instructions on those offenses was error that left the jury no choice but either to turn him loose or convict him of capital murder. In the course of affirming petitioner's conviction and death sentence, the State Supreme Court found that the facts of this case clearly do not support or warrant the instruction for manslaughter or simple murder. The court cited and quoted a prior noncapital [state-court] decision, which construed a state statute and concluded that an instruction should be refused if it would cause the jury to ignore the primary charge or if the evidence does not justify submission of a lesser-included offense. The court also cited [a state-court] aggravated-assault case rejecting an instruction for simple assault.

Petitioner sought certiorari from this Court, arguing that his death sentence is unconstitutional under [a] rule of our capital jurisprudence . . . . We granted certiorari, but asked the parties to address the following additional question: "Was petitioner's federal constitutional claim properly raised before the Mississippi Supreme Court for purposes of 28 U.S.C. § 1257?" Our answer to that question prevents us from reaching petitioner's constitutional claim.

Congress has given this Court the power to review "[f]inal judgments or decrees rendered by the highest court of a State in which a decision could be had . . . where any . . . right . . . is *specially set up or claimed* under the Constitution or the treaties or statutes of . . . the United States." Under that statute and its predecessors, this Court has almost unfailingly refused to consider any federal-law challenge to a state-court decision unless the federal claim was either addressed by or properly presented to the state court that rendered the decision we have been asked to review.

Petitioner's brief in the State Supreme Court did not properly present his claim as one arising under federal law. In the relevant argument, he did not cite the Constitution or even any cases directly construing it, much less any of this Court's cases. . . . As we recently explained in a slightly different context, a litigant wishing to raise a federal issue can easily indicate the federal law basis for his claim in a state-court petition or brief by citing in conjunction with the claim the federal source of law on which he relies or a case deciding such a claim on federal grounds, or by simply labeling the claim "federal." In the context of § 1257, the same steps toward clarity are just as easy to take and are generally necessary to establish that a federal question was properly presented to a state court. Petitioner did none of these things.

Petitioner also contends that he raised his federal claim by implication because the state-law rule on which he relied was "identical" or "virtually identical" to the constitutional rule . . . . Assuming, without deciding, that identical standards might overcome a petitioner's failure to identify his claim as federal, Mississippi's rule regarding lesser-included-offense instructions is not identical [to the federal rule] . . . .

Petitioner suggests that we need not treat his failure to present his federal claim in state court as jurisdictional. Notwithstanding the long line of cases clearly stating that the presentation requirement is jurisdictional, a handful of exceptions . . . have previously led us to conclude that this is an unsettled question. As in prior cases, however, we need not decide today whether our requirement that a federal claim be addressed or properly presented in state court is jurisdictional or prudential, because even treating the rule as purely prudential, the circumstances here justify no exception.

Accordingly, we dismiss the writ of certiorari as improvidently granted.

Fox Film Corp. v. Muller (1935)

This is an action brought in a Minnesota state court of first instance by the Film Corporation against Muller, to recover damages for an alleged breach of two contracts by which Muller was licensed to exhibit certain moving picture films belonging to the corporation. Muller answered, setting up the invalidity of the contracts under the Sherman Anti-Trust Act. It was and is agreed that these contracts are substantially the same as the one involved in [a previous litigation], that petitioner was one of the defendants in that action; and that the arbitration clause, paragraph 18 of each of the contracts sued upon, is the same as that held in that case to be invalid. In view of the disposition which we are to make of this writ, it is not necessary to set forth the terms of the arbitration clause or the other provisions of the contract.

The court of first instance held that each contract sued upon violated the Sherman Anti-Trust Act, and dismissed the action. In a supplemental opinion, that court put its decision upon the grounds, first, that the arbitration plan is so connected with the remainder of the contract that the entire contract is tainted; and, second, that the contract violates the Sherman Anti-Trust law. The state Supreme Court affirmed. We granted certiorari . . . .

In its opinion, the state Supreme Court, after a statement of the case, said: "The question presented on this appeal is whether the arbitration clause is severable from the contract, leaving the remainder of the contract enforceable or not severable, permeating and tainting the whole contract with illegality and making it void." That court then proceeded to refer to and discuss a number of decisions of state and federal courts, some of which took the view that the arbitration clause was severable, and others that it was not severable, from the remainder of the contract. After reviewing the opinion and decree of the federal District Court in the Paramount Case, the lower court reached the conclusion that the holding of the federal court was that the entire contract was illegal; and upon that view and upon what it conceived to be the weight of authority, held the arbitration plan was inseparable from the other provisions of the contract. Whether this conclusion was right or wrong we need not determine. It is enough that it is, at least, not without fair support.

Respondent contends that the question of severability was alone decided and that no federal question was determined by the lower court. This contention petitioner challenges, and asserts that a federal question was involved and decided. We do not attempt to settle the dispute; but, assuming for present purposes only that petitioner's view is the correct one, the case is controlled by the settled rule that where the judgment of a state court rests upon two grounds, one of which is federal and the other nonfederal in character, our jurisdiction fails if the nonfederal ground is independent of the federal ground and adequate to support the judgment. . . .

Whether the provisions of a contract are nonseverable, so that if one be held invalid the others must fall with it, is clearly a question of general and not of federal law. The invalidity of the arbitration clause which the present contracts embody is conceded. It was held invalid by the federal District Court in the Paramount Case, and its judgment was affirmed here. The question, therefore, was foreclosed; and was not the subject of controversy in the state courts. In that situation, the primary question to be determined by the court below was whether the concededly invalid clause was separable from the other provisions of the contract. The ruling of the state Supreme Court that it was not, is sufficient to conclude the case without regard to the determination, if, in fact, any was made, in respect of the federal question. It follows that the nonfederal ground is adequate to sustain the judgment.

The rule [that] our jurisdiction attaches where the nonfederal ground is so interwoven with the other as not to be an independent matter, does not apply. The construction put upon the contracts did not constitute a preliminary step which simply had the effect of bringing forward for determination the federal question, but was a decision which automatically took the federal question out of the case if otherwise it would be there. The nonfederal question in respect of the construction of the contracts and the federal question in respect of their validity under the Anti-Trust Act were clearly independent of one another. The case, in effect, was disposed of before the federal question said to be involved was reached. A decision of that question then became unnecessary; and whether it was decided or not, our want of jurisdiction is clear.

Writ dismissed for want of jurisdiction.

Michigan v. Long (1983)

Justice O'CONNOR delivered the opinion of the Court.

In *Terry v. Ohio*, we upheld the validity of a protective search for weapons in the absence of probable cause to arrest because it is unreasonable to deny a police officer the right to neutralize the threat of physical harm when he possesses an articulable suspicion that an individual is armed and dangerous. We did not, however, expressly address whether such a protective search for weapons could extend to an area beyond the person in the absence of probable cause to arrest. In the present case, respondent David Long was convicted for possession of marijuana found by police in the passenger compartment and trunk of the automobile that he was driving. The police searched the passenger compartment because they had reason to believe that the vehicle contained weapons potentially dangerous to the officers. We hold that the protective search of the passenger compartment was reasonable under the principles articulated in *Terry* and other decisions of this Court. We also examine Long's argument that the decision below rests upon an adequate and independent state ground, and we decide in favor of our jurisdiction.

I

Deputies Howell and Lewis were on patrol in a rural area one evening when, shortly after midnight, they observed a car traveling erratically and at excessive speed. The officers observed the car turning down a side road, where it swerved off into a shallow ditch. The officers stopped to investigate. Long, the only occupant of the automobile, met the deputies at the rear of the car, which was protruding from the ditch onto the road. The door on the driver's side of the vehicle was left open.

Deputy Howell requested Long to produce his operator's license, but he did not respond. After the request was repeated, Long produced his license. Long again failed to respond when Howell requested him to produce the vehicle registration. After another repeated request, Long, whom Howell thought "appeared to be under the influence of something," turned from the officers and began walking toward the open door of the vehicle. The officers followed Long and both observed a large hunting knife on the floorboard of the driver's side of the car. The officers then stopped Long's progress and subjected him to a *Terry* protective pat-down, which revealed no weapons.

Long and Deputy Lewis then stood by the rear of the vehicle while Deputy Howell shined his flashlight into the interior of the vehicle, but did not actually enter it. The purpose of Howell's action was to search for other weapons. The officer noticed that something was protruding from under the armrest on the front seat. He knelt in the vehicle and lifted the armrest. He saw an open pouch on the front seat, and upon flashing his light on the pouch, determined that it contained what appeared to be marijuana. After Deputy Howell showed the pouch and its contents to Deputy Lewis, Long was arrested for possession of marijuana. A further search of the interior of the vehicle, including the glovebox, revealed neither more contraband nor the vehicle registration. The officers decided to impound the vehicle. Deputy Howell opened the trunk, which did not have a lock, and discovered inside it approximately 75 pounds of marijuana.

The Barry County Circuit Court denied Long's motion to suppress the marijuana taken from both the interior of the car and its trunk. He was subsequently convicted of possession of marijuana. The Michigan Court of Appeals affirmed Long's conviction, holding that the search of the passenger compartment was valid as a protective search under *Terry* and that the search of the trunk was valid as an inventory search. The Michigan Supreme Court reversed. The court held that the sole justification of the *Terry* search, protection of the police officers and others nearby, cannot justify the search in this case. The marijuana found in Long's trunk was considered by the court below to be the "fruit" of the illegal search of the interior, and was also suppressed.

We granted certiorari in this case to consider the important question of the authority of a police officer to protect himself by conducting a *Terry*-type search of the passenger compartment of a motor vehicle during the lawful investigatory stop of the occupant of the vehicle.

II

Before reaching the merits, we must consider Long's argument that we are without jurisdiction to decide this case because the decision below rests on an adequate and independent state ground. The court below referred twice to the state constitution in its opinion, but otherwise relied exclusively on federal law.[3]

> [3] On the first occasion, the court merely cited in a footnote both the state and federal constitutions. On the second occasion, at the conclusion of the opinion, the court stated: "We hold, therefore, that the deputies' search of the vehicle was proscribed by the Fourth Amendment to the United States Constitution and art. 1, § 11 of the Michigan Constitution."

Long argues that the Michigan courts have provided greater protection from searches and seizures under the state constitution than is afforded under the Fourth Amendment, and the references to the state constitution therefore establish an adequate and independent ground for the decision below.

It is, of course, incumbent upon this Court to ascertain for itself whether the asserted non-federal ground independently and adequately supports the judgment. Although we have announced a number of principles in order to help us determine whether various forms of references to state law constitute adequate and independent state grounds, we openly admit that we have thus far not developed a satisfying and consistent approach for resolving this vexing issue. . . .

This *ad hoc* method of dealing with cases that involve possible adequate and independent state grounds is antithetical to the doctrinal consistency that is required when sensitive issues of federal-state relations are involved. Moreover, none of the various methods of disposition that we have employed thus far recommends itself as the preferred method that we should apply to the exclusion of others, and we therefore determine that it is appropriate to reexamine our treatment of this jurisdictional issue in order to achieve the consistency that is necessary.

The process of examining state law is unsatisfactory because it requires us to interpret state laws with which we are generally unfamiliar, and which often, as in this case, have not been discussed at length by the parties. Vacation and continuance for clarification have also been unsatisfactory both because of the delay and decrease in efficiency of judicial administration, and, more important, because these methods of disposition place significant burdens on state courts to demonstrate the presence or absence of our jurisdiction. Finally, outright dismissal of cases is clearly not a panacea because it cannot be doubted that there is an important need for uniformity in federal law, and that this need goes unsatisfied when we fail to review an opinion that rests primarily upon federal grounds and where the *independence* of an alleged state ground is not apparent from the four corners of the opinion. We have long recognized that dismissal is inappropriate where there is strong indication that the federal constitution as judicially construed controlled the decision below.

Respect for the independence of state courts, as well as avoidance of rendering advisory opinions, have been the cornerstones of this Court's refusal to decide cases where there is an adequate and independent state ground. It is precisely because of this respect for state courts, and this desire to avoid advisory opinions, that we do not wish to continue to decide issues of state law that go beyond the opinion that we review, or to require state courts to reconsider cases to clarify the grounds of their decisions. Accordingly, when, as in this case, a state court decision fairly appears to rest primarily on federal law, or to be interwoven with the federal law, and when the adequacy and independence of any possible state law ground is not clear from the face of the opinion, we will accept as the most reasonable explanation that the state court decided the case the way it did because it believed that federal law required it to do so. If a state court chooses merely to rely on federal precedents as it would on the precedents of all other jurisdictions, then it need only make clear by a plain statement in its judgment or opinion that the federal cases are being used only for the purpose of guidance, and do not themselves compel the result that the court has reached. In this way, both justice and judicial administration will be greatly improved. If the state court decision indicates clearly and expressly that it is alternatively based on bona fide separate, adequate, and independent grounds, we, of course, will not undertake to review the decision.

This approach obviates in most instances the need to examine state law in order to decide the nature of the state court decision, and will at the same time avoid the danger of our rendering advisory opinions. It also avoids the unsatisfactory and intrusive practice of requiring state courts to clarify their decisions to the satisfaction of this Court. We believe that such an approach will provide state judges with a clearer opportunity to develop state jurisprudence unimpeded by federal interference, and yet will preserve the integrity of federal law. It is fundamental that state courts be left free and unfettered by us in interpreting their state constitutions. But it is equally important that ambiguous or obscure adjudications by state courts do not stand as barriers to a determination by this Court of the validity under the federal constitution of state action.

The principle that we will not review judgments of state courts that rest on adequate and independent state grounds is based, in part, on the limitations of our own jurisdiction. The jurisdictional concern is that we not render an advisory opinion, and if the same judgment would be rendered by the state court after we corrected its views of federal laws, our review could amount to nothing more than an advisory opinion. Our requirement of a "plain statement" that a decision rests upon adequate and independent state grounds does not in any way authorize the rendering of advisory opinions. Rather, in determining, as we must, whether we have jurisdiction to review a case that is alleged to rest on adequate and independent state grounds, we merely assume that there are no such grounds when it is not clear from the opinion itself that the state court relied upon an adequate and independent state ground and when it fairly appears that the state court rested its decision primarily on federal law.

Our review of the decision below under this framework leaves us unconvinced that it rests upon an independent state ground. Apart from its two citations to the state constitution, the court below relied *exclusively* on its understanding of *Terry* and other federal cases. Not a single state case was cited to support the state court's holding that the search of the passenger compartment was unconstitutional. Indeed, the court declared that the search in this case was unconstitutional because "[t]he Court of Appeals erroneously applied the principles of *Terry v. Ohio* . . . to the search of the interior of the vehicle in this case." The references to the state constitution in no way indicate that the decision below rested on grounds in any way *independent* from the state court's interpretation of federal law. Even if we accept that the Michigan constitution has been interpreted to provide independent protection for certain rights also secured under the Fourth Amendment, it fairly appears in this case that the Michigan Supreme Court rested its decision primarily on federal law.

Rather than dismissing the case, or requiring that the state court reconsider its decision on our behalf solely because of a mere possibility that an adequate and independent ground supports the judgment, we find that we have jurisdiction in the absence of a plain statement that the decision below rested on an adequate and independent state ground. It appears to us that the state court felt compelled by what it understood to be federal constitutional considerations to construe its own law in the manner it did. . . .

The decision of the Michigan Supreme Court is reversed, and the case is remanded for further proceedings not inconsistent with this opinion.

Justice STEVENS, dissenting.

The jurisprudential questions presented in this case are far more important than the question whether the Michigan police officer's search of respondent's car violated the Fourth Amendment. The case raises profoundly significant questions concerning the relationship between two sovereigns—the State of Michigan and the United States of America.

The Supreme Court of the State of Michigan expressly held "that the deputies' search of the vehicle was proscribed by the Fourth Amendment of the United States Constitution and *art. 1, § 11 of the Michigan Constitution.*" The state law ground is clearly adequate to support the judgment, but the question whether it is independent of the Michigan Supreme Court's understanding of federal law is more difficult. Four possible ways of resolving that question present themselves: (1) asking the Michigan Supreme Court directly, (2) attempting to infer from all possible sources of state law what the Michigan Supreme Court meant, (3) presuming that adequate state grounds are independent unless it clearly appears otherwise, or (4) presuming that adequate state grounds are *not* independent unless it clearly appears otherwise. This Court has, on different occasions, employed each of the first three approaches; never until today has it even hinted at the fourth. In order to "achieve the consistency that is necessary," the Court today undertakes a reexamination of all the possibilities. It rejects the first approach as inefficient and unduly burdensome for state courts, and rejects the second approach as an inappropriate expenditure of our resources. Although I find both of those decisions defensible in themselves, I cannot accept the Court's decision to choose the fourth approach over the third—to presume that adequate state grounds are intended to be dependent on federal law unless the record plainly shows otherwise. I must therefore dissent.

If we reject the intermediate approaches, we are left with a choice between two presumptions: one in favor of our taking jurisdiction, and one against it. Historically, the latter presumption has always prevailed. . . .

Even if I agreed with the Court that we are free to consider as a fresh proposition whether we may take presumptive jurisdiction over the decisions of sovereign states, I could not agree that an expansive attitude makes good sense. It appears to be common ground that any rule we adopt should show respect for state courts, and a desire to avoid advisory opinions. And I am confident that all members of this Court agree that there is a vital interest in the sound management of scarce federal judicial resources. All of those policies counsel against the exercise of federal jurisdiction. They are fortified by my belief that a policy of judicial restraint—one that allows other decisional bodies to have the last word in legal interpretation until it is truly necessary for this Court to intervene—enables this Court to make its most effective contribution to our federal system of government.

The nature of the case before us hardly compels a departure from tradition. These are not cases in which an American citizen has been deprived of a right secured by the United States Constitution or a federal statute. Rather, they are cases in which a state court has upheld a citizen's assertion of a right, finding the citizen to be protected under both federal and state law. The complaining party is an officer of the state itself, who asks us to rule that the state court interpreted federal rights too broadly and "overprotected" the citizen.

Such cases should not be of inherent concern to this Court. The reason may be illuminated by assuming that the events underlying this case had arisen in another country, perhaps the Republic of Finland. If the Finnish police had arrested a Finnish citizen for possession of marijuana, and the Finnish courts had turned him loose, no American would have standing to object. If instead they had arrested an American citizen and acquitted him, we might have been concerned about the arrest but we surely could not have complained about the acquittal, even if the Finnish Court had based its decision on its understanding of the United States Constitution. That would be true even if we had a treaty with Finland requiring it to respect the rights of American citizens under the United States Constitution. We would only be motivated to intervene if an American citizen were unfairly arrested, tried, and convicted by the foreign tribunal.

In this case the State of Michigan has arrested one of its citizens and the Michigan Supreme Court has decided to turn him loose. The respondent is a United States citizen as well as a Michigan citizen, but since there is no claim that he has been mistreated by the State of Michigan, the final outcome of the state processes offended no federal interest whatever. Michigan simply provided greater protection to one of its citizens than some other State might provide or, indeed, than this Court might require throughout the country.

I believe that in reviewing the decisions of state courts, the primary role of this Court is to make sure that persons who seek to *vindicate* federal rights have been fairly heard. . . . I am confident that a future Court will recognize the error of this allocation of resources. When that day comes, I think it likely that the Court will also reconsider the propriety of today's expansion of our jurisdiction.

The Court offers only one reason for asserting authority over cases such as the one presented today: an important need for uniformity in federal law that goes unsatisfied when we fail to review an opinion that rests primarily upon federal grounds and where the independence of an alleged state ground is not apparent from the four corners of the opinion. Of course, the supposed need to review an opinion clashes directly with our oft-repeated reminder that our power is to correct wrong judgments, not to revise opinions. The clash is not merely one of form: the need for uniformity in federal law is truly an ungovernable engine. That same need is no less present when it is perfectly clear that a state ground is both independent and adequate. In fact, it is equally present if a state prosecutor announces that he believes a certain policy of nonenforcement is commanded by federal law. Yet we have never claimed jurisdiction to correct such errors, no matter how egregious they may be, and no matter how much they may thwart the desires of the state electorate. We do not sit to expound our understanding of the Constitution to interested listeners in the legal community; we sit to resolve disputes. If it is not apparent that our views would affect the outcome of a particular case, we cannot presume to interfere.

Finally, I am thoroughly baffled by the Court's suggestion that it must stretch its jurisdiction and reverse the judgment of the Michigan Supreme Court in order to show respect for the independence of state courts. Would we show respect for the Republic of Finland by convening a special sitting for the sole purpose of declaring that its decision to release an American citizen was based upon a misunderstanding of American law?

I respectfully dissent.

Walker v. Martin (2011)

This case concerns California's time limitation on applications for postconviction (habeas corpus) relief. The question presented: Does California's timeliness requirement qualify as an independent state ground adequate to bar habeas corpus relief in federal court?

California does not employ fixed statutory deadlines to determine the timeliness of a state prisoner's petition for habeas corpus. Instead, California directs petitioners to file known claims "as promptly as the circumstances allow." Petitioners are further instructed to state when they first learned of the asserted claims and to explain why they did not seek postconviction relief sooner. Claims substantially delayed without justification may be denied as untimely. . . .

Petitioner below, respondent here, Charles W. Martin, presented the claims at issue—all alleging ineffective assistance of counsel—in a habeas petition filed in the California Supreme Court nearly five years after his conviction became final. He stated no reason for the long delay. . . . [T]he court denied Martin's petition [as untimely]. In turn, the U.S. District Court for the Eastern District of California dismissed Martin's federal habeas petition raising the same ineffective assistance claims. Denial of Martin's state-court petition as untimely, the District Court held, rested on an adequate and independent state ground, *i.e.*, Martin's failure to seek relief in state court "without substantial delay."

The U.S. Court of Appeals for the Ninth Circuit reversed the District Court's decision. Contrasting the precision of "fixed statutory deadlines" with California's proscription of "substantial delay," the appeals court held that California's standard lacked the clarity and certainty necessary to constitute an adequate state bar.

. . . . [W]e hold that California is not put to the choice of imposing a specific deadline for habeas petitions (which would almost certainly rule out Martin's nearly five-year delay) or preserving the flexibility of current practice, but only at the cost of undermining the finality of state court judgments. In so ruling, we stress that Martin has not alleged that California's time bar, either by design or in operation, discriminates against federal claims or claimants.

I

While most States set determinate time limits for collateral relief applications, in California, neither statute nor rule of court does so. Instead, California courts apply a general "reasonableness" standard to judge whether a habeas petition is timely filed. The basic instruction provided by the California Supreme Court is simply that a habeas petition should be filed as promptly as the circumstances allow.

California's collateral review regime differs from that of other States in a second notable respect: All California courts have original jurisdiction in habeas corpus proceedings, thus no appeal lies from the denial of a petition for writ of habeas corpus. A prisoner whose petition has been denied by the superior court can obtain review of his claims only by the filing of a new petition in the Court of Appeal. The new petition, however, must be confined to claims raised in the initial petition.

Because a habeas petitioner may skip over the lower courts and file directly in the California Supreme Court, that court rules on a staggering number of habeas petitions each year.[2] . . .

[2] In fiscal year 2008–2009, the California Supreme Court issued dispositions in 3,258 original habeas actions. . . . During a similar time period, a total of 2,210 habeas cases were on this Court's docket.

II
A

A federal habeas court will not review a claim rejected by a state court if the decision of the state court rests on a state law ground that is independent of the federal question and adequate to support the judgment. The state-law ground may be a substantive rule dispositive of the case, or a procedural barrier to adjudication of the claim on the merits.

Ordinarily, a state prisoner seeking federal habeas relief must first exhaust the remedies available in the courts of the State, thereby affording those courts the first opportunity to address and correct alleged violations of the prisoner's federal rights. The adequate and independent state ground doctrine furthers that objective, for without it, habeas petitioners would be able to avoid the exhaustion requirement by defaulting their federal claims in state court. Accordingly, absent showings of "cause" and "prejudice," federal habeas relief will be unavailable when (1) a state court has declined to address a prisoner's federal claims because the prisoner had failed to meet a state procedural requirement, and (2) the state judgment rests on independent and adequate state procedural grounds.

B

To qualify as an "adequate" procedural ground, a state rule must be firmly established and regularly followed. A discretionary state procedural rule can serve as an adequate ground to bar federal habeas review. A rule can be firmly established and regularly followed even if the appropriate exercise of discretion may permit consideration of a federal claim in some cases but not others.

California's time rule, although discretionary, meets the "firmly established" criterion . . . . The California Supreme Court, as earlier noted, framed the timeliness requirement for habeas petitioners in a trilogy of cases. Those decisions instruct habeas petitioners to allege with specificity the absence of substantial delay, good cause for delay, or eligibility for one of four exceptions to the time bar. And California's case law made it altogether plain that Martin's delay of nearly five years ranked as "substantial."

Martin nevertheless urges that California's rule is too vague to be regarded as "firmly established." "[R]easonable time" period and "substantial delay," he maintains, are meaningless terms. We disagree. Indeterminate language is typical of discretionary rules. Application of those rules in particular circumstances, however, can supply the requisite clarity.

Congressional statutes and this Court's decisions, we note, have employed time limitations that are not stated in precise, numerical terms. Former Federal Habeas Corpus Rule 9(a), for example, set no fixed time limit on submission of habeas petitions. The Rule permitted dismissal of a state prisoner's petition when it appeared that delay in commencing litigation prejudiced the State in its ability to respond. To stave off dismissal, the petitioner had to show that he could not earlier have known, by the exercise of reasonable diligence, the grounds on which he based the petition. In [another case], we instructed district courts, when employing stay and abeyance procedure, to place reasonable time limits on a petitioner's trip to state court and back. . . .

Nor is California's time rule vulnerable on the ground that it is not regularly followed. Each year, the California Supreme Court summarily denies hundreds of habeas petitions by citing [untimeliness]. On the same day the court denied Martin's petition, it issued 21 other [such] summary denials. In reasoned opinions, too, California courts regularly invoke [untimeliness precedent] to determine whether a habeas petition is time barred.

Martin argued below that California's time bar is not regularly followed in this sense: Use of summary denials makes it impossible to tell why the California Supreme Court decides some delayed petitions on the merits and rejects others as untimely. We see no reason to reject California's time bar simply because a court may opt to bypass the [untimeliness] assessment and summarily dismiss a petition on the merits, if that is the easier path.

The Ninth Circuit concluded that California's time bar is not consistently applied because outcomes under the rule vary from case to case. For example, in *People v. Fairbanks*, a one-year delay was found substantial, while in *In re Little*, a delay of 14 months was determined to be insubstantial.

A discretionary rule ought not be disregarded automatically upon a showing of seeming inconsistencies.[7] Discretion enables a court to home in on case-specific considerations and to avoid the harsh results that sometimes attend consistent application of an unyielding rule.

[7] Closer inspection may reveal that seeming inconsistencies are not necessarily arbitrary or irrational. *Fairbanks* and *Little* are illustrative. In *Fairbanks*, the court found that petitioner did not act diligently when she waited to withdraw her guilty plea until one year after learning that revocation of her driver's license was irreversible. In *Little*, a *pro se* prisoner claimed that his trial counsel should have raised a posttraumatic stress disorder defense. Although the filing delay was 14 months, the court entertained it on the merits. Given the discrete context in which each case arose, the two decisions present no square conflict.

A state ground, no doubt, may be found inadequate when discretion has been exercised to impose novel and unforeseeable requirements without fair or substantial support in prior state law. Martin does not contend, however, that in his case, the California Supreme Court exercised its discretion in a surprising or unfair manner.

Sound procedure often requires discretion to exact or excuse compliance with strict rules, and we have no cause to discourage standards allowing courts to exercise such discretion. . . .

C

Today's decision, trained on California's timeliness rule for habeas petitions, leaves unaltered this Court's repeated recognition that federal courts must carefully examine state procedural requirements to ensure that they do not operate to discriminate against claims of federal rights. On the record before us, however, there is no basis for concluding that California's timeliness rule operates to the particular disadvantage of petitioners asserting federal rights.

For the reasons stated, we find no inadequacy in California's timeliness rule generally or as applied in Martin's case. The judgment of the United States Court of Appeals for the Ninth Circuit is therefore *Reversed.*

Exxon Mobile v. Saudi Basic Industries (2005)

This case concerns what has come to be known as the *Rooker-Feldman* doctrine, applied by this court only twice. Variously interpreted in the lower courts, the doctrine has sometimes been construed to extend far beyond the contours of the *Rooker* and *Feldman* cases, overriding Congress's conferral of federal-court jurisdiction concurrent with jurisdiction exercised by state courts, and superseding the ordinary application of preclusion law pursuant to 28 U.S.C. § 1738.

Rooker was a suit commenced in Federal District Court to have a judgment of a state court, adverse to the federal court plaintiffs, "declared null and void." In *Feldman*, parties unsuccessful in the District of Columbia Court of Appeals (the District's highest court) commenced a federal-court action against the very court that had rejected their applications. Holding the federal suits impermissible, we emphasized that appellate jurisdiction to reverse or modify a state-court judgment is lodged, initially by § 25 of the Judiciary Act of 1789, and now by 28 U.S.C. § 1257, exclusively in this Court. Federal district courts, we noted, are empowered to exercise original, not appellate, jurisdiction. Plaintiffs in *Rooker* and *Feldman* had litigated and lost in state court. Their federal complaints, we observed, essentially invited federal courts of first instance to review and reverse unfavorable state-court judgments. We declared such suits out of bounds, *i.e.,* properly dismissed for want of subject-matter jurisdiction.

The *Rooker-Feldman* doctrine, we hold today, is confined to cases of the kind from which the doctrine acquired its name: cases brought by state-court losers complaining of injuries caused by state-court judgments rendered before the district court proceedings commenced and inviting district court review and rejection of those judgments. *Rooker-Feldman* does not otherwise override or supplant preclusion doctrine or augment the circumscribed doctrines that allow federal courts to stay or dismiss proceedings in deference to state-court actions. . . .

II

In 1980, two subsidiaries of petitioner Exxon Mobil Corporation (then the separate companies Exxon Corp. and Mobil Corp.) formed joint ventures with respondent Saudi Basic Industries Corp. (SABIC) to produce polyethylene in Saudi Arabia. Two decades later, the parties began to dispute royalties that SABIC had charged the joint ventures for sublicenses to a polyethylene manufacturing method.

SABIC preemptively sued the two ExxonMobil subsidiaries in Delaware Superior Court in July 2000 seeking a declaratory judgment that the royalty charges were proper under the joint venture agreements. About two weeks later, ExxonMobil and its subsidiaries countersued SABIC in the United States District Court for the District of New Jersey, alleging that SABIC overcharged the joint ventures for the sublicenses. ExxonMobil invoked subject-matter jurisdiction in the New Jersey action under 28 U.S.C. § 1330, which authorizes district courts to adjudicate actions against foreign states.

In January 2002, the ExxonMobil subsidiaries answered SABIC's state-court complaint, asserting as counterclaims the same claims ExxonMobil had made in the federal suit in New Jersey. The state suit went to trial in March 2003, and the jury returned a verdict of over $400 million in favor of the ExxonMobil subsidiaries. SABIC appealed the judgment entered on the verdict to the Delaware Supreme Court.

Before the state-court trial, SABIC moved to dismiss the federal suit, alleging, *inter alia,* immunity under the Foreign Sovereign Immunities Act of 1976. The Federal District Court denied SABIC's motion to dismiss. SABIC took an interlocutory appeal, and the Court of Appeals heard argument in December 2003, over eight months after the state-court jury verdict.

The Court of Appeals, on its own motion, raised the question whether "subject matter jurisdiction over this case fails under the *Rooker-Feldman* doctrine because ExxonMobil's claims have already been litigated in state court." The court did not question the District Court's possession of subject-matter jurisdiction at the outset of the suit, but held that federal jurisdiction terminated when the Delaware Superior Court entered judgment on the jury verdict. The court rejected ExxonMobil's argument that *Rooker-Feldman* could not apply because ExxonMobil filed its federal complaint well before the state-court judgment. The only relevant consideration, the court stated, is whether the state judgment precedes a federal judgment on the same claims. If *Rooker-Feldman* did not apply to federal actions filed prior to a state-court judgment, the Court of Appeals worried, "we would be encouraging parties to maintain federal actions as 'insurance policies' while their state court claims were pending." Once ExxonMobil's claims had been litigated to a judgment in state court, the Court of Appeals held, *Rooker-Feldman* precluded the federal district court from proceeding.

ExxonMobil, at that point prevailing in Delaware, was not seeking to overturn the state-court judgment. Nevertheless, the Court of Appeals hypothesized that, if SABIC won on appeal in Delaware, ExxonMobil would be endeavoring in the federal action to "invalidate" the state-court judgment, "the very situation," the court concluded, "contemplated by *Rooker-Feldman's* 'inextricably intertwined' bar." . . .

Rooker and *Feldman* exhibit the limited circumstances in which this Court's appellate jurisdiction over state-court judgments, 28 U.S.C. § 1257, precludes a United States district court from exercising subject-matter jurisdiction in an action it would otherwise be empowered to adjudicate under a congressional grant of authority, *e.g.*, § 1330 (suits against foreign states), § 1331 (federal question), and § 1332 (diversity). In both cases, the losing party in state court filed suit in federal court after the state proceedings ended, complaining of an injury caused by the state-court judgment and seeking review and rejection of that judgment. Plaintiffs in both cases, alleging federal-question jurisdiction, called upon the District Court to overturn an injurious state-court judgment. Because § 1257, as long interpreted, vests authority to review a state court's judgment solely in this Court, the District Courts in *Rooker* and *Feldman* lacked subject-matter jurisdiction.[8]

> [8] Congress, if so minded, may explicitly empower district courts to oversee certain state-court judgments and has done so, most notably, in authorizing federal habeas review of state prisoners' petitions. 28 U.S.C. § 2254(a).

When there is parallel state and federal litigation, *Rooker-Feldman* is not triggered simply by the entry of judgment in state court. This Court has repeatedly held that the pendency of an action in the state court is no bar to proceedings concerning the same matter in the Federal court having jurisdiction. Comity or abstention doctrines may, in various circumstances, permit or require the federal court to stay or dismiss the federal action in favor of the state-court litigation. *See, e.g.*, *Colorado River Water Conservation Dist. v. United States*; *Younger v. Harris*; *Burford v. Sun Oil Co.*; *Railroad Comm'n of Tex. v. Pullman Co.* But neither *Rooker* nor *Feldman* supports the notion that properly invoked concurrent jurisdiction vanishes if a state court reaches judgment on the same or related question while the case remains *sub judice* in a federal court.

Disposition of the federal action, once the state-court adjudication is complete, would be governed by preclusion law. The Full Faith and Credit Act requires the federal court to give the same preclusive effect to a state-court judgment as another court of that State would give. Preclusion, of course, is not a jurisdictional matter. In parallel litigation, a federal court may be bound to recognize the claim- and issue-preclusive effects of a state-court judgment, but federal jurisdiction over an action does not terminate automatically on the entry of judgment in the state court.

Nor does § 1257 stop a district court from exercising subject-matter jurisdiction simply because a party attempts to litigate in federal court a matter previously litigated in state court. If a federal plaintiff presents some independent claim, albeit one that denies a legal conclusion that a state court has reached in a case to which he was a party, then there is jurisdiction and state law determines whether the defendant prevails under principles of preclusion.

This case surely is not the paradigm situation in which *Rooker-Feldman* precludes a federal district court from proceeding. ExxonMobil plainly has not repaired to federal court to undo the Delaware judgment in its favor. Rather, it appears ExxonMobil filed suit in Federal District Court (only two weeks after SABIC filed in Delaware and well before any judgment in state court) to protect itself in the event it lost in state court on grounds (such as the state statute of limitations) that might not preclude relief in the federal venue. *Rooker-Feldman* did not prevent the District Court from exercising jurisdiction when ExxonMobil filed the federal action, and it did not emerge to vanquish jurisdiction after ExxonMobil prevailed in the Delaware courts.

* * *

For the reasons stated, the judgment of the Court of Appeals for the Third Circuit is reversed, and the case is remanded for further proceedings consistent with this opinion.

Allen v. McCurry (1980)

Justice STEWART delivered the opinion of the Court.

At a hearing before his criminal trial in a Missouri court, the respondent, Willie McCurry, invoked the Fourth and Fourteenth Amendments to suppress evidence that had been seized by the police. The trial court denied the suppression motion in part, and McCurry was subsequently convicted after a jury trial. The conviction was later affirmed on appeal. . . .

[Then] he sought federal-court redress for the alleged constitutional violation by bringing a damages suit under 42 U.S.C. § 1983 against the officers who had entered his home and seized the evidence in question. We granted certiorari to consider whether . . . the state courts' partial rejection of McCurry's constitutional claim [w]as a collateral estoppel defense to the § 1983 suit against them for damages.

I

In April 1977, several undercover police officers, following an informant's tip that McCurry was dealing in heroin, went to his house in St. Louis to attempt a purchase. Two officers, petitioners Allen and Jacobsmeyer, knocked on the front door, while the other officers hid nearby. When McCurry opened the door, the two officers asked to buy some heroin "caps." McCurry went back into the house and returned soon thereafter, firing a pistol at and seriously wounding Allen and Jacobsmeyer. After a gun battle with the other officers and their reinforcements, McCurry retreated into the house; he emerged again when the police demanded that he surrender. Several officers then entered the house without a warrant, purportedly to search for other persons inside. One of the officers seized drugs and other contraband that lay in plain view, as well as additional contraband he found in dresser drawers and in auto tires on the porch.

McCurry was charged with possession of heroin and assault with intent to kill. At the pretrial suppression hearing, the trial judge excluded the evidence seized from the dresser drawers and tires, but denied suppression of the evidence found in plain view. McCurry was convicted of both the heroin and assault offenses.

McCurry subsequently filed the present § 1983 action for $1 million in damages against petitioners Allen and Jacobsmeyer, other unnamed individual police officers, and the city of St. Louis and its police department. The complaint alleged a conspiracy to violate McCurry's Fourth Amendment rights, an unconstitutional search and seizure of his house, and an assault on him by unknown police officers after he had been arrested and handcuffed.

The petitioners moved for summary judgment. The District Court apparently understood the gist of the complaint to be the allegedly unconstitutional search and seizure and granted summary judgment, holding that collateral estoppel prevented McCurry from relitigating the search-and-seizure question already decided against him in the state courts.

The Court of Appeals reversed the judgment and remanded the case for trial. . . .

II

The federal courts have traditionally adhered to the related doctrines of res judicata and collateral estoppel. Under res judicata, a final judgment on the merits of an action precludes the parties or their privies from relitigating issues that were or could have been raised in that action. Under collateral estoppel, once a court has decided an issue of fact or law necessary to its judgment, that decision may preclude relitigation of the issue in a suit on a different cause of action involving a party to the first case. As this Court and other courts have often recognized, res judicata and collateral estoppel relieve parties of the cost and vexation of multiple lawsuits, conserve judicial resources, and, by preventing inconsistent decisions, encourage reliance on adjudication.

In recent years, this Court has reaffirmed the benefits of collateral estoppel in particular, finding the policies underlying it to apply in contexts not formerly recognized at common law. Thus, the Court has eliminated the requirement of mutuality in applying collateral estoppel to bar relitigation of issues decided earlier in federal-court suits, and has allowed a litigant who was not a party to a federal case to use collateral estoppel "offensively" in a new federal suit against the party who lost on the decided issue in the first case. But one general limitation the Court has repeatedly recognized is that the concept of collateral estoppel cannot apply when the party against whom the earlier decision is asserted did not have a full and fair opportunity to litigate that issue in the earlier case.

The federal courts generally have also consistently accorded preclusive effect to issues decided by state courts. Thus, res judicata and collateral estoppel not only reduce unnecessary litigation and foster reliance on adjudication, but also promote the comity between state and federal courts that has been recognized as a bulwark of the federal system. *See Younger v. Harris*.

Indeed, though the federal courts may look to the common law or to the policies supporting res judicata and collateral estoppel in assessing the preclusive effect of decisions of other federal courts, Congress has specifically required all federal courts to give preclusive effect to state-court judgments whenever the courts of the State from which the judgments emerged would do so:

[J]udicial proceedings [of any court of any State] shall have the same full faith and credit in every court within the United States and its Territories and Possessions as they have by law or usage in the courts of such State. . . .

28 U.S.C. § 1738 (1976). It is against this background that we examine the relationship of § 1983 and collateral estoppel, and the decision of the Court of Appeals in this case.

III

. . . . [T]he legislative history of § 1983 does not in any clear way suggest that Congress intended to repeal or restrict the traditional doctrines of preclusion. The main goal of the Act was to override the corrupting influence of the Ku Klux Klan and its sympathizers on the governments and law enforcement agencies of the Southern States, and of course the debates show that one strong motive behind its enactment was grave congressional concern that the state courts had been deficient in protecting federal rights. But in the context of the legislative history as a whole, this congressional concern lends only the most equivocal support to any argument that, in cases where the state courts have recognized the constitutional claims asserted and provided fair procedures for determining them, Congress intended to override § 1738 or the common-law rules of collateral estoppel and res judicata. Since repeals by implication are disfavored, much clearer support than this would be required to hold that § 1738 and the traditional rules of preclusion are not applicable to § 1983 suits.

As the Court has understood the history of the legislation, Congress realized that in enacting § 1983 it was altering the balance of judicial power between the state and federal courts. But in doing so, Congress was adding to the jurisdiction of the federal courts, not subtracting from that of the state courts. The debates contain several references to the concurrent jurisdiction of the state courts over federal questions, and numerous suggestions that the state courts would retain their established jurisdiction so that they could, when the then current political passions abated, demonstrate a new sensitivity to federal rights.

. . . . In short, the federal courts could step in where the state courts were unable or unwilling to protect federal rights. This understanding of § 1983 might well support an exception to res judicata and collateral estoppel where state law did not provide fair procedures for the litigation of constitutional claims, or where a state court failed to even acknowledge the existence of the constitutional principle on which a litigant based his claim. Such an exception, however, would be essentially the same as the important general limit on rules of preclusion that already exists: Collateral estoppel does not apply where the party against whom an earlier court decision is asserted did not have a full and fair opportunity to litigate the claim or issue decided by the first court. But . . . Congress [never] intended to allow relitigation of federal issues decided after a full and fair hearing in a state court simply because the state court's decision may have been erroneous.

The Court of Appeals in this case . . . . concluded that since *Stone v. Powell* had removed McCurry's right to a hearing of his Fourth Amendment claim in federal habeas corpus, collateral estoppel should not deprive him of a federal judicial hearing of that claim in a § 1983 suit.

Stone v. Powell does not provide a logical doctrinal source for the court's ruling. This Court in *Stone* assessed the costs and benefits of the judge-made exclusionary rule within the boundaries of the federal courts' statutory power to issue writs of habeas corpus, and decided that the incremental deterrent effect that the issuance of the writ in Fourth Amendment cases might have on police conduct did not justify the cost the writ imposed upon the fair administration of criminal justice. The *Stone* decision concerns only the prudent exercise of federal-court jurisdiction under 28 U.S.C. § 2254. It has no bearing on § 1983 suits or on the question of the preclusive effect of state-court judgments.

The actual basis of the Court of Appeals's holding appears to be a generally framed principle that every person asserting a federal right is entitled to one unencumbered opportunity to litigate that right in a federal district court, regardless of the legal posture in which the federal claim arises. But the authority for this principle is difficult to discern. It cannot lie in the Constitution, which makes no such guarantee, but leaves the scope of the jurisdiction of the federal district courts to the wisdom of Congress. And no such authority is to be found in § 1983 itself. For reasons already discussed at length, nothing in the language or legislative history of § 1983 proves any congressional intent to deny binding effect to a state-court judgment or decision when the state court, acting within its proper jurisdiction, has given the parties a full and fair opportunity to litigate federal claims, and thereby has shown itself willing and able to protect federal rights. And nothing in the legislative history of § 1983 reveals any purpose to afford less deference to judgments in state criminal proceedings than to those in state civil proceedings. There is, in short, no reason to believe that Congress intended to provide a person claiming a federal right an unrestricted opportunity to relitigate an issue already decided in state court simply because the issue arose in a state proceeding in which he would rather not have been engaged at all.

Through § 1983, the 42d Congress intended to afford an opportunity for legal and equitable relief in a federal court for certain types of injuries. It is difficult to believe that the drafters of that Act considered it a substitute for a federal writ of habeas corpus, the purpose of which is not to redress civil injury, but to release the applicant from unlawful physical confinement, particularly in light of the extremely narrow scope of federal habeas relief for state prisoners in 1871.

The only other conceivable basis for finding a universal right to litigate a federal claim in a federal district court is hardly a legal basis at all, but rather a general distrust of the capacity of the state courts to render correct decisions on constitutional issues. It is ironic that *Stone v. Powell* provided the occasion for the expression of such an attitude in the present litigation, in view of this Court's emphatic reaffirmation in that case of the constitutional obligation of the state courts to uphold federal law, and its expression of confidence in their ability to do so.

The Court of Appeals erred in holding that McCurry's inability to obtain federal habeas corpus relief upon his Fourth Amendment claim renders the doctrine of collateral estoppel inapplicable to his § 1983 suit. Accordingly, the judgment is reversed, and the case is remanded to the Court of Appeals for proceedings consistent with this opinion.

It is so ordered.

Justice BLACKMUN, with whom Justice BRENNAN and Justice MARSHALL join, dissenting.

. . . . The Court today holds that notions of collateral estoppel apply with full force to this suit brought under 42 U.S.C. § 1983. In my view, the Court, in so ruling, ignores the clear import of the legislative history of that statute and disregards the important federal policies that underlie its enforcement. It also shows itself insensitive both to the significant differences between the § 1983 remedy and the exclusionary rule, and to the pressures upon a criminal defendant that make a free choice of forum illusory. I do not doubt that principles of preclusion are to be given such effect as is appropriate in a § 1983 action. In many cases, the denial of res judicata or collateral estoppel effect would serve no purpose and would harm relations between federal and state tribunals. Nonetheless, the Court's analysis in this particular case is unacceptable to me. It works injustice on this § 1983 plaintiff, and it makes more difficult the consistent protection of constitutional rights, a consideration that was at the core of the enacters' intent. Accordingly, I dissent.

In deciding whether a common-law doctrine is to apply to § 1983 when the statute itself is silent, prior cases uniformly have accorded the intent of the legislators great weight. . . . Although the legislators of the 42d Congress did not expressly state whether the then existing common-law doctrine of preclusion would survive enactment of § 1983, they plainly anticipated more than the creation of a federal statutory remedy to be administered indifferently by either a state or a federal court. The legislative intent, as expressed by supporters and understood by opponents, was to restructure relations between the state and federal courts. Congress deliberately opened the federal courts to individual citizens in response to the States' failure to provide justice in their own courts. Contrary to the view presently expressed by the Court, the 42d Congress was not concerned solely with procedural regularity. Even where there was procedural regularity, which the Court today so stresses, Congress believed that substantive justice was unobtainable. The availability of the federal forum was not meant to turn on whether, in an individual case, the state procedures were adequate. Assessing the state of affairs as a whole, Congress specifically made a determination that federal oversight of constitutional determinations through the federal courts was necessary to ensure the effective enforcement of constitutional rights.

That the new federal jurisdiction was conceived of as concurrent with state jurisdiction does not alter the significance of Congress's opening the federal courts to these claims. Congress consciously acted in the broadest possible manner. The legislators perceived that justice was not being done in the States then dominated by the Klan, and it seems senseless to suppose that they would have intended the federal courts to give full preclusive effect to prior state adjudications. That supposition would contradict their obvious aim to right the wrongs perpetuated in those same courts.

I appreciate that the legislative history is capable of alternative interpretations. See the Court's opinion. I would have thought, however, that our prior decisions made very clear which reading is required. The Court repeatedly has recognized that § 1983 embodies a strong congressional policy in favor of federal courts' acting as the primary and final arbiters of constitutional rights. . . .

The Court now fashions a new doctrine of preclusion, applicable only to actions brought under § 1983, that is more strict and more confining than the federal rules of preclusion applied in other cases. . . . [T]he Court states that the collateral-estoppel effect of prior state adjudication should turn on only one factor, namely, . . . a "full and fair opportunity" to litigate th[e] issue in the earlier case. If that one factor is present, the Court asserts, the litigant properly should be barred from relitigating the issue in federal court. One cannot deny that this factor is an important one. I do not believe, however, that the doctrine of preclusion requires the inquiry to be so narrow, and my understanding of the policies underlying § 1983 would lead me to consider all relevant factors in each case before concluding that preclusion was warranted. . . .

[T]he process of deciding in a state criminal trial whether to exclude or admit evidence is not at all the equivalent of a § 1983 proceeding. The remedy sought in the latter is utterly different. In bringing the civil suit the criminal defendant does not seek to challenge his conviction collaterally. At most, he wins damages. In contrast, the exclusion of evidence may prevent a criminal conviction. A trial court, faced with the decision whether to exclude relevant evidence, confronts institutional pressures that may cause it to give a different shape to the Fourth Amendment right from what would result in civil litigation of a damages claim. Also, the issue whether to exclude evidence is subsidiary to the purpose of a criminal trial, which is to determine the guilt or innocence of the defendant, and a trial court, at least subconsciously, must weigh the potential damage to the truth-seeking process caused by excluding relevant evidence.

A state criminal defendant cannot be held to have chosen voluntarily to litigate his Fourth Amendment claim in the state court. The risk of conviction puts pressure upon him to raise all possible defenses. He also faces uncertainty about the wisdom of forgoing litigation on *any* issue, for there is the possibility that he will be held to have waived his right to appeal on that issue. The deliberate bypass of state procedures, which the imposition of collateral estoppel under these circumstances encourages, surely is not a preferred goal. To hold that a criminal defendant who raises a Fourth Amendment claim at his criminal trial freely and without reservation submits his federal claims for decision by the state courts is to deny reality. The criminal defendant is an involuntary litigant in the state tribunal, and against him all the forces of the State are arrayed. To force him to a choice between forgoing either a potential defense or a federal forum for hearing his constitutional civil claim is fundamentally unfair.

I would affirm the judgment of the Court of Appeals.

Habeas Corpus

Introduction

The Constitution protects the historic writ of habeas corpus, which gives courts the power to direct the custodian of a person to bring the person to court to determine if the custodianship is lawful. The classic habeas case is a person convicted of a crime who challenges the conviction as unlawful. Habeas thus implicates many of the other topics an themes covered in this book, including federalism, separation of powers, efficiency, and the role of the courts. Consider the following questions:

- Why is habeas specifically enshrined in the Constitution? What does it say about the supremacy of federal law and, to some extent, of federal courts?

- What policies and policy tensions exist in federal habeas-review of state-court detentions? Has Congress struck the right balance?

- In what ways are habeas doctrine consistent or inconsistent with related but non-habeas topics covered elsewhere in this book?

United States Constitution

Article 1, § 9, cl. 2. The privilege of the writ of habeas corpus shall not be suspended, unless when in cases of rebellion or invasion the public safety may require it.

United States Code

28 U.S.C. § 2254.

(a) The Supreme Court, a Justice thereof, a circuit judge, or a district court shall entertain an application for a writ of habeas corpus in behalf of a person in custody pursuant to the judgment of a State court only on the ground that he is in custody in violation of the Constitution or laws or treaties of the United States.

(b)(1) An application for a writ of habeas corpus on behalf of a person in custody pursuant to the judgment of a State court shall not be granted unless it appears that—(A) the applicant has exhausted the remedies available in the courts of the State; or (B)(i) there is an absence of available State corrective process; or (ii) circumstances exist that render such process ineffective to protect the rights of the applicant. . . .

(d) An application for a writ of habeas corpus on behalf of a person in custody pursuant to the judgment of a State court shall not be granted with respect to any claim that was adjudicated on the merits in State court proceedings unless the adjudication of the claim—(1) resulted in a decision that was contrary to, or involved an unreasonable application of, clearly established Federal law, as determined by the Supreme Court of the United States; or (2) resulted in a decision that was based on an unreasonable determination of the facts in light of the evidence presented in the State court proceeding.

(e)(1) In a proceeding instituted by an application for a writ of habeas corpus by a person in custody pursuant to the judgment of a State court, a determination of a factual issue made by a State court shall be presumed to be correct. The applicant shall have the burden of rebutting the presumption of correctness by clear and convincing evidence. . . .

Boumediene v. Bush (2008)

Justice KENNEDY delivered the opinion of the Court.

Petitioners are aliens designated as enemy combatants and detained at the United States Naval Station at Guantanamo Bay, Cuba. There are others detained there, also aliens, who are not parties to this suit.

Petitioners present a question not resolved by our earlier cases relating to the detention of aliens at Guantanamo: whether they have the constitutional privilege of habeas corpus, a privilege not to be withdrawn except in conformance with the Suspension Clause, Art. I, § 9, cl. 2. We hold these petitioners do have the habeas corpus privilege. Congress has enacted a statute, the Detainee Treatment Act of 2005 (DTA) that provides certain procedures for review of the detainees' status. We hold that those procedures are not an adequate and effective substitute for habeas corpus. Therefore § 7 of the Military Commissions Act of 2006 (MCA) operates as an unconstitutional suspension of the writ. We do not address whether the President has authority to detain these petitioners nor do we hold that the writ must issue. These and other questions regarding the legality of the detention are to be resolved in the first instance by the District Court.

I

Under the Authorization for Use of Military Force (AUMF), the President is authorized to use all necessary and appropriate force against those nations, organizations, or persons he determines planned, authorized, committed, or aided the terrorist attacks that occurred on September 11, 2001, or harbored such organizations or persons, in order to prevent any future acts of international terrorism against the United States by such nations, organizations or persons.

The Deputy Secretary of Defense established Combatant Status Review Tribunals (CSRTs) to determine whether individuals detained at Guantanamo were "enemy combatants," as the Department defines that term. A later memorandum established procedures to implement the CSRTs.

Interpreting the AUMF, the Department of Defense ordered the detention of these petitioners, and they were transferred to Guantanamo. Some of these individuals were apprehended on the battlefield in Afghanistan, others in places as far away from there as Bosnia and Gambia. All are foreign nationals, but none is a citizen of a nation now at war with the United States. Each denies he is a member of the al Qaeda terrorist network that carried out the September 11 attacks or of the Taliban regime that provided sanctuary for al

Qaeda. Each petitioner appeared before a separate CSRT; was determined to be an enemy combatant; and has sought a writ of habeas corpus in the United States District Court for the District of Columbia.

Congress passed the DTA. Subsection (e) of § 1005 of the DTA amended 28 U.S.C. § 2241 to provide that "no court, justice, or judge shall have jurisdiction to hear or consider . . . an application for a writ of habeas corpus filed by or on behalf of an alien detained by the Department of Defense at Guantanamo Bay, Cuba." Section 1005 further provides that the Court of Appeals for the District of Columbia Circuit shall have "exclusive" jurisdiction to review decisions of the CSRTs.

In *Hamdan*, the Court held this provision did not apply to cases (like petitioners') pending when the DTA was enacted. Congress responded by passing the MCA, which again amended § 2241. The text of the statutory amendment is discussed below.

The Court of Appeals concluded that MCA § 7 must be read to strip from it, and all federal courts, jurisdiction to consider petitioners' habeas corpus applications; that petitioners are not entitled to the privilege of the writ or the protections of the Suspension Clause; and, as a result, that it was unnecessary to consider whether Congress provided an adequate and effective substitute for habeas corpus in the DTA. We granted certiorari.

II

As a threshold matter, we must decide whether MCA § 7 denies the federal courts jurisdiction to hear habeas corpus actions pending at the time of its enactment. We hold the statute does deny that jurisdiction, so that, if the statute is valid, petitioners' cases must be dismissed. . . .

IV

. . . . We hold that Art. I, § 9, cl. 2, of the Constitution has full effect at Guantanamo Bay. If the privilege of habeas corpus is to be denied to the detainees now before us, Congress must act in accordance with the requirements of the Suspension Clause. This Court may not impose a *de facto* suspension by abstaining from these controversies. The MCA does not purport to be a formal suspension of the writ; and the Government, in its submissions to us, has not argued that it is. Petitioners, therefore, are entitled to the privilege of habeas corpus to challenge the legality of their detention.

In light of this holding the question becomes whether the statute stripping jurisdiction to issue the writ avoids the Suspension Clause mandate because Congress has provided adequate substitute procedures for habeas corpus. The Government submits there has been compliance with the Suspension Clause because the DTA review process in the Court of Appeals provides an adequate substitute. Congress has granted that court jurisdiction to consider "(i) whether the status determination of the [CSRT] . . . was consistent with the standards and procedures specified by the Secretary of Defense . . . and (ii) to the extent the Constitution and laws of the United States are applicable, whether the use of such standards and procedures to make the determination is consistent with the Constitution and laws of the United States." . . .

A

Our case law does not contain extensive discussion of standards defining suspension of the writ or of circumstances under which suspension has occurred. This simply confirms the care Congress has taken throughout our Nation's history to preserve the writ and its function. Indeed, most of the major legislative enactments pertaining to habeas corpus have acted not to contract the writ's protection but to expand it or to hasten resolution of prisoners' claims.

There are exceptions, of course. Title I of the Antiterrorism and Effective Death Penalty Act of 1996 (AEDPA) contains certain gatekeeping provisions that restrict a prisoner's ability to bring new and repetitive claims in "second or successive" habeas corpus actions. We upheld these provisions against a Suspension Clause challenge in [prior cases]. The provisions at issue in [them], however, did not constitute a substantial departure from common-law habeas procedures. The provisions, for the most part, codified the longstanding abuse-of-the-writ doctrine. AEDPA applies, moreover, to federal, postconviction review after criminal proceedings in state court have taken place. As of this point, cases discussing the implementation of that statute give little helpful instruction (save perhaps by contrast) for the instant cases, where no trial has been held.

Here we confront statutes, the DTA and the MCA, that were intended to circumscribe habeas review. Congress's purpose is evident . . . from the unequivocal nature of MCA § 7's jurisdiction-stripping language ("No court, justice, or judge shall have jurisdiction to hear or consider an application for a writ of habeas corpus . . .") . . . .

When Congress has intended to replace traditional habeas corpus with habeas-like substitutes, . . . it has granted to the courts broad remedial powers to secure the historic office of the writ. . . . In contrast the DTA's jurisdictional grant is quite limited. The Court of

Appeals has jurisdiction not to inquire into the legality of the detention generally but only to assess whether the CSRT complied with the standards and procedures specified by the Secretary of Defense and whether those standards and procedures are lawful. If Congress had envisioned DTA review as coextensive with traditional habeas corpus, it would not have drafted the statute in this manner. . . . [M]oreover, there has been no effort to preserve habeas corpus review as an avenue of last resort. No saving clause exists in either the MCA or the DTA. And MCA § 7 eliminates habeas review for these petitioners. . . . To the extent any doubt remains about Congress's intent, the legislative history confirms what the plain text strongly suggests: In passing the DTA Congress did not intend to create a process that differs from traditional habeas corpus process in name only. It intended to create a more limited procedure. . . . It is against this background that we must interpret the DTA and assess its adequacy as a substitute for habeas corpus.

B

We do not endeavor to offer a comprehensive summary of the requisites for an adequate substitute for habeas corpus. We do consider it uncontroversial, however, that the privilege of habeas corpus entitles the prisoner to a meaningful opportunity to demonstrate that he is being held pursuant to "the erroneous application or interpretation" of relevant law. And the habeas court must have the power to order the conditional release of an individual unlawfully detained-though release need not be the exclusive remedy and is not the appropriate one in every case in which the writ is granted. These are the easily identified attributes of any constitutionally adequate habeas corpus proceeding. But, depending on the circumstances, more may be required.

Indeed, common-law habeas corpus was, above all, an adaptable remedy. Its precise application and scope changed depending upon the circumstances. It appears the common-law habeas court's role was most extensive in cases of pretrial and noncriminal detention, where there had been little or no previous judicial review of the cause for detention. Notably, the black-letter rule that prisoners could not controvert facts in the jailer's return was not followed (or at least not with consistency) in such cases.

The idea that the necessary scope of habeas review in part depends upon the rigor of any earlier proceedings accords with our test for procedural adequacy in the due process context. This principle has an established foundation in habeas corpus jurisprudence as well.

Accordingly, where relief is sought from a sentence that resulted from the judgment of a court of record, . . . considerable deference is owed to the court that ordered confinement. Likewise in those cases the prisoner should exhaust adequate alternative remedies before filing for the writ in federal court. Both aspects of federal habeas corpus review are justified because it can be assumed that, in the usual course, a court of record provides defendants with a fair adversary proceeding. In cases involving state convictions this framework also respects federalism; and in federal cases it has added justification because the prisoner already has had a chance to seek review of his conviction in a federal forum through a direct appeal. The present cases fall outside these categories, however, for here the detention is by executive order.

Where a person is detained by executive order, rather than, say, after being tried and convicted in a court, the need for collateral review is most pressing. A criminal conviction in the usual course occurs after a judicial hearing before a tribunal disinterested in the outcome and committed to procedures designed to ensure its own independence. These dynamics are not inherent in executive detention orders or executive review procedures. In this context the need for habeas corpus is more urgent. The intended duration of the detention and the reasons for it bear upon the precise scope of the inquiry. Habeas corpus proceedings need not resemble a criminal trial, even when the detention is by executive order. But the writ must be effective. The habeas court must have sufficient authority to conduct a meaningful review of both the cause for detention and the Executive's power to detain.

To determine the necessary scope of habeas corpus review, therefore, we must assess the CSRT process, the mechanism through which petitioners' designation as enemy combatants became final. Whether one characterizes the CSRT process as direct review of the Executive's battlefield determination that the detainee is an enemy combatant-as the parties have and as we do-or as the first step in the collateral review of a battlefield determination makes no difference in a proper analysis of whether the procedures Congress put in place are an adequate substitute for habeas corpus. What matters is the sum total of procedural protections afforded to the detainee at all stages, direct and collateral.

Petitioners identify what they see as myriad deficiencies in the CSRTs. The most relevant for our purposes are the constraints upon the detainee's ability to rebut the factual basis for the Government's assertion that he is an enemy combatant. As already noted, at the CSRT stage the detainee has limited means to find or present evidence to challenge the Government's case against him. He does not have the assistance of counsel and may not be aware of the most critical allegations that the Government relied upon to order his detention. The detainee can confront witnesses that testify during the CSRT proceedings. But given that there are in effect no limits on the admission of hearsay evidence—the only requirement is that the tribunal deem the evidence relevant and helpful—the detainee's opportunity to question witnesses is likely to be more theoretical than real.

Even if we were to assume that the CSRTs satisfy due process standards, it would not end our inquiry. Habeas corpus is a collateral process that exists, in Justice Holmes's words, to cut through all forms and go to the very tissue of the structure. It comes in from the outside, not in subordination to the proceedings, and although every form may have been preserved opens the inquiry whether they have been more than an empty shell. Even when the procedures authorizing detention are structurally sound, the Suspension Clause remains applicable and the writ relevant. This is so . . . even where the prisoner is detained after a criminal trial conducted in full accordance with the protections of the Bill of Rights. . . .

Although we make no judgment as to whether the CSRTs, as currently constituted, satisfy due process standards, we agree with petitioners that, even when all the parties involved in this process act with diligence and in good faith, there is considerable risk of error in the tribunal's findings of fact. This is a risk inherent in any process that, in the words of the former Chief Judge of the Court of Appeals, is closed and accusatorial. And given that the consequence of error may be detention of persons for the duration of hostilities that may last a generation or more, this is a risk too significant to ignore.

For the writ of habeas corpus, or its substitute, to function as an effective and proper remedy in this context, the court that conducts the habeas proceeding must have the means to correct errors that occurred during the CSRT proceedings. This includes some authority to assess the sufficiency of the Government's evidence against the detainee. It also must have the authority to admit and consider relevant exculpatory evidence that was not introduced during the earlier proceeding. Federal habeas petitioners long have had the means to supplement the record on review, even in the postconviction habeas setting. Here that opportunity is constitutionally required.

Consistent with the historic function and province of the writ, habeas corpus review may be more circumscribed if the underlying detention proceedings are more thorough than they were here. The extent of the showing required of the Government in these cases is a matter to be determined. We need not explore it further at this stage. We do hold that when the judicial power to issue habeas corpus properly is invoked the judicial officer must have adequate authority to make a determination in light of the relevant law and facts and to formulate and issue appropriate orders for relief, including, if necessary, an order directing the prisoner's release.

C

We now consider whether the DTA allows the Court of Appeals to conduct a proceeding meeting these standards. We are obligated to construe the statute to avoid constitutional problems if it is fairly possible to do so. There are limits to this principle, however. The canon of constitutional avoidance does not supplant traditional modes of statutory interpretation. We cannot ignore the text and purpose of a statute in order to save it.

The DTA does not explicitly empower the Court of Appeals to order the applicant in a DTA review proceeding released should the court find that the standards and procedures used at his CSRT hearing were insufficient to justify detention. This is troubling. Yet, for present purposes, we can assume congressional silence permits a constitutionally required remedy. In that case it would be possible to hold that a remedy of release is impliedly provided for. The DTA might be read, furthermore, to allow the petitioners to assert most, if not all, of the legal claims they seek to advance, including their most basic claim: that the President has no authority under the AUMF to detain them indefinitely. (Whether the President has such authority turns on whether the AUMF authorizes—and the Constitution permits—the indefinite detention of "enemy combatants" as the Department of Defense defines that term. Thus a challenge to the President's authority to detain is, in essence, a challenge to the Department's definition of enemy combatant, a standard used by the CSRTs in petitioners' cases.) At oral argument, the Solicitor General urged us to adopt both these constructions, if doing so would allow MCA § 7 to remain intact.

The absence of a release remedy and specific language allowing AUMF challenges are not the only constitutional infirmities from which the statute potentially suffers, however. The more difficult question is whether the DTA permits the Court of Appeals to make requisite findings of fact. The DTA enables petitioners to request review of their CSRT determination in the Court of Appeals; but the "Scope of Review" provision confines the Court of Appeals's role to reviewing whether the CSRT followed the standards and procedures issued by the Department of Defense and assessing whether those standards and procedures are lawful. Among these standards is the requirement that the conclusion of the Tribunal be supported by a preponderance of the evidence allowing a rebuttable presumption in favor of the Government's evidence.

Assuming the DTA can be construed to allow the Court of Appeals to review or correct the CSRT's factual determinations, as opposed to merely certifying that the tribunal applied the correct standard of proof, we see no way to construe the statute to allow what is also constitutionally required in this context: an opportunity for the detainee to present relevant exculpatory evidence that was not made part of the record in the earlier proceedings.

On its face the statute allows the Court of Appeals to consider no evidence outside the CSRT record. In the parallel litigation, however, the Court of Appeals determined that the DTA allows it to order the production of all reasonably available information in the possession of the U.S. Government bearing on the issue of whether the detainee meets the criteria to be designated as an enemy combatant, regardless of whether this evidence was put before the CSRT. The Government disagrees with this interpretation. For present purposes, however, we can assume that the Court of Appeals was correct that the DTA allows introduction and consideration of relevant exculpatory evidence that was reasonably available to the

Government at the time of the CSRT but not made part of the record. Even so, the DTA review proceeding falls short of being a constitutionally adequate substitute, for the detainee still would have no opportunity to present evidence discovered after the CSRT proceedings concluded.

Under the DTA the Court of Appeals has the power to review CSRT determinations by assessing the legality of standards and procedures. This implies the power to inquire into what happened at the CSRT hearing and, perhaps, to remedy certain deficiencies in that proceeding. But should the Court of Appeals determine that the CSRT followed appropriate and lawful standards and procedures, it will have reached the limits of its jurisdiction. There is no language in the DTA that can be construed to allow the Court of Appeals to admit and consider newly discovered evidence that could not have been made part of the CSRT record because it was unavailable to either the Government or the detainee when the CSRT made its findings. This evidence, however, may be critical to the detainee's argument that he is not an enemy combatant and there is no cause to detain him.

This is not a remote hypothetical. One of the petitioners, Mohamed Nechla, requested at his CSRT hearing that the Government contact his employer. The petitioner claimed the employer would corroborate Nechla's contention he had no affiliation with al Qaeda. Although the CSRT determined this testimony would be relevant, it also found the witness was not reasonably available to testify at the time of the hearing. Petitioner's counsel, however, now represents the witness is available to be heard. If a detainee can present reasonably available evidence demonstrating there is no basis for his continued detention, he must have the opportunity to present this evidence to a habeas corpus court. Even under the Court of Appeals's generous construction of the DTA, however, the evidence identified by Nechla would be inadmissible in a DTA review proceeding. The role of an Article III court in the exercise of its habeas corpus function cannot be circumscribed in this manner.

By foreclosing consideration of evidence not presented or reasonably available to the detainee at the CSRT proceedings, the DTA disadvantages the detainee by limiting the scope of collateral review to a record that may not be accurate or complete. In other contexts, *e.g.*, in post-trial habeas cases where the prisoner already has had a full and fair opportunity to develop the factual predicate of his claims, similar limitations on the scope of habeas review may be appropriate. In this context, however, where the underlying detention proceedings lack the necessary adversarial character, the detainee cannot be held responsible for all deficiencies in the record.

. . . . Petitioners have met their burden of establishing that the DTA review process is, on its face, an inadequate substitute for habeas corpus. Although we do not hold that an adequate substitute must duplicate § 2241 in all respects, it suffices that the Government has not established that the detainees' access to the statutory review provisions at issue is an adequate substitute for the writ of habeas corpus. MCA § 7 thus effects an unconstitutional suspension of the writ. In view of our holding we need not discuss the reach of the writ with respect to claims of unlawful conditions of treatment or confinement.

VI
A

In light of our conclusion that there is no jurisdictional bar to the District Court's entertaining petitioners' claims the question remains whether there are prudential barriers to habeas corpus review under these circumstances.

The Government argues petitioners must seek review of their CSRT determinations in the Court of Appeals before they can proceed with their habeas corpus actions in the District Court. As noted earlier, in other contexts and for prudential reasons this Court has required exhaustion of alternative remedies before a prisoner can seek federal habeas relief. Most of these cases were brought by prisoners in state custody, and thus involved federalism concerns that are not relevant here. But we have extended this rule to require defendants in courts-martial to exhaust their military appeals before proceeding with a federal habeas corpus action. . . .

In cases involving foreign citizens detained abroad by the Executive, it likely would be both an impractical and unprecedented extension of judicial power to assume that habeas corpus would be available at the moment the prisoner is taken into custody. If and when habeas corpus jurisdiction applies, as it does in these cases, then proper deference can be accorded to reasonable procedures for screening and initial detention under lawful and proper conditions of confinement and treatment for a reasonable period of time. . . . The cases before us, however, do not involve detainees who have been held for a short period of time while awaiting their CSRT determinations. Were that the case, or were it probable that the Court of Appeals could complete a prompt review of their applications, the case for requiring temporary abstention or exhaustion of alternative remedies would be much stronger. These qualifications no longer pertain here. In some of these cases six years have elapsed without the judicial oversight that habeas corpus or an adequate substitute demands. And there has been no showing that the Executive faces such onerous burdens that it cannot respond to habeas corpus actions. To require these detainees to complete DTA review before proceeding with their habeas corpus actions would be to require additional months, if not years, of delay. The first review applications were filed over a year ago, but no decisions on the merits have been issued. While some delay in fashioning new procedures is unavoidable, the costs of delay can no longer be borne by those who are held in custody. The detainees in these cases are entitled to a prompt habeas corpus hearing.

Our decision today holds only that the petitioners before us are entitled to seek the writ; that the DTA review procedures are an inadequate substitute for habeas corpus; and that the petitioners in these cases need not exhaust the review procedures in the Court of Appeals before proceeding with their habeas actions in the District Court. The only law we identify as unconstitutional is MCA § 7. Accordingly, both the DTA and the CSRT process remain intact. Our holding with regard to exhaustion should not be read to imply that a habeas court should intervene the moment an enemy combatant steps foot in a territory where the writ runs. The Executive is entitled to a reasonable period of time to determine a detainee's status before a court entertains that detainee's habeas corpus petition. The CSRT process is the mechanism Congress and the President set up to deal with these issues. Except in cases of undue delay, federal courts should refrain from entertaining an enemy combatant's habeas corpus petition at least until after the Department, acting via the CSRT, has had a chance to review his status. . . .

* * *

In considering both the procedural and substantive standards used to impose detention to prevent acts of terrorism, proper deference must be accorded to the political branches. Unlike the President and some designated Members of Congress, neither the Members of this Court nor most federal judges begin the day with briefings that may describe new and serious threats to our Nation and its people. The law must accord the Executive substantial authority to apprehend and detain those who pose a real danger to our security.

Officials charged with daily operational responsibility for our security may consider a judicial discourse on the history of the Habeas Corpus Act of 1679 and like matters to be far removed from the Nation's present, urgent concerns. Established legal doctrine, however, must be consulted for its teaching. Remote in time it may be; irrelevant to the present it is not. Security depends upon a sophisticated intelligence apparatus and the ability of our Armed Forces to act and to interdict. There are further considerations, however. Security subsists, too, in fidelity to freedom's first principles. Chief among these are freedom from arbitrary and unlawful restraint and the personal liberty that is secured by adherence to the separation of powers. It is from these principles that the judicial authority to consider petitions for habeas corpus relief derives.

Our opinion does not undermine the Executive's powers as Commander in Chief. On the contrary, the exercise of those powers is vindicated, not eroded, when confirmed by the Judicial Branch. Within the Constitution's separation-of-powers structure, few exercises of judicial power are as legitimate or as necessary as the responsibility to hear challenges to the authority of the Executive to imprison a person. Some of these petitioners have been in custody for six years with no definitive judicial determination as to the legality of their detention. Their access to the writ is a necessity to determine the lawfulness of their status, even if, in the end, they do not obtain the relief they seek.

Because our Nation's past military conflicts have been of limited duration, it has been possible to leave the outer boundaries of war powers undefined. If, as some fear, terrorism continues to pose dangerous threats to us for years to come, the Court might not have this luxury. This result is not inevitable, however. The political branches, consistent with their independent obligations to interpret and uphold the Constitution, can engage in a genuine debate about how best to preserve constitutional values while protecting the Nation from terrorism.

It bears repeating that our opinion does not address the content of the law that governs petitioners' detention. That is a matter yet to be determined. We hold that petitioners may invoke the fundamental procedural protections of habeas corpus. The laws and Constitution are designed to survive, and remain in force, in extraordinary times. Liberty and security can be reconciled; and in our system they are reconciled within the framework of the law. The Framers decided that habeas corpus, a right of first importance, must be a part of that framework, a part of that law.

The determination by the Court of Appeals that the Suspension Clause and its protections are inapplicable to petitioners was in error. The judgment of the Court of Appeals is reversed. The cases are remanded to the Court of Appeals with instructions that it remand the cases to the District Court for proceedings consistent with this opinion.

Chief Justice ROBERTS, with whom Justice SCALIA, Justice THOMAS, and Justice ALITO join, dissenting.

Today the Court strikes down as inadequate the most generous set of procedural protections ever afforded aliens detained by this country as enemy combatants. The political branches crafted these procedures amidst an ongoing military conflict, after much careful investigation and thorough debate. The Court rejects them today out of hand, without bothering to say what due process rights the detainees possess, without explaining how the statute fails to vindicate those rights, and before a single petitioner has even attempted to avail himself of the law's operation. And to what effect? The majority merely replaces a review system designed by the people's representatives with a set of shapeless procedures to be defined by federal courts at some future date. . . .

Habeas is most fundamentally a procedural right, a mechanism for contesting the legality of executive detention. The critical threshold question in these cases, prior to any inquiry about the writ's scope, is whether the system the political branches designed protects whatever rights the detainees may possess. If so, there is no need for any additional process, whether called "habeas" or something else.

Remarkably, this Court does not require petitioners to exhaust their remedies under the statute; it does not wait to see whether those remedies will prove sufficient to protect petitioners' rights. Instead, it not only denies the D.C. Circuit the opportunity to assess the statute's remedies, it refuses to do so itself: the majority expressly declines to decide whether the CSRT procedures, coupled with Article III review, satisfy due process. It is grossly premature to pronounce on the detainees' right to habeas without first assessing whether the remedies the DTA system provides vindicate whatever rights petitioners may claim. If the CSRT procedures meet the minimal due process requirements . . . and if an Article III court is available to ensure that these procedures are followed in future cases, there is no need to reach the Suspension Clause question. Detainees will have received all the process the Constitution could possibly require, whether that process is called "habeas" or something else. The question of the writ's reach need not be addressed. This is why the Court should have required petitioners to exhaust their remedies under the statute. If the collateral review procedures Congress has provided-CSRT review coupled with Article III scrutiny-are sound, interference by a federal habeas court may be entirely unnecessary. The only way to know is to require petitioners to use the alternative procedures Congress designed. The Court's refusal to require petitioners to exhaust the remedies provided by Congress violates the traditional rules governing our decision of constitutional questions. . . .

Justice SCALIA, with whom THE CHIEF JUSTICE, Justice THOMAS, and Justice ALITO join, dissenting.

Today, for the first time in our Nation's history, the Court confers a constitutional right to habeas corpus on alien enemies detained abroad by our military forces in the course of an ongoing war. THE CHIEF JUSTICE's dissent, which I join, shows that the procedures prescribed by Congress in the Detainee Treatment Act provide the essential protections that habeas corpus guarantees; there has thus been no suspension of the writ, and no basis exists for judicial intervention beyond what the Act allows. My problem with today's opinion is more fundamental still: The writ of habeas corpus does not, and never has, run in favor of aliens abroad; the Suspension Clause thus has no application, and the Court's intervention in this military matter is entirely *ultra vires*. . . .

America is at war with radical Islamists. The enemy began by killing Americans and American allies abroad: 241 at the Marine barracks in Lebanon, 19 at the Khobar Towers in Dhahran, 224 at our embassies in Dar es Salaam and Nairobi, and 17 on the USS Cole in

Yemen. On September 11, 2001, the enemy brought the battle to American soil, killing 2,749 at the Twin Towers in New York City, 184 at the Pentagon in Washington, D. C., and 40 in Pennsylvania. It has threatened further attacks against our homeland; one need only walk about buttressed and barricaded Washington, or board a plane anywhere in the country, to know that the threat is a serious one. Our Armed Forces are now in the field against the enemy, in Afghanistan and Iraq. Last week, 13 of our countrymen in arms were killed. The game of bait-and-switch that today's opinion plays upon the Nation's Commander in Chief will make the war harder on us. It will almost certainly cause more Americans to be killed. That consequence would be tolerable if necessary to preserve a time-honored legal principle vital to our constitutional Republic. But it is this Court's blatant *abandonment* of such a principle that produces the decision today.

In the long term, then, the Court's decision today accomplishes little, except perhaps to reduce the well-being of enemy combatants that the Court ostensibly seeks to protect. In the short term, however, the decision is devastating. At least 30 of those prisoners hitherto released from Guantanamo Bay have returned to the battlefield. Some have been captured or killed. But others have succeeded in carrying on their atrocities against innocent civilians. In one case, a detainee released from Guantanamo Bay masterminded the kidnapping of two Chinese dam workers, one of whom was later shot to death when used as a human shield against Pakistani commandoes. Another former detainee promptly resumed his post as a senior Taliban commander and murdered a United Nations engineer and three Afghan soldiers. Still another murdered an Afghan judge. It was reported only last month that a released detainee carried out a suicide bombing against Iraqi soldiers in Mosul, Iraq. These, mind you, were detainees whom *the military* had concluded were not enemy combatants. Their return to the kill illustrates the incredible difficulty of assessing who is and who is not an enemy combatant in a foreign theater of operations where the environment does not lend itself to rigorous evidence collection. Astoundingly, the Court today raises the bar, requiring military officials to appear before civilian courts and defend their decisions under procedural and evidentiary rules that go beyond what Congress has specified. As the Chief Justice's dissent makes clear, we have no idea what those procedural and evidentiary rules are, but they will be determined by civil courts and (in the Court's contemplation at least) will be more detainee-friendly than those now applied, since otherwise there would no reason to hold the congressionally prescribed procedures unconstitutional. If they impose a higher standard of proof (from foreign battlefields) than the current procedures require, the number of the enemy returned to combat will obviously increase.

But even when the military has evidence that it can bring forward, it is often foolhardy to release that evidence to the attorneys representing our enemies. And one escalation of procedures that the Court *is* clear about is affording the detainees increased access to witnesses (perhaps troops serving in Afghanistan?) and to classified information. During the

1995 prosecution of Omar Abdel Rahman, federal prosecutors gave the names of 200 unindicted co-conspirators to the "Blind Sheik's" defense lawyers; that information was in the hands of Osama Bin Laden within two weeks. In another case, trial testimony revealed to the enemy that the United States had been monitoring their cellular network, whereupon they promptly stopped using it, enabling more of them to evade capture and continue their atrocities. . . .

Williams v. Taylor (2000)

Justice STEVENS announced the judgment of the Court and delivered the opinion of the Court with respect to Parts I, III, and IV, and an opinion with respect to Parts II and V.*

> * Justice SOUTER, Justice GINSBURG, and Justice BREYER join this opinion in its entirety. Justice O'CONNOR and Justice KENNEDY join Parts I, III, and IV of this opinion.

The questions presented are whether Terry Williams's constitutional right to the effective assistance of counsel as defined in *Strickland v. Washington* was violated, and whether the judgment of the Virginia Supreme Court refusing to set aside his death sentence "was contrary to, or involved an unreasonable application of, clearly established Federal law, as determined by the Supreme Court of the United States," within the meaning of 28 U.S.C. § 2254(d)(1). We answer both questions affirmatively.

I

On November 3, 1985, Harris Stone was found dead in his residence on Henry Street in Danville, Virginia. Finding no indication of a struggle, local officials determined that the cause of death was blood alcohol poisoning, and the case was considered closed. Six months after Stone's death, Terry Williams, who was then incarcerated in the "I" unit of the city jail for an unrelated offense, wrote a letter to the police stating that he had killed "that man down on Henry Street" and also stating that he "did it" to that "lady down on West Green Street" and was "very sorry." The letter was unsigned, but it closed with a reference to "I cell." The police readily identified Williams as its author, and, on April 25, 1986, they obtained several statements from him. In one Williams admitted that, after Stone refused to lend him a couple of dollars, he had killed Stone with a mattock and taken the money from his wallet. In September 1986, Williams was convicted of robbery and capital murder.

At Williams's sentencing hearing, the prosecution proved that Williams had been convicted of armed robbery in 1976 and burglary and grand larceny in 1982. The prosecution also introduced the written confessions that Williams had made in April. The prosecution described two auto thefts and two separate violent assaults on elderly victims perpetrated after the Stone murder. On December 4, 1985, Williams had started a fire outside one victim's residence before attacking and robbing him. On March 5, 1986, Williams had brutally assaulted an elderly woman on West Green Street—an incident he had mentioned in his letter to the police. That confession was particularly damaging because other evidence established that the woman was in a vegetative state and not expected to recover. Williams had also been convicted of arson for setting a fire in the jail while awaiting trial in this case.

Two expert witnesses employed by the State testified that there was a high probability that Williams would pose a serious continuing threat to society.

The evidence offered by Williams's trial counsel at the sentencing hearing consisted of the testimony of Williams's mother, two neighbors, and a taped excerpt from a statement by a psychiatrist. One of the neighbors had not been previously interviewed by defense counsel, but was noticed by counsel in the audience during the proceedings and asked to testify on the spot. The three witnesses briefly described Williams as a "nice boy" and not a violent person. The recorded psychiatrist's testimony did little more than relate Williams's statement during an examination that in the course of one of his earlier robberies, he had removed the bullets from a gun so as not to injure anyone.

In his cross-examination of the prosecution witnesses, Williams's counsel repeatedly emphasized the fact that Williams had initiated the contact with the police that enabled them to solve the murder and to identify him as the perpetrator of the recent assaults, as well as the car thefts. In closing argument, Williams's counsel characterized Williams's confessional statements as "dumb," but asked the jury to give weight to the fact that he had "turned himself in, not on one crime but on four . . . that the [police otherwise] would not have solved." The weight of defense counsel's closing, however, was devoted to explaining that it was difficult to find a reason why the jury should spare Williams's life.[2]Document5zzFN_F0042

[2] In defense counsel's words: "I will admit too that it is very difficult to ask you to show mercy to a man who maybe has not shown much mercy himself. I doubt very seriously that he thought much about mercy when he was in Mr. Stone's bedroom that night with him. I doubt very seriously that he had mercy very highly on his mind when he was walking along West Green and the incident with Alberta Stroud. I doubt very seriously that he had mercy on his mind when he took two cars that didn't belong to him. Admittedly it is very difficult to get us and ask that you give this man mercy when he has shown so little of it himself. But I would ask that you would."

The jury found a probability of future dangerousness and unanimously fixed Williams's punishment at death. The trial judge concluded that such punishment was proper and just and imposed the death sentence. The Virginia Supreme Court affirmed the conviction and sentence. It rejected Williams's argument that when the trial judge imposed sentence, he failed to give mitigating weight to the fact that Williams had turned himself in.

State Habeas Corpus Proceedings

In 1988 Williams filed for state collateral relief in the Danville Circuit Court. . . . Based on the evidence adduced after two days of hearings, Judge Ingram found that Williams's conviction was valid, but that his trial attorneys had been ineffective during sentencing. Among the evidence reviewed that had not been presented at trial were documents prepared in connection with Williams's commitment when he was 11 years old that dramatically described mistreatment, abuse, and neglect during his early childhood, as well as testimony that he was borderline mentally retarded, had suffered repeated head injuries, and might have mental impairments organic in origin. The habeas hearing also revealed that the same experts who had testified on the State's behalf at trial believed that Williams, if kept in a structured environment, would not pose a future danger to society.

Counsel's failure to discover and present this and other significant mitigating evidence was below the range expected of reasonable, professional competent assistance of counsel. Counsel's performance thus did not measure up to the standard required under the holding of *Strickland v. Washington*, and if it had, there is a reasonable probability that the result of the sentencing phase would have been different. Judge Ingram therefore recommended that Williams be granted a rehearing on the sentencing phase of his trial.

The Virginia Supreme Court did not accept that recommendation. Although it assumed, without deciding, that trial counsel had been ineffective, it disagreed with the trial judge's conclusion that Williams had suffered sufficient prejudice to warrant relief. Treating the prejudice inquiry as a mixed question of law and fact, the Virginia Supreme Court accepted the factual determination that available evidence in mitigation had not been presented at the trial, but held that the trial judge had misapplied the law in two respects. First, . . the court held that it was wrong for the trial judge to rely on mere outcome determination when assessing prejudice. Second, it construed the trial judge's opinion as having adopted a *per se* approach that would establish prejudice whenever any mitigating evidence was omitted.

The court then reviewed the prosecution evidence supporting the future dangerousness aggravating circumstance, reciting Williams's criminal history, including the several most recent offenses to which he had confessed. In comparison, it found that the excluded mitigating evidence—which it characterized as merely indicating that numerous people, mostly relatives, thought that defendant was nonviolent and could cope very well in a structured environment, barely would have altered the profile of this defendant that was presented to the jury. On this basis, the court concluded that there was no reasonable possibility that the omitted evidence would have affected the jury's sentencing recommendation, and that Williams had failed to demonstrate that his sentencing proceeding was fundamentally unfair.

Having exhausted his state remedies, Williams sought a federal writ of habeas corpus pursuant to 28 U.S.C. § 2254. After reviewing the state habeas hearing transcript and the state courts' findings of fact and conclusions of law, the federal trial judge agreed with the Virginia trial judge: The death sentence was constitutionally infirm.

After noting that the Virginia Supreme Court had not addressed the question whether trial counsel's performance at the sentencing hearing fell below the range of competence demanded of lawyers in criminal cases, the judge began by addressing that issue in detail. He identified five categories of mitigating evidence that counsel had failed to introduce,[4] and he rejected the argument that counsel's failure to conduct an adequate investigation had been a strategic decision to rely almost entirely on the fact that Williams had voluntarily confessed.

> [4] "(i) Counsel did not introduce evidence of the Petitioner's background. . . . (ii) Counsel did not introduce evidence that Petitioner was abused by his father. (iii) Counsel did not introduce testimony from correctional officers who were willing to testify that defendant would not pose a danger while incarcerated. Nor did counsel offer prison commendations awarded to Williams for his help in breaking up a prison drug ring and for returning a guard's missing wallet. (iv) Several character witnesses were not called to testify. . . . [T]he testimony of Elliott, a respected CPA in the community, could have been quite important to the jury. . . . (v) Finally, counsel did not introduce evidence that Petitioner was borderline mentally retarded, though he was found competent to stand trial."

According to Williams's trial counsel's testimony before the state habeas court, counsel did not fail to seek Williams's juvenile and social services records because he thought they would be counterproductive, but because counsel erroneously believed that state law didn't permit it. Counsel also acknowledged in the course of the hearings that information about Williams's childhood would have been important in mitigation. And counsel's failure to contact a potentially persuasive character witness was likewise not a conscious strategic choice, but simply a failure to return that witness's phone call offering his service. Finally, even if counsel neglected to conduct such an investigation at the time as part of a tactical decision, the District Judge found, tactics as a matter of reasonable performance could not justify the omissions.

Turning to the prejudice issue, the judge determined that there was a reasonable probability that, but for counsel's unprofessional errors, the result of the proceeding would have been different. He found that the Virginia Supreme Court had erroneously . . . modified the

Strickland standard for determining prejudice, and that it had made an important error of fact in discussing its finding of no prejudice. Having introduced his analysis of Williams's claim with the standard of review applicable on habeas appeals provided by 28 U.S.C. § 2254(d) the judge concluded that those errors established that the Virginia Supreme Court's decision was contrary to, or involved an unreasonable application of, clearly established Federal law within the meaning of § 2254(d)(1).

The Federal Court of Appeals reversed. It construed § 2254(d)(1) as prohibiting the grant of habeas corpus relief unless the state court "decided the question by interpreting or applying the relevant precedent in a manner that reasonable jurists would all agree is unreasonable." Applying that standard, it could not say that the Virginia Supreme Court's decision on the prejudice issue was an unreasonable application of the tests . . . . It explained that the evidence that Williams presented a future danger to society was simply overwhelming, . . . and it characterized the state court's understanding of the facts in this case as reasonable.

We granted certiorari, and now reverse.

II

In 1867, Congress enacted a statute providing that federal courts shall have power to grant writs of habeas corpus in all cases where any person may be restrained of his or her liberty in violation of the constitution, or of any treaty or law of the United States. Over the years, the federal habeas corpus statute has been repeatedly amended, but the scope of that jurisdictional grant remains the same. It is, of course, well settled that the fact that constitutional error occurred in the proceedings that led to a state-court conviction may not alone be sufficient reason for concluding that a prisoner is entitled to the remedy of habeas. On the other hand, errors that undermine confidence in the fundamental fairness of the state adjudication certainly justify the issuance of the federal writ. The deprivation of the right to the effective assistance of counsel recognized in *Strickland* is such an error.

The warden here contends that federal habeas corpus relief is prohibited by the amendment to 28 U.S.C. § 2254 enacted as a part of the Antiterrorism and Effective Death Penalty Act of 1996 (AEDPA). The relevant portion of that amendment provides: "(d) An application for a writ of habeas corpus on behalf of a person in custody pursuant to the judgment of a State court shall not be granted with respect to any claim that was adjudicated on the merits in State court proceedings unless the adjudication of the claim—(1) resulted in a decision that was contrary to, or involved an unreasonable application of, clearly established Federal law, as determined by the Supreme Court of the United States."

In this case, the Court of Appeals . . . . read the amendment as prohibiting federal courts from issuing the writ unless: (a) the state court decision is in square conflict with Supreme Court precedent that is controlling as to law and fact or (b) if no such controlling decision exists, the state court's resolution of a question of pure law rests upon an objectively unreasonable derivation of legal principles from the relevant Supreme Court precedents, or if its decision rests upon an objectively unreasonable application of established principles to new facts. Accordingly, it held that a federal court may issue habeas relief only if the state courts have decided the question by interpreting or applying the relevant precedent in a manner that reasonable jurists would all agree is unreasonable.

We are convinced that that interpretation of the amendment is incorrect. It would impose a test for determining when a legal rule is clearly established that simply cannot be squared with the real practice of decisional law. It would apply a standard for determining the reasonableness of state-court decisions that is not contained in the statute itself, and that Congress surely did not intend. And it would wrongly require the federal courts, including this Court, to defer to state judges' interpretations of federal law.

As the Fourth Circuit would have it, a state-court judgment is unreasonable in the face of federal law only if all reasonable jurists would agree that the state court was unreasonable. Thus, in this case, for example, even if the Virginia Supreme Court misread our [precedent], we could not grant relief unless we believed that none of the judges who agreed with the state court's interpretation of that case was a "reasonable jurist." But the statute says nothing about "reasonable judges," presumably because all, or virtually all, such judges occasionally commit error; they make decisions that in retrospect may be characterized as "unreasonable." Indeed, it is most unlikely that Congress would deliberately impose such a requirement of unanimity on federal judges. As Congress is acutely aware, reasonable lawyers and lawgivers regularly disagree with one another. Congress surely did not intend that the views of one such judge who might think that relief is not warranted in a particular case should always have greater weight than the contrary, considered judgment of several other reasonable judges.

The inquiry mandated by the amendment relates to the way in which a federal habeas court exercises its duty to decide constitutional questions; the amendment does not alter the underlying grant of jurisdiction in § 2254(a). When federal judges exercise their federal-question jurisdiction under the "judicial Power" of Article III of the Constitution, it is "emphatically the province and duty" of those judges to "say what the law is." *Marbury v. Madison.* At the core of this power is the federal courts' independent responsibility— independent from its coequal branches in the Federal Government, and independent from the separate authority of the several States—to interpret federal law. A construction of AEDPA that would require the federal courts to cede this authority to the courts of the States would be inconsistent with the practice that federal judges have traditionally followed in discharging their duties under Article III of the Constitution. If Congress had intended to require such an important change in the exercise of our jurisdiction, we believe it would have spoken with much greater clarity than is found in the text of AEDPA. . . .

The message that Congress intended to convey by using the phrases "contrary to" and "unreasonable application of" is not entirely clear. The prevailing view in the Circuits is that the former phrase requires *de novo* review of "pure" questions of law and the latter requires some sort of "reasonability" review of so-called mixed questions of law and fact.

We are not persuaded that the phrases define two mutually exclusive categories of questions. Most constitutional questions that arise in habeas corpus proceedings—and therefore most "decisions" to be made—require the federal judge to apply a rule of law to a set of facts, some of which may be disputed and some undisputed. For example, an erroneous conclusion that particular circumstances established the voluntariness of a confession, or that there exists a conflict of interest when one attorney represents multiple defendants, may well be described either as "contrary to" or as an "unreasonable application of" the governing rule of law. In constitutional adjudication, as in the common law, rules of law often develop incrementally as earlier decisions are applied to new factual situations. But rules that depend upon such elaboration are hardly less lawlike than those that establish a bright-line test.

. . . . The statutory text likewise does not obviously prescribe a specific, recognizable standard of review for dealing with either phrase. Significantly, it does not use any term, such as *de novo* or "plain error," that would easily identify a familiar standard of review. Rather, the text is fairly read simply as a command that a federal court not issue the habeas writ unless the state court was wrong as a matter of law or unreasonable in its application of law in a given case. The suggestion that a wrong state-court "decision"—a legal judgment rendered after consideration of *facts and law*—may no longer be redressed through habeas (because it is unreachable under the "unreasonable application" phrase) is based on a mistaken insistence that the § 2254(d)(1) phrases have not only independent, but mutually exclusive, meanings. Whether or not a federal court can issue the writ under the unreasonable application clause, the statute is clear that habeas may issue under § 2254(d)(1) if a state-court "decision" is contrary to clearly established Federal law. We thus anticipate that there will be a variety of cases, like this one, in which both phrases may be implicated.

Even though we cannot conclude that the phrases establish a body of rigid rules, they do express a mood that the Federal Judiciary must respect. In this respect, it seems clear that Congress intended federal judges to attend with the utmost care to state-court decisions, including all of the reasons supporting their decisions, before concluding that those proceedings were infected by constitutional error sufficiently serious to warrant the issuance of the writ. . . . On the other hand, it is significant that the word "deference" does not appear in the text of the statute itself. Neither the legislative history nor the statutory text suggests any difference in the so-called "deference" depending on which of the two phrases is implicated. Whatever "deference" Congress had in mind with respect to both phrases, it surely is not a requirement that federal courts actually defer to a state-court application of the federal law that is, in the independent judgment of the federal court, in error. . . .

Our disagreement with the Court about the precise meaning of the phrase "contrary to," and the word "unreasonable," is, of course, important, but should affect only a narrow category of cases. The simplest and first definition of "contrary to" as a phrase is "in conflict with." In this sense, we think the phrase surely capacious enough to include a finding that the state-court "decision" is simply "erroneous" or wrong. (We hasten to add that even "diametrically different" from, or "opposite" to, an established federal law would seem to include "decisions" that are wrong in light of that law.) And there is nothing in the phrase "contrary to"—as the Court appears to agree—that implies anything less than independent review by the federal courts. Moreover, state-court decisions that do not "conflict" with federal law will rarely be "unreasonable" under either the Court's reading of the statute or ours. We all agree that state-court judgments must be upheld unless, after the closest examination of the state-court judgment, a federal court is firmly convinced that a federal constitutional right has been violated. Our difference is as to the cases in which, at first blush, a state-court judgment seems entirely reasonable, but thorough analysis by a federal court produces a firm conviction that that judgment is infected by constitutional error. In our view, such an erroneous judgment is "unreasonable" within the meaning of the Act even though that conclusion was not immediately apparent.

In sum, the statute directs federal courts to attend to every state-court judgment with utmost care, but it does not require them to defer to the opinion of every reasonable state-court judge on the content of federal law. If, after carefully weighing all the reasons for accepting a state court's judgment, a federal court is convinced that a prisoner's custody—or, as in this case, his sentence of death—violates the Constitution, that independent judgment should prevail. Otherwise the federal "law as determined by the Supreme Court of the United States" might be applied by the federal courts one way in Virginia and another way in California. In light of the well-recognized interest in ensuring that federal courts interpret federal law in a uniform way, we are convinced that Congress did not intend the statute to produce such a result.

III

In this case, Williams contends that he was denied his constitutionally guaranteed right to the effective assistance of counsel when his trial lawyers failed to investigate and to present substantial mitigating evidence to the sentencing jury. The threshold question under AEDPA is whether Williams seeks to apply a rule of law that was clearly established at the time his state-court conviction became final. That question is easily answered because the merits of his claim are squarely governed by our holding in *Strickland v. Washington*.

. . . . It is past question that the rule set forth in *Strickland* qualifies as "clearly established Federal law, as determined by the Supreme Court of the United States." . . . This Court's precedent dictated that the Virginia Supreme Court apply the *Strickland* test at the time that court entertained Williams's ineffective-assistance claim. And it can hardly be said that recognizing the right to effective counsel breaks new ground or imposes a new obligation on the States. Williams is therefore entitled to relief if the Virginia Supreme Court's decision rejecting his ineffective-assistance claim was either "contrary to, or involved an unreasonable application of," that established law. It was both.

IV

. . . . The record establishes that counsel did not begin to prepare for that phase of the proceeding until a week before the trial. They failed to conduct an investigation that would have uncovered extensive records graphically describing Williams's nightmarish childhood, not because of any strategic calculation but because they incorrectly thought that state law barred access to such records. Had they done so, the jury would have learned that Williams's parents had been imprisoned for the criminal neglect of Williams and his siblings, that Williams had been severely and repeatedly beaten by his father, that he had been committed to the custody of the social services bureau for two years during his parents' incarceration (including one stint in an abusive foster home), and then, after his parents were released from prison, had been returned to his parents' custody.

Counsel failed to introduce available evidence that Williams was borderline mentally retarded and did not advance beyond sixth grade in school. They failed to seek prison records recording Williams's commendations for helping to crack a prison drug ring and for returning a guard's missing wallet, or the testimony of prison officials who described Williams as among the inmates least likely to act in a violent, dangerous or provocative way. Counsel failed even to return the phone call of a certified public accountant who had offered to testify that he had visited Williams frequently when Williams was incarcerated as part of a prison ministry program, that Williams seemed to thrive in a more regimented and structured environment, and that Williams was proud of the carpentry degree he earned while in prison.

Of course, not all of the additional evidence was favorable to Williams. The juvenile records revealed that he had been thrice committed to the juvenile system—for aiding and abetting larceny when he was 11 years old, for pulling a false fire alarm when he was 12, and for breaking and entering when he was 15. But as the Federal District Court correctly observed, the failure to introduce the comparatively voluminous amount of evidence that did speak in Williams's favor was not justified by a tactical decision to focus on Williams's voluntary confession. Whether or not those omissions were sufficiently prejudicial to have affected the outcome of sentencing, they clearly demonstrate that trial counsel did not fulfill their obligation to conduct a thorough investigation of the defendant's background.

We are also persuaded, unlike the Virginia Supreme Court, that counsel's unprofessional service prejudiced Williams within the meaning of *Strickland.* After hearing the additional evidence developed in the postconviction proceedings, the very judge who presided at Williams's trial, and who once determined that the death penalty was just and appropriate, concluded that there existed a reasonable probability that the result of the sentencing phase would have been different if the jury had heard that evidence. We do not agree with the Virginia Supreme Court that Judge Ingram's conclusion should be discounted because he apparently adopted a *per se* approach to the prejudice element that placed undue emphasis on mere outcome determination. Judge Ingram did stress the importance of mitigation evidence in making his outcome determination, but it is clear that his predictive judgment rested on his assessment of the totality of the omitted evidence rather than on the notion that a single item of omitted evidence, no matter how trivial, would require a new hearing.

The Virginia Supreme Court's own analysis of prejudice reaching the contrary conclusion was thus unreasonable in at least two respects. First, as we have already explained, the State Supreme Court mischaracterized at best the appropriate rule, made clear by this Court in *Strickland*, for determining whether counsel's assistance was effective within the meaning of the Constitution. While it may also have conducted an outcome determinative analysis of its own, it is evident to us that the court's decision turned on its erroneous view that a mere difference in outcome is not sufficient to establish constitutionally ineffective assistance of counsel. Its analysis in this respect was thus not only "contrary to," but also, inasmuch as the Virginia Supreme Court relied on the inapplicable exception . . . , an "unreasonable application of" the clear law as established by this Court.

Second, the State Supreme Court's prejudice determination was unreasonable insofar as it failed to evaluate the totality of the available mitigation evidence—both that adduced at trial, and the evidence adduced in the habeas proceeding in reweighing it against the evidence in aggravation. This error is apparent in its consideration of the additional mitigation evidence developed in the postconviction proceedings. The court correctly found that as to "the factual part of the mixed question," there was "really . . . n[o] . . . dispute" that available mitigation evidence was not presented at trial. As to the prejudice determination comprising the "legal part" of its analysis, it correctly emphasized the strength of the prosecution evidence supporting the future dangerousness aggravating circumstance.

But the state court failed even to mention the sole argument in mitigation that trial counsel did advance—Williams turned himself in, alerting police to a crime they otherwise would never have discovered, expressing remorse for his actions, and cooperating with the police after that. While this, coupled with the prison records and guard testimony, may not have overcome a finding of future dangerousness, the graphic description of Williams's childhood, filled with abuse and privation, or the reality that he was "borderline mentally retarded," might well have influenced the jury's appraisal of his moral culpability. The circumstances recited in his several confessions are consistent with the view that in each case his violent behavior was a compulsive reaction rather than the product of cold-blooded premeditation. Mitigating evidence unrelated to dangerousness may alter the jury's selection of penalty, even if it does not undermine or rebut the prosecution's death-eligibility case. The Virginia Supreme Court did not entertain that possibility. It thus failed to accord appropriate weight to the body of mitigation evidence available to trial counsel.

V

In our judgment, the state trial judge was correct both in his recognition of the established legal standard for determining counsel's effectiveness, and in his conclusion that the entire postconviction record, viewed as a whole and cumulative of mitigation evidence presented originally, raised a reasonable probability that the result of the sentencing proceeding would have been different if competent counsel had presented and explained the significance of all the available evidence. It follows that the Virginia Supreme Court rendered a "decision that was contrary to, or involved an unreasonable application of, clearly established Federal law." Williams's constitutional right to the effective assistance of counsel as defined in *Strickland v. Washington* was violated.

Accordingly, the judgment of the Court of Appeals is reversed, and the case is remanded for further proceedings.

Justice O'CONNOR delivered the opinion of the Court with respect to Part II (except as to the footnote), concurred in part, and concurred in the judgment.[*]

[*] Justice KENNEDY joins this opinion in its entirety. THE CHIEF JUSTICE and Justice THOMAS join this opinion with respect to Part II. Justice SCALIA joins this opinion with respect to Part II, except as to the footnote.

. . . . The Court holds today that the Virginia Supreme Court's adjudication of Terry Williams's application for state habeas corpus relief resulted in just such a decision. I agree with that determination and join Parts I, III, and IV of the Court's opinion. Because I disagree, however, with the interpretation of § 2254(d)(1) set forth in Part II of Justice Stevens's opinion, I write separately to explain my views. . . .

II

A

. . . . Justice STEVENS's opinion in Part II essentially contends that § 2254(d)(1) does not alter the previously settled rule of independent review. Indeed, the opinion concludes its statutory inquiry with the somewhat empty finding that § 2254(d)(1) does no more than express a mood that the Federal Judiciary must respect. For Justice STEVENS, the congressionally enacted mood has two important qualities. First, federal courts must attend to every state-court judgment with utmost care by carefully weighing all the reasons for accepting a state court's judgment. Second, if a federal court undertakes that careful review and yet remains convinced that a prisoner's custody violates the Constitution, that independent judgment should prevail. . . Justice Stevens's interpretation of § 2254(d)(1) gives the 1996 amendment no effect whatsoever. . . .

Justice STEVENS arrives at his erroneous interpretation by means of one critical misstep. He fails to give independent meaning to both the "contrary to" and "unreasonable application" clauses of the statute. By reading § 2254(d)(1) as one general restriction on the power of the federal habeas court, Justice STEVENS manages to avoid confronting the specific meaning of the statute's "unreasonable application" clause and its ramifications for the independent-review rule. It is, however, a cardinal principle of statutory construction that we must give effect, if possible, to every clause and word of a statute. Section 2254(d)(1) defines two categories of cases in which a state prisoner may obtain federal habeas relief with respect to a claim adjudicated on the merits in state court. Under the statute, a federal court may grant a writ of habeas corpus if the relevant state-court decision was either (1) "*contrary to . . .* clearly established Federal law, as determined by the Supreme Court of the United States," or (2) "*involved an unreasonable application of . . .* clearly established Federal law, as determined by the Supreme Court of the United States."

. . . . The word "contrary" is commonly understood to mean diametrically different, opposite in character or nature, or mutually opposed. The text of § 2254(d)(1) therefore suggests that the state court's decision must be substantially different from the relevant precedent of this Court. . . . A state-court decision will certainly be contrary to our clearly established precedent if the state court applies a rule that contradicts the governing law set forth in our cases. Take, for example, our decision in *Strickland v. Washington*. If a state court were to reject a prisoner's claim of ineffective assistance of counsel on the grounds that the prisoner had not established by a preponderance of the evidence that the result of his criminal proceeding would have been different, that decision would be diametrically different, opposite in character or nature, and mutually opposed to our clearly established precedent because we held in *Strickland* that the prisoner need only demonstrate a reasonable probability that the result of the proceeding would have been different. A state-court decision will also be contrary to this Court's clearly established precedent if the state court confronts a set of facts that are materially indistinguishable from a decision of this Court and nevertheless arrives at a result different from our precedent. Accordingly, in either of these two scenarios, a federal court will be unconstrained by § 2254(d)(1) because the state-court decision falls within that provision's "contrary to" clause.

On the other hand, a run-of-the-mill state-court decision applying the correct legal rule from our cases to the facts of a prisoner's case would not fit comfortably within § 2254(d)(1)'s "contrary to" clause. Assume, for example, that a state-court decision on a prisoner's ineffective-assistance claim correctly identifies *Strickland* as the controlling legal authority and, applying that framework, rejects the prisoner's claim. Quite clearly, the state-court decision would be in accord with our decision in *Strickland* as to the legal prerequisites for establishing an ineffective-assistance claim, even assuming the federal court considering the prisoner's habeas application might reach a different result applying the *Strickland* framework itself. It is difficult, however, to describe such a run-of-the-mill state-court decision as diametrically different from, opposite in character or nature from, or mutually opposed to *Strickland,* our clearly established precedent. Although the state-court decision may be contrary to the federal court's conception of how *Strickland* ought to be applied in that particular case, the decision is not mutually opposed to *Strickland* itself.

Justice STEVENS would instead construe § 2254(d)(1)'s "contrary to" clause to encompass such a routine state-court decision. That construction, however, saps the "unreasonable application" clause of any meaning. If a federal habeas court can, under the "contrary to" clause, issue the writ whenever it concludes that the state court's *application* of clearly established federal law was incorrect, the "unreasonable application" clause becomes a nullity. We must, however, if possible, give meaning to every clause of the statute. Justice STEVENS not only makes no attempt to do so, but also construes the "contrary to" clause in a manner that ensures that the "unreasonable application" clause will have no independent meaning. We reject that expansive interpretation of the statute. Reading § 2254(d)(1)'s "contrary to" clause to permit a federal court to grant relief in cases where a state court's error is limited to the manner in which it *applies* Supreme Court precedent is suspect given the logical and natural fit of the neighboring "unreasonable application" clause to such cases.

. . . [A] state-court decision can involve an "unreasonable application" of this Court's clearly established precedent in two ways. First, a state-court decision involves an unreasonable application of this Court's precedent if the state court identifies the correct governing legal rule from this Court's cases but unreasonably applies it to the facts of the particular state prisoner's case. Second, a state-court decision also involves an unreasonable application of this Court's precedent if the state court either unreasonably extends a legal principle from our precedent to a new context where it should not apply or unreasonably refuses to extend that principle to a new context where it should apply.

A state-court decision that correctly identifies the governing legal rule but applies it unreasonably to the facts of a particular prisoner's case certainly would qualify as a decision involving an unreasonable application of clearly established Federal law. . . .

B

There remains the task of defining what exactly qualifies as an "unreasonable application" of law under § 2254(d)(1). The Fourth Circuit held . . . that a state-court decision involves an "unreasonable application of . . . clearly established Federal law" only if the state court has applied federal law in a manner that reasonable jurists would all agree is unreasonable. The placement of this additional overlay on the "unreasonable application" clause was erroneous. . . .

Defining an "unreasonable application" by reference to a reasonable jurist . . . is of little assistance to the courts that must apply § 2254(d)(1) and, in fact, may be misleading. Stated simply, a federal habeas court making the "unreasonable application" inquiry should ask whether the state court's application of clearly established federal law was objectively unreasonable. The federal habeas court should not transform the inquiry into a subjective one by resting its determination instead on the simple fact that at least one of the Nation's jurists has applied the relevant federal law in the same manner the state court did in the habeas petitioner's case. The "all reasonable jurists" standard would tend to mislead federal habeas courts by focusing their attention on a subjective inquiry rather than on an objective one. . . .

The term "unreasonable" is no doubt difficult to define. That said, it is a common term in the legal world and, accordingly, federal judges are familiar with its meaning. For purposes of today's opinion, the most important point is that an *unreasonable* application of federal law is different from an *incorrect* application of federal law. . . . In § 2254(d)(1), Congress specifically used the word "unreasonable," and not a term like "erroneous" or "incorrect." Under § 2254(d)(1)'s "unreasonable application" clause, then, a federal habeas court may not issue the writ simply because that court concludes in its independent judgment that the relevant state-court decision applied clearly established federal law erroneously or incorrectly. Rather, that application must also be unreasonable. . . .

Throughout this discussion the meaning of the phrase "clearly established Federal law, as determined by the Supreme Court of the United States" has been put to the side. That statutory phrase refers to the holdings, as opposed to the dicta, of this Court's decisions as of the time of the relevant state-court decision. . . . § 2254(d)(1) restricts the source of clearly established law to this Court's jurisprudence.

In sum, § 2254(d)(1) places a new constraint on the power of a federal habeas court to grant a state prisoner's application for a writ of habeas corpus with respect to claims adjudicated on the merits in state court. Under § 2254(d)(1), the writ may issue only if one of the following two conditions is satisfied—the state-court adjudication resulted in a decision that (1) was contrary to clearly established Federal law, as determined by the Supreme Court of the United States, or (2) involved an unreasonable application of clearly established Federal law, as determined by the Supreme Court of the United States. Under the "contrary to" clause, a federal habeas court may grant the writ if the state court arrives at a conclusion opposite to that reached by this Court on a question of law or if the state court decides a case differently than this Court has on a set of materially indistinguishable facts. Under the "unreasonable application" clause, a federal habeas court may grant the writ if the state court identifies the correct governing legal principle from this Court's decisions but unreasonably applies that principle to the facts of the prisoner's case.

III

Although I disagree with Justice STEVENS concerning the standard we must apply under § 2254(d)(1) in evaluating Terry Williams's claims on habeas, I agree with the Court that the Virginia Supreme Court's adjudication of Williams's claim of ineffective assistance of counsel resulted in a decision that was both contrary to and involved an unreasonable application of this Court's clearly established precedent. Specifically, I believe that the Court's discussion in Parts III and IV is correct and that it demonstrates the reasons that the Virginia Supreme Court's decision in Williams's case, even under the interpretation of § 2254(d)(1) I have set forth above, was both contrary to and involved an unreasonable application of our precedent. . . .

Made in the USA
Middletown, DE
29 December 2021

57274110R00300

ISBN 9781719216333